THE ENCYCLOPEDIA OF

CIVIL RIGHTS
IN AMERICA

THE ENCYCLOPEDIA OF CIVIL RIGHTS IN AMERICA

Volume 3

Price, U.S. v. – Zoot suit riots

Editors

David Bradley
College of William and Mary

Shelley Fisher Fishkin
University of Texas at Austin

SHARPE REFERENCE
An imprint of M.E. Sharpe, INC.

1998 Library Reference Edition published by Sharpe Reference

Sharpe Reference is an imprint of M.E. Sharpe, INC.

M.E. Sharpe, INC.
80 Business Park Drive
Armonk, NY 10504

Library of Congress Cataloging-in-Publication Data

The Encyclopedia of Civil Rights in America / editors, David Bradley, Shelley Fisher Fishkin.
p.   cm.
Includes bibliographical references and indexes.
ISBN 0-7656-8000-9 (set : alk. paper)
1. Afro-Americans—Civil rights—History—Encyclopedias.
2. Civil rights movements—United States—History—Encyclopedias.
3. Civil rights—United States—History—Encyclopedias.
I. Bradley, David, 1950-   .
II. Fishkin, Shelley Fisher.
E185.61.E544 1998
323.1′196073—dc21
97-25376
CIP

Printed and bound in the United States of America

The paper used in this publication meets the minimum requirements of the American National Standard for Information Sciences—Permanence of Paper for Printed Library Materials, ANSI Z39.48-1984

10 9 8 7 6 5 4 3 2 1

Frontispiece: In an effort to desegregate Central High School in Little Rock, Arkansas, National Guard troops escort African American students inside the school in 1957. (*AP/Wide World Photos*)

Project and Development Editor: R. Kent Rasmussen   *Research Supervisor:* Jeffry Jensen
Photograph Editor: Karrie Hyatt   *Acquisitions Editor:* Mark Rehn
Production Editor: Yasmine A. Cordoba   *Layout:* James Hutson

Cover and page design: Lee Goldstein

CONTENTS

THE ENCYCLOPEDIA OF

CIVIL RIGHTS

IN AMERICA

Price, United States v.

1966: Civil rights case in which perpetrators of the MISSISSIPPI CIVIL RIGHTS WORKERS MURDERS were convicted under a federal statute.

Following the arrest of three civil rights workers in MISSISSIPPI in 1964, three police officers and fifteen private citizens planned and carried out their execution. The police and their accomplices released the civil rights workers from jail, then shot them to death as escapees. The U.S. SUPREME COURT declared that the victims had been denied DUE PROCESS under the terms of the CIVIL RIGHTS ACT OF 1866. That act made it a federal crime for state officials to deny a person any of the rights and privileges guaranteed by the U.S. Constitution because of race. The Court went on to explain that the actions of the private citizens who willfully participated with the state official also came under the scope of the act.

—Thomas J. Mortillaro

Prisoner rights

Rights of persons imprisoned after being convicted of crimes.

There are those who would assert that the notion of "prisoner rights" is a contradiction in terms because persons convicted of crimes should have no rights. For much of U.S. history this attitude was shared by all three branches of government. Prisoners in the United States do have constitutional RIGHTS, but they are greatly diminished.

The Hands-off and Rights Periods Until the early 1960's efforts by prisoners to get COURTS to extend to them the same basic rights that other citizens enjoy under the Constitution, such as FREE SPEECH, freedom of RELIGION, freedom from cruel and unusual punishments, and DUE PROCESS of law were mostly unsuccessful. The era in which U.S. courts refused to recognize that prison inmates had any rights and viewed them as virtual slaves of the state has often been called the "Hands-off Period." In contrast, through the 1960's and 1970's—a period that known the "Rights Period"—federal courts began to recognize that inmates retained their constitutional rights, even though convicted of crimes and incarcerated in prison. This trend began in the lower federal courts but soon won recognition in the U.S. SUPREME COURT as well. However, the courts were careful to recognize that these rights retained by inmates were much less extensive than those of free citizens because prisoners had to be restricted by the legitimate administrative needs of the prisons. These needs include such matters as maintaining security and order within the prisons, rehabilitating inmates, and preventing the infiltration of drugs and other contraband into the prisons.

The Deference Period After the late 1970's U.S. courts in general and the Supreme Court in particular became less inclined to rule in favor of inmates than they were during the Rights Period. This last, contemporary period has been referred to as the "Deference Period"—a name chosen because of the tendency of the courts to "defer" to the judgment of corrections officials before making decisions in prisoner rights cases. The Supreme Court has stressed that courts lack the special knowledge and abilities that are critical to managing the unusual environment that exists inside prisons and jails. The Supreme Court has also made it clear that it believes courts should be cautious about using the Constitution to overturn the actions of corrections officials.

In typical modern prisoner rights cases inmates contend that an action taken by corrections officials that has been harmful to them is prohibited by the Constitution. Since the beginning of the Deference Period, courts not only have usually ruled against inmates bringing such suits, they also have established constitutional standards making it more difficult for inmates to win future suits as well.

Individual Rights The U.S. Constitution, especially its BILL OF RIGHTS, has established certain basic rights of individuals that may not be violated by the government. In the prison environment, the most important of these are the rights to free speech and expression, freedom of religion, freedom to associate with others, and freedom from unreasonable searches. The Supreme Court has usually ruled in favor of inmates contending that actions by prison officials have violated their basic rights. For example, the Court ruled that a prison may refuse to allow Muslim inmates assigned to outside work details to return to their prisons on Friday afternoons to observe their weekly religious rituals.

The Court has also permitted prisons to prohibit inmates from organizing unions within prisons. It has given them broad discretion in prohibiting inmates from receiving certain publications, allowed

Inmates of State Prisons in 1992

California	109,496	Mississippi	9,083
New York	61,736	Wisconsin	9,054
Texas	61,178	Colorado	8,997
Florida	48,302	Arkansas	8,433
Michigan	39,019	Oregon	6,596
Ohio	38,378	Nevada	6,049
Illinois	31,640	Kansas	6,028
Georgia	25,290	Iowa	4,518
Pennsylvania	24,974	Delaware	3,977
New Jersey	22,653	Minnesota	3,822
Virginia	21,199	New Mexico	3,271
Louisiana	20,810	Hawaii	2,926
North Carolina	20,455	Alaska	2,865
Maryland	19,977	Rhode Island	2,775
South Carolina	18,643	Utah	2,699
Alabama	17,453	Nebraska	2,565
Arizona	16,477	Idaho	2,475
Missouri	16,198	New Hampshire	1,777
Oklahoma	14,821	West Virginia	1,745
Indiana	13,166	Montana	1,553
Tennessee	11,849	Maine	1,515
Connecticut	11,403	South Dakota	1,487
District of Columbia	10,875	Vermont	1,267
Kentucky	10,364	Wyoming	1,022
Massachusetts	10,056	North Dakota	464
Washington	9,959		

Source: Data are from U.S. Department of Justice, Bureau of Justice Statistics, *Prisoners in 1992* (bulletin NCJ-141784). Washington, D.C.: U.S. Government Printing Office, 1993.

officials to search cells without warrants and without specific reasons for expecting to find contraband materials, permitted officials to conduct strip searches of inmates who may have had physical contact with visitors ("contact visits"), ruled that inmates do not have a constitutional right to contact visits, permitted prison bans on correspondence with inmates in other prisons, and upheld prison regulations prohibiting the press from interviewing inmates of their choice.

In some cases the Supreme Court has ruled in favor of inmates. For example, the Court ruled that inmates who are members of minority religions must be extended the same freedoms to engage in their religious practices as are extended to inmates who adhere to more widely followed religions. The Court has also held that prisons may not prohibit inmates from receiving outside mail without important reasons for doing so, and that they may not prohibit inmates from marrying.

The Supreme Court has treated certain inmates differently from others determining the constitutional test to be applied in these cases. Generally, when the Court has identified an individual right as fundamental, it has subjected any actions taken by government that impinge upon that right to increased scrutiny (often referred to as the strict scrutiny test). This means that in deciding whether a government action is constitutional, the government must demonstrate that it had a compelling reason for its action, that its action was necessary in light of this compelling government need, and that it could not have taken any other action to accomplish its compelling need that would have had less impact on the rights of inmates.

In 1987 the Court made it clear that it would not use a strict scrutiny approach in individual rights cases involving prisoners. The Court indicated that a prison regulation impinging on inmates' constitutional rights was valid so long as it was reasonably related to legitimate prison interests (often referred to as the rational basis test). This approach has been a much easier standard for the government to satisfy than the strict scrutiny approach. Under the rational basis test, the burden rests with inmates to demonstrate that a prison had no rational reason for its actions, or if it did have such a rational reason, that its actions were not reasonably related to that reason.

In 1993 Congress passed the Religious Freedom Restoration Act (RFRA). This brief act requires all courts to apply the strict scrutiny approach whenever a government action places a substantial burden on any person's free exercise of religion. The new law appeared to make it easier for inmates to win cases in which they allege that actions by prison officials have interfered with their freedom of worship.

Due Process Issues The DUE PROCESS clauses of the Constitution's Fifth and FOURTEENTH AMENDMENTS prohibit states from depriving people of life, liberty, or property without due process of law. Prison inmates have often argued that when prisons take administrative actions that affect them in ways they consider undesirable, they are being deprived of liberty and are therefore entitled to certain procedural protections before these unfavorable actions may be taken. The due process issues raised in these cases usually concern two questions. First is whether prisons must hold hearings of some sort before taking adverse administrative actions, such as transferring inmates to other institutions or to

Overcrowding, as in this infirmary of the Massachusetts Correctional Institute in 1987, has been a root cause of the problems in American prisons. (*AP/Wide World Photos*)

mental institutions, or placing inmates in administrative or punitive segregation (commonly called "solitary confinement"), and awarding of some other disciplinary action.

The second concern is the question of whether inmates are entitled to hearings before administrative actions can be taken, and, if so, what kinds of procedural protections must be extended to them at such hearings. For example, should inmates be entitled to be represented by counsel? May they call witnesses? Are they entitled to confront persons who testify against them?

The rules developed by the Supreme Court to answer the first due process question have been ambiguous and difficult to apply to real-life situations. The Court has ruled that inmates can acquire a liberty interest in one of two ways. One way is directly under the clauses themselves. This liberty interest arises when the administrative action taken falls outside the conditions of confinement usually associated with a prison sentence. For example, the Court has decided that moving inmates to less pleasant living arrangements within a prison is well within ordinary terms of confinement, but transferring inmates to mental hospitals for confinement is not.

A second way that inmates can acquire a liberty interest is when states do something to create a liberty interest. In one case, the Supreme Court indicated that this state-created liberty interest arises when a prison imposes a hardship on an inmate that is not usually part of a prisoner's existence in prison. The Court also held in this case, that imposition of thirty days of solitary confinement on an inmate for misconduct was not harsh enough to constitute an unusual and significant hardship. Since this was a new standard, the Court has not yet decided a case in which it has found that an administrative sanction imposed by a prison was harsh enough to constitute an unusual and significant hardship.

If a prison's administrative action does create one of these two types of liberty interests, the second due process question arises: What kinds of procedural protections must be extended to inmates before the kind of administrative action at issue is imposed? The Supreme Court has answered this question on a case-by-case basis by examining the particular administrative actions at issue and then determining what procedural protections are required before they may be taken. As a general rule,

it can be said that the more severe an action is, the greater the protections that must be extended to inmates before that action may be taken. For example, before "good-time" credits may be forfeited for misconduct, inmates must be informed of the allegations against them; also, they must be given hearings at which they must usually be permitted to call witnesses and introduce documentary evidence; they must be given statements of the evidence being used against them; and they must be given the prisons' reasons for their administrative actions in writing. However, inmates have no right to be represented by counsel at their hearings.

The Court has viewed transfers to mental institutions as more severe actions than depriving inmates of good-time credits. For this reason, inmates must be represented by counsel at hearings before such transfers can be imposed.

Cruel and Unusual Punishment The Eighth Amendment to the Constitution prohibits the imposition of cruel and unusual punishment. This provision has been used successfully by inmates to challenge medical treatments, the conditions in which inmates live, and the use of force by prison staff. In medical treatment cases, inmates have been able to win when they can prove that a prison was deliberately indifferent to their serious medical needs. Thus, for example, a prison may not ignore an inmate's need for an appendectomy.

In conditions of confinement cases, inmates have been able to win when they have proven that prisons were deliberately indifferent to living conditions that deprived them of a basic necessity of life. For example, a prison may not knowingly provide its inmates with an inadequate diet.

In use of force cases, inmates have been able to win when they can prove that the use of force against them was applied maliciously and sadistically by prison staff for the purpose of inflicting harm. For example, in restoring order during a prison riot, guards may not shoot inmates who do not reasonably appear to present a danger to the guards.

Access to the Courts Inmates often want to use the court system to appeal their criminal convictions, to complain about the conditions in which they are confined (or about some action taken by prison officials), or to deal with personal claims that have nothing to do with their confinement, such as divorce actions or claims for personal injuries suffered before or during their confinement. Since the beginning of the Rights Period, courts have generally been protective of inmates in this area. Supreme Court decisions appeared to indicate that prisons had to provide inmates with either an adequate law library or a legal assistance program that inmates could utilize to get their claims to court. However, the Court later seemed to have backed off from this approach. Although the precise holding of the Court is unclear, the Court made it clear that the prisons' constitutional duty is only to provide meaningful access to the courts. The Court indicated that this does not mean that prisons must "enable the prisoner to discover grievances, and to litigate effectively once in court."

Furthermore, the duty to provide meaningful access extends only to inmate claims relating to the legality of their convictions and to aspects of their confinement. It does not extend to purely personal claims arising outside the prison context.

Although it can no longer be said that prison inmates have no rights, the extent of those rights are greatly diminished because of their status as inmates. In addition, they face an uphill battle in asserting these diminished rights because they need only be provided minimal legal assistance or resources.

SUGGESTED READINGS:

Boston, John, and D. Manville. *Prisoners Self-Help Litigation Manual.* 2d ed. New York: Oceana Publications, 1995. Written for prisoners who must file their own prisoner rights lawsuits by two lawyers experienced in bringing prisoner rights suits.

Branham, Lynn, and Sheldon Krantz. *Sentencing, Corrections, and Prisoners' Rights in a Nutshell.* 4th ed. St. Paul, Minn.: West Publishing, 1994. Summary of laws relating to prisoner rights; written for law students, but in a style that the general public can understand.

Call, Jack. "The Supreme Court and Prisoners' Rights," *Federal Probation* 59, no. 1 (March, 1995). Survey of U.S. Supreme Court cases dealing with prisoners rights.

Del Carmen, Rolando, Susan Ritter, and Betsy Witt. *Briefs of Leading Cases in Corrections.* Cincinnati, Ohio: Anderson Publishing, 1993. Summaries of the most important cases on prisoner rights.

Mushlin, Michael. *Rights of Prisoners.* 2d ed. Colorado Springs, Colo.: Shepard's/McGraw-Hill, 1995. Comprehensive discussion of prisoner rights with annual supplements.

Palmer, John. *Constitutional Rights of Prisoners.* 4th ed. Cincinnati, Ohio: Anderson Publishing, 1991. Combination of text discussing the courts' treatment of the rights of prisoners and lengthy excerpts from important court decisions.

Rudovsky, David, Alvin Bronstein, Edward Koren, and Julia Cade. *The Rights of Prisoners.* 4th ed. Carbondale: Southern Illinois University Press, 1988. Part of a series about individual rights published for the general public by the American Civil Liberties Union.

—Jack E. Call

Privacy rights

The right to be safe from intrusions, especially by the government, into personal matters.

The right to privacy is thought of as a general right that encompasses a number of different interests. Although privacy is clearly in the liberal individualist tradition, it is strangely absent in the writings of classic liberals such as John Locke, Wilhelm von Humboldt, and John Stuart Mill. This may be the result of the fact that there were fewer threats to privacy in earlier times than in the more pressured, crowded, and technologically advanced modern world. It may also be that privacy received protection under a different guise or as a by-product of defending individual liberty. In any case, protection against invasions of privacy by direct appeal to a right of privacy has remained unique to American jurisdictions among English COMMON LAW countries. Furthermore, the articulation and defense of privacy as a right has been developed most fully in American law and by American judges and legal scholars.

Supreme Court Justice Louis BRANDEIS, in his famous dissenting opinion in the 1928 wiretapping case of *Olmstead v. United States*, spoke of the right to privacy in terms of the right to be left alone:

The makers of our Constitution undertook to secure conditions favorable to the pursuit of happiness. They recognized the significance of man's spiritual nature, of his feelings and of his intellect. . . . They sought to protect Americans in their beliefs, their thoughts, their emotions, and their sensations. They conferred, as against the government, the right to be let alone—the most comprehensive of rights and the right most valued by civilized men.

The identification of the right to privacy as the right to be let alone by Brandeis and others has not been without its critics, who point out that the identification is at once too broad and too narrow. That is, some invasions of privacy can be undertaken without hindering persons—such as videotaping their behavior with hidden cameras. By contrast, some forms of not letting persons alone—such as striking them with a pipe—do not seem to be invasions of privacy. Although widely recognized as a significant civil right, the right to privacy has been open to diverse definitions and interpretations.

Development The varying character of the right to privacy has been reflected in its development in American law. A statement and defense of the right is found in the classic essay "The Right to Privacy," published in 1890 by Louis Brandeis and Samuel Warren. They claimed that many recognized legal actions or torts were not so much based on property rights as on the more important principle of individual privacy. The impetus for their defense of privacy was the outrage experienced by the Warrens, a prominent Boston family, at the press coverage of their social activities, especially the wedding of their daughter. Their contention aroused great interest and support, and after some early setbacks, courts and legislatures in the United States moved to afford legal protection for the tort right of privacy. In New York a young woman discovered that a milling couple had used her picture on an advertising flyer, with the caption "Flour of the Family" below the picture. She sued for the use of her image without her consent. A New York appeals court rejected her claim and the thesis of the Warren-Brandeis article. In response, New York's legislature passed a law making it a crime and a tort to use a person's name or likeness for commercial purposes without the person's consent.

The early right to privacy recognized by law was quite narrow, but it gradually expanded to cover other types of violations of privacy, including intrusion on a person's seclusion or solitude, public disclosure of private facts about a person, publicity that places an individual in a false light, as well as the commercial appropriation of a person's name or picture. These privacy concerns are related to, though clearly not identical with, constitutional protections found in the Fourth Amendment guarantee against unreasonable searches and seizures and the Fifth Amendment guarantee against self-incrimination. Such privacy interests are often brought together under the label "information privacy."

Information Privacy Alan Westin's 1967 book *Privacy and Freedom* defined privacy as "the claim of individuals to determine for themselves when, how, and to what extent information about them is communicated to others." This is a fairly typical definition of privacy, which places information control at the center of privacy concerns. The definition, when "information" is taken liberally, captures an important set of interests that people have about the acquisition and communication of information about themselves. People have argued that their privacy is violated not only by unauthorized disclosure of personal information, such as that contained in medical or educational records, but also by unauthorized observation, by surveillance or videotaping, or by wiretapping of conversations. People are especially concerned about the unauthorized gathering and disseminating of personal or intimate information and about intrusions into places of seclusion. The Supreme Court has come to extend the reach of the Fourth Amendment protection against unreasonable searches and seizures to settings in which individuals have an expectation of privacy, such as a public telephone booth (but not, for example, a gym locker in a high school). Advancing technology provides continuing challenges to this concept of privacy.

Privacy and Autonomy In the 1965 case of GRISWOLD V. CONNECTICUT, the U.S. Supreme Court invalidated a Connecticut law prohibiting the use of contraceptives. Justice William O. Douglas, writing the majority opinion, asserted that the law violated a right to privacy implicit in the Constitution. Douglas alluded to concern about intrusive evidence gathering that the enforcement of such a law might occasion; he asked rhetorically: "Would we allow the police to search the sacred precincts of marital bedrooms for telltale signs of the use of contraceptives?" It is clear that the primary focus of the right is the liberty or autonomy of people to make personal decisions. Douglas emphasized that married couples should be free to make decisions about contraceptive use and ultimately procreation without governmental interference. In a later case

Members of the National Organization for Women march for privacy rights in a Christopher Street march in 1976. (*Betty Lane*)

extending the right to privacy to cover distribution of contraceptives to single persons, Justice William Brennan stated: "If the right to privacy means anything, it is the right of the individual, married or single, to be free from unwarranted governmental intrusion in matters so fundamentally affecting a person as the decision whether to bear or beget a child."

U.S. Courts, including the Supreme Court, have extended the right to privacy in various ways, although its precise contours have remained unclear and its application to certain activities has remained controversial. The Supreme Court has sometimes identified the core areas of this constitutional right to privacy as encompassing decisions relating to marriage, family, home, procreation, and child rearing and education. The Court's 1973 ROE V. WADE decision, which struck down a Texas law restricting abortion, is perhaps the Court's most politically controversial privacy decision. The Court has also invalidated laws placing restrictions on people's

right to marry, on zoning ordinances that are overly restrictive in their definitions of "family," and on the application of obscenity statutes to possession and use in the home.

In the mid-1970's the Supreme Court began growing more cautious in recognizing new privacy claims. In a decision in the 1986 case of *Bowers v. Hardwick*, the Court refused to extend the right to privacy to protect homosexuals from prosecution under state sodomy laws. Justice Byron White, writing for the majority, insisted that there is no constitutional right to engage in homosexual sodomy, noting that such conduct bears no relationship to privacy concerns previously recognized by the Court, namely, "marriage, family, and procreation." Justice Harry Blackmun in his dissenting opinion offered an alternative, more expansive interpretation of the right to privacy. He suggested that it has two aspects, place and decisional; the former protects private places, while the latter protects individual autonomy with respect to private and intimate decisions. A number of state courts, beginning with the New Jersey supreme court's famous decision in the 1976 Karen Quinlan case, based the right of individuals to refuse medical treatment on the right to privacy. People may decide to refuse or discontinue even life-preserving or life-prolonging treatments, especially of an invasive or intrusive kind. In 1988 the U.S. Supreme Court took up the issue for the first time, and it acknowledged a right of competent persons to refuse medical treatment. The Court, however, grounded the right in the liberty guarantee of the FOURTEENTH AMENDMENT'S DUE PROCESS CLAUSE, rather than regarding it as encompassed by the constitutional right to privacy.

SUGGESTED READINGS:

Inness, Julie. *Privacy, Intimacy, and Isolation*. New York: Oxford University Press, 1992.

Pennock, John, and J. Roland Chapman, eds. *Privacy*. New York: Lieber-Atherton, 1971.

Schoeman, Ferdinand, ed. *Philosophical Dimensions of Privacy*. New York: Cambridge University Press, 1984.

Shattuck, John. *Rights of Privacy*. Chicago: National Textbook, 1977.

Warren, Samuel, and Louis Brandeis. "The Right to Privacy." *Harvard Law Review* 4 (1890).

Westin, Alan. *Privacy and Freedom*. New York: Atheneum, 1967.

—*Mario F. Morelli*

Private clubs

Private-membership social organizations which have been exempted from certain provisions of federal nondiscrimination laws

Efforts to break down racial discrimination in public ACCOMMODATIONS AND FACILITIES began when CONGRESS passed the CIVIL RIGHTS ACT OF 1875. That ambitious piece of RECONSTRUCTION ERA legislation declared it illegal for any hotel, inn, theater, restaurant, or other business serving the public to exclude service because of race, color, or previous condition of servitude. After Reconstruction ended, however, the U.S. SUPREME COURT held the public accommodations section of the act unconstitutional in 1883, arguing that the Fourteenth AMENDMENT'S EQUAL PROTECTION CLAUSE could be applied only in cases involving state discrimination.

Efforts to combat discrimination resumed nearly a century later, when Congress passed the CIVIL RIGHTS ACT OF 1964. That act prohibited discrimination or segregation based on race, color, religion, or national origin at places of public accommodation when those operations affect commerce. However, the law left open certain ambiguities about how its provisions applied to essentially private facilities, such as country clubs, fraternal organizations, and other membership bodies. In 1968 federal courts began hearing cases addressing the question of what constituted "private" clubs. For example, in *Stout v. Young Men's Christian Association* (1968) and *Nesmith v. Young Men's Christian Association* (1968), federal district courts in Alabama and North Carolina determined that the small numbers of white applicants certain clubs rejected for membership was a major factor in determining that the clubs were not private. A year later, in *Daniel v. Paul*, the U.S. Supreme Court ruled that merely because a club did not investigate applicants before admitting them to membership did not support the club's claim of private status. Also in 1969, a district court in Georgia ruled in *Wesley v. Savannah* that private clubs and establishments clearly not open to the general public were not subject to the public accommodations provision of the Civil Rights Act.

Wright v. Cork Club, a 1970 district court case in Texas, held that to be considered private, a club must have a permanent mechanism to screen, select, or reject applicants on any basis, or on no basis at all; also, private clubs had to limit use of their facilities and services strictly to members and their bona fide guests, be controlled by members through general meetings or other forms permitting them to select and otherwise choose the officers. Moreover, the clubs had to be nonprofit, operate solely for the benefit of their members, and direct all their publicity solely to their members. In *United States v. Johnson Lake, Inc.* (1970), a district court in Alabama ruled that a club formed primarily to exclude AFRICAN AMERICANS on account of race was not a private club under the law.

Two years later, in another Alabama case, *Smith v. Young Men's Christian Association of Montgomery, Inc.*, a court ruled that the YMCA, which had a history of freely admitting to membership almost everyone who applied, gained a large share of its revenue from the public, that it was neither owned nor governed by its members, so it totally failed to meet private club status. A Florida case concerning the Biscayne Bay Yacht Club in 1973 concerned the fact that the city of Miami leased publicly owned land to a private club that excluded African Americans and Jews. In that case, the court ruled that the club's discriminatory policies violated the Fourteenth Amendment, because its lease created an unacceptable "symbiotic relationship" between it and the state.

In another Florida case, *Solomon v. Miami Woman's Club* (1973), a district court decided that even though the club sponsored facilities in state parks for handicapped persons, co-chaired the city bicentennial celebration, was statewide in size, and used the name of a city in its name, not every contract between a state and a private club necessarily made the club subject to the Fourteenth Amendment's anti-discrimination clause.

In *Anderson v. Pass Christian Isles Golf Club, Inc.* (1974), a federal appeals court in Mississippi ruled that a private golf club's arrangements with local hotels for hotel patrons to use its golf course destroyed its private club status; the court ordered the golf club to accept all hotel patrons without regard to their race. In *United States v. Slidell Youth Football Association* (1974) a district court in Louisiana established that the burden of establishing an association as a private club rests on the association itself.

State Action and Private Clubs The leading case involving private club discrimination was the Supreme Court's decision in *Moose Lodge No. 107 v. Irvis* (1972). A Pennsylvania statute required private clubs holding state liquor licenses to enforce club bylaws. Moose Lodge No. 107 had an openly discriminatory rule against admitting African Americans. State law required the Moose lodge to enforce that statute. When Leon Irvis, the black guest of a member attempted to purchase a drink and was refused, he sued. When his case reached the Supreme Court, the Court ruled that no state action had been taken against him because the state was not "a partner or joint venturer in the club."

In *Roberts v. United States Jaycees* (1984) the U.S. Supreme Court rejected the national Jaycees' argument that its members' First Amendment freedom of association had been violated by a Minnesota statute defining discrimination as any action denying any person "full and equal enjoyment of goods, services, facilities, privileges, advantages, and accommodations of a place of public accommodation because of race, color, creed, religion, disability, national origin or sex." National Jaycee bylaws limited membership to men between the ages of eighteen and thirty-five. Two Minnesota Jaycee chapters sought changes in local bylaws to conform, and the national Jaycees sought charter revocations. The Court stated the right to associate is not absolute, that Minnesota had a compelling interest to enforce antidiscrimination. The Jaycees provided no argument that admitting women to full membership would inhibit their ability to pursue civic, charitable, lobbying and fund-raising activities. Three years later the Court applied this principle to Rotary International in *Board of Directors of Rotary International v. Rotary Club of Duarte* (1987). In 1988 the Court extended the same arguments to all-male clubs in New York, requiring them to admit women applicants to their membership.

SUGGESTED READINGS:

Ducat, Craig R. *Constitutional Interpretation.* 6th ed. St. Paul, Minn.: West Publishing, 1996.

O'Brien, David M. *Constitutional Law and Politics: Civil Rights and Civil Liberties.* New York: W. W. Norton, 1991.

Stephens, Otis H., Jr., and John M. Sheb II. *American Constitutional Law.* St. Paul, Minn.: West Publishing, 1993.

—*Sam W. McKinstry*

Procedural rights

Methods for protecting individuals from the arbitrary abridgement of their rights by public officials.

Procedural rights, sometimes called criminal rights, protect individuals suspected of criminal activity from the arbitrary abridgement of their constitutional rights and liberties without DUE PROCESS of law. Most procedural rights are outlined in the Fourth, Fifth, Sixth, and Eighth amendments of the BILL OF RIGHTS. Examples include the right to COUNSEL and the protection against DOUBLE JEOPARDY. Procedural rights are usually distinguished from SUBSTANTIVE RIGHTS essential for the preservation of personal liberty such as the First Amendment freedoms of religion, speech, and press.

—*Thomas J. Mortillaro*

Project Confrontation

1963: SCLC desegregation campaign in BIRMINGHAM, ALABAMA.

Also known as the Birmingham Confrontation, or Project C, Project Confrontation was a campaign of civil demonstrations instigated when the Reverend Fred Shuttlesworth of Birmingham, acting on behalf of a group of black clergy and lay people, invited the SOUTHERN CHRISTIAN LEADERSHIP CONFERENCE (SCLC) to his city to lead protest marches and other actions against racial segregation. The campaign was directed at desegregating the lunch counters of downtown department stores. It began at the beginning of April, 1963, with SIT-INS at the counters conducted by college students, and escalated in the following days with protest marches. When peaceful marchers were violently attacked by police under the direction of Police Commissioner T. Eugene (Bull) Connor on April 7, 1963, the ensuing publicity made the campaign the subject of national debate and outrage. It also forced the attention of federal officials, including Attorney General Robert F. KENNEDY and President John F. KENNEDY.

Despite a court injunction ordering the protesters to desist, Martin Luther KING, Jr., and Ralph David ABERNATHY led additional marches. They and others were then arrested and jailed on Good Friday, April 12, 1963. While in solitary confinement, King wrote a manifesto in favor of direct action which became famed as the "LETTER FROM A BIRMINGHAM JAIL."

In late April James BEVEL organized children's marches, which, it was hoped, would be immune from police violence. On May 2, 1963, he began leading a series of peaceful marches of young people starting from Birmingham's Sixteenth Street Baptist Church and passing through the city. On May 3 a procession of youngsters was attacked by Bull Connor's police, who used dogs and fire hoses set at such high pressures that they knocked protesters from their feet. The courage of the young people of Birmingham under these conditions invigorated the morale of the campaign, however, and many parents who had previously declined to become involved were inspired to join the protests. Hundreds of schoolchildren continued to participate in the marches; by May 7, more than two thousand protesters had been arrested and jailed.

Project C ended in compromise with the Birmingham Truce Agreement of May 10, 1963, in which local whites pledged to hire African Americans to work in the downtown stores and to end segregated practices in offering services within the stores. The project dramatically publicized the gravity of repression of civil rights in the South, and, through King's letter and the involvement of children, made a moral case for direct action.

—*Barbara Bair*

Protest music

During periods of political or social upheaval, it has been common for songs to speak critically about existing conditions.

In the United States protest music has grown out of the various folk music traditions that were brought to this country. The two major sources of American folk music traditions are Anglo-Celtic and sub-Saharan African. The settlers who came to North America from the British Isles brought with them a rich variety of music, including ballads and sea chanteys.

Africans who were forcibly brought to the New World and put INTO SLAVERY also came with musical traditions that ran deep. The slaves astonished their captors with their melding of movement with music. In time, they began to create new musical styles. While the European slave owners attempted to destroy anything that related to the slaves' African roots, the slaves found ways of incorporating European musical forms into their own music and produced fresh and vital musical styles. During the eighteenth century, slaves began to express themselves musically through the new folk musical form of the spiritual. After they were introduced to Christianity by their European captors, they made spirituals a way of interpreting their bondage from a religious perspective. For example, many early black spirituals compared the sufferings of slaves to those that Jesus endured. However, it was necessary for the spirituals to contain coded language in order not to anger slave owners. For example, the word "Jesus" commonly represented "freedom." While spirituals expressed the slaves' torment through a religious idiom, there were also secular musical forms employed in which the slaves could vent other concerns.

The African slaves produced a rich selection of songs both for work and for recreational situations.

Pete Seeger performs at the Rally for Detente in New York City in 1975. (*AP/Wide World Photos*)

Because the oppressive nature of slavery did not permit many other satisfactory forms of expression, music became one of the slaves' most important outlets. Some of the secular songs had their words changed so that they could fit more appropriately in a church setting.

Music of the Twentieth Century While the anti-slavery songs of the eighteenth and nineteenth centuries spoke poignantly about the need for change, it was not until the twentieth century that the most overt protest songs were written. In the early part of the century, protest songs were sung by gospel, blues, and country singers. During the Depression years of the 1930's many singers wrote songs that spoke out against injustice. One of the most influential singers of this period was Woody Guthrie. With the advent of union organizing and the conflicts that arose between labor and management, a new contingent of protest singers was brought to the forefront, including Guthrie. Some of his most important songs included "Tom Joad," "Talking Dust Bowl Blues," and "Blowin' Down This Road." While racial prejudice was still commonplace in America, many white and African American singers joined ranks. This became more common during the turbulent 1960's.

AFRICAN AMERICANS began vocally to protest their second-class status during the mid-1950's in the southern states. With the rise of the CIVIL RIGHTS MOVEMENT and U.S. involvement in the Vietnam War during the 1960's, music gained ever-increasing importance as an avenue for expression of radical concepts of the day. One of the most famous protest songs of the period was "WE SHALL OVERCOME." The song was based on a nineteenth century black spiritual, but its words were changed to fit the occasion. Protest songs were often used to energize people to act. Songs of freedom were sung at rallies, church services, marches, and in jails.

In addition to such folk singers as Pete Seeger, Joan Báez, Buffy Sainte-Marie, Bob Dylan, Judy Collins, and Joni Mitchell, African American gospel singers such as Mahalia Jackson, Fannie Lou Hamer, and Guy Carawan sang in support of the Civil Rights movement. The songs that became staples of the movement included "O Freedom," "We'll Never Turn Back," "Ain't Nobody Gonna Turn Me Around," and "If You Miss Me from the Back of the Bus." A Bob Dylan song, "Blowin' in the Wind," became popular both in the Civil Rights movement and in the antiwar movement. With such lyrics as "how many deaths will it take til he knows that too many people have died," and "how many years can some people exist before they're allowed to be free," "Blowin' in the Wind" captured the sentiments of the activists of the period. Protest songs crossed over into various musical forms, including folk, gospel, popular, and rock. The turmoil of the times inspired songwriters to write songs that expressed their concerns for the issues of the day.

SUGGESTED READINGS:

Carawan, Guy, and Candie Carawan, eds. *Sing for Freedom: The Story of the Civil Rights Movement Through Its Songs*. Bethlehem, Pa.: Sing Out, 1990.

Fowke, Edith, and Joe Glazer. *Songs of Work and Protest*. New York: Dover, 1973.

Rodnitzky, Jerome L. *Minstrels of the Dawn: The Folk-Protest Singer as a Cultural Hero*. Chicago: Nelson-Hall, 1976.

Seeger, Pete, and Bob Reiser. *Everybody Says Freedom*. New York: Norton, 1989.

Walker, Wyatt T. *"Somebody's Calling My Name": Black Sacred Music and Social Change*. Valley Forge, Pa.: Judson, 1979.

—*Jeffry Jensen*

Providence race riots

1824: White-on-black VIOLENCE following the freeing of area slaves.

In October, 1824, two years after the state of Rhode Island ended SLAVERY, a riot erupted in Hardscrabble, near the location where the religious reformer Roger Williams had founded Providence with the goal of freedom and equality. Fearing that newly freed African Americans would move into their city, a mob of forty white men, armed with clubs and axes, destroyed about twenty black residences. Although the blacks tried to defend themselves, no one was seriously injured. When several whites were brought to trial the defense attorneys argued that their clients had performed a worthwhile service by ridding the area of a public nuisance. A similar riot occurred in the city seven years later when a barroom brawl erupted into another white mob action.

—*Duncan R. Jamieson*

Puerto Rican Legal Defense and Education Fund

PRLDEF: Puerto Rican advocacy group founded in 1972.

The PRLDEF was founded in New York City in 1972 by Jorge L. BATISTA, Victor Marrero, and César A. Perales to protect the rights of Puerto Ricans and other LATINOS in the United States. The group has strived to ensure equal protection under the law through advocacy and litigation. It has argued cases before the U.S. SUPREME COURT concerning such issues as discrimination and BILINGUAL EDUCATION. It has also repeatedly sued New York City to expand Latino representation in the city's civil service departments, and it has challenged discrimination against Latinos in public and private housing. The group's Voting Rights Projects have worked successfully to increase the number of Latino elected officials in the northeastern United States.

—*Christopher E. Kent*

Q

Quota systems

Government or corporate policies of basing decisions on such matters as hiring and promoting, college admissions, or the awarding of contracts on fixed numerical ratios of members of designated groups.

Not long after major civil rights legislation began to make an impact on public life during the late 1960's claims were heard that government programs ranging from AFFIRMATIVE ACTION in the workplace, school BUSING designed to achieve racial balance, and set asides in government contracting and subcontracting, were leading to "quota systems." To critics of these programs, a desirable state of affairs, equality of opportunity, was giving way to a questionable one: equal outcomes, or equality of result—in which achieving specific goals was taken as a measure of the effectiveness of combating DISCRIMINATION.

Charges that government programs directed against discrimination have led to quota systems have frequently been viewed as not only untrue, but inflammatory—less a reflection of the actual state of affairs than of those making the charges. In the first major study of the remedies for racial discrimination as they stood in the early 1970's, Harvard sociologist Nathan Glaser observed that having begun the battle against discrimination in the workplace and in educational opportunities, "we then began an extensive effort to record the race, color, and (some) national origins of just about every student and employee and recipient of government benefits or services in the nation." The pivotal issues revolved around such practices as federally mandated goals and timetables, inclining employers and contractors away from colorblind hiring and toward preferential policies requiring a "good faith effort" to achieve specific numerical results.

A Second Civil Rights Vision? The stated purpose of such key civil rights legislation as the CIVIL RIGHTS ACT OF 1964 and the VOTING RIGHTS ACT OF 1965 was to remove the barriers that had blocked AFRICAN AMERICANS and other minorities from full participation in the political and economic life of the country. However, it soon became clear to civil rights leaders of the time that merely removing barriers would not by itself put an end to the poverty in which much of the black community was mired. By the mid-1960's the CIVIL RIGHTS MOVEMENT was changing its focus from ending legal discrimination to lifting African Americans out of poverty and placing them where they would have been, had there been no discrimination. In short, the nation saw the emergence of a "second" civil rights vision. If the first vision aimed to end overt discrimination, the second aimed at achieving results for those in targeted groups.

A key concept of this second vision is the "shackled runner," first articulated by President Lyndon B. JOHNSON in a commencement address at Howard University in 1965. Johnson contended that

> you do not wipe away the scars of centuries by saying now you're free to go where you want and do as you desire. . . . You do not take a person who for years has been hobbled by chains and liberate him, bring him up to the starting line of a race and then say, you're free to compete with all the others, and justly believe that you have been completely fair.

Opening the gates, the speech concluded, was insufficient if some could not run through them. Jesse JACKSON later made the idea that African Americans were "shackled runners" one of his key premises in calling for more government efforts to aid their efforts to advance economically. Ensuing civil rights policy increasingly incorporated the notion that merely ending discrimination was insufficient for justice; it was necessary to provide a remedy for its past effects.

This remedy meant, however, setting aside for the time being the ideal of a colorblind legal system. It would be necessary, as Glazer had observed, to take race into account in order to rectify the effects of RACISM both past and present. Thus the country more and more pursued policies that mandated specific goals as a condition for saying that civil rights efforts were substantive and not merely verbal gestures. As Whitney YOUNG, then head of the NATIONAL URBAN LEAGUE put it, a "decade of discrimination in favor of Negro youth [is necessary to remedy] 300 years of deprivation." One of the first officials of the federal EQUAL EMPLOYMENT OPPORTUNITY COMMISSION (EEOC), Alfred Blumrosen, took the first step of "broadening" the concept of discrimination to include any institutional practice that adversely affected a minority group. This position contrasted with the civil rights act's narrow definition that sanctioned intentional discrimination by individuals against other individuals, something that was difficult to prove. "Disparate impact," as this idea would soon become known, soon became the key to proving discrimination for legal purposes. The only alternative, however, was to require preferential treatment as official policy as part of a general a shift of focus to results that could only be measured numerically.

The Philadelphia Plan and Beyond In 1967 the Johnson administration ordered contractors in Philadelphia and Cleveland to submit affirmative action plans indicating minority representation in all phases of federally contracted construction work. The key feature of these plans was their "manning tables," which stated the number of minorities to be hired. Two years later, the Nixon administration's Department of Labor drew up the official Philadelphia Plan, a set of directives mandating specific goals and timetables for increasing the representation of minorities in the construction industry in Philadelphia and three other cities, based on their supposed availability in the applicant pool, subject to compliance review.

Critics of the Philadelphia Plan charged that it violated both the nondiscrimination requirements of Title VII of the Civil Rights Act of 1964, as well as the act's repudiation of preferential treatment. The administration stood its ground against Congress, including the Senate Appropriations Committee. In 1969 President Richard M. NIXON's Executive Order 11478 established "a continuing affirmative action" program for recruitment, hiring, and promotion of minorities in the civil service. Attorney General John Mitchell drew attention to the change in the legal meaning of discrimination. About a year later, the U.S. Supreme Court, in its GRIGGS V. DUKE POWER CO. (1971) decision, lent official credence to the disparate impact doctrine and the idea that visible, measurable goals were needed to ensure that discrimination was indeed being remedied. The key phrase was that Title VII forbade not only overt discrimination, but also any practice "fair in form but discriminatory in operation."

As the 1970's progressed, increasing pressure from government agencies required more and more employers to hire women and minorities so that their work forces would reflect the proportions of women and minorities in the general population. In 1977 President Jimmy CARTER signed the Public Works Employment Act (PWEA) which included as a provision a set aside of 10 percent of its four-billion-dollar appropriation to "minority business enterprises" (MBEs). The Supreme Court of the time was upholding these laws as constitutional. In the case of *United Steelworkers of America v. Weber* (1979) a white male denied admission to a training program allegedly on account of his race had charged the employer with having set up an illegal quota in violation of Title VII solely to avoid disparate-impact litigation. By a 5-4 vote, the Supreme Court disagreed. A year later, in *Fullilove v. Klutznick* (1980), the Court ruled, 6-3, in response to a similar challenge that the PWEA set aside was acceptable, reflecting the broadened interpretation of discrimination and the increasing commitment by government to preferential treatment.

Set-Asides in Higher Education Admissions Policies Higher education had long been a focal point of efforts to increase minority representation. By the early 1970's major educational institutions had begun setting aside admission slots for minorities—a practice that seemed to some to be as questionable as earlier discrimination had been. The 1978 BAKKE CASE (*Regents of the University of California v. Bakke*) became the landmark Supreme Court decision that would determine the legality of COLLEGE AND UNIVERSITY affirmative action programs for years after. This decision came about when Allan Bakke, a white male, was rejected for admission to the medical school of the University of California's Davis campus two years in succession. Bakke had higher test scores than some minority students who were admitted under the school's affirmative action plan, which set aside sixteen of one hundred seats for minority group members. In its decision, a highly divided Supreme Court voted 5-4 to strike down the school's existing affirmative action plan as an illegal and unconstitutional quota system.

Despite the Court's *Bakke* decision, five justices stated that "race can be a factor," one of many, in a college's or university's decision about who to admit. However, the Court did not specify how much of a factor race could be, thus permitting the classification of applicants by race to continue. The justices also disagreed over the legal justification for the use of race as a valid criterion for admission into a college or university professional program. However, they agreed on the broadened meaning of discrimination and hence implicitly on the need to reject colorblindness. As Justice Blackmun stated in his separate opinion on *Bakke*, "to treat some [minorities] equally, we must treat them differently."

After *Bakke* many professional schools, especially law schools, continued setting aside certain numbers of places for minority applicants. It was not always clear what these numbers were, however, because most schools kept their admissions policies secret. They were outraged at incidents such as one that occurred at one law school in 1991, when a third-year student published an exposé in the school's student weekly that drew attention to the practice in a place where it came to public attention.

As a result of such incidents the term "race-norming" gained currency in the early 1990's to describe the practice of relativizing admissions standards to groups so that members of groups compete only against members of the same group for admission. Race-norming allowed schools to retain the practice of setting aside a given percentage of seats for minorities, with the result that average admissions tests scores for minorities were often considerably lower than those for whites (ASIAN AMERICAN test scores, however, were generally higher than those of whites).

In 1996 a Fifth Circuit Court decision, in *Hopwood v. University of Texas*, effectively overruled the *Bakke* case's arguments in the states under its jurisdiction. The court found in favor of Cheryl Hopwood, a white woman who had sued the University of Texas law school on grounds it had rejected her application for admittance because of its affirmative action plan to increase ethnic diversity among its student body. In the law school admissions policy that *Hopwood* challenged, African Americans and Latinos were competing only against each other for a predesignated 5 and 10 percent, respectively, of the roughly five hundred available seats. Minority applications were processed by a special subcommittee, and no one compared all the law school's applications against a single, uniform standard. Shortly before *Hopwood* was to go to the Supreme Court, the law school abandoned this practice; hence, the Supreme Court

refused to rule and let the lower court's decision in favor of the plaintiffs stand. This decision only applied to three states, however, leaving the ultimate fate of numerical set-asides undecided.

Government Contracting and Set-Asides It is important not to confuse a government program whose aim is merely to increase the number of women and members of minority groups who participate with programs mandating specific numerical ratios of minority participation. As public policies designed to advance the representation of women and minorities in industries such as construction developed, legislation was occasionally passed that did indeed mandate specific numerical ratios. For example, in government contracting in the construction industry, such legislation often made primary contractors scramble both to meet designated quotas and to find subcontractors qualified to do the work.

An example of a law that had this result was the Surface Transportation Assistance Act (STAA), also known as the Highway Improvement Act of 1982, which President Ronald REAGAN signed to go into effect in 1983. Section 105(f) of this law introduced a numerical ratio:

> Except to the extent that the Secretary determines otherwise, not less than 10 percent of the amounts authorized to be appropriated under this Act shall be expended with small business concerns owned and controlled by socially and economically disadvantaged individuals as defined by section 8(d) of the Small Business Act.

The phrase "socially and economically disadvantaged individuals" meant minorities and women. Major professional organizations in the construction industry were able to document that many people lost their businesses, despite being low bidders, because they lost subcontracted work to officially designated minority business enterprises as a result of efforts to meet the 10 percent quota.

In 1987 a new piece of legislation made the ratio more specific still. The Surface Transportation and Uniform Relocation Assistance Act of 1987, section 106(c), offered women-owned and minority-owned firms a combined goal of 10 percent of contracts, with 5 percent designated to each. By 1989 thirty-six states and 190 local governments had adopted set-asides, earmarking percentages of government funds for public works projects of various sorts to minority business enterprises, which included enterprises owned by women.

As evidence of technically illegal preferential policies began to surface more and more frequently, such laws were challenged in court. In 1989 the Supreme Court upheld a lower court decision in *Richmond v. J. A. Croson Co.*, which struck down a 30-percent quota. Later that same year, the Court handed down several more such decisions the best known of which were *Wards Cove Packing Co. v. Atonio* and *Martin v. Wilkes*. The Court was increasingly unwilling to sanction numerical ratios as a means of increasing women and minority representation in construction.

Nevertheless, such laws retained support in civil rights circles, in which it was generally denied that they created quota systems. In 1990 a new civil rights act surfaced in Congress. One of its express purposes was to overturn decisions such as *Croson* and *Wards Cove*. President George BUSH vetoed the bill on the grounds that it would create quota systems because employers would have to attempt to fill quotas to avoid potentially business-destroying litigation. However, the following year Congress resurrected what became the CIVIL RIGHTS ACT OF 1991, adding strong provisions on SEXUAL HARASSMENT in the wake of the Senate's Clarence Thomas hearings in fall of that year. The new law also contained a provision that banned the kind of race-norming encountered previously. This version President Bush signed.

However, the Supreme Court was not yet finished. Only four years later the Court heard the case of *Adarand Constructors v. Peña* (1995). In this landmark decision the Court mandated that "strict scrutiny" needed to be applied in any circumstance taking race into account as a positive factor; the taking of race into account must serve a "compelling government interest" as a condition of its constitutionality. This decision heralded the beginning of the federal government's break with quota systems.

Pulling Back from Quota Systems During the mid-1990's matters began to come to a head. The *Hopwood* case had gotten a great deal of publicity while still on its way to the Supreme Court. In 1994 Republicans took control of Congress for the first time in forty years, an election attributed to a backlash by "angry white men" against real or perceived quota systems. The following spring, President Bill CLINTON ordered a review of all affirmative action programs. Two California professors drafted what became known as the CALIFORNIA CIVIL RIGHTS INITIATIVE, billed as a return to the Civil Rights Act of 1964 and the original meaning of discrimination. They began to collect signatures to get it on the state ballot. A slow dismantling of quota systems had begun. On July 20, 1995, the University of California's Board of Regents took a historic vote in the face of massive protests—including a sit-in led by Jesse Jackson—to end the use of race as an admissions criterion. The university thus became the first of many institutions that would rethink their affirmative action programs. With the Supreme Court's decision to let stand the lower court decision in *Hopwood*, the way stood open for more court challenges to quota systems as means of achieving diversity.

SUGGESTED READINGS:

Bast, Diane, et al. *Disadvantaged Business Set-Aside Programs: An Evaluation.* Chicago: Heartland Institute, 1989.

Detlefson, Robert. *Civil Rights Under Reagan.* San Francisco, Calif.: ICS Press, 1991.

Dreyfuss, Joel. *The Bakke Case: The Politics of Inequality.* New York: Harcourt Brace Jovanovich, 1979.

Eastland, Terry. *Counting by Race: Equality from the Founding Fathers to Bakke and Weber.* New York: Basic Books, 1979.

_____. *Ending Affirmative Action: The Case for Colorblind Justice.* New York: Basic Books, 1996.

Kaminer, Wendy. *A Fearful Freedom: Women's Flight from Equality.* Reading, Mass.: Addison-Wesley, 1990.

Lynch, Frederick R. *Invisible Victims: White Males and the Crisis of Affirmative Action.* Westport, Conn.: Greenwood Press, 1989.

Roberts, Paul Craig, and Stratton, Lawrence M. *The New Color Line: How Quotas and Privilege Destroy Democracy.* Washington, D.C.: Regnery, 1995.

Sowell, Thomas. *Preferential Policies: An International Perspective.* New York: Morrow, 1990.

Taylor, Jared. *Paved with Good Intentions: The Failure of Race Relations in America.* New York: Carroll and Graf Publishers, 1992.

Yates, Steven. *Civil Wrongs: What Went Wrong with Affirmative Action.* San Francisco, Calif.: ICS Press, 1994.

—*Steven Yates*

R

Race riots

Civil disturbances pitting rival racial or ethnic groups against each other.

The mixing of different ethnic and racial groups has historically created opportunities for violent confrontations between groups in the United States. When such confrontations involve large numbers of people for extended periods of time, they have typically been described as "race riots." Injury, death, looting, and arson are their usual ingredients.

Race riots have not been limited to fighting among any pair of racial or ethnic groups. In the nineteenth century, American race riots involved native-born white Americans against IRISH AMERICAN immigrants. More commonly, however, white Americans turned violently on their nonwhite neighbors, as in PROVIDENCE, Rhode Island, where whites fought AFRICAN AMERICANS in 1824, and in CINCINNATI, Ohio, where whites drove African American residents out of the city in 1829. White

In 1968, a soldier stands guard on a deserted street in Washington, D.C., after riots caused a 4:00 P.M. curfew to be imposed. (*AP/Wide World Photos*)

violence was also occasionally directed against other ethnic groups. In the late nineteenth century it often involved native-born whites attacking different groups of ASIAN AMERICANS. In 1885, for example, white miners in ROCK SPRINGS, Colorado, killed eighty-five CHINESE mine workers. That same year white residents of TACOMA, Washington, turned against their Chinese neighbors. Until the mid-twentieth century, race riots were most commonly characterized by white Americans entering poor areas of cities to attack MINORITY GROUPS.

The Twentieth Century The changing economic conditions following U.S. involvement in WORLD WAR I contributed to a major race riot in EAST ST. LOUIS, Illinois, in 1917, when whites turned on the African American community. Similar racial violence arose in the early years of WORLD WAR II in DETROIT and CHICAGO. Not all this violence was directed against African Americans. In Los Angeles, for example, white servicemen attacked MEXICAN AMERICANS in what became known as the ZOOT SUIT RIOT of 1943.

During the years after World War II riots shifted in nature, with the subordinate group members more likely precipitating the violence in their own neighborhoods. While the earlier riots may have had more planning and premeditation, the major civil disorders of the 1960's and after were spontaneous outbreaks, usually touched off by incidents that were seemingly minor, compared to the anger they unleashed.

During the summers of 1960's cities from New York to Los Angeles and from Detroit to Memphis erupted repeatedly in racial violence. Most of these riots began following relatively minor incidents involving whites and African Americans. Such incidents typically brought to the surface anger arising from years of DISCRIMINATION and abuse. Most of the time when the violence was precipitated by the subordinate group against the dominant group, as was the case with the riots of the 1960's and after, the major underlying cause was racism. Years of prejudice and discrimination built up until an incident provided a spark. Frequently the police departments were made up almost entirely of members of the dominant group. Seen by whites as representing law and order, those same police were seen by African Americans and Latinos as representing repression and harassment.

Another way to examine the underlying causes of the 1960's riots is through television. A relatively new medium of entertainment during the 1960's, it reached nearly every household in the United States, no matter how poor or deprived. While its entertaining shows provided a chance to escape for a while, those same shows, and the commercials which sponsored them, also sent a message of prosperity and affluence. To those trapped in sweltering apartments in inner city neighborhoods it must have been difficult to watch other people live seemingly idyllic existences on television, while being bombarded by commercials promising a good life unattainable in the slum.

SUGGESTED READINGS:

Finkelman, Paul, ed. *Lynching, Racial Violence, and Law.* New York: Garland, 1992.

Gale, Dennis E. *Understanding Urban Unrest: From Reverend King to Rodney King.* Thousand Oaks, Calif.: Sage Publications, 1996.

Grimshaw, Allen D., ed. *Racial Violence in the United States.* Chicago: Aldine, 1969.

Kerner, Otto. *Report of the National Advisory Commission on Civil Disorders.* New York: New York Times Company, 1968.

Shapiro, Herbert. *White Violence and Black Response: From Reconstruction to Montgomery.* Amherst: University of Massachusetts Press, 1988.

—*Duncan R. Jamieson*

Racism

Belief in the innate superiority of one race over others; often used to justify discriminatory and oppressive practices directed at racial and ethnic minorities.

At its most basic level, the notion of human inequality and of the existence of "superior" and "inferior" races appears to have derived from human distrust and fear of people of different physical characteristics. Racism may be understood as a system of privilege for the dominant and allegedly superior racial group and of punishment for the subordinate and so-called inferior groups. Manifestations of racism range from overt, institutionalized variants involving genocide or enslavement of entire peoples to more subtle versions. In instances of the latter, members of certain races and their customs and habits are portrayed in stereotypical fashions, or in styles that lack sensitivity toward the cultural and behavioral qualities of the group. The history of Europe and the United States is replete with examples of racial oppression and persecution. Throughout the history of the United States, racism has appeared as a major obstacle to the various attempts to extend CIVIL RIGHTS and CIVIL LIBERTIES to all citizens.

Basic Assmptions Fundamental to all racist thinking is the belief that humankind consists of superior and inferior races and that much of human behavior is a function of a person's racial affinity. In the mind of the racist, physical differences are associated with differences in mental capacities. Therefore, the cultural and intellectual achievements of the various peoples of the world are seen as products of their racial qualities. Racist thinkers thus explain the creation of great empires and great scientific cultural achievements as expressions of the strength and vitality of a superior race. Likewise, the degraded political, social, and economic positions of racial and ethnic minorities are explained as the natural consequence of their inferior racial qualities. Similar arguments have been used in the United States to justify the denial of civil rights to AFRICAN AMERICANS and other minorities. Most racists also believe that race mixing will inevitably lead to a debasement of the superior race and ultimately to the decline of civilization. For that reason they consider it imperative that the purity of the superior race be maintained at all cost.

Race and Myth All racial thinking is based on the erroneous belief that "race" itself is a scientifically valid concept. Although this notion was accepted in some scientific circles in the nineteenth century, modern scientists have used the term "race" only in a narrow biological sense to denote groups of populations constituting the species *homo sapiens*. They point out that human genetic variability among the populations of Africa, Asia, and Europe is in fact not much greater than the genetic variability *within* these same populations. The only effective characteristics for race classification are anatomical and physiological, and there is no evidence that race mixture produces inferior progeny. Although in a biological sense humankind indeed consists of distinctive populations, there is no reliable evidence to suggest linkages between physical characteristics and mental capacities, and—by extension—cultural achievements. In view of the limited usefulness and the ambiguity of the term "race," the authors of the United Nations Educational, Scientific and Cultural Organization docu-

ment *The Race Concepts: Results of an Inquiry* (1950) suggested that the word be replaced by "ethnic group."

The term "race" as used by racial thinkers, in fact, is not so much a rational concept as a powerful myth, based often on fiction and on half-truths. One of the most dangerous racial myths, for example, is the notion of the existence of a superior "Aryan" race. This myth originated in the mistaken belief that a linguistic affinity between Sanskrit (the language of the sacred Hindu writings) and the languages of Western Europe constituted evidence of a biological relationship between the Arya people of India and the peoples of Western Europe. This myth became the inspiration for other similar myths, among them the Anglo-Saxon and the Nordic myths.

History of Racism Modern racism, and with it the discussion about higher and lower races, received a powerful stimulus from the European subjugation of large parts of Africa and Asia in the eighteenth and nineteenth centuries. Bewildered by the diversity of peoples in other parts of the world, European scientists and pseudo-scientists attempted to classify the various peoples of the world on the basis of a variety of physiological and anatomical characteristics. There was little consensus, however, and scientists at various times argued for the existence of from four to thirty-five different "races." The growing popularity of the concept of evolution, as popularized by the advocates of Social Darwinism, further fueled the debate during the late nineteenth century by suggesting that it was only natural that superior races should dominate weaker, inferior races.

Racial myths in the United States, notably the Anglo-Saxon and Nordic myths, came in handy in the defense of SLAVERY. Proclaiming the superiority of the "Nordic race," the amateur anthropologist Madison Grant warned in *The Passing of a Great Race* (1916) of the dangers of race mixture and advocated that African Americans be isolated in large colonies where they could be employed as laborers. Others, such as the publicist and lawyer Lothrop Stoddard, author of *Revolt Against Civilization: The Menace of the Under-Man* (1922), argued that racially inferior peoples threatened to destroy American civilization. Most followers of the Nordic myth warned against foreign IMMIGRATION, claiming that it would lead to a debasement of the American population. Racist ideas of that type often combined with anti-Semitic beliefs to provide ample ammunition for WHITE SUPREMACIST organizations, such as the KU KLUX KLAN and the American Nazi Party.

From Reconstruction to World War I The principal obstacle in the efforts to extend civil rights to all U.S. citizens was the notion that persons of color should not be entitled to the same rights and privileges as whites. While in the case of AMERICAN INDIANS white prejudice appears to have been more cultural than racial, the resulting policies were no less devastating. Considered a backward people by most whites, Native Americans found themselves removed to RESERVATIONS, where under a system of paternalistic tutelage they were denied even the elementary right of self-determination.

For African Americans the end of slavery did not result in the end of institutionalized racism. A wide variety of SEGREGATION policies and JIM CROW LAWS sought to nullify much of the progress they had made toward civil and political equality. By the same token, the activities of the Ku Klux Klan and other white supremacist organizations attested the continued existence of a virulent brand of racism. Still, the destruction of the power of southern slaveholding states and the ratification of the THIRTEENTH, FOURTEENTH, and FIFTEENTH AMENDMENTS to the U.S. CONSTITUTION laid the groundwork for a common national citizenship for African Americans and whites and, indirectly, for all other races. While the passage of the CIVIL RIGHTS ACT OF 1875 represented a high point in the struggle for civil rights, the U.S. SUPREME COURT declared the law unconstitutional in 1883. What followed was a long period of judicial retrenchment and congressional inactivity. In 1896 the U.S. Supreme Court, in PLESSY V. FERGUSON set a precedent for the SEPARATE-BUT-EQUAL PRINCIPLE that would remain valid for more than fifty years.

Among other groups which fell short of the Anglo-Saxon or Nordic norms, MEXICAN AMERICANS experienced widespread job discrimination as well as considerable POLICE BRUTALITY, especially in Texas and in California. Racial factors, in addition to economic factors, also affected the treatment of ASIAN AMERICANS. White laborers and small businessmen resented competition from CHINESE AMERICANS and fomented anti-Chinese riots that persuaded CONGRESS to pass the CHINESE EXCLUSION ACT OF 1882. In addition to the exclusionary provision, the act also declared Chinese residents of the United States ineligible for citizenship. JAPANESE AMERICANS experienced similar opposition from white labor groups and from white farmers who resented competition.

Racial prejudice was not confined to persons of color but also surfaced in response to a wave of white immigration from Southern and Central Europe in the late nineteenth century. The new arrivals—Italians, Greeks, Slavs, Germans, Jews, and ROMAN CATHOLICS—found themselves under attack from the American nativist movement. Traditional anti-Catholicism and anti-Semitism combined with the notion of the physical, mental, and moral inferiority of the newcomers to impart a conviction in nativist quarters that the new immigrants represented a threat to the United States.

From World War I to the 1960's The mass migration of African Americans from the South to the North that began during the decade of World War I, as well as the role of the United States in World War II, greatly affected racial attitudes in the twentieth century. Although African Americans could vote in the North, organize protests, and thus bring their political power to the attention of white politicians, their presence also generated animosities and helped in the revival of Ku Klux Klan activities. The resulting acts of VIOLENCE, including LYNCHINGS, were even directed against returning African American servicemen. The various programs of the New Deal of the 1930's may have helped indirectly to combat racism; however, it was largely the threat of a march on Washington, D.C., organized by African Americans that persuaded President Franklin D. Roosevelt to issue an executive order outlawing discrimination in defense industries and in government offices.

The fact that the United States was fighting World War II against avowedly racist regimes while its own army was racially segregated and thousands of American citizens had been deprived of their civil rights in the JAPANESE AMERICAN INTERNMENT called for a re-examination of the role of racism in American society. The grisly images of the Holocaust further dealt a serious blow to racist ideologies and contributed to renewed efforts by the executive and the judicial branches of the federal government to combat racism. Thus President Harry S TRUMAN's Committee on Civil Rights called for an end to segregation in American life while the president himself took steps to end segregation in the MILITARY.

At the same time, organizations such as the multiracial NATIONAL ASSOCIATION FOR THE ADVANCEMENT of Colored People (NAACP) and the younger Congress of Racial Equality made their impact felt. The 1950's also witnessed the rise to prominence of several African American leaders, among them Martin Luther King, Jr., and his Southern Christian Leadership Conference. Other nonwhite ethnic and racial minorities, such as Asian Americans, Native Americans, and Mexican Americans pursued equality and compensatory justice within their own civil rights movements. Despite a general decline in racist sentiment, the South, in particular, continued its segregationist policies.

The landmark Supreme Court decision in Brown v. Board of Education (1954), loudly decried by southern legislators, served as a milestone in the efforts of the Court to destroy the legacy of *Plessy v. Ferguson*. Its impact at the time, however, was limited. Generally, the presidency of Dwight D. Eisenhower was marked by complacency and governmental unwillingness to combat racism. Opposition from the political Right to an extension of civil rights to all Americans, however, provided the stimulus for the militancy of the 1960's, which was marked by sit-ins, freedom riders, and demonstrations such as the confrontations at Birmingham, Alabama, in April of 1963.

From the 1960's to the 1990's The most important turning point in the battle against racism came with the Civil Rights Act of 1964 and the Voting Rights Act of 1965. Through a skillful use of grants, a rapidly expanding federal government managed to obtain the cooperation of reluctant state and municipal governments in implementing the act while the newly created Equal Employment Opportunities Commission (EEOC) could pronounce on discriminatory practices. At the same time, however, concerns were voiced that some of the practices of the EEOC could lead to reverse discrimination.

By the late 1960's and the early 1970's Native American activists also called attention to the plight of their people by means of a series of demonstra-

Participants in a 1993 march commemorating the thirtieth anniversary of Martin Luther King, Jr.'s March on Washington stress the need to continue fighting against racism. (*AP/Wide World Photos*)

tions such as the takeover of ALCATRAZ ISLAND in 1969 and the seizure of the small town of WOUNDED KNEE on the Pine Ridge Reservation in South Dakota in 1973. Native American leaders voiced their concern over such issues as TERMINATION POLICY, while asking for an increase in congressional appropriations to a level enjoyed by other segments of American society. Asian Americans and Mexican Americans also benefited from the general decline in overt racism. Special restrictions on Asian immigration were removed and Latinos saw some improvement in the area of EMPLOYMENT DISCRIMINATION. The Civil Rights Act of 1964 made it illegal for employers to discriminate on the basis of national origin, while the Immigration Reform and Control Act of 1986 allowed for the legalization of certain undocumented immigrants.

The 1990's were marked by increasing popular awareness of the manifestations of racism in all aspects of public life. Renewed efforts to bring about a greater measure of equality through a variety of programs, such as AFFIRMATIVE ACTION, however, ran into considerable opposition, leaving the matter once again to the courts. Occasional outbreaks of racially motivated violence, the continued activities of white supremacist organizations, and other manifestations of racial discrimination supported the notion that racism remained endemic in many segments of American society.

SUGGESTED READINGS:

Montagu, Ashley. *Man's Most Dangerous Myth: The Fallacy of Race.* 5th ed. New York: Oxford University Press, 1974. Discourse on fallacies of racial thinking.

Myrdal, Gunnar. *An American Dilemma: The Negro Problem and Modern Democracy.* New York: Harper & Brothers, 1944. Exhaustive study of virtually all aspects of the problems of African Americans, exploring the contrast between American democratic ideals and the actual behavior of whites toward African Americans.

Poliakov, Leon. *The Aryan Myth: A History of Racist and Nationalist Ideas in Europe.* New York: New American Library, 1974. Traces the origins and evolution of the Aryan myth in the West and its relation to pseudo-scientific race theories.

Ropers, Richard H., and Dan J. Pence. *American Prejudice: With Liberty and Justice for Some.* New York: Plenum Press, 1995. Focuses on the pervasiveness of racism in American society and analyzes rationalizations for racism and prejudice.

Shipman, Pat. *The Evolution of Racism: Human Differences and the Use and Abuse of Science.* New York: Simon and Schuster, 1994. Excellent discussion of the history of evolution and of racism from the time of Charles Darwin to the present.

Sniderman, Paul M., and Thomas Piazza. *The Scar of Race.* Cambridge, Mass.: Belknap Press of Harvard University Press, 1993. Based on public opinion surveys during the 1980's and 1990's, this volume addresses the question of how Americans are dealing with the race issue and how it affects their political thinking.

Sowell, Thomas. *Race and Culture: A World View.* New York: Basic Books, 1994. Argues that existing internal cultural values of ethnic and racial minorities play a major role in determining their social status.

Takaki, Ronald T. *Iron Cages: Race and Culture in Nineteenth Century America.* New York: Alfred A. Knopf, 1979. Comparative analysis of the experience of African Americans, Native Americans, Mexicans, and Asians within a broad social, political, and economic context.

West, Cornel. *Race Matters.* Boston: Beacon Press, 1993. Collection of essays on topics such as black leadership, the new black conservatism, the legacy of Malcolm X, and racial reasoning.

—*Helmut J. Schmeller*

Ramírez, Henry M.

Born May 29, 1929, Walnut, Calif.: MEXICAN AMERICAN politician and officer in the U.S. COMMISSION ON CIVIL RIGHTS.

Henry Ramírez's civil rights activism dates back to the 1950's, when as a high school teacher he founded New Horizons, a program organized to steer young Chicanos away from street life and toward education. As the son of Mexican immigrants, and a former MIGRANT WORKER and aimless teenager himself, Ramírez had found his own way off the streets through education.

In 1968 Ramírez was appointed to the U.S. Commission on Civil Rights as director of its Mexican American Studies Division. Three years later he was appointed chairman of President Richard M. NIXON's Cabinet Committee on Opportunities for

Spanish-Speaking People. In this role, he was a visible Mexican American presence in Washington, a reminder to government authorities of the influence and needs of Spanish-speaking people. He continued to maintain contact with young people, encouraging them not to give up on their flawed but educable government.

—Cynthia A. Bily

Randolph, A. Philip

Apr. 15, 1889, Crescent City, Fla.—May 16, 1979, New York, N.Y.: AFRICAN AMERICAN labor leader and civil rights activist.

Often called the "father" of the modern CIVIL RIGHTS MOVEMENT, A. Philip Randolph was one of the first persons to link the African American struggle for civil rights with the battle over trade unionism. Randolph introduced a variety of tactics, ideological beliefs, and confrontational strategies that were later adopted by other civil rights leaders including Martin Luther KING, JR. As a labor leader, Randolph promoted the idea of economic self-sufficiency and legitimized the use of economic boycotts as a tactical weapon. His skills as a motivational and charismatic speaker demonstrated how civil rights leaders could utilize the power of public opinion to garner support for racial equality. His success in pursuing a nonviolent approach to change persuaded others to work within the American judicial and legislative systems. Most importantly, however, Randolph was willing to accept financial and political support from white liberals, but he convinced many prominent African American leaders that they should not rely on white activists, but instead, that they themselves should assume full responsibility for the leadership and direction of the Civil Rights movement.

The Formative Years Born in Florida, Randolph enjoyed many benefits not available to most African American youths. His father, a preacher, was an outspoken critic of southern SEGREGATION, and both his parents insisted that their sons obtain good educations and develop a strong sense of racial pride. Randolph and his brother, James, learned to read before entering school, and their parents constantly reminded them that they should never accept the belief that African Americans were second-class citizens. James died young, but the training Randolph received from his parents paved the way for his future success as a civil rights leader.

In 1903 Randolph entered the prestigious Cookman Institute in Jacksonville, Florida. After graduation, he became increasingly frustrated since African Americans were only being hired for manual labor positions in the South. He spent several summers in New York attempting to find a better job, and in 1911 he resettled in the city. Yet as numerous southern blacks would discover, emigration to the North did not always produce financial success or political equality. Randolph could only find jobs as a waiter, elevator operator, or porter. These experiences convinced him to become actively involved in labor organizations. He helped form an Elevator and Switchboard Operators Union and became involved with socialist political causes. In 1913 he married Lucille Campbell Greene, who introduced him to another African American activist, Chandler Owen. Over the following decade Owen and Randolph would emerge as the leading black intellectuals in New York. Both men became members of the Socialist Party and embraced Marxist doctrines. In November, 1917, they founded a magazine called *The Messenger* and began a systematic attack upon black leaders who relied on white liberals.

After the United States entered WORLD WAR I in 1917, Randolph and Owen accepted the Socialist Party's stance that workers should not fight since the war only benefitted rich capitalist interests. *The Messenger* argued that African American workers should not fight to make the world safe for democracy since they had been denied democracy at home. Throughout the war, both men labored for black unionism and the Socialist Party, and in 1920 Randolph was the party's candidate for state comptroller. By the mid-1920's however, the Socialist Party had come under vicious attacks from the state attorney general's office, and *The Messenger* faced bankruptcy. However, Randolph's wartime experiences firmly established him as the leading spokesperson for African American unionism in the 1920's.

The Brotherhood of Sleeping Car Porters In August, 1925, Randolph assumed leadership of the Brotherhood of Sleeping Car Porters (BSCP), whose members performed domestic chores on railroads. The Pullman Company, which employed more than twelve thousand African American men as porters, enjoyed a positive reputation among many prominent African Americans because it was the largest employer of African Americans in the United States. Pullman's reputation only improved after it granted porters a wage increase in 1924; however, a small group of respected porters in New York concluded that true economic equality could only occur if the porters rejected their dependence upon Pullman's company union and organized an independent trade union. Uncertain of their own leadership abilities and afraid that trade union activity might cost them their jobs, they needed a leader who could not be disciplined by the Pullman Company. Aware of Randolph's record of economic radicalism and his work with *The Messenger*, the porters selected him as their general organizer; for the next twelve years, Randolph devoted his life to the BSCP.

During this period, Randolph built a national organization with local BSCP chapters located throughout the country. While he left rank-and-file recruitment work to his lieutenants, he demonstrated all of the outstanding characteristics of a charismatic leader. His confidence and persistence kept the union alive. Although its membership remained limited and opposition continued to mount, Randolph exuded confidence and never wavered in his commitment to African American unionism and economic equality.

Randolph overcame numerous obstacles in his struggle to gain recognition for the BSCP as the sole legitimate collective bargaining agent for the sleeping car porters. He had to overcome the strength of Pullman's company union—the Employees Representation Plan (ERP). He had to counterbalance the muscle of Pullman's financial resources that could purchase support from African American NEWSPAPERS and politicians. He also had to overcome a lack of African American interest in trade unionism generally, as well as the racist attitudes of white labor leaders and counter the conservative advice given by prominent black leaders who relied on white paternalism. Moreover, Randolph had constantly to struggle for funding because few BSCP members could afford to pay union dues. Finally, he had to protect union members who faced acts of physical terror and termination for joining the BSCP. Through all this Randolph persevered. Viewing his union as a civil rights campaign, as well as a labor organization, Randolph used the BSCP to focus national attention on African American civil rights and racial injustice.

A. Philip Randolph in 1937, around the time that the Pullman Company finally recognized the Brotherhood of Sleeping Car Porters. (*Schomburg Center for Research in Black Culture, New York Public Library*)

Randolph had three goals for his union: to convince Pullman to accept it as the sole collective bargaining agent for its porters and maids, to win the union's acceptance and recognition from white labor leaders, and to establish himself as a national figure and thereby gain support from key black leaders and organizations. He achieved some early success when the NATIONAL ASSOCIATION FOR THE ADVANCEMENT OF COLORED PEOPLE (NAACP) endorsed the BSCP and granted it some financial support in 1925. The NAACP's secretary James Weldon JOHNSON often spoke at BSCP meetings, and its prominent intellectual leader, W. E. B. DU BOIS, often promoted Randolph's cause in the NAACP journal, *The Crisis*. Maintaining that the Pullman company was guilty of a national conspiracy to undermine the BSCP, Du Bois attacked the company for firing BSCP members and charged that it was steadily victimizing porters with its oppressive practices. Although the BSCP remained a struggling, nearly bankrupt union, the NAACP's endorsement, coupled with Du Bois' vehement defense, helped establish Randolph's legitimacy in the African American community.

In 1927 Randolph acquired another ally when a leading black newspaper, the CHICAGO DEFENDER, reversed its position and sanctioned the BSCP. Randolph had courted the *Defender* since 1925 and considered its blessing vital for his cause. At times he boasted that the BSCP would eventually destroy the paper and its editor-owner, Robert S. Abbott. It appears that the *Defender* ended its opposition to Randolph only after it lost financial backing from Pullman. Although other black newspapers continued to criticize Randolph, the *Defender*'s endorsement furthered Randolph's quest for legitimacy.

Another success occurred in 1929 when the American Federation of Labor (AFL) granted the BSCP several local charters in its organization. Randolph was disappointed by the AFL's refusal to grant the BSCP national recognition, but its limited affiliation with the AFL allowed Randolph to present his agenda at AFL national conventions and helped him develop relationships with other leaders in the national labor movement. In 1932 United Mine Workers president John L. Lewis got his union to pass a resolution at its annual meeting that provided the BSCP with financial contributions from the AFL. Although Randolph still faced significant opposition from other white labor leaders, he had begun to pave the way for the BSCP's eventual full incorporation into the AFL.

Randolph's greatest problem remained the strength of the ERP and Pullman's ability to intimidate porters. Most porters were unreceptive to unionism and believed that their best chance for advancement rested with the ERP. Throughout the 1920's Pullman granted minor wage and benefit concessions to the porters; Randolph maintained that these improvements resulted from BSCP pressure, but many porters disagreed. Workers who joined the union, moreover, faced physical terror.

For example, porter J. H. Wilkins of Kansas City was forcibly removed from his train and lynched in Georgia in 1930. With NAACP support, Randolph arranged mass protest demonstrations after Wilkins' lynching, but most porters naturally were afraid of becoming victims of similar VIOLENCE. Consequently, BSCP membership steadily dropped from a high of 4,632 in 1928 to 658 in 1933.

Meanwhile, however, the BSCP benefitted significantly from the election of Franklin D. Roosevelt and the introduction of New Deal legislation in 1933. The following year CONGRESS passed the Amended Railway Labor Act that outlawed the ERP. While the Pullman company challenged this law in the courts, Randolph secured federal mediation. In 1935 the majority of porters selected the BSCP as its bargaining agent. Following a successful certification election, the union was welcomed into the AFL. When the U.S. SUPREME COURT upheld the Railway Act in 1937, Pullman was forced to negotiate with the BSCP. On August 25, 1937—twelve years to the day after the BSCP was founded—Randolph signed a collective bargaining agreement with Pullman.

The March on Washington Movement The coming of WORLD WAR II in Europe helped carry American industry out of its Great Depression slump. An abundance of new jobs was created in the defense industry, but African Americans initially failed to benefit from the wartime prosperity. Following the passage of the Selective Service Act in September, 1940, Randolph led a group of black leaders to Washington to discuss this issue with President Roosevelt. Convinced that the White House was offering only symbolic promises, Randolph threatened to lead more than 100,000 African Americans in a mass march on Washington to protest unfair labor practices and segregation in the MILITARY. After all, he argued, why should African Americans be subjected to the draft when they could not get high-paying jobs at home and were denied the same rights as white soldiers.

By March, 1941, Randolph's plans for his March on Washington movement were generating great concern in Washington. Roosevelt realized that it would be disastrous for the United States if racial tensions were to erupt at home while it was attacking Hitler's racial policies abroad. As a result, Roosevelt issued EXECUTIVE ORDER 8802 and created the wartime Fair Employment Practices Committee (FEPC) that outlawed racial discrimination in defense industries. Although he failed to eliminate segregation in the armed forces, Randolph's actions produced significant economic gains for African Americans during the war. By the end of 1944 almost two million African Americans were working in defense factories, shipyards, and steel mills. Although many black workers were unable to gain access to skilled training, Randolph's pressure tactics led to several mass rallies, and the FEPC conducted several public hearings and reviewed thousands of complaints during the war.

This action also firmly established Randolph as a leading civil rights leader. His tactics of nonviolent CIVIL DISOBEDIENCE and mass protest were ultimately adopted by a host of postwar leaders, including Martin Luther KING, JR. Randolph helped shape the postwar agenda that called for the full implementation of the FOURTEENTH and FIFTEENTH AMENDMENTS to the Constitution and the end of JIM CROW practices in America. His March on Washington movement convinced other black leaders that, with the emergence of the African American urban working class during World War II, unprecedented victories could be attained in the postwar Civil Rights movement.

Modern Civil Rights Activist Randolph remained one of the key figures in the Civil Rights movement until his health failed in the late 1960's. He was actively involved in ending segregation in the armed forces during the Korean War, he helped desegregate southern schools following the Supreme Court's *Brown v. Board of Education* decision in 1954, and he convinced the Democratic Party to allow King to speak before its national convention in 1956. He worked with King through the 1950's; both men met with President Dwight D. EISENHOWER to discuss civil rights in 1958, and they picketed the 1960 Democratic Convention to protest presidential candidate John F. KENNEDY's ineffective civil rights record.

Randolph and King's most important collaboration culminated in the 1963 MARCH ON WASHINGTON. Selected to head the march, both Randolph and King coordinated their efforts in order to mobilize support for President Kennedy's pending civil rights legislation. While this event is often remembered for King's rousing "I HAVE A DREAM" SPEECH, Randolph also inspired the marchers with his own "Tribute to Women" speech. Revealing his progressive stance on gender issues, Randolph acknowledged the efforts of women activists such as Rosa

PARKS and he invited Marian Anderson and Mahalia Jackson to sing at the event. Randolph's and King's contributions to the event helped lead to Congress' passage of the CIVIL RIGHTS ACT OF 1964 and the VOTING RIGHTS ACT OF 1965, which finally guaranteed African Americans the rights granted in the Fourteenth and Fifteenth Amendments to the Constitution.

Aware of the fact that he was nearing the end of his career, Randolph founded the A. Philip Randolph Institute in 1964. He was pleased with the civil rights legislation that followed the March on Washington but understood that African Americans still had to fight for its implementation. Through his institute, he hoped to promote black labor activity and to further African American political power through voter registration drives. In 1968 because of failing health, he resigned as president of the BSCP and retired from the AFL-CIO executive council. He died in 1979; ten years later his face appeared on a U.S. postage stamp honoring Black Heritage Month.

SUGGESTED READINGS:

Anderson, Jervis. *A. Philip Randolph: A Biographical Portrait.* New York: Harcourt Brace Jovanovich, 1972.

Branch, Taylor. *Parting the Waters: America in the King Years, 1954-1963.* New York: Simon & Schuster, 1988.

Davis, Daniel S. *Mr. Black Labor: The Story of A. Philip Randolph, Father of the Civil Rights Movement.* New York: E. P. Dutton, 1972.

Harris, William H. *Keeping the Faith: A. Philip Randolph, Milton P. Webster, and the Brotherhood of Sleeping Car Porters, 1925-37.* Urbana: University of Illinois Press, 1977; reprint ed., 1991.

Pfeffer, Paula A. *A. Philip Randolph, Pioneer of the Civil Rights Movement.* Baton Rouge: Louisiana State University Press, 1990.

—*Robert D. Ubriaco, Jr.*

Rankin, Jeannette

June 11, 1880, near Missoula, Mont.—May 18, 1973, Carmel, Calif.: American WOMEN'S RIGHTS activist, pacifist, and first woman member of CONGRESS.

Rankin's place in the history of women's rights was secured in 1916 upon her election to the U.S.

Jeannette Rankin accepting an award from the National Organization for Women in 1972, a year before she died. (*Betty Lane*)

House of Representatives as its first female member. A Republican from Montana, she initially served one term, during which she voted against U.S. entry into WORLD WAR I. After winning a second term in 1940 she maintained her strong pacifist stance by being the only representative to vote against declaring war on Japan in December, 1941. She later also actively opposed the Vietnam War.

—*M. Casey Diana*

Raza Unida Party, La

MEXICAN AMERICAN rights organization founded in 1970.

Dissatisfied with both the Democratic and Republican political parties, Mexican Americans conceived of an alternative party to express the political aspirations of their people—La Raza Unida Party. It was organized primarily by the efforts of José Angel Gutierrez in 1970. Through its efforts Mexican Americans were elected for the first time to positions on the school board and city council of Crystal City, Texas. In June, 1972, the party held its first national convention.

Perhaps the party's most notable achievement occurred in the 1972 Texas gubernatorial election. La Raza Unida Party put forth a gubernatorial candidate, Ramsey Muniz, who received more than 214,000 votes. Although this figure constituted only a little more than 6 percent of the entire statewide vote, it caused the Democratic Party to win its narrowest victory ever over a Republican candidate. Moreover, in 1977 La Raza Unida helped defeat an immigration reform bill proposed by President Jimmy CARTER's administration. After the party's influence peaked during the 1970's, it waned considerably.

—*Michael R. Candelaria*

Reagan, Ronald

Born Feb. 6, 1911, Tampico, Ill.: Fortieth PRESIDENT of the United States (1981-1989).

A former governor of California, Ronald Reagan frequently voiced support for equal opportunity and civil rights while he was president of the United States during the 1980's. However his legislative and administrative records indicate his opposition to an active federal government role in pro-

moting and expanding civil rights. He appointed members of the EQUAL EMPLOYMENT OPPORTUNITY COMMISSION (EEOC) and other equal employment opportunity and civil rights bodies who were at best weak supporters of EEOC AFFIRMATIVE ACTION policies and were sometimes vocal opponents. Reagan's policy emphasis during his eight years in office was greater state and local responsibility for public decisions of all kinds, including affirmative action. Whether his intent was simply to pass decision-making authority onto state and local officials or to eliminate the policies by entrusting them to people who were not supporters is uncertain. Whatever his motives, the impact of his policies was a general lessening of support for equal employment opportunity and affirmative action programs.

—*William L. Waugh, Jr.*

Real estate boards

Community bodies that coordinate local real estate practices among real estate agents and government agencies.

Mortgage bankers, real estate developers, and local government officials have long organized real estate boards to coordinate community plans for economic development, review proposed changes in zoning laws, and support a healthy business climate. Such boards have also often served as agents of racial SEGREGATION when community leaders have sought to maintain the racial status quo. In the past especially informal agreements among board members promoted practices such as fostering RESTRICTIVE COVENANTS, "redlining," which limited certain groups of prospective buyers to specific neighborhoods, and "blockbusting." Blockbusting is achieved when real estate agents conspire artificially to inflate selling prices of houses, while moving as many minority families into a neighborhood as possible. Once a block has a majority of minority home owners, the market prices of its homes abruptly plummet, making it unlikely that its new owners will ever be able to resell them for as much as they paid for them. By the 1990's reforms in the regulation of real estate brokers prohibited many past discriminatory practices, but real estate boards could still provide the means by which unethical brokers could circumvent the law.

—*Nancy Farm Mannikko*

Reconstruction era

1866-1877: Period after the CIVIL WAR during which the Union government controled the defeated South and attempted to extend full civil rights to the region's AFRICAN AMERICANS

During the Civil War 170,000 African Americans fought on the side of the northern states against the Confederacy. The THIRTEENTH AMENDMENT freed the slaves in 1865. After northern victory, institutions and state governments were established in the South with the purpose of institutionalizing the end of the rebellion. One aspect the North's policy was to institutionalize the freedom of the African Americans of the South. Abraham LINCOLN's difficult policy of magnanimity came to an end after his assassination. John Wilkes Booth, after fatally wounding Lincoln, leaped onto the stage of the Ford Theater and shouted in Latin "Thus always with tyrants." The assassination inflamed northern passions to punish and change the South. Revelations of the Andersonville prison camp also raised a fury in the North. Union prisoners had been treated cruelly by southern captors, with the result that the camp commander and several other subordinates were hanged in the northern capital. Lincoln had argued earlier that the South had never left the Union and that the Civil War was really an illegal rebellion waged by disloyal, selfish interests. Lincoln believed that once loyal governments were restored and the South recognized the end of slavery, then the wounds would be healed and an attempt toward establishing equality could begin. With Lincoln's death, however, most Republicans decided that the South would have to be remade or reconstructed.

The FOURTEENTH AMENDMENT to the Constitution was ratified in 1868. This amendment was ratified in order to unite the nation on the basis of freedom of speech, liberty to travel and seek work, and equal citizenship for all regardless of race. Also important was the establishment of the FREEDMEN'S BUREAU in 1865. The Freedmen's Bureau had a mandate to ease the transition from slavery by providing food, transportation, shelter, pieces of land, and whatever it took to aid African Americans in the transition from slavery to equality.

Johnson and the Republicans The presidency of Andrew Johnson was highly significant for the Reconstruction era. He was a Democrat from Tennessee and the only senator from the South to remain loyal to the federal government. Therefore Lincoln made him vice president in 1864 despite Johnson's racist views. Johnson was of humble origins; he had made good by attacking the planter class, claiming that they were responsible for the South seceding from the nation. Johnson always remained a southerner at heart who feared that Republicans and their industrial supporters would ruin southern culture. Therefore Johnson began to issue many pardons to wealthy upper-class southerners, who had some time before learned how to flatter him, and appealed to his insecurities. Johnson also let new governments form in the

Key Events of the Reconstruction Era

1865	Thirteenth Amendment, abolishing slavery, is ratified; Union government creates the Freedmen's Bureau; Ku Klux Klan is organized in Tennessee.
1866	Congress passes the Civil Rights Act of 1866; forerunner of Fisk University is founded for black students in Nashville, Tennessee.
1867	Congress passes the first Reconstruction Act, dividing the former Confederacy into five military districts and imposing military governors.
1867	Ku Klux Klan holds its first national convention in Nashville, Tennessee.
1867	Federal government opens forerunner of Howard University for blacks in Washington, D.C.
1868	Fourteenth Amendment, granting former slaves full citizenship, is ratified.
1869	First of twenty-two black African Americans to serve in Congress between 1869 and 1880 enters the House of Representatives.
1870	Fifteenth Amendment, guaranteeing that no American citizen can be denied the right to vote on the basis of race or previous servitude, is ratified.
1870	Congress passes the Enforcement Act to impose criminal sanctions on violations of the Fifteenth Amendment.
1873	U.S. Supreme Court rules that the Fourteenth Amendment's due process clause does not protect rights under state laws in the *Slaughterhouse Cases*.
1875	Congress passes a sweeping civil rights act outlawing segregation in public accommodations and transportation and guaranteeing African Americans the right to serve in juries.
1876	Disputed presidential election of Rutherford B. Hayes triggers the end of the Reconstruction era.
1877	Northern Republicans and southern Democrats work out a compromise that permits the uncontested inauguration of Rutherford B. Hayes.
1877	After Hayes is inaugurated he withdraws the last Union troops from the South, formally ending Reconstruction.

South under very loose regulations. Alexander Stephens, for example, was given a pardon and allowed to be elected senator to the national legislature although he had been the vice president of the Confederacy. The South responded to Johnson's leniency by enacting the infamous BLACK LAWS. The black laws placed free African Americans into a position closely resembling slavery. Blacks could not vote, interracial marriages were forbidden, segregated facilities became specified for the first time on a legal basis, and African Americans could not assemble after sunset. To provide the planters with a labor force, the black laws maintained that vagrants or the unemployed could be arrested and put to work. Normally, local sheriffs enforced the black laws against African Americans and rarely bothered whites who broke the laws against, for example, vagrancy. Thus the Reconstruction era was a mix of northern attempts (some half-hearted) at being punitive, at providing for the welfare of the newly

freed, and at mending fences, and of concerted southern efforts to reassert local control and to deny blacks their civil rights.

Sharecropping began to replace slave labor. This happened partially because blacks did not have the cash to buy land or supplies. They wanted to remain on the land of the planters in return for favorable conditions. Satisfied to have the same labor force as before, the planters and smaller agriculturalists encouraged blacks to stay on in return for unsatisfactory conditions that almost resembled slavery. For example, liens were taken out on crops, of which nearly two-thirds went to the landowners. It became very difficult for sharecroppers to leave plantations and farms even if they had the means, because sharecroppers were generally deeply in debt to their landlords and were, by the black codes, subject to arrest and return if they attempted to flee their debts.

Congress soon began to take issue with Johnson's

More than twenty African Americans were elected to Congress during Reconstruction, but after Reconstruction ended black representation virtually disappeared. (*Associated Publishers*)

policies. In early 1866, Johnson informed Congress that all the southern states were ready to rejoin the Union. Radical Republicans, many of whom had been abolitionists before the Civil War, protested Johnson's policies as being intended to, in his words, "keep the South a white man's country." Radical Republicans began to spread rumors that the president was a drunk. Others claimed that Johnson and his son were picking up prostitutes and bringing them to the White House. In July, 1866, Congress enlarged and expanded the scope of the Freedmen's Bureau, a problack federal organization, over Johnson's veto. The Freedmen's Bureau built schools, hospitals, and other public facilities. More than 450,000 sick people of both races were treated in Freedmen's Bureau hospitals. The new agency also intervened into labor disputes so that former slaves might be paid fairly and work under better conditions. Nearly 250,000 African Americans were attending school soon after the bureau began its efforts, and new universities established specifically for African Americans also opened. The Freedmen's Bureau was the largest federal agency ever established and thus was a controversial issue in an era when the national government still maintained a relatively small presence in social matters.

Johnson, meanwhile, successfully led ten of the eleven southern states in not accepting the Fourteenth Amendment. The president's attitude resulted in the amendment being blocked from ratification until 1868. Radical Republicans convinced northern voters that Johnson's position as well as the hostile attitude of the South meant that the Civil War was not over. The result was that the Republicans triumphed during the congressional elections of the fall of 1866. Republicans also won all the gubernatorial elections as well as two-thirds of the Congress.

Congressional Reconstruction With enough votes to override a presidential veto, the Republican Congress declared that the government in every southern state except Tennessee was illegal. Furthermore, the South would have to be returned to outright military rule. Congress created five military districts in which Union generals exercised power. The main concern of the northern generals was that the South write new state constitutions. The new constitutions would contain provisions that would enable African Americans to take part in elections. Constitutional conventions were legally committed to enacting laws that would officially give the vote to blacks and that would ratify the Fourteenth Amendment. When a majority of registered voters did not turn out to ratify the constitutions, Congress changed election laws so that new constitutions could be written regardless of how small voter turnout was. Blacks participated but formed the majority of a constitutional convention in only one state, South Carolina. The constitutions written at this time usually were copied from northern models. They were a notable advance in terms of civil rights in America because the new constitutions allowed African Americans to take part in elections and established equality before the law. Southern governments, as a result of their new constitutions, became committed to the construction of hospitals and asylums, relief to the poor, and aid to the handicapped. The first divorce laws soon were passed and women received property rights. The new constitutions initiated prison reform as well as tax reform on an equitable basis. Uncultivated land was put on the market. Appointive offices now became elective so as to eliminate oligarchies. Other reforms inspired by the new constitutions were public works programs, which resulted in the construction of harbors, roads, and bridges. State-supported education also brought solid results. A huge project to build new public schools resulted in African American school attendance increasing to forty percent by the 1880's.

By 1870, all southern states were allowed to return to the Union legally by sending in elected congressional representatives and senators. Two African Americans served in the national senate and twenty were elected to congress.

Not all the reforms were executed perfectly. Although southerners would later consider Republican rule during Reconstruction a horror story, the shortcomings were exaggerated greatly in traditional histories. Carpetbaggers, usually Union army veterans and northern opportunists, arrived in the South for postwar political and economic profit. White southerners who cooperated with the northerners were called scalawags. Scalawags were normally poor southern whites who cooperated with the Reconstruction governments to get land from weakened planters or to settle personal scores. The basic fear of most southerners was that of blacks becoming organized politically. The resentment against scalawags and carpetbaggers, therefore, took on a highly emotional tone, although many carpetbaggers and scalawags had few direct interests in the situation of African Americans. Another resentment was the corruption that took place in most southern governments. It should be kept in mind that the national government was plagued by corruption as well. Southerners tended to overlook the fact that blacks did not control any of the southern governments during Reconstruction.

In Louisiana, congressmen voted themselves hams and bottles of champagne to go along with inflated stationery allowances. South Carolina voted one thousand dollars to its speaker of the house so that he could pay his losses at the horse tracks. On the whole, however, Reconstruction governments achieved positive results in the area of public services.

The Tilden-Hayes Election Congress passed a Tenure of Office Act in March, 1867, which prohibited the president from removing officials appointed with the advice as well as consent of the senate without that body's approval. This was done to keep reconstruction officials on the job. Republicans feared that Johnson would interfere with the pace of civil rights reform. When Johnson caught secretary of war Stanton conniving with Congress, Stanton was fired. Congress then attempted to impeach Johnson in 1868 but the vote was one short of the necessary two-thirds for conviction. Ulysses S. Grant then won the 1868 presidential election with the help of African American voters awarded the franchise because of the FIFTEENTH AMENDMENT.

Another vital piece of Reconstruction civil rights legislation, the Fifteenth Amendment forbids any state from depriving citizens of their right to vote. Ratified in 1870, the Fifteenth Amendment prohibits the denial of suffrage because of race, color, or previous condition of servitude. Famous for his drinking and bluntness, Grant was a successful general who had led his troops to victory. As president, however, he appointed yes-men who heaped praise on the president while looting the national treasury. Enormously popular in the North, Grant once received $100,000 from the city of New York for winning the Civil War. As the corruption was revealed, Grant's popularity declined. The Democrats found they had a chance of winning after they nominated Samuel J. Tilden, a young and dynamic reformer. His opponent was Rutherford B. Hayes, a Union general who was dull and uninspiring.

In the 1876 presidential election, Hayes was proclaimed the winner after a questionable election. Tilden unquestionably received more popular votes but the Republicans claimed that votes in Florida, South Carolina, and Louisiana were fraudulent, with the result that a Republican victory in each of the three states was granted. This shaky procedure enabled Hayes to have an electoral majority, and a phony commission upheld the Republican victory. Southern politicians protested strongly and demanded a public recounting of the votes in the three disputed states, which certainly would have resulted in Hayes's losing. Therefore, a deal was made between the parties that Hayes could be president in return for Union troops' being pulled out of the South in early 1877. Hayes kept his word and the departure of the federal troops resulted in an effective end of Reconstruction throughout the South.

VIOLENCE AND TERRORISM and KU KLUX KLAN intimidation ended any opposition to a Democratic takeover. Northerners had begun to lose interest in Reconstruction, instead becoming fascinated with the westward expansion and industrialization. Democrats quickly acted to severely limit the civil rights of African Americans throughout the South.

Results of Reconstruction The Republicans brought reform to the South; when they left, there was a backlash. The redemptionists were Democrats who appealed to whites by promising a return to something akin to the antebellum years. Discrimination became blatant against African Americans as well as MEXICAN AMERICANS. LYNCHINGS were rarely investigated. Segregation became official with the JIM CROW LAWS. POLL TAXES discouraged voter participation, especially by the poor. The South stagnated politically and economically. Democrats controlled the region until the 1960's.

SUGGESTED READINGS:

Foner, Eric. *Reconstruction: America's Unfinished Revolution, 1863-1877.* New York: Alfred A. Knopf, 1988.

Litwack, Leon. *Been in the Storm So Long: The Aftermath of Slavery.* New York: Random House, 1979.

McPherson, James M. *Ordeal by Fire: The Civil War and Reconstruction.* New York: Random House, 1982.

Moneyhon, Carl. *Republicanism and Reconstruction Texas.* Austin: University of Texas Press, 1979.

—Douglas W. Richmond

Redress movement

1976-1986; Campaign to win REPARATIONS from the federal government for JAPANESE AMERICAN INTERNMENT during WORLD WAR II.

The redress movement—or reparation movement, as it was originally called—began on the West Coast during the late 1960's, when a few JAPANESE AMERICANS called for restitution for their internment during World War II. The JAPANESE AMERICAN CITIZENS LEAGUE (JACL) decided to press for CONGRESS to create a commission to study the issue and make recommendations. After the government completed such a study, members of JACL would

The redress movement was undertaken to fight for compensation for the wrongs suffered by Japanese Americans forcibly removed from their homes and deprived of their civil rights during World War II. (*National Archives*)

be able approach Congress for redress measures themselves.

Many Japanese Americans were undecided on what goals to set, if any. Some thought that asking for a specific dollar figure in reparations payments would merely trivialize the suffering they had endured because of internment. Others thought that even asking for redress would be a disgrace. In 1970 the JACL passed the first of three resolutions calling for reparations. In 1974 the organization designated the reparations question as its highest priority and created the NATIONAL COMMITTEE FOR REDRESS. At the conclusion of their 1978 convention in Salt Lake City, Utah, the JACL unanimously passed a resolution that $25,000 should be paid to each internee or their heirs. Meanwhile, Japanese Americans who disagreed with the JACL's approach formed several other redress organizations, including the NATIONAL COUNCIL FOR JAPANESE AMERICAN REDRESS and the NATIONAL COALITION FOR REDRESS/ REPARATIONS.

—Larry N. Sypolt

Reed v. Reed

1971: U.S. SUPREME COURT decision that began an era of heightened scrutiny in SEX DISCRIMINATION cases by declaring, "to give a mandatory preference to members of either sex over members of the other, merely [for administrative convenience] is to make the very kind of arbitrary legislative choice forbidden by the EQUAL PROTECTION CLAUSE of the Fourteenth Amendment."

After Sally Reed and Cecil Reed were divorced, each of them filed a petition seeking to administer the estate of their adoptive son, Richard, who had died without a will in Ada County, Idaho. A probate court appointed Cecil Reed administrator of the estate, following Idaho statutes that placed mothers and fathers in the same class, while requiring that in choosing among members of the same class, "males must be preferred to females." Sally Reed appealed the decision, asserting that Idaho's preference for male administrators violated the EQUAL PROTECTION CLAUSE of the U.S. Constitution.

U.S. courts had historically treated sex discrimination by states as permissible, so long as there was some kind of rational basis for such behavior. Consistent with precedent, Idaho's supreme court upheld the statute, noting that it had the advantages of reducing workloads of probate courts, eliminat-

ing hearings, helping to avoid intrafamily controversy. The court also concluded that the law was reasonable in assuming that men were likely to make better estate administrators because they were more likely to be sophisticated in business affairs. After Sally Reed took her case to the U.S. Supreme Court, in *Reed v. Reed*, the Court purported to apply the traditional "rational-basis" test. Although Idaho's supreme court had set forth a rational basis for the states discriminatory statute, a unanimous U.S. Supreme Court rejected that basis as insufficient on November 22, 1971.

The ruling articulated no new standard, but it clearly departed from the traditional analysis by making "rational basis" a more difficult standard to meet. Five years later, in *Craig v. Boren* the Court recognized that a higher standard had been set in *Reed v. Reed* and it formally adopted an intermediate level of scrutiny for sex-based classifications challenged under the equal protection clause.

—Craig W. Allin and Elizabeth A. Sparks

Rehabilitation Act of 1973

1973: Federal law prohibiting DISCRIMINATION on the basis of disability in federally funded activities.

Often called the "declaration of independence," "BILL OF RIGHTS" or "gateway to equality" for all Americans with disabilities, Section 504 of the Rehabilitation Act of 1973 was the first federal law guaranteeing full CIVIL RIGHTS protections in all areas of life for people with disabilities. President Gerald Ford delegated responsibility for implementing Section 504 to the Department of Health, Education, and Welfare. Regulations were drafted through the Office for Civil Rights, but were only signed into law in April, 1977, after a nationwide demonstration led by the AMERICAN COALITION OF CITIZENS WITH DISABILITIES.

—Gerald S. Argetsinger

Reitman v. Mulkey

1967: U.S. SUPREME COURT decision striking down a California referendum designed to abolish HOUSING DISCRIMINATION.

By upholding the opinion of California's supreme court, which had found repeal of the state's fair housing code to be unconstitutional, the U.S. Supreme Court reaffirmed the principle of equity in housing opportunity. In 1964 Californians voted by a 2-1 majority to repeal their state's fair housing code, known as the Rumford Act. This action—which many observers labeled evidence of the white backlash against the increasingly vocal black CIVIL RIGHTS MOVEMENT—was immediately challenged in the courts. However, it took three years to resolve. Even after the U.S. Supreme Court's 1967 decision, Republican governor Ronald REAGAN, an opponent of open housing laws, encouraged state lawmakers to draft legislation permitting racial discrimination in housing. It would take passage of the federal Fair Housing Act of 1968 to halt state efforts to permit discrimination based on race.

—*Nancy Farm Mannikko*

Religion, freedom of

Fundamental right guaranteed by the FIRST AMENDMENT to the U.S. CONSTITUTION, but containing indirect limitations due to an inconsistent history of judicial interpretations of that right.

The right of religious freedom has long been considered one of the most fundamental and cherished rights of American citizens, justly deserving its place as the first enumerated (or specifically named) right in the Constitution's BILL OF RIGHTS. Surveys of general public opinion have consistently shown throughout American history that religious freedom is valued more than any other right, including those of free speech and free press, which follow it within the text of the First Amendment. The opportunity to practice one's religion freely and openly has continually been named as a chief reason why persons of all religious persuasions have left their native lands for the American shores, and thus the history of America itself is in large part the story of a multiplicity of religious traditions taking root in American soil. To speak of religious

The First Amendment

Congress shall make no law respecting an establishment of religion, or prohibiting the free exercise thereof; or abridging the freedom of speech, or of the press, or the right of the people peaceably to assemble, and to petition the Government for a redress of grievances.

freedom, however, either as an "absolute" right which may never be violated, or to characterize American history as having safeguarded this right from its beginnings is to claim more than the record itself is able to bear.

Colonial Attitudes Concerning Religious Establishment The first settlers in British North America were interested not so much in maintaining freedom of religion as purity of religion. The Puritans of Plymouth and Massachusetts Bay embarked from their native England in order to establish societies based on their own conceptions of the perfect religious state, a "city on a hill" which reflected their conviction that their God had called them as a covenant people as he had once called the Israelites of old. Although it was true that Puritans in England had been harassed and persecuted for practicing their faith, and that their move to the New World would mean a freedom to practice their religion openly that they did not enjoy at home, the early New England colonists had no intention of sharing their new freedom by allowing adherents of other religious traditions to practice those traditions in their midst. What Quakers, Baptists, Antinomians, and others soon found was that the earliest English settlers of New England were determined to establish Puritanism as an official and exclusive religion, supported both by public funds and by laws designed to protect its singular status. In other words, the intention of the original colonists was not "freedom of religion" but rather the "establishment" of religion, through which one form of religious tradition was given preferential treatment over all others.

Exclusive religious establishment was not confined just to the New England colonies. In the southern colonies of Virginia, the Carolinas, and even Maryland, the Church of England worked hard to establish its exclusive rights over the religious sphere of colonial society. As with Puritanism in New England, the Church of England was publicly supported in the southern colonies through taxation and laws that guaranteed its dominance over all matters coming within its purview. An example can be found in marriage laws: Even though there existed from an early period pastors of such religious traditions as the Baptists and the Presbyterians, only pastors affiliated with the Church of England could legally officiate over marriages. Such laws as this, along with similar laws which forced nonmembers to support Church of England parishes through tax revenues, gave Anglican pastors and parishes advantages not shared by any other religion. Even in Maryland, which had originally been founded as a haven for persecuted ROMAN CATHOLICS from England and which boasted in its "Act Concerning Religion" of 1649 one of the earliest provisions for religious toleration found in the American colonies, there eventually was passed legislation which established the Church of England as the "official" religion, to the point where Roman Catholics were pushed into the margins and forced to practice their religion secretly.

"Liberty in Religious Concernments" Only in Rhode Island and the middle colonies of Pennsylvania and New Jersey was anything like true religious freedom to be found. Rhode Island had been established by exiles from Puritan Massachusetts Bay, such as Roger Williams, who were determined that members of all religions, Christian and non-Christian alike, should be able to practice their faiths openly and without threat of persecution. The colony soon became home to a number of religious traditions not welcome elsewhere in New England, including Quakers, Baptists, and even JEWS. The RHODE ISLAND CHARTER of 1663, which made the colony a royal protectorate, included in its text the affirmation that "a most flourishing civil state may stand and best be maintained . . . with a full liberty in religious concernments." Such convictions also governed the colonies of New Jersey and especially Pennsylvania, both established by groups of Quakers who had suffered at the hands of Anglicans in England and Puritans in America, and who therefore understood the value of religious freedom. To these colonies came a diversity of religious traditions, some from Europe such as Mennonites and other ANABAPTIST groups, and others from neighboring colonies where religious establishment of a particular tradition made the practice of other faiths difficult or impossible. But even here, freedom of religion was not synonymous with religious toleration or in every way absolute: Although he himself had suffered arrest, trial, and condemnation in Massachusetts Bay, Roger Williams had nothing good to say about the Quakers and other followers of other faiths who inhabited the Rhode Island colony. Even in Pennsylvania, Roman Catholics were prohibited from holding public office on account of their non-Protestant faith.

Changing Attitudes Toward Religious Freedom It would take a generation whose attitudes had been tempered by revolution to introduce into the American social landscape the idea of religious freedom as a fundamental right. Patriots of every religious persuasion took up arms in support of the revolutionary cause, in part because they had grown weary of having the support of publicly established religion forced on them without their consent. Even before the Revolutionary War, citizens in both New England and in the colonial South had begun to protest the mandatory taxation for the support of established churches and pastors. In some New England communities, local citizens were given the option of choosing a pastor other than Congregationalist as the object of public support, while in other communities in both New England and the southern colonies, tax payments could be specified for the support of one's local church, rather than for the officially established church. Quakers, who as a matter of religious conviction refused to support any other except their own meetings, were increasingly exempted from establishment laws, thus introducing the notion of voluntarism into the American religious vocabulary. By the time of the Revolution, voluntarism had gone from a novel idea to a watchword, and the impetus that would lead to the language of the First Amendment was born.

The movement toward religious freedom actually began not with the framing of the U.S. Constitution, but with the individual states. While religious establishment would remain the norm in many of the New England states, in Virginia, New York, Pennsylvania, New Jersey, and the Carolinas provisions guaranteeing religious freedom were made prominent parts of new state CONSTITUTIONS. The process of framing Virginia's constitution led to the writing—by such luminaries as Thomas JEFFERSON and James Madison—of declarations of religious freedom that destroyed forever in that state any official preference for one religious tradition over any other. In his "Memorial and Remonstrance Against Religious Assessments" (1785) Madison argued against the continuance of any form of religious establishment, and he was a vigorous advocate of Jefferson's "Bill for the Establishment of Religious Freedom," which Virginia's legislature adopted in 1786. As a result, all religious traditions in Virginia would henceforth compete on a level playing field, with voluntary support of local churches and pastors the norm rather than the exception.

Ironically, because of such provisions in early

state constitutions, there was little consideration at first of including in the new federal Constitution a guarantee of religious freedom. Even Madison, who had played a large part in the passage of such a guarantee in Virginia, saw little reason for any language at all about religion, apart from a provision found in Article VI of the U.S. Constitution banning religious tests for public offices; in his mind, the new government would have no jurisdiction whatever in religious matters. A number of states, however, refused to ratify the new constitution unless it guaranteed certain fundamental rights, including religious freedom. It was this, rather than positive conviction on the matter, that led to the passage of the First Amendment as part of the Bill of Rights.

The Religion Clauses of the First Amendment The FIRST AMENDMENT contains two separate, yet related, clauses that together were intended to guarantee religious freedom. The establishment clause states that "Congress shall make no law regarding an establishment of religion," while the free exercise clause that follows adds, "or prohibiting the free exercise thereof . . ." The establishment clause prohibits Congress from passing any law that sets up a particular religion as "official," therefore giving it preference over any other, the free exercise clause prevents Congress from actions that would interfere with the religious beliefs or practices of any individual citizen or group; however, some actions might be taken to hinder a religion if a compelling interest were found to justify such an action.

The original assumption behind the First Amendment's two religion clauses was that the prohibition against establishment would automatically lead to the free exercise of religion by rendering the government powerless to take any action whatever that could affect religion. Citizens would thus be free to hold whatever religious convictions they wished (or practice no religion at all) without threat of governmental interference.

Originally, the provisions of the First Amendment applied only to the federal government; the individual states could pass whatever laws they wished concerning religion. Some states, particularly in New England, continued the practice of religious establishment well into the nineteenth century; a few states, including New Hampshire and Maryland, did not abolish all religious tests for state office until well into the twentieth century. It was

not until 1940, when the provisions of the Fourteenth Amendment were applied to states in the U.S. Supreme Court's *Cantwell v. Connecticut* decision, that the establishment and free exercise clauses of the First Amendment were made universal. Even so, there remained much debate about what the First Amendment actually guaranteed. Some historians and jurists, including Chief Justice William Rehnquist, have asserted that the establishment clause only forbids government preference of one religion over another, but that the Framers of the Bill of Rights never intended that government should withhold all support from all religions. Those of the "nonpreferentialist" view point to declarations of many participants in the constitutional discussions of that period to the effect that religion was an important thread in the fabric of American society, and that governments, state and federal, had the obligation to see religion remain vital and healthy. Consequently, Rehnquist and others have suggested that it would be permissible for the government to give aid to all religions equally, rather than be governed by the "wall of separation" demanded by their opponents.

On the other side of the debate, there are those who insist that the legislative history of the passage of the religion clauses of the First Amendment makes clear that it was indeed "strict separation," rather than nonpreference, that governed the thinking of the Framers of the Bill of Rights, in particular because they rejected earlier drafts of the amendment that would have specifically allowed for such nonpreferential support. Although debate has raged in both scholarly journals and court opinions, it appears that those advocating strict separation in religious matters have largely carried the day.

A Push Toward Christian Conformity Regardless of which view is correct as to the intent of the Framers, judicial interpretations of the establishment and free exercise clauses have been characterized as both inconsistent and confusing. As a result, this most fundamental of civil rights has been regarded as by no means universal or absolute. Although Jefferson attempted during his presidency to maintain his strict "wall of separation" between government and religion, even extending to the refusal to proclaim national days of thanksgiving and prayer, he nevertheless felt no compunction in maintaining the right of the federal government to take steps to christianize AMERICAN INDIANS. A similar attitude was applied later in the nine-

Freedom to practice religion was important to African Americans even during the era of slavery, when camp meetings such as this offered a welcome contrast to the restrictions they faced in their secular lives. (*Library of Congress*)

teenth century against the MORMONS because of their practice of polygamy, with the result that the largely Mormon territory of Utah was delayed in its admission to the Union as a state. It was not until the Mormons themselves voluntarily gave up the practice that the way was cleared for Utah's application to be approved. Certain utopian groups such as the Oneida community of New York were also harassed because of their practices that ran contrary to the religious sentiments of the surrounding society. In Oneida's case, it was the notion of "scientific breeding" that led to opposition because it allowed for multiple marriage partners within the community itself. Indeed, the nineteenth century has often been termed the "Protestant century," because the nation's religious attitudes came primarily from evangelical Protestantism, and those who differed in any way from those attitudes would inevitably become objects of determined and even violent opposition.

Nowhere was such opposition more evident than in the cases of the religions of African Americans and immigrant communities. Whether in slave quarters on southern plantations or in cities of the North, wherever free blacks attempted to worship according to their own consciences, white Protestants opposed their doing so—backed by laws. Similar opposition was also experienced by immigrant ROMAN CATHOLICS and JEWS, who were equally opposed by Protestant nativists who felt threatened by the immigrants' increasing numbers. Even though both cases also involved social and economic issues, the limiting of religious freedom nevertheless was an important part of the story.

Constitutional Test Cases The twentieth century has witnessed the continuing of many of the previous themes, particularly in the increasing number of establishment and free exercise cases which have been argued before the U.S. Supreme Court. Central to this confusion has been the fact that the Founders' assumption that nonestablishment would guarantee free exercise has been contradicted in many cases, resulting in problems that the Founders could not have anticipated. Moreover, many important test cases involving the two First Amendment religion clauses have been brought by religious minority groups whose convictions and practices had not previously been considered by mainstream American religion or society. These factors, among others, have led to much of the confusion with which the court system and society in general has struggled.

A sampling of court cases is illustrative. In *West Virginia State Board of Education v. Barnette* (1943), for example, the Supreme Court reversed the stand it had taken in *Minersville School District v. Gobitis* (1940), which allowed the government to require schoolchildren to salute the flag. The government may reimburse parents for fees paid to transport their children to private religious schools (*Everson v. Board of Education*, 1947), and may also require local school boards to lend textbooks to students in such schools (*Board of Education v. Allen*, 1968). The government may allow release time for religious instruction given away from school (*Zorah v. Clauson*, 1952), but not on school grounds themselves (*McCollum v. Board of Education*, 1948). On the other hand, schools may not discriminate against a student club on the basis of its religious content (*Board of Education v. Mergens*, 1990). School prayer has been consistently barred (*Engel v. Vitale*, 1962), as has Bible reading (*Abington v. Schempp*, 1963), the posting of the Ten Commandments (*Stone v. Graham*, 1980), and moments of silence (*Wallace v. Jaffree*, 1985). A particularly important set of standards for the setting of such boundaries was defined in *Lemon v. Kurtzman* (1971), which banned public school teachers from teaching secular subjects in private religious schools. The so-called "Lemon test" requires that government actions have a specifically secular purpose, that they do not advance religion, and that they not entangle the government in religious matters. The Lemon test has been employed by the Court in its decisions concerning religious issues ever since.

Three cases touching on the religious practices of minority groups have caused a great deal of debate among both jurists and the public at large. Two of these cases involved Native American religious groups. In *Lyng v. Northwest Indian Cemetery Protective Association* (1988), the Court refused to block the federal government from building a road near land which was considered sacred by Native American tribes, even though building such a road would hinder the practice of religious rituals connected with that land. In *Employment Division v. Smith* (1990) the Court upheld the right of a state to refuse unemployment benefits for Native Americans fired from their jobs because of their use of hallucinogenic drugs in connection with certain religious ceremonies. Similarly, the Court in *Goldman v. Weinberger* (1986) refused to reverse an air force prohibition on officers' wearing Jewish yarmulkes while on duty. On the other hand, in two cases dealing with Sabbath restrictions (*Sherbert v. Verner*, 1963, and *Thomas v. Review Board*, 1981), the Court sided with two persons who had been denied unemployment compensation because they refused to work on Saturdays for religious reasons.

What Is Religious Freedom? Although the First Amendment asserts in both its establishment and free exercise clauses a seemingly absolute right to religious freedom, the actual application of those clauses suggests that there are limits on religious freedoms. The Framers of the First Amendment believed that government had no jurisdiction over religious matters whatever, but the Supreme Court's record in such matters suggests that government may indeed "advance religion," so long as it does so indirectly. On the other hand, it may hinder religious practice if it believes there is a compelling social interest that warrants such action. Perhaps the inconsistency of the Court's decisions ultimately rests with the ambiguity of the language of the establishment and free exercise clauses themselves. The Founders indeed hoped for a society in which religious freedom was guaranteed, but they left it to later generations to decide just what religious freedom really means.

SUGGESTED READINGS:

Alley, Robert. *School Prayer: The Court, the Congress, and the First Amendment*. New York: Prometheus Books, 1994. Discusses the history of one of the most difficult First Amendment questions to arise in recent history.

Barker, Lucius, and Twiley Barker. *Civil Liberties and the Constitution*. Englewood Cliffs, N.J.: Prentice Hall, 1990. Survey of civil rights cases that have come before the Supreme Court, including cases on religion.

Berns, Walter. *The First Amendment and the Future of American Democracy.* New York: Basic Books, 1976. Includes a defense of the nonpreferentialist view.

Curry, Thomas. *The First Freedoms: Church and State in America to the Passage of the First Amendment.* New York: Oxford University Press, 1986. History of the movement from religious establishment to religious freedom.

Levy, Leonard. *The Establishment Clause: Religion and the First Amendment.* New York: Macmillan, 1986. Makes a case against the nonpreferentialist view of the establishment clause.

Malbin, Michael. *Religion and Politics: The Intentions of the Authors of the First Amendment.* Washington, D.C.: American Enterprise Institute, 1978. Modern defense of the nonpreferentialist position.

Pfeffer, Leo. *Church, State, and Freedom.* Boston: Beacon Press, 1967. Classic discussion of the separationist viewpoint.

—*Robert C. Davis*

Reparations

Compensatory payments made to redress past injustices.

Whereas many CIVIL RIGHTS issues concern the conditions existing in a society at a current moment, the notion of reparations focuses on past injustices. The principle of reparations has a long history in international relations; however, payment of reparations by a government to its own citizens is less common. The U.S. government has instituted highly publicized reparations programs for a small number of groups of its citizens.

The Logic of Reparations Reparations can achieve at least two distinct goals. Most simply, they may serve to compensate persons who sustained some injury caused by a government or society. For example, in the mid-1990's the U.S. government considered compensating about seven hundred persons who were physically harmed because they had been subjected to government radiation experiments without their knowledge. This "restitution" principle is the least controversial justification for reparations, largely because it is consistent with the American principle of justice toward all persons. However, it is difficult to calculate monetary restitution for intangible injustices, such as DISCRIMINATION

or internment. More problematic is the making of restitution after a victim's death.

Alternatively, reparations have been seen as penances paid by governments or societies for injustices committed in their name. Matters of calculating exact compensation and identifying personal injuries are less relevant in this "atonement" principle. It is the act of paying reparations, rather than their amount, that is important. By its nature, the atonement principle lends itself to matters of group justice and civil rights. Payments might go to descendants of victims or to members of a racial or ethnic group that earlier experienced injustice. The emphasis on penitence and the weaker injury claims held by the beneficiaries make reparations according to the atonement principle more controversial.

American Reparations Payments Numerous calls have been made for the U.S. government to make reparations payments to ethnic and racial groups. Three cases in the twentieth century have stood out. AMERICAN INDIANS have long sought compensation for the U.S. government seizures of lands on which they lived for generations. An early form of compensation offered by the government was the system of Indian RESERVATIONS. This was never deemed to be entirely satisfactory by the American Indians themselves, however, and the government continued to relocate tribes and seize additional lands into the early twentieth century. In 1946 an Indian Claims Commission was established to adjudicate claims relating to the seizure of Indian property and the failure to fulfill treaty obligations. Most claims have been considered according to the restitution principle. In addition, the U.S. SUPREME COURT in 1989 required the federal government to pay $122 million to eight Sioux tribes whose lands had been seized in 1877.

The federal policy of JAPANESE AMERICAN INTERNMENT and confiscation of internees' property during WORLD WAR II gave rise decades later to new reparations claims through the REDRESS MOVEMENT. Although the government initially argued that the wartime relocation and internment were necessary to prevent espionage and sabotage, it eventually acknowledged that the action had been a gross violation of the internees' civil rights. The CIVIL LIBERTIES ACT OF 1988 authorized payment of twenty thousand dollars to each surviving internee. Although the recipients had been interned on the basis of their Japanese ancestry, it was their individual injuries, rather than their membership in an oppressed group, that determined their eligibility for reparations payments.

Most controversial have been calls for reparations to AFRICAN AMERICANS, such as those made by REPUBLIC OF NEW AFRICA. Some trace the promise of reparations to Abraham LINCOLN, whose idea to give each emancipated slave forty acres and a mule died with Lincoln himself after the Civil War. Many advocates of reparations have continued to believe that the unpaid work performed by generations of African Americans held in SLAVERY requires payment by white society. Although all former American slaves have long since died, some people still see reparations to African Americans to be necessary to atone for past injustice. An additional rationale for reparations holds that because living African Americans continue to suffer from the legacies of slavery and past discrimination, they themselves deserve restitution. Still others argue that because a large part of the nation's wealth was made possible by slave labor, part of that wealth rightfully belongs to the descendants of slaves.

Reparations for African Americans have been endorsed by the NATIONAL ASSOCIATION FOR THE ADVANCEMENT OF COLORED PEOPLE, black leaders such as the Reverend Jesse JACKSON and Nation of Islam leader Louis FARRAKHAN, local government bodies such as the city council of Detroit, and coalitions such as the National Coalition of Blacks for Reparations in America. A number of legislative proposals have been introduced in the U.S. CONGRESS to establish reparations commissions and make reparations payments. Nevertheless, near the end of the twentieth century it seemed unlikely that any such program would soon be implemented. Reasons included the fact that the cost of such a program would be prohibitively high, given the number of potential recipients and the scale of the claims being made (up to $275,000 per person). More than this, American public opinion still overwhelmingly rejected claims that a fiduciary link exists between contemporary African Americans and those who suffered under slavery.

SUGGESTED READINGS:

Collins, Daisy. "The United States Owes Reparations to Its Black Citizens." *Howard Law Journal* 16 (Fall, 1970).

Ellen, David. "Payback Time." *The New Republic* (July 31, 1989).

Healey, Jon. "Congress Ponders Compensation for Radiation Test Subjects." *Congressional Quarterly Weekly Report* 52, no. 1 (1994).

Nagata, Donna K. "The Japanese-American Internment: Perceptions of Moral Community, Fairness, and Redress." *Journal of Social Issues* 46, no. 1 (1990).

—*Steve D. Boilard*

Reproductive rights

Rights relating to individual choices about procreation, contraception, ABORTION, and sterilization.

Virtually all societies place limits on reproductive rights. In most Western countries, however, procreation is considered fundamental to survival of society. Procreation was ruled a basic CIVIL RIGHT by the U.S. SUPREME COURT in *Skinner v. Oklahoma* (1942); a broadening interpretation of reproductive choice has been evident since that time. The marital relationship has been viewed as a zone of PRIVACY protected by the Ninth Amendment (*Griswold v. Connecticut*, 1965); it is that same right of privacy that has protected a woman's right to choose to terminate a pregnancy (ROE V. WADE, 1973). Claims of reproductive freedom have extended to four aspects of reproduction: conception, gestation, labor, and child rearing.

The Conflict Women's search for autonomy and self-identity has caused the modern American family unit to evolve. The traditional role of women as companions to their husbands and bearers of children changed as women entered the workforce in increasing numbers. A marked decrease in fertility and the recognition that women had the absolute right to control their own bodies followed. Through the last three decades of the twentieth century, the issue of privacy versus governmental intrusion has brought to light additional dimensions of the social rights of individuals. Because it involves some of the most hotly contested and most politically and socially divisive issues of the late twentieth century, individual autonomy has been pitted against the opinion that the government should play a role in regulating sexual behavior, promote social morality, and protect third persons. Courts have generally applied a balancing test that weighs a state's infringement of personal autonomy against the legitimate state interest in taking such action. Much of constitutional law in this area has focused on finding an acceptable balance between private rights and the public good. Technological advances in science, medicine, and genetics also have forced society and the government to confront these and other collateral issues, such as surrogate motherhood and the use of fetal tissue for experimentation and treatment.

Historical Background Legal regulation of abortion was virtually nonexistent before the twentieth century. In premodern societies, abortion and infanticide were the chief means of limiting population growth; contraception was relatively infrequent.

In post-Revolutionary America, abortion early in pregnancy was neither prohibited nor uncommon. Until 1821 no state had enacted a statute regulating or outlawing the procedure. Each state was governed by English common law, which permitted abortion until "quickening," when the first fetal movement was perceived by the mother, generally between the fourth and sixth months of pregnancy. Due to then liberal attitudes toward sexuality, and because abortion before quickening was thought to present little danger to the health of the woman, first trimester and many second trimester abortions faced only minor, if any, legal regulations or resistance.

The subsequent decline in the U.S. birth rate suggests an increased use of BIRTH CONTROL and abortion. Sought primarily by the wealthy as well as by single women, abortion was not considered a moral issue, but rather a subject discussed behind closed doors. During the second half of the nineteenth century, changes in the social order and a shift in demographics from rural to urban contributed to changing patterns of fertility, social roles, and moral values. The popular press carried advertisements for abortifacients and remedies to relieve "menstrual blockage" or "obstruction" primarily caused by pregnancy. "Clinics for ladies" to treat menstrual "irregularities" remained confidential, but became common. Home remedies designed to induce miscarriages became popular, ranging from strenuous exercise to soap solutions and mild poisons to the physical introduction of sharp objects, such as coat hangers, into the uterus.

By 1900 every state had laws prohibiting the use of drugs or instruments to bring about abortion at any stage of pregnancy, unless necessary to save the life of the woman. Medical practitioners were thrust into the abortion debate out of concern for the physical safety of abortions, a desire to police the profession and eliminate competition from homeopaths, apothecaries, and other self-professed "healers," and an overall wish to upgrade the standards of medical education and practice.

Between the end of the nineteenth century and 1960, abortion became a medical issue. Laws permitting abortion only to "save the life of the woman" were vague, arbitrary, and not evenhandedly applied. There was an absence of agreed-upon criteria against which "life" was to be defined. Public discussion of abortion was rare due to the "delicate" nature of public sensibilities; privately, however, an underground network sharing names of illegal abortionists and abortion techniques evolved. Until the 1960's, moreover, medical control of abortion remained basically unchallenged, partly because the procedure was still available to members of the upper class, and also because women were excluded from medical decision making because they lacked the knowledge to challenge medical decisions. The ultimate and unquestioned authority rested with medical practitioners. Those most affected were poor women and women of color. Unable to afford safe abortions, they were forced to choose between dangerous abortions and unwanted babies.

Civil Rights and Reform One effect of the CIVIL RIGHTS MOVEMENT was to awaken the public to the injustices, inequities, and deprivations suffered by women because they are women. The assertion of WOMEN'S RIGHTS and sexual freedom, as well as changing sexual mores and the new freedom promised by birth control pills and intrauterine devices (IUDs), gave women more control over their familial choices. Women began entering the workforce in large numbers. Those who valued childbearing—but only on their own terms—began to claim that abortion is a woman's right, and one integrated into their right of equality. In their quest for self-identification, women began claiming their right as autonomous beings to control their own bodies. They therefore argued it was their individual decision to choose when, if at all, to bear children, and whether an abortion was appropriate.

The women's movement broke down the barriers of social and economic inequality and highlighted the fact that the traditionally subordinated status of women was outmoded. Legislative reform of abortion laws, which began in the 1950's, accelerated between 1967 and 1973. The thrust of these reforms was to create exceptions to strict prohibitions on abortion, making it legal in cases of serious fetal defects, or when physicians considered it necessary to protect pregnant women's mental or physical health, and also in cases of rape or incest.

The turning point for reproductive choice as an issue took place at the 1967 national conference of the NATIONAL ORGANIZATION FOR WOMEN (NOW) led by Betty Friedan, who pushed to include the "right of women to control their reproductive lives" in NOW's Women's Bill of Rights. The National Association for the Repeal of Abortion Laws (NARAL) was created in 1968. After 1973 it became the NATIONAL ABORTION AND REPRODUCTIVE RIGHTS ACTION LEAGUE, the principal national lobbying group for grassroots pro-choice organizations in the United States. A broad coalition group, it is dedicated to protecting the right of choice for all childbearing women. In 1985 it claimed 250,000 members.

Other reform efforts followed. The Presidential Advisory Council on the Status of Women, appointed by President Lyndon B. JOHNSON, issued a report in 1968 calling for repeal of all abortion laws. Planned Parenthood supported repeal of criminal abortion statutes in 1969, and the Commission on Population Growth issued a report in 1972 favoring abortion reform. Between 1967 and 1973, nineteen states reformed their abortion laws.

Roe v. Wade On January 22, 1973, in one of the most controversial court decisions in American history, the U.S. Supreme Court extended the right of privacy to a woman's decision to terminate her pregnancy. By a 7-2 vote, the Court ruled in *Roe v. Wade* that because the right of privacy was fundamental, only the most compelling reasons permit government interference with the exercise of that right. The Court also answered the claim of anti-abortion ("pro-life") activists that abortion destroys life, ruling that an unborn fetus is not a person entitled to FOURTEENTH AMENDMENT guarantees of life and liberty because the word "person" in that amendment is used in the postnatal sense only. By 1996, however, at least thirty states allowed prosecution for criminally causing death or injury to the viable fetus of another, thereby expanding the concept of fetal rights.

For ease of reference, the Supreme Court divided the term of the pregnancy into "trimesters." During the first trimester, the woman herself in con-sultation with her physician, can decide whether

Should Abortion Be Legalized?

In 1993 the Gallup Poll asked a cross section of Americans this question: "Do you think abortions should be legal under any circumstances, legal only under certain circumstances, or illegal in all circimstances?" These are the results.

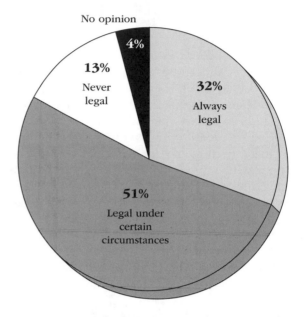

Source: U.S. Department of Justice, Bureau of Justice Statistics, *Sourcebook of Criminal Justice Statistics—1993*. Washington, D.C.: U.S. Government Printing Office, 1994. Primary source, *The Gallup Poll Monthly*, April, 1993.

to terminate her pregnancy without government interference. During the second, the government can regulate abortion only to preserve and protect the health of the woman. During the third trimester, when the fetus is viable, or capable of meaningful life outside the womb (defined as at twenty-three and one-half or twenty-four weeks' gestation in 1973), the government's interest in protecting fetal life becomes more compelling as the pregnancy advances. Only then can the government ban abortion.

The Court argued that although the government does have an interest in protecting prenatal life, that interest must be balanced against a woman's right to privacy. The Court found the right of privacy broad enough to protect a woman's exclusive claim on her body, thereby considerably expanding the scope of that right. RIGHTS, however, are not absolute. As the pregnancy advances, the state's interest in protecting prenatal life becomes more compelling and the woman's privacy interest diminishes.

Pro-life Activism Opponents to *Roe v. Wade* attempted to erode the sweeping reform that ensued. States enacted restrictions on abortion in the form of obligatory waiting periods, consent requirements from male partners, or parents in the cases of minors, bans on Medicaid funding, medical testing requirements, and facility restrictions. In each case, the constraints were tested in the courts, but *Roe v. Wade*, while eroded, was not overturned.

The White House also entered the fray. In 1976 Henry Hyde, a Republican Congressman from Illinois, attached to a budget bill signed by President Jimmy CARTER an amendment that prohibited the federal government from allowing federal Medicaid funds to be used to pay for abortions. This meant that poor women could not have abortions paid for by government health plans. After 1980 federal funds for abortions became available only in cases in which the lives of pregnant women were at stake. In 1993 the House of Representatives voted by a large margin to retain the Hyde Amendment, but modified it to provide payment for abortions in cases of rape or incest.

In 1980 then-presidential candidate Ronald REAGAN promised to choose only anti-*Roe v. Wade* judges to fill Supreme Court vacancies if he were elected. As president he imposed a gag order on abortion counseling at government facilities. His successor as president, George BUSH, prohibited scientific research on aborted fetal tissue and the importing and the prescribing of the French drug RU-486, which promised to make early abortions safe and inexpensive. When President Bill CLINTON took office in 1993, he rescinded the gag rule on abortion counseling at government-supported hospitals and stopped the bans on fetal tissue research and importing RU-486.

Emotional marches followed in which pro-life advocates carried placards with photographs of fetuses, and pro-choice advocates carried posters showing bloody coat hangers symbolizing the era prior to the legalization of abortion. Pro-lifers used aggressive methods to prevent abortion, such as picketing clinics and the homes of staff workers,

Participants in a pro-life rally in New York City in 1977 carry signs expressing many of the sentiments identified with their movement. (*Betty Lane*)

staging demonstrations, stalking and shouting at patrons, throwing plastic models of fetuses, harassing clinic employees, chaining themselves to doors, and lying prostrate in driveways and streets. Clinics were vandalized and bombed and several ABORTION CLINIC MURDERS occurred. Similar demonstrations and violence occurred around the nation on the twenty-fourth anniversary of *Roe v. Wade* in 1997.

One of the organizations attracting national attention was OPERATION RESCUE, headquartered in Binghamton, New York. It was founded in 1986 by Randall Terry, a former car salesman turned Fundamentalist Christian speaker. The group was dedicated to stopping women from getting abortions by blockading clinic entrances in major cities. After its activities peaked in 1988-1989, they steadily declined. Lawsuits and a number of multimillion dollar fines had a tempering effect on its activities and membership, as have disputes among its own leaders. The most notorious of its clinic blockades occurred in ATLANTA, GEORGIA, during the 1988 Democratic National Convention and in 1991 in Wichita, Kansas. At the 1992 Democratic National Convention in New York City, a member of the group attempted to hand presidential candidate Bill Clinton a fetus. Although Terry was not physically present at the time of that incident, he was convicted of aiding and abetting in the disruption that ensued and was sentenced to five months in prison.

Birth Control Controversies The controversy over birth control was never as intensely vocal or emotional as that over abortion. The birth control movement reflected the changing social environment and the growing emancipation and independence of women. Birth control technology and capability have expanded rapidly, especially with the introduction of methods ranging from IUDs and birth control pills, to injectable contraceptives, reversible implants placed under the skin, "morning after" pills, medicated vaginal rings containing absorbable steroids, and biodegradable systems. Birth control pills, first approved for use in 1960, revolutionized birth control methods as a result of their easy accessibility, simplicity, and effectiveness.

In 1961 Estelle Griswold and Charles Lee Buxton openly challenged a Connecticut state law that outlawed contraceptives and made their use a criminal offense. Connecticut had generally not enforced this law against individual physicians, sellers, or married couples. The law affected mainly the poor, barring their access to the same birth control coun-

seling and supplies available to the middle class. Two earlier attempts to challenge Connecticut's law had failed. In November, 1961, Griswold and Buxton opened a birth control clinic amid publicity. Shortly thereafter, they were arrested for dispensing birth control information and instructions to a married couple in violation of the Connecticut statute.

After being found guilty in a state court and fined, Griswold and Buxton appealed their case to the U.S. Supreme Court, urging it to declare Connecticut's law unconstitutional. In a 7-2 decision, the Court held, in GRISWOLD V. CONNECTICUT, that the Connecticut law forbidding use of contraceptives intruded on the right of marital privacy implicitly guaranteed under the U.S. Constitution. This case represented the first time that the Court formally recognized a constitutional right of privacy—which is among the rights not specifically enumerated in the Constitution. It then remained for the Court to define this right. Justice William O. Douglas, writing for the majority, recognized that because the marital relationship lay within a zone of privacy derived from the First, Third, Fourth, Fifth, Ninth, and Fourteenth amendments to the Constitution, it should be protected from state and federal interference.

The immediate consequence of the *Griswold* decision was the repeal of birth control statutes in Connecticut and thirteen other states. This led to a dramatic increase in the number of women who gained access to birth control devices and counseling. *Griswold* was, however, confined to traditional notions of contraception by married persons. In 1972 the Supreme Court held that the privacy guarantee also extended protection to contraception by single persons; in 1977, this right was held to extend to minors.

These court decisions have demonstrated a general legal response to a changing social environment. Restrictive birth control prohibitions were either replaced by more flexible regulations or were eliminated totally. Meanwhile, increased sexual permissiveness developed in society as the women's movement gained momentum and open cohabitation among unmarried couples was no longer prohibited. Many college dormitories were sexually integrated and sex and emotional intimacy became increasingly dissociated. Women began claiming sexual fulfillment as an integral part of their existence, separate and apart from their traditional procreative roles.

Sterilization Voluntary sterilization for purposes of fertility control was a development of the second half of the twentieth century. Sterilization for eugenic reasons, however, has existed since the early part of the twentieth century. Voluntary sterilization has become legal in all fifty states, but with some restrictions, such as age, spousal or parental consent, and waiting periods. The federal government has funded approximately 10 percent of all voluntary sterilizations for the poor annually.

SUGGESTED READINGS:

Blanchard, Dallas A. *The Anti-Abortion Movement and the Rise of the Religious Right*. New York: Twayne, 1994. Examines the development of the pro-life movement, its leaders, and the various organizations involved in its existence. Includes a detailed abortion history.

Blank, Robert, and Janna C. Merrick. *Human Reproduction, Emerging Technologies, and Conflicting Rights*. Washington, D.C.: Congressional Quarterly Press, 1995. Examines modern reproduction issues from a public policy perspective, focusing on how new technology has reshaped the debate.

Brodie, Janet Farrell. *Contraception and Abortion in Nineteenth Century America*. Ithaca, N.Y.: Cornell University Press, 1994. Carefully researched and detailed historical chronology of nineteenth century information on reproductive control.

Domino, John C. *Civil Rights and Liberties: Toward the Twenty-first Century*. New York: HarperCollins, 1994. Useful legal perspective on major civil rights and liberties issues.

Luker, Kristin. *Abortion and the Politics of Motherhood*. Berkeley: University of California Press, 1984. Important detailed sociological and historical study with copious notes and extensive bibliography.

McCorvey, Norma, with Andy Meisler. *I Am Roe: My Life, "Roe v. Wade," and Freedom of Choice*. New York: HarperCollins, 1994. The plaintiff in *Roe v. Wade* writes about her life within the social and historical context of the times.

Tribe, Laurence H. *Abortion: The Clash of Absolutes*. New York: W. W. Norton, 1990. Scholarly but readable work by a noted constitutional scholar discussing the historical and cultural aspects of abortion and the clash between the "absolutes" of life and liberty guaranteed in the U.S. Constitution.

—*Marcia J. Weiss*

Republic of New Africa

RNA: Revolutionary AFRICAN AMERICAN group formed in 1968 to demand REPARATIONS and land entitlements from the federal government.

RNA's formal establishment was dramatic: Several hundred BLACK NATIONALISTS, summoned by activists Robert F. WILLIAMS, Gaidi Obadele (Milton Henry), and Imari Abubakari Obadele (Richard Henry), gathered in Detroit to declare their independence from an oppressive government—the United States of America. They hoped to form an autonomous republic for African Americans within the Deep South. The new organization soon had members and supporters throughout the United States, including COMMUNIST PARTY leader Angela DAVIS and other well-known politicians.

The RNA demanded that the U.S. government pay $400 billion in reparations for the centuries of oppression suffered by African Americans, and that the government turn over to African Americans Alabama, Georgia, Louisiana, Mississippi, and South Carolina—the region considered to be the black "homeland" territory in the United States. With that money and land, RNA would form a separate nation based on the principles of *ujamaa*, or "communitarianism."

Well armed, the organization was prepared for battle if it became necessary. On its first anniversary, an RNA conference held in a Detroit church was stormed by police, who fired hundreds of rounds of ammunition into the church and found their fire returned. Four RNA members were wounded and one police officer killed; three RNA members were tried and acquitted of murder. In 1971 a police raid on RNA headquarters in Jackson, Mississippi, resulted in the death of another police officer and the arrest and conviction of eleven RNA members, including provisional president Imari Obadele. In 1977 Obadele filed suit from federal prison, demanding the release of records of the FEDERAL BUREAU OF INFORMATION (FBI) proving that RNA had been infiltrated and subverted by the antiradical program of the FBI.

Though it had once been among the most influential black nationalist groups, the RNA gradually became less important, but still claimed several thousand members into the 1990's.

—*Cynthia A. Bily*

Reservations, Indian

Tract of land on which one or more AMERICAN INDIAN tribes live that are held in trust by the U.S. federal government.

Indian reservations are administered directly by the Bureau of Indian Affairs under the Department of the Interior. The U.S. government has recognized 510 Indian tribes and Alaskan (Inuit) groups located on 278 hundred tracts of land so designated by executive order, statue, or treaty, all of which fall under federal trusts. The largest reservation is the 14-million-acre Navaho Reservation.

Colonial Antecedents During the colonial period in British North America, Britain was content to leave Indian-white relations to the jurisdiction of local governments. The only requirement was that settlers and colonies were to compensate Indians for any land they acquired, and then only with the permission of the British government. By 1756, because of the extent and complexity of legal transactions, the British crown had appointed two Indian superintendents to negotiate and regulate trade with the American Indians; one for the northern territory and one for the southern regions.

Because British and colonial relations with Indian tribes were crucial for appropriating land, promoting economic growth, and the further expansion of trade, the British government annually sent three thousand pounds to the governors of South Carolina and Georgia to maintain the loyalty of the Cherokees, Choctaws, Chickasaws, and Creeks. The British government also supported numerous Indian tribes in the northeast in maintaining trade routes and in restricting further colonization by the French. This support, and even recognition of Indian political and legal independence, changed when the British defeated the French in the Great War for Empire (1756-1763). De facto Indian rights, regarding negotiation and land purchase, did continue, and compensation by the British for land loss was usually in the form of trade goods, such as beads, firearms, and metal implements.

During this period the British government established a territorial division for Anglo-American land purchase and Indian settlement within the thirteen colonies. The Proclamation of 1763 established a line along the crest of the Appalachian Mountains, mainly in an effort to control colonial expansion west of the demarcation and to maintain the sovereignty of numerous transwestern Indian nations.

American Colonial Land Policy After the American Revolutionary War (1775-1783), the notion of Manifest Destiny and an overwhelming desire by colonists for acquiring more land became apparent. Consequently, the Continental Congress attempted, on August 7, 1786, to control Indian affairs with an Ordinance for the Regulation of Indian Affairs to prevent further encroachment upon Indian land by settlers. Despite the belief of many social, church, and political leaders who accepted the psychic unity of humanity, the major concern of the Congress was that Indian land not be sold to a European power.

Eventually, the situation of unmitigated fraud, skirmishes, and displacement of Indians became so apparent that President George Washington's cabinet sought to protect Indian rights. As a consequence, under Secretary of State Thomas JEFFERSON and Secretary of War Henry Knox, who both believed that Indians possessed the natural rights of humanity, the rights of Indians were recognized when the government determined European settlers had the right to purchase land from Indians, who had the right to sell.

Indian Removal Policy As early as 1802, Andrew Jackson and other Tennessee land owners had commenced, through bribery, force, and fraud, to force cessions of Indian lands, thereby commencing the process of removing many thousands of Indians from most of Alabama, a fifth of Georgia, and half of Mississippi to Oklahoma, a region west of the Mississippi River designated as Indian Territory. Furthermore, in his 1829 inaugural address, President Andrew Jackson called for the passage of a Removal Act. Congress approved the act on May 28, 1830. The bill offered fair value exchange for lost territory, granted tribes absolute ownership of their new lands, made provisions for aid and assistance during Indian migration, and promised protection to Indian emigrants from hostile western Indians. The Removal Act encouraged and successfully accommodated colonial expansion that was being brought about by the American industrial revolution of the 1820's and 1830's, which created the need for more territory and for access to newly discovered resources, particularly for cotton and tobacco lands. Large-scale cash crop farming required even further exploitation of "unused" native lands. Colonial expansion continued with forced relocation of the indigenous people. The Bureau of Indian Affairs, established in 1824 under the aus-

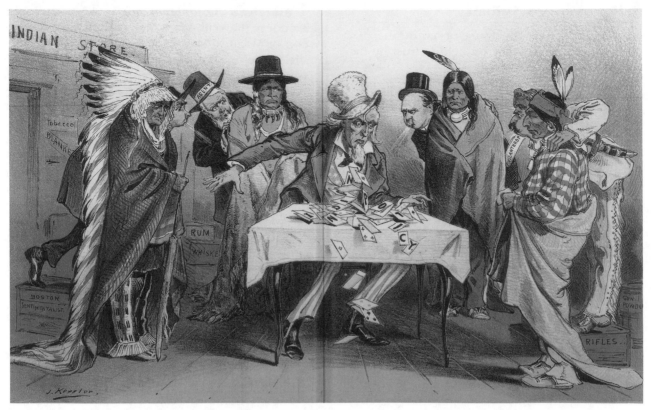

Cartoonist Joseph Keppler parodied the federal government's inconsistent Indian policy in his *Puck* magazine. (*Library of Congress*)

pices of the War Department, reflected the hostility between whites and Indians.

Government Policies The philanthropy and Manifest Destiny policy of dealing with Indian problems was essentially one of segregation, whereby Indian tribes would be confined to designated areas, presumably for protection from the devastating effects of white civilization. The continued relocation and concentration of tribes in the West was, it was also assumed, to be accompanied by the work of religious societies that would civilize Indians by means of vocational training, education, Christianization, commerce, and agriculture. It was believed that control and enlightenment of the Indians could only be achieved if they were no longer nomadic and instead worked as farmers on allotted areas of land that whites did not want.

Probably the greatest legal benefactor for Indian CIVIL RIGHTS, concerning treaty rights, sovereignty of Indian nations, law and order, and title of land, was Chief Justice John Marshall, best known for three decisions that became the basis of many subsequent civil rights litigations. In *Johnson and Gra-*

ham's Lessee v. McIntosh (1823), Marshall maintained that all Indians did not possess unqualified sovereignty, and the fundamental principle of discovery did not give discoverers exclusive title to aboriginal lands. Arguing the *Cherokee Nation v. Georgia* (1831) case, Marshall contended that the Cherokee nation, although a state, was not a foreign state, but a domestic dependent nation, and that the court had no original jurisdiction. In *Worcester v. Georgia* (1832), Marshall argued that the state of Georgia had no right to impose its authority on the Cherokee or their territory.

Historical Development of Reservations By the 1860's, the established territories of American Indians were being occupied by white settlers, miners, ranchers, loggers, missionaries, and the military who were stationed to protect the numerous exploitative economic ventures of the settlers. The 1862 Homestead Act opened Indian land to white homesteaders in Kansas and Nebraska, and after the Civil War many soldiers and their families also settled in the West. The traditional ways of Indian life, once dependent upon a high degree of mobility had, in most cases, changed radically. By the 1870's, all Indians had been assigned to reservations, and tribes were no longer treated as independent states but rather as domestic dependencies. Unfortunately, most reservations were desolate tracts of marginal rural land, areas generally without an adequate ecological basis to maintain self-sufficient communities.

Many political and social leaders were of the opinion that assimilation of Indians was fundamental if they were to survive in the dominant culture. Therefore the United States government and other leaders sought to replace Indian communal values with capitalistic values and a sense of individualism. In 1887 President Grover Cleveland signed the General Allotment Act, sometimes called the Dawes Act, which subdivided reservations and allotted enrolled members of tribes 40- to 160-acre parcels of land. As part of the act, tribal land holdings in excess of the individual allotments would be sold. Before the repeal of the Allotment Act in 1934, during the New Deal of social reform, Indians lost more than 90 million acres of land that came under white ownership, approximately 2.3 percent of the United States' land. It should be noted that from 1887 to 1934, through confiscation, fraud, trickery, treaty violation, and government decree, Indians lost approximately 86 million of the 138 million acres they had been promised by treaties. Many administrators and politicians believed that the Dawes Act would effectively dismantle the reservations and develop a sense of community by creating individually owned lands, thereby fostering a sense of economic competition within and between once traditional kin and ethnic groups. In 1924 all Indians twenty-one and older were made citizens and granted the right to vote.

Indian Reorganization Act of 1934 John Collier, a major figure in Indian reform, was the architect of the INDIAN REORGANIZATION ACT, or Wheeler-Howard Act. The act has been criticized for its paternalism and met with active opposition from some Indian leaders and dissenting bureaucrats, but the act did aid Indians in sharing in various New Deal programs. The trend toward assimilation was stopped by this bill. Its main elements were an immediate end to the allotment policy; a multimillion dollar credit fund to encourage Indian businesses and farms; an Indian legal and court system with Indian judges for nonfederal crimes; the recruitment of Indians within the Bureau of Indian Affairs; reorganization to foster self-governance; and establishment of a means for pooling land resources that could be corporate entities.

From 1934 to 1947 the Indian land base increased by 3.7 million acres. Concomitantly, many advances in civil rights were made in the areas of education, health and medical programs, revitalization of traditional skills and arts, freedom of practicing traditional spiritual rituals, and restoring tribal integrity. During this critical period, tribal governments, in concert with the first pan-Indian group, the National Congress of American Indians (formed in 1944 by a group of acculturated Indians) commenced to foster national and regional organizations that eventually encouraged self-government. The later establishment of the AMERICAN INDIAN MOVEMENT in 1968 was rejected by many Indians as being too radical and as interfering in internal tribal affairs, but the Senate Foreign Relations Committee was obliged to acknowledge the group and to make concessions after the 1972 occupation of the Washington Bureau of Indians Affairs building and the 1973 takeover of WOUNDED KNEE in South Dakota.

Reservation Termination and Relocation After World War II, increasing dissatisfaction with the Bureau of Indian Affairs and emerging attitudes regarding equal rights for minority groups led to the concept of assimilation again becoming popular. From these urges arose what has come to be called TERMINATION POLICY, which advocated ending the reservation system. House resolution 698 was passed on July 1, 1952. This law directed the Committee on Interior and Insular Affairs to review whether the Bureau of Indian Affairs had adequately studied if tribes could "determine their qualifications for management of their own affairs without further supervision of the Federal Government." With growing pressure from Indian protermination factions, Congress, on July 1, 1953, passed the termination bill HR Concurrent Resolution 108. With passage of the bill, a tribe could sell its land, thus terminating the reservation. The most noted cases were the Klamath and Menominee reservations. Some terminated areas came under state jurisdiction, supervision, and help. The termination policy proved inadequate in establishing tribal economic independence.

In the late 1950's, with low on-reservation employment, many Indians relocated to urban centers in search of employment and higher education. In

1951, the Bureau of Indian Affairs created employment assistance, job training programs, and offered assistance in finding housing. Many Indians felt dissatisfaction, frustration, and alienation off the reservation, and returned home. Some Indians, however, returned to their respective reservations to practice their new occupational and professional knowledge.

Contemporary Reservation Revitalization With the failure of termination policy, the concept of self-government was revitalized with various legislative and judicial acts, such as The Elementary and Secondary Education Act of 1965, the 1968 AMERICAN INDIAN CIVIL RIGHTS ACT, The Indian Education Act of 1972 (which acknowledged the special educational needs of children of low-income families), and the Indian Self-Determination and Educational Act of 1975. Other civil rights legislation were the Equal Employment Opportunity Act, the Voting Rights Act, the Fair Housing Act, and Equal Employment Opportunity Act. The Tax Status Act of 1982 authorized tribes to be treated as states. As a consequence of these civil rights decisions, the right to maintain distinct sociocultural and political communities became foremost in tribal agendas.

In the late 1990's, after approximately 350 years of colonization, various state and federal governments were still legally and ethically unresolved regarding many of the legal problems of ceded lands and compensation for lands and resources wrested away from American Indians.

SUGGESTED READINGS:

Cohen, Felix. *Handbook of Federal Indian Law.* Albuquerque: University of New Mexico Press, 1971.

Deloria, Vine, Jr., ed. *American Indian Policy in the Twentieth Century.* Norman: University of Oklahoma Press, 1985.

Hoxie, Frederick E. *A Final Promise: The Campaign to Assimilate the Indians, 1880-1920.* New York: Cambridge University Press, 1995.

Kappler, Charles J., ed. *Indian Affairs: Laws and Treaties.* 5 vols. Washington: Government Printing Office, 1904-1941. Reprint. New York: AMS Press, 1971.

Rogan, Paul. *Fathers and Children: Andrew Jackson and the Subjugation of the American Indian.* New York: Alfred A. Knopf, 1975.

Utley, Robert M. *The Indian Frontier of the American West 1846-1890.* Albuquerque: University of New Mexico Press, 1984.

Washburn, Wilcomb E. *Red Man's Land—White Man's Law: A Study of the Past and Present Status of the American Indian.* New York: Charles Scribner's Sons, 1971.

Wax, Murray L. *Indian Americans.* Redwood Cliffs, N.J.: Prentice-Hall, 1971.

—*John Alan Ross*

Restrictive covenants

Private agreements appended to residential property sales requiring home buyers not to resell their property to members of certain groups.

Property owners in suburban subdivisions and city neighborhoods alike have often entered into collective agreements designed to preserve the value of their real estate. These formal contracts, or covenants, spell out mutually agreed-upon standards for aspects of housing that are not covered by state or city building codes. A neighborhood association, for example, may draw up a covenant that specifies which colors can be used to paint houses or that forbids installation of certain types of lawn decorations, such as plastic pink flamingos. In the past, restrictive covenants often forbade property owners from selling their property to members of certain ethnic or religious groups, such as AFRICAN AMERICANS or ROMAN CATHOLICS; however, the U.S. SUPREME COURT ruled that such restrictions were a violation of the Constitution in SHELLEY V. KRAEMER (1948) and BARROWS V. JACKSON (1953).

—*Nancy Farm Mannikko*

Reverse discrimination

DISCRIMINATION that allegedly occurs to members of majority groups as a result of policies designed to counteract historical discrimination against MINORITY GROUP members.

Discrimination is generally understood as the unjust denial of benefits or rights to persons on the basis of their race, gender, national origin, or other considerations relating their membership in identifiable groups. In the context of the history of civil rights in America, reverse discrimination can be understood as another term for AFFIRMATIVE ACTION. Those who favor affirmative action policies tend to use the term "affirmative action," while opponents tend to call such policies "reverse discrimination." Critics prefer the term "reverse discrimination" because it emphasizes the similarities among historically institutionalized forms of discrimination, such as JIM CROW LAWS, and the discrimination involved in affirmative action itself. On the other hand, supporters of affirmative action contend that although reverse discrimination might produce some injustice, overall it is not morally wrong. In a judicial setting, the most famous challenge to affirmative action as a form of reverse discrimination came with the BAKKE CASE, decided by the U.S. SUPREME COURT in 1978. During the 1990's additional rulings in court cases involving challenges by nonminorities to affirmative action policy have sparked further debate over whether this remedy for discrimination can be constitutionally justified.

Objections to Reverse Discrimination Historically, white males have been the primary beneficiaries of institutionalized discrimination in America; women and minority groups, particularly AFRICAN AMERICANS, have suffered the most from its negative effects. With the implementation of government policies such as affirmative action, designed to right the balance against the lingering negative effects of the social injustice caused by SLAVERY and other forms of discrimination, women and racial minorities have received benefits such as increased opportunities in employment and education. Those who believe that affirmative action is reverse discrimination argue that such policies fail to right the balance but rather tip it in the other direction, allowing some women and racial minorities to enjoy the benefits of discrimination, while white males and some white women become its new victims. Affirmative action as reverse discrimination allows gender and race to be considered in the granting of university admissions and employment opportunities to women and minorities.

Central to the claim that reverse discrimination is morally unjust is the perception that affirmative action has moved in a direction unintended by President Lyndon B. JOHNSON, who through executive orders during the 1960's brought the policy of affirmative action into being. Johnson sought to accelerate the process of achieving equality of opportunity in employment, which was the aim of Title VII of the CIVIL RIGHTS ACT OF 1964. He did not explicitly conceive of affirmative action programs as providing preferential treatment for women and racial minorities, but the U.S. Department of LABOR,

to whom responsibility fell for the administration of employment-related affirmative action programs, developed procedures to monitor compliance with affirmative action that appeared to shift the focus of affirmative action in the direction of preferential treatment. These procedures called for all federal contractors to develop goals related to the hiring of members of underrepresented groups in the workplace, as well as timetables for this hiring to occur, in order to achieve a more balanced representation of women and racial minorities.

Given this need to meet goals and timetables to achieve a more representative workforce, affirmative action as preferential treatment does permit the hiring of less qualified applicants for positions over more qualified applicants on the basis of race or gender. Since hiring decisions were based on race or gender during the period of U.S. history when SEGREGATION was enforced, those who condemn reverse discrimination point to this similarity as evidence for the injustice of reverse discrimination. Another similarity opponents of affirmative action find between reverse discrimination and historical discrimination is that both treat individuals not on the basis of their merits as individuals but on the basis of their membership in certain groups. A third popular criticism of reverse discrimination is that racial and gender-based preferential treatment is actually harmful to the groups it wishes to benefit, since it opens successful women or racial minority members to the suspicion that their success is based on affirmative action, rather than their own competency and efforts.

The Bakke Case A well-known legal challenge to reverse discrimination occurred in the case of *Regents of the University of California v. Bakke*, decided by the U.S. SUPREME COURT in 1978. A white male, Bakke was twice denied admission to the University of California at Davis Medical School, which had a preferential admissions program in effect in order to increase the representation of racial minorities in its student body. As admission to the places in the medical school set aside under this program was restricted to nonwhites, Bakke was not allowed to compete for any of them. He then contended that he had been rejected on the basis not of his qualifications, but of his race.

By a 5-4 margin the Supreme Court agreed with Bakke, and ordered him admitted to the medical school. It held the university's special admissions program to be illegal, since it excluded some applicants from consideration simply because of their race. The Court stopped short, however, of declaring preferential treatment itself to be a violation of the FOURTEENTH AMENDMENT'S guarantee of equal protection under the law. It affirmed that it may be constitutionally permissible to take race into account in making university admissions decisions, so long as race is not taken to be the key element in these decisions. In this way—so the Court reasoned—race could count in admissions, while at the same time applicants could be considered on an individual basis. There is educational value in a university's having a diverse student body, the Court agreed, so affirmative action in support of this goal was held to be constitutionally legitimate.

Arguments for Reverse Discrimination The argument that gender and racial diversity is a valuable element in educational institutions and in the workplace is often used in defense of affirmative action. With the population of American society as diverse as it is, it is argued, reverse discrimination can serve a social good by bringing people of different racial groups into situations where as they work and learn with each other. The prejudices of sexism and RACISM that some might bring to these situations could conceivably disappear.

Those who condemn reverse discrimination tend to do so on the basis of its similarities to historical discrimination; those who believe reverse discrimination is a fair public policy tend to emphasize the differences between historical discrimination and reverse discrimination. Proponents point out that during the period of U.S. history when women and racial minorities were barred from education and from jobs, they were also viewed by members of the dominant class as inferior. The practice of reverse discrimination does not, however, stamp any group as inferior. Backers of reverse discrimination

Representative Melvin Watt, whose North Carolina congressional district had been drawn to strengthen minority voting power, was concerned that he might lose his seat if the Supreme Court ruled that the district had to be redrawn so as not to discriminate against white voters in 1993. (*AP/Wide World Photos*)

admit that the practice can lead to unjust treatment of individual white males, but emphasize that unlike historical discrimination reverse discrimination does not aim to exclude any particular group from consideration for employment or educational opportunities.

The Future of Reverse Discrimination In the mid-1990's, a series of judicial rulings on affirmative action served to limit its use in the workplace and in educational settings. In 1995 the Supreme Court let stand two lower-court rulings that found affirmative action to have discriminated against white males. In one of these cases, a 1981 affirmative action plan that ensured African American firefighters in BIRMINGHAM, ALABAMA, would receive one out of every two promotions was ruled illegal. In 1996, in a direct challenge to the *Bakke* decision, a federal appeals court found in favor of Cheryl Hopwood, a white woman who had sued the University of Texas law school on grounds that she was rejected for admittance as a result of the university's affirmative action plan to increase ethnic diversity among its student body.

Even before the Hopwood decision, the University of California system decided to eliminate preferences in admission based on race, gender, or ethnicity. California's state proposition 209, an initiative to make the practice of preferential treatment illegal, was passed by California voters in November, 1996. Such challenges served to make the future of affirmative action uncertain, suggesting that other models of affirmative action might be developed to take its place.

SUGGESTED READINGS:

Boxhill, Bernard. *Blacks and Social Justice.* Totowa, N.J.: Rowman & Allenheld, 1984.

Cohen, Carl. *Naked Racial Preference: The Case Against Affirmative Action.* Lanham, Md.: Madison Books, 1995.

Cohen, Marshall, et al. *Equality and Preferential Treatment.* Princeton, N.J.: Princeton University Press, 1977.

Fullinwider, Robert K. *The Reverse Discrimination Controversy.* Totowa, N.J.: Rowman & Littlefield, 1980.

Rosenfeld, Michael. *Affirmative Action and Justice: A Philosophical and Constitutional Inquiry.* New Haven, Conn.: Yale University Press, 1991.

—*Diane P. Michelfelder*

Reynolds v. Sims

1964: U.S. SUPREME COURT decision requiring Alabama to reapportion its legislative voting districts according to the principle of "one man, one vote."

By the mid-1960's many claims against state apportionment plans had been brought before federal COURTS. However, the Supreme Court's *Reynolds* decision stands out because of the "one man, one vote" principle articulated by Chief Justice Earl WARREN. Warren declared that the basic aim of legislative apportionment is "fair and effective representation" for all citizens. As a result of this holding, states were compelled by court orders to devise their reapportionment plans so that every citizen had an equal vote in the political process, regardless of their geographical residence.

—*Angelyque P. Campbell*

Rhode Island Charter

1663: Colonial charter establishing Rhode Island as a separate colony, with freedom of RELIGION guaranteed for all citizens.

Although by no means the only early American experiment in religious freedom—or even the most famous—the colony of Rhode Island was nevertheless notable for its success in the face of persistent and determined opposition. Derided by its neighbors and given to contentiousness and disorganization within its own ranks, Rhode Island still managed to emerge as an important example of government-guaranteed religious freedom prior to the ratification of the First Amendment to the U.S. CONSTITUTION.

A Colony of Nonconformists Liberty of conscience was the root issue that first set the founder of Rhode Island, Roger Williams, against the religious and political leadership of the early New England Puritans. A religious nonconformist in a day when conformity was prized, Williams arrived in Massachusetts Bay in 1631 to become pastor in Boston. He refused the pulpit, however, when the congregation rejected his demands that they completely separate themselves from any contact with the Church of England. Williams then moved to neighboring Plymouth, where he served as pastor for two years but found even the more strict separatists of that colony to be overly lenient.

In 1634 Williams was to become pastor of the church in Salem. However, by then he had expanded his criticisms of the colony's leadership by charging them with too much political interference in strictly religious affairs and stating that colonial land had been expropriated illegally from local Indian tribes. He was tried by the Massachusetts General Court and expelled from the colony, a decision that the Massachusetts leadership assumed would silence Williams permanently. It had the opposite effect.

In 1636 Williams and a few followers decided to establish their own colony at the headwaters of Narragansett Bay. On land deeded to him by local Indians, Williams and his followers established the colony of Providence, later to be known as the Providence Plantations. He was soon followed in turn by other expatriates from Massachusetts Bay, and by 1642 three other towns had been established as well. In 1644 Williams went to England to secure a charter for the new colony, primarily as a legal barrier against the attempts of Massachusetts Bay and the colony of Connecticut to interfere with internal matters. With the assistance of such notable Puritans as John Milton, he managed to obtain a charter from the commissioners of the Westminster Parliament, though it was never signed by King Charles I, who was then beleaguered by Oliver Cromwell's Puritan revolution.

By this time, the tradition of religious freedom for which Rhode Island later became famous was already in force as Quakers, JEWS, Baptists, and others not welcome in the other Puritan colonies found a haven in the colony's various towns. Religious freedom was automatically equated with religious toleration; Williams himself had nothing good to say about the beliefs of the Quakers residing in his colony, but neither they nor any other groups were hindered from the practice of their particular faiths. Some of the oldest churches and synagogues in America were established in Newport and Providence.

Securing a Royal Charter By 1647 the towns of the Rhode Island Colony had banded together to establish a formal government that Williams himself led off and on for the next several years. However, internal strife and continuing threats from other colonies hampered Rhode Island's efforts at stability, despite its parliamentary charter status. Throughout the decade of the 1650's, Williams' colleague John Clarke had remained in England in order to press

Rhode Island's case for a more stable and permanent charter but was hindered from doing so by the chaos of English politics. In 1662, however, John Winthrope, Jr., of Connecticut arrived in England seeking a charter for that colony which, if successful, would have meant the annexation of much of Rhode Island's territory. Redoubling his efforts, Clarke eventually took advantage of the collapse of Cromwell's government and the restoration of the monarchy to induce King Charles II to grant a permanent royal charter in 1663. That charter remained in force until the American Revolution.

Prominent in that document was official recognition of Rhode Island's long-standing tradition of religious freedom, which had been an important part of the colony's success. The charter's text made reference to the colonists' own affirmation that "a most flourishing civil state may stand and best be maintained with a full liberty in religious concernments." Ironically, this courageous experiment in religious liberty was largely unknown and overlooked in the later constitutional debates that led to the passage of the First Amendment, particularly in comparison with its larger colonial neighbor to the south, Pennsylvania. Later, however, Rhode Island's story became a shining example of the power of religious freedom, and its story has cast a long shadow over the subsequent interpretation of the constitutional amendment whose guarantee of this fundamental civil right has become its legacy.

SUGGESTED READINGS:

Curry, Thomas. *The First Freedoms: Church and State in America to the Passage of the First Amendment.* New York: Oxford University Press, 1986.

Gaustad, Edwin. *Liberty of Conscience: Roger Williams in America.* Grand Rapids, Mich.: William B. Eerdmans, 1991.

—*Robert C. Davis*

Right to die

The right to freedom of choice in determining the timing and manner of one's own death.

Advances in health care technology in the late twentieth century have created a number of new legal issues and ethical dilemmas. Widespread desire for equal access to HEALTH CARE has been one such concern. A related concern has been the question of whether individual persons have the right to refuse health care. The right to die has broad philosophical implications, including the hypothetical right of the young, healthy, or able-bodied to commit suicide. Legal debate has, however, focused on the rights of the elderly and seriously ill to control their own deaths. Legal terminology relating to these issues has been unusually problematic. Indeed, definitions of death itself have radically changed as improved resuscitative methods and brain-monitoring technologies have developed. The use of the general phrase "right to die" itself reflects this lack of definition.

By one definition, the "right to die" means the right to refuse medical treatment. One of the earliest controversies over extending this definition grew out of the case of a long comatose patient named Karen Anne Quinlan, whose family sought to refuse treatment on her behalf because she could not do so herself. In 1976 the family won the right from New Jersey's supreme court to disconnect her life-support equipment. Ironically, after she was taken off the equipment, she remained alive—but still comatose—another nine years.

"Right to die" has come to encompass withholding assisted feeding, suicide, assisted suicide, and euthanasia (or mercy killing). Legal and ethical concerns differ for each of these cases, yet the phrase "right to die" is often used without these distinctions being made.

Legal Foundations Nothing in the original U.S. CONSTITUTION supports the right to die. However, some right-to-die advocates find such a right in the later BILL OF RIGHTS in the implied intent of the Constitution's Framers. The Ninth Amendment, for example, guarantees rights "retained by the people" even when not specifically enumerated in the Constitution. This amendment has been interpreted to provide PRIVACY RIGHTS. Right-to-die advocates argue that privacy rights include the intimate nature of such decisions as death. In 1996, however, a federal appeals court in San Francisco ruled that there was a constitutional right to die.

In June, 1997, the U.S. Supreme Court handed down a landmark decision, ruling unanimously that there is no federal constitutional right to die. The decision did not, however, debar the states from enacting their own right-to-die laws.

Many of the acts associated with the right to die involve the taking of life, so there are strong legal arguments against such a right. Euthanasia is legally considered a form of murder. Suicide and assisted

U.S. Opinion on Medically Assisted Suicide

In 1994 the Gallup Poll asked a cross section of Americans if they approved of physician-assisted suicide for persons suffering great pain with no hope of improvement. The poll got these results:

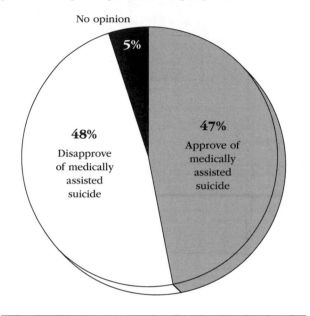

Source: George Gallup, Jr., ed., *The Gallup Poll: Public Opinion, 1994* (Wilmington, Del.: Scholarly Resources, 1995).

suicide have been more legally complex. The physician Jack Kevorkian, who has participated in many assisted suicides, has been credited with raising public awareness of assisted suicide. As a result of his participation in more than twenty-five well-publicized suicides, several state legislatures have passed laws banning assisted suicide, although the state of Oregon passed a statute allowing it. These laws have faced extensive court challenges. After 1991 Kevorkian himself faced criminal prosecution for murder. In a unique application of English COMMON LAW, he was tried in 1996 for feloniously violating a common law proscription against assisted suicide. The dismissal of the murder charge and his acquittal in other cases reflected the uncertainty of public opinion. While not necessarily showing legal approval of his actions, jurors consistently refused to send him to prison.

In this complicated legal environment, right-to-die advocates have developed legal tools for persons who wish to assert this right, at least regarding refusing medical care when rendered incompetent by a medical condition. "Living wills" specify in advance the conditions under which persons would

Dr. Jack Kevorkian, who continued to assist terminally ill persons in committing suicide during the 1990's in the face of repeated attempts to prosecute him for murder. (*AP/Wide World Photos*)

refuse life-sustaining treatment. Living wills have not always been honored, however, for such reasons as uncooperative families or medical personnel. Their reluctance to comply with the living wills has often resulted from the ambiguity of the documents themselves, which cannot anticipate and specify all possible circumstances. Actual decisions, then, have been fraught with moral and legal complications, with the risk that wrong decisions might result in lawsuits, if not criminal prosecutions.

The Case for the Right to Die Advocates for the right to die focus on how people die in the midst of life-prolonging technology. Improved technology typically increases duration of life at the expense of quality. Many people express horror at the idea of spending weeks or months lingering in hospitals with hopeless terminal conditions, kept alive by machines. Immobility, pain, and lack of personal freedom have led many patients to ask for deaths that they are not allowed. Health care workers point out that they themselves are legally and ethically obligated to preserve life. Many medical conditions may steadily worsen so that death may be certain for months, or even years, before it comes. Even in cases in which the illness is not terminal—for example in some cases of multiple sclerosis—some patients prefer death.

In addition to humane concerns for patients' welfare, right-to-die advocates also point to the emotional and financial burdens experienced by patients' families. Not only must families watch their loved ones' suffering, but their grief is prolonged, interfering with jobs and the needs of other family members. The drain on financial resources may last for years after death finally takes place.

There are additional questions about the burden on society created by prolonging an unwanted life. Hospitals, insurance agencies, and government programs bear an increasing share of health care costs, all of which are passed on to the public. Advanced medical technology is not only expensive but limited by availability and location. Many who need access to health care are unable to obtain it.

At the beginning of the twentieth century, most Americans died in their own homes. Near the century's end, most deaths occurred in hospitals or nursing homes. Research on the fear of death has shown that those with terminal illnesses or those of advanced age do not always fear death itself. What they fear is painful or lingering death, or dying alone. The prolongation of unwanted lives impairs all life, by making death unnatural and fearsome.

The Case Against the Right to Die Many critics of the right to die have opposed only some actions that fall under that term. Opposition to euthanasia is common, for example, whereas support for the right to refuse life-prolonging treatment is widespread. The strongest critics of the general right to die argue the "slippery slope" analogy: Once the sacred and, for doctors, professional obligation to sustain life is breached, it will be difficult to prevent broader application than originally intended. Critics frequently cite the case of the Netherlands, where euthanasia is legal with patient consent, but where accusations have been made of cases of euthanasia without consent. The difficulty, as reflected in the opposition of the American Medical Association to assisted suicide, is that in real life, situations typically exceed the law's ability to define concepts such as consent.

Not only can consent be difficult to define, but so are such terms as "terminal condition," "pain," and "quality of life." Terms that seem clear-cut to lay people, such as "persistent vegetative state" for comatose persons, are ambiguous in practice. Consent becomes complex not only for those rendered incompetent by their medical conditions, but also for persons with mental disabilities and for minors. Concern is expressed here with the more generally noncontroversial withholding of treatment.

The DISABILITY RIGHTS MOVEMENT has expressed concern with the right to die, not only on behalf of the mentally disabled and children, but of competent adults with physical disabilities. The concern is that, once legally recognized, the right to die would become an obligation to die. Critics point out that, for example, the Holocaust did not only claim the lives of Jews. People with physical and mental disabilities were among the first to be murdered. Advocates for people with disabilities point to alternatives to suicide and assisted suicide that they claim are often ignored.

Depression associated with chronic pain and disability can be either short-term or chronic. Suicide attempts are associated more with short-term acute depression than with chronic depression. Diagnoses (being told one is depressed) or changes in conditions can trigger or aggravate transient emotional problems. Moreover, chronic depression can be effectively treated with counseling, support groups, psychotherapy, and medication. Most important, pain can also be effectively treated in many of the terminally ill, although physicians are poorly trained in palliative care.

The hospice movement has promoted a variety of approaches for humane treatment of the terminally ill, including counseling for patients and families, assistance with home health care and aggressive palliative care. Hospice activists have promoted many causes associated with the right to die, such as living wills, but they are recognized by right to die critics as offering an appropriate alternative to precipitating death. Hospice care is restricted to patients with terminal diagnoses.

SUGGESTED READINGS:

Biskup, Michael, and Carol Wekesser, eds. *Suicide: Opposing Viewpoints*. San Diego: Greenhaven Press, 1992.

Davidson, Glen W., ed. *The Hospice: Development and Administration*. New York: Harper & Row, 1985.

Dudley, William, ed. *Death and Dying: Opposing Viewpoints*. San Diego: Greenhaven Press, 1992.

Humphrey, Derek. *Final Exit: The Practicalities of Self-Deliverance and Assisted Suicide for the Dying*. Eugene, Oreg.: Hemlock Society, 1991.

Kevorkian, Jack. *Prescription—Medicide: The Goodness of Planned Death*. Buffalo, N.Y.: Prometheus Books, 1991.

Koop, C. Everett. *The Right to Live, the Right to Die*. Wheaton, Ill.: Tyndale House, 1976.

—*Nancy E. Macdonald*

Rights definitions

Codifications of the liberties and privileges accorded to each person in a society by laws, moral codes, political covenants, or fundamental principles.

Few elements of social discourse arouse as much impassioned confusion as rights. Philosophers complain that Americans often do not understand what they are doing when they assert manifold rights. The proliferating assertions of rights since World War II have created a rhetorical morass because no universally held definition of rights, or even a rational method for achieving a definition, exists. Appeals to specific rights and to types of rights have, however, proven useful in mediating conflict. Deciding who has rights can be more peaceful than resorting to might. In this sense, philosophers generally agree, all rights are CIVIL RIGHTS because they are a means to assess responsibilities, safeguard citizens' welfare, and resolve specific social and political disputes peacefully.

There is much less agreement about how rights are to perform civil functions, in part because of the historical development of rights. The concept of rights derives from the ancient theory of natural law, which holds that each person has the innate ability to choose rationally in accordance with universal moral principles. Citizens' rights in the modern sense evolved after philosophers of the eighteenth and nineteenth centuries emphasized individualism in political theory. Originally, rights served to protect people from power arbitrarily exercised by their government; this idea is expressed, for example, in the DECLARATION OF INDEPENDENCE. In the twentieth century, however, rights also began to be invoked to protect one group from dominance by another. For example, women asserted the right to employment opportunities equal to those of men. Rights have also been asserted to mediate conflicting motives of individuals, such as when a terminally ill patient's desire for physician-assisted suicide in order to exercise the RIGHT TO DIE conflicts with the physician's oath against aiding death. The evolving, expanding conceptions of rights have complicated attempts to work out a comprehensive theory of rights that satisfies philosophers, legal professionals, social activists, and politicians.

Classifications of rights have caused some of the conceptual difficulty. At least four classifying principles are apparent in debates about rights. First, rights may be active or passive; that is, a right may entitle one either to act or to be the recipient of another's action. Second, rights may be classified by the type of right-holder, for example: American Indian rights, CHILDREN'S RIGHTS, or VICTIMS' RIGHTS). Third, rights may be specific or general; there is the specific right to sell one's property and the general right to own property. Fourth, rights may be classified by the basis of justification for a right. For example, a right may derive from universal principles, from a specific society's morality, or from laws.

In addition to difficulties of classification, philosophers disagree whether a right empowers a right-holder's ability to choose (choice or will theory) or defends the right-holder's interests or access to benefits (interest or benefit theory), although the interest theory has predominated. A further complicating factor comes from arguments by philoso-

A sign carried in a New York City civil rights demonstration in 1991 sums up the varieties of rights concerning modern Americans. (*Betty Lane*)

phers who emphasize the good of a community over that of its individual members, as do communist and some socialist theorists; they deny the existence of individual rights or subordinate them to communal harmony.

Most discussions of rights, however, concern ways of justifying them in order to clarify how to apply them. In this light, the formula of legal theorist Wesley N. Hohfeld isolates basic elements of a definition: "A" has a right to do "X" against "B" by virtue of "Y." "A" is the right-holder, "B" is the person, group, or institution that must respect the right, "X" is a specific action, such as voting or owning a firearm, and "Y" is the principle of justification. As political philosophy has changed, "Y" has as well. The justifications most frequently appealed include God, nature as an abstract principle, human nature, morality, custom, civil covenants, and law.

Natural Rights Various philosophers and theologians have held that certain rights belong to every person because they either are God-given or are of the fundamental order of nature. In either case, such rights are universal and, having existed before societies or governments, are superior to customs and laws. Most prominent among political philosophers who discussed the idea was John Locke. Locke's *Two Treatises on Government* (1690) lists life, liberty, and property as among the natural rights protecting a person from tyranny. Locke's ideas profoundly influenced the founders of the United States, who listed the rights to life, liberty, and the pursuit of happiness in the Declaration of Independence. No government, the declaration argues, can deprive its citizens of these rights because they were given by the "Creator." The U.S. CONSTITUTION, in turn, specifies individual CIVIL LIBERTIES, such as freedom of ASSEMBLY and freedom of RELIGION, in the BILL OF RIGHTS, which was ratified in 1791. Similarly, the revolutionary French Assembly founded its Declaration of the Rights of Man and of the Citizen (1789) on the rights to liberty, property, security, and resistance to oppression.

Human Rights The idea of natural rights fell from favor as political philosophies moved away from justifications based upon divinity or upon nature in the abstract. The modern descendant of natural rights is human rights. Human rights automatically belong to people simply because they are human. Human rights are universal moral standards that must be met if one is treated as fully human. Although somewhat vague, the definition promotes several crucial ideas: that humans are distinct in nature (human rights need not apply to animals), that there is a minimum set of conditions that enable people to fulfill their humanness, and that human rights are independent of and have priority over national mores and laws. Human rights, like natural rights, can be taken away by no group or government. Modern political thinkers therefore consider human rights extralegal and an argument of last resort to protect people when all local moral and legal approaches have failed.

Attempts to enumerate human rights have raised considerable controversy, especially after claims based upon human rights entered international politics. The United Nation's Universal Declaration of Human Rights (1948) provides basic definitions in twenty-one articles. Some articles are general, promoting personal liberties such as FREE SPEECH and travel, and some are quite specific, including a worker's right to a regular vacation. The international reaction to the declaration underscores the difficulty with human rights. Differing political ideologies have prompted varied interpretations of some of these rights, and even rejection when they appear to inhibit a government's control of its citizens. The final three articles, the right to education, employment, and an adequate standard of living, although widely supported, have also attracted criticism because in many cases they are simply impracticable. An impoverished nation may not be able to afford to provide education, employment, and an "adequate" living, even by local standards, to everyone. Since the declaration does not mandate a means of enforcing its provisions, some nations pay it little more than lip service or use it to criticize the internal affairs of other nations.

Moral Rights Justification of rights based upon specific customs and moral codes underlies the idea of moral rights. As happens with the more general conception of human rights, some vagueness attends moral rights because the elements of custom and morality are not always clearly articulated, making it difficult to identify the specific moral principle that gives meaning to a moral right. For this reason, some social theorists reject moral rights as a useful concept for practical civil affairs. For example, Jeremy Bentham, an influential English philosopher, dismissed moral rights as "nonsense upon stilts."

Most philosophers, however, recognize that morality, however vaguely conceived, can foster a recognition of rights in specific cases. This recognition typically occurs when some action is owed to one person by another even though no contract or law requires it. For example, a divorce settlement might leave the children of a marriage in the father's custody but with no requirement of child support payments from the mother. Still, based on the moral principle that parents should share in raising children, she might recognize the child's right to her support—even feel pressure from others to do so—and send money to her former husband.

Civil Rights The lack of clear formulation of moral rights prompted the scorn of logical positivists such as Bentham. They insist that a right only exists if it is enforceable and that it is enforceable only if it is explicitly justified by a political covenant or the law. For legislators, judges, lawyers, and rights activists, concerned with justifying specific rights claims, the positivist position has had considerable attraction. History has seen a steady accumulation of codified rights. In the United States, those rights that apply equally to all citizens in all states are civil rights in the strictest sense.

Civil rights comprise civil liberties and property rights, political rights, welfare rights, and, to some, social and economic rights. Civil liberties and property rights draw justification from political covenants. In the United States, citizens often refer to civil rights as constitutional rights because the Bill of Rights lists many important protections. Civil rights specifically mentioned in the Bill of Rights include the right to petition the government for a redress of grievances, protection from unreasonable search and seizure, and the right to DUE PROCESS and a speedy trial. Political rights empower citizens to participate in government. The Constitution, its FIFTEENTH AMENDMENT, its NINETEENTH AMENDMENT, and its TWENTY-SIXTH AMENDMENT define who is eligible to vote and forbid various attempts to discourage voters, such as by the imposition of POLL TAXES. Other provisions indicate who is eligible, and therefore has the right, to run for political office.

Welfare rights are ENTITLEMENTS for people unable to provide some basic necessity for themselves. Typically, federal or state legislation creates welfare rights, but they derive ultimately from the social philosophy that the needy have a moral right to society's assistance. Government programs that give the poor food or food stamps, pay for medical care, and provide job training are the practical result. Finally, social rights and economic rights also depend upon legislative acts for enforcement; such acts are often very controversial because they challenge assumptions about race and class, political power, or economic theory. For example, laws regarding equal rights for minority groups, as codified in the various federal civil rights acts and applied in AFFIRMATIVE ACTION programs, laws regarding a MINIMUM WAGE, and laws regarding strikes have all been made in a context of controversy. Social reform organizations such as the NATIONAL ASSOCIATION FOR THE ADVANCEMENT OF COLORED PEOPLE and the NATIONAL ORGANIZATION FOR WOMEN usually make it their goal to secure reform by having new civil rights explicitly incorporated into a political covenant (for example, the proposed EQUAL RIGHTS AMENDMENT) or legislative act.

Legal Rights Legal rights are those justified by statutes in federal, state, or local law or specified in contracts. The distinction between legal rights and civil rights is not always sharp, although generally legal rights tend to be more specific. Furthermore, considerable ambiguity plagues the word "right" in legal and civil issues, as Hohfeld points out in *Fundamental Legal Conceptions as Applied in Judicial Reasoning* (1964). According to Hohfeld, people use the word "right" in four distinct senses: a claim, a privilege, a power, and an immunity. A legal claim requires some action for the benefit of the right-holder from a second party, who has a correlative duty to perform it. For example, a person who buys a car can demand possession of the car from the seller, who has a legal duty to comply. A legal privilege exists for right-holders to perform some action when they have no legal duty to a second party to refrain from that action. Workers can form LABOR UNIONS, for example, as long as no laws forbid it. A right-holder has a legal power over a second party concerning some legal relation when the right-holder can effect a change in that relation. A married couple changes a legal relation to children upon adopting them, and a person making out a will changes the obligations to those who are named to receive bequests. A right-holder has a legal immunity from a second party concerning a legal relation if the second party has no power to change that relation. One person, for example, may not arbitrarily silence another; the freedom of speech provision in the First Amendment prohibits Congress from passing a law granting individuals that power.

Hohfeld insists that one person's right involves a correlative duty on the part of another, an idea that has guided most subsequent legal theorists. The reciprocating rights and duties of each citizen hold society together through a network of relations. Philosophers have pointed out that some commonly espoused rights do not logically impose clear correlative duties. This is especially true of human rights. A person's right to education does not make clear who must provide it or what the education should entail. The right to pursue happiness does not impose on others the duty to help—at most, it forbids interference, the absence of action, which some political thinkers call a negative duty.

Non-Human Rights In addition to rights of humans, other rights have been championed. Initiatives to shield animals from mistreatment (animal rights), to rescue endangered species and deteriorating ecosystems (environmental rights), or to forbid ABORTION (sometimes called fetal rights) cannot, however, logically appeal to the right-holder (the owner of the horse, the landowner or hunter, the pregnant woman). Proponents of non-human rights variously base their arguments upon, to cite three arguments: first, some aspect of natural principle, such as the sacredness of all life; second, morality, such as the proscription against cruelty or killing in the case of animal and fetal rights; or third, civil rights, as when a degraded ecosystem threatens the health and livelihood of people living in it.

SUGGESTED READINGS:

Coleman, Jules L., ed. *Rights and Their Foundations*. New York: Garland, 1994. Fifteen essays by legal scholars and philosophers about legal approaches to the theory of rights and their importance to the law.

Donnelly, Jack. *Universal Human Rights in Theory and Practice*. Ithaca, N.Y.: Cornell University Press, 1989. Examines the definition and theory of human rights, cultural relativism, and problems in social reform and politics.

Hohfeld, Wesley N. *Fundamental Legal Conceptions as Applied in Judicial Reasoning*. New Haven, Conn.: Yale University Press, 1964. Often-cited classic in defining rights.

Lomasky, Loren E. *Persons, Rights, and the Moral Community*. New York: Oxford University Press, 1987. Criticizes the proliferation of rights claims not based clearly on moral principles. Discusses how basic rights, exercised with restraint, can support a flexible, just society.

Shute, Stephen, and Susan Hurley, eds. *On Human Rights*. New York: Basic Books, 1993. Eight essays by philosophers and social critics about the theory of human rights, civil rights, rights and economics, the politics of rights, and women's rights.

Thomson, Judith Jarvis. *The Realm of Rights*. Cambridge, Mass.: Harvard University Press, 1990. Clarifies and modifies Hohfeld's distinctions among rights as claims, privileges, powers, and immunities in order to identify basic general rights.

Wellman, Carl. *A Theory of Rights*. Totowa, N.J.: Rowman & Allanheld, 1985. Clear exposition of legal rights that interprets Hohfeld's treatment of rights as claims, powers, privileges, and immunities in order to aid practical judicial reasoning.

White, Alan R. *Rights*. Oxford, England: Clarendon Press, 1984. Scrutinizes the concept of rights and the various definitions and types of rights in order to demonstrate how they come from differing approaches to goodness, necessity, or obligation.

—*Roger Smith*

Robeson, Eslanda Cardozo Goode

Dec. 15, 1896, Washington, D.C.—Dec. 13, 1965, New York, N.Y.: Civil rights activist, author, and wife of Paul ROBESON.

Proud of her black heritage, Eslanda Robeson especially cherished the memory of her paternal grandfather, Francis Lewis Cardozo, who had served as secretary of state and secretary of the treasury in South Carolina during the RECONSTRUCTION ERA.

Upon graduation from high school at the age of sixteen, Robeson won a full scholarship to the University of Illinois, where she enrolled in domestic science courses. Discovering that she preferred chemistry, she made that her major; she transferred to Columbia University for her senior year, graduat-

ing in 1917. Afterward she was hired by Presbyterian Hospital to prepare tissue slides for pathological diagnosis—a job that made her the first black on the hospital's professional staff. She met Paul Robeson at the hospital in 1920, when he was hospitalized for a severe football injury; they were married on August 17, 1921. Eslanda encouraged Paul to undertake an acting and concertizing career and accompanied him as his manager on his trips abroad during the 1920's and 1930's.

Writing About Blacks Robeson's book *Paul Robeson, Negro* (1930), published simultaneously in London and New York, was planned as a civil rights document as well as a biography. Chapters on her husband's early life and college career described difficulties faced by blacks growing up in the officially free, but heavily segregated, northern states. A chapter on Harlem in the 1920's portrayed the vigorous black cultural community that had grown up, unhindered by restraints imposed in the surrounding white world. Robeson passionately denounced the lawlessness and lynching that marred white relations with blacks in the South and praised Paul for using his music and art to show white audiences, who knew nothing of black life, that African Americans lived fully human lives.

In London Eslanda became fascinated with Africa; from 1935 to 1937 she studied anthropology at University College, London, and the London School of Economics, specializing in the field of African cultures. In 1936 she spent three months traveling in Africa, going from Cape Town to Swaziland, Uganda, and the Belgian Congo. After the Robesons returned to the United States in 1939, Robeson enrolled in the Hartford Seminary Foundation and completed a Ph.D. in anthropology in 1945. That same year she published *African Journey*, based on the diary she had kept in 1936. Her book denounced the exploitation of Africans that she had witnessed and used her striking photographs from the trip to portray her African hosts as dignified and intelligent human beings.

Robeson joined with the white novelist Pearl Buck in 1949 to write *American Argument*, a dialogue on RACISM. The book contrasted Buck's experience growing up as a white child among nonwhite people in China with Robeson's experience growing up as a young black in white America. Together they denounced colonial exploitation of native peoples and racial inequality in the United States.

Political Activism   During the 1930's, as the political situation in Europe worsened, Robeson became an ardent antifascist and praised the Soviet Union for its opposition to Adolf Hitler and to European colonialism. She and her husband made several trips to the Soviet Union during the 1930's and were impressed by the relative absence of racial prejudice there.

During the 1940's Robeson became a successful lecturer before college and church audiences, speaking out on race relations, colonialism, and African affairs. During the Cold War between the Soviet Union and the United States, the Robesons re-affirmed their faith in Soviet good intentions. They openly criticized the U.S. government for supporting colonial regimes in Africa and Asia and for doing too little to combat racism at home. Robeson helped organize the national convention of Henry Wallace's Progressive Party in 1948 and ran as the party nominee for secretary of state of Connecticut in 1948, and for Congress in 1950.

Political activity created personal hardships for the Robesons. Veterans' groups organized violent protests to prevent Paul from giving concerts, and many cities and towns barred him from appearing on stage or in concert halls. As a result, the family income fell drastically. From 1950 to 1958 the U.S. Department of State refused to issue the Robesons passports on the grounds that their presence overseas would endanger American national security. On July 7, 1953, Eslanda was called to testify as a hostile witness by Senator Joseph McCarthy's Senate Investigative Committee. Although she refused to discuss her political views as a matter of constitutional right and vigorously attacked the committee as racist, its members did not cite her for contempt. Not until 1962, with her passport regained and the constitutional issues less pressing, would she sign an oath that she had never been a member of any communist party.

In the late 1950's Robeson wrote a series of articles on African affairs that were syndicated by the Associated Negro Press. At the time of her 1965 death (from cancer) she was at work on books dealing with the recent history of the Congo (now Zaïre) and the politics of race in America.

SUGGESTED READINGS:

Duberman, Martin Bauml. *Paul Robeson*. New York: Alfred A. Knopf, 1988.
Gilliam, Dorothy Butler. *Paul Robeson: All-American.*
Washington, D.C.: New Republic Books, 1976.
Hoyt, Edwin P. *Paul Robeson: The American Othello*. Cleveland: World Publishing, 1967.
—*Milton Berman*

Robeson, Paul

Apr. 9, 1898, Princeton, N.J.—Jan. 23, 1976, Philadelphia, Pa.: AFRICAN AMERICAN actor, singer, and civil rights activist.

A towering, multitalented figure in modern American culture, Robeson earned a law degree from Columbia University during the early 1920's, while he played professional football. During the 1920's and 1930's he earned a reputation as a powerful singer and talented actor and appeared in concerts, on the stage, and in films. During this same period, he developed an interest in his African heritage; in 1934 he traveled to the Soviet Union, where he was impressed by the fact that African Americans were treated as equals. Unaware of the terror of Joseph Stalin's Soviet regime, Robeson was captivated by life under communism. After the outbreak of Spain's civil war in 1936, Robeson declared his support for the socialist Popular Front against Francisco's Franco's fascist forces.

The Politicization of Robeson's Art   Robeson reached the highpoint of his performing career when he played the lead in a Broadway production of William Shakespeare's *Othello* in 1943-1944. During the following years, he began to politicize his concerts by presenting speeches advocating racial equality and workers' rights. While his remarks were tolerated through 1946, the outbreak of the Cold War and reports of his confrontational meeting with President Harry S TRUMAN turned American opinion against Robeson. Not interested in accommodating to the prevailing political realities, Robeson marginalized himself further when he supported the presidential aspirations of Henry Wallace in 1948 and attended the procommunist Congress of the World Partisan of Peace in Paris in 1949.

After Robeson returned to the United States in June, 1949, he was notified that his contract for more than eighty concerts had been canceled. In response to the mounting popular opposition to him, Robeson became more adamant in his demands for racial and economic justice. On August 27, 1949, he was scheduled to present a concert in Peekskill, New York, but the event was

Singer-actor Paul Robeson, whose refusal to disavow communism nearly wrecked his career. (*Associated Publishers*)

canceled when a conservative demonstration against his appearance resulted in a riot among protesters and those who wished to hear Robeson sing. Robeson denounced the riot and the failure of the police to protect his supporters and scheduled another Peekskill concert for early September. With support from union workers, the concert was held, but the tense situation degenerated into violence as the concert ended and the audience began to leave. Once again, demonstrators attacked those who attended; more than 150 people were injured and extensive property damage resulted.

Robeson and his supporters were not responsible for the Peekskill riots, but his name was afterward identified with violence; consequently, he found even more doors closed to him. While his talent as a singer was recognized, American audiences no longer would tolerate his left-wing rhetoric. Many of his friends thought that his spirit was broken by the aftermath of Peekskill. In 1950 he planned to abandon the United States for what he thought would be sympathetic Great Britain, but his request for a renewal of his passport was denied. The period from 1950 to 1955 was characterized by Robeson's isolation. A target of surveillance by the Federal Bureau of Investigation and other law enforcement agencies, and denounced by Roy Wilkins of the National Association for the Advancement of Colored People, Robeson found himself a casualty of the Cold War within the United States.

As African Americans began to realize returns on their long struggle for civil rights and to awaken to the leadership of Martin Luther King, Jr., few Americans, black or white, were receptive to Robeson. In 1958, when he was finally granted a passport, he went to England, expecting he would be welcomed; however, the British gave him a cold reception and he quietly moved on to the communist-bloc countries of Eastern Europe. In Budapest, Sophia, Warsaw, and the other Eastern European capitals, he was received enthusiastically. He enjoyed a revival of his performing career, but even this was cut short by his failing health and that of his wife, Essie. A planned tour of Australia and New Zealand was curtailed when the Robesons' physical conditions worsened. After his health was partly restored, he returned to the United States. During 1964 and 1965 he presented several concerts, but his energy was gone. Essie's death in December, 1965, shattered Robeson. Three years later he moved to Philadelphia, where he lived with his sister; his public career was over. After suffering a stroke in December, 1975, he died the following month.

SUGGESTED READINGS:

Davis, Lenwood G. *A Paul Robeson Research Guide: A Selected, Annotated Bibliography.* Westport, Conn.: Greenwood Press, 1982.

Duberman, Martin B. *Paul Robeson.* New York: Alfred A. Knopf, 1989.

Ramdin, Ron. *Paul Robeson: The Man and His Mission.* London: P. Owen, 1987.

Robeson, Paul. *Here I Stand.* Boston: Beacon Press, 1971.

—*William T. Walker*

Robinson, Aubrey E., Jr.

Born Mar. 30, 1922, Madison, N.J.: AFRICAN AMERICAN civil rights attorney and federal judge.

In his first years as a practicing attorney—one of only a few African American attorneys in Washington, D.C.—Robinson began making a name for himself as a civil rights advocate. During the 1950's he was general counsel, and then director, of the American Council on Human Rights, and he also served on the boards of directors of such organizations as the Family Services Association of America and the Interreligious Commission on Race Relations. However, he made his greatest contributions in the U.S. district court in Washington, D.C., where he was appointed judge in 1966 and chief judge in 1982.

During more than twenty years as a judge, Robinson made many rulings with important rights implications. For example, he limited the right of the government to use wire taps in investigating narcotics cases, he upheld the rights of women workers to seek redress for SEXUAL HARASSMENT, he overturned an Air Force ban on Jewish officers' wearing yarmulkes, and he declared that the public must be awarded access to tape recordings secretly made by President Richard M. NIXON. He also spoke out against congressionally enacted mandatory minimum sentences and in support of more presidential appointments of black federal judges; and he oversaw the creation of a federal public defender's office and a group of volunteer lawyers to help prisoners with their civil complaints. He also appointed a controversial mental health "special master," an outside specialist responsible for the district's mental health services, and created elaborate security measures to protect terrorists and drug lords facing trial.

Robinson retired as chief judge in 1992 at the mandatory retirement age of seventy; however, he continued in the advisory role of senior judge.

—*Cynthia A. Bily*

Robinson, Jackie

Jan. 31, 1919, Cairo, Ga.—Oct. 24, 1972, Stamford, Conn.: Major league baseball player and civil rights advocate.

The first AFRICAN AMERICAN to play major league baseball in the twentieth century, Robinson broke the color barrier in 1947. He had first attracted attention as a four-sport athlete at the University of California at Los Angeles (UCLA) from 1939 to 1941. While there, in addition to playing baseball, he twice led the southern division of the Pacific Coast Conference in basketball scoring, was an All-American running back on the football team, and won the national college long-jump championship in track and field.

Two years after leaving UCLA, Robinson was drafted into the Army. During his Army service he challenged racial SEGREGATION practices on MILITARY bases. Initially denied entry into the army's officer candidate school because of his race, Robinson challenged his exclusion and was eventually commissioned a second lieutenant. He later faced court martial charges for insubordination arising out of an incident in which he refused to move to the back of a segregated military bus in Texas. After he was acquitted he received an honorable discharge.

Following his Army service, Robinson played one season of baseball with the Kansas City Monarchs in the Negro Baseball Leagues. At that time, major league baseball excluded black players pursuant to an unwritten agreement among the owners

Jackie Robinson, the first African American to play major-league baseball in the modern era, in 1951. (*National Baseball Library, Cooperstown, N.Y.*)

dating back to the nineteenth century. After the war, however, pressure to integrate baseball was steadily increasing as many critics complained of the hypocrisy of requiring African Americans to fight for their country while denying them the opportunity to play "the national pastime."

Branch Rickey, president of the Brooklyn Dodgers baseball team, decided to challenge the exclusion of black players and selected Robinson to break the color line. Although Robinson was arguably not the best black baseball player at that time, Rickey admired his maturity and his experience of competing in interracial settings at UCLA, as well as his competitive fire. In August, 1945, he signed Robinson to play with the Montreal Royals, the Dodgers' top minor league club. After leading the Montreal Royals to the International League championship in 1946 and winning the league batting championship, Robinson joined the Brooklyn Dodgers in the spring of 1947, thereby breaking the ban on black players in the major leagues.

Robinson's Rookie Season During his first year as a second baseman with the Dodgers, Robinson experienced extraordinary verbal and physical abuse from white players. Pitchers threw balls at his head, while opposing baserunners cut him with their spikes. Off the field, Robinson received scores of death threats. Although he had a fiery temper and enormous pride, he refused to retaliate and instead took out his frustrations on the field. His aggressive playing style—particularly in baserunning—helped to win games for the Dodgers. Despite the great pressures on him during his rookie season, Robinson led the Dodgers to their first National League championship in six years and a berth in the World Series. He also led the league in stolen bases and was named rookie of the year. Overnight, he captured the hearts of black America and attracted thousands of new spectators to major league games. His success paved the way for other black baseball players. By the end of the 1947 season, two other major league teams had signed black players, and by the early 1950's, most other major league teams had done likewise.

Robinson played ten years for the Brooklyn Dodgers—primarily as a second baseman—during which time the Dodgers won six National League pennants and one World Series. He had an array of skills, but was particularly known as a daring base runner, stealing home plate nineteen times in his career and five times in one season. In 1962 Robin-

son became the first black player to win election to the Baseball Hall of Fame.

Off the field, Robinson, unlike many other black ballplayers, was an outspoken critic of segregation, challenging the exclusion of blacks from management positions in baseball. After his retirement from baseball in 1957, Robinson continued his civil rights advocacy and became an active promoter of black-owned businesses. He conducted frequent fundraising events for the NATIONAL ASSOCIATION FOR THE ADVANCEMENT OF COLORED PEOPLE (NAACP) and other civil rights causes and organizations. Through the 1960's he wrote a regular newspaper column in which he criticized the persistence of racial injustice in various aspects of American life.

Probably no other athlete has made a greater impact on American SPORTS than Robinson. His personal success opened the door to other black baseball players and helped pave the way for the acceptance of black athletes in other professional sports. From the late 1940's until his death in 1972, Robinson was one of the most important symbols of the virtue of racial integration in American life.

SUGGESTED READINGS:

Falkner, David. *Great Time Coming: The Life of Jackie Robinson from Baseball to Birmingham.* New York: Oxford University Press, 1995.

Robinson, Jackie, with Alfred Duckett. *I Never Had It Made.* New York: Putnam, 1972.

Tygiel, Jules. *Baseball's Great Experiment: Jackie Robinson and His Legacy.* New York: Oxford University Press, 1983.

—*Davison M. Douglas*

Robinson, Jo Ann Gibson

Born April 17, 1912, Culloden, Ga.: AFRICAN AMERICAN educator and civil rights advocate.

By profession a college teacher, Jo Ann Gibson Robinson has been best known for her work in connection with the 1955 MONTGOMERY BUS BOYCOTT. However, before Rosa PARKS defied a JIM CROW LAW that required African Americans to give up their bus seats to white passengers, Robinson had struggled to abolish this law. While teaching in the English department at Alabama State College in Montgomery, she had been president of an organization of middle-class black women called the Women's Political Council (WPC). During the early 1950's the

WPC had lobbied the city against the seating policy and had threatened a boycott. When Parks's arrest finally galvanized attention on the seating law, Robinson and the WPC were crucial in organizing and helping to sustain the long boycott that ensued.

—*Timothy L. Hall*

Robinson, Randall

Born July 6, 1941, Richmond, Va.: Political activist.

A graduate of Harvard University Law School, Randall Robinson worked initially as a civil rights attorney and subsequently as a congressional aid. In this latter capacity he traveled to South Africa as part of a congressional delegation in the 1970's and eventually became a strong critic of South Africa's apartheid policies. By 1977 he was executive director of TRANSAFRICA, a lobbying group for African and Caribbean causes that he helped to found. In 1984 he achieved national attention by organizing a year-long series of daily protests of apartheid in front of South Africa's Washington, D.C., embassy building. These and other protests were instrumental in CONGRESS' eventual passage of the Comprehensive Anti-Apartheid Act of 1986, which implemented U.S. sanctions against South Africa until 1991, when South African leader Nelson Mandela was released from prison.

—*Timothy L. Hall*

Robinson, Rubye Doris Smith

Apr. 25, 1942, Atlanta, Ga.—Oct. 7, 1967, Atlanta, Ga.: AFRICAN AMERICAN civil rights activist and one of the founders of the STUDENT NON-VIOLENT COORDINATING COMMITTEE (SNCC).

As a sophomore at Spelman College in ATLANTA, GEORGIA, Rubye Doris Smith participated in the GREENSBORO SIT-INS of 1960. This activity motivated her to join in other integration efforts. Her SNCC activities included participation in FREEDOM RIDES, community-action organizing, and voter registration drives across the South. Arrested numerous times for these activities, she introduced the "jail-without-bail" tactic to help focus national NEWS MEDIA attention on SNCC efforts. This tactic gave nation-wide press coverage to those civil rights protesters who elected to serve their entire sentences rather than pay nominal fines for their protest activities.

As Smith's experience broadened, so did her methods of protest. She regarded nonviolence as a situational tactic rather than a general one. The espousal of such a philosophy put her at odds with the SOUTHERN CHRISTIAN LEADERSHIP CONFERENCE (SCLC) and Martin Luther KING, JR., who advocated a policy of nonviolent protest only. Smith's political savvy, however, influenced SNCC to change its direction. She gained support for her situational tactics by going to Africa, where she witnessed the success of techniques she advocated at first hand. She returned from Africa with a growing commitment to BLACK NATIONALISM. Her ability to alter and modify political directions also led her to challenge SNCC's male-dominated leadership. She participated in a sit-in at James FORMAN's office to focus attention on the limited role of women in the organization's leadership; however, her attempts to correct gender inequalities within SNCC were not meant to alter the goal of the organization: immediate improvement of black life in America.

Smith's energy and focus allowed her to play a major role in the transformation of SNCC to the new direction of black nationalism. She was a dedicated freedom fighter, who made everything, including her personal life, secondary to the organization. In 1964 she married another SNCC veteran, Cliff Robinson, and gave birth to a son, Kenneth Toure, named for the president of Guinea, West Africa. Back at work in just two days, she continued to remain active in organizational activities until her untimely death from lymphoma in 1967.

—*Thomas J. Edward Walker and Cynthia Gwynne Yaudes*

Rock Springs riot

1885: RACE RIOT against CHINESE mineworkers in Wyoming Territory.

Ethnic tension rose in the small Wyoming coal-mining camp as the coal deposits played out and economic uncertainty loomed. A fistfight between whites and Chinese miners developed into a full-scale riot in which twenty-eight Chinese men were killed and fifteen wounded. Whites drove the remainder of the Chinese community into the hills, where some fifty of them died from starvation and exposure.

This contemporary print of the massacre of Chinese mine workers at Rock Springs was drawn from a photograph taken on the scene by a U.S. infantry trooper. (*Bancroft Library, University of California*)

In addition to the economic insecurity and RA-CISM that underlay the riot, the federal government's CHINESE EXCLUSION ACT, which Congress had passed in 1882, helped to fuel anti-Chinese hostility throughout the United States. Although an investigation by the Chinese consul showed racism to be the riot's underlying cause, U.S. president Grover Cleveland refused to admit any government responsibility. However, he did recognize the inhumanity of the actions and authorized an indemnity of $150,000 to be paid for the loss of life and property.

—*Duncan R. Jamieson*

Roe v. Wade

1973: Landmark U.S. Supreme Court ruling overturning state laws forbidding ABORTION.

In this historic decision the Supreme Court ruled, on January 22, 1973, that the constitutional right to PRIVACY was broad enough to encompass a woman's right to terminate her own pregnancy. In so deciding, the Court invalidated all state laws restricting abortions prior to the moment when the fetus becomes viable. The Court declined to specify exactly when human life begins, but it did specifically state that the "person" guaranteed the right to life and liberty in the FOURTEENTH AMENDMENT did not include the unborn. Under *Webster v. Reproductive Health Services* (1989), the Court later upheld a Missouri law requiring the testing of all fetuses five months and older for viability.

For many years the Supreme Court remained true to *Roe v. Wade* by consistently ruling abortion legal. Abortion became a realistic option for many women, as its cost was reduced and it was made more accessible. An antiabortion backlash, however, advocated recriminalizing abortion, and many so-called pro-life politicians were elected to office. They passed legislative agendas that placed obsta-

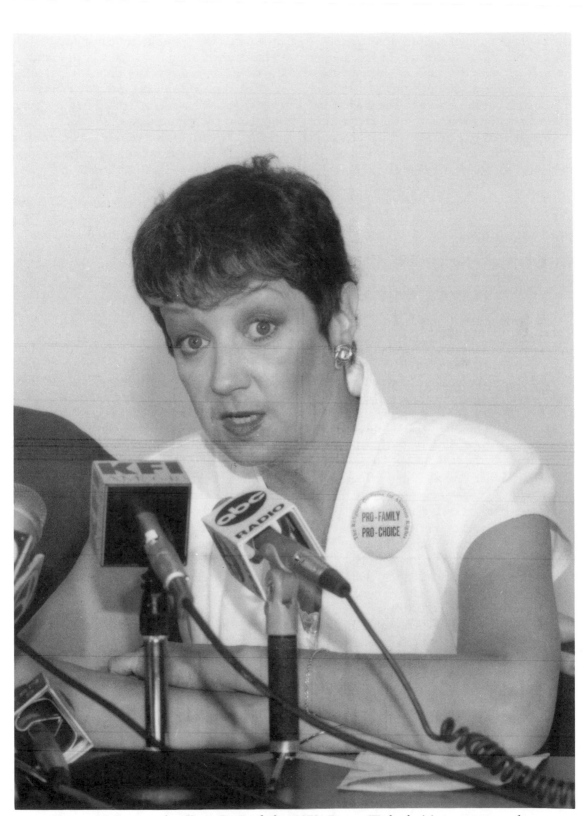

Norma McCorvey, the "Jane Roe" of the 1973 *Roe v. Wade* decision, expresses her disappointment at the Supreme Court's movement away from legal abortions in the late 1980's. (*AP/Wide World Photos*)

cles in the paths of women seeking abortions.

During the mid-1990's the proposed Freedom of Choice Act (FCA) was designed to prevent states from defining unreasonable cutoff dates after which a woman could not abort a pregnancy and outlaws state laws that prohibit abortion. Passage of the bill was expected to ensure that the REPRODUC-TIVE RIGHTS guarantees of *Roe v. Wade* would not be completely abandoned.

—*Marcia J. Weiss*

Roman Catholics

Members of the largest religious denomination in the United States—a church with significant and growing social and political influence.

The story of the Catholic experience in the United States is one of evolution from enclaves of poor and persecuted immigrants concerned with establishing and protecting their own civil rights to that of a powerful organized constituency playing a leading role in the debate over the CIVIL RIGHTS of other groups. The landmark of Catholic ascendance in U.S. history was the narrow electoral victory of President John F. KENNEDY in 1960. Kennedy's election demonstrated that Catholics had achieved acceptance in mainstream American culture. While the civil rights of Catholics were assured, the 1960's ushered in new debates over the civil rights of African Americans, women, and homosexuals in which Catholic leaders would play key roles.

One complexity in understanding Roman Catholic positions on civil rights is the emergence of three distinct but related factions within the United States in the twentieth century. The "official" position of the Roman Catholic Church on social matters such as civil rights is expressed by its bishops and cardinals. However, the laity, common Catholics who are neither ordained nor members of religious orders, are a separate group that has not always complied with all aspects of official Catholic teaching. Their independence is known as "Americanism" within the church and can be reflected in the participation of some lay Catholics in civil rights efforts not supported by the official church leadership. A third, and somewhat distinctively American Catholic faction are theologians. Influenced by the U.S. system of higher education which has stressed ACADEMIC FREEDOM, and which has been supported

by numerous Catholic colleges and universities, Catholic theologians emerged in the latter half of the twentieth century as independent thinkers and leaders. These modern Catholic factions in the United States have often disagreed on matters of social and civic importance.

The Civil Rights of Immigrant Catholics The first group of English Catholic colonists settled in Maryland in 1634, but the cultural and social foundation of what became the United States was predominately Protestant. DISCRIMINATION against the Catholic minority did not appear to be widespread until the first half of the nineteenth century when that small minority suddenly became a multitude. During the 1820's, 54,000 Catholics immigrated to the United States. That number increased to 700,000 during the 1840's; in the second half of the nineteenth century nearly five million Catholics entered the country.

The nineteenth century saw a great deal of social upheaval as the demographics of the United States changed. IRISH, German, Italian, Polish, and other EUROPEAN Catholics flocked to the United States seeking a better life. However, each new wave of Catholic immigrants brought a backlash of discrimination and persecution that included EMPLOYMENT DISCRIMINATION and social ostracization. It is difficult fully to separate anti-immigrant persecution from anti-Catholic sentiments during that period. Reasons given for anti-Catholic bias often included distrust of the Catholic desire for private schools, the concentration of wealth in the hands of the bishops, and the membership of many immigrant Catholics in questionable urban political organizations.

During the 1830's nativist feelings and actions swept through the large eastern urban areas, where most new immigrants settled. When anti-Catholic violence erupted, Catholic bishops responded by reaffirming the compatibility of being both American and Catholic. The response of Catholics under persecution was to become more "parochial" through the creation of Catholic newspapers and schools. During the 1850's the Know-Nothing Party emerged with the expressed purpose of excluding Catholics from public office and ultimately expelling them from the country. Typical of popular sentiment of the time, one writer during this period accused Catholic domestic servants—who were predominantly immigrant women—of being spies for the pope. During the 1880's the American Protective Association was formed; its members promised never to vote for a Catholic, never to hire a Catholic, and never to join Catholics in a LABOR STRIKE.

The Twentieth Century The new century brought a new threat to the rights and freedoms of American Catholics: the KU KLUX KLAN. While the Klan is primarily associated with persecution of African Americans, many historians believe that Catholics held an even more prominent position among the Klan's many enemies. The Klan characterized Catholicism as a threat to national autonomy and the American way of life. The impact of organizations such as the Klan, along with events such as the defeat of Catholic candidate Alfred E. Smith in the presidential election of 1928, maintained Catholic identification with a minority status, despite the growing numbers, economic power, and political status of American Catholics.

Two figures who recognized that reconciling the American ethos with the Catholic tradition was crucial for guaranteeing the civil liberties of Catholics were John A. Ryan and John Courtney Murray. An economist by training, Ryan championed working-class rights by authoring significant works on economic justice and promoting legislation to protect workers and provide a MINIMUM WAGE. Ryan joined the national board of the AMERICAN CIVIL LIBERTIES UNION; through such secular associations, he was able to promote connections between Catholic values and wider social concerns. Murray was a theologian, whose principal concern was religious liberty in the United States. Prior to Murray's work, Catholic social reformers—including Ryan—believed a close relationship between religion and the state was the ideal. Murray, however, sided with the Framers of the U.S. CONSTITUTION on the value of a clear separation of church and state. This view brought criticism and censorship from the Vatican, but Murray was ultimately vindicated as the Catholic Church later largely adopted his position.

New Catholic Immigrants The latter half of the twentieth century continued to find the rights of immigrant Catholics at issue. However, instead of an influx from European nations, Catholic immigration during this period was primarily from Asian countries, MEXICO, Cuba, and Puerto Rico, as well as from Central and South America. With European Catholics already well established in the American mainstream, these new waves of immigrant Catholics faced little conflict because of anti-Catholicism; however, they were subject to the nativism and resulting discrimination experienced by previous generations of immigrants. The U.S. LATINO Catholic population alone grew from about 4.9 million in 1960 to 13.3 million in 1987, representing about 20 percent of the total American Catholic population.

In 1962, Arizona-born Mexican American César CHÁVEZ established the NATIONAL FARM WORKERS ASSOCIATION, which worked to improve the difficult working conditions and financial stability of the predominantly Catholic Hispanic farmworkers. The character of Chávez's organization was distinctively Catholic; it included liturgies, fasting, and prayer vigils, as well as the support of many Catholic priests and bishops. At the close of the twentieth century Catholic pluralism was reflected in the hard-fought achievement of civil liberty and assimilation into the highest levels of U.S. society by previous immigrant groups, as well as the ongoing struggle of new immigrant Catholics.

Catholicism and the Civil Rights Movement Records of AFRICAN AMERICAN Catholics in North America date back to the sixteenth century. Nevertheless, the Catholic Church in America had little impact on the treatment of blacks in the slave trade. Because the church was made up of immigrant populations struggling for their own civil rights, its members were reluctant to raise objections to the treatment of blacks for fear of retribution. At the time of Emancipation only about 5 percent of the 4.5 million African Americans were Catholic. Many black Catholics were connected with the church merely because their masters were Catholic. Freedom brought a large black exodus from Catholicism.

In the post-Civil War era the Catholic Church in the United States made several declarations concerning opening its faith to blacks; however, SEGREGATION was also tolerated. Many separate black Catholic Churches were created. In 1889 the Congress of Colored Catholics met to discuss strategies for meeting the spiritual and social needs of the black Catholic community. The overall record of the Catholic Church on the issue of race relations for most of the twentieth century was mixed. While several official statements were made on behalf of the rights of African Americans, little by way of resources was devoted to assistance. The 1940's through the 1960's witnessed a dramatic rise in the African American population with no equivalent rise in black Catholics or programs for evangelization of the black community.

The CIVIL RIGHTS MOVEMENT of the 1960's came at a time of Catholic ascendance in the social fabric of the United States. This ascendance included the development of a vocal Catholic Left. Both black and white Catholics joined the Civil Rights movement and called for greater equality within the structure of the church. The controversy and infighting of the Catholic Church reflected the tension in the society at large, and many church leaders resisted the Civil Rights movement. In 1963 William DuBay, a priest, made headlines by accusing Cardinal James Francis McIntyre of Los Angeles of persecuting priests, seminarians, and lay people who joined the Civil Rights movement.

In 1968 the Black Catholic Clergy Caucus accused the American Catholic Church of being a white racist institution. The group demanded greater representation at all levels of decision making and greater self-determination for black Catholic communities. The church responded to such claims by issuing specific statements on the issues of RACISM in 1966, 1968, and 1979. However, these statements fell short of supporting the acts of CIVIL DISOBEDIENCE in which many Catholics felt compelled to participate. For example, many priests and nuns were involved in the 1965 marches at SELMA.

Changes in the racial makeup of Catholic leadership came slowly. In 1965 the first African American bishop since the mid-nineteenth century was appointed. By 1984 ten American bishops were black. When Pope John Paul II visited the United States in 1987 he gave a special audience to African American Catholic leaders. In 1988 Eugene Marino of Atlanta became the nation's first African American archbishop. For many African Americans the changes were coming too slowly, however. In 1989 charismatic Washington, D.C., priest George Stallings broke from the Catholic Church to join the separatist African American Catholic Church.

Catholicism and the Women's Movement While African Americans and immigrant populations struggled within the Catholic Church and society for equal rights, women posed a unique civil rights issue within Catholicism. The church's social teaching called for the fundamental equality of all people, however its theological tradition prevented it from ordaining women to the priesthood and therefore excluded women from many positions of leadership. This tension was particularly strong in the United States because of the power of the WOMEN'S RIGHTS movement and because of the legacy of the Civil Rights movement.

In addition to issues of equality, the church's staunch opposition to ABORTION and artificial contraception brought it into further opposition to the women's movement. In the eyes of many women, Roman Catholicism was opposed to women's rights. For example, the church lobbied against the EQUAL RIGHTS AMENDMENT. However, numerous Catholic women believed that gender inequality was generated by misinterpretation of the Christian message and so they sought a more egalitarian understanding of the faith.

In the 1960's a distinct Catholic feminism developed which manifested itself in feminist theologians and the formation of organizations advocating women's rights and women's spirituality. The post–World War II era found women who were given jobs during the war longing to maintain employment. After a brief drop in the 1950's, the percentage of women working outside the home would rise for the next four decades. In the 1950's the Catholic Church took a strong stand against women's paid employment, arguing that it symbolized the moral decay of the family. In the 1960's Catholic feminist theologians in the United States such as Mary Daly and Rosemary Radford Ruether began to identify sexism within the teaching of the Catholic Church and called for change. The statements of the Catholic Church from the 1950's to the 1970's demonstrate a shift in approaching women's rights from advocating exclusive motherhood to supporting greater career freedom. Nevertheless, the church's internal leadership restrictions remained.

Perhaps the most dramatic representation of the American Catholic women's movement occurred in 1979 when Pope John Paul II was visiting the United States. In Washington, D.C., before a large audience, Sister Theresa Kane, the president of the Leadership Conference of Women Religious, challenged the pope to address the injustices faced by women in the church. No such public challenge of a pope had been recorded in modern times. In the two decades that followed that meeting no significant change in the status of women in the Catholic Church occurred. Nevertheless, Catholic women in America continued actively to assert their rights. Numerous Catholic feminist organizations formed, including Catholics for a Free Choice (1974), which

The Roman Catholic Church's refusal to condone any form of artificial contraception or abortion has created a major rift within its membership. (*Betty Lane*)

sought reproductive rights, and the Women's Ordination Conference (1974). In the 1980's and 1990's some Catholic women grew impatient waiting for the church to change its stance on reproductive and leadership issues. Some left for other denominations, while others formed new spiritual communities.

Catholicism and Gay Rights Just as race, gender, and sexual orientation presented unique challenges and issues to society, the GAY RIGHTS movement posed difficult challenges for the American Catholic Church. Catholic moral theology regards all sexual acts that are not procreative and unitive as sinful. Beginning in the 1970's, the gay rights movement in the United States brought a discussion of the Catholic position to the fore. Liberal and conservative elements in Catholicism debated what, if any, rights and legitimacy should be extended to homosexuals.

In 1969 a group of Catholic homosexuals formed Dignity, an organization dedicated to gay advocacy within the church and the protection of gay civil rights in society. Other progressive organizations within Catholicism supported the gay movement. In 1975 the American Theological Society issued a statement charging that the Church's stigmatization of homosexuals was partially to blame for the oppression of gays in society. However, the official position of the Catholic Church remained staunchly opposed to granting rights to homosexuals. A 1986 papal letter condemning homosexuality resulted in the subsequent expulsion of many Dignity groups from local parishes in the United States.

In light of the AIDS crisis, Catholic Church leaders attempted to distinguish between homosexual orientation and homosexual acts. Homosexual orientation was perceived to be not always a matter of choice, while homosexual acts were chosen and immoral in the eyes of the Church. This distinction allowed for the American Catholic Church to justify ministry to homosexuals suffering from AIDS while maintaining a strict condemnation of homosexual behavior. However, many who sympathized with the gay rights movement found the distinction damaging to the efforts to protect the civil rights of homosexuals.

SUGGESTED READINGS:

Carey, Patrick W. *The Roman Catholics.* Westport, Conn.: Greenwood Press, 1993. Concise history of Roman Catholicism in the United States from European discovery through the 1980's with biographical sketches of key Catholic leaders.

Curran, Charles E. *American Catholic Social Ethics: Twentieth-Century Approaches.* South Bend, Ind.: University of Notre Dame Press, 1982. Review of the significant Catholic movements and figures working for social change in the United States.

Davis, Cyprian. *The History of Black Catholics in the United States.* New York: Crossroad, 1992. Historical overview of the experience of African Americans in the American Catholic Church.

Hennesey, James. *American Catholics: A History of the Roman Catholic Community in the United States.* New York: Oxford University Press, 1981. Comprehensive history of Catholicism in the United States from the colonial period to the 1970's.

Kowalewski, Mark R. *All Things to All People: The Catholic Church Confronts the AIDS Crisis.* New York: State University of New York Press, 1994. Utilizing the context of the AIDS epidemic, an exploration of the Catholic Church's teaching on homosexuality combining theological analysis with sociological investigation.

Maxwell, John. *Slavery and the Catholic Church.* Chichester: Barry Rose Publishers, 1975. Reviews the Roman Catholic Church's historical response to slavery.

Weaver, Mary Jo. *New Catholic Women: A Contemporary Challenge to Traditional Religious Authority.* Bloomington, Ind.: Indiana University Press, 1995. Historical examination of the feminist challenge to Roman Catholicism in the United States.

—*Maurice Hamington*

Roque Espiritu de la Ysla v. United States

1935: California and federal court ruling denying naturalization rights to a Filipino immigrant.

After the Philippines were taken over by the United States at the end of the Spanish-American War of 1898, the Filipinos were given the status of American nationals. They could travel freely between the United States and their own country, but they were ineligible to become U.S. citizens. With some encouragement from the American government and employers, a number of Filipinos came to the United States as students and sugar plantation workers. During the Great Depression, however, several thousand Filipino workers were sent home in a repatriation program.

Roque Espiritu de la Ysla was among the Filipinos who came to the United States. When California's supreme court turned down his application for U.S. CITIZENSHIP, he appealed to the U.S. SUPREME COURT. He argued that because he was a citizen of a country that owed allegiance to the United States, he should have the same constitutional protections as those born in the United States and that he was therefore entitled to the same citizenship rights. When the Supreme Court refused to hear his case, it in effect denied naturalization and citizenship rights to all Filipinos.

—Shakuntala Jayaswal

Runyon v. McCrary

1976: U.S. SUPREME COURT decision ruling unconstitutional the exclusion of children by private commercial schools on the basis of race.

A private school in Arlington, Virginia, that was part of a nonprofit association of private schools, had a policy denying admission to AFRICAN AMERICANS. In response to a challenge by parents of students who were denied admission, the Supreme Court held on June 25, 1976, that such practices constituted unacceptable racial discrimination in the contractual relationship between the parents and the educational institution.

—Marcia J. Weiss

Rust v. Sullivan

1991: U.S. Supreme Court decision upholding a government ban forbidding family planning agencies from providing counseling or information relating to ABORTION.

In a 5-4 decision involving pro-life policy making, the Court held on May 23, 1991, that President George BUSH could deny federal funds to any organization that mentioned abortion as a reproductive option. The president's authority derived from Health and Human Services (HHS) administrative regulations issued in 1988 (Title X of the Public Health Service Act). Opponents of this decision argued that it violated the constitutional guarantees of free speech and privacy and that it had a chilling effect on speech.

In the fall of 1991 Congress passed an appropriation bill containing a provision that effectively overturned the *Rust* decision by countermanding the HHS regulations in dispute. However, President Bush vetoed the bill, and Congress failed to overturn his veto. After President Bill CLINTON took office in 1993, he lifted the disputed regulations.

—Marcia J. Weiss

Rustin, Bayard

Mar. 17, 1910, West Chester, Pa.—Aug. 24, 1987, New York, N.Y.: Civil rights and war-resistance activist and pacifist theoretician.

Rustin was one of the founders of the SOUTHERN CHRISTIAN LEADERSHIP CONFERENCE (SCLC) and a key organizer of the 1963 MARCH ON WASHINGTON. The son of West Indian immigrants, he was raised in a Quaker household in the United States. He was committed to peaceful tactics for social change. He believed throughout his career in building coalitions among African Americans, white liberals, and labor unions on religious and pacifist principles. His activism linked the civil rights and peace movements.

Rustin was a member of the Young Communist League when he became a youth organizer for the March on Washington planned by A. Philip RANDOLPH in 1941. The 1941 march was directed at winning FAIR EMPLOYMENT PRACTICES from the federal government. Rustin later utilized his experience working with Randolph in the 1940's to organize the 1963 March on Washington.

Rustin went from his work with Randolph in the 1940's to the staff of the Fellowship of Reconciliation (FOR). He was also involved in the founding of the CONGRESS OF RACIAL EQUALITY (CORE), along with James FARMER and George Houser in 1942, and he served as one of the organization's field secretaries. CORE was committed to using nonviolent methods to protest public SEGREGATION and to win passage of civil rights laws. Rustin was arrested in 1942 for civil disobedience when he refused to move to the back of a segregated bus. While working on civil rights issues, he remained a sincere pacifist. He encouraged draft resistance and was imprisoned as a conscientious objector from 1943 to 1945. He later became an officer in the War Resisters League and he worked with organizations working to end racial segregation in the MILITARY. In 1947 he organized the Journey of Reconciliation, a FOR/CORE project designed to test Supreme Court rulings regarding segregated TRANSPORTATION. The Journey of Reconciliation tactic of filling buses with African American riders set a precedent for the later FREEDOM RIDERS of 1961. Arrested in North Carolina in 1947 because of his FOR activism, Rustin was sentenced to work on a chain gang. He wrote a series of exposés about his experience that helped abolish the state's chain gang system.

Rustin began a close partnership with Martin Luther KING, JR., in 1955 and was King's special assistant until 1960. He was an important strategist in the MONTGOMERY BUS BOYCOTT and was one of the group of activists who developed the SCLC. He planned demonstrations for civil rights at the national conventions for both major national political parties in 1960 and masterminded the 1963 March on Washington and the 1964 boycott of New York City public schools.

Changing Views Rustin's views began to be rejected by younger, more militant activists in the 1960's. These activists challenged his continued commitment to nonviolence and integration and rejected the tactics used by leaders in the first years of the civil rights movement in favor of a new politics of BLACK POWER. Rustin continued to advocate peaceful means for change and multiracial activism, but shifted the focus of his own activism to class rather than racial issues, working to alleviate economic inequity in American society and to lessen the burden of poverty on people of all races.

His relative conservatism within the Civil Rights movement was reflected in his opposition to the POOR PEOPLE'S CAMPAIGN of 1967 (he argued that the use of mass civil disobedience, rather than passive resistance or peaceful marches, would lead to repression and backlash) and the 1983 Jobless March on Washington.

Rustin was president of the A. Philip Randolph Institute in New York from 1963 to 1979, cochairing the organization until his death. At the institute he spearheaded coalition campaigns with the UNITED FARM WORKERS OF AMERICA, labor unions, and Jewish and educational groups. He also was a strong supporter of African independence movements, including the movement for peaceful liberation in South Africa.

Rustin was also a champion of GAY RIGHTS. His own homosexuality had earlier been a divisive factor in the inner circle around Martin Luther King, Jr., because it was seen as a potential source for governmental blackmailing of the movement, including the sullying of King's own reputation. In the 1970's Rustin advocated the gay liberation movement as an extension of the earlier Civil Rights movement, but was nevertheless criticized by many gay activists for not taking a stronger stand.

Rustin wrote many publications on activism and rights issues, including *Fear, Frustration, Backlash: The New Crisis in Civil Rights* (1966), *Which Way Out?* (1967), *A Word to Black Students* (1970), *Strategies for Freedom: The Changing Patterns of Black Protest* (1976), and *South Africa: Is Peaceful Change Possible?*, a report coauthored with others for the New York Friends Group in 1984.

—*Barbara Bair*

S

Salinas lettuce strike

1934: Labor walkout by Filipino farmworkers in California.

This month-long farmworker strike was an important incident in the history of Filipino labor, as it demonstrated the possibility of success for ethnic agricultural labor groups.

The Filipinos who worked in the lettuce fields of Salinas, California, included leaders who had gained experience organizing workers in the sugarcane fields of Hawaii. Their efforts to negotiate for better wages and working conditions during the summer of 1934 proved alarming to the local growers who then attempted to find replacement Filipino workers to avert a strike. However, the Filipino Labor Union (FLU) joined with the Vegetable Packers Association, an AFL affiliate, to present a strong front in the strike that started in August, 1934. However, after they succeeded in shutting down the lettuce fields, there was a split between the two groups. The AFL threatened to withdraw support if the Filipinos did not give up what AFL members thought were unreasonable demands and if they did not accept union leadership.

The FLU voted to continue the strike, although the Vegetable Packers Association broke off its connection. The Filipinos then experienced an increase in violence aimed at them. Meanwhile, the Monterey County Industrial Relations Board unilaterally announced that the strike was over. The Filipinos' decision to continue the strike caused riots and brought out more anti-Filipino campaigns on several fronts, including charges that the FLU was communist. Under the leadership of its president, Rufo Canete, the FLU organized a day of unity and announced a new strike by MEXICAN and Filipino workers.

This solidarity only brought more violence from the locals, this time in the form of firebombs, followed by the county sheriff accusing the FLU president of intimidating Filipino contract workers.

Canete eventually settled the strike, winning higher wages and recognition of the FLU as the legitimate union of the farmworkers.

—*Shakuntala Jayaswal*

Salvador Roldan v. Los Angeles County

1933: California court decision exempting Filipinos from the ANTIMISCEGENATION statute prohibiting marriages between persons classified as "white" and those classified as "Mongolian."

After a Los Angeles county clerk refused Salvador Roldan, a Filipino, a license to wed a woman of European descent, Roldan challenged the refusal and brought the case before the district court of appeals. The court considered the case, however, not as to the constitutionality of the antimiscegenation laws, but rather on the basis of whether the legislature, which had enacted the prohibition against white-Mongolian marriages, would have intended the inclusion of Filipinos in the term "Mongolian."

The court based its decision exclusively upon the usage of the term at the time the amendments were made. Reviewing the racial categories accepted at the time, the court found that the commonly accepted classifications distinguished between "Malay" and "Mongolian," and that a Filipino would have been considered "Malay." The pivotal factor persuading the court that members of the Malay race were not intended as objects of the legislators' antimiscegenation laws was a recognition that the laws were adopted in order to prevent the marriage of whites with CHINESE AMERICANS in an effort to inhibit Chinese immigration during the latter half of the nineteenth century. The court thus decided in favor of the plaintiff. A few months after the decision, however, the state legislature added the category "Malay" to the antimiscegenation statute.

—*Elizabeth R. Moore*

Salvatierra v. Independent School District

1930: Federal court decision ruling against SEGREGATION of MEXICAN AMERICANS because they were considered members of the "white race."

In this U.S. federal appeals court decision, the court ruled that because Mexican American chil-

Margaret Sanger, the founder of Planned Parenthood. (*AP/Wide World Photos*)

dren are "white," Texas could not segregate them in schools. However, the court did not rule against the principle of segregation itself. The court also allowed that segregating Mexican American children in the three youngest grade levels was a reasonable exercise of the school board's discretion, and that it was not for the court to look more deeply into the administrative affairs of the school authorities absent specific allegations of wrongdoing or injury.

—*Marcia J. Weiss*

Sanger, Margaret

Sept. 14, 1879, Corning, N.Y.—Sept. 6, 1966, Tucson, Ariz.: BIRTH CONTROL pioneer and founder of Planned Parenthood.

A pioneer in birth control and WOMEN'S RIGHTS, New York City public health nurse Margaret Sanger sought to establish a system of clinics where women could obtain reliable birth control services. Although she did not persuade Congress to repeal the Comstock Act of 1873, which prohibited interstate transport of contraceptive information and devices, she began to change public attitudes about birth control and the right of women to control their own reproductive lives.

Sanger opened her first clinic in 1916 in a Brooklyn tenement, where she distributed handbills providing birth control information in English, Yiddish, and Italian. Her clinics also served as educational centers at which private medical practitioners were instructed in contraceptive techniques, a subject not taught in medical schools at the time.

—*Marcia J. Weiss*

Satow, Masao

Feb. 14, 1908, San Mateo, Calif.—March 3, 1977. National director of the JAPANESE AMERICAN CITIZENS LEAGUE (JACL).

The holder of a theology degree from Princeton, Satow was active in the JACL from the early 1930's. Following his release from the JAPANESE AMERICAN INTERNMENT, he gained a national position with the Young Men's Christian Association and in 1946 became national secretary—and subsequently director—of the JACL until 1973.

—*Charles A. Desnoyers*

School discrimination

DISCRIMINATION directed against minority groups in public primary and secondary schools.

The history of racial SEGREGATION in American education has been influenced by different causal factors at various times. Prior to the Civil War, any rudimentary education received by AFRICAN AMERICANS was on a segregated basis depending on the will of white slave owners. After the war the SOUTHERN STATES endorsed segregation in their public schools. In many states African American families paid taxes to support white education, while their own children were barred from the schools. Sometimes they were required to pay twice: for black schools and white schools. Even that, however, did not guarantee schools for their children. In some border states, permissive segregation was incorporated into statutes. Some NORTHERN STATES also segregated their public schools; however, such discrimination was usually at the discretion of local school boards. In any case, HOUSING DISCRIMINATION in most northern cities and economic factors created segregated neighborhoods that produced segregated schools.

Discrimination against minorities was also reflected in COLLEGE AND UNIVERSITY enrollments. The failure of institutions of higher learning to enroll minority students was usually attributed to the students' inadequate secondary school preparation, rather than to active discrimination by the institutions themselves.

Some schools for African Americans in the South were established by northern white philanthropists, Christian missionaries, or by southern African Americans themselves. The FREEDMEN'S BUREAU, created by CONGRESS in 1865, helped people recently liberated from SLAVERY and white refugees with necessities such as food, clothing, and shelter. In 1866 education was added to the mission of the bureau; two years later a new law provided that the bureau's educational work was to continue until the states made adequate provisions for educating freedmen at public expense. During the period of missionary and bureau schooling, black and white children attended separate schools. The pattern of segregation and inequality established during the RECONSTRUCTION ERA was strengthened in the early twentieth century South. As late as 1920, 85 percent of all black pupils in the South were enrolled in only the first four grade levels. In 1916 there were

Key Events in Public School Desegregation

1896	U.S. Supreme Court's *Plessy v. Ferguson* verdict defines separate-but-equal doctrine, which is later used to justify school segregation.
1899	The Court's *Cumming v. Richmond County Board of Education* decision permits a school district to provide a high school for whites without providing one for African Americans.
1927	In *Gong Lum v. Rice* the Court allows a state to segregate Chinese American students in "colored" schools instead of "white" schools.
1939	NAACP Legal Defense and Educational Fund (LDF) is formed to oppose racially discriminatory laws; after winning legal victories in higher education cases, the LDF begins assault on public school segregation.
1954	Supreme Court's *Brown v. Board of Education of Topeka, Kansas* decision finds that racial segregation in public schools violates the Fourteenth Amendment's equal protection clause because segregated schools are "inherently unequal."
1955	The Court's second opinion in *Brown v. Board of Education* ("*Brown II*") orders public schools to desegregate "with all deliberate speed."
1957	When Arkansas uses National Guard troops to block black pupils from integrating a Little Rock high school, President Dwight D. Eisenhower federalizes the guard and sends additional troops to Little Rock to ensure that the school is peacefully integrated.
1958	Supreme Court's *Cooper v. Aaron* decision rejects an attempt to delay public school desegregation because of potential racial turmoil.
1964	In *Griffin v. Prince Edward County School Board* the Court rules that a school district cannot simply close its public schools to avoid desegregating them.
1968	In *Green v. County School Board* the Court finds that a school district's "freedom of choice" does not satisfy its obligation to desegregate its schools.
1971	In *Swann v. Charlotte-Mecklenburg Board of Education* the Court authorizes busing to desegregate school districts.
1974	In *Lau v. Nichols* the Court rules that a school district's failure to provide bilingual education for Chinese American students violates federal civil rights law.
1982	In *Plyler v. Doe* the Court rules that denial of public education to illegal aliens violates the equal protection clause.
1991	In *Board of Education of Oklahoma City Public Schools v. Dowell* the Court rules that a school district is entitled to have a desegregation order lifted when it has complied in good faith with a desegregation decree since it was entered and when vestiges of past discrimination have been eliminated to the extent practicable.

only sixty-seven African American public schools with fewer than twenty thousand students.

School Discrimination and the Courts Between 1896, when the U.S. SUPREME COURT passed down its PLESSY V. FERGUSON decision, affirming the SEPARATE-BUT-EQUAL DOCTRINE, and 1930, only three cases dealing with black education came before the Supreme Court, and none of these dealt with school segregation. In CUMMING V. RICHMOND COUNTY BOARD OF EDUCATION (1899), the Court allowed the Richmond, Virginia, school board to close its lone public high school for African Americans, while still maintaining its white high schools. In *Berea College v. Kentucky* (1908), the Court allowed the state of Kentucky to outlaw racially integrated instruction in private colleges operating under state charters. In GONG LUM V. RICE (1927), the Court held that states could segregate a "Mongolian" girl from "Caucasian" schools and compel her to attend a school for black children. Segregation of that type was practiced in many states. During the 1930's and 1940's, the education cases with which the Supreme

Court dealt concerned discrimination against minority applicants to graduate and professional schools.

By the late 1940's the NATIONAL ASSOCIATION FOR THE ADVANCEMENT OF COLORED PEOPLE LEGAL DEFENSE FUND (LDF) had scored several notable successes in the struggle against racial segregation in higher education and it decided to take on the larger issue of segregation in public schools. Under the leadership of future Supreme Court justice Thurgood MARSHALL the LDF filed five separate discrimination suits that were combined into the single case, BROWN V. BOARD OF EDUCATION OF TOPEKA, KANSAS, which the Supreme Court decided in 1954. These cases challenged existing patterns of segregation and discrimination that pervaded public school systems throughout the South and its border regions, including Kansas. Following the strong lead of Chief Justice Earl WARREN, the Court voted unanimously to strike down segregation in all public schools. A watershed case in American education, the Court's *Brown* decision also ranks as one of the most important and far-reaching decisions ever rendered by the Supreme Court.

The Aftermath of Brown In compliance with the *Brown* decision, school DESEGREGATION began in the fall of 1954 in a few large cities, such as Wil-mington, Delaware; Baltimore, Maryland; and Washington, D.C., and in certain counties in Missouri, Arkansas, and West Virginia. The next year the Supreme Court issued a follow-up decision, the so-called "implementation decision"—which has

For many African Americans in the South, the reality of "separate-but-equal" educational facilities meant school houses such as this late Depression-era building. (*Library of Congress*)

been dubbed *Brown II*—ordering that desegregation advance "with all deliberate speed." However, the actual logistics of implementing school desegregation on a massive scale remained troublesome. By the fourth anniversary of the original *Brown* decision, only ten out of seventeen states had even begun the desegregation process.

In the fall of 1958 desegregation was halted in LITTLE ROCK, ARKANSAS, and several counties of Virginia. Seven states were willing to eliminate public schools altogether rather than to integrate. In the light of the disruption in Little Rock, the local school board petitioned the federal courts for a temporary suspension of its desegregation plan in order to achieve calm. This request was rejected by the Supreme Court in COOPER V. AARON. It was not until the 1960's that desegregation finally began to advance significantly.

Equal Protection, Segregation, and Education
The CIVIL RIGHTS ACT OF 1964 was a watershed for the CIVIL RIGHTS MOVEMENT and the culmination of decades of activity dealing with racial equality. The act was especially important in the implementation of school desegregation. The key section of the 1964 act was its Title VI, which empowered the federal government to cut off funding to school districts practicing racial discrimination. This law rested on the legal premise that children compelled by compulsory state attendance laws to attend segregated schools were being deprived of EQUAL PROTECTION of the laws. Moreover, the fact that the students might be assigned to attend certain schools on considerations of geography rather than those of race, did not make the schools they attended any less inferior or such classifications any less illegal, unless it could be shown that no reasonable classification would alleviate the inequality. If a school system used race to classify its pupils, such a classification scheme was automatically regarded as unconstitutional. Regardless of the basis of classification, if it resulted in racial segregation, it was considered suspect and the school board and the state had to demonstrate a compelling interest with no suitable alternative. Under the federal law, states were required to provide equal educational opportunities to all pupils, and they had an affirmative constitutional obligation to eliminate segregation, regardless of how it came about.

De jure SEGREGATION in schools is that which is mandated by law or created by the deliberate actions of school officials; under court rulings, it is regarded as automatically unconstitutional. De facto segregation is that which arises naturally from social and geographical conditions, such as segregated housing patterns. Since no overt intent to discriminate might exist, it is not necessarily unconstitutional. In SWANN V. CHARLOTTE-MECKLENBURG BOARD OF EDUCATION (1971) the Supreme Court held that using BUSING to achieve racial balance was a permissible tool for eliminating de jure segregation. As a result, mandatory reassignment or "forced busing" plans were implemented throughout the country during the early 1970's. However, the Court's 1973 KEYES V. DENVER SCHOOL DISTRICT NUMBER ONE decision blurred the distinction between de jure and de facto segregation. In MILLIKEN V. BRADLEY the following year, the Court addressed the validity of cross-district or interdistrict consolidation to remedy de jure segregation in a single district in Detroit. That decision required states to assert a positive policy of placement of students or facilities to achieve integration. Quotas or percentages (also called "goals" or "set-asides") might be used, but could not be the sole determinant.

The Mid-1970's through the 1990's In the two decades that passed after *Milliken*, little progress was made in desegregating public schools in urban areas. Desegregation and busing questions continued to be perplexing, and the Supreme Court vacillated in specific desegregation cases, while continuing to uphold the distinction between de jure and de facto segregation. Between *Milliken* and 1979, the court seemed to move away from mandating busing and other remedial programs. For example, in *Pasadena City Board of Education v. Spangler* and *Austin Independent School District v. United States*, both in 1976, the Court ruled that once a desegregation plan had achieved a unitary school system, no further remedial action was necessary. In 1979, however, in *Columbus Board of Education v. Penick* and in *Dayton Board of Education v. Brinkman*, extensive desegregation remedies were approved based on the impact of past school board actions and omissions. The following year, in *Delaware State Board v. Evans* (1980), the Court let stand a decision to order interdistrict school busing for Wilmington.

By 1980 opposition to court-ordered busing was mounting. Violent protests erupted in Boston's white ethnic neighborhoods; whites in Los Angeles withdrew from the public school system; and Washington State sought to restrict mandatory busing plans. Congress sought to reduce court-ordered desegregation by proposing laws to restrict the jurisdiction of the federal courts to order transportation plans to achieve racial desegregation. Alternative, voluntary solutions were implemented, including "magnet" and "alternative" schools, faculty and staff training, and remedial programs.

In its rulings during the 1990's, the Supreme Court reduced the role of the federal courts over matters dealing with school desegregation. On authority of the Supreme Court's OKLAHOMA CITY BOARD OF EDUCATION V. DOWELL (1991) and *Freeman v. Pitts* (1992) decisions, federal judges could discontinue ongoing supervision of racial desegregation in districts in basic compliance with court orders to desegregate. In *Missouri v. Jenkins* (1995), the Supreme Court placed limits on federal judicial authority that usurped local control over education in order to desegregate the Kansas City, Missouri, schools.

Mexican American Schooling Mexican American school children have faced discriminatory treatment similar to that of African American children. For example, during the 1820's and 1830's, ROMAN CATHOLIC missions in California operated schools in which AMERICAN INDIANS and mestizo children attended alongside white children. However, after the missions became secularized in the 1840's increasing numbers of whites came to California and set up voluntary schools for their children to which Native Americans were not admitted.

From 1846 to 1848 former Mexican nationals residing in the United States were guaranteed the rights of citizens, but were regarded as cheap, exploitable labor. They occupied low social ranks; education mirrored their low social position. In 1871 the first public school for the Spanish-speaking population was established in New Mexico. Although repeatedly petitioned to do so, it was not until 1898 that Congress made a small land grant to help finance higher education. The territory's first school law was passed in 1891; it provided for a seven-month compulsory school term, but no school tax. Funds were to come from licensing and fines from gambling and alcohol.

Similar patterns of educational deprivation and failure existed in Texas, where children were assigned to schools on the basis of their ethnicity rather than ability. Discrimination against Mexican Americans in the schools included denial of equal allocations and distribution of financial resources.

Historically, Texas educators viewed public education as a vehicle for Americanization of "foreign elements." Some parts of the state did not originally provide public education for Mexican Americans. After Mexican Americans were finally admitted to public schools, local authorities established separate "Mexican" schools that were explicitly sanctioned by the state's constitution. Mexican American segregation was authorized until 1930, and segregation of Mexican Americans was not repudiated as an expression of official state policy until 1948.

In 1929 a federal appeals court decision in Texas, SALVATIERRA V. INDEPENDENT SCHOOL DISTRICT, set the pattern of the next forty years. Absent a statute allowing segregation of LATINOS, any attempts by local officials to segregate pupils exceeded their powers. Where there was no proof of intent to discriminate, however, the court decision regarded segregation of the first three grade levels as a reasonable exercise of a school board's discretion. In that case as well, Mexican Americans were acknowledged as members of the "white race." Therefore, they were entitled to equal treatment with other "whites."

A Ninth Circuit California case, MÉNDEZ V. WESTMINSTER SCHOOL DISTRICT (1946), held that segregation of Mexican American children was unconstitutional absent a law expressly permitting that practice. Arbitrary segregation was held to violate the FOURTEENTH AMENDMENT in DELGADO V. BASTROP INDEPENDENT SCHOOL DISTRICT (1948). The problem, however, was not corrected because guidelines for ensuring compliance were not provided, and school segregation continued. In *Hernandez v. Texas* (1954)—the only Mexican American discrimination case decided by the Supreme Court—Latinos were held to be among those protected by the Fourteenth Amendment because their systematic exclusion from JURY DUTY violated the amendment's EQUAL PROTECTION CLAUSE. In that decision the Court recognized Latinos as an identifiable class.

Another federal court decision, *Hernandez v. Driscoll* (1957), made it unlawful to segregate Hispanics in the first grade absent standardized tests. Many school districts continued to operate with gerrymandered zoning and "freedom-of-choice" plans until the early 1970's, when courts ordered establishment of unitary school systems and the dismantling of dual systems.

American Indian Schooling During the first century of the republic, Native American education was primarily an instrument of military strategy. During the 1770's the new American government made the first government expenditure on Native American education in an effort to pacify New England Indians and thereby help ensure the conquest of Indian lands to the west. After 1819 the federal government signed contracts with church missionaries to operate schools for Indians. Many tribes were eager for modern education, so long as it did not threaten the loss of their own cultural heritage.

Direct formal relations between Indian tribes and the federal government began with the Treaty of Fort Laramie in 1851. Over the following fifteen years, Indian parents began requesting that federal authorities provide schools for their children, but the requests went unanswered. In 1866 a new treaty was signed under which the United States agreed to increase spending on various Indian matters, including education. Four years later the first federal school for Indians was opened on a RESERVATION; however, it closed only six months later because its building was needed for other purposes. In 1875 new government schools for Indians were opened, with instruction in the native languages. By 1880, however, instruction was exclusively in English. Increasingly antagonistic toward the federal schools, parents began stopping their children from attending. The government responded by withholding food rations from the families until they sent their children to school. By the 1930's the government policy had shifted to enrolling Indian children in regular public schools. Schooling was most successful among southern Indians, the so-called Five Civilized Tribes (Cherokee, Creek, Chickasaw, Choctaw, and Seminole), settled between Tennessee and Mississippi at the end of the American Revolution.

SUGGESTED READINGS:

Alexander, Kern, and M. David Alexander. *American Public School Law*. 3d ed. St. Paul, Minn.: West Publishing, 1992. Traces the evolution of education law with commentary and edited case excerpts.

Rangel, Jorge C., and Carlos M. Alcala. "Project Report: De Jure Segregation of Chicanos in Texas Schools." *Harvard Civil Rights-Civil Liberties Law Review* 7, no. 2 (March, 1972). Historical analysis of legal segregation and educational discrimination of Latino children in Texas.

Rossell, Christine H. *The Carrot or the Stick for School Desegregation Policy*. Philadelphia: Temple University Press, 1990. Provides details on magnet schools and voluntary and mandatory busing plans.

Van Geel, Tyll. *The Courts and American Education Law*. Buffalo, N.Y.: Prometheus Books, 1987. Contains a chapter on segregation based on race and gender.

Weinberg, Meyer. *A Chance to Learn: The History of Race and Education in the United States*. Cambridge, England: Cambridge University Press, 1977. Historical sources documenting social science research on the education of African American, Mexican American, American Indian, and Puerto Rican children.

_____. *The Search for Quality Integrated Education: Policy and Research on Minority Students in School and College*. Westport, Conn.: Greenwood Press, 1983. Highlights various research and studies on minority groups from a historical perspective.

—*Marcia J. Weiss*

Scott Act

1888: Amendment to the CHINESE EXCLUSION ACT OF 1882.

This federal law intensified the severity of the Chinese Exclusion Act by barring the re-admission to the United States of CHINESE possessing certificates entitling them to return that had been issued under the 1882 act. Although the new law violated provisions of the 1880 federal treaty with China, the U.S. SUPREME COURT upheld it as a justifiable exercise of the sovereign power of the United States to exclude ALIENS.

—*Milton Berman*

Scottsboro Nine

Nine young AFRICAN AMERICANS who were convicted of raping two white women in Scottsboro, Alabama, in 1931.

On March 25, 1931, a group of white boys entered the Stevenson, Alabama, train station and claimed that they had been thrown off a freight train by a group of young African Americans. After the white boys pressed charges, the freight train was stopped at Paint Rock, Alabama. Twelve people—nine black youths (ranging in age from thir-

Haywood Patterson, a Scottsboro defendant, escaped from prison fifteen years after his conviction in 1933. (*National Archives*)

teen to twenty), one white youth, and two white women—were found hitching rides on the train. All were arrested and taken to nearby Scottsboro. After their arrest, the two women claimed they had been raped by the blacks. Acting on their own outrage and fear of possible mob violence, county officials decided to try the African American youths quickly.

Obtaining a lawyer for the black youths was difficult. Judge Alfred E. Hawkins tried to appoint every member of the Jackson County bar to the defense without success. Finally, Milo C. Moody, a seventy-year-old lawyer in need of money, agreed to take the case. Moody was described by some as senile and incapable, hardly adequate counsel. A black church group from Chattanooga hired Stephen R. Roddy, an alcoholic real estate lawyer, to replace Moody.

The nine defendants were divided into four groups for trial at the request of the prosecution. The trials proceeded, with Roddy as a reluctant defense lawyer, later assisted by Moody. Evidence failed to corroborate the accounts of the alleged rapes. Medical testimony indicated that the rapes could not have occurred in the time frame described by the women. The women showed no signs of physical abuse and their testimonies were rife with contradictions. Victoria Price, one of the women, changed her testimony several times. Additionally, the prosecution's "eyewitnesses" were extremely improbable.

The four trials were finished in only four days. Eight of the youths were found guilty and sentenced to death by electrocution. The remaining youth's trial was declared a mistrial because one juror held out for life imprisonment rather than CAPITAL PUNISHMENT.

The NATIONAL ASSOCIATION FOR THE ADVANCEMENT OF COLORED PEOPLE (NAACP) and the International Labor Defense (ILD) were among the outside groups closely observing the situation in Scottsboro. The NAACP and the ILD engaged in a bitter struggle to gain victories in the subsequent legal appeals for the Scottsboro Nine and the ILD emerged as the victor. The ILD lawyers argued three major points in the appeals, which reached the U.S. SUPREME COURT twice. The lawyers' arguments concerned the denial of right to adequate counsel, the hurried pace and hostile setting of the trials, and the absence of blacks on the Jackson County jury rolls.

In the first appeal to the Supreme Court, the Court ordered a retrial on the basis that the defendants had been denied DUE PROCESS when they were not provided adequate defense counsel. The Court used the INCORPORATION DOCTRINE to apply the Sixth Amendment, which guarantees the defendant the assistance of counsel, to the state of Alabama. This ruling established a precedent for future cases by broadening the scope of defendants' rights protected under the auspices of due process.

In the second appeal to the Supreme Court, the Court ruled on the exclusion of blacks from juries in Alabama. Based on the *prima facie* case presented regarding the systematic and unjust exclusion of blacks from jury rolls, the Court declared that the defendants had been denied civil rights guaranteed to them by the EQUAL PROTECTION CLAUSE of the FOURTEENTH AMENDMENT. The Court also stated that the denials of county officials were not adequate defense against a *prima facie* case of discrimination. Another legal precedent was thus established. The appeals process failed, however, to obtain the young men's freedom but the trials, along with the subsequent struggles by a broad coalition of concerned groups to free the defendants, became symbols in the broader struggle for civil rights in the South. The events brought to light the racial injustice practiced within the judicial system in the South.

Ultimately, all of the Scottsboro defendants were freed. In 1936 agreements were reached to drop charges against Olen Montgomery, Roy Wright, Willie Roberson, and Eugene Williams. In 1943 Charlie Weems was released by the Alabama Parole Board. Three years later, the board released Ozie Powell

and paroled Clarence Norris. Haywood Patterson gained his freedom by escaping from prison in 1948 and fleeing to Detroit, from which the governor of Michigan refused to extradite him. Andrew Wright was the last of the Scottsboro Nine to achieve his freedom. He was released from prison on June 9, 1950.

SUGGESTED READINGS:

Carter, Dan T. *Scottsboro: A Tragedy of the American South*. Baton Rouge: Louisiana State University Press, 1969.

Chalmers, Allan K. *They Shall Be Free*. Garden City, N.Y.: Doubleday, 1951.

Crenshaw, Files, and Kenneth A. Miller. *Scottsboro: The Firebrand of Communism*. Montgomery, Ala.: Brown Printing Co., 1936.

Hays, Arthur Garfield. *Trial by Prejudice*. New York: Covici-Friede, 1933.

Tindall, George Brown. *The Emergence of the New South, 1913-1945*. Baton Rouge: Louisiana State University Press, 1967.

—*Alvin M. Pettus*

Seale, Bobby

Born October 22, 1936, Dallas, Tex.: Cofounder of the BLACK PANTHER PARTY.

After trying his hand as a comedian and poet, Bobby Seale flirted with AFRICAN AMERICAN student organizations at Merritt College in Oakland, California, where he had been a student. However, he became disenchanted with the organizations and dubbed them "armchair revolutionaries" because they only talked about problems instead of taking action. Along with Huey P. NEWTON, he founded the Black Panther Party in Oakland in 1966 and assumed the position of chairman.

Although Newton was the party's recognized leader, Seale was its most fiery orator and its best organizer. He helped implement many of the programs that the party provided to the community, such as the breakfast program for schoolchildren and free clinics for people unable to pay for medical assistance. As a former serviceman Seale exhibited a steely resolve and intimidating presence that played into the white stereotype of what a militant Black Panther looked like.

In 1973 Seale ran for mayor of Oakland. Despite a lack of campaign resources, he placed second behind a white Republican. Seale eventually quit the Black Panther Party, citing personal and ideological differences with Newton. Years later, he earned a bachelor's degree at Temple University and became a sought-after speaker and lecturer at universities across the country.

—*Judson L. Jeffries*

Segregation

Physical separation of persons in schools, housing, and other social contexts on the basis of characteristics such as their race, religion, or national origin.

The institution of SLAVERY implanted in the American consciousness ideas about sharp distinctions among races. Moreover, whites branded AFRICAN AMERICANS as a race inferior. The slavery of African Americans itself was taken as proof of white superiority. Even the nation's SUPREME COURT fell under the sway of this perverse reasoning when it declared, in the DRED SCOTT CASE (1857), that African Americans could not be citizens of the United States because they were by nature inferior to whites. Although the RECONSTRUCTION ERA witnessed some efforts to eradicate the invidious racial distinctions set in place by the nation's history of slavery, ultimately these distinctions found new life in various forms of racial segregation that survived until the middle of the twentieth century.

The Rise of Segregation The Reconstruction era saw important steps taken to heal the separation of races inflicted upon the nation by slavery.

In 1890 San Francisco became the first major U.S. city to enact a segregation ordinance—designed to restrict Chinese residents to the "Chinatown" district—but a local court quickly struck down the law. (*Asian American Studies Library, University of California at Berkeley*)

The THIRTEENTH AMENDMENT (1865) abolished slavery itself. The EQUAL PROTECTION clause of the FOURTEENTH AMENDMENT (1868) abolished the various BLACK LAWS adopted in the south after the Civil War. Southern states intended these laws, which deprived newly freed African Americans of important economic rights such as freedom of contract, to create a kind of perpetual economic segregation between whites and African Americans. The black laws would have consigned African Americans to a perpetual economic underclass. Another clause of the Fourteenth Amendment stipulated that all persons born in the United States were citizens, thus welcoming African Americans back into the fold of citizenship from which the *Dred Scott* decision had banished them.

The FIFTEENTH AMENDMENT (1870) guaranteed the right to vote without respect to race or "previous condition of servitude." This guarantee removed African Americans from the constitutional status of second-class citizens by protecting their fundamental right to participate in the democratic process. Finally, as the Reconstruction era was ending, Congress passed the CIVIL RIGHTS ACT OF 1875, which made a variety of facilities such as restaurants, hotels, and modes of transportation freely available to individuals without regard to their race. If the constitutional amendments of the Reconstruction period effected a kind of political integration of whites and blacks, the Civil Rights Act of 1875 attempted to accomplish a social integration of the races.

Reconstruction progress toward racial integration collapsed during the 1880's, however. The Supreme Court held in the *Civil Rights Cases* (1883) that Congress had no power to restrict private discrimination in which resulted in racial segregation. By this holding, the Court stripped Congress of power to prevent racial segregation effected by private owners of facilities such as restaurants and hotels. Moreover, in PLESSY V. FERGUSON (1896), the Court concluded that even government-sponsored segregation in railway carriages did not violate the equal protection clause of the Fourteenth Amendment. *Plessy* granted a constitutional blessing to official segregation, and in the following years southern states would seize upon the SEPARATE-BUT-EQUAL PRINCIPLE to justify laws requiring racial segregation in a host of contexts, from restaurants and factories to cemeteries and drinking fountains. Ultimately, even the "equal" portion of the "separate but equal" principle showed itself to be a hollow

promise. In CUMMING V. RICHMOND COUNTY BOARD OF EDUCATION (1899), the Court upheld a local school district policy of providing whites but not blacks with the opportunity to attend high school. Although African Americans bore the brunt of segregationists laws and policies, they were not alone. CHINESE AMERICANS, for example, were also the objects of segregation practices. In GONG LUM V. RICE (1927), for example, the Supreme Court upheld the constitutionality of MISSISSIPPI's segregation of Chinese Americans from whites in public school.

The Abolition of Official Segregation The Supreme Court's *Plessy v. Ferguson* decision established the "separate but equal" principle that guided constitutional law for almost sixty years. Eventually, however, the Court reconsidered its *Plessy* holding and in the middle of the twentieth century began dismantling the elaborate framework of segregation that had penetrated the South especially so pervasively. Segregation's demise began when the Court recalculated the "equal" element of the "separate but equal" principle and determined that makeshift programs offered to blacks in graduate areas such as law were not equal to those offered white counterparts. This failure of equality, the Court held in cases such as *Missouri ex rel. Gaines v. Canada* (1938) and SWEATT V. PAINTER (1950), violated the Fourteenth Amendment's equal protection clause. Four years after the decision in *Sweatt*, however, the Court dealt a crushing blow to segregation by ruling in BROWN V. BOARD OF EDUCATION (1954), that segregation in public schools was inherently unequal and thus a violation of the equal protection guarantee. During the years immediately following its *Brown* decision, the Court summarily invalidated one variety of segregation after another. It banned officially mandated segregation in public facilities and invalidated the sexual segregation represented by state statutes—called "ANTIMISCEGENATION" LAWS—that prohibited racial intermarriages. Moreover, although the Court interpreted the Fourteenth Amendment's equal protection clause to forbid official segregation—rather than private acts of racial discrimination—it held in SHELLY V. KRAEMER (1948) that the Constitution barred courts from enforcing the racially discriminatory private RESTRICTIVE COVENANTS that reinforced patterns of residential segregation.

Remedies for Segregation In the public schools of the South especially, years of segregation had created dual systems of SCHOOLS: schools for whites, on one hand, and schools for blacks on the other hand. When the Supreme Court declared segregation in public schools unconstitutional, it did not simply ban future attempts to maintain separate schools. Rather, the Court ordered segregated school districts to undo the effects of prior official segregation by dismantling the dual school systems and replacing them with racially unitary systems. The task of implementing DESEGREGATION fell mainly to the lowest federal courts, which for at least two decades after the original *Brown* decision had to overcome seemingly endless recalcitrance on the part of school districts hostile to desegregation efforts. The authority of lower federal courts to order a wide range of remedies was sweeping but not unlimited. Although federal judges could order controversial desegregation remedies such as BUSING, they could only do so for demonstrated instances of official or "de jure" SEGREGATION, as opposed to segregation that occurred without official participation, called "de facto" segregation.

Even as late as the 1990's segregation remained within some public institutions of the South. In *United States v. Fordice* (1992), the Supreme Court found that the state of Mississippi's system of higher education still employed various practices that had been originally implemented to reinforce racial segregation and that still had that effect. More commonly, however, the 1990's witnessed increasing efforts by school districts to end the ongoing supervision of their schools by federal courts. In OKLAHOMA CITY BOARD OF EDUCATION V. DOWELL (1991), the Supreme Court held that desegregation orders were intended to be temporary and that school districts that had complied with these orders over time could, in some circumstances, be relieved from further desegregation efforts.

SUGGESTED READINGS:

Barnes, Catherine A. *Journey from Jim Crow: The Desegregation of Southern Transit*. New York: Columbia University Press, 1983.

Finkelman, Paul, ed. *The Age of Jim Crow: Segregation from the End of Reconstruction to the Great Depression*. New York: Garland, 1992.

Lofgren, Charles A. *The Plessy Case: A Legal-Historical Interpretation*. New York: Oxford University Press, 1987.

McMillen, Neil R. *Dark Journey: Black Mississippians in the Age of Jim Crow*. Urbana, Ill.: University of Illinois Press, 1989.

Massey, Douglas S., and Nancy A. Denton. *American Apartheid: Segregation and the Making of the Underclass*. Cambridge, Mass.: Harvard University Press, 1993.

Rasmussen, R. Kent. *Farewell to Jim Crow: The Rise and Fall of Segregation in America*. New York: Facts On File, 1997.

Williamson, Joel. *The Crucible of Race: Black-White Relations in the American South Since Emancipation*. New York: Oxford University Press, 1984.

Woodward, C. Vann. *The Strange Career of Jim Crow*. 3d rev. ed. New York: Oxford University Press, 1974.

—*Timothy L. Hall*

Segregation, de facto and de jure

Distinction between racial SEGREGATION *not* resulting from deliberate government action and that resulting from official action.

De jure segregation, which means segregation "by law," is segregation brought about by deliberate government attempts to separate individuals on the basis of race. JIM CROW LAWS are the most overt forms of de jure segregation. De facto segregation, on the other hand, means segregation "by the facts"; it is racial separation caused by individual choices and cultural practices, rather than direct official actions.

Under the U.S. CONSTITUTION government may not compel different races of people to live in different neighborhoods; however, the Constitution does not preclude members of particular racial groups from congregating in particular neighborhoods. Some observers have argued that de facto segregation has arisen in the United States out of the country's history of de jure segregation. Nevertheless, the COURTS have maintained a distinction between these two forms of segregation in determining when the Constitution has been violated.

Distinctions between de jure and de facto segregation have appeared most prominently in school desegregation cases. In this context, the Supreme Court has held that de jure, but not de facto, segregation violates the EQUAL PROTECTION CLAUSE of the FOURTEENTH AMENDMENT. Furthermore, the Court ruled in MILLIKEN V. BRADLEY (1974) that federal courts have power to desegregate schools and other public facilities only after finding that government has engaged in de jure segregation. Once a court discovers that a school district has been the object of de jure segregation policies, then a federal court has power to counteract both the effects of de jure *and* de facto segregation in public schooling. Moreover, according to the Court's decision in *Washington v. Seattle School District No. 1* (1982), individual school districts are free to undertake voluntary measures to end de facto as well as de jure segregation.

—*Timothy L. Hall*

Selma, Alabama, march

1965: Mass demonstration planned by Martin Luther KING, JR., to dramatize the demands of AFRICAN AMERICANS for VOTING RIGHTS in the South.

After Congress passed the landmark CIVIL RIGHTS ACT OF 1964, the CIVIL RIGHTS MOVEMENT, under the leadership of Martin Luther King, Jr., focused on its next legislative goal—getting CONGRESS to pass a strong voting rights law designed to end discrimination against African Americans. In the early 1960's voting registration for African Americans in the rural South was almost nonexistent. King, along with civil rights leaders from the SOUTHERN CHRISTIAN LEADERSHIP CONFERENCE (SCLC) and the STUDENT NON-VIOLENT COORDINATING COMMITTEE (SNCC), chose Selma, Alabama—situated in the heart of the southern black belt—as the starting point for their voting rights campaign.

The campaign began in January, 1965. Each day when African Americans marched to Alabama's Dallas County Court House to register to vote, they were met with club-swinging state troopers on horseback who beat and arrested them. King himself was among the demonstrators arrested. The decision to march from Selma to Montgomery, Ala-

Alabama state troopers break up the civil rights march in Selma in March, 1965. (*AP/Wide World Photos*)

bama's capital, was in response to the shooting death of a black demonstrator in nearby Marion. Shot in the stomach by a state trooper, Jimmie Lee Jackson died a week later. King wanted to march to Montgomery to deliver a petition to Alabama governor George Wallace protesting Jackson's death and the arrest of more than one thousand black demonstrators. Wallace issued an order prohibiting the march and gave state troopers the authority to use whatever measures they deemed necessary to prevent it.

Bloody Sunday On Sunday, March 7, 1965, demonstrators began what was to become the first of three attempts to march to Montgomery. About six hundred African Americans, carrying bedrolls and knapsacks, stepped out of Brown Chapel African Methodist Episcopal Church in a long column for the four-day march to Montgomery, fifty miles away. The marchers were led by the SCLC's Hosea WILLIAMS and SNCC's John Robert LEWIS. That day King remained in ATLANTA, GEORGIA, to minister to his congregation.

As the marchers reached the crest of Selma's Edmund Pettus Bridge, they were met by state troopers wearing helmets and gas masks. When the marchers refused to turn back, the command to attack was given. Many marchers turned and ran, to escape tear gas and lawmen charging against them on horseback with their nightsticks, chains, and electric cattle prods.

Despite a temporary federal restraining order on marching, the civil rights demonstration—this time led by King himself—tried a second time on Tuesday, March 9, to march to Montgomery. About a quarter of a mile into the march King decided not to proceed and led the marchers back to Brown Chapel. That night three white Unitarian ministers were assaulted by local whites. Among the victims was the Reverend James J. Reeb, who died two days later. Calling Reeb's death and the events in Selma an American tragedy, President Lyndon B. JOHNSON delivered a nationwide television address to a joint session of Congress to request the passage of a strict voting rights bill.

On Wednesday, March 17, a federal judge ruled that the Selma-to-Montgomery march could proceed. Although the ruling cleared the way for the march, Governor Wallace refused to provide the marchers with police protection. President Johnson, therefore, federalized the Alabama National Guard and ordered it to oversee the march.

The March to Montgomery The Selma-to-Montgomery march finally got underway on Sunday, March 21. More than three thousand marchers of all races and occupations moved along Route 80 with armed troops standing at intervals along the road. At night the marchers slept in tents they pitched along the road. By the time they reached the outskirts of Montgomery on the fourth day, their number had increased to twenty-five thousand. On Thursday, March 25, they reached the capital, where King addressed the crowd as millions watched on television.

The triumphant mood of the march was short-lived, however. That same evening, four members of the KU KLUX KLAN shot and killed a white woman, Viola Liuzzo, who was transporting marchers from Montgomery back to Selma. Liuzzo's killers were quickly arrested, and President Johnson again went on national television to condemn the shooting and call for an investigation of the Klan.

On Friday, August 16, five months after the Selma-to-Montgomery march, President Johnson signed the federal VOTING RIGHTS ACT OF 1965 into law. During the following year nine thousand African Americans registered to vote in Alabama's Dallas County.

SUGGESTED READINGS:

Fager, Charles E. *Selma, 1965: The March That Changed the South*. Boston: Beacon Press, 1985.

Siegel, Beatrice. *Murder on the Highway: The Viola Liuzzo Story*. New York: Four Winds Press, 1993.

Vivian, Octavia, ed. *How We Got over the Bridge to Freedom: Looking Back and Moving Forward, a Mini-History of the Voting Rights Struggle in the Alabama Black Belt*. Montgomery, Ala.: National Celebration of the Right to Vote Committee, 1990.

Wexler, Sanford. *The Civil Rights Movement: An Eyewitness History*. New York: Facts on File, 1993.

—*Eddith A. Dashiell*

Separate-but-equal principle

Constitutional doctrine arising in 1896 that gave legal sanction to racial SEGREGATION so long as the segregated races had access to facilities considered "equal."

The abolition of SLAVERY in the wake of the Civil War did not produce equality for newly freed AFRICAN AMERICANS. The South responded to the new-found freedom of African Americans by enforcing a separation of whites and African Americans that would maintain the perceived superiority of the white race. Although the FOURTEENTH AMENDMENT'S EQUAL PROTECTION CLAUSE might have been thought of as abolishing precisely this kind of legally enforced inferior status, the U.S. SUPREME COURT originally interpreted it otherwise. Responding to southern JIM CROW LAWS requiring segregated cars for whites and blacks on railways, the Court ruled, in PLESSY V. FERGUSON (1896), that this segregation did not offend the equal protection clause. Favored with this blessing, southern states gradually expanded the scope of segregation to include racial separation across a wide range of social institutions. Jim Crow reigned in parks and golf courses, jails and prisons, film theaters and restaurants. Most significantly, southern states enforced racial segregation in schools, colleges, and universities.

The separate-but-equal principle purported to grant African Americans equal facilities, even though enforced separation branded them as socially inferior. The equality supposedly accorded African Americans was often pure fiction, however. Especially in educational institutions, African Americans invariably suffered inferior opportunities in inferior facilities. In some contexts, such as graduate programs, southern states did not bother to create even inferior opportunities for African Americans. Threatened with litigation, states might respond, as Texas did with respect to the University of Texas Law School, by creating a token professional program for African Americans. In SWEATT V. PAINTER (1950), however, the Supreme Court signaled that it would no longer turn a completely blind eye to fictional claims of separate equality. There the Court held that a hastily created black law school established by the state of Texas to avoid admitting an African American to the University of Texas Law School was not equal to the educational experience accorded white law students. *Sweatt* suggested that certain educational intangibles made a separate law school inherently unequal.

That pronouncement ultimately reached its full bloom in BROWN V. BOARD OF EDUCATION OF TOPEKA, KANSAS (1954). In *Brown* the Court announced that segregated public schools were inherently unequal. Subsequently, in a series of decisions announced without opinions, the Court declared unconstitutional officially sanctioned segregation across a wide spectrum of public facilities and institutions,

thus permanently burying the separate-but-equal principle.

—*Timothy L. Hall*

Serna v. Portales

1974: Federal court decision affirming a BILINGUAL EDUCATION policy in New Mexico.

In this decision a federal circuit court in New Mexico held that a school district was not meeting the educational needs of its MEXICAN AMERICAN pupils by failing to implement bilingual education and other programs designed to enhance educational opportunities of Mexican-American children.

—*Marcia J. Weiss*

Sex discrimination

Unequal treatment of persons on the basis of their sex.

Societies have long acknowledged that women and men are biologically different, and have consequently given them different social, economic, and political rights and responsibilities. As Western societies have become more sensitive to their own violations of the rights of members of recognizable groups and categories of persons, many elements of the differential treatment of men and women have become regarded as forms of sex discrimination.

The U.S. Constitution In 1787, when future president John Adams was participating in the convention that framed the U.S. CONSTITUTION, his wife, Abigail Adams, wrote to him, encouraging him to "remember the Ladies, and be more generous and favourable to them than your ancestors." She wanted the Framers to include rights for women in the new constitution, but her request was ignored. The document the convention produced made no direct reference to sex. By its silence the Constitution implicitly adopted the prevailing view that women existed primarily as children and wives in families headed by men. The Constitution left questions of VOTING RIGHTS to the states, thereby implicitly ratifying the rules in every state that denied women the vote. General WOMAN SUFFRAGE was not achieved until ratification of the NINETEENTH AMENDMENT in 1920. Throughout American history WOMEN'S RIGHTS generally have differed from those of men.

In the aftermath of the CIVIL WAR, fundamental changes were made in the U.S. Constitution. A particularly significant change was adoption in 1868 of the Fourteenth Amendment's EQUAL PROTEC-TION CLAUSE, which declared that "no State shall . . . deny to any person within its jurisdiction the equal protection of the laws." However, it would be more than one hundred years before the U.S. SUPREME COURT recognized the applicability of this command to sex discrimination. Meanwhile, the Court's nineteenth century decisions perpetuated discriminatory treatment of women, particularly in the workplace. In 1873, for example, the Court upheld an Illinois statute that forbade married women from practicing law as attorneys. In support of the Court's decision, Justice Samuel Freeman Miller wrote that

> the natural and proper timidity and delicacy which belongs to the female sex evidently unfits it for many of the occupations of civil life. . . . The paramount destiny and mission of woman are to fulfil the noble and benign offices of wife and mother. This is the law of the Creator.

A year later the Supreme Court ruled that state laws restricting the vote to men did not violate the equal protection clause.

Early in the twentieth century several states passed protective laws, generally limiting the number of hours women and children were allowed to work. Whether intended or not, a natural consequence of such laws was to make it less attractive for potential employers to hire women than men. When maximum-hours legislation was challenged in *Muller v. Oregon* (1908), the Supreme Court unanimously upheld the law. The Court argued that physical structure and maternal functions differentiated women from men and justified legislation to protect women, even if similar legislation to protect men might be unconstitutional.

The same state laws were challenged as violating the equal protection clause. Men sought to overturn laws that discriminated in favor of women, and women sought to overturn laws that restricted their employment opportunities. For most of the twentieth century the Supreme Court routinely upheld the challenged discriminations. Classifications based on sex—like most legal classifications—were constitutionally permissible so long as they had a "rational basis." A state could satisfy the rational basis test for a discriminatory law if it could give some plausible reason for the discrimination; the reason did not have to be persuasive. As late as 1961 the Supreme Court, under Chief Justice Earl WARREN, unanimously upheld a Florida statute that excluded women from JURY DUTY unless they specifically requested inclusion on the jury lists.

Legislative Prohibition of Sex Discrimination
The modern era of sex discrimination legislation began with the federal EQUAL PAY ACT OF 1963 and the CIVIL RIGHTS ACT OF 1964. The Equal Pay Act prohibited discrimination in wage compensation on the basis of sex. However, its importance was quickly overshadowed by the far broader, but unanticipated, sex-discrimination provisions of the Civil Rights Act. Title VII of the civil rights bill before Congress in January, 1964, sought to prohibit EM-PLOYMENT DISCRIMINATION based on race, color, religion, or national origin. During House debate on the bill, an amendment prohibiting discrimination based on sex was offered by Howard W. Smith of Virginia. As chair of the House rules committee, Smith had for years been a chief obstacle to passage of any civil rights legislation. Since a federal law prohibiting sex discrimination in employment would have voided the many state laws then providing special protections to women, Smith assumed that if his amendment passed there would be additional opposition to the civil rights bill as a whole. Smith was wrong. His amendment was hailed by the few women members of Congress, and women's groups across the nation became a major new constituency in support of the legislation.

In its final form, Title VII applied the same broad antidiscrimination language to sex that it applied to race, color, religion, and national origin. Those provisions were later supplemented. For example, Title IX of the Education Amendments of 1972 prohibited sex discrimination in a variety COLLEGE educational programs receiving federal financial assistance. A particularly noticeable result was a significant increase in athletic opportunities for college women. Another example is the Pregnancy Discrimination Act of 1978, which expanded the definition of sex discrimination to include discrimination related to pregnancy and childbirth; the CIVIL RIGHTS ACT OF 1991 expanded the remedies available to women whose rights under this law were violated to include compensatory and punitive damages and recovery of attorney's fees. The

Family and Medical Leave Act of 1993 provided assurance that jobs would be held for employees whose family and child-rearing needs required them to take temporary leaves from their employment.

Most states have also adopted comprehensive FAIR EMPLOYMENT PRACTICES LAWS that prohibit discrimination based on sex. Their coverages have varied, but many of these laws have covered at least some employers that are not covered by the federal law's Title VII. A number of states have also gone further than Title VII by prohibiting discrimination based on marital status or sexual orientation.

At the federal level laws prohibiting workplace sex discrimination have been enforced primarily by the EQUAL EMPLOYMENT OPPORTUNITY COMMISSION (EEOC), which has interpreted the sex discrimination prohibitions of Title VII broadly. In 1980 the commission issued guidelines defining SEXUAL HARASSMENT and declaring it a violation of Title VII. In 1986 the U.S. Supreme Court had occasion to consider whether sexual harassment did indeed violate Title VII. In MERITOR SAVINGS BANK V. VINSON, and again in *Harris v. Forklift Systems, Inc.* (1993), the Court affirmed the EEOC guidelines.

Constitutional Law and Sex Discrimination
Quite apart from enforcing statutory prohibitions against sex discrimination, the U.S. Supreme Court has, since 1970, applied the EQUAL PROTECTION CLAUSE of the FOURTEENTH AMENDMENT to narrow the range of permissible discriminations based on sex. The Court's initial departure from its traditional "rational basis" analysis occurred in REED V. REED (1971), in which the Court overturned an Idaho statute that preferred men to women in naming the executors of estates. The Court acknowledged the rational-basis test, but rejected a perfectly plausible rationale supplied by the state as arbitrary and forbidden by the equal protection clause. The Court was clearly prepared to be more skeptical of the constitutionality of sex-based discriminations than it had been historically.

A few years later, in the case of FRONTIERO V. RICHARDSON (1974), eight Supreme Court justices agreed to strike down federal laws allocating military benefits in a way that discriminated on the basis of sex. Four of them were prepared to declare that governmental classifications based on sex—like those based on race—were inherently suspect and therefore subject to strict judicial scrutiny. This would have been a huge step. Under rational-basis review the burden of proof is on a statute's challenger, and any plausible rationale by the government is sufficient to save a challenged statute. By contrast, under strict scrutiny the burden of proof is on the government to demonstrate that the discrimination is necessary to achieve a compelling government interest and that such discrimination is narrowly tailored for that purpose. Indeed, the government's burden under strict scrutiny is so great that challenged statutes have almost always fallen. However, at that time there was not a majority of justices willing to take so large a step.

At the time of the Court's *Frontiero v. Richardson* decision, the states were considering ratification of the EQUAL RIGHTS AMENDMENT (ERA). If that proposed amendment had been adopted, the Constitution would have required equal rights for women and Court action would have become unnecessary. However, by the time the ERA missed its deadline for ratification, the Court's opportunity had passed.

In a number of cases in 1974 and 1975 the Supreme Court struck down various statutes discriminating on the basis of sex, while managing to avoid the question of whether rational-basis analysis or strict scrutiny was the proper test. In 1976 the Court split the difference. An Oklahoma statute set the minimum legal age for purchasing beer at twenty-one for males and eighteen for females. In *Craig v. Boren* that year the Court voided the statute, concluding that *Reed v. Reed* and its progeny stood for the proposition that classifications based on sex deserved an intermediate level of scrutiny. In the opinion of the Court: "To withstand constitutional challenge . . . classifications by gender must serve important governmental objectives and must be substantially related to achievement of those objectives."

The Court's selection of intermediate scrutiny for classifications based on sex left some discriminatory practices in place. In *Michael M. v. Superior Court of Sonoma County* (1981) a badly divided court upheld a California statutory rape law that held males, regardless of their age, solely and criminally liable for intercourse with underage females. In *Rostker v. Goldberg* the same year the Court upheld the military CONSCRIPTION against the charge that drafting men but not women violated equal protection. Many military job specialties opened to women in later years, but their continuing exclusion from most combat units—like the sex-based labor laws of the past—has both protected women and limited their career opportunities.

In other areas of law the Court's intermediate scrutiny of sex-based classifications has resulted in significant change. For example, under the rule of *J.E.B. v. Alabama ex rel. T.B.* (1994) states may not exercise peremptory challenges to dismiss persons from JURY DUTY solely on the basis of their sex. In public COLLEGES AND UNIVERSITIES traditional bastions of single-sex education have been integrated by court action. For example, the Supreme Court ordered the Mississippi University for Women to admit a male applicant to its nursing program in 1982, and in 1996 it required Virginia Military Institute to admit women.

Sex Discrimination in the 1990's The Civil Rights Act of 1991 created the Glass Ceiling Commission to study and report on the status of women and minorities in the workplace. Its 1995 report provides a useful overview of sex discrimination in employment during the early 1990's. The commission found that women in the workforce had proportionately more college and advanced degrees than men. Despite their apparent educational advantages, however, women held only 3 to 5 percent of senior-level jobs in major corporations and they were represented on only 10 percent of major corporation boards. Of *Fortune Magazine*'s top one thousand companies only two had female chief operating officers. Moreover, women's pay lagged behind that of men. Female managers earned 15 to 50 percent less than their male counterparts. Women holding M.B.A. degrees from the top twenty college programs were paid 12 percent less than their male counterparts during their first year on the job. Female professionals and managers worked disproportionately in the lower-paid public and not-for-profit sectors. In the private sector, the commission concluded that equally qualified women were denied advancement into senior management on the basis of sex.

By the early 1990's sex discrimination was a topic of controversy in arenas as diverse as athletics, criminal justice, education, law, medical research, military service, politics, and religion.

SUGGESTED READINGS:

Babcock, Barbara Allen, et al. *Sex Discrimination and the Law: History, Practice, and Theory*. Boston: Little, Brown, 1996.

Boumil, Marcia Mobilia. *Law and Gender Bias*. Littletown, Colo.: F. B. Rothman, 1994.

Dusky, Lorraine. *Still Unequal: The Shameful Truth About Women and Justice in America*. New York: Crown Publishers, 1996.

Federal Glass Ceiling Commission. *Good for Business: Making Full Use of the Nation's Human Capital*. Washington, D.C.: Government Printing Office, 1995.

Friedman, Sara Ann. *Work Matters: Women Talk About Their Jobs and Their Lives*. New York: Viking Press, 1996.

Goldstein, Leslie Friedman. *Contemporary Cases in Women's Rights*. Madison: University of Wisconsin Press, 1994.

Jamieson, Kathleen Hall. *Beyond the Double Bind: Women and Leadership*. New York: Oxford University Press, 1995.

Katz, Montana, and Veronica Vieland. *Get Smart! What You Should Know (but Won't Learn in Class) about Sexual Harassment and Sex Discrimination*. New York: Feminist Press at the City University of New York, 1993.

Minson, Jeffrey. *Questions of Conduct: Sexual Harassment, Citizenship, Government*. New York: St. Martin's Press, 1993.

Morewitz, Stephen John. *Sexual Harassment and Social Change in American Society*. San Francisco: Austin and Winfield, 1996.

—*Craig W. Allin and Elizabeth A. Sparks*

Sexual harassment

A form of illegal SEX DISCRIMINATION in the workplace.

The concept of "sexual harassment" in the workplace developed around the same time that the EQUAL RIGHTS AMENDMENT was being considered for ratification. However, legal prohibitions against such behavior go back at least as far as the CIVIL RIGHTS ACT OF 1964. The EQUAL EMPLOYMENT OPPORTUNITY COMMISSION (EEOC), which was made responsible for enforcing the relevant parts of the civil rights legislation, determined that harassment based on sex is a form of sex discrimination prohibited under Title VII of the Civil Rights Act. According to guidelines that the EEOC published in November, 1980:

Unwelcome sexual advances, requests for sexual favors, and other verbal or physical conduct of a sexual nature constitute sexual harassment when

(1) submission to such conduct is made either explicitly or implicitly a term or condition of an individual's employment, (2) submission to or rejection of such conduct by an individual is used as the basis for employment decisions affecting such individual, or (3) such conduct has the purpose or effect of unreasonably interfering with an individual's work performance or creating an intimidating, hostile, or offensive working environment.

Harassment of the first and second types is called "quid pro quo" harassment (from the Latin for "something for something") because something is demanded in return for the economic benefits of work. In cases of sexual favors in return for promotion, victims may include not only the employee propositioned but also other employees whose job prospects were affected. Harassment of the third type is called "hostile environment" harassment. Here there is no quid pro quo.

The SUPREME COURT has decided two significant cases involving hostile environment harassment. In MERITOR SAVINGS BANK V. VINSON (1986) the Court supported the EEOC's conclusion that hostile environment sexual harassment violates Title VII. Seven years later in *Harris v. Forklift Systems, Inc.* the Court determined that victims do not have to prove psychological injury to demonstrate an impermissible hostile environment. Speaking for a unanimous Court, Justice Sandra Day O'CONNOR said that "so long as the environment would reasonably be perceived, and is perceived, as hostile and abusive, there is no need for it also to be psychologically injurious."

Most complaints of sexual harassment have involved women as victims and men as perpetrators, but the law protects both men and women and does not require that the person doing the harassing be of the opposite sex. Sexual harassment does

During Associate Justice Clarence Thomas' Senate confirmation hearings in 1991, University of Oklahoma law professor Anita Hill raised issues of sexual harassment in the workplace that tainted Thomas' confirmation and helped focus national attention on the issue. (*AP/Wide World Photos*)

require that victims be treated differently because of their sex. Differential treatment based on sexual preference is not covered by the law. A difficult issue in enforcing the law is determining whether sexual conduct is "unwelcome." In assessing cases the EEOC examines the totality of circumstances, including the nature of the sexual advances and the contexts in which alleged incidents have occurred. Also difficult is determining whether a work environment is "hostile." In *Harris* the Supreme Court concluded that an environment is hostile when "a reasonable person would find [it] hostile or abusive," and the victim also perceives it that way. Factors may include the frequency and severity of discriminatory conduct, whether it is physically threatening or humiliating, and whether it unreasonably interferes with an employee's work performance.

Although the Supreme Court has held that employers are not automatically liable for all instances of sexual harassment occurring in their workplaces, employer liability is broad. Employers have usually been held responsible for the actions of their supervisory personnel, and they themselves have been held liable for sexual harassment in instances when they have known about it—or should have known about it—and have failed to take immediate corrective action. Under Title VII employers have an affirmative duty to eradicate hostile or offensive work environments.

—*Craig W. Allin and Elizabeth A. Sparks*

Sharpton, Alfred, Jr.

Born Oct. 3, 1954, Brooklyn, N.Y.: Civil rights activist, minister, and founder of the National Youth Movement.

The Reverend Alfred Sharpton, Jr., capped a career of social activism and agitation in September, 1996, with his announcement that he would attempt to oust New York City mayor Rudolph Giuliani in the 1997 elections. Sharpton said he hoped to focus the mayoral debate on POLICE BRUTALITY, overcrowding in public schools, and the dearth of high-level jobs held by blacks in the city. It was not Sharpton's first bid for public office. In 1992 and 1994 he ran unsuccessfully in the Democratic primaries for the U.S. Senate. It was also not the first time that Sharpton thrust himself into the public eye over race issues.

Ordained as a Pentecostal minister at the age of ten, Sharpton worked as a promoter during the 1970's for the soul singer James Brown, who became a surrogate father to him. As a fourteen-year-old, Sharpton worked under the Reverend Jesse JACKSON as a youth organizer for Operation Breadbasket, organizing a boycott of a clothing store that had no African Americans on its board. A few years later he founded the National Youth Movement, mobilizing young people to march against and BOY-COTT corporations that discriminated against minorities. He first gained national attention in December, 1986, following a killing in the Howard Beach section of Queens, New York. A black man, Michael Griffith, was killed by a car after being chased onto a Queens highway by white men. Sharpton organized a motorcade and marches through the neighborhood and successfully pressed for the appointment of a special prosecutor.

Sharpton has attracted criticism for some of his other activism—most notably for his support of Tawana Brawley, a teenager from upstate New York who alleged she had been raped in 1987 by five white men. Sharpton accused police of a cover-up, but a special grand jury later ruled that the girl's allegations were false. Sharpton also was criticized in 1995 for making racially charged statements about a Jewish clothing store owner in Harlem. The owner's store was later set on fire and eight people were killed.

—*Christine Harvey*

Shelley v. Kraemer

1948: U.S. SUPREME COURT decision banning states from enforcing racially motivated RESTRICTIVE COVENANTS.

The arguments presented to the Supreme Court in *Shelley v. Kraemer* involved several cases, including one originating in Missouri and one in Michigan, where white property owners had obtained court orders to remove African Americans from recently purchased homes. In both cases the sellers of the properties in question had signed restrictive covenants in which they pledged to sell to whites only. Attorneys for the NATIONAL ASSOCIATION FOR THE ADVANCEMENT OF COLORED PEOPLE (NAACP) had been preparing to argue a case challenging the constitutionality of racially restrictive covenants for almost twenty years. Only two previous cases involving restrictive covenants had come before the U.S. Supreme Court. In both (*Corrigan and Curtis v. Buckley*, 1926, and *Hansberry v. Lee*, 1940) the Court's decisions had sidestepped questions about the constitutionality of the covenants themselves.

Although none of the cases associated with *Shelley* matched the profile of the ideal case NAACP attorney Thurgood MARSHALL had hoped for, the timing proved right. Liberal Democrats in President Harry S TRUMAN's administration opposed restrictive covenants and urged the president to support the NAACP brief. Truman, who had just received the report of a national commission investigating civil rights in the United States, conferred with his solicitor general, Clark Clifford, and with officials in the JUSTICE DEPARTMENT. On October 30, 1947, Attorney General Tom Clark announced that the Justice Department would become involved in *Shelley v. Kraemer*. After consulting with other government departments, such as Interior, the Justice Department filed an *amicus curiae* (friend of the court) brief condemning restrictive covenants as being damaging to the country.

Not surprisingly, the Court ruled in favor of the victims of restrictive covenants. However, with *Shelley* the Court edged only a little closer to dealing directly with racial issues in HOUSING DISCRIMINATION. The Court stopped short of outlawing racial clauses in restrictive covenants, but did bar states from enforcing them. That is, private property owners could still create and sign restrictive covenants that barred certain classes of prospective buyers, but compliance had to be voluntary. If an owner violated the terms of a covenant, neighbors could no longer ask for relief in the form of court orders removing unwanted new neighbors from their property. The question of whether aggrieved neighbors could sue for perceived damages was, however, left open until 1953. At that time the Supreme Court's decision in BARROWS V. JACKSON banned the use of racial clauses in restrictive covenants entirely.

—*Nancy Farm Mannikko*

Shuttlesworth, Fred L.

Born Mar. 18, 1922, Mt. Meigs, Ala.: AFRICAN AMERICAN baptist minister and civil rights leader.

Fred Shuttlesworth was a key participant in efforts during the turbulent 1950's and 1960's to abolish SEGREGATION in the South. A pastor of sev-

eral Baptist churches, he also participated in several important civil rights organizations. After the state of Alabama banned the NATIONAL ASSOCIATION FOR THE ADVANCEMENT OF COLORED PEOPLE (NAACP) from the state, Shuttlesworth helped organize and was named president of the Alabama Christian Movement for Human Rights. He also helped organize the SOUTHERN CHRISTIAN LEADERSHIP CONFERENCE (SCLC), for which he served as secretary, and he was a close friend of Martin Luther KING, JR.

Shuttlesworth's efforts to end discrimination in the buses of BIRMINGHAM, ALABAMA, resulted in the destruction of his home by dynamite, but this attack did not blunt his zeal for civil rights protest. Over the following years he vigorously campaigned against segregation despite being beaten and arrested on more than one occasion. During the 1960's he moved to Cincinnati, Ohio, to serve as pastor of a Baptist church there. By the mid-1990's he was pastor of the Greater New Light Baptist Church and director of the Shuttlesworth Housing Foundation, an organization that assisted low-income families to purchase homes.

—*Timothy L. Hall*

Sit-ins

Nonviolent, direct-action tactic used by civil rights protest movements to force change, particularly during the early 1960's.

Sit-ins first caught the nation's attention when four African American students from North Carolina Agricultural and Technical College sat at the "whites-only" lunch counter of a Woolworth's store in downtown Greensboro, North Carolina, on February 1, 1960, and refused to move unless they were served. The students did not invent the tactic, however. Other American civil rights protesters had earlier adapted it from the struggle led by Mohandas GANDHI against British imperialism in India, but it soon became the potent symbol of a new, more assertive era of civil rights activism on the part of younger activists.

Origins of the Sit-in Movement In the South and in many border states in the early 1960's it was illegal for blacks and whites to sit together in public places such as bus stations, restaurants, and lunch counters. When the North Carolina A&T students staged their sit-in demonstration, similar demonstrations against JIM CROW LAWS had already taken place in at least sixteen other American cities; however, none of those other protests had the consequences that the GREENSBORO SIT-INS would have. Within days demonstrations modeled on the Greensboro sit-ins spread across the state, and indeed throughout the segregated South. College and high school students initiated approximately seventy sit-ins in the two months after Greensboro. The SOUTHERN CHRISTIAN LEADERSHIP CONFERENCE attempted to harness the energy of the new movement and to impose a degree of organization on the young protesters almost immediately. In April the SCLC convened a student conference at Shaw University in Raleigh, North Carolina, under the direction of Ella BAKER and the Reverend James Lawson, a movement organizer from Nashville, Tennessee. The STUDENT NON-VIOLENT COORDINATING COMMITTEE (SNCC), a new, more confrontational civil rights organization made up of a younger constituency than the older organizations, emerged from this conference.

Before Greensboro sit-ins were usually organized by established civil rights organizations such as the NATIONAL ASSOCIATION FOR THE ADVANCEMENT OF COLORED PEOPLE (NAACP) and the CONGRESS OF RACIAL EQUALITY (CORE). They were almost always sanctioned, if not led, by black CHURCHES and recognized leaders in the African American community. These demonstrations were the result of intense planning. Lawson, for example, taught workshops in Nashville on the philosophy and history of nonviolent protest before leading sit-ins. SNCC, however, was a new generation of activists born after World War II who were impatient for change in the segregated South. While its leaders planned protests as carefully as their predecessors, they also planned more of them and were less likely to compromise on their goals.

The initial Greensboro sit-in seemed on its surface to be an impromptu event that would have been unlikely to sustain its own momentum, much less inspire other protests. But while Ezell Blair, Jr. (later Jibreel Khazan), Franklin McCain, Joseph McNeil, and David Richmond sat down at the Woolworth's counter without prior training in nonviolent protest and without specific larger goals in mind, they did share a background in an organized movement center. Each of them had grown up in North Carolina. A lawyer associated with the NAACP named Floyd MCKISSICK had led organized sit-ins there in the late 1950's, and all four students were acquainted with him through the NAACP Youth Council. The Greensboro protesters were also acting on a new tradition of nonviolent direct action that was emerging from the MONTGOMERY BUS BOYCOTT and desegregation of public schools.

The Sit-ins' Spread During the eighteen months following Greensboro an estimated seventy thousand African Americans and thousands of white sympathizers participated in sit-ins. At least 141 college students and 58 professors lost their positions for taking part in them. Scores of restaurants and lunch counters throughout the South were forced to desegregate. Sit-in participants put their physical safety on the line in every demonstration. Hecklers waving Confederate flags confronted the Greensboro students before a bomb threat closed the store down. In Montgomery, Alabama, protest leaders had their phones tapped and students faced police armed with rifles, shotguns, and tear gas. In Chattanooga, Tennessee, whites threw dishes at protesters and even used a bullwhip on one student. Nashville counterdemonstrators stubbed out cigarettes on protesters' backs. In Jackson, Mississippi, demonstrators were smeared with ketchup and mustard, threatened with knives and nooses, and then brutally assaulted for several minutes before a store manager bothered to call local police. In Houston, Texas, whites kidnapped a black sit-in participant, carved "KKK" on his chest, and hung him by his knees from a tree.

The violence that sit-in protesters encountered was a stark contrast to the quiet dignity that they were trained to display. Two of the main goals of each protest were to assert the essential humanity of African Americans that segregation denied and to bring attention to that denial. Mass NEWS MEDIA made these tactics especially effective in convincing Americans of the injustice of Jim Crow; enraged segregationist counterdemonstrators whose actions were caught by national news cameras did little to help their cause in the nation at large. Another main goal of individual sit-ins was to demonstrate to local business owners how economically destructive segregation could be. Sit-ins were often accompanied by economic BOYCOTTS, and where they were effective the reasons for success were more likely to be economic than humanitarian.

Success of the Sit-in Movement The tactic of the sit-in spread to other areas after 1960, most famously that of interstate travel. FREEDOM RIDERS began to protest segregated seating on Greyhound buses in 1961. Protests of this type continued in the Civil Rights movement at least until 1964, when President Lyndon B. JOHNSON signed into law the CIVIL RIGHTS ACT OF 1964 that made segregation of public facilities illegal. Afterward, Native American activists, Chicano activists, prisoners, feminists, and even antiabortion activists have used sit-ins to bring attention to their causes.

SUGGESTED READINGS:

Carson, Clayborne. *In Struggle: SNCC and the Black Awakening of the 1960s*. Cambridge, Mass.: Harvard University Press, 1981.

Chafe, William. *Civilities and Civil Rights: Greensboro, North Carolina, and the Black Struggle for Freedom*. New York: Oxford University Press, 1980.

Morris, Aldon. *The Origins of the Civil Rights Movement: Black Communities Organizing for Change*. New York: Free Press, 1984.

Proudfoot, Merrill. *Diary of a Sit-In*. Chapel Hill: University of North Carolina Press, 1962.

Williams, Juan. *Eyes on the Prize: America's Civil Rights Years, 1954-1965*. New York: Penguin Books, 1987.

Wolff, Miles. *Lunch at the 5 & 10*. Chicago: Ivan R. Dee, 1990.

J. Todd Moye

Slavery

Exploitative system of labor and social organization that subordinated AFRICAN AMERICANS— particularly in the SOUTHERN STATES—from the seventeenth century to the end of the CIVIL WAR.

Through much of human history certain classes of people have been forced to labor for the benefit of others as slaves. Persons held as slaves were typically regarded as property that could be bought and sold and they possessed few, if any, rights. In British North America, and later in the United States, slavery evolved into a system that melded slavery with race. After brief attempts to enslave AMERICAN INDIANS, British settlers turned exclusively to enslaving persons of African ancestry. By 1861 the words "slave" and "negro" were virtually synonymous.

Legally and practically, the institution of slavery was riddled with contradictions and ambiguities. Slaves were human beings who were accorded some legal rights; however, at the same time they were legally regarded as property, and legal codes gave property a privileged position. This contradiction forced slave owners to perform mental gymnastics in order to justify slavery morally when it came under attack in the late eighteenth century. This duality of person-property contributed to the outbreak of the Civil War.

Beginnings of North American Slavery African American slavery began in the early seventeenth century. In 1619 a Dutch ship swapped twenty Africans for provisions at the British colony of Jamestown, Virginia. These Africans were treated as indentured servants, but other Africans who followed them experienced varying degrees of freedom. In 1660 Virginia instituted a slave code that defined slavery. The code linked the legal status of children to that of their mothers, and that status extended throughout a person's lifetime. The code permitted white slave owners to profit from their lust by impregnating their slave women to produce new slave progeny.

During the seventeenth century, British landowners seemed to prefer white indentured servants over black Africans. However, the improved economic conditions and increased political stability in Restoration England after 1660 reduced the supply of white workers willing to migrate to North America as indentured servants. Under the indenture system, indentured servants were given full freedom after completing their terms of indentures. In contrast, under the slave system slaves were to work for their entire lives.

Historians have not fully agreed on why Africans, rather than other peoples, were enslaved. Several reasons may be advanced, however. Cultural factors played a large role. British settlers regarded Africans as "black"—a term symbolizing darkness and evil, and themselves as "white"—which symbolized purity or divinity. Cultural chauvinism also placed Africans at a disadvantage: The British regarded themselves as Christian and "civilized," while Africans were "heathen" and "barbarian." Moreover, as Africans assumed increasing responsibility for menial labor in the colonies, British settlers came to associate such work with Africans.

White settlers had little trouble acquiring Africans to work as slaves. However, it proved more difficult to resolve the ethical and legal contradictions in regarding slaves simultaneously as human beings and property. In the theocentric world of the seventeenth century, acceptance of the idea that slaves possessed souls and could go to heaven constituted the highest recognition that they were indeed human beings. Nevertheless, in 1667, the Virginia Colony determined that slaves who became Christians did not become free persons. At the same time the courts could not readily give range to the full implications of slaves being persons without interfering with the property rights of their owners. For example, the laws allowed slave families to be split up when their members were sold separately.

Slave codes gradually developed legal fictions to protect the lives of slaves from wanton cruelty and from murder. The slaves themselves created certain customary rights in their relationships with individual masters. Slaves worked sufficiently hard to see that the agricultural or industrial enterprises of their masters continued to function, for slaves and masters alike had to eat. However, slaves could and did engage in work stoppages or slowdowns in the face of what the slaves themselves regarded as unacceptable treatment.

The Eighteenth Century The moral contractions posed by slavery continued to vex slave owners through the eighteenth century, a time in which North American slavery underwent critical transformations. Slavery always involved the constants of coercion and salability, but it varied in practice over time and in various places making the differences among different slave enterprises as important as the similarities. For example, slavery existed in New England, the mid-Atlantic Coast colonies, and the southern colonies, but there were important variations in the slave systems of each region.

In New England slaves played only a small role in the economy. They were fewer in number than in the southern colonies and they mostly worked as artisans or as hands on small family farms—often in relative isolation from other slaves. In the middle colonies, slaves sometimes were congregated in port cities such as New York or Philadelphia, where they worked as sailors and longshoremen. They had close contact with one another. In the Hudson Valley of New York, for example, slaves worked on large agricultural enterprises similar to those in the Deep South. In the Chesapeake Bay region slavery evolved slowly throughout the seventeenth century, while in the Carolinas, owners imported the system full-blown from Barbados. Slaves made up 70 percent of the Carolinas' population in 1720. Carolina slave codes were consequently harsh, limiting unsupervised slave gatherings and severely punishing rebellions. During the eighteenth century these re-

Key Events in the History of African American Slavery

1619	Africans are brought to Virginia as indentured servants.
1641	Massachusetts Bay Colony legalizes slavery.
1662	Virginia legislature rules that offspring of mixed-race unions are slave or free according to the mother's status.
1667	Virginia rules that becoming a Christian does not make a slave free.
1691	Virginia restricts manumissions to prevent growth of a free black class.
1712	Slave revolt in New York inspires tougher slave codes and new restrictions on free black ownership of property.
1775	First abolitionist organization in the United States, the Pennsylvania Society for the Abolition of Slavery, is formed.
1777	Vermont becomes the first state to abolish slavery; North Carolina toughens restrictions on manumission.
1783	Massachusetts abolishes slavery by judicial decision.
1787	Northwest Ordinance prohibits slavery in the Northwest Territory.
1793	As northern states are abolishing slavery, invention of the cotton gin enhances cotton plantation productivity, making slavery much more profitable to maintain in the South; federal government passes Fugitive Slave Law.
1808	Importation of slaves into the United States is outlawed.
1820	Missouri Compromise admits Missouri to the Union as a slave state, while prohibiting slavery in northern states.
1822	Denmark Vesey leads a slave insurrection in Charleston, South Carolina.
1830	Slavery is virtually abolished throughout the North.
1831	Nat Turner leads massive slave revolt in Virginia.
1832	New England Anti-Slavery Society is organized.
1842	In *Prigg v. Pennsylvania* the U.S. Supreme Court invalidates a state law against removing African Americans from the state by force to reenslave them because the law violates the fugitive slave clause of the Constitution.
1856	South Carolina governor James H. Adams argues for the repeal of the federal law prohibiting importation of slaves.
1857	Supreme Court's *Dred Scott* decision invalidates the Missouri Compromise and rules that residence in a free state does not make a slave free.
1859	John Brown stages raid on federal arsenal at Harper's Ferry, Virginia, to capture arms for his abolition work.
1861	Civil War begins.
1863	Abraham Lincoln issues the Emancipation Proclamation.
1865	Thirteenth Amendment abolishes slavery throughout the United States.

gional differences persisted and contributed at the century's end to the gradual elimination of slavery from the New England and middle colonies and its confinement to the South.

Although Europe carried about twelve million Africans into slavery, barely a twentieth of these people were taken to British North America, or the late United States. Moreover, although the United States outlawed importing slaves in 1808, the county had the largest slave population in the world in 1860. Elsewhere in the Western Hemisphere, most of the slaves were male and were literally worked to death, making continual slave importation necessary. In contrast, ratio of men and women slaves in the United States had become even during the eighteenth century, allowing procreation to occur on a regular basis.

The equalization of male and female slave numbers compelled vital changes in slavery. It made possible slave families, although these lacked legal sanction. After 1750 an increasing majority of slaves in British North America were not born in Africa but in the New World. As a result—especially on large plantations—a creole slave culture evolved, one that allowed the slaves to survive the crushing trauma of enslavement. Slave parents reared children, taught them life skills through folk tales, and gave them a sense of identification—as human beings, as members of families, and as expatriates of Africa. In the process, regional and cultural distinctions imported from Africa yielded to amalgamation in the United States. Slaves retained an awareness of their African heritage, even as they imbibed European ways, creating a culture that was truly African American.

During the eighteenth century a racial caste system evolved, especially in the southern colonies. Although an anomalous class of free African Americans existed—mostly in cities—law and social custom presumed that persons with black skins were slaves until proven otherwise. Colonies passed harsh laws punishing MISCEGENATION, lest racial intermixing blur the lines of racial caste. To control free African Americans and respect the property rights of slave owners at the same time, laws governing emancipation became strict. In Virginia, for example, masters had the right to free their slaves, but freed slaves had twelve months to leave the state.

In part, this caste system reflected internal concerns in colonies with large slave majorities overwhelming local white control, but it crystallized further in response to the greatest challenge to slavery in the eighteenth century—the American Revolution. Among the inalienable RIGHTS specified in the DECLARATION OF INDEPENDENCE that set colonies on the road to creating the United States, one finds "liberty," a right all people possessed. The owners of slaves struggled mightily among the apparent incongruities of liberty as a human right, slaves as persons, and their own interests in property and social control.

The northern states responded to moral and economic arguments against slavery and passed laws abolishing slavery within their own borders. In 1787 the national government passed the Northwest Ordinance, banning slavery from the federal territories north of the Ohio River. Over the next several decades slavery became an institution peculiar to the southern states. Free blacks in cities developed institutions such as CHURCHES that became voices for emancipation. Many whites assumed that slavery would soon come to an end after President Thomas JEFFERSON signed a bill ending the importation of slaves from abroad effective January 1, 1808.

From Independence to Civil War After the importation of slaves into the United States ended, slavery not only persisted, but also flourished. The development of the cotton gin, which separated seeds from cotton fiber, made cotton cultivation more profitable. Cotton cultivation expanded deep into the South, where armies of African American slaves busied themselves clearing lands for the planting and harvesting of this white gold. Slavery extended into the future states of Alabama and MISSISSIPPI, and even flourished in Kentucky, where slaves often labored to grow hemp for rope making.

One of the ironies of slavery in the period before the Civil War was that as planters gained greater wealth and power and the slave system matured, the slaves themselves enjoyed greater material comfort. Their housing and diets sometimes were comparable to those of average white southerners. However, the slave system itself hardened, adding new restrictions on slaves activities and making emancipation appear all but impossible. In Mississippi, for example, slaves could not congregate by themselves in groups of more than five. After Nat Turner's 1831 slave rebellion, in which sixty Virginia whites were slain, many states passed new laws or strengthened old ones that forbade the teaching of slaves to read.

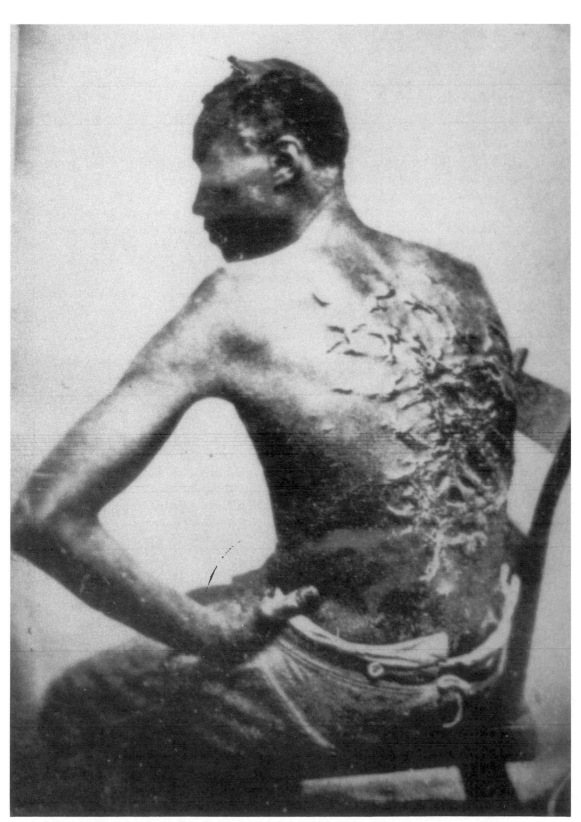

The whipping scars on this Louisiana man attest the lack of rights held by persons under chattel slavery. (*National Archives*)

Law courts continued to grapple with questions about what rights slaves had. They generally agreed that the law protected slaves from being murdered or excessively punished. The courts did sentence white defendants who killed slaves and did not, as in colonial times, merely require convicted white murderers to compensate the owners of the slaves whom they killed. Although persons who committed crimes against slaves had much less to fear from the law than those who committed similar crimes against whites, violence against slaves met with swifter and surer justice in the antebellum South than in any other slave society at the time.

Even if courts assumed the responsibility for protecting the lives of slaves, in most other cases slaves did not enjoy basic human rights such as livelihood and control over their own persons. Because slaves remained the property of their masters, the masters had the right to all the bounty that the slaves's labor produced. Frederick DOUGLASS noted with disdain that when he had been a slave, he had to turn over his wages to his master in Baltimore. However, it was the crime of rape, which many women slaves endured, that was the most vexing violation of slaves' human rights. Female slaves were the private property of their masters, to be exploited as the masters saw fit. Ravished slave women had no recourse at law.

Not all interracial sexual relationships were coerced, however, and more than a few masters genuinely disdained sexual violence against slave women. Apart from murder and extreme material cruelty, the more positive treatment of slaves depended entirely on the goodwill of their masters.

Daily Life Under Slavery The rationale behind slavery involved economic productivity—particularly in agricultural work. Slave owners used their slaves in a variety of ways. Most slave owners had only a few slaves, who worked alongside them in their fields or houses. Many such slaves lived under the same roofs as their masters. On larger units of production, where twenty or more slaves resided, slavery took on a much different character. On larger farms slaves usually lived in special quarters with other slaves and were under less close supervision of their owners. They mended clothes, tilled garden plots, reared children, and engaged in religious exercises. Studies of slave life have noted that slaves developed a view of themselves quite distinct from those held by their masters. The slaves dreamed of freedom, identified contradictions in

their masters' views of African Americans as perpetual slaves, and adjudged their masters guilty of egregious wrongs.

Slaves usually began working at sunup. Adult men and women tilled fields of cottons, tobacco, rice, and corn under the eyes of overseers and drivers—who were often trusted slaves. Masters organized slave labor in two general ways. In the gang system, groups of slaves performed ad hoc chores throughout the work day; in the task system, slaves were assigned specific jobs and were relieved of duty once those jobs were finished. Masters routinely ignored gender differences when they assigned tasks. All hands picked cotton, but men generally did the plowing, while the women did the hoeing.

Slaves too young to work were placed under the care of slaves too old to work. As early as age five, young slaves performed household chores or transported small items to the fields. By age twelve, most male slaves were assigned to the fields or to permanent duty in the big houses. Slave children often played with the children of their masters and learned through such interaction that their status differed greatly. For example, the male children of masters usually began wearing trousers around the age of five, while male slave children continued to wear oversized shirts as outer garments. Black and white children usually ceased to associate with each other by the time they were teenagers.

Many masters claimed that slavery was a more humane labor system than a system based on free labor because slaves were fed, clothed, and sheltered throughout their lives, even when they became too old to work. In practice, however, cradle-to-grave care was not always provided. Occasionally, masters simply allowed slaves to starve to death after they became too old to work productively.

Attempts at Reform During the 1850's some southerners attempted to reform the slave codes, to bring them into line with the inflated claims of slave owners that southern slavery was humane. Some southerners proposed repealing laws forbidding teaching slaves to read, as well as enacting new laws that would legitimize slave marriages. However, the outbreak of the Civil War in 1861 made continued discussion on these points moot.

In its essence, slavery involved slaves and masters in a relationship tied to the production of goods or produce in local areas. However, disputes over the perpetuation of slavery increasingly occupied the national agenda and led ultimately to the secession of eleven southern states from the Union and a bloody civil war. In a legal sense, it was the duality of slave as person and slave as property that made slavery an issue with which the national government had to deal.

Although federal law in 1793 provided for the return of runaway slaves, whites in the free states increasingly refused to sanction their return to slavery. This reality compelled slave owners to draft stronger FUGITIVE SLAVE LAWS and made northerners view the federal government as a creature of the slave owners. Moreover, as the United States expanded to the west, northern states sought to prevent extending slavery to the newly settled lands. Southerners pointed to the Fifth Amendment, which forbade Congress from making laws that seized property without due process of law, and argued that excluding slavery from federal territories was unconstitutional. In 1820 Congress had barred slavery from lands in the Louisiana Purchase above the line of 36° 30′ north latitude, as part of the Missouri Compromise.

In 1857 the U.S. SUPREME COURT issued a ruling on the constitutionality of the Missouri Compromise. In the DRED SCOTT CASE, the Court affirmed that Congress could not deny slave holders the right to take their property into any federal territory. In this case, the court ignored the human facet of slavery. In ruling that in the United States slaves "had no rights which the white man was bound to respect," the Court clearly sided with the notion that slaves were property. Moreover, the Court explicitly ruled that African Americans could not be citizens of the United States, even if individual states conferred citizenship on them. Many citizens in the free states rejected the Court's decision. In 1860 their votes elected the Republic Party candidate, Abraham LINCOLN, to the PRESIDENCY. The Republicans pledged to bar slavery from the federal territories, the Supreme Court's opinion notwithstanding. Seven states seceded from the Union immediately after Lincoln's election, a testimony to the power of the contradictory reality of human and property rights implicit in slavery to affect the stability of the United States.

SUGGESTED READINGS:

Blassingame, John W. *The Slave Community: Plantation Life in the Antebellum South*. New York: Oxford University Press, 1972. Surveys life in slave quarters and how their structures allowed slaves to survive slavery.

Boles, John B. *Black Southerners, 1619-1869*. Lexington, Ky.: University Press of Kentucky, 1984. Highly readable survey of slavery in the South.

Fehrenbacher, Don E. *The Dred Scott Case: Its Significance in American Law and Politics*. New York: Oxford University Press, 1978. Complete study of the Dred Scott case as a legal and political issue.

Gates, Henry Louis, Jr., ed. *The Classic Slave Narratives*. New York: Mentor, 1987. The personal memoirs of four former slaves.

Genovese, Eugene D. *Roll, Jordan, Roll: The World the Slaves Made*. New York: Pantheon, 1974. Penetrating Marxian analysis of slavery.

Kolchin, Peter. *American Slavery, 1619-1877*. New York: Hill & Wang, 1993. Compares American slavery with that in other societies.

Kulikoff, Allan. *Tobacco and Slaves: The Development of Southern Cultures in the Chesapeake, 1680-1800*. Chapel Hill: University of North Carolina Press, 1986. Emphasizes how slavery changed over time in a given place.

Morris, Thomas D. *Southern Slavery and the Law, 1619-1860*. Chapel Hill: University of North Carolina Press, 1996. Complete analysis of the laws governing slavery.

—*Edward R. Crowther*

Sleepy Lagoon case

1942-1943: Los Angeles murder case that prompted anti-MEXICAN AMERICAN violence and rioting.

In early August, 1942, José Díaz, a Mexican American youth, was found dead on the outskirts of Los Angeles in a gravel pit known as Sleepy Lagoon that was frequented by young Mexican Americans. Díaz's skull had been fractured but no conclusive evidence that he was murdered was ever found. Nevertheless, Los Angeles police arrested twenty-three other Mexican American youths and one Anglo, charging them all with murder. Despite the lack of evidence, a jury found most of the arrested youths guilty of assault or first- or second-degree murder the following January. The unfair verdicts prompted Carey McWILLIAMS and others concerned about LATINO rights to form the Sleepy Lagoon Defense Committee; in October, 1944, an appeals court overturned the convictions and freed all the youths. Meanwhile, the press played up the case by stereotyping Mexican Americans as dangerous ruffians and turning the word "Mexican" into a synonym for lawlessness. Racial tensions rose in Los Angeles and events soon led to the ZOOT SUIT RIOTS, in which servicemen on leave and in mobs attacked Mexican American youths at will without police retribution.

—*Michael R. Candelaria*

Smith v. Allwright

1944: U.S. SUPREME COURT decision banning all-white primaries.

Thurgood MARSHALL of the NATIONAL ASSOCIATION FOR THE ADVANCEMENT OF COLORED PEOPLE (NAACP) brought action against representatives of the Democratic Party on behalf of Mr. Lonnie E. Smith, a black resident of Houston, Texas, who had been denied the right to vote in a primary election. In 1941 the Court had upheld federal criminal charges against party election supervisors in *United States v. Classic* because the U.S. CONSTITUTION authorized Congress to regulate primaries as well as general elections if "the primary is by law made an integral part of the election machinery." Using this rationale, the Court found the electoral scheme in Texas constituted state action because it delegated power from the state to political parties to set the qualifications for primary elections of state and national officials. The Court reserved political parties' right to set general membership criteria, but declared that if the criteria were essential to voting in primaries to select nominees for general elections, then the party would be considered an actor of the state, and as such its actions would be found to be unconstitutional. In holding that the rules of the Democratic Party excluding African Americans from voting in primary elections violated the FIFTEENTH AMENDMENT, the Court overruled its 1935 *Grovey v. Townsend* decision.

—*Angelyque P. Campbell*

Snake River massacre

1887: Mass murder of thirty-one CHINESE AMERICAN miners by whites near Hells Canyon, Idaho.

The 1880's saw VIOLENCE directed at Chinese in the American West on an unprecedented scale. In

1880 a riot destroyed the Chinese community in Denver, Colorado. In 1885 the city of TACOMA, WASHINGTON, expelled its entire Chinese community. However, these incidents paled before the ROCK SPRINGS, WYOMING, massacre of September, 1885, in which twenty-eight Chinese coal miners were killed.

In nearby Idaho, where Chinese miners made up a significant portion of the settler population, the anti-Chinese violence also had been fueled by greed. In May, 1887, a Chinese mining camp near Hells Canyon on the Snake River was attacked by whites demanding gold they believed the Chinese had hidden nearby. Thirty-one Chinese men were stabbed, shot, or tortured to death. An indemnity for the Chinese contained in a draft immigration treaty the following year was rejected by both the U.S. Congress and the Chinese Foreign Office.

—*Charles A. Desnoyers*

Social Security Act

1935: Federal law designed to provide for long-term economic security and welfare for all American citizens.

When President Franklin D. Roosevelt signed the Social Security Act into law, the act launched and shaped welfare policies of the modern United States. As much as any other New Deal legislation, the Social Security Act was a landmark with significant economic, social, and political consequences. It marked a transition away from the more conservative and market-oriented economic policies that had dominated programs and attitudes during the late nineteenth and early twentieth centuries. It also marked the first significant federal involvement in the fight against poverty. The Social Security Act dealt directly with the economic condition of people; the act came to symbolize the transition toward a more activist and more progressive role for the public sector. The impetus toward the adoption of these policies can be seen in part as a direct response to the economic crisis brought on by the Great Depression (1929-1939), a depression that was historically significant for its severity and its duration. As the Depression dragged on, lost and inadequate incomes resulting from either unemployment or other economic inequities caused serious and widespread hardship. Specific groups bore a disproportionate burden of the economic and social costs of the Depression. The Social Security Act provided more consistent and adequate provisions for many groups that had historically experienced EMPLOYMENT DISCRIMINATION and thus endured a larger share of the economic distress of the Depression.

The historic act shifted the obligation for social welfare from the various states to the federal government and created a government pension and insurance program financed by worker payroll taxes. Payroll taxes are levied as a percentage of wages and salaries and are collected from employees and employers. The reliance upon these taxes ultimately led the social security system to be managed as a pay-as-you-go system. The reliance upon the pay-as-you-go method of finance in essence dispels one of the more persistent myths about the social security system, namely that the contributions of individual workers are being accumulated in a fund for that own worker's retirement or use. The social security system is historic because it was designed and implemented as a national system and not as an individual retirement or insurance account. The Social Security Act established a Social Security Board to administer the programs that would help stabilize the economy by providing income assistance and promoting the public's general welfare. The legislation was debated and formed in the midst of the Depression and as such was intended to provide for the general well-being by improving the material circumstances of the nation's most economically vulnerable citizens: the elderly, the unemployed, the disabled, and the poor. The Social Security Act increased investments, established an unemployment compensation program, provided aid to the blind and disabled, set up old-age and survivor's benefits, and created a system of more consistent and adequate assistance programs for mothers and children.

Provisions of the Social Security Act The legislation that established the social security system, along with all of the subsequent amendments to the act, created a number of programs. There are so many programs that there is no consensus about which part of the legislation is the most important. During the drafting of the legislation it was thought that the establishment of a federal-state program of unemployment compensation would be the act's most meaningful and interesting part. In the years after enactment, other parts of the legislation have turned out to be more controversial and thus have

generated more interest and debate.

The Social Security Act set up cash benefits in the form of either social insurance programs or public assistance programs. Social insurance programs provide benefits on the basis of prior contributions or services. Pensions for retired workers, Old Age Survivor's and Disability Insurance, and UNEMPLOYMENT BENEFITS for those temporarily out of work are all social insurance programs. Public assistance programs provide benefits on the basis of a "means-tested" need. Aid to Dependent Children, Old-Age Assistance, and Aid to the Blind are all public assistance programs. There were efforts to incorporate health insurance as part of the Social Security Act of 1935 but attempts to include it encountered such forceful and direct opposition from the medical profession that it was ultimately dropped. It is also noteworthy that most of the means-tested programs in the American welfare system provide either subsidies or in-kind assistance rather than cash payments. In aggregate terms, cash payments in social insurance programs are significantly higher than total cash payments in public assistance programs.

Given that the legislation largely defined the role of the federal government's involvement in the economic lives of many people and businesses, it is not surprising that there have been several significant amendments to the Social Security Act of 1935. For example, in 1939 Congress amended the old-age insurance program so that it provided some economic security to the family members of workers. Consequently, after the 1939 amendments more women and children were covered by social security. After 1939, the social security system formally adopted a pay-as-you-go financing arrangement. Amendments in the 1950's increased benefits paid along with the rate of the payroll tax and extended coverage to include farmworkers and household domestics. In 1962 Congress included a provision dealing with unemployed fathers and renamed the ADC program. The new name was AID TO FAMILIES WITH DEPENDENT CHILDREN (AFDC). AFDC is the program commonly referred to as welfare. In 1965 Congress added Medicaid and Medicare to the Social Security program. Medicaid provides assistance with hospital and medical costs for the poor, and Medicare provides assistance for the disabled and the elderly.

Significantly, many of these programs were established as ENTITLEMENTS. Under the entitlement system, any person who meets the criteria as specified by Congress is entitled to receive benefits. The reason for establishing a program as an entitlement is to protect it from the politics of the appropriation process. Entitlement programs are part of the mandatory spending portion of the budget. Other entitlements in the federal budget include such things as the interest paid on the national debt, veteran's benefits, and some farm price supports. Before the passage of the Social Security Act, many insurance and assistance programs either did not exist at all or were inadequately and inconsistently funded in various states. In 1935, for example, only twenty-eight states had some sort of old-age assistance legislation. Less than 3 percent of persons over age 65 were receiving public aid in January, 1935. Despite the apparent connection between paid employment and economic stability only Wisconsin had an unemployment-insurance law in 1935. The Social Security Act of 1935 was the first national unemployment insurance program. It provided grants-in-aid to states, which then administered the program and paid benefits according to their own state guidelines.

The Role of the Courts The Social Security Act helped to reshape the role of the federal government as well as the relationship between the federal government and the states. Questions therefore arose as to the act's constitutionality. The "general welfare" phrase in the Constitution clearly gives the government the power to promote the general welfare. It was not at all clear, however, if that power extended to the provisions of the Social Security Act. In two companion decisions handed down in 1937, the U.S. SUPREME COURT upheld the Social Security Act. The constitutionality of establishing a federal law to provide for unemployment compensation was narrowly upheld in *Steward Machine Co. v. Davis*. The Court decided that Congress had the right to levy a tax in order to provide for the nation's general welfare. In a related decision, *Helvering v. Davis*, the Supreme Court upheld the old-age benefits provisions of the Social Security Act. The majority decision in the Helvering case, written by Justice Benjamin N. Cardozo, held that the distress of the Depression was so harsh that it required a concerted federal effort. A system that permitted some states to fund programs while other states did not would almost certainly be deficient and would leave many states and many of its citizens and businesses at a distinct disadvantage.

SUGGESTED READINGS:

Abramovitz, Mimi. *Under Attack, Fighting Back: Women and Welfare in the United States*. New York: Monthly Review Press, 1996.

Altmeyer, Arthur J. *The Formative Years of Social Security*. Madison: University of Wisconsin Press, 1966.

Cloward, Richard, and Frances Fox Piven. *Regulating the Poor: The Functions of Public Welfare*. New York: Random House, 1971.

Gordon, Linda. *Pitied but Not Entitled: Single Mothers and the History of Welfare 1890-1935*. Cambridge, Mass.: Harvard University Press, 1994.

Marmor, Theodore R., and Jerry L. Mashaw, eds. *Social Security: Beyond the Rhetoric of Crisis*. Princeton, N.J.: Princeton University Press, 1988.

Marmor, Theodore R., Jerry L. Mashaw, and Philip L. Harvey. *America's Misunderstood Welfare State: Persistent Myths, Enduring Realities*. New York: Basic Books, 1990.

Witte, Edwin E. *The Development of the Social Security Act*. Madison: University of Wisconsin Press, 1963.

—*Timothy E. Sullivan*

Society of American Indians

SAI: Pantribal AMERICAN INDIAN rights and improvement organization founded in 1911.

SAI was established in Columbus, Ohio, in 1911 by six distinguished Native Americans: Laura M. Cornelius (Oneida), Charles Eastman (Dakota Sioux), Carlos Montezuma (Yavapai), Charles Daganett (Peoria), Thomas L. Sloan (Omaha), and Henry Standing Bear (Sioux). Although the society generally advocated assimilation, it believed that American Indian culture contained beneficial values, and its leaders sought to convince non-Indians to respect Native American achievements and accept the concept of Indians as functioning and worthy participants in American society.

During its thirteen-year existence the society sought to improve Indian education and worked to better conditions on the reservations. However, factionalism and strife over issues such as peyote use led to the organization's decline and eventual demise in 1924.

—*David A. Crain*

Southeast Asian Americans

Immigrant refugee populations of Southeast Asians who have resettled in the United States.

Following the end of the Vietnam War in 1975, significant numbers of Southeast Asian refugees immigrated to the United States. These refugee groups, composed primarily of Cambodians, Laotians, and Vietnamese, brought with them historical and cultural traditions that sometimes brought them into conflict with the cultural patterns and the laws of the dominant American society. These conflicts often involved perceived inconsistencies in U.S. constitutional law. For example, the First Amendment of the U.S. CONSTITUTION protects freedom of RELIGION. Many Laotians burn paper at their funerals; however, in California burning paper at funerals is considered a violation of local fire codes. Some immigrant Laotian leaders (especially those from the highland Hmong), who were familiar with American constitutional law, believed that their rights to freedom of religious expression had been subverted through the implementation of local law.

The problem of upholding civil rights for Southeast Asian Americans has sometimes required compromising constitutional law, local law, and traditional Southeast Asian cultural norms. In some cases in which American law does not formally sanction certain Southeast Asian customs—such as arranged or forced marriages—informal solutions have been found. In many cases, however, resolutions have been difficult to obtain.

Social and Legal Discrimination Cultural differences have sometimes led to precarious conflicts. Situations involving various forms of discrimination have stimulated social scientists to ask important questions regarding the nature of prejudice that has often been aimed at Southeast Asian Americans. Often, as a result of stereotypes ascribed to Southeast Asian Americans, both social and legal discrimination has occurred. According to some historians, this represents a perpetuation of anti-Asian prejudices that can be traced back to anti-JAPANESE sentiments that emerged during and after World War II. During the late 1940's and early 1950's, for example, many Filipinos—most of whom were migrant workers—were thought by Americans to be Japanese and were consequently stigmatized. Although Filipinos are culturally and linguistically unrelated to the Japanese, few Americans could see the difference.

Other forms of discrimination have affected later immigrants to the United States. EMPLOYMENT DISCRIMINATION in particular has been widespread. Some social scientists have pointed out that many employers refuse to hire Southeast Asian immigrants. Explanations for not hiring these people have ranged from concerns over the immigrants' lack of English fluency to stereotypes of Southeast Asians as "dirty" and "lazy." Employers who have hired Southeast Asian Americans have, however, generally found that the stereotypes are groundless. Moreover, research has shown that Southeast Asians as a group tend to acquire English language proficiency in comparatively short periods of time.

Charges of welfare fraud have been common as well. To illustrate, many Anglo-Americans have assumed incorrectly that Indochinese immigrants (Cambodians, Hmongs, Miens, and Vietnamese) have accumulated fortunes by stealing funds from the government through misappropriation of welfare money. Those making such charges have suggested that some immigrant families own expensive computers, large cars and boats, but otherwise appear to be living in poverty. Author Tricia Knoll has observed that, while some cases of fraud have reached the courts, the illusion that welfare fraud has been committed by Southeast Asians has, in part, arisen from cases in which extended families pool their resources in order to make large purchases. In most such cases a larger number of persons use the purchased items than would be normal for most Anglo-American families.

More subtle forms of discrimination have been directed at Southeast Asian Americans. A few religious organizations that sponsor resettlement programs for various Southeast Asian communities have been charged with actively criticizing and denouncing the traditional religious beliefs and practices of Southeast Asian Americans. Knoll has referred to this type of discrimination as "abuse of sponsorship status."

Still other forms of discrimination can be found in laws that have been established to set policy for refugees. The Refugee Act of 1980, for example, defined U.S. policy toward immigrant refugees. The Refugee Act was established largely to manage the increasing influx of Southeast Asians who had immigrated to the United States following the end of the Vietnam War. While the policies laid the foundation for a more coherent plan for managing incoming refugees, many of the policies betrayed subtle forms of discrimination. For example, refugees eligible for cash assistance could also receive medical aid. However, "jeopardy" situations could often arise if recipients took low-paying jobs with little or no medical benefits. Because such recipients were considered technically employed, medical benefits could be—and often were—cut off.

Cultures in Conflict Many of the conflicts that have emerged between Southeast Asians and the dominant society of the United States stem from fundamental cultural differences. As previously mentioned these cultural differences sometimes resulted in violence, litigation, and ongoing tensions between Southeast Asians and non-Asian Americans. For example, many Southeast Asian Americans have continued to follow traditional cultural forms of family organization. Among most of the groups emphasis is placed on the extended family as the most recognizable and cohesive social unit. This emphasis contrasts sharply with the North American ideal of the nuclear family. Also, most

Southeast Asian societies traditionally trace their descent through the male line and give ultimate public authority to the male head of the household. Thus, when public functionaries must intervene in the family affairs of Southeast Asians the potential for violating their cultural taboos is high. For example, when school officials call the mothers of pupils to consult on school matters they violate the Southeast Asian custom of contacting the male heads of households first.

Because of these differences, matters such as setting up businesses, applying for federal assistance, and dealing with various public institutions have been fraught with problems. Education, for example, involves the constitutional right to a free and open public education. Some social scientists have pointed out the curriculum and instructional strategies employed by most schools in the United States tend to favor styles of instruction tailored exclusively to Anglo-American students. For exam-

Laotian American Hmong children in a dance troupe in Sacramento, California, in 1990. (*Eric Crystal*)

ple, American teachers, when questioning students, will often ask for volunteers to answer. Anglo-American students are used to responding to teachers informally so they have little problem volunteering answers. For Southeast Asians, however, talking to a teacher is considered a highly formal matter. These students will often wait until they are explicitly or directly called upon before responding. In many cases this never occurs; thus, in many instances, Southeast Asian students are subtly omitted from classroom interactions.

Cultural practices involving religious use of drugs has sometimes placed Southeast Asians in conflict with U.S. law. The use of opium, for example, is common in parts of Southeast Asia—particularly in the highlands of Laos. Traditional shamans from Laos occasionally use opium in religious contexts to assist them in penetrating the spirit world. Many shamans continued to use opium after coming to the United States. With the commitment of federal task forces against the use of illegal drugs, traditional drug uses have been rendered outside the law. Some Southeast Asian leaders have argued that their use of substances for religious purposes is protected under federal law by citing the AMERICAN INDIAN RELIGIOUS FREEDOM ACT of 1978.

Civil Rights: Cases and Issues Because readily available resolutions to complex conflicts are not often obtainable, numerous cases have found their ways into the U.S. court system. A few cases will be illustrative.

In Cambodia's traditional Hmong culture most marriages are arranged. When a potential marriage is proposed, the families of the initiate bride and groom will meet and negotiate a bride price. Many young American Hmong have rejected this form of marriage arrangement favoring American courting practices instead. During the 1980's several cases involving conflicts between traditional courtship practices and U.S. law reached the courts. In each case adult Hmong males were charged with abduction. In actuality, these Hmong males were merely following traditional Hmong rules for courting. Although abduction rarely occurs, even in traditional circumstances, it is still viewed as normal by many Hmong. Abduction occurs when two families have agreed upon a marriage, but the designated bride rejects the selected groom. Because a formal agreement has been established between the families, the groom, according to Hmong folk law, has the right to abduct the bride. Some Hmong females who

have been abducted in the United States have taken their cases to court. In most abduction cases penalties against the abductors have been lenient and cultural counseling, designed to convey American modes of courting, has been established as part of the resolution process.

In California in 1989 a welfare fraud case was brought against an Iu Mien (a highland Laotian group) family. Part of the charge involved the contention that the names of more people were entered on the welfare application form as family members than were actually living in the household of the person applying. Here again, differing cultural emphases played a role. The Mien, like many other Southeast Asians, do not associate the family with a single household. Instead a single extended family may comprise forty to one hundred people who may be living in as many as ten households. In this particular case the state was able to make its case against this family despite the obvious cultural differences involved.

During the late 1970's and early 1980's a series of conflicts broke out between Vietnamese fishermen and Texas fishermen in Seabrook, Texas, on Galveston Bay. When Vietnamese refugees first began commercial fishing in Texas' coastal waters they did not fully understand federal and state laws for regulating catch limits. As a result, they sometimes took larger catches than they were allotted by law. This angered local Texans who complained that Vietnamese fishermen were engaging in "unfair competition," and several demonstrations broke out to protest their fishing practices. At one point the KU KLUX KLAN got involved in anti-Southeast Asian public demonstrations. In 1979 at Seadrift, Texas, tensions reached a peak resulting in the death of a Texas crabber. Two Vietnamese brothers were accused of the crime, but were later acquitted when a jury ruled that the two had acted in self-defense. After that period Vietnamese fishermen followed fish and game laws more closely but continued to outproduce their Texas counterparts because of their collective work ethic. Although fewer conflicts have been reported, sentiment against Vietnamese fishermen in Texas remained strong.

Steps Toward Resolutions As the numbers of Southeast Asian immigrants increases and as more cases involving interpretations of civil law arise, resolutions to these conflicts are being found. Numerous Mutual Assistance Associations (MAAs) have been organized to mitigate financial and legal problems encountered by Southeast Asian Americans. In addition, lawyers specializing in the rights of immigrants have been taking on these types of cases in increasing numbers. These legal specialists are often called in by sponsoring agencies to handle cases where cultural differences wind up in litigation.

The area that has perhaps seen the most progressive changes has been education. In California, Minnesota, North Carolina, and Wisconsin serious efforts have been made to accommodate increasing numbers of Southeast Asian students. The central thrust of these new programs is to enhance instruction for non-English speaking Southeast Asian students so that all language minority students might benefit. In fact BILINGUAL EDUCATION was established in 1974 in the case of LAU V. NICHOLS. This case was argued not on the basis of its educational worth, but on its merits to ensure that all students have the same access to education. Thus, bilingual education was established on the basis of civil rights. The subsequent development of bilingual education as well as the continued growth of various "English as a second language" approaches has greatly benefited Southeast Asian Americans.

Perhaps the most dramatic relief efforts have been organized by various international agencies to help Cambodian refugees. UNICEF, the American Friends Service Committee, and other similar agencies have combined relief efforts in Cambodia with domestic programs in the United States. These efforts have resulted in establishing refugee status for many Cambodians. Although some members of Congress opposed giving refugee status to many of the Cambodians who were fleeing their home country, the overwhelming sentiments favoring refugee status outweighed the opposition largely because news of the "killing field" genocide that occurred in Cambodia from 1976 through 1979 had been covered extensively in the NEWS MEDIA. By obtaining refugee status and by subsequently im- migrating to the United States, these Cambodian Americans were guaranteed protection under the U.S. Constitution.

SUGGESTED READINGS:

Caplan, Nathan, John K. Whitmore, and Marcella H. Choy. *The Boat People and Achievement in America: A Study of Family Life, Hard Work, and Cultural Values.* Ann Arbor: University of Michigan Press, 1991. Study of the achievements of Vietnamese immigrants, with special attention to their academic performance.

Freeman, James M. *Hearts of Sorrow: Vietnamese-American Lives.* Stanford, Calif.: Stanford University Press, 1982. Examination of problems Vietnamese Americans have faced in adjusting to life in the United States

Haines, David W. *Refugees as Immigrants: Cambodians, Laotians, and Vietnamese in America*, edited by David W. Haines. Totowa, N.J.: Rowman & Littlefield, 1989. Collection of articles on themes ranging from immigrant welfare status to education.

Knoll, Tricia. *Becoming American: Asian Sojourners, Immigrants, and Refugees in the United States.* Portland, Oreg.: Coast to Coast Books, 1982. Describes a wide range of topics relating to various Southeast Asian American immigrant populations.

Strand, Paul J., and Woodrow Jones, Jr. *Indochinese Refugees in America.* Durham, N.C.: Duke University Press, 1985. Examination of the cultural adaptation of Cambodians, Laotians, and Vietnamese in the United States.

Tapp, Nicholas. *Sovereignty and Rebellion: The White Hmong of Northern Thailand.* New York: Oxford University Press, 1989. This study examines the political and economic hardships that led to the White Hmong exodus from Southeast Asia.

Trueba, Henry T. Lila Jacobs, and Elizabeth Kirton. *Cultural Conflict and Adaptation: The Case of Hmong Children in American Society.* New York: Falmer Press, 1990. Close examination of Hmong children in American schools.

—Michael Shaw Findlay

Southern Christian Leadership Conference

SCLC: Civil rights organization founded in 1957 and led by Martin Luther KING, JR., Ralph ABERNATHY, and others.

The SCLC was founded by King and a group of more than sixty fellow African American ministers in ATLANTA, GEORGIA, who met in a conference organized by Bayard RUSTIN in January, 1957. Formed in the wake of the MONTGOMERY BUS BOYCOTT, the SCLC was dedicated to using nonviolent direct action to confront and change racist practices across the SOUTHERN STATES. It soon became one of the most important organizations of the CIVIL RIGHTS MOVEMENT.

Origins and Plan The idea of the SCLC originated with Rustin, Stanley Levison, and Ella BAKER, all seasoned activists with the CONGRESS OF RACIAL EQUALITY (CORE), the Fellowship of Reconciliation, the NATIONAL ASSOCIATION FOR THE ADVANCEMENT OF COLORED PEOPLE (NAACP), and other rights groups, but the main strength of the organization came from the wellspring of religious leadership in the South. The SCLC was structured as an umbrella organization. At the top was an organizing committee or governing board of national leaders, all of whom were black, most of whom were ministers, and almost all of whom were male and from the South. They coordinated the work of regional organizers and local affiliates in order to bring protests such as the Montgomery boycott to many southern communities.

The local chapters, each with its own concerns and agendas, sent delegates to SCLC conventions. The delegates would network and receive training and support at the meetings, while overall goals and policies would be set during the convention proceedings. The delegates would then return to their hometowns to carry out SCLC mass actions, often with help from the national leaders, such as King himself, and from regional organizers who would travel where they were needed to help lead protest actions.

The SCLC was strongly influenced by the ideas of Mohandas GANDHI, who advocated the use of mass action and peaceful resistance to bring about change in India. Part of its strategy was the willingness of SCLC activists to undergo arrests and jailings in CIVIL DISOBEDIENCE of repressive laws. The SCLC's legal defense wing, which helped arrested protesters, was named the Gandhi Society.

Campaigns and Goals The campaigns of the SCLC were specifically designed to expose and end practices of JIM CROW segregation and discrimination in TRANSPORTATION, employment, customer service, and other areas of public, work, and social life. They were also planned to challenge racist laws that denied full citizenship rights and social opportunities to African Americans, and to pressure federal, state, and local officials to pass new laws that would ensure equal rights.

Local affiliates were organized around activist churches or other social groups, such as benevolent societies, civic organizations, voter registration groups, and fraternal orders, that were willing to provide meeting places and bases for civil rights activities. Individual members belonged to their local organizations—not the national SCLC—and those groups in turn were affiliated with the SCLC. National leadership was provided first by King, and after King's death, by Ralph David Abernathy, along with a cadre of close advisers and strategists, regional organizers, and leaders of specific campaigns, including Rustin, Baker, Levison, Andrew YOUNG, Hosea WILLIAMS, Septima Poinsette CLARK, Fred L. SHUTTLESWORTH, Jesse JACKSON, Dorothy Cotton, James BEVEL, James L. Lawson, Jr., and many others. These leaders successfully combined popular grassroots forms of activism with high-level political strategy.

As the organization and its staff grew, its activities conducted at the local level became very diverse, instigated as much by rank-and-file activists and regional organizers as by the national leadership. These activities sometimes brought the SCLC into local rivalry with other civil rights groups, including the NAACP, although many of the SCLC's founders had come out of the NAACP, and efforts were made to reduce competition between the two groups. The loose and varied structure of the SCLC often brought charges that it was chaotic and poorly organized. Indeed, the organization employed what one historian called a "hit-and-run" strategy, in which activists moved from one confrontation to another, and in which some campaigns were proposed but not carried out, or begun and abandoned in order to focus finances and energies on others that seemed more likely to bring success. Local SCLC affiliates also had to find a balance between exposing extreme white supremacists through public protest and encouraging greater exertion of rights among African Americans with avoiding retaliatory white violence against demonstrators or the people who had to remain living in targeted communities. Despite the SCLC's many local programs and its own fluctuating nature, it was the key campaigns of direct action for which it became best known.

Key Campaigns A primary goal of the SCLC was to use local actions to reach beyond the South and state or local authority to attract national publicity to civil rights abuses and provoke federal intervention against local white supremacist practices. This tactic of the SCLC has been called the "Second Reconstruction." Several major SCLC actions helped sway national public opinion and federal action in favor of the passage of federal civil rights acts. These included PROJECT CONFRONTATION

In 1995 the Green County, Alabama, branch of the Southern Christian Leadership Conference conducted a march emulating—on a small scale—the Million Man March held in Washington, D.C., two months earlier. (*AP/Wide World Photos*)

in Birmingham and other lunch counter sit-ins and marches, which helped lead to the CIVIL RIGHTS ACT OF 1964, and the VOTER EDUCATION PROJECT, which encouraged passage of, and then built upon, the VOTING RIGHTS ACT OF 1965. The Voter Education Project was a massive drive using volunteers to go door to door and to speak at local meetings to encourage African American citizens to register to vote despite intimidation from whites. Septima Poinsette Clark was the major force behind the SCLC's Citizenship Education Program, which conducted week-long workshops for rural blacks to enable them to educate others on political processes and to aid them in registering to vote. Other key campaigns were undertaken in Albany, Georgia; St. Augustine, Florida; and Selma, Alabama.

The organization was invigorated by the participation of student and teenage volunteers, who began working for the SCLC as well as in the sit-ins and freedom rides organized through CORE in the early 1960's. Student activism also led to another rivalry within the Civil Rights movement with the formation of the STUDENT NON-VIOLENT COORDINATING COMMITTEE (SNCC) in 1960. It was not until Birmingham in 1963 that the SCLC, and King's leadership, became truly pivotal.

A series of SCLC campaigns focused on Washington, D.C., including the Prayer Pilgrimage that took place soon after the SCLC's founding, which brought King into the national limelight, and the MARCH ON WASHINGTON of 1963, during which King delivered his famous "I HAVE A DREAM" speech. In the mid-1960's the SCLC began to expand its scope beyond the South to focus on northern urban communities. It also began to emphasize the problem of poverty and inequities in the overall economic system of the United States, in addition to specific civil rights. The last major campaign instigated by King before his assassination was the POOR PEOPLE'S CAMPAIGN of April-June 1968. Carried out under the presidency of Abernathy, this campaign included a new march on Washington and encampment where the 1963 mass rally had taken place near the Washington Monument.

Decline of the Movement In the few years immediately following King's 1968 death, many key leaders in SCLC, including Jesse Jackson, left the organization. Jackson had been a major figure in the CHICAGO branch of Operation Breadbasket, one of SCLC's last high-profile campaigns of the late 1960's. The SCLC staff dwindled after the Poor People's Campaign, and SCLC finances reached a point of collapse, but the organization continued to work on school desegregation, labor rights, and other issues in the South into the early 1970's.

SUGGESTED READINGS:

Branch, Taylor. *Parting the Waters: America in the King Years, 1954-1963*. New York: Simon and Schuster, 1988. Chronicles the life of Martin Luther King, Jr., against the backdrop of civil rights politics from the events leading up to the Montgomery bus boycott through the 1963 March on Washington.

Fairclough, Adam. *To Redeem the Soul of America: The Southern Christian Leadership Conference and Martin Luther King, Jr.* Athens: University of Georgia Press, 1987. History of the SCLC from its origins through the administration of Ralph David Abernathy.

Freedman, Jill. *Old News: Resurrection City*. New York: Grossman, 1970. Photographic essay on the Resurrection City encampment in Washington, D.C., and the Poor People's Campaign of 1968.

Garrow, David J. *Bearing the Cross: Martin Luther King, Jr., and the Southern Christian Leadership Conference*. New York: William Morrow, 1986. Detailed biography of King in the context of SCLC activism.

Grant, Joanne. *Fundi: The Story of Ella Baker*. New York: Fundi Productions, 1981. 45 min. Videocassette/film on the life of Ella Baker, who helped conceive the idea of the SCLC and later supported the Student Non-Violent Coordinating Committee's autonomy from SCLC.

Peake, Thomas R. *Keeping the Dream Alive: A History of the Southern Christian Leadership Conference from King to the Nineteen-Eighties*. New York: Peter Lang, 1987. History of the development of the SCLC, the "Second Reconstruction" era of activism, and the leadership of the movement after the assassination of King.

—*Barbara Bair*

Southern states

The southeastern portion of the United States in which SLAVERY remained legal until after the CIVIL WAR.

The southern states have a special significance for CIVIL RIGHTS issues. Before the Civil War in the mid-nineteenth century, slavery was heavily concentrated in the southeastern United States. Indeed, most of the southern states attempted to secede from the United States in large part out of fear that the institution of slavery would be endangered if they remained in the Union. After the war, the first federal CIVIL RIGHTS ACT was passed to establish the rights of recently freed slaves. During the late nineteenth and early twentieth centuries, legal DISCRIMINATION against minorities, primarily AFRICAN AMERICANS, was most obvious in the southern states. Throughout U.S. history, moreover, the majority of AFRICAN AMERICANS have lived in the South. As a result, the South was the primary focus of the CIVIL RIGHTS MOVEMENT of the mid-twentieth century.

Historians and other social scientists vary somewhat in their designations of which American states are "southern." The term is often used only for the eleven states that formed the Confederate States of America: Alabama, Arkansas, Florida, Georgia, Louisiana, Mississippi, North Carolina, South Carolina, Tennessee, Texas, and Virginia. However, the "border states" of Delaware, Kentucky, Maryland, Missouri, and West Virginia are also often classified as southern states. Many of those who study the region further distinguish between the "Deep South" and the "Peripheral South." Alabama, Georgia, Louisiana, Mississippi, and South Carolina are the states most frequently considered part of the Deep South. The Peripheral South consists of surrounding states, usually including Arkansas, Florida, North Carolina, Tennessee, Texas, and Virginia. The Deep South has the heaviest concentration of the African American population, and whites in the Deep South have, historically, shown greatest commitment among white Americans to support racial DISCRIMINATION and SEGREGATION. Between 1790 and 1860 people of African ancestry made up about one-third of the population of the southern states. However, more than half of the populations of Louisiana and South Carolina during that period were black, while African Americans made up only about one-fifth of the populations of Kentucky and Tennessee.

Slavery in the Southern States Africans were brought to Virginia as early as 1619. Although slavery existed in almost all parts of colonial North America, Virginia was the first area in which slavery became an important part of the economy. Tobacco, long used by AMERICAN INDIANS, became popular among Europeans in the 1600's, and the market for this American plant continued to grow over the

centuries. Some parts of Virginia, notably the Shenandoah Valley, were settled by small farmers, who needed to work their own lands and to make these lands produce crops with maximum efficiency. Those small farmers had little use for slaves, since people who are forced to work do not make efficient workers. Much of Virginia, however, was settled by planters given huge grants of land by the British crown or by the royal governors of the colony. The planters, with their great stretches of property, could afford to grow tobacco, which rapidly wears out the land. Their agricultural techniques were wasteful, chiefly involving just the clearing of smaller trees from hardwood forests, planting and harvesting quantities of tobacco for three years or so, and then moving on to new fields. For this kind of agriculture, labor efficiency was not vital; it was sufficient to have large numbers of workers. Therefore, Virginia became the center of slavery in early colonial North America.

During the early 1790's, at the same time slavery was being abolished in most of the northern states, Eli Whitney invented the cotton gin, a machine for separating seeds from cotton. At the same time, James Watt, in England, invented a machine for spinning, weaving, and printing cotton fabric. These inventions made another plantation crop, cotton, highly profitable and created a new demand for slave labor in Alabama, Georgia, and Mississippi, where land was available and suitable to cotton. Exporting slaves to other southern states rapidly became a central part of Virginia's economy.

South Carolina and Louisiana also became part of the southern slave economy, with slaves growing Louisiana's profitable sugar cane crop in addition to cotton. These two states were the only ones to hold significant numbers of free blacks, primarily in South Carolina's port city of Charleston and in Louisiana's port city of New Orleans. Although only small numbers of southern plantation owners held many slaves, these plantation owners controlled the politics of their states.

The years before the Civil War saw several slave revolts, most notably the famous revolt led by Nat Turner in 1831. The revolts sparked fear among white southerners and led them to sharply limit the rights of African Americans. It became illegal in all southern states to teach slaves to read or write. Both enslaved and free African Americans were forbidden to gather together, even for religious services, without a white person present. The fear that led to these initial attempts to control blacks continued to fuel southern resistance to civil rights for blacks through much of the region's history.

Reconstruction and Civil Rights During the period of RECONSTRUCTION following the Civil War, Union troops occupied most of the South and slaves were freed by the THIRTEENTH AMENDMENT. With the backing of the Union government, some African Americans were elected to public office. African Americans were most influential in Louisiana and in South Carolina—the only states with substantial numbers of well-educated people of African ancestry. Southern whites struck back, however. They attempted to control their freed slaves and to force them to continue doing plantation type labor through regulations known as BLACK LAWS, or black codes. The first states to pass black laws, in 1865, were MISSISSIPPI and South Carolina. Mississippi's laws required all African Americans to show proof of their employment for the coming year each January. African Americans were forbidden to leave their jobs before the end of a contract. Those who were unemployed or judged to be disorderly could be prosecuted for vagrancy. South Carolina's laws forbade blacks to hold any job except farmer or servant and required them to sign annual contracts and to work from sunup until sundown. As in Mississippi, unemployed African Americans were considered guilty of vagrancy.

Almost all of the states of the former Confederacy enacted similar laws. Louisiana required work from all family members of former slave families and gave employers complete control over labor disputes. Florida's law made blacks who broke labor contracts subject to public whipping. The southern states were, however, forced to repeal the black laws by the end of 1866, as a result of northern opposition. Southern resistance to allowing African Americans to claim their place in society led the northern-controlled Congress to pass the CIVIL RIGHTS ACT OF 1866. Passed over the veto of President Andrew Johnson, the act declared that all people born in the United States, except for untaxed Indians, were American citizens and held all of the rights of CITIZENSHIP. Despite this legislation, most southern states retained strict vagrancy laws, based on the black laws, and these were enforced almost exclusively against blacks. By these kinds of legal strategies, the former slaves were retained as cheap agricultural labor, even after the formal end of slavery.

Southern Redemption and the Segregation Era In 1877 newly elected president Rutherford B. Hayes withdrew all remaining federal troops from the southern states, effectively ending civil rights enforcement. Throughout the South, "redeemer" governments, which sought to return to white control, took power with the end of Reconstruction. The KU KLUX KLAN and other terrorist organizations helped by keeping black voters away from the polls. South Carolina elected Wade Hampton as its redeemer governor, and his government became an example for other southern states. Hampton was committed to the idea of paternalism, of restricting political participation to "qualified" African Americans who would accept the position of their race in southern society.

This type of paternalism was followed by state laws that attempted to take away the VOTING RIGHTS of African Americans altogether. Property and educational qualifications, POLL TAXES, GRANDFATHER CLAUSES, and other means of restricting voting virtually eliminated blacks from voting in Mississippi by 1890, in South Carolina by 1895, and in Louisiana by 1898. These laws also often had the effect of limiting participation by poorer whites. Mississippi, for example, cut back the total number of voters in the state by about 70 percent between the end of Reconstruction and the early 1890's. In 1897 Louisiana had 130,000 registered black voters and 164,000 registered white voters. By 1904 there were only a little more than 1,000 registered black Louisianians and 92,000 registered white voters.

Under slavery, white and black southerners had lived in close proximity to each other. By the end of the nineteenth century, however, segregation emerged as a southern white strategy for controlling blacks. Between 1880 and WORLD WAR I, all of the southern states enacted laws dictating the separation of the races. Segregation laws were passed gradually and differed from community to community, making it difficult for traveling blacks to predicate what would be acceptable in different places. For example, a young man who was traveling by train from Raleigh, North Carolina, to Nashville, Tennessee, in 1892, found himself threatened with a police beating and jail in Chattanooga, Tennessee. He had just left a railroad station in which drinking fountains were not segregated and, without knowing, drank from a "whites only" fountain in Chattanooga.

In 1896 a Louisiana segregation law became the

legal basis of segregation throughout the South and in the states of Oklahoma and Arizona. During that year the U.S. Supreme Court ruled that a Louisiana law requiring the racial segregation of railroad passenger cars was constitutional in Plessy v. Ferguson. This established the separate-but-equal principle. Legal segregation was most thorough and detailed in the states of the Deep South. In 1922, for example, the state of Mississippi passed a law requiring that taxicabs be racially segregated. In 1932 Atlanta, Georgia, passed a law requiring that black and white baseball teams play in fields that were separated by at least two city blocks.

Laws relegating African Americans to the status of second-class citizens through segregation and restriction of participation in public life were known as Jim Crow laws. Although the Deep South had the most restrictive legislation, limits were placed on the civil rights of blacks throughout the southern states. When, the struggle against such laws began in the mid-twentieth century, it provoked a reaction throughout the South, but the reaction was especially intense in the Deep South.

The Dixiecrats The first stirrings of the modern Civil Rights movement began during World War II. Early U.S. government efforts to secure civil rights for minorities provoked an immediate political response from the states of the South. After the war President Harry S Truman showed some support for racial equality, and the Truman administration allowed the Justice Department to provide support for school desegregation in important court cases. In 1947 Truman appointed a committee to study civil rights in order to find ways of improving the lives of African Americans. The following year, under pressure from civil rights activists, he issued Executive Order 9981, which substantially desegregated the military.

President Truman's mild advocacy of civil rights for blacks angered many white southern voters and southern politicians. Three days after the Democratic Party nominated Truman for another term in 1948, delegates from the southern states met in Birmingham, Alabama, to organize the States' Rights Party. Also known as the Dixiecrat Party, it made racial segregation a fundamental part of its platform. The Dixiecrats nominated Governor Strom Thurmond of South Carolina as their presidential candidate and Governor Fielding Wright of Mississippi as their candidate for vice-president. Although Truman carried most of the southern

states in the election, the segregationist Dixiecrats won South Carolina, Mississippi, Alabama, and Louisiana.

Integration of Southern Schools In 1954, in the case of *Brown v. Board of Education of Topeka, Kansas*, the U.S. Supreme Court ruled that the separate-but-equal principle, the basis of legal segregation, was unconstitutional. The following year the Court called for the desegregation of schools "with all deliberate speed." In response, Robert D. Patterson, a plantation manager in the Mississippi Delta, founded a new organization known as the Citizens' Council of America. Its goal was to prevent the desegregation of southern schools by lawful opposition. Council branches rapidly spread throughout the South, eventually encompassing a total membership of 300,000.

The political leaders of the southern states became increasingly outspoken in their support of segregation. In Congress, Virginia senator Harry F. Byrd led a group of nineteen senators and eighty-one representatives—all from the states of the former Confederacy—in issuing a declaration condemning the *Brown* decision. In southern state politics, segregation became a hot political issue. Southern moderates were pushed out of the way by ardent segregationists. Mississippi governor James P. Coleman, Alabama governor James Folsom, and Louisiana governor Earl Long, all moderates on race issues, were succeeded by the loudly self-proclaimed segregationist governors: Ross Barnett, elected in Mississippi in 1956; John Patterson, elected in Alabama in 1958; and Jimmie Davis, elected in Louisiana in 1960. The Citizens' Councils were especially active in the election of Barnett, who thereafter staked his political future on segregationism.

Even southern politicians who were initially inclined to be sympathetic to integration often became passionate anti-integrationists in order to appeal to white voters. In Virginia, Governor Thomas B. Stanley, who at first approved the *Brown* decision, spoke against it. In Arkansas, the racially moderate governor Orval Faubus became famous for his opposition to integration. Both Virginia and Arkansas, states in the Peripheral South, were centers of early southern resistance to integration.

The Virginia state government announced a policy of "massive resistance" to integration. In 1956 the state's General Assembly, acting under the leadership of Senator Byrd, issued a resolution adopting the doctrine of "interposition." This doctrine meant that states had the right to "interpose," or intervene, between the federal government and local institutions, such as schools. Interposition became a legal justification for opposition to federal intervention for the sake of civil rights, and the doctrine was afterward adopted by Alabama, Georgia, South Carolina, Mississippi, and Louisiana.

Arkansas showed that a state could attempt to use force, as well as legal doctrines, to oppose integration. During 1956, governors in Kentucky and Tennessee had used state police and national guardsmen to control violent mobs opposed to the integration of schools. Governor Allan Shivers of Texas had also used police powers to respond to anti-integrationist violence, but Governor Shivers, instead of enforcing school integration, delayed it for a year. Arkansas governor Faubus, who happened to be seeking re-election, decided that he could use Shivers' strategy to promote himself as a segregationist in the views of white voters. Faubus ordered Arkansas National Guardsmen to bar nine black students from entering LITTLE ROCK's Central High School. When the local school board sought to ignore the troops and desegregate the school in spite of Faubus, white mobs gathered in front of the school, harassing the black pupils who sought admission. President Dwight D. EISENHOWER reluctantly ordered the Arkansas National Guard into federal service and sent a detachment of federal troops to Little Rock to enforce compliance with the law.

In Louisiana Governor Jimmie Davis attempted to take personal control of schools in New Orleans in 1961 to prevent their integration. He backed down, however, when a federal circuit court of appeals ordered him to cease interfering. In that same year, Georgia governor Ernest Vandiver allowed the peaceful integration of Atlanta schools. By the end of 1961 only Alabama, Mississippi, and South Carolina still had public schools that were completely segregated by race.

Civil Rights Protests and Southern Responses
One of the earliest mass protest campaigns to achieve legal equality outside of the school system for southern blacks occurred in 1955 in Alabama, in the city of Montgomery, where the young minister Dr. Martin Luther KING, JR., led the ensuing MONTGOMERY BUS BOYCOTT to protest segregation in public transportation. This successful boycott led similar activities to spread throughout the South. In 1960 college students took up seats at a Woolworth's lunch counter in Greensboro, North Carolina, and refused to leave until served. The lunch counter SIT-IN movement quickly spread to other cities in the South, followed by FREEDOM RIDES to desegregate interstate TRANSPORTATION in the South, and by voter registration drives.

The strategy for change in the South employed by King and other civil rights leaders involved both economic and political tactics. Economically, the boycotts and sit-ins aimed at pushing southern business leaders to reach agreements with protesting African American citizens. Politically, the crises produced by clashes between activists and conservative southern governments attracted the attention of nonsoutherners and provoked increased intervention by the federal government.

Segregationist feelings were never shared by all white southerners. Especially in urban areas, many whites were willing to come to terms with black demands for social and political equality. This was particularly true among businesspersons, whose businesses suffered from social disruption. During 1963 protests in BIRMINGHAM, ALABAMA, for example, white merchants and manufacturers called for accommodation with black community leaders. Birmingham commissioner of public safety Eugene "Bull" Connor, with the support of Alabama governor George Wallace, successor of Ross Barnett, called in state troopers and put down demonstrations by force. However a new city administration, supported by Birmingham business leaders, agreed to desegregate lunch counters and public facilities and to stop discriminating against blacks in hiring.

Economic pressure would only work in states that had white leaders who were willing to compromise. Texas, with a rapidly expanding economy and influential business leaders, showed a willingness to compromise with civil rights pressures. Mississippi, however, largely rural and by many measures the poorest state in the nation, remained deeply committed to Jim Crow traditions. Only bringing in influences from other parts of the country could change places such as Mississippi.

The police violence in Birmingham—widely viewed on nationwide television—made much of America sympathetic to the civil rights struggle. In Mississippi a sniper murdered activist Medgar EVERS in 1963. Not long afterward, the peaceful MARCH ON WASHINGTON intensified the image of an innocent people oppressed by southern violence. By 1964

Alabama governor George Wallace's campaign for the U.S. presidency in 1968 was one of the last significant manifestations of southern segregationist politics. (*AP/Wide World Photos*)

the U.S. Congress was inspired to pass a new CIVIL RIGHTS ACT, which prohibited many forms of discrimination. Southern congressmen, led by senators Richard Russell of Georgia, James Eastland of Mississippi, and Sam Ervin of North Carolina tried unsuccessfully to block the act.

Mississippi's resistance to change made it a national center of civil rights efforts. In 1964 white and black college students travelled there for the Freedom Summer project, which involved establishing black schools and helping Mississippi blacks register to vote. Mississippi provoked national outrage when three of these young people, two white and one black, were murdered. In the same year, angry Mississippi whites burned thirty black homes and thirty-five black churches. A 1965 voter registration drive in Alabama created further national outrage. To dramatize the movement in Alabama, Martin Luther King, Jr., planned a march from SELMA to the state capital in Montgomery. Governor George Wallace refused to give the march a permit and marchers were savagely attacked by state troopers and a sheriff's posse.

The violence in Alabama and Mississippi led to another major piece of federal legislation: the VOTING RIGHTS ACT OF 1965, designed to prohibit discrimination in states where less than 50 percent of the citizens were registered to vote. Virginia, North Carolina, South Carolina, Georgia, Alabama, Mississippi, and Louisiana were the states chiefly affected by the Voting Rights Act.

Continuing Struggle in the New South The legal violation of black civil rights in the South largely ended by the 1970's. Between 1964 and 1993 the number of black elected officials in the United States increased from 170 to about 8,000, with two-thirds of the black elected officials in 1993 coming from the southern states. The major southern cities of Atlanta, New Orleans, Birmingham, and Richmond all had black mayors in the 1990's. Nevertheless, both white racial politics and illegal violations of black civil rights continued to pose problems. In Louisiana's 1991 gubernatorial elections, for example, an estimated 60 percent of white voters voted for David Duke, a former Ku Klux Klan leader. A wave of burnings of black churches swept the Deep South in the summer of 1996, suggesting that Klan-style terrorism continued to be practiced by some whites. For all of the progress under law, race remained a major southern civil rights problem.

SUGGESTED READINGS:

Black, Earl. *Southern Governors and Civil Rights: Racial Segregation as a Campaign Issue in the Second Reconstruction.* Cambridge, Mass.: Harvard University Press, 1976. History of how southern governors made political use of the segregation issue.

Chalmers, David M. *Hooded Americanism: The First Century of the Ku Klux Klan, 1865-1965.* New York: Doubleday, 1965. History of the Klan from Reconstruction to the Civil Rights movement.

Foner, Eric. *Reconstruction: America's Unfinished Revolution, 1863-1877.* New York: Harper & Row, 1988. Detailed history of the Reconstruction era as an attempt at achieving racial justice in America.

Roland, Charles P. *The Improbable Era: The South Since World War II.* Lexington: University of Kentucky Press, 1975. Overview of Southern politics, culture, and society from the late 1940's to the early 1970's.

Williamson, Joel. *The Crucible Within: Black-White Relations in the American South Since Emancipation.* New York: Oxford University Press, 1984. Study of how race relations in the South after the Civil War shaped modern ideas of race.

Woodward, C. Vann. *The Strange Career of Jim Crow.* 3d ed. New York: Oxford University Press, 1966. Classic history of Jim Crow laws in the South.

Young, Andrew. *An Easy Burden: The Civil Rights Movement and the Transformation of America.* New York: HarperCollins, 1996. Memoir of an African American civil rights activist who became mayor of Atlanta, a congressman, and U.S. ambassador to the United Nations.

—*Carl L. Bankston III*

Southwest Voter Registration Project

SVREP: LATINO pro-voting rights organization formed in 1974.

Founded by Chicano activist William VELÁSQUEZ in San Antonio, Texas, the SVREP was a grassroots organization whose primary goal was to encourage MEXICAN AMERICANS, AFRICAN AMERICANS, and AMERICAN INDIANS in the Southwest to participate in the political process. To encourage members of these minorities to vote, it has participated in litigation to safeguard VOTING RIGHTS, and it created the Southwest Voter Research Institute in 1986. The institute monitors voting patterns, studies the effect of public policies on the minority communities, and testifies in lawsuits involving voting issues.

In its original and major purpose, the SVREP has conducted hundreds of voter registration drives in fourteen western states. These have involved recruiting, training, and developing local volunteers, who mobilize voters, build coalitions, and network with leaders. The SVREP also has a program to encourage citizenship so that former noncitizens can vote; in large cities it has worked with businesses and other organizations to register voters.

In 1995 President Bill CLINTON presented the Presidential Medal of Freedom, the highest civilian honor, to the widow of the founder of SVREP, William Velásquez, in recognition of his commitment to democracy.

—Shakuntala Jayaswal

Sports, professional

Athletic competition, on either an individual or a team basis, involving direct monetary compensation.

The professional sports world has been the setting for the discussion of a variety of rights issues. Some, such as controversies over the participation of AFRICAN AMERICANS and other ethnic minorities, have mirrored larger social currents. Others, notably debates over the economic and personal freedoms of athletes, have concerned more insular topics. Because of the highly public nature of many professional sports, however, virtually all such issues—whether reflecting broader social realities or restricted to more narrow concerns—have been the subject of widespread interest.

Issues of Ethnic and Minority Participation
Members of ethnic minorities long faced barriers to participation in the world of professional sports; there, as in most other parts of American life, the most virulent discrimination was typically directed against African Americans.

From the outset, African Americans faced discrimination in professional baseball. The first major league, which operated from 1871 to 1875, the National Association, and the National League, established in 1876, excluded black players; however, by the 1880's, black players had joined otherwise all-white professional teams. Bud Fowler, the first black professional player, competed in numerous white minor leagues from 1878 through 1887. Brothers Moses Fleetwood Walker and Welday Walker briefly played major-league baseball for the Toledo Mudhens of the American Association in 1884. Players and spectators received them well, except in Baltimore and Louisville; however, Toledo later released the Walkers amid threats from anonymous sources.

Moses Fleetwood Walker and pitcher George Stovey of the Newark International League team provoked controversy in 1887 by forming professional baseball's first all-black battery. Several white players threatened to quit if they were allowed to continue playing. Chicago White Stockings manager Cap Anson refused to let his team compete against Newark unless the battery was benched. The International League's board of directors, therefore, prohibited any subsequent contracts with black players. The "gentleman's agreement" excluded all black players from organized baseball.

By the 1920's, segregated Negro Leagues were formed. The Negro National League, organized by Rube Foster, operated almost continuously from 1920 through 1948, while the Negro American League, Eastern Colored League, East-West League, and Negro Southern League lasted shorter durations. The Negro Leagues produced such legendary players as Satchel Paige, Josh Gibson, Cool Papa Bell, and numerous others who would have starred in the major leagues except for the racial ban. Negro League teams typically struggled financially, suffered discrimination at certain hotels and restaurants, and traveled in unreliable, cramped vehicles.

Organized baseball desegregated following World War II. By 1945 more liberal public attitudes, the beginnings of the CIVIL RIGHTS MOVEMENT, the increased voting strength of blacks in northern cities, the black press, the undeniable talents of black players, and government pressure combined to spur integration. Brooklyn Dodgers co-owner Branch Rickey selected star shortstop Jackie ROBINSON of the Kansas City Monarchs to break organized baseball's color line. In August, 1945, Rickey told Robinson about his plans at a conference in New York. He insisted that Robinson concentrate on performing well on the field and have "guts enough not to fight back" against the caustic criticism, hate mail, and threats that he might face. Robinson vowed to not flinch or respond publicly.

Robinson signed with the Montreal Royals, the Dodgers' top minor-league affiliate, in October, 1945, and confronted discrimination from the time he began spring training in Florida in 1946. Upon joining the Dodgers in 1947, Robinson was taunted by teammates and faced considerable prejudice from opposing players, executives, and spectators. Some opposing players threatened to strike if Robinson played, but National League president Ford Frick quelled such moves by promising to suspend any player who refused to play with Robinson. Nevertheless, some players spiked Robinson hard when sliding into second base and tagged him hard when he attempted to steal, and some pitchers tried to bean him. Fans wrote crank notes threatening his life, called him names, and hurled racial epithets. In Philadelphia, a black cat was thrown at him while he was on the playing field.

Robinson reacted calmly without retaliating, becoming one of the best and most exciting major-league players. He earned Rookie of the Year honors in 1947 and led the National League in batting in 1949, winning the Most Valuable Player award. The following year, he became the first African American selected to participate in a major league All-Star Game. He helped the Dodgers win six pennants and became the first black elected to the National Baseball Hall of Fame. His pioneering accomplishments enabled other blacks to enter professional baseball. The Cleveland Indians signed outfielder Larry Doby in August, 1947, integrating the American League. Blacks joined the St. Louis Browns in 1947 and New York Giants in 1949. By 1950 nine blacks were playing in the major leagues, nearly half with the Dodgers. Roy Campanella, Willie Mays, Ernie Banks, Hank Aaron, Roberto Clemente, Frank Robinson, Bob Gibson, Juan Marichal, and others soon attained stardom.

Nevertheless, prejudice continued to plague major-league baseball; not until 1959 did the Boston Red Sox, the last major-league team to integrate, sign an African American. By 1971, however, blacks made up about 25 percent of National League rosters and 18 percent of American League rosters.

Yet African Americans did not secure any executive position in major-league baseball until Monte Irvin served as public-relations representative in the commissioner's office from 1968 to 1982. Blacks have since served as major-league executives, coaches, and managers. The Cleveland Indians, in 1975, made Frank Robinson the first African American major-league manager; Larry Doby, Maury Wills, Cito Gaston, Dusty Baker, and Don Baylor have also managed major-league clubs. Hank Aaron has served as vice president of the Atlanta Braves, and Bill White and Leonard Coleman have held the NL presidency. Nevertheless, critics have continued to charge that African Americans are dramatically underrepresented in baseball's managerial and executive positions.

Professional Boxing Professional boxing, by contrast, has provided greater mobility for blacks. Southern plantation owners often pitted their biggest slaves in the ring. Virginian Tom Molyneaux and other slaves gained their freedom by defeating fellow slaves in bouts on which slave owners bet heavily. George Dixon held the featherweight crown from 1892 to 1900, Joe Walcott dominated the welterweight division from 1896 to 1906, and Joe Gans held the lightweight title from 1902 to 1908.

Racial tensions flared, however, when controversial Jack Johnson became the first African American heavyweight champion in 1908. When Johnson retained the heavyweight title by dominating popular white ex-champion Jim Jeffries in July, 1910, in Las Vegas, whites in several cities organized race riots. Johnson's flamboyant personal lifestyle, which included marriages to several white women, also infuriated whites. Johnson lost his title at Havana, Cuba, in April, 1915, when Jess Willard knocked him out.

Joe Louis, the next black heavyweight champion, symbolized racial harmony to whites and racial progress to African Americans. Louis held the heavyweight crown from 1937 to 1949, appearing respectful of his fallen opponents in the ring and docile and deferential to whites outside the ring. White Americans, especially outside the South, praised him for being modest and unassuming. Louis particularly gained popularity among whites after knocking out German Max Schmeling in the first round of their June, 1938, fight in New York City. Many Americans viewed Schmeling's defeat as a triumph of American values over Nazi racism and totalitarianism.

Muhammad Ali, three-time heavyweight champion from 1964 to 1978, achieved more notoriety than any other African American athlete. His boxing style appealed to boxing fans, while his flamboyant personality enhanced his celebrity status. As Cassius Clay, he stirred controversy by bragging, prancing, and even predicting the round in which he would knock out opponents. In 1965, he joined the Nation of Islam and changed his name to Muhammad Ali. Many young African Americans hailed Ali's religious commitment, but most whites found the move threatening. Ali was convicted of draft evasion in 1967, when he refused to serve in the Vietnam War. Boxing authorities revoked his heavyweight title. Vietnam War critics saw him as a hero, but war supporters denounced him as a traitor. In 1970, the U.S. Supreme Court unanimously reversed Ali's conviction, enabling him to resume his boxing career.

Professional Football Integration of professional football occurred slowly. Charles Follis, the first black professional player, competed as running back for the Shelby Athletic Association in Ohio from 1902 to 1906. During the next decade, Charles "Doc" Baker and Henry McDonald also pioneered as African American professional players. The newly formed American Professional Football Association (APFA) and National Football League (NFL) included only thirteen African Americans between 1920 and 1933. Black stars included Paul Robeson, Duke Slater, and halfback Fritz Pollard, who overcame blatant discrimination to help the Akron Pros attain a share of the 1920 APFA title. In 1921, Akron appointed Pollard head coach, making him the first African American mentor of a major team sport. Pollard later coached the Milwaukee Badgers and Hammond Pros.

NFL rosters carried only two blacks by 1933. In an October, 1933, contest, Lester Caywood of the Cincinnati Reds punched an African American, Joe Lillard of the Chicago Cardinals. Lillard retaliated with an uppercut, causing ejection of both players. By an owners' agreement, African Americans were subsequently banned from the NFL for more than a decade.

The NFL and the newly formed All-American Football Conference (AAFC) both integrated in 1946. When the NFL's ban on African Americans was lifted, the Los Angeles Rams signed running back Kenny Washington and end Woody Strode; during the next three years, however, only the New York Giants and Detroit Lions followed suit. From the outset, the AAFC allowed its teams to sign blacks. Lineman Bill Willis and back Marion Motley joined the Cleveland Browns. Both quickly won all-league honors their first season, convincing

other teams to desegregate. Motley became the first black elected to the Pro Football Hall of Fame. The American Football League, established in 1960, integrated more quickly, with forty-six blacks by its third year.

Blacks achieved NFL stardom despite other forms of discrimination. Jim Brown of the Cleveland Browns became football's premier running back, setting numerous rushing records, and other blacks starred at running back, end, safety, and cornerback; however, few were allowed to become quarterbacks, centers, linebackers, kickers, or punters. No NFL club employed an African American quarterback until the Buffalo Bills signed James Harris in 1969. Moreover, the NFL did not integrate completely until 1962, when running back Bobby Mitchell joined the Washington Redskins. By then, NFL rosters listed 100 blacks.

As in baseball, African Americans in football moved slowly into administrative positions. Buddy Young served as NFL director of player relations from 1964 to 1983, while Gene Upshaw became head of the NFL Players Association in 1983. Bobby Mitchell was named assistant general manager of the Washington Redskins in 1981. Several NFL clubs named blacks to assistant coaching positions by the 1980's, but only two appointed African Americans as head coaches. Art Shell, the first modern NFL African American head coach, guided the Los Angeles and Oakland Raiders from 1989 through 1994, while Dennis Green became head coach of the Minnesota Vikings in 1992.

Professional Basketball Segregation likewise long prevailed in professional basketball. The American Basketball League, organized in 1925, and the Basketball Association of America (BAA), established in 1946, excluded black teams. The African American New York Rens, formed by Bob Douglas in 1923, battled the all-white Original Celtics for professional basketball supremacy in the 1920's but faced discrimination in housing, restaurants, and elsewhere. Nevertheless, the Rens in 1932 became the first African American team to garner a professional title in any organized sport. The Harlem Globetrotters, formed in 1927 by white Abe Saperstein, dazzled crowds during a grueling schedule of one-night performances and helped to spread basketball internationally. Saperstein, however, allegedly collaborated with owners of white teams to keep out blacks so the Globetrotters could sign them.

In 1946, the National Basketball League (NBL) briefly integrated. Pop Gates signed with the Tri Cities Blackhawks and Dolly King with the Rochester Royals; however, they lasted only one NBL season, partly because of a fight between Gates and Chick Meehan of the Syracuse Nationals. The rival BAA desegregated in 1948, when six blacks joined the Chicago Stags.

The National Basketball Association (NBA) was integrated in 1950, when Chuck Cooper joined the Boston Celtics, Earl Lloyd the Washington Capitols, and Sweetwater Clifton the New York Knickerbockers; the St. Louis Hawks, the last all-white NBA team, did not sign black players until 1959. By that time NBA rosters included twenty-three blacks. By 1970, blacks made up nearly 60 percent of all NBA players and 54 percent of all American Basketball Association (ABA) players. African American stars such as Bill Russell, Wilt Chamberlain, Elgin Baylor, Oscar Robertson, Julius Erving, Kareem Abdul-Jabbar, Magic Johnson, and Michael Jordan became some of the most dominant players in basketball history.

Unlike their baseball and football counterparts, NBA teams have made significant progress in hiring blacks as head coaches and executives. In 1966, the Boston Celtics made Bill Russell the first African American NBA coach. Russell guided the Celtics to two NBA titles in three seasons. Lenny Wilkens coached four different teams, setting an NBA mark for most career victories. By the mid-1990's, at least sixteen other blacks had coached NBA clubs. Wayne Embry, the first African American NBA executive, served as general manager of the Milwaukee Bucks from 1977 to 1985 and of the Cleveland Cavaliers from 1986 to 1995.

Other Professional Sports African Americans also encountered roadblocks in several other sports. In horse racing, Isaac Burns Murphy, Willie Simms, Jimmy Winkfield, and other black jockeys performed so well in the late nineteenth century that jockey clubs eventually denied them licensing. Bicycling organizations discriminated against African American riders, although Marshall Taylor garnered three straight national titles near the turn of the century. The elite socioeconomic class status of tennis and golf long deterred blacks from making much impact in either sport. In the 1950's, 1960's, and 1970's, Althea Gibson and Arthur Ashe captured U.S. Open and Wimbledon tennis titles, while Charles Sifford and Calvin Peete enjoyed some success on the professional golf circuit. In the mid-1990's, amateur champion Tiger Woods turned professional and took the golf world by storm, becoming one of the best-known athletes in the world almost overnight.

Other Ethnic Groups Although African Americans have been the targets of the most severe and widespread discrimination in American sports, members of other minority groups have also had to struggle to achieve acceptance as professional athletes. In the early years of the twentieth century, American Indian Jim Thorpe was widely acclaimed to be the world's greatest athlete; although he achieved his greatest fame as an amateur competing in Olympic track and field events, Thorpe later played major-league baseball and went on to an even more successful career as a pioneer of professional football. Thorpe, his teammate John "Chief" Meyers, and such other notable Native Americans as Charles Albert "Chief" Bender, "Indian" Bob Johnson, and Allie "Superchief" Reynolds helped to give professional baseball a partially integrated character in the years before the breaking of the sport's color line in 1947. So did Latino players such as Adolfo "Dolf" Luque and Vernon "Lefty" Gomez and Jewish players such as Hank Greenberg, who also endured racial taunts and other forms of discrimination as baseball stars of the first half of the twentieth century.

Other Rights Issues Although matters of race were still being debated in the professional sports world at the close of the twentieth century, other rights topics had come to the fore by the early 1970's. Most notable were issues of economic and personal rights, particularly in regard to player freedom of movement in the major team sports.

As the leading American team sport for most of the twentieth century, baseball long set the pattern followed by other professional sports. During the infancy of professional baseball in late nineteenth century, early team owners had dealt with the threat of competing leagues by introducing the notorious "reserve clause"—which bound a player to his team until he was released or traded at the team's discretion—as part of the standard player contract. In concert with a 1922 Supreme Court ruling that baseball was a sport, not a business, and was therefore exempt from federal antitrust laws, the reserve clause gave team owners overwhelming bargaining strength in their dealings with players. Players who were unhappy with their salaries or who wished to

Baseball star Curt Flood, pictured here in 1959, lost his 1972 challenge to Major League Baseball's reserve clause; however, his personal sacrifice led to a different court challenge that brought a revolution in the rights of players. (*AP/Wide World Photos*)

change teams had no real recourse; they could refuse to play, but such holdouts, though common, were seldom effective.

By the late 1960's, however, major-league players had formed an effective union led by former United Steelworkers of America labor lawyer Marvin Miller. The union soon began to shift the balance of power toward the players. A successful players' strike at the beginning of the 1971 season won concessions from the owners on pension issues; the union also encouraged Curt Flood, a star outfielder who had refused to accept a trade from the St. Louis Cardinals to the Philadelphia Phillies, to contest the trade in court as a violation of his rights. The issue was eventually decided by the U.S. SUPREME COURT, which in 1972 ruled against Flood on the basis of the 1922 decision. In 1975, however, the union won a landmark victory by attacking on a different front: Rather than arguing that the reserve clause was illegal, union lawyers persuaded an independent arbitrator that the clause's language bound players to their teams for a period of only one year. The decision ushered in the era of free agency, through which players could sell their services to the teams of their choosing; as a result, salaries skyrocketed, and players for the first time in nearly a century enjoyed a degree of freedom in choosing their employers.

Although many fans decried the effects of free agency, players and their representatives simply defended it as the extension into the sports world of rights unthinkingly enjoyed by workers in other fields. Soon, free agency debates were raging in the other major team sports, which had their own limitations on player movement. National Football League players won free agency in 1976 but then unwisely negotiated it away; as a consequence, football salaries lagged far behind baseball salaries, even though pro football had overtaken pro baseball in popularity. Not until the late 1980's did NFL players win back free agency rights, as the consequence of protracted legal maneuverings that required the dissolution of the players' union. Although player representatives in baseball, football, basketball, and other team sports typically negotiated some restrictions on player movement with team owners to preserve league stability (and to limit the supply of players, an important factor in the escalation of salaries), the 1970's and 1980's in general stand as the era of the professional team athlete's emancipation.

SUGGESTED READINGS:

Ashe, Arthur R., Jr. *A Hard Road to Glory: A History of the African American Athlete Since 1946.* New York: Warner Books, 1988.

Chalk, Ocania. *Pioneers of Black Sport: The Early Days of the Black Professional Athlete in Baseball, Basketball, Boxing, and Football.* New York: Dodd, Mead, 1975.

Miller, Marvin. *A Whole Different Ball Game: The Sport and Business of Baseball.* Secaucus, N.J.: Carol Publishing Group, 1991.

Peterson, Robert W. *Cages to Jumpshots: Pro Basketball's Early Years.* New York: Oxford University Press, 1990.

_____. *Only the Ball Was White.* Englewood Cliffs, N.J.: Prentice-Hall, 1970.

Tygiel, Jules. *Baseball's Great Experiment: Jackie Robinson and His Legacy.* New York: Oxford University Press, 1983.

—*David L. Porter and Christopher E. Kent*

Stanton, Elizabeth Cady

Nov. 12, 1815, Johnstown, N.Y.—Oct. 26, 1902, New York, N.Y.: Founder of the nineteenth century WOMEN'S RIGHTS movement.

The daughter of a lawyer and judge, Elizabeth Cady grew up occasionally overhearing discussions in her home of cases involving women made destitute because they had no legal RIGHTS. She later attended Troy Female Academy, led an active social life, and married Henry Stanton, a leader in the ABOLITIONISM movement. For their wedding trip they attended a World Anti-Slavery Convention in London, where a controversy erupted over seating female delegates and guests. In the end both were seated behind a curtain and denied participation. Elizabeth met the famous woman delegate Lucretia MOTT, and the two planned for the future a challenge to discrimination against women. In 1848 they organized the first women's rights convention at Seneca Falls, New York. As the climax, the Seneca Falls DECLARATION OF SENTIMENTS was approved, including—at Elizabeth's insistence—a demand for WOMAN SUFFRAGE.

Thereafter Stanton, together with Susan B. ANTHONY, led the woman suffrage movement for the rest of the century. They organized the NATIONAL WOMAN SUFFRAGE ASSOCIATION in 1869 and then its

Elizabeth Cady Stanton (right) and her lifelong associate in the women's rights movement, Susan B. Anthony. (*Library of Congress*)

similarly named successor, the National American Woman Suffrage Association, in 1890. Stanton also championed numerous other rights for women, including marriage and divorce reform and changes in laws on property ownership.

—*Elizabeth C. Adams*

State v. Young

1919: U.S. SUPREME COURT decision outlawing discrimination in JURY DUTY.

Despite such early Supreme Court rulings against jury-selection discrimination as *United States v.* MULLANY (1808) and STRAUDER V. WEST VIRGINIA (1880), discrimination against African Americans remained rampant throughout the SOUTHERN STATES. The Court's *State v. Young* decision reaffirmed that African Americans could not be systematically excluded from juries. However, because there was no effective mechanism for enforcement of the decision, this decision—like its predecessors—had little practical effect in the South. In 1935 the Court reaffirmed *State v. Young* in *Norris v. Alabama*—a decision that overturned the conviction of the SCOTTSBORO NINE in Alabama.

—*Christopher E. Kent*

Stevens, Thaddeus

Apr. 4, 1792, Danville, Vt.—Aug. 11, 1868, Washington, D.C.: Republican congressional leader during the CIVIL WAR era.

As chairman of the House of Representatives' powerful Ways and Means Committee during the Civil War, and as leader of both the Republican Party and its Radical wing in the early years of RECONSTRUCTION, Thaddeus Stevens was a dynamic force directed toward slave emancipation with protected civil rights, land grants, and educational opportunities. His leadership position was based, in part, on finely honed rhetorical talents. Political enemies felt the cutting edge of his razor-sharp wit and invective. His leadership was also based on his political skills in formulating, passing, and enforcing major legislation such as the FOURTEENTH AMENDMENT, the CIVIL RIGHTS ACT OF 1866, and the Military Bill for Reconstruction. For some he became a champion of meaningful emancipation, for others he was the incarnation of all Reconstruction evils.

Born with a clubfoot, Stevens experienced cruel taunts in his adolescence that made him sensitive to inequality. He also experienced poverty. His hardworking mother enabled him to be educated at the Peacham Academy of Vermont and at Dartmouth College. That education was his passport out of poverty was a fact Stevens never forgot.

Early Career In 1816 Stevens set up a law practice in Gettysburg, Pennsylvania. Prospering, he entered politics and was elected in 1833 to the Pennsylvania legislature on the anti-Masonic ticket. By the time he left, in 1841, his attention had turned to other causes. He fought for extending free public school education to all of Pennsylvania. Stevens also fought against proslavery bills in the legislature and used his legal practice to defend runaway slaves, usually at his own expense. In 1837 he vainly fought to protect the VOTING RIGHTS of free Pennsylvania AFRICAN AMERICANS.

Elected as a Whig to the U.S. House of Representatives in 1848 and 1850, Stevens denounced the Compromise of 1850 with its provision to return fugitive slaves. In castigating SLAVERY and ridiculing Southern myths about "the happy slave," Stevens made many enemies. Dissatisfied with the crumbling Whig Party, he left politics. However, enthused about the formation of the new Republican Party, he helped organization efforts in Pennsylvania's Lancaster County. In 1858 he returned to Congress. His early speeches attacking slavery and the DRED SCOTT CASE nearly caused rioting on the House floor.

Civil War and Reconstruction With the outbreak of the Civil War, Stevens moved into the powerful position of chairman of the House Ways and Means Committee. In that position he took strong stands advocating the recruitment of southern slaves into the Union Army and confiscating rebel property. His continual urging of noncompliance with the FUGITIVE SLAVE ACT resulted in legislation forbidding the return of fugitive slaves in March, 1862; the legislation may be considered as the first act of emancipation. Despite opposition from the border states, Stevens' lobbying for the recruitment of black troops came to fruition in July, 1862.

Fearing that President Abraham Lincoln would vacillate on the issue, Stevens fought for the THIRTEENTH AMENDMENT that abolished slavery, as well as the FIFTEENTH AMENDMENT that later guaranteed black suffrage. He also supported creating free schools for former slaves and giving forty acres of land to each liberated slave.

Following Lincoln's assassination, Stevens emerged as both the most influential Republican and the spokesman for treating the former Confederacy as conquered provinces under congressional supervision—a position antithetical to new president Andrew Johnson's plans. In late 1865 Stevens helped set up the joint House-Senate Committee on Reconstruction, which then dominated. Two months later he was in open battle with Johnson over the FREEDMAN'S BUREAU bill and the Civil Rights bill which would make it a criminal offense to deny African Americans any state or federal right accorded to whites. Stevens got Congress to pass both bills over Johnson's veto. He also played a major role in blocking the seating of former Confederate leaders in Congress. Meanwhile, he conceived and piloted through Congress the Fourteenth Amendment.

Following a major Republican victory in the election of 1866, and in the wake of growing violence directed against blacks in the South, Stevens gained passage of a Reconstruction bill that divided the former Confederacy (except Tennessee) into five military districts, each administered by a Union general. Black suffrage would be enforced, with voter registration taking place through the Freedmen's Bureau. However, Stevens' bill to compensate former slaves with forty acres of land failed to gain adequate support.

Weak and near death, Stevens nevertheless mustered his remaining strength to bring a House resolution of impeachment against President Johnson. He died ten days after the Senate trial failed to convict by one vote. He chose burial in a racially integrated cemetery, under a simple monument in which were carved words that he himself had penned:

I repose in this quiet and secluded spot,
not from any natural preference for solitude,
but finding other cemeteries
limited by charter rules as to race,
I have chosen this that I might illustrate in death
the principles which I advocated through a long life,
Equality of man before his Creator.

SUGGESTED READINGS:

Brodie, Fawn. *Thaddeus Stevens: Scourge of the South*. New York: Norton, 1959.

Current, Richard. *Old Thad Stevens: A Story of Ambition*. Madison: University of Wisconsin Press, 1942.

Korngold, Ralph. *Thaddeus Stevens: A Being Darkly Wise and Rudely Great*. New York: Harcourt, Brace, 1955.

—*Irwin Halfond*

Stone, Lucy

Aug. 13, 1818, Coy's Hill, near West Brookfield, Mass.—Oct. 18, 1893, Dorchester, Mass.: Abolitionist, publisher, and WOMEN'S RIGHTS activist.

One of the first feminist leaders in the United States, Lucy Stone became the first Massachusetts woman to earn a college degree, at Ohio's Oberlin College in 1847. Shortly after graduation, she obtained a lecturing position with the American Anti-Slavery Society. In 1847 she led a women's rights convention in Massachusetts. Her lecture inspired John Stuart Mill to write "The Enfranchisement of Women" and prompted Susan B. ANTHONY to join the cause of women's rights.

After Stone's marriage to Henry Blackwell, she kept her own name as a protest against laws that restricted married women. By the turn of the century, the nickname "Lucy Stoners" was applied to members of the women's rights movement, but particularly to married women who kept their own names.

Lucy Stone, founder of the American Women Suffrage Association. (*Library of Congress*)

Stone founded the American Woman Suffrage Association (AWSA) in 1869, an organization that sought state legislation to grant women the vote. When it merged in 1890 with the NATIONAL WOMAN SUFFRAGE ASSOCIATION, advocating instead a constitutional amendment granting women new rights, it formed the National American Woman Suffrage Association (NAWSA). Stone became chairman of the executive committee, and Elizabeth Cady STANTON served as the first president. In 1870 Stone founded the *Women's Journal*, a weekly suffragist publication. She and her husband edited the journal. True to Stone's rebellious nature, she became the first person to be cremated in New England after she died.

—*M. Casey Diana*

Strauder v. West Virginia

1880: U.S. SUPREME COURT ruling that race was not to be used to debar citizens from JURY DUTY.

Strauder was an AFRICAN AMERICAN who had been convicted of murder in a West Virginia court by an all-white jury. Afterward he asserted that his constitutional rights under the FOURTEENTH AMENDMENT had been violated by a state statute which provided that "all white male persons who are twenty-one years of age shall serve as jurors." On March 1, 1880, the U.S. Supreme Court reversed Strauder's conviction and held that the statute violated the Fourteenth Amendment's EQUAL PROTECTION CLAUSE because it overtly discriminated against nonwhites. The Court further ruled that appellants need not show that such statutes had discriminatory impacts on the outcomes of their trials, as they were automatically void. Strauder was thus not required to prove that he might not have been convicted if there had there been African Americans on his jury.

—*David R. Sobel*

Student Non-Violent Coordinating Committee

SNCC: Civil rights organization founded by AFRICAN AMERICAN college students in North Carolina in 1960.

After students of North Carolina A&T College staged the successful GREENSBORO SIT-INS in Febru-

ary, 1960, local college students formed SNCC (usually pronounced *snick*) to coordinate further protest demonstrations against SEGREGATION. SNCC went on to play a key role in the CIVIL RIGHTS MOVEMENT of the early 1960's. Its first major innovation came in 1961 when it sent FREEDOM RIDERS into the Deep South to test TRANSPORTATION discrimination and to encourage African Americans to assert their VOTING RIGHTS. The freedom rides also promoted community awareness about the political, economic, and social plight of black Americans in general. Other early SNCC projects included taking over certain political initiatives from other civil rights organizations. From the CONGRESS OF RACIAL EQUALITY, SNCC took responsibility for the administration of its black voter registration project in MISSISSIPPI.

SNCC's most valuable contribution was the building of political institutions that paralleled those dominated by southern whites. During its eight-year existence, it created a cultural awareness that RACISM was a part of the American conscience, that it was more than a regional phenomenon, and that all Americans—particularly the young—should organize to combat it. Entering the scene when few protest movements were centrally focused, SNCC brought the energy of youthful volunteers.

Key figures involved in SNCC's creation included SOUTHERN CHRISTIAN LEADERSHIP CONFERENCE veteran Ella BAKER; Rubye Doris SMITH, a participant in the Greensboro sit-ins; and John Robert LEWIS, an organizer of lunch counter sit-ins in Nashville, Tennessee. Lewis was unanimously elected SNCC's chairperson in 1963. SNCC membership eventually included some of the most active civil rights figures of the period, such as James FORMAN, who joined the organization in 1961 as its executive secretary; Robert Parris MOSES, who became SNCC's chief organizer that same year; H. Rap BROWN, the Alabama State Project Coordinator in 1964; and Stokely CARMICHAEL, who replaced Lewis as chairperson in 1966.

From SNCC's beginning, its members suffered greatly for their activities. Civil rights demonstrations were frequently dangerous, especially those calling for an end to racial discrimination in transportation facilities in the South. Many of SNCC's freedom riders, who violated southern legal and social codes, were viciously beaten and arrested by authorities. SNCC volunteers suffered physical abuse and received death threats from local white

H. Rap Brown (at microphones) at a press conference for the Student Non-Violent Coordinating Committee. (*Library of Congress*)

citizens who gathered in violent opposition to their protests. SNCC's determination to continue organized protest in the face of such opposition came from the individual courage and idealism of its members and the solid group political strategy of the organization.

As SNCC's pursuit for equal rights broadened, it became apparent to many within the organization that if it were to achieve its goals, it had to open its membership to white Americans. The decision to do this caused much debate within the organization. After a close vote in 1964, SNCC formally invited northern white students to assist in its voter registration efforts in Mississippi, and to participate in the creation of "Freedom Schools" that would teach the idea that racism was morally wrong.

The ensuing expansion of SNCC membership caused those who stood firmly against integration to reaffirm their resolve. Renewed opposition took many forms, including violent social and political responses. In the summer of 1964 three of SNCC's new northern members were victims of the MISSISSIPPI CIVIL RIGHTS WORKERS MURDERS. Later that same tragic summer, the MISSISSIPPI FREEDOM DEMOCRATIC PARTY delegates were rebuffed in their effort to be seated as the official Mississippi delegation to the Democratic Party national convention.

The Shift to Black Power After the Democratic Party convention, a growing atmosphere of governmental indifference to white violence against African Americans contributed to a rise in black militancy within SNCC. This fact, coupled with the refusal by the white political power structure to allow black access to the political policy-making center, inspired an ideological turmoil within the organization that eventually led to the organization's demise. By 1966 disillusion and frustration with the slowness of integration fragmented group solidarity. In this climate, many black civil rights activists began accepting the idea that if political change were to take place, African Americans must take power for themselves. Militant leaders of previously isolated groups in many of America's black communities called upon black Americans to use whatever means were required, including violence, to effect a black separation from the white culture. Responding in support of these influences and encouraged by the successes of recent freedom movements on the African continent, SNCC changed political direction.

The idea of "BLACK POWER" terrified white Americans, who interpreted it as a signal for racial warfare. Whites and moderate African Americans who had remained in SNCC became fearful of the new ideology's influence. When the organization began negotiations with the more militant BLACK PANTHER PARTY to form an alliance in 1968, many moderates left the group. As the organization increasingly articulated revolutionary views and showcased black firebrands, it mirrored the increasing frustrations of many groups that were seeking change during the 1960's.

While the pursuit of noble ideals and the achievement of political reform had been psychologically fulfilling, the experience for many veteran SNCC members was anything but politically gratifying. Procedural rights had been granted for the previously disenfranchised; legal segregation was abolished; a black consciousness was included in American electoral politics; and white America was alerted to the idea that black America would no longer accept the status quo. However, substantive equality for black Americans was not yet a reality, impeded by a political, economic, and social system defined and controlled by white America. In the end, disillusioned and disappointed, SNCC members looked elsewhere for personal political gratification, generally in the areas of mainstream political activity or in the separatist movements of BLACK NATIONALISM. By the end of 1968, SNCC had all but collapsed.

SUGGESTED READINGS:

Brown, H. Rap. *Die Nigger Die*. New York: Dial Press, 1969.

Burner, Eric. *And Gently Shall He Lead: Robert Parris Moses and Civil Rights in Mississippi*. New York: New York University Press, 1994.

Carmichael, Stokely, with Charles V. Hamilton. *Black Power: The Politics of Liberation in the United States*. Rev. ed. New York: Random House, 1992.

Carson, Clayborne. *In Struggle: SNCC and the Black Awakening of the 1960's*. Cambridge, Mass.: Harvard University Press, 1995.

Forman, James. *The Making of Black Revolutionaries*. New York: Open Hand Publishing, 1972.

Stoper, Emily. *The Student Non-Violent Coordinating Committee: The Growth of Radicalism in Civil Rights Organization*. Brooklyn, N.Y.: Carlson Publishers, 1989.

—Thomas J. Edward Walker and Cynthia Gwynne Yaudes

Substantive rights

Constitutional guarantees of personal liberties such as free speech, privacy, travel; distinguished from PROCEDURAL RIGHTS.

Many, if not most, Americans would agree on the importance of fundamental individual rights such as FREE SPEECH, travel, privacy, and personal liberty. The U.S. SUPREME COURT has sought to protect fundamental CIVIL RIGHTS, which belong to all free citizens, from violation by legislatures, executive departments, and lower court opinions. The DUE PROCESS clauses of the Fifth Amendment and FOURTEENTH AMENDMENT to the U.S. CONSTITUTION guarantee that federal and state governments shall deprive no person of "life, liberty or property, without due process of law." DUE PROCESS of law serves to protect two important but different kinds of rights—substantive and procedural

PROCEDURAL RIGHTS, or procedural due process, include the right to fair, just, and unbiased treatment by government officials. For example, AFRICAN AMERICANS were unfairly denied the equal protection of the laws guaranteed by the Fourteenth Amendment until after the Supreme Court's ruling in BROWN V. BOARD OF EDUCATION OF TOPEKA, KANSAS (1954). Racially separate schools in SOUTHERN STATES and the District of Columbia were inherently unequal and, thus, an unconstitutional violation of civil rights and DUE PROCESS of law. In another example, Colorado's Amendment Two declared that gays and lesbians would not have any particular protections from the law. The Supreme Court ruled in 1996 that Colorado's amendment violated provisions of the Fourteenth Amendment by targeting a single group.

Substantive due process grants citizens an expectation to be free of arbitrary bureaucratic regulations and unreasonable content in the law. Substantive rights include such personal liberties as the freedom to travel, to marry any person of one's own choosing, to bear or not to bear children, to worship a god or gods according to one's conscience, to associate with others, to live with members of one's family, and to be free of coerced sterilization. The right to choose a marriage partner is an example of a substantive right. In 1967 the Supreme Court struck down a Virginia MISCEGENATION law forbidding interracial marriage in LOVING V. VIRGINIA. The freedom to marry is recognized as a vital personal right essential to the pursuit of happiness by free men and women.

The Supreme Court at one time used substantive rights arguments to strike down utility rates regulation and laws that placed conditions on contracts, minimum wages, and hours. Its 1905 *Lochner v. New York* decision typified the era between the 1890's and 1937, in which substantive rights were considered more important than opposing community benefits. Asserting health reasons, New York's state legislature sought to limit the number of hours that bakers could work each week. The Supreme Court treated the state's maximum-hours legislation as an unconstitutional interference with the substantive right of an individual to enter into a contract.

Around the same time, however, the Court upheld another state's law limiting the working hours of women. In *Muller v. Oregon* (1908) the Court saw women's maternal responsibilities and their presumed physical vulnerabilities as compelling reasons for the state to protect them, thus limiting their substantive right to make contracts to work. During the Depression of the 1930's, with new justices sitting on it, the Court generally chose not to continue to substitute its judgment about the reasonableness of business regulation for that of legislative bodies.

The Right to Privacy The most important substantive rights may be PRIVACY RIGHTS. Privacy is controversial because the Constitution does not specifically mention a right to it. Nor do nearly all state CONSTITUTIONS (an exception is California's constitution) or documents such as the DECLARATION OF INDEPENDENCE. The Supreme Court nevertheless invalidated a state law that prohibited married couples from using contraceptives as an interference with the right of privacy, a right that was cited as older than the BILL OF RIGHTS. This decision was reached in GRISWOLD V. CONNECTICUT (1965). The right to privacy and BIRTH CONTROL was declared to be an unenumerated (unlisted) and implied right of the Third, Fourth, Fifth, and Ninth amendments to the Constitution.

In ROE V. WADE (1973) the right to privacy was expanded to include a right to choose an ABORTION. A Texas law that forbade all abortions at any stage in a pregnancy, except to save a mother's life, was declared unconstitutional. The substantive right of privacy encompassed a woman's decision to terminate her pregnancy. As with other substantive rights, constitutional limitations apply to the right of privacy. Congressional and state legislative refusal to fund abortions for poor women (*Harris v. McRae*, 1980) and federal regulations that ban doctors at federally financed family planning clinics from counseling women on abortion (*Rust v. Sullivan*, 1991) do not, the Court has ruled, infringe the right to privacy or REPRODUCTIVE RIGHTS. In 1992 the Supreme Court recognized the state legislatures' interest in potential (fetal) life while still upholding a substantive right to an abortion.

SUGGESTED READINGS:

Barnett, Randy E., ed. *The Rights Retained by the People: The History and Meaning of the Ninth Amendment*. Fairfax, Va.: George Mason University Press, 1989.

Fisher, Louis, and Neal Devins. *Political Dynamics of Constitutional Law*. 2d ed. St. Paul, Minn.: West Publishing, 1996.

Murphy, Walter F., James E. Fleming, and Sotirios A. Barber. *American Constitutional Interpretation*. 2d ed. Westburn, N.Y.: Foundation Press, 1995.

Tribe, Laurence H. *The Constitutional Protection of Individual Rights: Limits on Government Authority*. Mineola, N.Y.: Foundation Press, 1978.

—*Steve J. Mazurana*

Supreme Court, U.S.

The highest court in the federal court system, the Supreme Court interprets the U.S. CONSTITUTION, limits the scope and power of the legislative and executive branches of the federal government, and makes rulings that affect the daily lives of Americans.

Although Article 3 of the U.S. Constitution, which created the Supreme Court, was a part of the document issued by the Constitutional Convention in 1787, the Court did not come into being until a bill of rights had been appended to the nation's founding document. The first ten amendments to the Constitution, known as the U.S. BILL OF RIGHTS, were intended to satisfy the governments of the states, some of which, wary of settling too much power on a centralized government, had initially refused to ratify the Constitution.

Thus the Supreme Court and the Bill of Rights were linked almost from the nation's inception. As Thomas JEFFERSON, one of the leading proponents of the Bill of Rights, said: "The Bill of Rights is necessary because of the legal check which it puts into the hands of the judiciary." The First Congress, which adopted the Bill of Rights, drafted primarily by James Madison, also fleshed out Article 3 with the Judiciary Act of 1789, fortifying the conception of the judicial branch by establishing a bench of six for the Supreme Court (a chief justice and five associate justices) and two subsidiary levels of judicial tribunals, consisting of primary district courts and circuit courts of appeals. Although the three-tiered structure of the federal judiciary has remained intact, the size of the Supreme Court bench has, since 1869, been nine seats.)

The Bill of Rights and the Fourteenth Amendment As originally conceived by Madison and others, the Bill of Rights was intended to apply only at the federal level. The question of whether its restrictions could be placed on state governments, however, was not addressed until 1833, when John Marshall, the nation's fourth chief justice, writing for a unanimous Court in BARRON V. BALTIMORE (1833), stated that the guarantees of the Bill of Rights applied only at the federal level. The issue apparently remained settled until the FOURTEENTH AMENDMENT was passed in the wake of the Civil War, granting former slaves the right to vote and, overturning the infamous DRED SCOTT CASE (1857), citizenship in both the United States and the individual states in which the former slaves resided. The Fourteenth Amendment also prohibits states from abridging the privileges or immunities granted citizens of the United States and from depriving persons of DUE PROCESS; these protections, along with the amendment's EQUAL PROTECTION CLAUSE, reopened the question of the scope of the Bill of Rights.

The Supreme Court's initial interpretation of the Fourteenth Amendment came in 1873 when, in the Slaughterhouse Cases, a majority of the justices held that governance of CIVIL RIGHTS—specifically those of black Americans—remained with the states. Four of the nine justices dissented from this view, but only insofar as they registered a belief that the Fourteenth Amendment was meant to secure the rights, not only of black but of all Americans. Among the privileges and immunities protected by the amendment, some dissenters maintained, was the right to labor; others added that the amendment's due process clause protected Americans from being arbitrarily deprived of their property by the state.

Economic v. Civil Rights The Slaughterhouse Cases proved to be a major setback to the advancement of civil rights. It was not until Justice Hugo L. Black spearheaded the so-called due process revolution in the middle of the twentieth century that the guarantees of the Bill of Rights were gradually incorporated into the Fourteenth Amendment. This investiture of federal oversight over state-imposed limits on the privileges and immunities of citizens became known as the INCORPORATION DOCTRINE, by which the Bill of Rights could be incorporated into the Fourteenth Amendment's protections. The Bill of Rights thereby became applicable at the state level.

Until the mid-twentieth century, however, the Court showed a strong inclination to interpret the Fourteenth Amendment narrowly. The civil rights cases (1883) nullified the thrust of the CIVIL RIGHTS ACTS OF 1866-1875 guaranteeing equal access to public accommodations; because of the Court's political orientation, it found that the Fourteenth Amendment only applied to state action, not to the acts of private parties such as hoteliers and restaurateurs. In PLESSY V. FERGUSON (1896), the Court applied similar logic to find that a state law requiring racial SEGREGATION on railroads did not violate the Fourteenth Amendment's equal protection clause, thus bringing the SEPARATE-BUT-EQUAL PRINCIPLE into being. Equal protection was denied women too: In *Bradwell v. Illinois* (1873) and MINOR V. HAPPERSETT (1875), the Court declined, respectively, to grant women the right to practice law and the right to vote.

During the half century following the Slaughterhouse Cases, the Court continued to expand the Fourteenth Amendment's protection of economic rights at the expense of civil rights. Adhering to a laissez-faire philosophy, the Court elevated freedom of contract to the status of orthodoxy in *Lochner v. New York* (1905), in which a state statute limiting work hours was struck down as unconstitutional. The Court retained its profoundly conservative orientation until President Franklin D. Roosevelt devised a court-packing plan in 1937 as a means of defeating the Court's hostility toward the New Deal. The justices backed down first, and Roosevelt did not reconfigure the Supreme Court. Subsequent Court endorsement of New Deal initiatives translated into a reevaluation of the Fourteenth Amendment, resulting not only in increased government regulation of business but also in increased scrutiny of state laws restraining CIVIL LIBERTIES. Whereas in *Palko v. Connecticut* (1937) the Court endorsed only a moderate theory of "selective incorporation," whereby those aspects of the Bill of Rights that are deemed to be "of the very essence of a scheme of ordered liberty" can be applied to the states, by mid-century the due process revolution was in full swing.

The Incorporation Doctrine Justice Benjamin N. Cardozo, writing for the eight-member majority in the Palko case, opined that whereas not all of the freedoms contained in the Second through the Eighth amendments applied at the state level, it was settled that those in the First Amendment, "the matrix, the indispensable condition" for almost every form of personal freedom, were incorporated into the Fourteenth Amendment. His was an idea first suggested by Justice Louis BRANDEIS in *Gilbert v. Minnesota* (1920), and later adopted by the Court in *Gitlow v. New York* (1925), which upheld the conviction of a Socialist Party spokesman under a state law prohibiting advocacy of subversion, but allowed for incorporation. In 1927 Brandeis went further. In his concurring opinion in *Whitney v. California*, he urged that Justice Oliver Wendell Holmes's "clear and present danger" doctrine, first formulated in *Schenck v. United States* (1919) as a test for determining the permissibility of government restrictions on speech, be converted into a constitutional rationale for protection of speech. The Founders' belief that "freedom to speak as you will and to speak as you think," he argued, "are indispensable to the discovery and spread of political truth."

Expansion of the incorporation doctrine to include other individual liberties proceeded fitfully. In 1923 in *Meyer v. Nebraska*, the Court struck down a state law that prohibited teaching foreign languages in elementary schools, declaring that the Fourteenth Amendment protects the right of individuals "generally to enjoy privileges, essential to the orderly pursuit of happiness by free men." In the first of the notorious SCOTTSBORO NINE cases, *Powell v. Alabama* (1932), the Fifth Amendment right to an fair trial was specifically applied to the states. But in *Corrigan and Curtis v. Buckley* (1926), the Court rejected due process arguments advanced to invalidate a local RESTRICTIVE COVENANT that prohibited real estate sales to AFRICAN AMERICANS.

Wartime Setbacks During the 1940's and early 1950's, civil liberties took a back seat to national security concerns. Wartime sentiments resulted in decisions such as *Minersville School District v. Gobitis* (1940), in which the Court held that schoolchildren could be expelled from public school for refusing to salute the flag, and *Korematsu v. United States* (1944), upholding the detention of Japanese Americans. The Cold War, too, took its toll on civil liberties: *Dennis v. United States* (1951), for example, permitted the federal government, under the Smith Act, to incarcerate Communist Party leaders on grounds that such persons were potentially subversive. In time all three decisions would be repudiated. The *Gobitis* decision was officially reversed in 1943; the *Korematsu* decision, although never overruled, was addressed in 1980, when Congress authorized payments of twenty thousand dollars each to survivors of the internment camps; and in 1957, in *Yakus v. United States*, the Court reversed its stance on the Smith Act and, effectively (although not officially), its ruling in the *Dennis* case.

The Due Process Revolution The advent of the modern due process revolution can be traced to a footnote in the otherwise forgettable *United States v. Carolene Products* (1938), in which Justice Harlan F. Stone indicated that the Court would employ more exacting scrutiny in examining the constitutionality of state laws affecting political rights and the rights of "insular" minorities. Then, in 1947, the revolution gained its intellectual leader when Justice Hugo Black, dissenting in *Adamson v. California*, argued that the Fourteenth Amendment required states to respect the guarantees of the Bill of Rights.

Black was a constitutional literalist whose philosophy of adhering to the original intent of the drafters of the Constitution had its greatest impact in the area of First Amendment law. His was the guiding spirit behind the reformation of state policies concerning establishment of religion, racial equality, and—in particular—criminal procedure that took place during the years the Supreme Court was led by Chief Justice Earl WARREN. In landmark cases such as *Mapp v. Ohio* (1961), GIDEON V. WAINWRIGHT (1963), and MIRANDA V. ARIZONA (1966), the Warren Court expanded the rights of criminal defendants by obliging states (which largely govern criminal law) to outlaw the use of improperly gathered evidence, to appoint counsel for indigent defendants, and to protect against the improper procurement of confessions before trial.

The Civil Rights Movement During the tenure of Earl Warren a CIVIL RIGHTS MOVEMENT on behalf of African Americans also took place, largely through the efforts of the NATIONAL ASSOCIATION FOR THE ADVANCEMENT OF COLORED PEOPLE (NAACP) and its chief advocate, Thurgood MARSHALL (who would

later become a Supreme Court justice). The Court took its initial step toward overruling the separate-but-equal doctrine in *Missouri ex rel. Gaines v. Canada* (1938), which required SOUTHERN STATES to provide equal facilities for blacks if they wished to maintain segregated schools, but BROWN V. BOARD OF EDUCATION OF TOPEKA, KANSAS (1954), one of the first cases decided by the Warren Court, spelled the end of state sanctioned segregation. *Brown II*, handed down the next year, outlined the means by which school integration was to be achieved "with all deliberate speed."

In cases such as *Heart of Atlanta Motel v. United States* (1964), outlawing segregation in public accommodations, the Warren Court upheld the CIVIL RIGHTS ACT OF 1964. Equally important were decisions such as GOMILLION V. LIGHTFOOT (1960), which reversed the Court's long-standing hands-off policy

Justices of the U.S. Supreme Court in 1993; seated (from left to right): Sandra Day O'Connor, Harry Blackmun, Chief Justice William Rehnquist, John Paul Stevens, and Antonin Scalia; standing: Clarence Thomas, Anthony Kennedy, David Souter, and Ruth Bader Ginsburg. (*AP/Wide World Photos*)

toward political redistricting, and BAKER V. CARR (1962), which laid the groundwork for the principle of "one person, one vote" later enunciated in *Gray v. Sanders* (1963).

The Right to Privacy Another civil-rights-era decision, *National Association for the Advancement of Colored People v. Alabama ex rel. Patterson* (1958), validated two rights that the Court found to be implicit in the words of the Constitution: the right of free association, which includes a second right, the right to privacy. PRIVACY RIGHTS had first been formulated in 1890 by Louis Brandeis, together with Samuel Warren, before the former joined the Court. It was not, however, formally adopted by the Supreme Court until 1965 when, in GRISWOLD V. CONNECTICUT, the right to privacy was accepted as the constitutional rationale for overturning a law against distributing contraceptives.

Although privacy rights have other constitutional applications, the *Griswold* case more or less wedded them to sexual matters. When the Court came to decide its watershed abortion case, ROE V. WADE, in 1973, it struck down state antiabortion statutes on grounds that they violated a woman's right to privacy. In 1986, when considering whether the Constitution protected consensual homosexual activity in *Bowers v. Hardwick*, the Court concluded that this type of sexual activity was not protected by the right to privacy.

Reaction to Rights Expansion The due process revolution and the Civil Rights movement, predictably, spawned a powerful backlash. In the aftermath of the progressive era that coincided with the tenure of Earl Warren and with several Democratic administrations, chief justices Warren Burger and William Rehnquist, both Republican appointees, presided over courts which were often concerned with curtailing what many regarded as the liberal excesses of the Warren Court. President Richard M. NIXON named Burger to head the Court specifically because of the latter's outspoken opposition to the exclusionary rule, enshrined in *Mapp v. Ohio*, and to the so-called Miranda rights. The debate over AFFIRMATIVE ACTION, which began in earnest with the BAKKE CASE, evolved into reverse discrimination cases such as WARDS COVE PACKING CO. V. ATONIO (1989). *Roe v. Wade* has proven to be both a political lightning rod and the target of a seemingly endless stream of subsequent litigation curtailing—if not completely outlawing—abortion.

SUGGESTED READINGS:

Epstein, Lee, and Thomas G. Walker. *Constitutional Law for a Changing America: Institutional Powers and Constraints.* Washington, D.C.: CQ Press, 1992.

Garraty, John A., ed. *Quarrels That Have Shaped the Constitution.* New York: Harper & Row, 1964.

Hall, Kermit L. et al., eds. *The Oxford Companion to the Supreme Court of the United States.* New York: Oxford University Press, 1992.

Paddock, Lisa. *Facts About the Supreme Court of the United States.* New York: H. W. Wilson, 1996.

Schwartz, Bernard. *A History of the Supreme Court.* New York: Oxford University Press, 1993.

Spaeth, Harold J. *Supreme Court Policy Making.* San Francisco: Freeman, 1974.

Wiecek, William M. *Liberty Under Law: The Supreme Court in American Life.* Baltimore: The Johns Hopkins University Press, 1988.

—Lisa Paddock

Swain v. Alabama

1965: U.S. SUPREME COURT decision affirming the right of attorneys to use peremptory challenges to remove AFRICAN AMERICANS from juries.

An African American convicted of rape in Alabama by an all-white jury, Swain asserted that his EQUAL PROTECTION rights had been violated by discrimination in the jury selection process. He contended that whereas African Americans represented 26 percent of persons eligible for JURY DUTY in Talladega County, where he had been tried, only 10-15 percent of persons called to jury service were black. He further charged that in his own trial the prosecutor used all of his preemptory challenges to eliminate black jurors completely. Moreover, no black person had ever served on a petit jury in the county.

On March 8, 1965, the Supreme Court affirmed Swain's conviction, holding that he had failed to establish a prima facie case of purposeful racial discrimination. To do so, he would have had to demonstrate that the peremptory challenge system as a whole was racially discriminatory. Swain failed to meet this standard because he failed to go beyond the facts of his case and "show the prosecutor's systematic use of peremptory challenges against Negroes over a period of time." The Court reasoned that the general scheme of peremptory challenges had independent value despite its inherently discretionary nature. The Court later reversed this decision in *Batson v. Kentucky* (1986).

—*David R. Sobel*

Swann v. Charlotte-Mecklenburg Board of Education

1971: U.S. SUPREME COURT decision endorsing BUSING as an appropriate means of achieving SCHOOL integration.

This case stemmed from a longstanding legal dispute over school DESEGREGATION in Charlotte, North Carolina, whose public schools were merged with those of surrounding Mecklenburg County. The district covered 550 square miles and contained 107 schools and 84,000 students—71 percent of whom were white and 29 percent AFRICAN AMERICAN. A court-ordered desegregation plan that required shifting students between city and county schools was not functioning well, so the issue of permissible remedies was addressed specifically.

On April 20, 1971, the Supreme Court found that a school board that had an established history of racially motivated institutional practices was guilty of de jure segregation. Permissible remedies included altering attendance zones; pairing, clustering, or grouping schools; and transportation of students to schools out of their own neighborhoods through busing. The Court further held that using mathematical ratios to achieve racial balance were permissible but not required. Every school in every community was not required to reflect the racial composition of the school system as a whole, so local district courts were permitted to be flexible in designed desegregation plans.

—*Marcia J. Weiss*

Sweatt v. Painter

1950: U.S. SUPREME COURT decision regarding the SEPARATE-BUT-EQUAL PRINCIPLE in COLLEGE AND UNIVERSITY EDUCATION.

In early 1946 Heman Marion Sweatt, an African American postman, applied to the University of Texas School of Law. Although Sweatt already possessed both a bachelor's degree from Wiley College and credit for graduate work he had completed at the University of Michigan, he was denied admission to the law school because of his race. Sweatt then filed a lawsuit in state court against the university, charging that rejection of his application on the basis of race violated his Fourteenth Amendment right to EQUAL PROTECTION under the law. A state judge ruled that the university must either admit Sweatt or establish a law school for African Americans that would offer training equivalent to that of the law school at the University of Texas. However, when the state created a law school for blacks in Houston, Sweatt refused to enrol in it and again filed a lawsuit. The Texas courts offered Sweatt no relief, and in March, 1949, his case came before the U.S. SUPREME COURT.

Thurgood MARSHALL, an attorney for the NATIONAL ASSOCIATION FOR THE ADVANCEMENT OF COLORED PEOPLE (NAACP), hoped that Sweatt's case would overturn the Court's 1896 decision in PLESSY v. FERGUSON, which had established the enduring principle that racial segregation was constitutional if separate facilities were equal. Marshall contended that the separate law facilities provided for black students in Texas were in no way equal to those available to white students. Marshall introduced a mass of sociological data to the Court—a strategy that would be successfully employed four years later in BROWN v. BOARD OF EDUCATION. He also obtained an *amicus* brief signed by almost two hundred law professors arguing that the separate-but-equal doctrine violated the Fourteenth Amendment. Though the Court ignored most of the sociological data, it agreed that the black law school was inferior to the University of Texas Law School. In a unanimous decision on June 5, 1950, the Supreme Court ordered the University of Texas to admit Sweatt to its school of law. After attending the law school for one year, he had to withdraw because of poor grades.

The Supreme Court's *Sweatt v. Painter* decision did not overturn the *Plessy* ruling, and the separate-but-equal doctrine remained in effect at most southern universities. The University of Texas continued to deny admission to black undergraduates, and permitted black graduate and professional students to take only those courses not available at black schools. However, Heman Sweatt's victory marked

The Supreme Court's *Sweatt v. Painter* decision struck a fundamental blow against racial discrimination in higher education. (*Library of Congress*)

the first time that the Court agreed that inferior institutions violated the separate-but-equal doctrine. In later years states with segregated institutions of higher education had either to increase their expenditures for black institutions or admit African Americans to programs formerly open only to whites.

—*Thomas Clarkin*

T

Tacoma incident

1885: Expulsion of the CHINESE AMERICAN residents of Tacoma, Washington, by whites.

During the 1880's Tacoma, Washington, had about seven thousand residents, of whom 10 percent were Chinese. In March, 1884, the local water company announced plans to hire Chinese laborers to install water pipes, although a recession had left many whites without employment. A labor union with both political and economic bases took control of the town and won control of the city government in the May elections. The city government then began restricting the rights of the Chinese, whom the whites blamed for their economic difficulties, despite the fact that the nation as a whole was in economic decline. The Chinese were first segregated and then encouraged to leave town entirely. On November 3, 1885, a white mob entered the Chinese neighborhood and forced the two hundred remaining residents to pack and leave Tacoma. Efforts by the expelled Chinese to bring legal action against the whites responsible for their expulsion failed in federal district court.

—*Duncan R. Jamieson*

Talton v. Mayes

1896: U.S. SUPREME COURT decision ruling that the U.S. BILL OF RIGHTS did not apply to AMERICAN INDIAN tribes or their courts.

Talton v. Mayes originated with the conviction of a Cherokee man for homicide, following his indictment by a grand jury that was composed, pursuant to Cherokee law, of five members. Noting that federal grand juries functioning under federal Fifth Amendment guarantees consisted of at least six jurors, Talton appealed his conviction. By an 8-1 majority, the Supreme Court ruled that the Fifth Amendment did not apply to Cherokee law. Although wards of the federal government, Indian tribes were not federal institutions. Even when the federal government chose to create courts and institutions on reservations, tribes retained their inherent, sovereign right to enact and adjudicate laws binding on tribal members except where those laws collided with federal laws specifically applicable to tribal governance. Hence, Bill of Rights provisions pertaining to the rights of criminally accused did not limit the actions of tribal courts.

Although the Talton case involved the procedural guarantees of the Bill of Rights and tribal institutions, the decision was widely interpreted to mean that the Bill of Rights did not restrain the actions of federal and state governments toward Native Americans. In 1968 Congress enacted the INDIAN BILL OF RIGHTS to provide Native Americans with some Bill of Rights' guarantees.

—*Joseph R. Rudolph, Jr.*

Taney, Roger Brooke

Mar. 17, 1777, Calvert County, Md.—Oct. 12, 1864, Washington, D.C.: Chief justice of the United States (1836-1864).

Roger Brooke Taney was descended from a long line of prominent and aristocratic tobacco growers who first settled in the Maryland tidewater region in the middle of the seventeenth century. Although Taney himself freed the slaves he had inherited, he never freed himself from the southerner's hostility toward the federal government's attempts to control the "peculiar institution," and this attitude would result in long-standing repercussions for his historical reputation.

A stalwart supporter of controversial President Andrew Jackson, Taney first came to Washington as Jackson's attorney general. Then, after two successive treasury secretaries refused to carry out Jackson's desire to destroy the Bank of the United States, the president turned to Taney, who as acting secretary of the treasury served as hatchet man. When Jackson tried to reward Taney with a U.S. SUPREME COURT appointment in 1835, the Senate balked. But a few months later, after an executive session during which no notes were taken, Taney's nomination was approved.

Taney succeeded John Marshall, the much-loved "Great Chief Justice," who left large shoes to fill. Nonetheless, Taney soon rose to the occasion. Although his opponents had feared that the Jack-

Chief Justice Roger Taney, author of the notorious *Dred Scott* decision. (*Supreme Court of the United States, Office of the Curator*)

sonian Democrat would try to reverse the advances in constitutional nationalism made under the Federalist Marshall, the Taney Court contributed to constitutional jurisprudence by emphasizing a more equitable sovereignty shared with state governments. Over time, Taney's leadership increased the prestige of the Court among the American people.

Unfortunately, toward the end of his tenure, Taney presided over the infamous *Dred Scott* case (1857), delivering an inflammatory opinion for the Court that hastened the onset of Civil War by declaring that people held in SLAVERY were not citizens and invalidating the Missouri Compromise. Taney lived for seven more years, during which he continued to lead a Supreme Court whose power and effectiveness had been utterly undermined. A century after his death, however, Taney's reputation had revived, and he was once more regarded as one of the Court's greatest justices.

—*Lisa Paddock*

Tang Tun v. Edsell

1912: U.S. SUPREME COURT ruling upholding the government's refusal to readmit a CHINESE AMERICAN after he visited China.

Tang Tun claimed to be a U.S. citizen who was born in Seattle in 1879. After visiting China and returning in 1897 without incident, he traveled to China and married in 1905, but was refused readmission to the United States as an ALIEN, and his claim of U.S. CITIZENSHIP was rejected. He appealed to the federal courts on May 11, 1912, but the Supreme Court reaffirmed the exclusive jurisdiction of immigration officials and refused to examine their decision.

—*Milton Berman*

Tape v. Hurley

1885: California Supreme Court decision mandating the right of public education for ASIAN AMERICANS

During the 1880's the superintendent of San Francisco public schools ordered Jennie M. A. Hurley, the principal of a city school, not to admit a CHINESE AMERICAN child named Mamie Tape. Tape's father, Joseph Tape, sued Hurley on the grounds that California's public schools were open to all children without regard to race. After Tape won in a municipal court, the school system appealed the case. In March, 1885, California's supreme court upheld the lower court's ruling. The San Francisco school board then negotiated a settlement with the Chinese consulate that led to the creation of a new, segregated public school for Asian pupils. This development marked the beginning of Asian American SEGREGATION in California schools.

—*Charles A. Desnoyers*

Termination policy

1950's-1960's: Federal policy designed to end the special legal status of AMERICAN INDIANS.

Despite the passage of the INDIAN REORGANIZATION ACT of 1934, considerable support for the earlier policy of assimilation and of opposition to the reservation system continued. In 1953 these views obtained the support of a congressional majority and a resolution was passed calling for an end to the wardship system and immediate termination of federal supervision over specific tribes deemed already able to support themselves.

As tribes began to calculate the costs of terminating their wardship relationship with the federal government, they united in opposing the policy. Joining them were numerous non-Indian civil rights organi-

COME TO DENVER.

THE CHANCE OF YOUR LIFETIME !

Good Jobs

    Retail Trade

    Manufacturing

    Government–Federal, State, Local

    Wholesale Trade

    Construction of Buildings, Etc.

Happy Homes

    Beautiful Houses

    Many Churches

    Exciting Community Life.

    Over Half of Homes Owned by Residents

    Convenient Stores–Shopping Centers

Training

    Vocational Training

        Auto Mech., Beauty Shop, Drafting,

        Nursing, Office Work, Watchmaking

    Adult Education

        Evening High School, Arts and Crafts

        Job Improvement, Home-making

Beautiful Colorado

    "Tallest" State, 48 Mt. Peaks Over 14,000 Ft.

    350 Days Sunshine, Mild Winters

    Zoos, Museums, Mountain Parks, Drives

    Picnic Areas, Lakes, Amusement Parks

    Big Game Hunting, Trout Fishing, Camping

Bureau of Indian Affairs poster designed to encourage American Indians to resettle in cities during the period when the termination policy was being implemented. (*National Archives*) zations. During the administrations of John F. KENNEDY and Lyndon B. JOHNSON, federal Indian policy shifted again, away from rapidly terminating the wardship system and toward helping tribes achieve a level of development that would make wardship unnecessary. By the time the termination policy was fully discarded, Native American groups had undertaken several direct action protests to dramatize their opposition to being terminated, and more than a hundred tribes had lost their ward status.

—*Joseph R. Rudolph, Jr.*

Terrace v. Thompson

1923: U.S. SUPREME COURT ruling affirming the constitutionality of the state of Washington's 1921 Alien Land Law.

Frank Terrace wanted to lease land to a JAPANESE national and sued Lindsay L. Thompson, the state attorney general of Washington, who threatened to prosecute under the 1921 law forbidding ALIENS who had not declared an intention to become citizens from owning or leasing land. Since Japanese persons were then ineligible for U.S. CITIZENSHIP they could not comply with the act. On November 12, 1923, the U.S. Supreme Court ruled that although aliens were entitled to protection under the DUE PROCESS and EQUAL PROTECTION CLAUSES of the U.S. Constitution, preventing them from owning land did not violate those clauses.

—*Milton Berman*

Terrell, Mary Church

Sept. 23, 1863, Memphis, Tenn.—July 24, 1954, Annapolis, Md.: AMERICAN civil rights and WOMEN'S RIGHTS activist.

Terrell excelled in many areas: education, teaching, writing, lecturing, and activism. For more than sixty years she championed education and racial and gender equality. After Terrell was graduated from Oberlin College in 1884, she taught at Wilberforce University in Ohio, then at M Street Colored High School in Washington, D.C. There she met Robert H. Terrell—Harvard University's first African American graduate. In 1895 Terrell became one of two women, and the first black person, appointed to the Washington, D.C., school board. Despite her privileged upbringing, Terrell could not escape seg-

regation or discrimination; thus, she devoted her life to furthering the rights of African American women.

Terrell recognized the power of the press. She wrote exposés of lynching and discrimination that appeared in black and in white periodicals.

Terrell helped found and became the first president (1896-1901) of the NATIONAL ASSOCIATION OF COLORED WOMEN (NACW)—the first national group organized and administered solely by black women. As president, Terrell created a program to help African American women become better wives and mothers. The NACW's motto, "Lifting as we climb," epitomized the group's effort to improve conditions within the African American community. The organization condemned LYNCHING and JIM CROW LAWS and advocated the WOMAN SUFFRAGE MOVEMENT.

In her distinguished career, Terrell addressed the International Congress of Women in Berlin in 1904, the International Congress of Women for Permanent Peace in Zurich in 1919, and the World Fellowship of Faith in London in 1937. During the early years of her activism she mainly employed interracial dialogue and moral persuasion; later, she adopted such strategies as picketing and boycotting. Her carefully orchestrated assault on illegal SEGREGATION in Washington, D.C., preceded the 1960's CIVIL RIGHTS MOVEMENT. When the case appeared before the U.S. SUPREME COURT, it ruled in Terrell's favor and ended discrimination in the nation's capital.

—*Heather M. Seferovich*

Thirteenth Amendment

1865: Amendment to the U.S. CONSTITUTION that definitively ended legal SLAVERY throughout the United States.

After Abraham LINCOLN issued the EMANCIPATION PROCLAMATION in 1863, the constitutional status of slavery remained undetermined. Legal slavery continued in the border states of Delaware, Kentucky, Maryland, and Missouri; because they had not seceded from the Union, the Emancipation Proclamation did not apply there. Furthermore, major questions remained concerning the permanence of the Emancipation Proclamation, even in those areas of the rebellious Confederacy. Lincoln had issued the Emancipation Proclamation under his authority as commander-in-chief. It was uncertain whether a measure issued under the emergency circumstances

Mary Church Terrell, founder of the National Association of Colored Women. (*Library of Congress*)

The Thirteenth Amendment

SECTION 1. Neither slavery nor involuntary servitude, except as a punishment for crime whereof the party shall have been duly convicted, shall exist within the United States, or any place subject to their jurisdiction.

SECTION 2. Congress shall have power to enforce this article by appropriate legislation.

of war would be considered permanent after the war ended.

Lincoln and many Republicans in Congress addressed the issue by proposing an amendment banning "slavery or involuntary servitude" in the United States, "except as a punishment for a crime." In this way, antislavery would be the law of the land: No state or "any place subject" to United States jurisdiction could create or maintain a slave system, and no individual could be held in slavery. However, conservatives in the House of Representatives blocked the passage of the amendment until Lincoln—who was re-elected to the PRESIDENCY in 1864—pressed reluctant Democrats and conservative Republicans to respect his electoral mandate. He even used his patronage power to appoint people to government posts in exchange for favorable votes by their congressmen on the amendment. In January, 1865, the House of Representatives approved the Thirteenth Amendment, which was then forwarded to the states for ratification. The states quickly affirmed the new amendment, the first in sixty years, in part out of tribute to Lincoln, who was assassinated in April. The amendment won final ratification on December 18, 1865.

The importance of this amendment is difficult to overstate. For the first time, the word "slavery" appeared in the U.S. Constitution, in a passage specifically banning it from the United States. The presence of this amendment strengthened the hands of both President Andrew Johnson, who succeeded Lincoln, and Congress in setting terms for RECONSTRUCTION, by which the seceding states were restored to a normal relationship with the national government. It was easier to require each of these states to draft a new state constitution specifically abolishing slavery in accordance with the federal Constitution. Along the border, slavery was neatly abolished without resorting to a program whereby owners of slaves received compensation or in which slavery was phased out gradually.

—*Edward R. Crowther*

Tiburcio Parrott, In re

1880: Federal court decision striking down a California state constitutional provision prohibiting corporations from employing ASIANS.

The discovery of gold in California in 1848 brought thousands of people from all over the country and from overseas, including many CHINESE. By 1879, however, the mining bubble had burst and many were left unemployed. A California constitutional convention convened in September, 1878, to deal with the specific problem of the Chinese. When it ended in March, 1879, it had resolved that corporations and almost all public agencies could not hire any Chinese to work, and it set forth that further Chinese IMMIGRATION to California should be discouraged.

The president and director of the Sulphur Bank Quicksilver Mining Company, Tiburcio Parrott, challenged the decision. When he was arrested for violating the new section of the California constitution, he sued in a U.S. circuit court. On March 22, 1880, the federal court agreed with Parrott that the California legislature had violated both the FOURTEENTH AMENDMENT of the Constitution and the Burlingame Treaty of 1868, an agreement between the governments of China and the United States. It declared that prohibiting the employment of Chinese was unconstitutional.

—*Shakuntala Jayaswal*

To Secure These Rights

1947: Report of President Harry S TRUMAN's committee on civil rights.

Prompted by renewed violence against African Americans during the months following World War II and by the continuation of SEGREGATION and other forms of DISCRIMINATION, President Truman created a Civil Rights Committee on December 5, 1946. Created by Executive Order 9808 and headed by Charles E. Wilson, the president of General Electric, the committee was to investigate federal, state, and local enforcement of the laws and to recommend ways of improving the protection of CIVIL RIGHTS.

In his assignment to the fifteen members of the committee, Truman referred to the failure of local law enforcement to protect people from murder, intimidation, and assault. While writing in general about "individuals" and "people," the president was reacting to the continuing problem posed by racial violence. Black Americans, even those returning from wartime military service in Europe and Asia, faced threats, attacks, and even LYNCHINGS. They needed, but did not always receive, protection from local sheriffs and courts; however, Truman explained, the FOURTEENTH AMENDMENT to the Constitution authorized "the Federal Government . . . to act when state or local authorities abridge or fail" to guarantee equal protection under the laws. Because the government was operating with "inadequate" civil rights statutes, the president argued that stronger, expanded measures were necessary to give the Department of Justice "the tools to do the job."

The Committee's Report After ten meetings between January and September, 1947, correspondence with 250 private organizations and individuals, and testimony from approximately forty witnesses, the committee delivered its far-reaching and ground-breaking report on October 29, 1947. *To Secure These Rights* urged the nation to strengthen six areas: protection of civil rights, the right to personal safety and security, citizenship rights, freedom of conscience and expression, the right to equal opportunity, and the building of public support for civil rights.

The report, which Truman later called "a charter of human rights for our time," focused on "four basic rights": those tied to personal safety, citizenship, freedom of conscience and expression, and equal opportunity. The authors of *To Secure These Rights* explained that they were both "shocked" and "ashamed" about much of what their investigation had uncovered. The "gulf between ideals and practice" was intolerable, they asserted. Because they saw "no essential conflict between freedom and government," they urged that the national government "take the lead" in ending the gulf. Citing the economic, moral, and international harm done to the country by its inadequate respect for and protection of civil rights, the committee made thirty-five recommendations. Among these were passage of a federal antilynching law; abolition of segregation, POLL TAXES, and RESTRICTIVE COVENANTS; creation of a permanent committee on FAIR EMPLOYMENT PRACTICES and a permanent commission on civil rights; desegregation of the MILITARY; revitalization of the civil rights division in the JUSTICE DEPARTMENT; and strengthening of federal civil rights statutes. The report also recommended REPARATIONS for victims of the JAPANESE AMERICAN INTERNMENT of World War II.

Reaction to these proposals was mixed. White southerners saw them as an attack on states' rights; northerners, labor leaders, and liberals praised the recommendations. Members of the white working class and others who helped make up the Democratic coalition forged in the 1930's by Franklin D. Roosevelt were not ready to fight for minority rights and did little to support enactment of the committee's ideas.

The Report's Impact Two months later Truman followed the report's recommendations by authorizing the Department of Justice to file an *amicus curiae* brief with the Supreme Court in SHELLEY V. KRAEMER. The national government was joining the fight against restrictive housing covenants. Then, on February 2, 1948, Truman sent a ten-point "minimum program" on civil rights to Congress. Among its ten proposals were a permanent civil rights commission and committee on fair employment practices, a federal law against lynching, and greater protection for VOTING RIGHTS, as well as settlement of the claims made by Japanese American internees. While the program did not go as far as *To Secure These Rights* advocated, it nonetheless led to angry denunciations from southern political leaders, and a Gallup poll taken in March indicated that Truman's program had only 6 percent support nationally, a fact that helped stop the president's extensive proposal from moving through Congress. Still, a president can issue executive orders, and Truman did so twice in order to take steps advocated in *To Secure These Rights*. EXECUTIVE ORDER 9980 created the Fair Employment Board to deal with discrimination against civil service employees, and EXECUTIVE ORDER 9981 led to the desegregation of the armed forces.

SUGGESTED READINGS:

Berman, William C. *The Politics of Civil Rights in the Truman Administration.* Columbus: Ohio State University Press, 1970.

Hamby, Alonzo L. *Man of the People: A Life of Harry S. Truman.* New York: Oxford University Press, 1995.

McCoy, Donald R. *The Presidency of Harry S. Truman.* Lawrence: University Press of Kansas, 1984.

—*Claudine L. Ferrell*

Toyota v. United States

1925: U.S. SUPREME COURT decision denying CITIZENSHIP to a JAPANESE veteran of the U.S. armed forces.

Born in Japan, Hidemitsu Toyota served for a decade in the U.S. Coast Guard. Because his time of service included the years 1917 and 1918, he applied for American citizenship under a 1918 law permitting naturalization of ALIENS who served in the U.S. military during WORLD WAR I. However, the long trend of restricting immigration and effectively preventing Asian naturalization—culminating in the Immigration Act of 1924—ultimately influenced the Supreme Court's 1925 decision against Toyota. The Court ruled that the 1918 law applied only to aliens already considered eligible for citizenship, not those barred or restricted on grounds of race or nationality, such as the Japanese.

—Charles A. Desnoyers

TransAfrica

Pan-Africanist lobbying organization founded in 1977.

Established by Randall ROBINSON to provide an AFRICAN AMERICAN voice in U.S. foreign policy, TransAfrica has lobbied the U.S. CONGRESS in support of African peoples throughout the world, particularly in Africa and the Caribbean. Through TransAfrica Forum, established in 1981, the organization has educated the public about the need for civil and HUMAN RIGHTS reforms and opportunities and has urged a stronger advocacy role for the United States on behalf of the world's black populations. By the late 1990's TransAfrica had more than eighteen thousand members receiving newsletters and action alerts from its national office in Washington, D.C. It has encouraged its members to pressure their congressional representatives to support progressive policies.

TransAfrica's earliest campaigns were in support of black majority rule in Southern Africa, first in Rhodesia, which became independent as Zimbabwe in 1980, and then in South Africa. In the early 1980's TransAfrica captured the attention and support of the American public with such highly visible efforts as a year-long CIVIL DISOBEDIENCE campaign at South Africa's Washington, D.C., embassy designed to call attention to that repressive apartheid system. The campaign helped lead to Congress' passage of the Anti-Apartheid Act of 1986.

While its anti-apartheid campaigns drew the most media attention, TransAfrica continued to lobby for aid for developing African and Caribbean nations, aid to refugees, and famine relief. The organization staged demonstrations, and called for sanctions against countries violating human rights. In 1990 TransAfrica introduced an International Careers Program to train African American students for foreign service. During the early 1990's TransAfrica helped persuade President Bill CLINTON to support restoring Haiti's democratically elected president to power.

TransAfrica has also occasionally criticized black leaders, such as the dictatorial rulers of Ethiopia, Kenya, and Zaire. In 1995 the forum launched a major campaign against the repressive military regime of Nigeria; by 1996 its campaign had drawn the support of Jesse JACKSON and other prominent African American figures, and TransAfrica again appeared to be on the verge of swaying American public opinion.

—Cynthia A. Bily

Transportation discrimination

Deenial of equal access, services, or treatment in modes of public transportation, such as coaches, boats, trains, and buses.

Throughout American history, members of MINORITY GROUPS have confronted systematic DISCRIMINATION and SEGREGATION on modes of transportation. In every region of the country, AFRICAN AMERICANS, LATINOS, and ASIAN AMERICANS have been denied equal access to systems of public conveyance. In the NORTHERN STATES the separation of whites and blacks on stagecoaches, steamboats, and trains was commonplace before the CIVIL WAR. During the 1830's and 1840's white and African American ABOLITIONISTS in Massachusetts moved to abolish JIM CROW transportation. Through consistent pressure, a change in public opinion, and proposed government intervention, railroad companies abandoned the practice in that state. In 1849 the noted black journalist Frederick DOUGLASS wrote that "not a single railroad can be found in any part of Massachusetts, where a colored man is treated and esteemed in any other light than that of a man and a traveler."

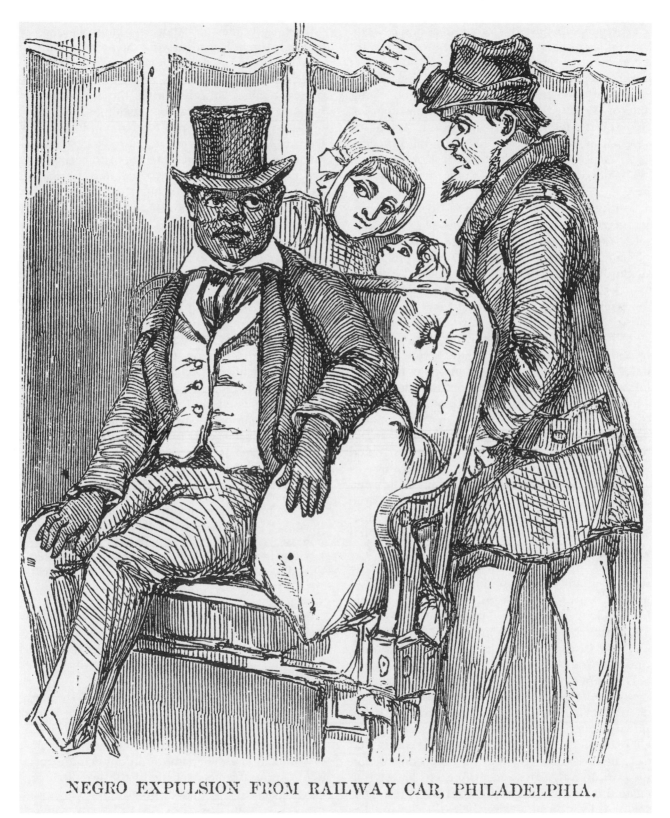

NEGRO EXPULSION FROM RAILWAY CAR, PHILADELPHIA.

One of the most visible forms of segregation was in public transportation. (*Library of Congress*)

Segregation persisted in other areas of the North. One English observer described the trend toward segregation as, "in effect, two nations—one white and another black—growing up together within the same political circle, but never mingling on a principle of equality." With the introduction of streetcars in Philadelphia in 1858, African Americans were permitted to ride on only the front platforms. This practice continued until a local ordinance in 1867 ended segregation in public transportation there.

Southern Patterns In the post-Civil War SOUTHERN STATES, the northern customs of segregation quickly spread throughout the region. For example, the state of MISSISSIPPI enacted a law that prohibited African Americans from riding in railroad cars "set apart, or used by, and for white persons." However, only a few other southern states passed similar laws during this period, and those laws that were passed were quickly overturned with the introduction of Radical Republican control of the southern states under RECONSTRUCTION. The separation of races that did take place in public transportation during Reconstruction were based on customs and patterns. As in the North, African Americans in the South often had to ride on the open platforms of streetcars, or in specially marked cars—some designated by black stars. Although they paid the same fare as whites, African Americans had to sleep on the open decks of steamboats and eat with members of the crew. On railroads they were barred from the first-class cars and were often assigned to unventilated boxcars with wooden planks as seats.

African American Response Also as in the North, blacks in the South did not quietly submit to the new Jim Crow measures. From the beginning, they challenged the system of separate transportation in the region's urban areas. In Nashville, Mobile, New Orleans, Richmond, Baltimore, and other southern cities, African Americans fought regulations, company mandates, and customs in streetcar segregation. "For as long as distinctions will be kept on in public manners," the editor of an African American NEWSPAPER wrote, "these discriminations will react on the decisions of juries and courts, and make impartial justice a lie." Under Reconstruction rule, African Americans successfully challenged segregation through court rulings and the decisions of Union Army officials. Nevertheless, following Reconstruction, the customs, practices, and laws of Jim Crow were quickly reinstated.

In 1881 Tennessee's state legislature passed the first permanent law separating the races in railroad cars for first-class passengers. Between 1887 and 1907 every other southern state, except Missouri, passed similar laws requiring the separation of races on trains and in railroad waiting rooms.

Plessy v. Ferguson and Reaction In 1891 New Orleans African Americans organized a citizen committee to devise a strategy to overturn a Louisiana law calling for SEPARATE-BUT-EQUAL facilities on all passenger trains in the state. The group hired a lawyer, who proposed a test case in the courts. A French-speaking Louisianan with one-eighth African blood, Homer Plessy, agreed to challenge the law. After Plessy was arrested for refusing to give up his seat in a white-only railroad coach, his case made its way to the U.S. SUPREME COURT. On May 18, 1896, the Court ruled, in PLESSY V. FERGUSON, that Louisiana's law had not violated Plessy's constitutional rights. This decision entrenched segregation in the South—leading to more laws separating blacks and whites in almost every walk of life.

Laws mandating racial discrimination on street cars were passed during the first decade of the twentieth century. A North Carolina law regarding public streetcars was typical of those found in southern states. It required that

> all street, inter-urban railway companies, engaged as common carriers . . . shall . . . set apart so much of the front portion of each car operated by them as shall be necessary, for occupation by the white passengers therein, and shall likewise provide and set apart so much of the rear part of said car as shall be necessary, for occupation by the colored passenger therein. . . .

Passengers or employees who violated the law were ejected and could be found guilty of a misdemeanor and fined up to fifty dollars and thirty days in jail. The only stipulation was for nonwhite nurses tending white children.

Even in the face of increasing violence by southern whites and the apparently conservative leadership of black educator Booker T. WASHINGTON, African Americans continued to fight actively against discrimination and separation in public transportation. During the first decade of the twentieth century, blacks led BOYCOTTS of streetcar lines in at least twenty-five southern cities. "In every city where it has been found advisable to separate the races in the street cars the experience has been the same," the Mobile *Daily Register* reported in 1903. "The negroes . . . have invariably declared a boycott." Using the same tactics that would be employed in the MONTGOMERY BUS BOYCOTT of some fifty years later, African Americans walked to work, school, or to shop in retail stores. They also called into service private carriages and horse for hire services to transport people across southern cities. In other areas of the region, community leaders formed rival transit companies and purchased motor buses. At first wildly popular among the black community, the boycotts cost white-owned streetcar companies thousands of dollars in lost revenue. The Houston, Texas, electric company reported that after five months, black protests had crippled their business. In Jacksonville, Florida, and in Montgomery and Mobile, Alabama, protesters forced the companies to abandon Jim Crow for a time (although they the policies were later quietly reinstated).

In 1907 Oklahoma passed a state law providing for segregated coaches. Five African Americans fought the law and sought a court injunction against the railway company. The resulting case, *McCabe v. Atchison, Topeka & Santa Fe Railway Company*, made its way to the U.S. Supreme Court, which unanimously ruled that the Oklahoma law applied only to commerce within the sate, and thus did not violate the U.S. CONSTITUTION's interstate commerce clause or the Fourteenth Amendment. Although African Americans continued to find segregated travel degrading and inconvenient, WORLD WAR I, the Great Depression, and other events interrupted organized agitation for the next twenty-five years.

New Activism With rising political status during the New Deal, African Americans again began actively to fight Jim Crow laws through the federal INTERSTATE COMMERCE COMMISSION and in the nation's court system. In April, 1937, Arthur Mitchell, a black member of the U.S. House of Representatives from Chicago, was denied Pullman accommodations while traveling by train to Hot Springs, Arkansas. Despite his having purchased a first-class ticket, he was ordered to the black coach to comply with local laws after the train crossed into Arkansas. Mitchell filed a complaint with the ICC, alleging unjust discrimination in providing accommodations to black passengers. In late 1938 the ICC dismissed his complaint, so he appealed the case to a federal district court in Chicago. That court upheld the ICC's decision, so the congress-

man next appealed to the U.S. Supreme Court. In *Mitchell v. United States* (1941), the Court ruled that segregated accommodations in interstate travel violated the Interstate Commerce Act because they were unequal to those provided to white passengers. "The discrimination shown," the Court ruled, "was palpably unjust and forbidden by the Act." The case paved the way for future efforts at ending Jim Crow transportation.

Calling for a "Double Victory" over racism abroad (against Germany and Japan) and at home, the fight to end segregation increasingly became a high priority for many African Americans during WORLD WAR II. The large crowds traveling on public transportation during the war years led to increasing tensions between whites and blacks. Incidents of shouting, shoving, and fighting on buses, streetcars, and trains became daily occurrences throughout most southern cities. During this time, the NATIONAL ASSOCIATION FOR THE ADVANCEMENT OF COLORED PEOPLE (NAACP) began a series of broad-based legal attacks on transportation discrimination in interstate travel and on other forms of segregation.

By this time a more liberal U.S. Supreme Court was willing to consider more cases in the areas of civil liberties and civil rights. In 1946 the Court handed down a landmark decision in MORGAN V. COMMONWEALTH OF VIRGINIA. Two years earlier, Irene Morgan, a black woman traveling from Baltimore to Virginia had refused to give up her seat on a Greyhound bus to a white couple and was convicted under Virginia law, which required all passengers on buses to "separate without discrimination" so that seats would never be occupied by "persons of different races at the same time." The Virginia NAACP argued before Virginia supreme court that the state law's provisions applied only to *intra*state travel and not to Morgan, who had been traveling between states. Virginia's supreme court rejected the request and the association's lawyers quickly appealed to the U.S. Supreme Court; this was the first segregated transportation case the NAACP brought to the Court. In a 7-1 vote, the Court, citing an undue burden on interstate travel, struck down the Virginia law that required segregation while traveling within the state.

New Tactics Despite the Supreme Court's *Morgan* decision, most southern states continued to enforce segregation on interstate and intrastate modes of mass transportation. Meanwhile, a new civil rights organization, the CONGRESS OF RACIAL

EQUALITY (CORE) sought to use nonviolent direct action to end segregation and racial discrimination in the region. CORE officials planned a "Journey of Reconciliation" (a model for the later FREEDOM RIDES) through the upper South to force implementation of the *Morgan* decision. Leaving Washington on April 9, 1947, two groups of black and white men spent two weeks riding through Virginia, North Carolina, Tennessee, and Kentucky on Trailways and Greyhound buses. By the end of their excursions, they had tested segregation ordinances some twenty-six times—leading to twelve arrests—and only one incident of violence.

By 1950 the U.S. Supreme Court struck down segregation in railroad dining cars under the Interstate Commerce Act in *Henderson v. United States*. The Court slowly and steadily continued to chip away at the walls of segregation and moved closer to striking at the heart of the *Plessy* decision. African Americans continued to hope for a broad ruling on segregation, while many white southerners began to grumble about federal government efforts to destroy states' rights.

In 1954 the Supreme Court announced its landmark ruling on public school segregation in BROWN V. BOARD OF EDUCATION OF TOPEKA, KANSAS. Although the case dealt specifically with the field of public education—striking down the principle of SEPARATE-BUT-EQUAL schools—the decision was the beginning of the end for constitutional support of Jim Crow laws. Chief Justice Earl Warren noted that "any language in *Plessy v. Ferguson* contrary to this finding is rejected." In the wake of the *Brown* decision and the Court's indication that the ruling would extend to other fields, the ICC ruled that the Jim Crow system separating interstate passengers on trains, buses, and in waiting rooms was unlawful and ordered strict new rules for integration by January 10, 1956. The segregated South, however, would have to be forced by direct action and economic boycott to comply.

Montgomery, Alabama Only a few days after the ICC's 1955 ruling, a black seamstress, Rosa PARKS quietly refused to give up her bus seat to a white man in Montgomery, Alabama. Arrested and jailed, she became a test case for leaders in the local black community who sought to end Jim Crow laws in Alabama's capital city. E. D. Nixon led the campaign to mount a legal challenge to the segregated bus system, and he solicited the help of two young ministers, Ralph ABERNATHY and Martin Luther KING, JR., to help lead a boycott of city buses. On December 5, 1955, the Montgomery bus boycott began as the city's black community began finding other means of getting to work.

Black leaders organized the Montgomery Improvement Association (MIA) and selected King as its leader. The young pastor quickly emerged as an inspiration to the black community and folk hero and media celebrity to many Americans—both black and white. King urged blacks in Montgomery to keep moving. "If you can't fly, run," he said, "if you can't run, walk; if you can't walk, crawl—but, by all means keep moving." The boycott's economic impact on the city's bus line was highly effective. Montgomery's black community forced the layoffs of several employees of the bus company, whose revenues steadily declined. In addition, business at many downtown stores declined.

The legal case behind the Montgomery bus boycott was *Browder v. Gayle* (1956), in which a federal district court ruled that bus segregation violated the U.S. Constitution. The court ruled in a two-to-one decision, that there was "no rational basis" upon which the separate-but-equal doctrine could be validly applied to public carrier transportation in Montgomery or in Alabama. After an appeal by the city, the Supreme Court affirmed the lower court's decision in the fall of 1956. After a 381-day boycott, African Americans had their first experiences riding in the fronts of buses.

The *Browder* decision convinced several other southern cities to desegregate their own bus lines voluntarily. Meanwhile, the black communities of several cities, such as Tallahassee, Florida, and Rock Hill, South Carolina, organized bus boycotts. African Americans also continued to challenge Jim Crow laws in railway transportation. The NAACP led the way in litigation—winning cases that ended transportation discrimination in Miami, Miami Beach, Tampa, New Orleans, and ATLANTA. Other cities, however, such as BIRMINGHAM, Mobile, and Memphis held on to segregation in public transportation until the end of the 1950's.

Sit-ins and Freedom Rides With the beginning of the student sit-in movement in 1960, the Civil Rights movement began a new phase of activism. Gone were the days of relying simply on court cases to fight Jim Crow. News of a direct-action campaign by students in Greensboro, North Carolina, in February, 1960, quickly spread across the South, and SIT-INS at lunch counters, restaurants, and waiting rooms in rail, bus, and air terminals became popular. By the end of 1960, the Supreme Court had handed down another landmark decision in *Boynton v. Virginia*—ruling that a restaurant located in a Trailways bus terminal serving interstate passengers could not refuse service to blacks. Thus by the early 1960's Jim Crow transit had been outlawed throughout the South. Regardless of the law, the customs continued and were often violently enforced.

To help make bus desegregation—and the *Boynton* decision—a reality, "instead of merely an approved legal doctrine," CORE again organized a bus trip through the region that was called a freedom ride. Among the participants were James FARMER, John Robert LEWIS, and James Peek. Throughout Alabama, the riders received brutal beatings at the hands of whites in Anniston, Birmingham, and Montgomery. When they finally reached Jackson, Mississippi, most of the riders were arrested. The violence that freedom riders experienced helped to persuade the administration of President John F. Kennedy to ask the ICC for new rules regarding segregation in transportation. These rules included a ban on segregation on interstate buses; the posting of signs declaring that "seating aboard this vehicle is without regard to race, color, creed or national origin, by order of the Interstate Commerce Commission"; and the forbidding of Jim Crow terminal facilities—including waiting rooms, rest rooms, and restaurants.

Although segregation continued for a few more years, legal transportation discrimination was effectively outlawed by the federal government. Passage of the CIVIL RIGHTS ACT OF 1964 prohibited racial discrimination in all public accommodations, and the long fight to end Jim Crowism in public transportation was effectively over.

SUGGESTED READINGS:

Ayers, Edward. *Promise of the New South: Life After Reconstruction*. New York: Oxford University Press, 1992. Contains several sections on segregation in southern transportation.

Barnes, Catherine A. *Journey from Jim Crow: The Desegregation of Southern Transit*. New York: Columbia University Press, 1983. Examines in detail the rise and demise of Jim Crow transit in the South.

Brook, Thomas, ed. *Plessy v. Ferguson: A Brief History with Documents*. Boston: Bedford Books, 1997. Documentary edition providing a history of the *Plessy* case, along with court documents, published responses to the decision, profiles of Supreme Court justices, and a chronology.

King, Martin Luther. *Stride Toward Freedom: The Montgomery Story*. New York: Harper & Row, 1958. King's own history of the Montgomery bus boycott.

Lofgren, Charles A. *The Plessy Case: A Legal Historical Interpretation*. New York: Oxford University Press, 1987. Examines the legal and historical ramifications of the *Plessy* decision.

Meier, August, and Elliott Rudwick. *CORE: A Study in the Civil Rights Movement, 1942-1968*. New York: Oxford University Press, 1973. Examines the role of CORE in combatting interstate transportation discrimination from the 1940's to the 1960's.

Rasmussen, R. Kent. *Farewell to Jim Crow: The Rise and Fall of Segregation in America*. New York: Facts On File, 1997. Survey of the history of segregation, with considerable attention to transportation issues.

Woodward, C. Vann. 3d ed. *The Strange Career of Jim Crow*. New York: Oxford University Press, 1974. The most important and influential book on the history of segregation in the South.

—*S. Jonathan Bass*

Trotter, William Monroe

April 7, 1872, Chillicothe, Ohio—April 7, 1934, Boston, Mass.: AFRICAN AMERICAN civil rights activist and journalist.

Trotter grew up in a home permeated by the principles of equality. His father James, born a slave in Mississippi, came of age in Ohio and served with the Massachusetts Fifty-fifth Regiment during the Civil War. His mother, Virginia Isaacs, was reared in Ohio as the daughter of slaves from Thomas Jefferson's Monticello plantation. His militant father, an affluent real estate dealer, worked as a black Democrat to change racial injustices. William grew up in a middle-class Hyde Park home in Boston's South End with mostly white friends and competitors. Elected president of his senior class, Trotter attended Harvard University becoming the first black Phi Beta Kappa and being graduated with honors in 1895. On June 27, 1899, he married the daughter of another racially militant family, Geraldine (Deenie) Pindell.

Becoming a Protest Journalist Trotter joined other race leaders referred to as the Boston Radicals, critics of Booker T. WASHINGTON's accommodationist approach to LYNCHING and DISFRANCHISEMENT in the South. In 1901 Trotter began publishing an African American newspaper, the BOSTON GUARDIAN, which became his voice. At the 1903 meeting of the National Negro Business League in Boston, Trotter was one of those arrested for disrupting the proceedings by asking questions of Washington. The event, which became known as the Boston Riot, to many was a demonstration of the ever-present threat to FREE SPEECH. Opponents of the arrests mobilized opposition to Washington's leadership. In September, 1903, Trotter organized and became president of the Boston Suffrage League, which called for federal antilynching legislation, federal aid to southern schools, an end to JIM CROW LAWS on interstate carriers, and enforcement of the FIFTEENTH AMENDMENT.

Formation of the Anti-Washington Movement Washington fought back by filing libel suits and by using his influence to withdraw support from Trotter's newspaper, which continued to lose money. To pay their mounting debts, the Trotters were forced to sell their home. Washington's continual use of power and white influence turned many African American leaders into opponents. In the summer of 1905, twenty-nine African American men secretly met at Fort Erie, Ontario, to form the NIAGARA MOVEMENT. These men endorsed the Declaration of Principles written by Trotter and his fellow Harvard classmate W. E. B. DU BOIS. The document demanded equal economic, social, political, and educational opportunities and an end to mob violence. Trotter became the head of the important Press and Public Opinion Committee, which sought out the support of federal legislators for just laws.

The Tuskegee Machine, one name for the support network behind Washington, infiltrated the Niagara Movement and opposed its direction. The machine discounted the Niagara Movement by publicly attributing the leadership to Trotter, pictured as an intolerant fanatic and the moving spirit behind the opposition to Washington. Undaunted, Trotter fought against the discharge of the soldiers involved in the BROWNSVILLE INCIDENT. Despite the powerful tactics used by the Bookerites, the Niagara Movement gained followers.

Trotter's political and personal opinions created conflict with other radical leaders. Feuds spilled

William Monroe Trotter, editor of the *Boston Guardian*. (*Schomburg Center for Research in Black Culture, New York Public Library*)

over into the columns of the *Boston Guardian*. Withdrawing from the Niagara Movement, Trotter forged in April, 1908, the Negro American Political League, which directed his agenda. Trotter attended and participated, in May, 1909, in the debates over resolutions of an interracial committee, but he was excluded from a Committee of Forty. Piqued, Trotter remained in Boston when the committee reconvened in 1910. At the 1910 meeting, the NATIONAL ASSOCIATION FOR THE ADVANCEMENT OF COLORED PEOPLE (NAACP) was created. Trotter gave support to NAACP campaigns only when the NAACP met his demands. He testified against a Massachusetts bill to prohibit interracial marriage and mobilized the community against the racist motion picture *The Birth of a Nation* (1915). Unlike the NAACP, Trotter protested segregated training camps during WORLD WAR I for African American officers.

He preferred to work through his all-black Negro American Political League (renamed the National Equal Rights League). In l913 and 1914, Trotter led delegations to meet with President Woodrow WILSON to stop segregation in federal offices. His argument in 1914 led to criticism of his lack of respect. During World War I, Trotter called for Wilson to add a fifteenth objective to his Fourteen Points—elimination of racial discrimination and for African American representation at the Peace Conference. Denied a passport by the American government, Trotter posed as a cook and shipped out on the *Yarmouth*, bound for Paris, where he influenced public opinion, but not the outcome of Versailles.

The Later Years Trotter returned to the United States in the summer of 1919, during which a series of race riots occurred in major cities. Without money and alienated, he led the National Equal Rights League push for federal antilynching legislation, for pardons for the remaining soldiers found guilty of inciting a riot in 1917, and for desegregated federal offices. Locally Trotter thwarted Boston attempts to segregate the freshman dormitories at Harvard University and to segregate City Hospital. Trotter died as a result of a fall from a roof on April 7, 1934.

SUGGESTED READINGS:

Fox, Stephen R. *The Guardian of Boston: William Monroe Trotter*. New York: Atheneum, 1971.
Sollors, Werner, ed. *Blacks at Harvard*. New York: New York University Press, 1993.
Wolseley, Roland E. *Black Achievers in American Journalism*. Nashville, Tenn.: James C. Winston, 1995.

—*Dorothy C. Salem*

Truman, Harry S

May 8, 1884, Lamar, Mo.—Dec. 26, 1972, Kansas City, Mo.: Thirty-third PRESIDENT of the United States (1945-1953).

President Truman's main contributions to civil rights were the executive orders he signed to establish merit as the basis for civil service employment (EXECUTIVE ORDER 9980, 1948) and to bar racial discrimination in the military (EXECUTIVE ORDER 9981, 1948). Truman inherited some of President Franklin D. Roosevelt's equal employment programs, including the Fair Employment Practices Commission created by Roosevelt's Executive Order 9346 (1943). The commission enjoyed only modest success but did encourage state officials to develop similar fair employment practices laws. Truman himself did not choose civil rights or equal oppor-

tunity as a policy focus, but he avoided racial conflicts that might interfere with the war effort and may have acted out of a sense of simple fairness in barring discrimination in the civil service and the armed forces.

—*William L. Waugh, Jr.*

Truth, Sojourner

c. 1797, Hurley, Ulster County, N.Y.—Nov. 26, 1883, Battle Creek, Mich.: Noted abolitionist speaker and advocate of AFRICAN AMERICAN rights.

Born into SLAVERY as the property of a wealthy Dutch patron and given the slave name of Isabella, Truth grew up speaking Dutch. She had several masters until she went to a household in New Paltz in 1810, where she bore at least five children, four of whom survived infancy. She escaped from her master in 1827, the year before mandatory emancipation freed the slaves in New York State. Known then as Isabella Van Wagener, she learned that her son had been sold illegally to the Deep South, and with the help of Quakers, she secured his freedom.

Around 1829 Truth went to New York City, where she worked as a domestic servant. A deeply religious woman, she heard voices and had visions, which she attributed to God. While she had been a member of an established religious denomination, she found the company of other mystics more satisfactory. In 1843 she heard a voice that commanded her to take the name Sojourner Truth and to become an itinerant preacher. Though illiterate, she had a broad knowledge of the Bible and preached a message that God's love should show itself through humankind's goodness and love for one another. A tall woman, she presented a commanding appearance.

In Northampton, Massachusetts, she encountered the abolitionist movement's more radical wing, led by William Lloyd Garrison, in 1843. Afterward she traveled throughout the East and Midwest speaking against slavery and racism. She often appeared on the same platform with other well-known abolitionists, such as Frederick DOUGLASS and Harriet Beecher Stowe. Being a woman and an African American made it exceptionally difficult for her to find places at which she could speak, and when she did, proslavery people and southern sympathizers often broke up the meetings.

Sojourner Truth met President Abraham Lincoln in 1864, when she encouraged him to allow more African Americans to enlist in the Union's armed forces. (*Library of Congress*)

At a convention in Worcester, Massachusetts, she learned of the women's rights movement and became an ardent advocate. She presented a speech containing her famous refrain—"and ain't I a woman"—during the 1851 women's rights convention in Akron, Ohio.

During the CIVIL WAR Truth actively solicited gifts of food and clothing for African American regiments fighting for the Union. In 1864 she met with Abraham LINCOLN, pleading that he allow more African Americans to enlist in the Union Army. She also nursed wounded soldiers.

—Duncan R. Jamieson

Tubman, Harriet

c. 1820, Bucktown, Md.—Mar. 10, 1913, Auburn, N.Y.: One of the most outstanding figures in the Underground Railroad.

An escaped slave herself, Harriet Tubman is credited with having led as many as three hundred African Americans out of SLAVERY. Born into slavery on Maryland's Eastern Shore, she served as a maid, children's nurse, field hand, and cook for her master. There an overseer fractured her skull when she was about thirteen.

In 1849, while Tubman was in her late twenties, her master died, and rumors arose that his slaves would be sent farther south. Fearing what might happen, Tubman escaped to Philadelphia, where she worked as a maid. During the next ten years, she made many forays into the South to lead her relatives and other African Americans to freedom. Her first trip, in 1851, took her to Baltimore, where she guided her own sister and two children to freedom. The next year she again went south, this time to bring her brother and his family north. In 1857 she hired a wagon and rescued her parents from the Eastern Shore. In all, she made nineteen trips to Maryland, sometimes working with the Underground Railroad. She was so successful that slaveholders posted rewards totaling forty thousand dollars for her capture. She also freed slaves in the North; on at least one occasion she led a crowd that took a fugitive slave from his captives and spirited him away to CANADA. Her exploits made her well known to leaders in the ABOLITIONIST movement who invited her to speak at their conventions.

When she escaped slavery herself she took up residence in St. Catherines, Ontario, where in 1858 she met and worked with John Brown. Having no pacifist inclinations herself, Tubman planned to assist Brown's raid on Harpers Ferry in October, 1859, but she arrived too late to participate. Her home in Canada represented the final destination for many of those she led from slavery.

During the CIVIL WAR Tubman served as a Union spy and scout in South Carolina, often going behind Confederate lines to gather military intelligence from fellow African Americans. She also worked as

Harriet Tubman, one of the most outstanding figures in the Underground Railroad, through which many slaves made their way to the North and freedom. (*Library of Congress*)

a nurse as well as assisting escaped slaves who came to the federal lines.

—*Duncan R. Jamieson*

Twenty-fourth Amendment

1964: Amendment to the U.S. CONSTITUTION abolishing POLL TAXES in federal elections.

The Twenty-fourth Amendment

SECTION 1. The right of citizens of the United States to vote in any primary or other election for President or Vice President, for electors for President or Vice President, or for Senator or Representative in Congress, shall not be denied or abridged by the United States or any State by reason of failure to pay any poll tax or other tax.

By the turn of the twentieth century, all of the former Confederate states assessed poll taxes as a precondition to voting. The taxes were deliberately used to make it more difficult for AFRICAN AMERICANS to register to vote. By the 1960's all the southern states had abandoned poll taxes except Alabama, Arkansas, MISSISSIPPI, Texas, and Virginia. Ratification of the Twenty-fourth Amendment in 1964 banned the use of poll taxes as a qualification for voting in federal elections. The VOTING RIGHTS ACT OF 1965 gave the U.S. attorney general power to challenge poll taxes as a voting prerequisite in state and local elections. As a result, the United States prevailed in HARPER v. VIRGINIA BOARD OF ELECTIONS (1966) to ban poll taxes as a precondition to voting in all elections.

—*Angelyque P. Campbell*

Twenty-sixth Amendment

1971: Amendment to the U.S. CONSTITUTION that extended VOTING RIGHTS to citizens between eighteen and twenty-one years old.

The Twenty-sixth Amendment

SECTION 1. The right of citizens of the United States, who are eighteen years of age or older, to vote shall not be denied or abridged by the United States or by any State on account of age.

Prior to ratification of the Twenty-sixth Amendment, every U.S. state required its citizens to be at least twenty-one years of age before they could register to vote. After the United States had been fighting the Vietnam War for several years, the national mood of the country reflected a new belief that if eighteen-year-olds were considered old enough to be drafted to fight and die for their country, they should also be recognized as adults at the voting booths. All states unanimously enacted legislation lowering the voting age from twenty-one to eighteen.

—*Angelyque P. Campbell*

U

Unemployment benefits

Government programs providing benefits to workers who have lost their jobs.

Holding paying jobs may be difficult for individuals with severe physical disabilities or for those who must care for dependent children, but many adults who can work endure poverty because jobs paying living wages are not available to all. Paradoxically, U.S. economic growth has given rise to the periodic and chronic unemployment of millions. The precise extent of joblessness in the United States is difficult to measure. Government estimates do not, for example, take into account underemployed workers (those who want to work full time but can find only part-time jobs), or discouraged workers (those who have given up searching for jobs). Official unemployment rates compiled by the federal Bureau of Labor Statistics are often criticized for underestimating the extent of unemployment. In June, 1992, for example, more than nine million people were officially counted as unemployed, but nongovernmental sources estimated their number to be as high as eighteen million. During the 1980's and 1990's, the official United States unemployment rate ranged from 4 to 11 percent of able-bodied workers.

Jobless workers often have limited resources to draw upon. Financial and emotional support may come from families, if it is available, or from networks of friends or local nonprofit charitable organizations. Unemployment compensation from the state is also an important source of temporary wage replacement support for workers who have become unemployed.

Unemployment Insurance Unemployment Insurance (UI) was established along with other social insurance programs under 1935's SOCIAL SECURITY ACT. The UI system is a federal- and state-run program overseen by the federal Department of Labor, which enforces broad laws that provide consistency from state to state. However, every state,

along with the District of Columbia, Puerto Rico, and the Virgin Islands, has leeway in determining most of the details of program qualification, operation, and administration. Thus, much variation exists throughout the country, and each year UI laws change as states enact new provisions concerning coverage, financing, and administration. In 1995, for example, nineteen states amended their laws to require that UI recipients who are close to exhausting their regular benefits participate in reemployment services, such as job-search assistance.

The UI system is funded by taxes on employers, who pay 6.2 percent on the first seven thousand dollars of each employee's covered wages annually. The unemployment premiums of individual employers reflect the number of workers that they have laid off in the past. The threat of high premiums can be seen as one preventative measure that discourages companies, however minimally, from casually laying off employees. Since laws designed to reduce unemployment are practically nonexistent in the United States, this administrative procedure is one of the few national measures that exists to control the rate of joblessness.

History of the Program Compared to other developed nations, the United States was slow to establish a UI program. By 1935, CANADA, Australia, and nineteen European countries already had UI plans operating. The earliest known plan was created in Switzerland in 1789. The first municipality to subsidize voluntary unemployment insurance plans was Dijon, France, in 1896. Similar arrangements were soon found in other European communities. By 1911, Great Britain had established the first national compulsory unemployment program.

At the beginning of the twentieth century few resources were available to unemployed persons in the United States. Popular ideas about "rugged individualism" placed the onus of joblessness on individual workers, and the unemployed were often regarded as lazy, dissolute, or inept workers. It was not until 25 percent of the U.S. workforce were out of work in 1933 that attitudes shifted. With so many people unable to support themselves and their families, rhetoric that had placed blame on unwilling workers was replaced by the idea that unemployment was an inherent feature of modern social and economic organization that would have to be dealt with using public resources.

As joblessness spread during the late 1920's and early 1930's, citizens became more outspoken in their demands for relief. Risking arrest and imprisonment, groups of workers increasingly organized forms of protest, including mass demonstrations at state capitals. Wisconsin passed the first unemployment insurance law in January, 1932. This act required that employers of ten or more workers contribute a small percentage of their payroll to a state-controlled fund. Many states were slow to develop UI programs because they feared they would discourage business investment, but by 1933 at least eighty-three UI bills had been introduced in twenty-three states. In April, 1935, New York became the second state to enact UI.

Threatened by growing agitation from desperate citizens, President Franklin D. Roosevelt and many congressional leaders were concerned with reemploying the jobless through temporary work relief programs such as the Works Progress Administration (WPA). Such programs paved the way for greater federal involvement in UI relief, and in 1935 the Social Security Act spelled out provisions for unemployment compensation. It was only after federal legislation, which included federal financial assistance to states, that UI state programs became widespread. Although membership by the states was not required, a federal unemployment tax imposed on each state's employers ensured that by 1938 every state had joined the system.

Patterns of Entitlement and Discrimination
In 1993 about 90 percent of all employed persons in the United States were covered by UI. Those not covered typically included workers on small farms, personal-service workers, part-time workers, workers who had been employed for less than a given number of weeks, workers who quit their jobs, and the self-employed. During the early 1990's one out of four unemployed workers was receiving UI benefits, but there was variation from state to state.

For workers to be eligible for UI in most states, they must earn a minimum amount for specified periods of time, and they must become unemployed through no fault of their own. They must also show that they are willing and able to work by demonstrating that they are actively seeking work. Every state has minimum and maximum levels of weekly benefits. Those who are not eligible for maximum benefits usually receive about 50 percent of their previous weekly earnings. In 1993 the average amount received was approximately $173 weekly and the average worker's duration of bene-

fits was 15.6 weeks. All but two states provided statutory maximums of twenty-six weeks in a benefit year. Massachusetts and Washington, with thirty-week maximums, were the exceptions. Through the federal-state extended benefits program, some workers are entitled to up to thirteen additional weeks of coverage when they exhaust their regular benefits.

Despite rising unemployment rates with longer durations of unemployment, the percentage of unemployed who received UI declined steadily during and after the 1970's. A number of factors contribute to the inability of the system to meet the needs of jobless workers, including tighter federal and state restrictions, productivity declines in the manufacturing sector and concomitant declines in unionization, increases in part-time employment and jobs in the service sector, increases in unemployment in states where the ratio of UI claimants to the total number of unemployed has traditionally been lower than average, and increases in the numbers of women workers and young workers—two groups historically underrepresented in the program.

The underrepresentation of women receiving UI benefits can be traced to the program's origins. When UI was developed, policy makers operated under the assumption that male family heads and full-time workers were the most deserving of employment-related assistance. Women and racial and ethnic minorities, who suffered labor market disadvantages by being excluded from well-paying and full-time jobs, were automatically marginalized by the program. A two-tiered, publicly subsidized benefit system was created that reinforced unequal work patterns in the private realm. Recipients of UI were labeled the deserving unemployed, and women workers, the main recipients of welfare, were stigmatized as undeserving, casual, or secondary workers. The disadvantaged status of women workers under UI has been further reinforced by disqualification rules such as earnings eligibility and requirements on availability to work. Other factors, such as sexual harassment and pregnancy discrimination, fuel higher quit rates and lower earnings among women, thus leading to fewer or no UI benefits.

SUGGESTED READINGS:

Abramovitz, Mimi. *Regulating the Lives of Women: Social Welfare Policy from Colonial Times to the Present*. Boston: South End Press, 1988.

Becker, Joseph M., ed. *In Aid of the Unemployed.* Baltimore: The Johns Hopkins University Press, 1965.

Fox Piven, Frances, and Richard A. Cloward. *Regulating the Poor: The Functions of Public Welfare.* New York: Vintage Books, 1971.

Kates, Nick, Barrie S. Greiff, and Duane Q. Hagen. *The Psychosocial Impact of Job Loss.* Washington, D.C.: American Psychiatric Press, 1990.

Pearce, Diana M. "Toil and Trouble: Women Workers and Unemployment Compensation." *Signs: Journal of Women in Culture and Society* 10, no. 3 (1985).

—*Eleanor Ann LaPointe*

United Farm Workers of America

UFW: LATINO-based farmworkers' LABOR UNION that formed in California during the early 1960's.

The United Farm Workers of America, which has operated under that name since 1972, is the most prominent and largest organization that grew out of efforts beginning in 1962 to unionize American farmworkers. The union developed through a series of organizations devoted to agricultural labor activism. Because all of these organizations were either founded and headed by César CHÁVEZ, or were created through mergers involving such organizations, they are often collectively called the UFW movement. Chávez was, indeed, the leader of all of these organizations, including the still-existing UFW itself, until his death in 1993. These organizing efforts were originally concentrated in California; eventually they involved farmworkers in the northwestern, north central, southwestern, and southeastern regions of the United States. The UFW has remained the largest farmworkers union in California.

Precipitating Conditions From the end of World War II until 1960 many people thought that conditions had become conducive to organizing American farmworkers. Partial mechanization had eliminated many of the worst jobs in the fields, leaving what some thought would be smaller, but more skilled, less easily replaceable, and more politically powerful workforces. Moreover, farmworker wages were substandard and living and working conditions were deplorable. In the face of the gains that had been made for other blue-collar occupations through unionization, there was a new expectation that a sense of solidarity would finally develop among the nation's farmworkers, and that effective political activism to better their conditions would result.

There were, however, several factors that mitigated against the formation of a powerful farmworkers union. Ironically, the same technological developments and living and working conditions that might have enhanced the appeal of union-organizing among farmworkers had also caused them to develop survival strategies that made organizing difficult. Having little job stability because of threats from mechanization and an abundance of cheap immigrant labor, and conditions that could hardly be worse in another agricultural employment setting, many workers responded by moving from job to job, adopting the lifestyle of MIGRANT WORKERS. Since many workers thought of their employment as only temporary, they had difficulty appreciating the appeal of pursuing the long-term goals of unions. It was also difficult for union organizers to contact both nomadic populations and farmworkers who stayed in the same locale, because the latter lived in isolated locations, usually on land that was privately owned by people or companies that would not allow organizers access.

Additionally, American farmworkers have traditionally come from diverse classes, races, and ethnic groups, and employers had learned how to exploit their differences in order to prevent development of worker solidarity. The same problem has plagued civil rights activism generally in the United States.

One of the most serious obstacles to the establishment of the farmworkers movement was opposition of the land owners. During this Cold War period, many employers pointed to the fact that the COMMUNIST PARTY had affiliated with unions in other industries during the Depression to argue that all unions contributed to the communist menace. At the same time, they organized their own associations to enhance their power in COLLECTIVE BARGAINING and with legislators, in order to promote antiunion laws. Before the 1960's these strategies effectively denied farmworkers what other industries recognized as the basic right to organize and bargain collectively.

One factor that made the agricultural employers' inflexible antiunion stance work was the existence of the bracero program. The "guest worker" program created by Congress in 1942 to address the farm labor shortages of World War II, the bracero program was originally scheduled to end in 1945. The program allowed for the importation of farmworkers from Mexico to the United States and for their return to Mexico after they had harvested American crops. Bracero wages were below even those paid to the indigenous American agricultural labor force, so growers used their lobbying power successfully to petition Congress for extensions of the program, and for the passage of Public Law 78, which made the program permanent in 1951. The program depressed farmworkers' wages, which continued to decline in relation to other blue-collar occupations. The braceros also provided growers with a tool for breaking labor strikes by American workers, although this practice was specifically prohibited under federal law. The number of bracero workers brought into the United States escalated from a wartime high of around fifty or sixty thousand annually to nearly half a million by the late 1950's, when the American labor shortages that had originally justified the program no longer existed. A large majority of braceros worked in California and Texas.

The widespread abuse of braceros coupled with their effect on American farmworkers eventually led to the program's demise. In the 1960's the CIVIL RIGHTS MOVEMENT expanded to embrace American farmworkers, who were predominantly members of minority groups—particularly MEXICAN AMERICANS— as well the most oppressed occupational group in the country. President John F. KENNEDY's pro-civil rights stance made it possible to focus public attention on foreign and domestic farmworkers' plight. The federal Department of LABOR bracero program supervisor publicly condemned it as "legalized slavery," and an anti-bracero movement that had Kennedy's support resulted in the abolition of Public Law 78 in 1964. Thus, the unique political climate of the 1960's finally made effective organization of American farmworkers possible for the first time.

Emergence of the UFW At the beginning of the 1960's, the situation of American farmworkers was much as it had been throughout the postwar era. In California and the Southwest, the largely Mexican American agricultural labor force was subjected to blatantly exploitative policies by growers, who were confident that law enforcement agencies and lawmakers would continue to ignore their engineering of labor surpluses to maintain pools of desperate unemployed workers who would readily cross picket lines, as well as their own often violent

intimidation of strikers. In order for an effective farmworkers movement to come into being it was necessary for the bracero program to end, for sympathy for farmworkers to develop among the American public, and for a charismatic leader to appear who could unify workers. César CHÁVEZ was that leader; his appearance also helped to bring about the other two preconditions for change.

In 1962 Chávez created the first of a series of organizations that later developed into the UFW movement. He used the political climate of the 1960's to gain support for his movement from civil rights and other social activists, students, organized labor, politicians, and other socially conscious Americans. However, the farmworkers themselves were on the frontlines of the movement in its infancy, and it was their sacrifices that brought in outside assistance.

The first large-scale collective action taken by the movement initially involved a labor strike against grape growers in the region around Delano, California, in 1965. The movement's leadership brought the strike to the attention of the national NEWS MEDIA, and all of America became aware of the workers' living and working conditions that led to their strike, the violent intimidation of strikers, and the use of strikebreaking workers, while the growers who perpetrated these actions successfully petitioned for court injunctions against the strikers. The heightened public awareness of the brutality and injustice suffered by farmworkers and Chávez's insistence on nonviolence gained sympathy for the movement from organizations and individuals whose financial contributions and political clout made its accomplishments possible. In fact, the concessions for workers gained through the five-year-long DELANO GRAPE STRIKE required a consumer BOYCOTT of grapes and products made from them that could not have been effective without the cooperation of large numbers of Americans who did not consider themselves political or labor activists.

The "Golden Age" and Decline The Delano strike and boycott were so successful that by the mid-1970's 85 percent of California's grapes were being picked by workers covered by UFW contracts. However, during these collective actions, an unanticipated and formidable foe to the movement emerged in the form of the well-established Western Conference of Teamsters. In his movement's early years, Chávez had rejected formal affiliation with mainstream organized labor because the legal

César Chávez and a UFW member during a strike. (*AP/Wide World Photos*)

restrictions attending such status would have eliminated such strategies as mass demonstrations and secondary product boycotts. Many Teamsters responded by expressing condescension toward the UFW movement's grass roots and social activism-oriented style.

After the movement's early organizing success, the Teamsters became its active competitor for farmworker contracts. Because the Teamsters were seen as more sympathetic to growers than UFW movement organizers, they had a competitive advantage in the fight to represent farmworkers due to their endorsement by employers. In fact, one of the UFW movement's best-known strikes targeted Salinas, California, lettuce growers who had contracts with the Teamsters. The 1970 SALINAS LETTUCE STRIKE involved workers who wanted UFW representation because the Teamsters had signed contracts with growers lacking important provisions without unionization elections or seeking input from their membership. In the Salinas strike and other union jurisdictional disputes, the Teamsters employed the same tactics as the growers to prevail in this union rivalry. As competition between the warring unions escalated at farm after farm, law enforcement officers often selectively arrested Chávez's followers, who were also terrorized by Teamster-hired thugs. By late 1973 UFW farmworkers had fourteen contracts with growers, compared to 305 contracts held by the Teamsters.

These setbacks influenced movement leaders to seek affiliation with mainstream organized labor. This was accomplished through the merger of Chávez's NATIONAL FARM WORKERS ASSOCIATION (NFWA) with an AFL-CIO-affiliated agricultural union in 1967. The resulting organization was the United Farm Workers Organizing Committee, which was formally renamed the United Farm Workers of America (UFW) in 1972.

Many of the UFW's most dramatic victories were due to its successful promotion of the passage of the Agricultural Labor Relations Act (ALRA) by the California state legislature in 1975. Edmund G. Brown, Jr., was elected governor in 1974 after a campaign in which he promised to address farmworker rights. The Agricultural Labor Relations Board (ALRB) established by this act mediated both disputes between growers and workers and between the rival unions, hoping to break the cycle of economic disruption and human suffering that seemed to be endless. The ALRA enjoyed the support of all parties: the UFW and its supporters, the Teamsters, and growers—each faction thinking that it would make a net gain from ALRB decisions.

Unexpected problems surfaced almost immediately. The ALRB's $1.3-million appropriation was dissipated during its first five months, as it decided more than a thousand cases involving impending worker strikes and held more than four hundred elections to decide which union would represent workers on particular farms. As a result, the board released most of its staff members and suspended its functions in February of 1976. It did not resume operations until July of that year, after the state legislature reinstated it and increased its funding.

The ALRB's shutdown provided an opportunity for those critical of its often prolabor decisions to engage in political maneuvering to change the makeup of the board. Growers felt betrayed because union-representation elections before and after the board's shutdown found workers voting for union affiliation in 80 to 90 percent of the cases. (After March, 1977, a jurisdictional agreement signed between the UFW and Teamsters left field organizing to the former and relegated industries' workers to the latter, leaving the UFW the only major farmworkers' choice). By most accounts, the board restructuring efforts were successful because there was still considerable pro-grower sympathy in the legislature. In any case, ALRB heard fewer cases each year after its reformation: only 122 in fiscal year 1977-1978, with the number dwindling each year thereafter.

The 1970's was the most successful period for UFW activism. Immediately prior to and after the ALRA's passage, the farmworkers movement obtained for its membership safer and more humane living and working conditions, a living-wage structure, basic benefits such as pensions and health insurance, and protection from dismissal or physical harm for lodging complaints against growers. Although union farms employed only 10 percent of California's agricultural labor force in the 1970's, thousands of other farmworkers received similar benefits because employers saw little reason to interrupt production for elections and negotiations that were likely to result in their workers gaining the same concessions anyway.

By the early 1980's, however, most of these gains were receding. Growers and their associations contributed heavily to the California gubernatorial campaign of George Deukmejian. After being elected,

Deukmejian virtually destroyed the effectiveness of the ALRB, from the UFW's perspective, by drastically reducing its budget, firing its administrative judges and investigators, appointing more pro-grower board members, and installing a general counsel who dismissed almost all union grievances. As a result, workers' benefits disappeared, wages fell sharply, worker health and safety issues were ignored, and, by some accounts, worker housing became worse than ever before.

By the mid-1990's, the UFW remained the largest union representing California's farmworkers. Most observers speculate that another golden era for the farmworkers movement would require a change in the social-political climate and a reversal of the great losses suffered by organized labor generally since 1980.

SUGGESTED READINGS:

Edid, Maralyn. *Farm Labor Organizing: Trends and Prospects*. Ithaca, N.Y.: IRL Press, 1994.

Gomez-Quinones, Juan. *Chicano Politics: Reality and Promise, 1940-1990*. Albuquerque: University of New Mexico Press, 1990.

Griswald del Castillo, Richard, and Richard A. Garcia. *Cesar Chavez: A Triumph of Spirit*. Norman: University of Oklahoma Press, 1995.

Jenkins, J. Craig. *The Politics of Insurgency: The Farm Worker Movement in the 1960's*. New York: Columbia University Press, 1985.

Levy, Jacques E. *Cesar Chavez: Autobiography of La Causa*. New York: W. W. Norton, 1975.

Matthiessen, Peter. *Sal Si Puedes: Cesar Chavez and the New American Revolution*. New York: Delta, 1971.

Mooney, Patrick H., and Theo J. Marjka. *Farmers' and Farm Workers' Movements: Social Protest in American Agriculture*. New York: Twayne, 1995.

—*Jack Carter*

United Nations

U.N.: International body comprising sovereign nations that was founded in 1947.

The United Nations came into existence on October 24, 1945, in the immediate aftermath of WORLD WAR II. It had originally been a group of twenty-six nations pledged to fight the Axis powers in World War II. Its Charter was drawn up by representatives of fifty nations in San Francisco. Its purposes have been to maintain international peace and security and to promote cooperation in international economic, social, cultural, and humanitarian issues. Civil rights are called HUMAN RIGHTS in the United Nations terminology.

The U.N. Structure The United Nations includes nearly all the nations of the world. Its secretary general is the chief administrative officer; included within that office is the U.N. Center for Human Rights and various regional commissions, part of whose duties include human rights issues. The secretary general has sponsored various conferences on human rights, including the World Conference on Human Rights in 1993 and the Fourth World Conference on Women in 1995.

The General Assembly, the principal organ of the United Nations, is composed of representatives from all member countries. Each country has one vote on all issues. The General Assembly makes nonbinding recommendations on international issues, including issues relating to human rights. The General Assembly has been active on some human rights issues, particularly South African apartheid. Through its law commissions and special committees, the General Assembly has sponsored various international conventions on human rights. Some of these have been ratified by enough countries to become international law. The only country that has not normally ratified such human rights conventions is the United States.

The Security Council is another principal organ composed of five permanent members—China, France, Russia, the United Kingdom, and the United States—and ten elected members. This council promotes international peace and security. It has sent peacekeeping military forces to countries such as Bosnia and Somalia. Observer missions have been sent to other nations to promote peace and human rights. In 1993 the Security Council created an international tribunal to prosecute violations of international humanitarian law. The first order of business of the tribunal was to prosecute persons responsible for human rights violations during the civil war after the breakup of the former Yugoslavia.

The International Court of Justice decides legal disputes between countries. While not as active in human rights issues as other United Nations organs, the court has issued opinions on apartheid in South Africa and on the convention on genocide as it relates to the former Yugoslavia.

Human Rights Organs The Economic and Social Council is a U.N. organ that promotes international cooperation on economic, social, cultural, and humanitarian problems. It is composed of U.N. members from fifty-four countries and is the principal policy-making organ on human rights. Its Commission on Human Rights promotes respect for basic rights, the prevention of discrimination, and the protection of minorities. It investigates specific human rights violations. It works on international conventions and declarations to legalize human rights issues. The Commission on the Status of Women promotes WOMEN'S RIGHTS in social, economic, and political realms. The right of women to live free of violence is also part of the charge of this commission. Included within the Economic and Social Council are a number of regional commissions, part of whose charge is the promotion of human rights in their assigned regions.

The International Labor Organization is a specialized agency of the United Nations. It promotes an International Labor Code through conventions and recommendations that set minimum labor standards. The labor code is extremely broad and includes basic human rights such as freedom of association, the right to form LABOR UNIONS, the right to LABOR STRIKES, the abolition of forced labor, and the elimination of all forms of discrimination in employment. The labor code also recognizes the right to a safe workplace.

The U.N. Charter Article 55 of the U.N. Charter commits member nations to promote universal respect for and observance of human rights and fundamental freedoms. This is to be done without distinction as to race, sex, language, or religion. The United Nations' Universal Declaration of Human Rights promotes rights and freedoms without distinction as to race, color, sex, language, religion, political or other opinion, national or social origin, property, birth, or other status. It recognizes rights to life, liberty, and security of the person. It prohibits slavery, servitude, torture, and cruel, inhuman, and degrading punishment. It grants equality before the law, a right to an effective remedy for violations of fundamental rights, fair and public hearings before impartial tribunals, and a presumption of innocence in criminal prosecution. Arbitrary interference with privacy, family, home, and correspondence is forbidden. Freedom of movement, residence, marriage, and property ownership is recognized. Freedom of thought, conscience, religion, opinion, expression, assembly, and association are

also recognized. A specific right to seek, receive, and impart information and ideas through any medium and regardless of international borders is recognized. Rights to take part in government, equal access to public services, universal and equal suffrage, periodic and genuine elections, and social security are recognized. Also recognized are rights to work, free choice of employment, just and favorable conditions of work, unemployment protection, equal pay for equal work, just remuneration for work, and the right to form trade unions. A right to education is recognized and parents are given the right to choose the kind of education to be given their children.

Other Conventions The Covenant on Civil and Political Rights created the United Nations Human Rights Commission. The covenant guarantees rights to life, liberty, freedom of movement, presumption of innocence, appeal of convictions, privacy, and other fundamental freedoms also recognized by the universal declaration. The covenant goes on to restrict the death penalty to only the most serious crimes. It grants freedom of marriage and provides that the obligations of marriage and family be shared equally between the partners. Certain CHILDREN'S RIGHTS are guaranteed. It also prohibits propaganda advocating war and hatred based on race, religion, national origin, or language. The covenant became international law in 1976 after receiving the necessary ratification from thirty-five countries.

The Covenant on Economic, Social, and Cultural Rights, if passed, would recognize rights to self-determination, wages sufficient for a minimal standard of living, equal pay for equal work, equal opportunity for advancement, compensation for maternity leave, a free primary education, and protection for intellectual property. The right to form trade unions and to strike would be recognized. The covenant would prohibit all forms of exploitation of children. The covenant had yet to be ratified in the late 1990's.

The Convention against Genocide declares genocide a crime under international law. Genocide is defined as acts intended to destroy a national, ethnic, racial, or religious group. The convention provides for trial by an international tribunal.

The Convention against Torture requires countries to make torture illegal and punish those who commit torture. Law enforcement and military personnel are to be trained to prevent torture. Allegations of torture are to be investigated and victims given compensation. The Convention on Elimination of Discrimination against Women is designed to eliminate all forms of SEX DISCRIMINATION and to enhance the status of women to a level of equality with men. Women are to have identical legal status with men. Women are specifically given rights to equal participation in government, education, employment, choice of profession, social security, and health care. Women are to have equal rights in marriage and all its incidents such as child custody. Discrimination based on marriage, pregnancy, or maternity is illegal. The Convention on the Rights of the Child bans discrimination against children and provides children with special rights and protections appropriate to their age.

SUGGESTED READINGS:

Alston, Philip. *The United Nations and Human Rights: A Critical Appraisal.* Oxford: Clarendon Press, 1992.

Donnelly, Jack. *International Human Rights.* Boulder, Colo.: Westview Press, 1992.

Janello, Amy, and Brennon Jones, eds. *A Global Affair: An Inside Look at the United Nations.* New York: Jones & Janello, 1995.

Muller, Robert. *Safe Passage into the Twenty-first Century: The United Nations' Quest for Peace, Equality, Justice, and Development.* New York: Continuum, 1995.

United Nations. *Basic Facts About the United Nations.* New York: Author, 1992.

Wronka, Joseph. *Human Rights and Social Policy in the Twenty-first Century.* Lanham, Md.: University Press of America, 1992.

—*David Paas*

Uno, Edison

Oct. 19, 1929, Los Angeles, Calif.—Dec. 24, 1976: JAPANESE AMERICAN rights activist and leader in the REDRESS MOVEMENT.

Edison Uno spent more than four years in relocation camps as a teenager because of the federal government's JAPANESE AMERICAN INTERNMENT program during WORLD WAR II. After the war he helped former internees win settlements in their loss claims, insisting that settlements be made in 1942 dollars and not at prevailing market value.

Uno led a drive to repeal Title 2 of the Internal Securities Act which had authorized retention camps. He also taught in the ethnic studies department of San Francisco State College during the 1960's, and was a member of San Francisco mayor Joseph Aliotio's crime commission. As an early advocate of REPARATIONS, Uno introduced a proposal at the 1970 national conference of the JAPANESE AMERICAN CITIZENS LEAGUE to ask Congress to compensate internment camp survivors for their losses and suffering during the war. For his work in this campaign, he received the Hearst Award as an outstanding civil libertarian.

—*Larry N. Sypolt*

V

Vasquez v. Hillery

1986: U.S. SUPREME COURT ruling condemning racial discrimination in the selection of grand juries.

Hillery was an AFRICAN AMERICAN convicted of murder in a California state court. Before his trial, he moved to quash his indictment on the grounds that African Americans were systematically excluded from grand juries. His motion was denied and he was convicted. Afterward, he unsuccessfully appealed his case through the state court system, then raised an EQUAL PROTECTION challenge in federal court. On January 14, 1986, the U.S. Supreme Court agreed with Hillery's allegations and upheld his challenge.

The Court recognized a long-standing principle requiring reversal of convictions of defendants indicted by grand juries from which members of their own race were systematically excluded. Although Hillery's conviction in a fair trial arguably removed any prejudice attributable to the grand jury process, the Court enforced its own rule on reversing cases where there had been intentional discrimination in grand jury selection. The Court commented that just as a conviction would be voided if a prosecutor charged the defendant on the basis of race, convictions in jury trials could not cure indictments tainted by racially exclusive grand juries.

—*David R. Sobel*

Velásquez, William

May 8, 1944, Orlando, Fla.—June 15, 1988, San Antonio, Tex.: MEXICAN AMERICAN rights activist

In 1970 Velásquez served as the field director of the Southwest Council of La Raza in Phoenix. The following year he became assistant director for the National Council of La Raza. In 1972 he founded the nonprofit SOUTHWEST VOTER REGISTRATION PROJECT in San Antonio, Texas; he served as its executive director for fourteen years. In this position he helped increase both the number of registered Latino voters and the number of Latino elected officials.

—*Michael R. Candelaria*

Vera Cruz, Philip Villamin

Dec. 25, 1904, Saoang, Philippines—June 11, 1994, Bakersfield, Calif.: Filipino American labor union official.

Born and raised in the Philippines, Vera Cruz had a little schooling but mainly worked in the fields. In 1926 he left for the United States, planning to earn money and return home. He worked throughout the western states at low-paying jobs, including farming, while finishing his own high school education and sending money home.

While working in the vineyards of California's San Joaquin Valley, Vera Cruz was active in efforts to organize farm labor. He joined the 1948 asparagus strike in Stockton and became a leader in the National Farm Labor Union (NFLU) during the 1950's and in the Filipino-dominated Agricultural Workers Organizing Committee (AWOC) in the 1960's. The most visible and successful effort to improve the working conditions of farmworkers in California started with the AWOC leading strikes against the grape growers of Coachella and Delano in 1965. The National Farm Workers Association, a predominantly MEXICAN AMERICAN union led by César CHÁVEZ then joined in. Their efforts to get union contracts attracted national figures such as Martin Luther KING, JR., and news media attention for the laborers.

Vera Cruz was one of the voices urging the two groups to merge, resulting in the UNITED FARM WORKERS (UFW) Organizing Committee, which was formalized in 1971, with him as second vice president. However, several conflicts—some interethnic, others ideological—led to his resigning from the UFW in 1977. Though he continued to support the labor movement and the UFW after his resignation, he had found during his tenure that the Filipinos tended to be submerged by the concerns of the Mexican Americans. For example, the Spanish language, which most Filipinos did not understand, was used at meetings. Moreover, the grassroots nature of the union was overshadowed by the presence of one charismatic leader—Chávez. The latter's

Philip Villamin Vera Cruz (right) shortly after his break from César Chávez. (*San Francisco Chronicle*)

support of Philippine president Ferdinand Marcos, whose dictatorship led to human rights abuses, disturbed Vera Cruz as well. Vera Cruz's death in 1994 ended a tradition of activists among the early Filipino immigrant laborers.

—*Shakuntala Jayaswal*

Victims' rights

Modern concept holding that victims of crimes should be permitted a greater role in the criminal justice system and should be compensated for the harm caused by the offender.

The modern CRIMINAL JUSTICE systems in which the state considers itself the victim when crimes are committed are a relatively recent development. In colonial America victims of crimes were themselves considered responsible for the investigation and prosecution of suspected offenders. They had to conduct their own investigations, pay for warrants to be issued, and hire attorneys to handle the prosecution. The sanctions then imposed on convicted offenders often involved restitution to the victims. After the Revolutionary War and ratification of the U.S. CONSTITUTION and the BILL OF RIGHTS, however, the government took over those responsibilities, particularly in felony cases. As criminal justice officials assumed these new roles, decisions regarding cases began to be based more on the protection of state interests than on those of the victims. The symbolic threat to the social order posed by crime was deemed to be more important than the suffering of individual victims.

Over time, the role of victims was limited to initiating investigations by bringing offenses to the attention of criminal justice officials, and testifying against defendants at court proceedings. To some extent, the victims' ability to make even these few contributions has depended on the needs of the police and prosecutors. At the same time that the role of the victim was declining, the rights of defendants expanded and became more clearly defined. The concept of victims' rights eventually arose because many victims of crime came to believe that they had been victimized twice—first by the offenders, then by a criminal justice system that did not significantly involve them in the process.

The victims' rights movement has been a true grassroots movement, consisting of a broad alliance of organizations interested in promoting the rights of crime victims. Most efforts to reform laws and provide victim services have resulted from the actions of local groups that developed in response to specific crimes, or sets of crimes, committed within local communities. The efforts of these groups have led to an expansion of the services available to victims of crime and laws designed to enhance their involvement in the criminal justice process.

The Concept of Victims' Rights Early discussions about victims' rights centered on the issue of compensation. Supporters offered two primary arguments in support of these programs: First, that they are humanitarian responses to help victims who cannot afford the expenses incurred due to their victimization; and second, that the losses suffered due to crimes should be spread over the entire society, so that individual victims would not be forced to bear the entire costs.

The concept was expanded in the early 1970's when feminists and rape victims staged urban rallies against the crime of rape. Their concerns centered on rape prevention and the ways in which police and prosecutors usually treated women who reported sexual attacks. Their efforts led to many

reforms, including passage of rape shield laws, provision of sensitivity training for police officers who deal with victims of sexual assault, and creation of rape crisis centers. Other groups followed, leading to the establishment of new programs providing victim assistance across the country. More important, the concept of victims' rights was expanded to encompass greater victim participation in the criminal justice process and protection of victims' privacy and safety, as well as compensation.

Legislation for Victims In the early 1980's President Ronald REAGAN appointed the President's Task Force on Victims of Crime to address the question of victim services. The task force made sixty-eight recommendations, including a proposal that the Sixth Amendment to the U.S. CONSTITUTION be amended to allow victims to be present and heard at all critical stages of judicial proceedings pertaining to their cases. Rather than amend the Constitution, Congress passed the 1984 Victims of Crime Act, which set up a federal fund for the compensation of crime victims and guaranteed victims several rights. These included the right to be treated with fairness and respect for the victims' dignity and privacy; reasonable protection from accused offenders; the right to be notified of court proceedings; the right to be present at all court proceedings related to the offense, unless the court determines that testimony by the victim would be materially affected if the victim heard other testimony at trial; the right to confer with prosecutors in cases; the right to restitution; and the right to information about the conviction, sentencing, imprisonment, and release of offenders.

Every state legislature has also provided some legal rights for crime victims as part of their state codes. For example, nearly all states require sex offenders to register their whereabouts after serving their sentences. Many states go further by making such information available to the communities

---

The Sixth Amendment to the U.S. Constitution

In all criminal prosecutions, the accused shall enjoy the right to a speedy and public trial, by an impartial jury of the State and district wherein the crime shall have been committed; which district shall have been previously ascertained by law, and to be informed of the nature and cause of the accusation; to be confronted with the witnesses against him; to have compulsory process for obtaining witnesses in his favor, and to have the assistance of counsel for his defence.

in which offenders reside. The rights provided by statute tend to be very specific, however, and do not necessarily apply to the victims of all crimes, or in all circumstances.

Many states have opted further to ensure the rights of crime victims by amending their CONSTITUTIONS. While the amendments vary from state to state, most provide victims with the right to be treated with dignity and respect and the right to be notified of, to be heard at, and to attend important criminal justice proceedings related to their cases. California led the nation by ratifying its own Victims' Rights Amendment in 1982. Many other states quickly followed suit.

The U.S. Supreme Court The U.S. SUPREME COURT has tried to balance the rights of victims with those guaranteed to offenders. This has been a difficult task, complicated by the fact that the legal issues that have been raised have come from a wide range of substantive areas (such as victim compensation, participation in court proceedings, and the safety and privacy of victims). Consequently, there has been a lack of consistency in the overall case law surrounding victims' rights. In some instances, the Court has even been inconsistent in its decisions regarding a specific issue. In 1987, for example, the Court held in *Booth v. Maryland* that victim impact statements created a constitutionally unacceptable risk that jurors would be swayed by the standing and reputation of victims in making decisions to impose CAPITAL PUNISHMENT. The justices did not believe that the "worth" of a victim was an appropriate factor for jurors to consider. In 1991, however, the Court reversed itself in *Payne v. Tennessee* by ruling that testimony by the survivors of murder victims is permissible at the penalty stage of capital trials. The majority of the Court argued that such testimony allows the jury to assess the harm resulting from the actions of the offender, a factor which has always been considered by courts to be important.

The Supreme Court has placed limitations on the ability of victims to obtain restitution and compensation from convicted offenders. In *Pennsylvania Department of Public Welfare v. Davenport*, for example, the Court held that offenders who declare bankruptcy do not have to pay restitution because such obligations are dischargeable debts. In addition, the Court has ruled that a federal judge cannot order a defendant to pay restitution if the charge involving that victim was dropped as part of a plea bargain (*Hughey v. United States*). In 1991 the Court held unconstitutional a New York State statute that confiscated fees and royalties gained by offenders through the sale of their stories to publishers and filmmakers and permitted victims to claim the confiscated funds. The justices argued that the goal of preventing offenders from profiting from their crimes and transferring their funds to their victims did not justify infringements of their First Amendment right to FREE SPEECH.

Concerns Over Victims' Rights Two issues have been raised regarding the victims' rights movement. First, critics worry that infringements of defendants' rights will occur in the process of protecting the rights of victims. In particular, critics believe that victim impact statements or the presence of victims and their families at court proceedings may unfairly sway juries toward conviction by injecting unfair emotionalism into hearings. Proponents, on the other hand, note that defendants' families are allowed to be present in courtrooms and testify on defendants' behalf without unduly influencing juries and suggest that victims deserve the same courtesy.

There is also concern over the financial impact of victim services on the criminal justice system. Critics note the lack of a solid funding base for victim compensation programs and the administrative costs associated with keeping victims informed of the various hearings. They argue that providing these services drains already limited court resources. Proponents counter that the costs of keeping victims informed is minimal and is outweighed by the benefits.

SUGGESTED READINGS:

Davis, R., B. Smith, and S. Hillenbrand. "Restitution: The Victim's Viewpoint." *The Justice System Journal* 15, 3 (1992).

Karmen, Andrew. *Crime Victims*. New York: Wadsworth Publishing, 1996.

Lurigio, Arthur, Wesley G. Skogan, and Robert C. Davis, eds. *Victims of Crime: Problems, Policies, and Programs*. Newbury Park, Calif.: Sage Publications, 1990.

Roberts, Albert R., ed. *Helping Crime Victims: Research, Policy, and Practice*. Newbury Park: Sage Publications, 1990.

Stark, James, and Howard W. Goldstein. *The Rights of Crime Victims*. New York: Bantam Books, 1985.

Viano, Emilio, ed. *The Victimology Handbook: Research Findings, Treatment, and Public Policy.* New York: Garland Publishing, 1990.

—*AnnMarie Kazyaka*

Violence and terrorism

Actual or threatened use of violence for purpose of denying the civil rights of members of certain groups.

The use of violence and terrorism as anti-civil rights weapons has been part of the fabric of American life from the era of slavery through modern times. The number of violent terrorist attacks and threats directed at AFRICAN AMERICANS, ROMAN CATHOLICS, JEWS, and members of other MINORITY GROUPS began increasing markedly in the 1950's and early 1960's.

The California attorney general's Commission on Racial, Ethnic, Religious, and Minority Violence has drawn up what is a generally accepted definition of hate violence. This definition encompasses acts of intimidation, harassment, physical force, or threat of physical force directed against any person, or family, or their property or advocate, motivated at least in part by hostility to their real or perceived race, ethnic background, national origin, religious belief, sex, age, disability, or sexual orientation. The definition applies when the acts are committed with the intention of causing fear or intimidation, or to deter the free exercise or enjoyment of any rights or privileges secured by the Constitution or the laws of the United States, or the state, whether or not performed under color of law.

Anti-Civil Rights Violence in the South The 1950's and early 1960's were marked by considerable anti-civil rights violence in the SOUTHERN STATES. Domestic terrorism began in response to the U.S. SUPREME COURT school desegregation decision in *Brown v. Board of Education* (1954). Just as the *Brown* decision inspired the CIVIL RIGHTS MOVEMENT to intensify the struggle to improve the political and social condition of African Americans, so did it begin to inspire violent opposition by extremist groups. White terrorists, often associated with the KU KLUX KLAN and neo-Nazis, repeatedly engaged in futile efforts to curtail the advance of the Civil Rights movement by burning churches and crosses, bombings, beatings, and killings. A vast majority of the perpetrators of these crimes were able to evade arrest by law enforcement officers and only rarely were convicted in southern courts.

Marshall Policy of Limited Federal Intervention Many proponents of racial equality in the South pushed for military intervention but Assistant Attorney General Burke Marshall, head of the Civil Rights Division of the Department of JUSTICE from 1961 to 1965, insisted that temporary federal intervention would not permanently curtail the violence. Marshall recognized that southern police often tolerated, and sometimes even participated in, attacks on African Americans and civil rights demonstrators, but he supported only limited federal power to back local law enforcement against terrorism. He stated that any government that relied upon a national police force would only temporarily succeed, and would itself soon become a threat to the liberties of all citizens. Marshall's philosophy that massive federal intervention should not replace local law enforcement remained during the KENNEDY and JOHNSON administrations, despite protests by the NATIONAL ASSOCIATION FOR THE ADVANCEMENT OF COLORED PEOPLE (NAACP) and other civil rights organizations.

The NAACP even adopted a quickly rejected resolution calling upon the federal government to take over the administration of the state of MISSISSIPPI. FEDERAL BUREAU OF INVESTIGATION (FBI) director J. Edgar Hoover remained a strong opponent of federal intervention. He voiced many concerns about what might follow if the FBI were called to police the South. The FBI did, however, manage to infiltrate the Ku Klux Klan in 1963; by 1965 it had informants in the top levels of seven of the Klan groups then in existence. During that year, the FBI claimed its agents comprised about a fifth of the estimated ten thousand members of the Klan.

One of the more notable events during the 1960's, when mobs of white racists terrorized African Americans and their supporters with impunity, occurred in 1961 in Montgomery, Alabama, where police failed to protect the FREEDOM RIDERS. The freedom rides had been initiated by the CONGRESS OF RACIAL EQUALITY (CORE); they involved racially mixed groups who rode interstate buses through the South to challenge local segregation laws. Four years later, continued local resistance to voter registration led to the strategy of petitioning Alabama governor George Wallace to provide protection during Martin Luther KING, JR.'s VOTING RIGHTS march from SELMA to Montgomery. Not only did Wallace

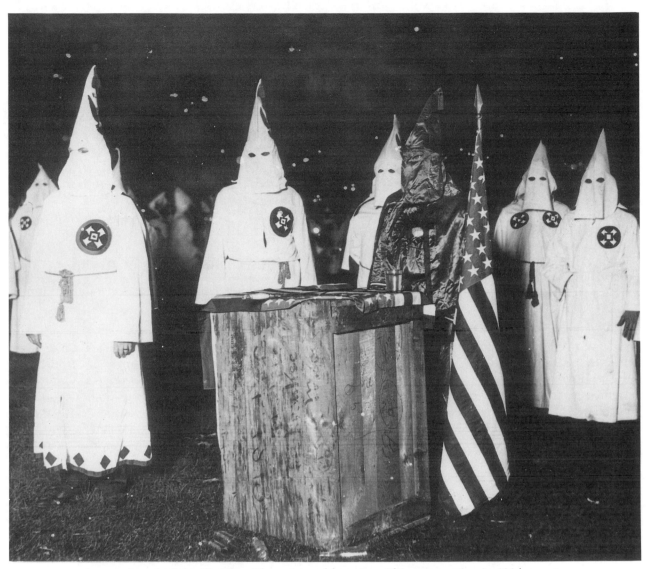

A central goal of the Ku Klux Klan, pictured here in a Chicago meeting in 1924, was to intimidate African Americans, Jews, and Roman Catholics through the implicit threat of violence. (*Library of Congress*)

refuse protection, but the march was brutally terminated by police just after it entered Montgomery. The local sheriff had his deputies use cattle prods, clubs, whips, and tear gas to dispel the nonviolent crowd. "Bloody Sunday" drew international exposure and was followed by a court-approved march order issued by federal district judge Frank Johnson in Montgomery.

Civil Rights of Violent Extremists The First Amendment rights of FREE SPEECH and free association apply to all American citizens, regardless of the views they hold or the messages they attempt to convey. The landmark case of *Brandenburg v. Ohio*

(1969) provided broad protection for the activities of extremist groups when the Supreme Court overturned a Ku Klux Klan leader's conviction for suggesting in a rally speech that it might become necessary to take revenge if the federal government continued to "suppress the white, Caucasian race." The Court held that the constitutional guarantees of free speech and free press do not permit the state or federal government to punish a group for advocating violence as a means of achieving a goal. Only when speech amounts to the actual planning or encouragement of imminent criminal conduct to the point where such conduct is likely to occur, can the government prohibit the speech itself, thus making a clear distinction between mere advocacy and actions.

The First Amendment also protects the wearing of Ku Klux Klan hoods, masks, military-style uniforms, swastikas, and other symbols, along with the distribution of racist, anti-Semitic, and anti-civil rights literature. Moreover, it protects the right of terrorist groups to demonstrate publicly, even in communities strongly opposed to the group's presence. However, when an organization's purpose is to engage in unlawful conduct, such as violence and intimidation, the compelling interests of the state in regulating such activities may outweigh all but the strongest free association claims. This doctrine has been successfully applied to obtain Ku Klux Klan membership lists.

Domestic terrorism incidents against persons or groups exercising their civil rights are no longer considered isolated events, but are due in part to a rapidly growing paramilitary movement among violent extremist groups. In militia camps in areas in the South and in Montana, members of violent extremist groups undergo paramilitary training in guerrilla war tactics, bomb detonation, and automatic weapons use, while talking of the inevitability of a final "race war." Growing racial tensions in many areas have been used as a shield for racist organizations to increase their maneuvers and recruiting efforts—which have been made easier through the Internet and other modern technology. The 1990's have seen an increase in racially motivated violence and terrorism against American minority groups exercising their civil rights such as Jews and homosexuals, as verified by sources such as the Anti-Defamation League and the Harvard Center for Criminal Justice.

SUGGESTED READINGS:

Abraham, Henry J. *Freedom and the Courts: Civil Rights and Liberties in the United States*. New York: Oxford University Press, 1967.

Belknap, Michael R. *Federal Law and Southern Order: Racial Violence and Constitutional Conflict in the Post-Brown South*. Athens: University of Georgia Press, 1995.

———. "Vindication of Burke Marshall: The Southern Legal System and the Anti-Civil-Rights Violence of the 1960's." *Emory Law Journal* 33 (Winter, 1984).

Jones, Charles H. "The Civil Rights Act of 1964 and Racially Motivated Violence." *Suffolk University Law Review* 18 (Winter, 1984).

Lee, Virginia N. "Legislative Responses to Hate-Motivated Violence: The Massachusetts Experience and Beyond." *Harvard Civil Rights-Civil Liberties Law Review* 25 (Summer, 1990).

Murphy, Paul L. *The Bill of Rights and American Legal History*. New York: Garland Publishing, 1990.

Powledge, Fred. *Free at Last?: The Civil Rights movement and the People Who Made it*. Boston: Little, Brown, 1991.

—*Daniel G. Graetzer*

Virginia Declaration of Rights

1776: Influential early state declaration of fundamental rights.

In May, 1776, American dissatisfaction with British rule moved the Second Continental Congress to urge the American colonies to reject British rule and set up independent governments. Virginia immediately followed this suggestion. During that same month, a Virginia convention instructed the colony's delegates to the Continental Congress to press for independence. Moreover, the convention appointed a committee to prepare a declaration of RIGHTS and a pattern for government. Among the committee members were George Mason, the principal architect of the Virginia Declaration, and future U.S. president James Madison. By June 12, 1776, the committee had produced a Declaration of Rights, which the convention adopted. Within two weeks, the convention also ratified a state constitution prepared by the committee.

The Declaration's Content The Virginia Declaration of Rights was based on British constitutional antecedents, such as the Magna Carta, and from the NATURAL RIGHTS theories of English philosopher John Locke. In ringing terms the declaration stated that "all men are by nature equally free and independent, and have certain inherent rights." These inherent rights required for personal security are based on certain fundamental premises of government, and the declaration enumerated these premises. First, the power of government is "vested in, and consequently derived from, the People." Second, government is instituted for the benefit of the people, and their interests are most secure when the form of government instituted is democratic.

Third, within the contemplated democratic form of government, no person or persons should have any peculiar privilege. Finally, a healthy democratic order requires that centers of governmental power—such as the legislative, executive, and judicial powers—be maintained "separate and distinct," and that legislative and executive positions be filled by regular elections. The declaration's articulation of the principle of separation of powers was the first appearance of this central value of the American political order in a constitution.

With these structural matters attended to, the declaration turned to enumerating fundamental rights, many of which were later restated in the U.S. CONSTITUTION and BILL OF RIGHTS. The declaration asserted a series of rights associated with criminal prosecutions, such as the right against excessive bail and fines and against cruel and unusual punishments; the right to a trial by jury in criminal and civil cases; the privilege against self-incrimination; and the right to due process of law, which the declaration articulated as the right not to be deprived of liberty "except by the law of the land or the judgment of peers."

The Virginia Declaration also spoke in support of the role of the "well-regulated Militia" in a free society, anticipating the Second Amendment to the U.S. Constitution, which guaranteed the right to bear arms. In addition, the declaration asserted certain fundamental freedoms that would find expression in the First Amendment to the U.S. Constitution: freedom of the press and freedom of religion. Although Mason crafted the main elements of the declaration's language, on one point at least, the views of his younger colleague, James Madison, prevailed. Mason's draft of the declaration mentioned religious freedom in terms of government tolerance of religion. However, Madison bridled at this reference to toleration, as though religious freedom depended on the good graces of government. He urged instead that the declaration articulate a right of the "free exercise of religion." On this point, the younger man prevailed over the elder, and the Virginia Declaration offered the assurance that "all men are equally entitled to the free exercise of religion, according to the dictates of conscience."

The Declaration's Influence Virginia's Declaration of Rights preceded the more famous Declaration of Independence by nearly two weeks. When delegates from the thirteen colonies attending the Continental Convention determined to sever ties with Britain, and Thomas JEFFERSON took pen in had to give expression to this severance, they doubtless had the words of Virginia's Declaration reverberating in their minds. Echoes of the Virginia Declaration can be heard in Jefferson's Declaration of Independence and in the Bill of Rights of the U.S. Constitution. Moreover, the Virginia Declaration of Rights strongly influenced many state CONSTITUTIONS.

SUGGESTED READINGS:

Davidow, Robert P., ed. *Natural Rights and Natural Law: The Legacy of George Mason*. Fairfax, Va.: George Mason University Press, 1986.

Pacheco, Josephine F., ed. *The Legacy of George Mason*. Fairfax, Va.: George Mason University Press, 1983.

Schwartz, Bernard. *The Great Rights of Mankind: A History of the Bill of Rights*. New York: Oxford University Press, 1977.

—*Timothy L. Hall*

Voter Education Project

VEP: Minority voter registration organization founded under the administration of the SOUTHERN REGIONAL COUNCIL in 1962.

The precise origins of VEP have been the subject of some debate, but the most accepted explanation credits President John F. KENNEDY's administration with inspiring the organization. Concerned with escalating VIOLENCE surrounding the CIVIL RIGHTS MOVEMENT's direct action campaign, Kennedy urged civil rights leaders to focus their efforts on voter registration instead of public demonstrations. Part of the rationale for focusing on voter registration stemmed from 1957 and 1960 voting laws that provided federal protection to persons registering, or assisting others to register, to vote. Following months of negotiations among the administration, civil rights leaders, and private foundations from the fall of 1961 to March, 1962, VEP was founded with nearly a million dollars in grants from the Taconic Foundation, the Stern Family Fund, and the Field Foundation under the administration of the biracial Southern Regional Council (SRC).

Early Years A tax-exempt organization, VEP utilized the infrastructure of the SRC, while maintaining its own autonomy to dispense funds to other civil rights groups. With a goal of increasing the number of registered AFRICAN AMERICAN voters in eleven SOUTHERN STATES, organizations such as the CONGRESS FOR RACIAL EQUALITY (CORE), the STUDENT NON-VIOLENT COORDINATING COMMITTEE (SNCC), the NATIONAL ASSOCIATION FOR THE ADVANCEMENT OF COLORED PEOPLE (NAACP), and the SOUTHERN CHRISTIAN LEADERSHIP CONFERENCE (SCLC), utilized their affiliations with VEP funding to conduct voter education and registration projects throughout the South.

Under the administration of Wiley Branton, an attorney from Pine Bluff, Arkansas, who served as legal counsel during the LITTLE ROCK, ARKANSAS, school DESEGREGATION case and as a CORE lawyer for the FREEDOM RIDERS, VEP helped to increase the number of southern black voters. Between 1962 and 1964 black voter registration in the south increased by 688,800, from approximately 25 percent of the eligible black voters to about 40 percent. This increase resulted mainly from efforts that focused

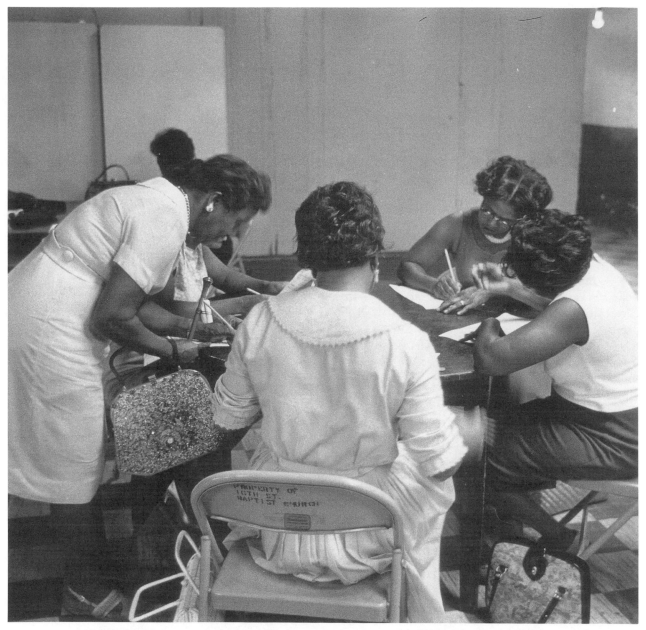

Alabama women preparing to register to vote study in the basement of Birmingham's Sixteenth Street Baptist Church in mid-1963. (*Library of Congress*)

on southern urban areas and the border states. Unfortunately, VEP-funded efforts of the COUNCIL OF FEDERATED ORGANIZATIONS (COFO) to increase the number of African American voters in MISSISSIPPI failed to meet with equal success.

COFO was a coalition of national and local civil rights organizations in Mississippi that distributed VEP funds among groups registering rural African Americans. At the beginning of the VEP and COFO effort, registered African American voters equalled only 5.3 percent of Mississippi's potential black vote. VEP and CORE efforts, under the direction of Robert Parris MOSES, COFO's voter registration field director and the director of SNCC's Mississippi Project, resulted in less than four thousand new voters being added to the roles between 1962 and 1963. This negligible increase, at a cost of fifty thousand dollars, ultimately resulted VEP's withdrawal from Mississippi in 1963.

Opposition to COFO attempts to register black voters in Mississippi took many forms. Registrars required African Americans to pass literacy and understanding tests that were not routinely required of white voters, registration dates and locations were often changed without notice. White landlords threatened to evict black tenants who attempted to exercise their VOTING RIGHTS and merchants refused to sell their products to blacks attempting to vote.

Vernon JORDAN, Jr., succeeded Branton as VEP administrator in 1965. Under his guidance more than a million additional African Americans were added to voter registration rolls throughout the South. Along with the increase in African American voters came increases of African Americans elected to county, city, state, and national offices. Jordan used VEP to counsel these newly elected black officials on the intricacies of political power. Accompanying the growth of African American political power came improvements in schools and living conditions for southern blacks. Also important as a result of increased African American political clout was an increase in police protection of black citizens from violence carried out by white supremacy groups.

The Final Years VEP separated from the SRC shortly after the Tax Reform Act of 1969, which prohibited voter registration agencies from accepting more than 25 percent of their funding from any single donor. Former SNCC chairman John Robert LEWIS assumed leadership of VEP in 1970. With its

goal of bringing black southerners into the political process by exercising their right to vote partially realized with the passage of the VOTING RIGHTS ACT OF 1965, VEP shifted focus to other minority groups. In 1971 it began voter education and registration efforts among MEXICAN AMERICANS in the Southwest. Through VEP's work thirty thousand Mexican Americans were added to Southwest voter roles in 1971.

With a recessionary national economy during the 1970's, VEP found funding increasingly difficult to obtain. Between 1972 and 1975 its funding dropped from $708,000 to $206,000. After continued financial difficulties VEP ceased operations in the late 1980's.

SUGGESTED READINGS:

Cutler, Bill. "Planting Seeds: The Voter Education Project." *Southern Exposure* 12 (February, 1984).

Forman, James. *The Making of Black Revolutionaries.* Washington, D.C.: Open Hand Publishing, 1985.

Haines, Herbert H. *Black Radical and the Civil Rights Mainstream.* Knoxville: University of Tennessee Press, 1988.

—*Paul Chandler Moulton*

Voting rights

The right of citizens of a democracy to elect their own representatives to govern them; limited in the early years of U.S. history to white males.

The steady expansion of voting rights in American history took two hundred years fully to develop; in its final stages it became one of the most distinctive features of the nation's twentieth century political history. Broadening the definition of who may vote has not always been easy. During the nineteenth century, it took the CIVIL WAR and passage of the THIRTEENTH, FOURTEENTH, and FIFTEENTH AMENDMENTS to the U.S. CONSTITUTION immediately after that war to pave the way for AFRICAN AMERICAN men who had been emancipated from SLAVERY to be able to vote.

During the twentieth century, it took the organized pressure of the CIVIL RIGHTS MOVEMENT during the 1950's and 1960's to overcome nearly a hundred years of massive resistance by the white people of the SOUTHERN STATES to the Civil War amendments and to African American voting. Not until the passage of the VOTING RIGHTS ACT OF 1965 did voting by African Americans in the South become a meaningful right on a large scale. Meanwhile, it took nearly fifty years of organized effort by women to amend the Constitution and gain for women the right to vote in 1920.

For AMERICAN INDIANS it also took until the twentieth century to gain the status of full U.S. citizenship and the right to vote. Other minority groups, such as ASIAN AMERICANS, and particularly CHINESE immigrants, were originally discriminated against, and denied the ability to vote. Again, meaningful change took place only in the twentieth century.

Early History During the British colonial period of the United States the right to vote was severely restricted. Prior to the independence of the United States, voting was essentially limited by law to white males who held property. Some British colonies also had religious tests. ROMAN CATHOLICS, for example, could not vote in some colonies, JEWS were barred from voting in others. Some colonies prohibited Quakers from voting, and Massachusetts and New Jersey both required that voters be members of an official state church. After the Revolution and adoption of the new CONSTITUTION in 1787, religious qualifications for voting were abolished, and property qualifications began to disappear. By custom, women were not permitted to vote. For purposes of determining the population bases for taxation and political representation, the Constitution specifically excluded Native Americans, and only three-fifths of each state's slave population were counted as persons. Neither slaves nor Indians could vote. In addition, all but one of the new states that came into the union between 1800 and 1860 specifically restricted the vote to whites, effectively guaranteeing that even free African Americans could not vote.

The U.S. Constitution gave individual states broad powers to set "the time, places, and manner of holding elections." Although this power was seemingly reasonable at the time, many southern states later came to use it as an excuse to discriminate against those they wished to keep voting. Fortunately, the same constitutional provision authorized Congress "to make or alter such state regulations by national law"; this provision eventually proved useful in overriding the states and broadening the scope of who could vote.

Voting rights in the United States have always been linked to CITIZENSHIP. In order to vote, one must be a citizen of the United States. When DRED SCOTT, a Missouri slave, tried to claim his freedom during the 1850's because he had lived in free territories, the U.S. SUPREME COURT not only denied his claim, but also ruled that African Americans could not be U.S. citizens. In 1868, after the South had lost the Civil War, the FOURTEENTH AMENDMENT conferred citizenship on former slaves; two years later the FIFTEENTH AMENDMENT specifically guaranteed to all citizens the right to vote, without regard to race, creed, or ethnicity.

African Americans in the South In the first decades after the Civil War, ever-growing numbers of African Americans began to vote. Under the victorious Union's RECONSTRUCTION plan, many African Americans in the South were elected to municipal and state offices and legislative bodies, as well as to the U.S. CONGRESS. However, with the withdrawal of federal troops from the South in 1877, the ascendancy of an anti-civil rights Supreme Court during the post-Reconstruction years, and a growing fear by many whites of the possibility of sharing political power with African Americans, black voting decreased as dramatically as it had arisen. In the South especially, states erected legal and official barriers to prohibit black voting. POLL TAXES requiring prospective voters to pay for the privilege cut down on voting by both poor whites and poor African Americans. After MISSISSIPPI passed the first poll tax law in 1890, other states quickly followed suit.

In 1901 the last African American elected to Congress saw his term expire; afterward, for nearly three quarters of a century, no other African Americans were elected to Congress from the Deep South. In many southern states, would-be voters had to pay poll taxes not only for the year in which they wished to vote, but also for all previous years in which they might have been eligible to vote. The Supreme Court held poll taxes as acceptable forms of state regulation of voting as late as 1937 and did not find them unconstitutional until 1966.

Other devices by which voting rights were formally restricted included grandfather clauses, literacy tests, and state manipulation of primary elections. Grandfather clauses permitted whites who would otherwise have been disqualified from voting by measures used to disqualify African Americans, by exempting them from other voting registration requirements if they could show they had

African Americans participating in their first election after passage of the Fifteenth Amendment. (*Associated Publishers*)

Voting rights

Federal Voting Rights Expansions

Date	Action	Significance
1870	Fifteenth Amendment	Guaranteed the vote to African American men.
1920	Nineteenth Amendment	Guaranteed the vote to women.
1961	Twenty-third Amendment	Gave residents of the District of Columbia the vote in presidential elections.
1964	Twenty-fourth Amendment	Outlawed use of poll taxes to restrict voting rights.
1965	Voting Rights Act	Outlawed use of tests to restrict voting rights.
1970	Voting Rights Act	Outlawed literacy tests.
1971	Twenty-sixth Amendment	Lowered the voting age in federal elections to eighteen.
1972	*Dunn v. Blumstein*	U.S. Supreme Court ruling banning the long residency requirements used by some states.
1975	Voting Rights Act	Required that voting information be bilingual in parts of twenty-four states.
1982	Voting Rights Act	Extended Voting Rights Act of 1965 twenty-five years.

grandparents who had been eligible to vote. Since virtually no African Americans in the South had grandparents who had been eligible to vote, grandfather clauses simply served as a technique for disqualifying blacks from voting without disqualifying whites.

The southern states and a few others, including Oklahoma, used a variety of tricks to avoid compliance with federal court decisions requiring them to allow African Americans to vote. In 1915, for example, when the Supreme Court ruled Oklahoma's grandfather clause unconstitutional, the state quickly passed a new law ordering electoral officials to register only those persons who had been voters in 1914—a time when few black Oklahomans were on the voting lists. This second law was allowed by the Supreme Court to stand until 1939.

The forms of literacy tests varied, but their common stated purpose was to require would-be voters to demonstrate that they could interpret provisions of state constitutions or laws before registering to vote. The real purpose of literacy tests, however, was to give registrars an additional excuse not to register African American voters. Administration of the tests was done in so arbitrary a manner that even illiterate whites passed, while black college instructors failed.

African Americans were also prevented from participating in meaningful elections by state control of primary elections. Because the southern states were united in their deep dislike for the Republican Party of President Abraham LINCOLN, for many years the region had only a single major political party: the Democratic Party. Consequently, meaningful electoral decisions were made only at the primary level. So few people voted Republican that winning a Democratic primary was considered tantamount to winning a general election. Some southern states passed laws restricting participation in their Democratic primaries to whites; when that technique was held unconstitutional, the states declared their state Democratic Party organizations to be private clubs, which were free of public regulation. Voting in the Democratic primaries then became private affairs, outside the control of federal courts, and the southern states could effectively keep their primaries closed to African American voters.

In addition to all the formal restrictions, the informal use of threats, violence, and economic coercion by whites against African Americans effectively frightened and discouraged many would-be black voters. The net effect of this denial of voting rights was to deprive African Americans of any ability to bring about changes in political power. From the lowest levels of government—which often denied African Americans such amenities as street lights, paved roads, sewers, and representation on school boards—to state legislatures without black representatives and national offices for which African Americans could not vote, the democratic remedy of the ballot box was largely closed to African Americans. Without the right to vote, who would listen to them?

After World War II As hundreds of thousands of African Americans who fought in WORLD WAR II returned home, a change began to take place. People who had risked their lives to defend democracy demanded that democracy be meaningful to them. They wanted, among other things, an unimpeded right to vote. Congress took a first step toward addressing the problems of African American voter registration when it passed the CIVIL RIGHTS ACT OF 1957. Although criticized by some as too weak, this act nevertheless was the first civil rights legislation passed by Congress in nearly a hundred years. It set up a bipartisan CIVIL RIGHTS COMMISSION to study racial problems and to make recommendations to Congress. The commission's first major report dealt with the abuse of voting rights in the South, and identified some of the problems with African American voter registration. The law also gave federal district courts greater authority to deal with any act of Congress involving civil rights, including the right to vote, and set up a new Civil Rights Division in the Department of JUSTICE. Within a decade of its creation, that new division became one of the most proactive agencies of the federal government in investigating and enforcing the right to vote.

The drive for realization of voting rights gained real momentum during the 1960's. Organizations such as the NATIONAL ASSOCIATION FOR THE ADVANCEMENT OF COLORED PEOPLE, which grew rapidly after World War II, and newer organizations, such as the SOUTHERN CHRISTIAN LEADERSHIP CONFERENCE, the CONGRESS FOR RACIAL EQUALITY, and the STUDENT NON-VIOLENT COORDINATING COMMITTEE pressed for change. Although some of these organizations were at first skeptical about the value of voting as a tool for change, almost all of them supported organized efforts to secure voting rights by the mid-1960's. These efforts included the VOTER EDUCATION PROJECT in the South; the Freedom Summer effort in Mississippi (which provoked the MISSISSIPPI CIVIL RIGHTS WORKERS MURDERS in 1964); and the famous protest march for voting rights to SELMA, ALABAMA, which culminated in severe beatings by the Selma police of marchers. Leaders such as Martin Luther KING, JR., James FARMER, Medgar EVERS, Fanny Lou HAMER, and scores of others joined the marches and worked for change. The net effect of this organized protest, widely publicized in the American and foreign NEWS MEDIA, was to make it increasingly difficult for both Congress and the executive branch of the federal government to ignore the barriers that still kept large segments of African Americans from being able to vote.

As part of the governmental response, Congress passed, and the states ratified in 1964, the TWENTY-FOURTH AMENDMENT, ending poll taxes in all federal elections—but not in state elections. At the time that amendment was passed, a 1937 Supreme Court ruling upholding the power of individuals to set all their own election procedures was still in effect. It would have been nearly impossible to pass an amendment regulating state voting requirements.

The single most important law affecting voting rights, the VOTING RIGHTS ACT OF 1965, was passed by Congress with the strong encouragement of President Lyndon B. JOHNSON in 1965. In that legislation, Congress set up procedures for registration in specified areas that had a record of using registration tricks to discriminate against African Americans. The thrust of this section of the act was to require these covered states and counties to submit any changes in their voting laws to the attorney general of the United States. Granting a federal official such power over state election procedures was unprecedented and it put real teeth into the new legislation. The attorney general could also appoint poll watchers and voting examiners to make sure that black voters were not intimidated or harassed. The act also prohibited devices such as literacy tests and forbade procedures such as GERRYMANDERING voting districts for racially discriminatory purposes.

Although the act did not prohibit state poll taxes, Congress directed the attorney general to bring suit against Alabama, Mississippi, Texas, and Virginia—the four states that still required payment of state poll taxes. In the ensuing litigation, the U.S. Supreme Court finally declared state poll taxes were unconstitutional in 1966.

Under the new law, registration of African Americans quickly jumped from 29 percent of those eligible to vote before the law was passed, to 60 percent. Before the Voting Rights Act only about 10 percent of the Deep South's registered voters were African Americans; by 1970 African Americans comprised 30 percent of the electorate in Mississippi, 25 percent in South Carolina, and 20 percent in Alabama, Georgia, and Louisiana. The Voting Rights Act also opened the door of the polls to other minorities. Moreover, it led to the election of significant numbers of minority office holders at all levels of government and ensured minorities a voice in government that had not been heard up until then.

Giving Meaning to Voting Rights The right to go to the polls and mark a ballot is only part of the right to vote. Once that door is opened, there are a number of problem areas concerning how the vote should be counted. Should all votes count equally? For example, should the vote of a city dweller, who is one of many, count the same as that of a country dweller, who is one of few? Should voting districts be drawn so that black or other minority voters form majorities that will increase the likelihood of their electing minority candidates? Among the voting rights questions that have been asked since the earlier barriers to voting were removed, these issues have remained among the most difficult and controversial voting problems to be resolved.

In a true democracy, the assumption is that each vote cast is equally meaningful—that one vote weighs neither more nor less than another. This theory has not, however, always held true in fact. It has taken a combination of court decisions and legislative actions to bring reality closer to the theory. In a series of far-reaching decisions during the 1960's, the U.S. Supreme Court recognized that the ways in which votes for representation are counted must be equal throughout each state. In *Baker v. Carr* (1962) the Court ruled that rural areas with small populations should not outweigh urban areas with larger populations. This decision—which Earl WARREN called the most important of his tenure as chief justice—required Tennessee to redraw its voting districts to reflect more accurately the fact that because its population had shifted from farms to cities between 1900 and 1960, its cities should have more electoral districts and its farms fewer, in order for city votes to count equally in political power.

As a result of these decisions, voting districts throughout the United States have been reassessed every ten years to determine whether their populations have remained stable. Where census counts have shown significant shifts, voting districts have been redrawn to reflect the changes in numbers. This procedure, called redistricting, has tended to shift voting power from rural to urban districts in most states.

The basic system of shifting voting power from the country to the city has been relatively straightforward. The main problems that redistricting has faced in the last decades of the twentieth century have had to do with race and ethnicity. In cities where members of a minority group are spread out among several voting districts, it has been difficult for minority candidates to be elected in any one of the districts in which members of the minority live. However, where minority group voters have been concentrated within single districts—no matter how peculiar their geographic shapes—it has been far more likely that minority candidates are elected.

Both the courts and the legislatures that draw electoral district lines have struggled greatly with these problems. The courts have tended to be become more restrictive, as they have been reluctant to uphold what they see as proportional representation of minorities by race. On the other hand, when courts have been convinced by legislatures that their reasons for drawing particular elective districts as they have are primarily political, not racial, the courts have tended to find the new district lines acceptable. By the late 1990's controversy over the legality of voting districts seemed destined to continue well into the twenty-first century.

SUGGESTED READINGS:

Arrington, Karen McGill, and William L. Taylor, eds. *Voting Rights in America: Continuing the Quest for Full Participation.* Washington, D.C.: Leadership Conference Education Fund and the Joint Center for Political and Economic Studies, 1992.

Bryson, Conrey. *Lawrence A. Nixon and the White Primary.* Rev. ed. El Paso: Texas Western Press, 1992.

Davidson, Chandler, and Bernard Grofman, eds. *Quiet Revolution in the South: The Impact of the Voting Rights Act, 1965-1990.* Princeton, N.J.: Princeton University Press, 1994.

Graham, Gene. *One Man, One Vote: Baker v. Carr and the American Levellers.* Boston: Atlantic Monthly Press, 1972.

Grofman, Bernard, ed. *Political Gerrymandering and the Courts.* New York: Agathon Press, 1990.

Hine, Darlene Clark. *Black Victory: The Rise and Fall of the White Primary in Texas.* Millwood, N.Y.: KTO Press, 1979.

Maveety, Nancy. *Representation Rights and the Burger Years.* Ann Arbor: University of Michigan Press, 1991.

Thernstrom, Abigail M. *Whose Votes Count? Affirmative Action and Minority Voting Rights.* Cambridge: Harvard University Press, 1987.

—*Dagmar S. Hamilton*

Voting Rights Act of 1965

1965: Federal legislation designed to eliminate discriminatory practices in voter registration in order to guarantee unhampered VOTING RIGHTS to all citizens.

Regarded as the measure that removed the final vestige of disfranchisement of African Americans, the Voting Rights Act provided direct federal action and enforcement to remove obstacles that had long prevented AFRICAN AMERICANS from voting. The various mechanisms that SOUTHERN STATES had employed to defy earlier federal voting rights legislation had long demonstrated the failure of the FIFTEENTH AMENDMENT to guarantee members of minorities unrestricted exercise of their voting rights. As late as the 1960's only 22.5 percent of African Americans eligible to vote in Alabama, Georgia, Louisiana, Mississippi, and South Carolina were registered to vote, and in MISSISSIPPI the figure was only 6.7 percent. Southern district courts, on which mostly conservative white male judges sat, additionally burdened prospective black voters, for whom the recourse of litigation often proved impossibly expensive and time-consuming.

President Lyndon B. JOHNSON vowed to enact a federal law that would end all political chicanery and subterfuges practiced by southern states to disfranchise African Americans since the Civil War a century earlier. At his urging CONGRESS passed the Voting Rights Act by a 328-74 vote in the House and a 79-18 vote in the Senate.

One key provision of the act (section 2), outlawed existing voting restrictions and racial GERRY-MANDERING that denied or abridged any adult citizen of the right to vote. Another provision (section 4) contained a triggering formula, that automatically abolished literacy tests or similar devices used as voting requirements in all states for five years.

The act initially targeted Alabama, Georgia, Louisiana, Mississippi, South Carolina, Virginia, and forty counties in North Carolina. The act's section 5 became its most important and most controversial provision. Under that section, the targeted states and counties were required to submit any changes in their voting laws to the U.S. attorney general for

President Lyndon B. Johnson signs the Voting Rights Act of 1965. (*AP/Wide World Photos*)

approval. This condition gave the JUSTICE Department authority to regulate the enforcement of the act in each covered jurisdiction. The act went so far as to allow the attorney general to appoint poll watchers and voting examiners at times when reinforcement was needed to ensure that blacks were able to register and vote without difficulty from officials or private citizens. One aspect of voting rights that the act did not address was poll taxes, which Texas, Alabama, Mississippi, and Virginia still used. However, the U.S. SUPREME COURT's ruling in HARPER V. VIRGINIA BOARD OF ELECTIONS in 1966 soon prohibited poll taxes in those states.

The increase in black voting participation in the southern states after the Voting Rights Act went into effect was phenomenal, especially in MISSISSIPPI, where the proportion of eligible black voters who were registered rose from 6.7 percent to 59.8 percent in 1967. The provisions in the act reflected the federal government's sentiment that access to the ballot would undo the disfranchisement experienced by blacks after Reconstruction ended. Many scholars have marked the passage of the Voting Rights Act as the "Second Reconstruction"—the reincorporation of blacks into political life.

—*Angelyque P. Campbell*

Voting Rights Act of 1975

1975: Federal legislation expanding key provisions of the VOTING RIGHTS ACT OF 1965.

On August 6, 1975, President Gerald Ford signed amendments to strengthen the Voting Rights Act of 1965. Despite the great increase in black participation in the electoral process in the SOUTHERN STATES since passage of the earlier law, voting discrimination continued to exist. The proportion of AFRICAN AMERICANS eligible to vote who were registered still lagged 10 percentage points behind that of whites. Out of 101 southern counties with majority black populations, thirty-eight had no elected black officials at any level of government, and another eleven majority-black counties had only one black elected official each. Of the sixteen African Americans then in CONGRESS, only two had been elected from southern states.

The 1975 law extended the scope of federal voting rights law to reach discrimination occurring in sixty-two additional political subdivisions, including some in the country's northern and western regions. The law was also written to increase voting participation of AMERICAN INDIANS and Spanish-speaking citizens, as well as African Americans. The act expressly banned literacy tests. One section of the act (Title II) expanded coverage of the original voting rights act to jurisdictions with significant disadvantaged language minorities. Another section (Title III) ordered a ten-year ban on English-only registration and elections in any district, 5 percent of whose eligible voters represent a single language minority.

—*Angelyque P. Campbell*

Voting Rights Act of 1982

1982: Federal legislation extending the VOTING RIGHTS ACT OF 1965.

During Warren Burger's tenure as chief justice of the United States, from 1969 to 1986, the U.S. SUPREME COURT began tackling more difficult issues concerning the protection of interest-group representation in VOTING RIGHTS litigation. At times, however, Court rulings from that period appeared to resist broadening the scope of the Voting Rights Act of 1965 to address issues of minority-vote dilution. Instead, the Court continued to apply the quantitative formula of the "one man, one vote" principle as resolutions to malapportionment cases, such as *City of Mobile v. Bolden* (1980), which held that the FIFTEENTH AMENDMENT applied only to access to the ballot, not to vote dilution, and that both the FOURTEENTH and Fifteenth Amendments required a showing of intent to discriminate. *Bolden* thus became a major setback in voting rights litigation.

In 1982 CONGRESS responded to the Court's *Bolden* decision with new amendments to the Voting Rights Act that sought to overcome the harsh effects of *Bolden*. These amendments extended the preclearance provision of section 5 and the language-minority provisions added in the 1975 amendments and amended section 2 of the act to state explicitly that proof of discriminatory rules was enough to substantiate a claim of vote dilution. Despite strong opposition from conservative administrators and congressional members to the new law's racial quota provisions, the amendments passed both houses of Congress and a Republican administration. The new provisions were extended through 2007.

—*Angelyque P. Campbell*

Wagner Act

1935: Federal legislation providing most American workers with the right to organize and bargain collectively through representatives of their own choosing.

Also known as the National Labor Relations Act (NLRA), this law articulated the rights of U.S. citizens to associate, organize, and designate representatives for the purpose of negotiating terms and conditions of employment. Its 1935 passage made those provisions the policy of the United States by establishing procedures for using the rights and by protecting those who chose to exercise them.

Historical Context Until its passage (and 1937 affirmation by the U.S. SUPREME COURT, which upheld its constitutionality), every twentieth century American president had endorsed COLLECTIVE BARGAINING but had done little to see it happen. The government's past policy stemmed from an interpretation of the Constitution that held that employers and employees had an "equality of right" that government could not disturb. Eventually, of course, LABOR UNIONS seemed necessary to balance the respective powers of employer and employee and establish an "equality of position," as Justice Oliver Wendell Holmes wrote, without which there could be no genuine liberty of contract.

The Wagner Act therefore set up a legal framework that committed government to favor workers and their chosen unions, and changed a long-held position of restraints, if not animosity, toward union activity. Although modified by the Taft-Hartley Act (1947) and Landrum-Griffin Act (1950), and by court rulings and employer actions, its basic legal framework remained intact. Its framework defined the rights of WORKERS on the job, listed a series of unfair labor practices, and empowered the National Labor Relations Board division of the U.S. Department of LABOR to supervise representative elections and hear unfair labor practice complaints. Under the law, workers had the right to form, join, or help labor organizations, and bargain collectively with employers without their interference, coercion, or restraint. Employers were required to bargain "in good faith" with unions certified to represent their employees about wages and fringe benefits, hours, and working conditions—including rules and changes in operations such as shutdowns or subcontracting work.

Senator Robert Wagner, the act's sponsor, argued for the connection to be found between economic and political democracy. He noted that

development of a partnership between industry and labor in the solution of national problems is the indispensable complement of political democracy. And that leads us to this all-important truth: There can be no more democratic self-government in industry without workers participating therein, than there could be democratic government in politics without workers having the right to vote. . . . That is why the right to bargain collectively is at the bottom of social justice for the worker, as well as the sensible conduct of business affairs. The denial of observance of this right means the difference between despotism and democracy.

Some businesses supported the law. For example, the Twentieth Century Fund—a group of business leaders embracing scientific management and mass consumption—sponsored a report on labor relations that supported the Wagner Act. The law—designed by Wagner, his economic adviser Leon Keyserling, Columbia University economist William Leiserson, and Brookings Institution economist Isador Lubin—in part sought to help ensure labor peace and to create consumers. Some of the nation's largest industrial firms, such as General Electric, RCA, and U.S. Steel soon recognized the wisdom of the Wagner Act and its effects. Workers got the right to unionize and likely press for higher wages, plus a relatively painless way to resolve grievances without resorting to STRIKES; industry got market controls and more potential customers. Moreover, the legal framework that the law provided for labor-management relations ensured that both employee and employer would be bound by the law—a condition that helped act as a guide and a restraint on bargaining adversaries.

Other businesses, however, initially ignored, resisted, and even disobeyed the Wagner Act until the Supreme Court's 1937 affirmation. "Industry, if it has any appreciation of its obligation to future generations, will fight this proposal to the very last," warned General Motors' Alfred P. Sloan. Sidney Hillman, a leader of the CONGRESS OF INDUSTRIAL ORGANIZATIONS explained that "High-priced counsel advised their clients to disobey it. They told them it would never get by the Supreme Court."

Although fundamental in its effect and groundbreaking in its scope, the Wagner Act had precedents—the Railway Labor Act of 1926, the Norris-LaGuardia Act of 1932, and the National Industrial Recovery Act (NIRA) of 1933. The Railway Labor Act was limited to the railroad industry, but established an early government preference for peaceful labor relations achieved through collective bargaining. Norris-LaGuardia limited judicial restraints on strikes and other job actions and prohibited "yellow-dog contracts" mandating a worker's pledge to not join a union as a condition of employment. The omnibus NIRA, passed as an attempt to escape the Great Depression, included the right for employees to organize and join unions (but without a key component: protecting workers from employer retaliation)—until the Supreme Court struck down that law in 1935.

The same year that the Wagner Act was enacted, there were immediate consequences. More than half of all work stoppages between 1935 and 1937 were prompted by employer refusals to recognize unions. Meanwhile, union membership grew dramatically: from three million members in 1933 to nine million in 1939—a figure representing one third of the U.S. labor force.

Limitations The Wagner Act has had certain limitations in the benefits that it has provided labor. Its enforcement mechanisms are weak; the NLRB can issue rulings but has no power to enforce them without court orders. Its process is rigid; some labor critics considered the Wagner Act a way that worker militancy was channeled away from grassroots organizing and into institutional bureaucracy. The law is slow; its administration takes time, and it can be manipulated by well-funded legal maneuvers. The law is limited; only employees of companies engaged in interstate commerce are covered, so farmworkers, workers with supervisory duties or in small businesses, domestic workers, public workers, and railroad workers have occasionally been excluded. Antiunion forces have not relented in their efforts to weaken or repeal federal labor law. Thirty antilabor bills were introduced in Congress in 1941 alone, and a handful have passed, further

weakening the Wagner Act. The most significant was the Taft-Hartley Act.

Taft-Hartley revived the judicial power to use court injunctions in strikes; it criminalized the closed shop (by which employers agree to hire only union members) and weakened union-shop language (by which employers agree that workers must remain union members as a condition of employment) by empowering states to criminalize them in so-called right-to-work laws. It also added six union unfair labor practices, encouraged employers to sue unions for losses stemming from illegal strikes or boycotts, outlawed sympathy strikes and most secondary BOYCOTTS, guaranteed employers "freedom of speech" in communicating with workers, and empowered the U.S. president to stop strikes by declaring national emergencies.

Despite these and other erosions of the Wagner Act, it has continued to function. Before it was enacted, employers could refuse to recognize unions, refuse to bargain with them, and refuse to live up to a labor contract unless workers' unions compelled them to. After the Wagner Act became law, employers were legally required to bargain in good faith with elected unions.

SUGGESTED READINGS:

Fraser, Steve. *Labor Will Rule: Sidney Hillman and the Rise of American Labor.* Ithaca, N.Y.: Cornell University Press, 1991.

Gross, James. *Broken Promise: The Subversion of U.S. Labor Relations Policy, 1947-1994.* Philadelphia: Temple University Press, 1995.

Silverberg, Louis, ed. *The Wagner Act: After Ten Years.* Washington, D.C.: Bureau of National Affairs, 1945.

Yates, Michael. *Labor Law Handbook.* Boston: South End Press, 1987.

—*Bill Knight*

Walters, Alexander

Aug. 1, 1858, Bardstown, Ky.—Feb. 2, 1917, New York, N.Y.: AFRICAN AMERICAN religious leader and civil rights activist.

Although born a slave in a back room of a hotel belonging to his mother's owner, Walters became one of the most influential black churchmen of his generation. He was educated for an African Methodist Episcopal Zion ministry at a rural school near his

Kentucky home. When he graduated in 1875 he had completed his formal education. Licensed to preach by the church in March, 1877, Walters rose rapidly through the clerical ranks, serving successive pastorates in Louisville, San Francisco, and Portland, Oregon. While serving as presiding elder in San Francisco, Walters represented California at the church's 1884 general conference, where he was elected first assistant secretary. In 1888 he moved to New York City to take over the pastorate of his historic Mother Zion Church. In 1891 the church's Board of Bishops sent Walters to London, England, to represent the church at the Ecumenical Conference. There he defended African American Methodists against derogatory allegations made by white American Methodists. In 1892 he was elected bishop of the AME Zion Church for the Seventh District.

Concerned about the worsening position of blacks in the last quarter of the nineteenth century, Walters supported Thomas T. FORTUNE, editor of the NEW YORK AGE, in calling for the organization of a National Afro-American League. The league's first convention, with delegates from local branches in both North and South, met in Chicago in 1890 and adopted a pledge to fight racial injustice through the courts and to use the press to influence popular opinion. Unable to raise funds for legal challenges to SEGREGATION, the league died after two years.

As state legislatures passed more discriminatory laws in the 1890's, barring blacks from voting and making segregation of the races ever more rigid, and as white mobs continued to lynch blacks accused of crimes, Walters grew increasingly worried and asked Fortune to call another meeting of black leaders. A convention in Rochester, New York, in September, 1898, renamed the league the National Afro-American Council, which became the largest organization of national African American leaders in the country.

National Afro-American Council Elected president of the council, Walters quickly denounced accommodationist responses to increasing segregation and disfranchisement. To him the real question was how blacks could secure the equal rights guaranteed in the Constitution; withdrawal from politics could not accomplish that. When supporters of a back-to-Africa movement asked the 1899 meeting of the council for its approval, Walters opposed the motion and responded with a powerful statement in favor of black rights within the United States.

Walters usually cooperated with Booker T. WASH-INGTON, who exerted significant influence on the members of the council. Cordiality ceased, however, when Walters proposed calling on Congress to enforce the section of the FOURTEENTH AMENDMENT that provided that states should have their congressional representations reduced in proportion to the extents that they barred blacks from voting. Washington vigorously objected and succeeded in having Walters removed as council president in 1902 and replaced by Fortune. After Fortune resigned in 1904, Walters again assumed the council presidency.

As Walters moved further from Washington's ideas on civil rights, he began to associate with W. E. B. DU BOIS and the NIAGARA MOVEMENT. The National Afro-American Council ceased to function after Walters left it in 1908. In 1909 he was one of seven blacks who helped organize the founding conference of the NATIONAL ASSOCIATION FOR THE ADVANCEMENT OF COLORED PEOPLE. He was elected vice-president of that organization in 1911.

Convinced that the Republican Party had abandoned blacks, Walters joined with Du Bois in urging blacks to vote for Woodrow WILSON in the 1912 presidential election. However, he was soon disillusioned by Wilson's decision to expand segregation of government facilities in Washington, D.C. Wilson offered Walters the post of U.S. minister to Liberia in 1915, but the latter declined in order to concentrate on his religious and civil rights work in the United States.

Walters' now-scarce autobiography, *My Life and Work*, published in 1917, the year of his death, includes texts of the powerful speeches in defense of black rights that he delivered before British and white American audiences.

SUGGESTED READINGS:

Harlan, Louis R. *Booker T. Washington: The Wizard of Tuskegee, 1901-1915*. New York: Harper & Row, 1983.

Thornbrough, Emma Lou. *T. Thomas Fortune: Militant Journalist*. Chicago: University of Chicago Press, 1972.

_____. "The National Afro-American League, 1887-1908." *Journal of Southern History* 37 (November, 1961).

Walls, William Jacob. *The African Methodist Episcopal Zion Church: Reality of the Black Church*. Charlotte, N.C.: American Methodist Episcopal Zion Publishing House, 1974.

—Milton Berman

Wards Cove Packing Co. v. Atonio

1989: U.S. SUPREME COURT ruling on employment discrimination.

In ruling in this decision that employers had to demonstrate the "business necessity" of employment practices adversely affecting minorities and other protected groups, the Supreme Court reversed its 1971 GRIGGS V. DUKE POWER COMPANY decision. *Wards Cove* required workers to prove actual DISCRIMINATION instead of simply relying on statistical evidence of the adverse impact of presumed discriminatory practices. Placing the burden of proof on employees made it easier for businesses practicing discrimination to justify their employment practices. Two years later, however, CONGRESS restored the *Griggs* standard for proving discrimination by passing the CIVIL RIGHTS ACT OF 1991.

—*William L. Waugh, Jr.*

Warren, Earl

Mar. 19, 1891, Los Angeles, Calif.—July 9, 1974, Washington, D.C.: Chief justice of the United States (1953-1969).

President Dwight D. EISENHOWER once remarked that appointing Earl Warren as chief justice was "the biggest damn-fool mistake I ever made." However, in 1953 Eisenhower was returning a political favor. During the preceding year's election Warren, then in his third term as a highly popular and effective Republican governor of California, was instrumental in helping Eisenhower win the Republican presidential nomination. Eisenhower in turn promised Warren the first vacancy on the U.S. SUPREME COURT. After Eisenhower was elected, he was slow to make good his promise, but when Chief Justice Fred Vinson died in 1953, Warren called in his favor.

Warren came to the Court with no prior judicial experience but with a gift for leadership. In short order he demonstrated an ability to lead the Court second only to that of John Marshall, the "Great Chief Justice" whose associate justices customarily agreed with his positions, issuing unanimous opinions. With patient determination Warren did the same, convincing the other eight justices of the importance of speaking out in a unanimous voice against racial SEGREGATION in BROWN V. BOARD OF EDUCATION (1954), one of the first cases that came before the Warren Court and, arguably, one of the most momentous cases ever decided by the Supreme Court.

The years Warren presided over the Court coincided with a generally progressive mood in American society, and the Warren Court is remembered for its consistent record of legal reform, particularly in the area of CIVIL RIGHTS. In matters of FREE SPEECH, church-state separation, political reapportionment, racial equality, and criminal procedure, Earl Warren and the Court he headed almost always sided with the individual.

And it was almost inevitable that a backlash would follow. After Warren retired, he was replaced by Warren Burger, chosen specifically for his outspoken opposition to the Warren Court's expansion of constitutional protections for criminal defendants. Burger, in turn, was succeeded by William Rehnquist, appointed by yet another Republican president to help roll back what many had come to view as the liberal excesses of the Warren era.

—*Lisa Paddock*

Washington, Booker T.

c. Apr. 5, 1856, near Hale's Ford, Va.—Nov. 14, 1915, Tuskegee, Ala.: AFRICAN AMERICAN educator and leader.

Born into SLAVERY, Washington went on to become a leading African American educator and nationally known spokesman on racial issues during the late nineteenth and early twentieth centuries. He grew up with only the name of "Booker" and added "Washington" when he enrolled in school. When he later discovered that his mother had given him the last name "Taliaferro," he added it as his middle name.

Boyhood and Young Adulthood Washington was born in a slave cabin on the two hundred-acre Virginia plantation of James Burroughs, who owned about ten slaves. After the CIVIL WAR and emancipation, Washington's mother took him to Malden, West Virginia, where he worked as a houseboy for a prominent white family. During his teenage years he worked in a local salt factory and in the nearby coal mines.

Washington developed a strong desire to learn to read, a privilege rarely extended to slave children. He later wrote that he determined when he was very young that if he accomplished nothing else in life, he "would in some way get enough education to enable me to read common books and newspapers." He received a rudimentary education at schools set up for African American children by the FREEDMEN'S BUREAU and set his sights on entering Hampton Normal and Agricultural Institute in Virginia, a post-secondary school established to educate former slaves and their children. In 1872 Washington set out for Hampton with only $1.50 in his pocket. He gained admission by cleaning rooms thoroughly enough to draw the attention and support of Mary Mackie, the schools' principal for women students. Washington's tuition at Hampton was paid by a northern benefactor, and he earned his room and board by working on campus as a janitor. At Hampton Washington took pride in both his academic work and the manual labor he performed to earn his bed and board; he later stated that the school taught him to love labor for its own sake and for the sense of self-reliance that it brought to him. Through hard work and academic zeal, Washington earned the respect of Hampton's director, General Samuel Armstrong.

In 1875 Washington graduated from Hampton and returned to Malden, West Virginia, to teach at the school that he had attended as a child. Four years later, after a year of study at Wayland Seminary in Washington, D.C., he returned to Hampton to work as a house father in a dormitory set aside for Native American students.

Washington's experiences during his youth shaped his attitude on civil rights issues as well as his theories of education. Because he had been freed from slavery as a child, he never developed the hatred for the institution expressed by former slaves such as Frederick DOUGLASS. Although Washington condemned slavery as a great moral wrong, he also described the institution as a school through which African Americans passed on their way to a better life. Nor did he harbor any bitter feelings against southern whites for embracing slavery. He often stated that he enjoyed serving whites as much as he enjoyed serving the members of his own race.

Throughout his youth Washington had achieved success through hard work and deference to influential white people. He came to believe that the freed slaves and their offspring could make economic, social, and political gains in the same way—by performing well at hard and humbling jobs and by accepting with patience and grace the indignities that were so often part of African American life at the turn of the twentieth century. At Hampton Washington also learned the value of education that focused more on trades than on academic subjects. He later wrote in his autobiography that the Hampton student "was constantly making the effort through the industries to help himself, and that very effort was of immense value in character-building." He came to believe that African Americans must prove themselves useful—indeed indispensable—in key trades before they could lay claim to the political and social privileges enjoyed by most white Americans.

Establishing Tuskegee Institute In May, 1881, General Armstrong asked Washington to serve as principal of a technical training school that was being formed for African American students by prominent white citizens of Tuskegee, Alabama. Washington readily accepted the offer, and the Tuskegee Normal School for Colored Youth opened on July 4, 1881. The institution began with thirty students in makeshift quarters, but Washington immediately drew plans for rapid expansion. With a $437 loan, he purchased for the school a one-hundred-acre farm and began a construction effort. By the time Tuskegee's first class graduated in 1885, the campus comprised a handful of buildings, including Porter Hall, Tuskegee's first permanent edifice. Washington began traveling around the United States giving speeches, raising funds, and recruiting faculty members for his school, which was later renamed Tuskegee Institute.

At Tuskegee, Washington implemented the educational and pedagogical theories that he had learned at Hampton Institute. Tuskegee emphasized the mastery of practical skills. Male students learned modern agricultural techniques, masonry, carpentry, and other practical skills that would ensure steady employment and income after graduation. Female students studied home economics and were trained for careers in nursing and teaching. Washington believed that academic knowledge alone did not provide students with a sound education; he wrote that "we must do something besides teach them mere books." He explained that a student with the ability to translate Greek sentences might not fulfill a need in the community, whereas a student with the ability to make bricks, houses, or wagons would surely be needed and appreciated. In addition, Washington emphasized the importance of personal hygiene and grooming.

Through the 1890's Tuskegee Institute acquired

Booker T. Washington, the leading African American spokesperson of the late nineteenth century. (*Library of Congress*)

additional land and added several buildings, all of which were constructed by Tuskegee students, reflecting the school's emphasis on hands-on learning. Meanwhile, Washington gained a national reputation as an educator and spokesman on issues concerning race. He became a speaker in great demand, addressing groups such as the National Education Association and delivering commencement addresses at prestigious universities. In 1896 he delivered the commencement address at Harvard University and received from Harvard an honorary master's degree. In 1898 President William McKinley visited Tuskegee and praised Washington's work.

Political and Social Beliefs Through his speeches and writings, Washington made known his views on issues concerning civil rights. Throughout his career, he preached the value of patience and humility; rather than agitate for equal social and political rights for African Americans, he urged that they should prove themselves through hard work and good citizenship. Only after African Americans proved themselves worthy citizens and productive members of society would they merit the full social and political benefits of American society.

On September 18, 1895, Washington spelled out his political and social theories in a speech at the Atlanta Cotton States and International Exposition, a celebration of the South's agricultural development. This speech—called by his critics the "ATLANTA COMPROMISE"—expressed his hope that the exposition would do more to "cement the friendship of the two races than any other occurrence since the dawn of freedom." He predicted "a new era of industrial progress" throughout the South, with African Americans playing a key role in that effort. He urged African Americans to look for achievement "in agriculture, mechanics, in commerce, in domestic service, and in the professions," and he predicted that they would prosper "in proportion as we learn to dignify and glorify common labour and put brains and skill into the common occupations of life." He added that "no race can prosper till it learns that there is as much dignity in tilling a field as in writing a poem." Washington concluded by suggesting that the "wisest among my race understand that the agitation of questions of social equality is the extremest folly, and that progress in the enjoyment of all the privileges that will come to us must be the result of severe and constant struggle rather than artificial forcing."

Washington also spelled out his political, social, and educational theories in his 1901 autobiography, *Up from Slavery*, which details the rags-to-riches tale of a man born in slavery who, through hard work and perseverance, achieved national prominence. The book was well received in its time and has sold millions of copies since its publication. For several decades Washington's autobiography was commonly included on high school history and English reading lists. Washington's other books include *Character Building* (1902), *Working with the Hands* (1904), and *My Larger Education* (1911).

Supporters and Critics Washington's message of patience and hard work was applauded by both white and black citizens throughout the United States. Theodore Roosevelt, Andrew Carnegie, Mark Twain, and William Taft became strong supporters of Washington and his work at Tuskegee Institute. Southern whites were especially pleased with Washington's advising African Americans to focus their efforts on attaining worthwhile labor, rather than on gaining their political and social rights. Grant money and contributions poured into Tuskegee Institute from across the United States.

However, praise for Washington's message was not unanimous. He was accused of making an unsatisfactory compromise with white America by accepting an inferior social and political position for African Americans in exchange for opportunities for economic achievement. His critics argued that providing African Americans with the skills for economic independence would not alone lead to the attainment of rights that would ensure equality for all African American citizens.

Less than a year after Washington delivered his Atlanta address, the U.S. SUPREME COURT, in PLESSY V. FERGUSON, created the SEPARATE-BUT-EQUAL doctrine, which allowed states to require separate public facilities for white and black citizens. Throughout the South, a wave of JIM CROW laws followed, segregating public transportation, train stations, public parks and beaches, golf courses, sports arenas, schools, and other public places. Washington's critics argued that his attitude on racial issues of patience and accommodation allowed discriminatory legislation to pass without criticism or impediment.

Foremost among Washington's critics was W. E. B. DU BOIS. In *The Souls of Black Folks* (1903) Du Bois declared that Washington "represents in Negro thought the old attitude of adjustment and submission." Du Bois saw the ideas in Washington's Atlanta address as merely "a gospel of Work and Money" that encouraged African Americans to forgo political power, civil rights, and opportunities for higher education. In contrast to Washington, Du Bois demanded for African Americans the right to vote, civic equality, and opportunities for higher academic education. In 1909 Du Bois helped to form the NATIONAL ASSOCIATION FOR THE ADVANCEMENT OF COLORED PEOPLE (NAACP), which demanded an immediate end to all forms of racial discrimination in the United States, a position that provided a strong counterpoint to the philosophy of moderation and gradualism espoused by Washington.

Defenders of Washington's philosophy argue that the economic needs of African Americans were more pressing than their need to attain political rights and social privileges. Moreover, his defenders point out that he did lobby to break down the barriers that kept African Americans away from the ballot box, and he preached against the most damaging aspects of life under Jim Crow, such as LYNCH-ING and the atrocities perpetrated by terrorist organizations such as the KU KLUX KLAN.

Washington has remained a controversial figure long after his death and has continued to prompt debate in the African American community. His place in the long struggle for African American civil rights is aptly depicted in a scene in Ralph Ellison's novel *Invisible Man* (1952). The novel's unnamed narrator attends Tuskegee Institute and comments on a bronze statue on campus portraying Washington holding a veil of ignorance above a kneeling slave. The narrator is uncertain whether Washington is lifting the veil, or lowering it.

SUGGESTED READINGS:

Bontemps, Arna. *Young Booker: Booker T. Washington's Early Days.* New York: Dodd, Mead, 1972.

Du Bois, W. E. B. *The Souls of Black Folk.* 1903. Reprint. New York: Penguin Books, 1989.

Franklin, John Hope, and Alfred A. Moss, Jr. *From Slavery to Freedom: A History of African Americans.* 7th ed. New York: McGraw-Hill, 1994.

Harlan, Louis R. *Booker T. Washington: The Making of a Black Leader, 1856-1901.* New York: Oxford University Press, 1972.

Smock, Raymond W., ed. *Booker T. Washington in Perspective: Essays of Louis R. Harlan.* Jackson: University Pres of Mississippi, 1988.

Washington, Booker T. *Up from Slavery.* 1901. Reprint. New York: W. W. Norton, 1996.

_____. *Character Building.* 1902. Reprint. New York: Haskell House Publishers, 1972.

—*James Tackach*

Watkins, Bruce R., Sr.

Mar. 20, 1924, Parkville, Mo.—Sept. 13, 1980, Kansas City, Mo.: AFRICAN AMERICAN civil rights activist and politician.

Watkins was a prominent local politician in Kansas City, Missouri, where he was elected one of the first African American city council members in 1963. He was also co-founder of a civil rights organization called Freedom, Inc., established in 1962. At the end of the 1970's he became the first African American candidate for mayor of Kansas City. Although he defeated the incumbent in the Democratic Party primary, he lost the general election. Thereafter, he worked for the Department of HOUSING AND URBAN DEVELOPMENT until his death of cancer in 1980.

—*Timothy L. Hall*

Watsonville incident

1930: Anti-Asian rioting by whites.

During the 1920's federal legislation greatly reduced foreign IMMIGRATION, making it difficult for many U.S. industries to meet their unskilled labor needs. Filipinos were then considered American nationals because the Spanish-American War had made the Philippines an American territory, so it was legal to import them to do agricultural work. In January, 1930, white residents of Watsonville, California, turned on the Filipino farmworkers who had recently come into their region. In the four-day riot that ensued, one Filipino was killed, forty-six were injured, and many of the rest were driven out of the area. Eight people were tried for rioting; four were convicted, but no one was tried for murder.

—*Duncan R. Jamieson*

Wattleton, (Alyce) Faye

Born July 8, 1943, St. Louis, Mo.: Reproductive rights activist and officer in Planned Parenthood Federation of America.

One of the most influential AFRICAN AMERICAN women in the field of REPRODUCTIVE RIGHTS, Wattleton trained as a nurse and worked as a maternity nursing instructor in Dayton, Ohio. While there, she first saw women who had undergone life-threatening illegal abortions. Later she attended Columbia University and earned a master of science degree in maternal and infant health care with certification as a nurse-midwife. While she interned at Harlem Hospital, the importance of women's access to safe abortions became clear to her.

In 1967 she moved to Ohio to work as consultant and assistant director of public health nursing services in Dayton's public health department. She joined the local Planned Parenthood board; the following year she became its executive director. Later she became president of the Planned Parenthood Federation of America (PPFA). During her tenure, federal Medicaid funding of abortions for the poor was cut off after the Hyde Amendment was enacted in 1976; it prohibited federal funding of abortions unless a mother's life was endangered.

Faye Wattleton, president of Planned Parenthood Federation of America from 1978 to 1992. (*Betty Lane*)

The Ronald REAGAN and George BUSH administrations' political agenda attempted to dismantle programs designed to confront inadequate health care for the poor and the homeless. Wattleton argued that the poor—like the rich—should have access to the full range of health services, among them reproductive freedom and choice.

Under Wattleton Planned Parenthood dedicated itself to creating a society in which unintended pregnancies are reduced through sex education and counseling about contraception and access to information and supplies. Its newspaper and television advertisements were often geared toward educating teenagers. Wattleton argued, however, that children needed to be educated about sexuality before they became adolescents.

—*Marcia J. Weiss*

Watts riots

1965: RACE RIOT that ravaged central Los Angeles, California.

During the two decades following World War II, the white, middle-class section of central Los Angeles known as Watts was gradually transformed into an AFRICAN AMERICAN community. As members of a predominantly black enclave within a city with a predominantly white city government, Watts residents came to resent mistreatment at the hands of the police department. During the mid-1960's incidents involving African Americans and officers of the Los Angeles Police Department who patrolled Watts caused tensions to mount. In August, 1965, police stopped a young black man for drunk driving and got into minor altercations with several bystanders watching the arrest. After the police left the scene, angry Watts residents began stoning passing cars, beating white motorists, and overturning cars and setting them on fire.

The actions the police took enraged the crowd, but the next day Watts became calm while community leaders attempted to mediate between the police and the residents. That night, however, violence again erupted, and again the police response failed to control the situation. On the morning of August 13, huge crowds converged on Watts's main business district, some two miles from the initial rioting, and began looting. Firebombing and attacks against white-owned businesses followed. The police requested assistance from the National Guard, and

National Guardsmen patrol riot-torn Watts district of Los Angeles. (*AP/Wide World Photos*)

after another thirty-six hours of rioting the police, supported by twelve thousand army personnel, restored order. Thirty-four deaths had resulted, hundreds more injuries, and approximately $35 million worth of property had been destroyed, making Watts the worst urban riot since the 1943 disturbance in DETROIT.

—*Duncan R. Jamieson*

"We Shall Overcome"

Song used as the anthem of the CIVIL RIGHTS MOVEMENT.

"We Shall Overcome" is perhaps the best-known song in American PROTEST MUSIC. Its genius lies in its simplicity, solemnity, and sureness of promise. The song touches a responsive chord in those facing oppression. According to singer Pete SEEGER, the song originated in either gospel songwriter Charles Tindley's "I'll Overcome Some Day," (1903) or the anonymously composed "I'll Be All Right." Which came first is uncertain; however, a form close to the modern song was being sung by the 1940's.

The song used the "shout" technique, a rapid beat accompanied by hand clapping, rather than the slow-moving mantra later familiar. One of its main features is its dynamic, adaptive nature. Its oldest and most familiar lines are "We shall overcome . . . We shall overcome some day," but it has adopted new verses for specific movements, with phrases such as "We will win our rights," "Black and white together," and "We are not afraid."

Highlander Folk School Impact "We Shall

Overcome" was first adapted for a social protest in the black churches of Charleston, South Carolina, where tobacco workers went on strike in 1945. The following year leaders of that protest took the song to Tennessee's Highlander Folk School, a training ground for labor union organizers. Founded by Zilphia Horton and Myles Horton, the school was dedicated to ending SEGREGATION and integrating society. Zilphia believed that music could unite groups and encouraged students to use the song in their labor strikes across the United States. It was at Highlander that popular white folksinger Pete Seeger first heard the song; he is credited with changing the words from "We will overcome" to "We *shall* overcome" and with adding a new verse that begins, "We'll walk hand in hand." However, many singers give more credit to Guy Carawan, a self-described white California hillbilly who directed music at the Highlander school in the mid-1950's, after Zilphia's death. A student of black gospel music, Carawan is credited with spreading the sound of songs such as "We Shall Overcome" and "Eyes on the Prize" throughout the South.

Transition to Civil Rights In an April, 1960, SIT-IN demonstration in Nashville, Tennessee, the song was sung for the first time in a civil rights protest. Bernard Lafayette, later of the STUDENT NON-VIOLENT COORDINATING COMMITTEE, believed that the song provided a confident framework to the nonviolent principles that they wanted to foster. Protesters were taught to cross their hands across their chests in order to hold the hands of the persons at their sides in order to emphasize their interconnectedness, and—in the words of one protester—to "wear down ugly by beauty, confront violence with love. " The FREEDOM RIDERS who began challenging TRANSPORTATION segregation laws in 1961 spread the song into the Deep South. Martin Luther KING, JR.'s August, 1963, MARCH ON WASHINGTON brought the song into the livingrooms of the entire nation as folksinger Joan BÁEZ enjoined marchers to join her in singing the anthem.

On March 7, 1965, responding to the need for continuing action to sustain Civil Rights movement support, King initiated an all-out drive for black voting registration by leading a protest march from SELMA to Montgomery, Alabama. Spurred by the VIOLENCE he witnessed along the way as unarmed marchers were brutally beaten President Lyndon B. JOHNSON delivered the VOTING RIGHTS ACT OF 1965 to Congress. In a compassionate speech accompany-

ing his presentation, Johnson said: "It is not just Negroes, but really it is all of us who must overcome the crippling legacy of bigotry and injustice. And we *shall* overcome."

Although rooted in African American traditions, "We Shall Overcome" has moved throughout the world to help fight dehumanizing conditions wherever found and has become the symbolic representation of social reform. From the United Farm Workers to the Nonviolent Northern Ireland Peace movement, from protesters in Lebanon and North Korea to South Africa and China, from causes as diverse as textile workers to women's rights and nuclear disarmament, the anthem has promoted a universal idea of overcoming injustice. Because of its simplicity, sheet music and scores are unnecessary; it needs only one person to teach it to thousands. In continuing the musical tradition of change, "We Shall Overcome" has continued to touch responsive chords to struggles against oppression.

SUGGESTED READINGS:

Denisoff, R. Serge. *Sing a Song of Social Significance.* Bowling Green, Ohio: Bowling Green University Popular Press, 1972.

Glazer, Tom, ed. *Songs of Peace, Freedom, and Protest.* New York: David McKay, 1970.

Seeger, Pete, and Peter Blood. *Where Have All the Flowers Gone: A Singer's Stories, Songs, Seeds, and Robberies.* Bethlehem, Pa.: Sing Out, 1993.

Silverman, Jerry. *Songs of Protest and Civil Rights.* New York: Chelsea House, 1992.

—*Beth M. Waggenspack*

Wells, Ida B.

July 16, 1862, Holly Springs, Miss.—Mar. 25, 1931, Chicago, Ill.: AFRICAN AMERICAN civil rights activist and journalist.

For forty years Ida Bell Wells (also known as Ida B. Wells-Barnett) was a voice for equality, justice, and human dignity. She forcefully articulated issues that stimulated the struggles for civil, political, and economic rights for African Americans. Her clarion calls awoke the conscience of the nation, and her progressive ideas of reform were at the forefront of the struggle for social justice.

Wells was born into SLAVERY a half year before Abraham LINCOLN issued the EMANCIPATION PROCLAMATION. At the age of sixteen she assumed guardianship of five siblings when her parents and a baby brother succumbed to yellow fever. After moving to Memphis, Tennessee, she spent the next years of her life teaching, furthering her education at Fisk University in Nashville, and developing her writing ability by participating in a lyceum at LeMoyne Normal Institute.

Voice for Civil Rights Wells matured during the RECONSTRUCTION ERA, but as she reached adulthood in the 1880's JIM CROW LAWS and a series of antiblack federal and local court decisions dissolved the protection afforded to African Americans by the CIVIL RIGHTS ACT OF 1875. The restitution of SEGREGATION in public TRANSPORTATION immediately affected her. On May 4, 1884, while she was traveling through Tennessee to a new teaching assignment on a first-class train ticket, a conductor told her to move from the "Ladies" car to the Jim Crow car. Wells vigorously resisted but was physically forced off the train. She then sued the Chesapeake, Ohio, and Southwestern Railroad. A lower court awarded her five hundred dollars, but Tennessee's supreme court later reversed the decision.

Discouraged by the outcome of her case, Wells inaugurated her struggle for civil rights by employing her journalistic skills. She became an editor of the *Evening Star* and another weekly, *The Living Way*. Under the pen name "Iola," she wrote a weekly column on everyday problems in African American life. Her early writings focused on her experience fighting Jim Crow laws and later evolved into broader issues concerning African Americans. Soon, she was contributing articles advancing the cause of civil rights to prestigious newspapers, as well as to small church-related newspapers.

Always the activist, Wells was elected secretary of the Colored Press Association (later known as the Afro-American Press Association) in 1887. By 1889 she owned part of the Memphis *Free Speech and Headlight*. As its editor, she was fearless. Her militant editorials protested racial injustices including DISFRANCHISEMENT, house burning, LYNCHING, and segregated schools. Pressing for equal rights and full citizenship, she joined the AFRO-AMERICAN LEAGUE, an organization founded by Fortune T. Thomas FORTUNE.

Voice Against Lynching In March, 1892, an event determined the future direction of all of Wells's energies. On the outskirts of Memphis, three black friends of hers who were outstanding community citizens opened a grocery store that competed successfully against a white grocery store across the street. Resentment grew between the two businesses until a minor riot resulted in the incarceration of Wells's friends. Later, a white mob stormed the county jail, removed the men, shot, and hanged them.

This event stimulated Wells to use her editorial voice to challenge the lynch law and to inform people that lynchings, which were usually justified by accusations of rape, were actually "an excuse to get rid of Negroes who were acquiring wealth and property." In the *Free Speech*, she entreated the black community to "leave a town which will neither protect our lives and property, nor give us a fair trial in the courts, but takes us out and murders us in cold blood." About two thousand people heeded her plea and left Memphis to move west, while those who remained staged a BOYCOTT of the streetcar line, driving it near to bankruptcy. Wells exploded the myth that vindicated lynching by stating that many sexual liaisons between black men and white women were of mutual consent. In response, a mob from the enraged white community destroyed her *Free Press* office in May, 1892, while she was attending the African Methodist Episcopal Church convention in Philadelphia. A white newspaper openly called for lynching and threatened Wells's life.

Wells, however, persisted in denouncing lynching. Writing for the NEW YORK AGE and other weekly African American NEWSPAPERS, she composed a series of articles detailing the lynchings of 728 black people during the decade before 1892. These articles revealed the evils and false reasoning associated with lynching, earned her a national audience, and were the basis of two pamphlets: *Southern Horrors: Lynch Law in All Its Phases* (1892) and *A Red Record: Tabulated Statistics and Alleged Causes of Lynchings in the United States, 1892-1893-1894* (1895).

From 1892 to 1895, Wells conducted antilynching speaking tours in the United States, England, and Scotland. One result was the formation of the British Anti-Lynching Society, which imposed international pressure on the problem. Similar societies originated in the United States. In 1893 Wells, who was offended that the World's Columbian Exposition in CHICAGO would not allow an African American pavilion, acquired financial help from Frederick DOUGLASS and published a widely read antilynching pamphlet, *The Reason Why the Colored American Is Not in the World's Columbian Exposition*. Additionally, she began a national movement against lynching by forming the NATIONAL ASSOCIATION OF COLORED WOMEN (NACW) in 1896. She also served as secretary of the National Afro-American Council from 1898 to 1902 and headed its antilynching speakers bureau. To protest a brutal lynching in South Carolina and to ask for national legislation to outlaw "the national crime," she personally led a delegation to meet President William McKinley in 1898. As a result, he made a speech against lynching, but the atrocities continued. Later, Wells conducted her own investigations of lynchings in Cairo and Springfield, Illinois, EAST ST. LOUIS, Illinois, Elaine, Arkansas, and Little Rock, Arkansas. She continued to fight for antilynching legislation through the remainder of her life.

Voice for Reform After the Columbian Exposition Wells had organized Illinois' first black women's club in CHICAGO. The organization, which carried her name, raised money to prosecute a police officer for killing an innocent black man on Chicago's West Side, helped establish the first black orchestra in Chicago, opened the first kindergarten for black children, and was a charter member of the Cook County Women's Clubs.

In 1895 Wells married Ferdinand L. Barnett, a Chicago lawyer, newspaper editor, and later assistant state attorney for Cook County. Although Wells was a devoted mother and homemaker, she persisted in her reform activities. She and her husband moved to the all-white East Side of Chicago and challenged RESTRICTIVE COVENANTS in housing. In 1910 she organized the young men of her Bible class at Grace Presbyterian Church in Chicago into the Negro Fellowship League, which provided housing and employment for black male immigrants. It flourished until the end of the decade when the Young Men's Christian Association for Black Men and the NATIONAL URBAN LEAGUE took over many of its functions. Wells was also active in the founding of the NATIONAL ASSOCIATION FOR THE ADVANCEMENT OF COLORED PEOPLE (NAACP) in 1910. In 1913 she became the first black woman probation officer in the nation, but she lost her appointment when a new city administration assumed power three years later.

Voice for Suffrage Wells believed that the vote was the key for African Americans to achieve economic, social, and political equity and reform. Upon arriving in Chicago, she had joined the NATIONAL WOMAN SUFFRAGE ASSOCIATION. When women received the vote in Illinois' local elections, she organized the Alpha Suffrage Club, the state's first suffrage organization for black women. In Chicago, she also marched with whites who were urging passage of a federal suffrage amendment and, in 1913, paraded in Washington, D.C. Later that year, she returned to Washington as a member of the executive committee of the National Equal Rights League.

In 1930 she ran for an Illinois state senate in the Republican primary as an independent. Defeated by the incumbent, Wells was disappointed that women voters had not responded to her. However, her boldness sometimes drove people away and affected her ability to reach her goals. For example, she broke with T. Thomas Fortune because of his inability to work with white reformers, and she was in constant conflict with the conciliatory diplomatic policies of Booker T. WASHINGTON. She supported the militant ideology of W. E. B. DU BOIS, but her inability to moderate her views diminished her leadership in the NACW and the NAACP.

Shortly before dying of uremia, Wells wrote in her autobiography: "All at once the realization came to me that I had nothing to show for all those years of toil and labor." Echoes of her voice, however, reverberate throughout the late twentieth century in various civil rights acts passed from 1957 to 1991, but especially the CIVIL RIGHTS ACT OF 1968 and the VOTING RIGHTS ACT OF 1965. A Chicago housing project, a residential national historic landmark, a commemorative marker on Beale Street in Memphis, and a postage stamp visibly mark her place in the history of the struggle for civil rights.

SUGGESTED READINGS:

Sterling, Dorothy. *Black Foremothers: Three Lives*. New York: Feminist Press, 1979.

Thompson, Mildred I. *Ida B. Wells-Barnett: An Exploratory Study of an American Black Woman, 1893-1930*. Brooklyn, N.Y.: Carlson Publishing, 1990.

Trimieu, Darryl M. *Voices of the Silenced: The Responsible Self in a Marginalized Community*. Cleveland, Ohio: Pilgrim Press, 1993.

Wells-Barnett, Ida B. *Crusade for Justice: The Autobiography of Ida B. Wells*. Edited by Alfreda M. Duster. Chicago: University of Chicago Press, 1970.

_____. *The Memphis Diary of Ida B. Wells*. Edited by Miriam DeCosta-Willis. Boston: Beacon Press, 1995.

_____. *Selected Works of Ida B. Wells-Barnett*. Compiled by Trudier Harris. New York: Oxford University Press, 1991.

—*Cassandra S. Gissendanner*

White, Walter Francis

July 1, 1893, Atlanta, Ga.—March 21, 1955, New York, N.Y.: Executive secretary of the NATIONAL ASSOCIATION FOR THE ADVANCEMENT OF COLORED PEOPLE (NAACP).

A light-skinned man of mixed-race background, White chose to identify with his African American heritage and devoted his life to the struggle for civil rights. He joined the NAACP as its assistant executive secretary in New York in 1918 and spent his

Although Walter White could have easily "passed" as a white person, he chose to be identified as an African American and worked tirelessly for the NAACP. (*Schomburg Center for Research in Black Culture, New York Public Library*)

entire career with the organization. He used his Caucasian appearance to infiltrate communities in the SOUTH in order to investigate LYNCHINGS and RACE RIOTS. Trusted by those who believed he was white, he was able to obtain inside information that he then publicized, propelling the NAACP's campaign against lynching and its push for the passage of antilynching legislation. His book *Rope and Faggot: A Biography of Judge Lynch* (1929) was widely read and influenced public opinion about lynching. White exposed the economic underpinnings of mob violence against blacks and linked lynching with the popularity of religious fundamentalism in the South, with its rejection of new ideas and sanctions against sexual freedoms. White was convinced that detailed exposure of racial violence would bring about public discussion of the practice and thus public outrage and reform.

When White became executive secretary of the NAACP in 1931, the association combined its investigations of violent incidents with ongoing lobbying of Congress to win federal antilynching laws. White specialized in administering the NAACP's legal committee, working closely with its head, Arthur B. Spingarn. During the Depression and the beginning of World War II he helped to build coalitions between the NAACP and other groups, including church, labor, and women's organizations that were working in support of New Deal-related reforms. They pressured the federal government to end POLL TAXES that discriminated against poor black voters, to desegregate the American MILITARY, and to make provisions for FAIR EMPLOYMENT PRACTICES for blacks in government-related work, as well as endorse the campaign to end lynching. White also supported the international pan-African movement and the decolonization of Africa.

White published his autobiography, *A Man Called White* (1948), and several other books. He also wrote a syndicated newspaper column, maintained a heavy speaking schedule, and hosted a radio show about public policies. All his activities were directed at keeping civil rights issues alive in the public mind. Although the administrative power White had within the NAACP decreased after 1950, he remained executive secretary until his death from a heart attack. His death occurred not long after the NAACP won important legal victories in its fight for school desegregation, a campaign that he had helped to structure.

—*Barbara Bair*

White supremacism

Belief that Christians of European ancestry are superior to members of other races, whom they should dominate.

White supremacism entered North America with the first European settlers. As early as the sixteenth century Europeans enslaved and murdered Native Americans and Africans. The belief that whites were superior to other people merely by virtue of their race, and that they were entitled to greater protection of the laws, still lingered among some Americans at the end of the twentieth century.

White Supremacism in American History Many of the first Europeans who settled in America believed that whites were culturally, spiritually, and perhaps even physically, more advanced than other races. These beliefs were used to justify the murder, conquest, and enslavement of Africans and Native Americans. Taken for granted in the early United States, white supremacism was supported by the legal system. Federal and state legislation permitted African American SLAVERY and racial discrimination. In cases such as the famous DRED SCOTT CASE (1857), the U.S. SUPREME COURT refused to grant nonwhites the same legal rights and protections to which whites were entitled.

By the mid-nineteenth century many white Americans opposed some of the trappings of white supremacism, such as slavery. This opposition was a major impetus behind the CIVIL WAR. After the war, amendments to the U.S. CONSTITUTION were passed that abolished slavery; granted citizenship to all people born in the United States, regardless of race; and provided for the equal protection of all citizens by the law. Congress also passed a series of CIVIL RIGHTS ACTS designed to provide federal protection for the former slaves. At the same time, however, the first organized white supremacist group, the KU KLUX KLAN (KKK), was created.

The first organized white supremacist group in America, the KKK was created shortly after the end of the Civil War. It soon engaged in a campaign to terrorize African Americans and keep them from gaining social, political, or economic power in the South. The Klan dissolved in the early 1870's, partly as a result of the federal civil rights laws and partly because it became less necessary after southern whites regained control of their state governments.

In the late nineteenth and early twentieth centuries, white supremacy remained a common belief in America. Laws were passed that made life for non-whites nearly as intolerable as it had been for African Americans under slavery. In 1896 the Supreme Court held, in PLESSY V. FERGUSON, that segregated facilities were not unconstitutional. People of color were also frequently subjected to POLL TAXES and other mechanisms that removed their ability to vote. White supremacism reached a peak in the early 1900's. This was caused, in part, by the great waves of IMMIGRATION that were occurring at the time, by nationalist feelings brought about by World War I, and by attempts of southern white aristocrats to defeat the agrarian Populists.

The KKK was reborn, reaching an all time high of perhaps four million members in 1925. This time, many of its members lived in the North, the Midwest, and the West. Animosity toward foreigners and people of color became so socially acceptable that President Warren G. Harding was sworn into the Klan in a ceremony at the White House. At least one Supreme Court justice was also a member of the Klan. The film *The Birth of a Nation*, which was released in 1915 and was wildly popular, consisted largely of Klan propaganda. White supremacy at this time was more than just a belief; it was also often the catalyst of racist actions. On a federal level, anti-immigration laws were passed, that discriminated against Jews and nonwhites. Many states also had ANTIMISCEGENATION LAWS, which provided for the criminal punishment of whites and people of color who intermarried.

White supremacists also terrorized and murdered people of color throughout the United States, sometimes even destroying entire communities. Between 1889 and 1941, nearly four thousand African Americans were victims of LYNCHING. Law enforcement personnel frequently turned a blind eye to these atrocities and sometimes even participated in them.

Although membership in the KKK shrank rapidly during the Depression, white supremacy remained a way of life in America. For example, most military units during World War II were segregated by race. In addition, thousands of JAPANESE AMERICANS who lived on the West Coast, most of whom were American citizens, were ordered into internment camps during the war. Many of these people lost their homes and businesses. American Jews were also often victimized by people who blamed them for the U.S involvement in the war, or who sympathized with Nazi ideals.

Significant gains were achieved for people of

color during the CIVIL RIGHTS MOVEMENT of the 1950's and 1960's. These gains came at great cost, however, as many of those who fought for civil rights were terrorized, beaten, or murdered by white supremacists. Across the South, black churches were bombed. In MISSISSIPPI, Emmett Till, a fourteen-year-old black youth was lynched merely because he had allegedly whistled at a white woman. In these cases, the wrongdoers were infrequently punished by a judicial system that was almost entirely white.

Change did come gradually. The U.S. Supreme Court finally overruled *Plessy v. Ferguson* and declared segregation unconstitutional. The Court also overturned antimiscegenation laws. Congress passed another series of civil rights acts, and the federal government stepped in to prosecute white supremacists who had not been prosecuted by the states. Change did not come easily, however; many Americans still believed in white supremacy.

The Late Twentieth Century The 1970's through the 1990's saw a change in the face of American white supremacy. A bewildering number of supremacist groups emerged, often with a tangled web of ties to one another. These groups were driven by different motives than earlier groups, were more often located in the West and Midwest than the South, and were often able to cloak their true intents. Nonetheless, like the old KKK, their primary goal was to ensure white supremacy. Examples of white supremacist groups of the late twentieth century include neo-Nazis, Christian Identity groups, militia groups, and skinheads.

One thread among these groups was the second resurgence of the KKK. Although its membership never approached what it had been in the 1920's, the Klan refused to disappear. Many Klan leaders went on to found other white supremacist groups, such as Tom Metzger of California. Others were elected to political office, such as David Duke of Louisiana. However, the Klan was partially crippled by lawsuits (including a seven-million-dollar judgment in favor of a woman whose son was lynched by Klan members) and was largely eclipsed by newer, more vital groups. A second thread of white supremacism was neo-Nazi groups. While Nazi ideologies had been popular among a few Americans as early as the 1930's, they became most popular in the 1970's. Groups of this kind, though primarily anti-Semitic, also disliked people of color.

A third thread of white supremacy is known as the Christian Identity Church movement, which preaches white supremacism as a primary tenet. Many Identity members believe that a cataclysmic race war will occur in the United States and that whites must be prepared to seize "their" territory. Most Identity groups are highly distrustful of the U.S. government, believing that it is dominated by Jews and other minorities. The Identity movement gained many members in the Midwest during the farm crisis of the 1980's; some farmers who were facing economic disaster found it easy to blame the government and minorities for their troubles. Identity groups included the Aryan Nations, which advocated dividing the United States into separate nations on the basis of race; the Order, which led a series of armed robberies and other criminal acts; and the Posse Comitatus, which advocated that all political power be vested at the county level.

A fourth thread of white supremacy has been the youth movement. In the 1980's, as America turned more and more toward a service economy and as many industrial jobs disappeared, some members of the working class became disillusioned. They saw America as no longer offering them opportunity. Young people were particularly disturbed, as they saw no future for themselves. Some of these youth were actively recruited into white supremacist groups, such as the skinheads and the White Aryan Resistance (WAR). Many of these groups took advantage of modern communication technology to spread their beliefs. WAR, for example, operated both a toll-free hotline and a site on the World Wide Web. Some of the youth groups were prone to violence. Others took to wearing suits and attempted to create an image of respectability.

A final thread in late-twentieth century white supremacism has been militias and other survivalist groups. These groups were often heavily armed and highly distrustful of the government. They have been responsible for acts of violence, as well as schemes to defraud the government and others out of money. They have often refused to pay taxes. In some cases, their members have declared themselves citizens of self-created countries, claiming to be immune from state and federal laws. While not all of these groups were racist, many were.

In sum, white supremacism had diversified greatly by the 1990's. Some supremacists sought to achieve respectability, often by emphasizing positions similar to those of the mainstream political Right. Their targets had also changed; while early Klan members focused on intimidating African

California Ku Klux Klan leader Tom Metzger made deportation of aliens a major plank in his failed effort to run for the U.S. Senate in 1982. (*AP/Wide World Photos*)

Americans, Roman Catholics, and Jews, the newer groups focused on gays, Asians, and Latinos.

Not all white supremacists have belonged to organized groups. Indeed, by the late twentieth century, it had often become difficult to differentiate some views of white supremacist groups from those of mainstream political groups. For example, many white supremacist groups supported eliminating AFFIRMATIVE ACTION, restricting immigration, reducing welfare, getting "tough on crime," and enacting ENGLISH-ONLY laws—just as many Democrats and Republicans did.

Several factors have contributed to the continuing existence of white supremacist beliefs. One is economics; people who face financial difficulties often look for someone to blame, and people of color are often easy to scapegoat. Another likely factor is parenting. Psychological research suggests that authoritarian parenting techniques are more likely to make children receptive to adopting prejudiced beliefs. Ignorance of other cultures and fear of the unknown have also played roles.

The effects of white supremacism have been profound in the United States, from slavery and murder to social and economic degradation. However, there have also been many attempts to combat these effects. These attempts have included establishment of civil rights and HATE CRIME laws; formation of antihate groups, such as the Southern Poverty Law Center's Klanwatch, the ANTI-DEFAMATION League, and the National Association for the Advancement of Colored People; and entire movements to secure civil rights for minority groups.

SUGGESTED READINGS:

Aho, James A. *The Politics of Righteousness: Idaho Christian Patriotism.* Seattle: University of Washington Press, 1990. Discussion of white supremacist groups in the western United States, such as the Order, the Identity Christians, and the Freemen.

Allport, Gordon W. *The Nature of Prejudice.* 1954. Rev. ed. New York: Addison-Wesley, 1979. Classic work on the psychological and sociocultural bases of prejudice.

Dees, Morris, and Steve Fiffer. *Hate on Trial: The Case Against America's Most Dangerous Neo-Nazi.* New York, Villard Books, 1993. Behind-the-scenes look at the case in which the Southern Poverty Law Center obtained a $12.5 million judgment against white supremacist Tom Metzger for the murder of an Ethiopian man.

Ezekiel, Raphael. *The Racist Mind: Portraits of American Neo-Nazis and Klansmen.* New York: Viking Press, 1995. Interviews with white supremacist group members.

Hamm, Mark S. *American Skinheads: The Criminology and Control of Hate Crime.* Westport, Conn.: Praeger, 1993. Sociological exploration of skinheads.

Klanwatch. *The Ku Klux Klan: A History of Racism and Violence.* Montgomery, Ala.: Author, 1982. Well-illustrated series of articles about the history and activities of the Klan.

Loewen, James W. *Lies My Teacher Told Me: Everything Your American History Textbook Got Wrong.* New York: New Press, 1995. Includes chapters on race relations in American history.

Ridgeway, James. *Blood in the Face: The Ku Klux Klan, Aryan Nations, Nazi Skinheads, and the Rise of a New White Culture.* New York: Thunder's Mouth Press, 1990. Descriptions of right-wing racist groups, with many excellent illustrations.

Stanton, Bill. *Klanwatch: Bringing the Ku Klux Klan to Justice.* New York: Mentor, 1992. Discussion of modern Klan activities and the attempts by the Southern Poverty Law Center to stop them.

—*Phyllis B. Gerstenfeld*

White v. Chin Fong

1920: U.S. SUPREME COURT ruling permitting a CHINESE resident to return to the United States after finding that his rights had been violated.

Chin Fong, a merchant who had traveled to China, was denied re-admission to the United States on the grounds that his original entry had been fraudulent. The U.S. Supreme Court ruled that under the applicable treaty with China he had the right to travel back and forth. Further, immigration officials had no authority to deny him that right by reconsidering the validity of his original entry.

—*Milton Berman*

Wilder, Douglas

Born Jan. 17, 1931, Richmond, Va.: AFRICAN AMERICAN civil rights activist and politician; the first black governor of Virginia.

The grandson of slaves, Wilder grew up in the capital city of the former Confederacy. He attended segregated Richmond schools and graduated from Virginia Union University. During the Korean War he won a Bronze Star for bravery and worked to gain promotions for black infantrymen. After earning his law degree at Howard University, he established a highly successful career as a trial lawyer.

In 1969 Wilder became the first African American elected to the Virginia state legislature since the RECONSTRUCTION ERA. He served for sixteen years in the state senate, where he sought the abolishment of racist lyrics in the official state song, worked against entrenched HOUSING DISCRIMINATION, and sought more jobs for minorities and union rights for government employees. Wilder also called for the end of CAPITAL PUNISHMENT, although later as governor he abandoned this position. He was ultimately successful in his struggle to establish a state holiday honoring Martin Luther KING, JR.

In 1985 he was elected Virginia's lieutenant governor with nearly 52 percent of the vote. He considered this victory to be the true breakthrough for blacks in his state. Running as an advocate of ABORTION rights, Wilder defeated Republican J. Marshall Coleman in 1985 to become the first black candidate ever elected governor of any American state. In the close contest he won more 40 percent of the state's white vote. As Virginia's governor Wilder established a reputation for moderation and fiscal austerity in budget matters.

In 1991 he made an unsuccessful bid for the Democratic party's presidential nomination. Prohibited by law from seeking a second consecutive term as governor, Wilder announced in 1993 that he would run for a seat in the United States Senate as an independent. In 1994 he withdrew and backed his political archrival, incumbent Democrat Charles S. Robb, who went on to defeat challenger Oliver North.

—*John E. Santosuosso*

Wiley, George

Feb. 26, 1931, Bayonne, N.J.—Aug. 8, 1973, Chesapeake Bay, Md.: Welfare rights activist and officer in the CONGRESS OF RACIAL EQUALITY (CORE).

Trained as an organic chemist, George Alvin Wiley was teaching chemistry at Syracuse University when he become chairman of Syracuse's CORE chapter in 1961. The following year he and local CORE activists challenged the Syracuse school dis-

George Wiley, a leading advocate of welfare rights during the 1960's. (*Library of Congress*)

trict, which they claimed engaged in de facto segregation of African American students. When the school district agreed to create an integration program in 1963, Wiley received credit for his determined and principled leadership. He caught the attention of CORE's national leaders, who invited him the next year to serve on the national council that formulated CORE policy. In November, 1964, Wiley accepted the position of CORE's national associate director. At that time CORE had severe financial problems and was racked by internal differences regarding organizational goals. Wiley struggled to resolve CORE's financial difficulties, but his continued commitment to racial integration ran counter to the growing influence of BLACK NATIONALISM and separatism within CORE. In 1968, after Wiley lost to Floyd MCKISSICK in his bid to become CORE's national director, he resigned from the organization.

Following his departure from CORE, Wiley became active in protecting the rights of families on welfare. He helped found the National Welfare Rights Organization (NWRO) in 1967. Under his leadership, the NWRO employed both legal and nonviolent protest strategies to ensure that welfare recipients received benefits to which they were legally entitled. After disputes within the NWRO led to Wiley's resignation as executive director in 1973, he founded the Movement for Economic Justice (MEJ), a group dedicated to resolving the inequitable distribution of wealth in the United States. The MEJ continued for three years after Wiley's death in a boating accident in 1973, finally closing its offices in 1976.

—*Thomas Clarkin*

Wilkins, Roy

Aug. 30, 1901, St. Louis, Mo.—Sept. 8, 1981, New York, N.Y.: AFRICAN AMERICAN civil rights activist and officer in the NATIONAL ASSOCIATION FOR THE ADVANCEMENT OF COLORED PEOPLE (NAACP).

A longtime leader of the NAACP, Wilkins was at the center of the CIVIL RIGHTS MOVEMENT. He successfully advocated nonviolent political action to achieve equal rights. Unlike most other civil rights leaders, Wilkins grew up in a stable, largely integrated environment in the Midwest. His generally positive experiences enabled him to see the potential and the benefits of integration. His American heartland background also led to his strong support for a system of law and lifelong adherence to the U.S. CONSTITUTION.

Wilkins' life did not start out that way, however. He was born into a poor family from rural MISSISSIPPI that had escaped the long, violent arms of southern racists by fleeing. Wilkins mother died when he was five; then he and two younger siblings were taken by a maternal aunt and uncle from St. Louis, Missouri, to Minnesota's St. Paul—a mainly white northern city with a sprinkling of generally integrated black families. There they were raised by Elizabeth and Sam Williams, well respected in the community; they were a working-class couple with solid middle-class values. All three Wilkins children went to college at a time when that was rare even for middle-class white families.

Wilkins grew up and thrived in this largely white environment. Most of his playmates and close friends were white, as were all his teachers. Some of his teachers took him under their wing because of his academic abilities, which were fostered by his aunt and uncle. As a youth he liked the police—a feeling he had to unlearn later in his life. Early on, Wilkins was drawn to writing. In high school he edited a school literary magazine and the yearbook. At the University of Minnesota he was a night editor of the university newspaper. In addition, through his college years he held a number of jobs, with the railroad and as a clean-up man in the stockyards. His early interest in writing and in communal affairs also landed him a job as editor of the weekly African American NEWSPAPER, *St. Paul Appeal*. At the same time, he served as secretary of a local NAACP chapter.

While in college Wilkins was deeply touched by the LYNCHING of three African American men in Duluth, Minnesota, close to his home. He not only used the theme in an oratory contest (in which he won third prize), but the event made the horror stories of the South real, making up for the general absence of unpleasant encounters with racism in his own life.

Early Professional Life Wilkins' interest in journalism and his growing interest in African American affairs led him to take a job in 1923 with the *Kansas City Call*, an important but underfunded African American weekly. Hard work led to his elevation as managing editor. He also courted and married Aminda (Minnie) Ann Badeau in 1929; his marriage lasted until his death fifty-two years later. Meanwhile, in Kansas City, Missouri, Wilkins experienced at first hand the oppression of African Americans. He described it as a JIM CROW town, through and through. It was there that he first suffered personally the indignities of SEGREGATION. As a result, he became more involved in city-wide NAACP activities, eventually serving as branch secretary. He organized a BOYCOTT of segregated theaters and campaigned for voters to reject bonds that supported segregation.

Through his roles as managing editor and chief editorial writer, NAACP functionary, and effective political activist he met a number of nationally prominent African American thinkers and organizational leaders. In 1931 NAACP executive secretary Walter WHITE asked Wilkins to serve as the organization's assistant secretary. Wilkins then moved to New York, where he spent the rest of his life, in a position that afforded him access to some of the most prominent and powerful people in the country.

View from the Top Over time, Wilkins became the dominant figure in the NAACP, the oldest, the largest, and arguably the most influential of the African American civil rights organizations. In addition to serving as the NAACP's executive secretary, he was given the important job of editor of the national magazine *The Crisis* when W. E. B. DU BOIS resigned in 1934; he held the position for fifteen years. In 1941 he became a consultant to the War Department on the training and placement of African Americans in the MILITARY. In April, 1945, he along with White and Du Bois were consultants to the American delegation at the UNITED NATIONS Conference in San Francisco. In the late 1940's he became a regular panel discussant on a New York weekly radio show, *Pride and Prejudice.* In 1949 and 1950 he was chairman of the National Emergency Civil Rights Mobilization, an umbrella organization composed of more than a hundred local and national groups.

Also in 1949, Wilkins was appointed the NAACP's acting executive secretary when White took a year-long leave of absence. When White died in 1955, Wilkins was appointed his permanent replacement. In August, 1963, he helped organize the seminal MARCH ON WASHINGTON, at which he was a featured speaker. He served on the important 1967 Presidential Commission on Civil Disorders. In 1968 he was chairman of the U.S. delegation to the International Conference on Human Rights.

Wilkins changed the NAACP, facilitating its growth and role as the preeminent civil rights organization. By keeping doors open to members of both the white and African American middle classes, Wilkins expanded the organization's membership and budget. To his success in lobbying, developing educational programs, and taking legal action, he added direct political action: protests, marches, sit-ins, economic boycotts, and voter-registration drives. Throughout his adult life, Wilkins fought for equal rights for African Americans. He pressed hard for a federal antilynching law; its failure was one of the most enduring disappointments and frustrations of his life. Nevertheless, it is clear that groups such as the NAACP helped lower the incidence of LYNCHING by raising levels of political protest and through public discussions in the Congress, where antilynching legislation was invariably blocked by southern filibusters.

Wilkins also personally participated in pushing the government to desegregate military facilities. He supported the efforts by A. Philip RANDOLPH to get the government to desegregate the defense industry. Along with others, Wilkins' efforts—expressed in countless meetings with both civil rights and government agencies—led to President Harry S Truman's 1948 EXECUTIVE ORDER 9981 to desegregate the armed services. Wilkins was strongly committed to eliminating EMPLOYMENT DISCRIMINATION. Beyond this, he pushed for equality across many spheres and was supportive of the judicial process that led to eliminating the legal barriers in politics, in the SCHOOLS, in HOUSING, in PUBLIC ACCOMMODATIONS, and in TRANSPORTATION. The NAACP was best known for its role in the Supreme Court's landmark BROWN V. BOARD OF EDUCATION OF TOPEKA, KANSAS (1954) decision, but it was a major force in every significant civil rights case during this period. Although Wilkins did not personally argue cases before the Court—as did Thurgood MARSHALL—or go out and organize in the field, he helped steer the course that led to the dramatic improvement of racial minorities.

Wilkins wore several hats. For many years he was a writer and an editor, working to present issues to the largely African American public. In addition, he oversaw the business work of the NAACP, and he helped keep alive and flourishing an organization that often faced serious financial strictures. Wilkins was also a key player in policy decisions—what areas to emphasize, how to reach alliances, whom to lobby, what political tactics to follow. For the most important protests and marches, his body was on the line; on several occasions he was arrested for CIVIL DISOBEDIENCE.

In addition, because of his writing and speaking abilities and his quiet and dignified demeanor, Wilkins was often an ambassador to the white world—both within the United States and to the world at large. He testified regularly before congressional committees and government agencies; he spoke before both Democratic and Republican platform committees in the 1960's; he conferred with every president from Harry S Truman to Gerald Ford; he appeared regularly on radio; and he wrote extensively for both African American and general publications.

Splits Within the Movement Wilkins' defining characteristics were commitment, longevity, stability, and political acumen. He was at the center of the action for a long time, and his support for the cause of civil rights was unswerving. He believed in support for integration, for liberal democracy, and for the United States. He wanted change to occur quickly but nonviolently, in part because he understood that with the escalation of violence, African Americans would ultimately be the losers. However, he was not a pacifist; he believed in self-defense but strongly preferred avoiding situations where it would be necessary. He kept the door open to white America, arguing that without some level of support, especially from the powerful, the progress of racial minorities would be limited. In all these ideas, he was steadfast.

As a result of his commitments, Wilkins was always battling somewhere. For most of his life he fought against white racists who opposed change and against so-called moderates who wanted to limit protest and who trusted in the system's ability to self-correct. He attacked the idea of "all deliberate speed" in the dismantling of segregation, noting that to racists, "slow going" meant "no going."

Wilkins and the mainstream Civil Rights movement also faced opponents on the left. From the 1930's through the 1950's, Wilkins did battle with members of the COMMUNIST PARTY who sought to channel discontent with the treatment of African Americans to a larger agenda of overthrowing capitalism. Wilkins distrusted communist denials of democratic processes, freedom, and religion, which were vitally important to African Americans.

Later, particularly starting in the mid-1960's, mainstream nonviolent groups, such as the NAACP and the NATIONAL URBAN LEAGUE, came increasingly under challenge from more militant organizations, such as the radicalized STUDENT NON-VIOLENT COORDINATING COMMITTEE (SNCC) and the CONGRESS OF RACIAL EQUALITY (CORE), two proponents of the BLACK POWER movement. New and young leaders, such as Stokely CARMICHAEL and H. Rap BROWN, wanted African Americans to have complete control over their political lives, so they forced whites out of their organizations. Quickly, the demand for African American autonomy expanded to economics, social relations, and culture—to the BLACK NATIONALISM of Du Bois and, among a small minority, the back-to-Africa movement of Marcus GARVEY. Perhaps most threatening thing to Wilkins was the Black Power movements's advocacy of violence.

Wilkins was a frequent target for black radicals because of his nonideological position, his acceptance of the American political system, his per-

ceived willingness to compromise, and his public role and the importance of his position among mainstream civil rights organizations. Because of the need to keep pro-civil rights forces together, Wilkins opposed Martin Luther KING, JR.'s transition to public antiwar protester. Wilkins himself did not support the war, but he thought the primary task of civil rights leaders was to promote the rights of African Americans; moreover, he was reluctant to condemn his ally Lyndon B. JOHNSON.

At one point the attacks on Wilkins became sufficiently threatening that he needed police protection. It must have been particularly demoralizing and personally insulting for him to be accused by young African Americans of being part of the American establishment when he had devoted his whole professional and private life to his race. Nevertheless, he maintained his decorum and civility without ever withdrawing from the cause. Almost by instinct, Wilkins opposed black separatism as he had opposed segregation of African Americans by whites. His main thrusts were on political equality and equal economic opportunity within the American democratic tradition. He argued that African Americans were citizens and as such were entitled to the full equal protection of the laws guaranteed by the FOURTEENTH AMENDMENT to the Constitution.

Wilkins was a political realist. African Americans were a small minority of the population (about 11 percent) and they could not impose change either through political or economic force or through armed rebellion, a scenario that frightened him. Their political leverage against Republican presidents was limited because they voted in large numbers for their Democratic opponents. They could not take over local political office until they first won the VOTING RIGHTS long denied them in the South despite the FIFTEENTH AMENDMENT. Even united, however, their economic power could not force large corporations to make dramatic changes in hiring procedures (this has changed over time), nor could they compel father-and-son trade unions to integrate completely. Moreover, as a leader of the most important civil rights organization, Wilkins had to worry about his own constituency and not alienating those with differences of opinion within the organization.

Although Wilkins grew up in an integrated and largely white environment, he lived most of his adult life within the African American community

Roy Wilkins, head of the National Association for the Advancement of Colored People from 1955 to 1977. (*Library of Congress*)

physically, socially, and culturally. During his eight years in Kansas City and for many years in Harlem, he lived in African American ghettos. It was only toward the end of his life—when Harlem had deteriorated seriously—that he moved to an integrated neighborhood in Queens. Throughout his adult life he was a member of the black African Methodist Episcopal Church. Although he had access to many white politicians and industry leaders, his main political and social confidantes were African American. His own musical tastes leaned toward an African American jazz. He was familiar with the main currents in African American literature and frequently attended black theater. Although he was committed to integration and—much more than most African Americans—felt comfortable in the larger American world, he lived much of his private adult life within the African American world.

Awards and Accomplishments For good reason, Roy Wilkins was often referred to as the senior statesman of the Civil Rights movement, sometimes called "Mr. Civil Rights." He was at the center of power longer than almost all other leaders. He had access to the highest levels of office—both governmental and business. He once remarked that President Lyndon B. Johnson said to him after one of countless discussions they had during the president's push for civil rights: "I'm always calling you. Why don't you call *me* more often?"

Wilkins' contributions benefitted both African Americans and the larger American citizenry. He was a lifelong activist who pushed hard for the elimination of injustice and for the leveling of the economic playing field. A testimony to his efforts is the fact that most of his political goals were accomplished: the end of lynching, elimination of segregated primaries, several powerful CIVIL RIGHTS ACTS, the widespread election of African Americans to political office, inclusion of African Americans in juries, legal representation of poor African Americans in the judicial system, integration of the armed services, and both FAIR EMPLOYMENT and fair HOUSING laws.

For his work, Wilkins received numerous accolades. Among them was the University of Minnesota's Outstanding Achievement Award (1960), the Spingarn Medal (1964), the U.S. Medal of Freedom (1968), and the Joseph Prize for Human Rights (1975). In partial recognition from those who knew him best, his own house, he was made director emeritus of the NAACP on his retirement in 1977.

SUGGESTED READINGS:

Cashman, Sean Dennis. *African-Americans and the Quest for Civil Rights, 1900-1990*. New York: New York University Press, 1991. Well-written and straight-forward narrative.

Meier, August, John Bracey, Jr., and Elliot Rudwick. *Black Protest in the Sixties*. New York: Markus Wiener Publishing, 1991. Collection of *New York Times Magazine* articles including one on Wilkins.

Ross, B. Joyce. *J. E. Spingarn and the Rise of the NAACP, 1911-1939*. New York: Atheneum, 1972. Useful inside account of the NAACP.

Weisbrot, Robert. *Freedom Bound: A History of America's Civil Rights Movement*. New York: Norton, 1990. Scholarly but readable, comprehensive history of the movement.

White, John. *Black Leadership in America: From Booker T. Washington to Jesse Jackson*. 2nd ed. London: Longman, 1990. Simple but useful overview of positions on integration and separation.

Wilkins, Roy. *Talking It Over: Selected Speeches and Writings*. Norwalk, Conn.: M & B Publishing, 1977. Wilkins' own speeches on a wide variety of topics.

Wilkins, Roy, with Tom Mathews. *Standing Fast: The Autobiography of Roy Wilkins*. New York: Viking Press, 1982. Best all-around source on Wilkins' life and thought.

—*Alan M. Fisher*

Williams, Franklin H.

Born Oct. 22, 1917, Flushing, N.Y.: NATIONAL ASSOCIATION FOR THE ADVANCEMENT OF COLORED PEOPLE (NAACP) officer and statesman.

Williams was the assistant special counsel of the NAACP from 1945 to 1950 and director of the NAACP's West Coast office in California from 1950 to 1959. Williams then embarked on a political career and became assistant attorney general of the state of California in 1959 to 1960. After the election of President John F. KENNEDY, Williams became African regional director of the Peace Corps, one of Kennedy's favorite programs of international outreach and volunteerism. Williams built on his international experience with the Peace Corps by becoming the United States representative to the United Nations Economic and Social Council in 1963.

During the administration of President Lyndon B. JOHNSON Williams was appointed U.S. ambassador to Ghana, remaining in that position until 1968. Williams worked to further the stature of African Americans in foreign service, and as an ambassador he headed the Association of Black Ambassadors and helped to chair the Council of American Ambassadors. In the latter part of his career, Williams turned to urban reform and international philanthropy as fields of activism. He became the director of the Urban Center at Columbia University and president of the influential Phelps-Stokes Fund, as well as a member of the board of directors of several major corporations.

—*Barbara Bair*

Williams, Hosea

Born Jan. 5, 1926, Attapulgus, Ga.: Civil rights activist and officer in the SOUTHERN CHRISTIAN LEADERSHIP CONFERENCE (SCLC).

Clergyman and publisher Hosea Williams was a key activist and leader in the SCLC. He took part in a string of SCLC actions, including major SIT-INS, BOYCOTTS, STRIKES, marches, and demonstrations, and was frequently jailed for his participation in SCLC causes. Among the actions in which he participated as an outside organizer were the demonstrations and sit-ins at St. Augustine, Florida, in 1964. During those actions Williams was arrested when he and others waded into the water at a segregated all-white beach. Soon afterward he was chosen to head SCLC's voter registration campaigns.

Williams was active in the movement registering voters in SELMA, ALABAMA, in 1965, and was walking at the head of the peaceful march there when it was attacked by state troopers. In the wake of Selma, Williams proposed and headed SCOPE, a campaign to recruit and send teams of hundreds of SCLC staff workers and volunteers into rural communities and cities of the South to register black voters. Williams was one of the founders, and the first president, of the ATLANTA branch of the SCLC from 1967 to 1969. He became SCLC national executive director in 1969, serving in that capacity until 1971. From 1970 to 1971 he was also regional vice president of the SCLC.

In 1961 Williams began publishing the *Crusader* newspaper, which he produced for many years; in 1972 he became the pastor of the Martin Luther King, Jr., People's Church of Love. He was elected to the Georgia state legislature in 1974 and became a member of the Atlanta city council after leaving state office. He was also an adviser to the president during the administration of Ronald REAGAN.

—*Barbara Bair*

Williams, Robert Franklin

Born 1925: NATIONAL ASSOCIATION FOR THE ADVANCEMENT OF COLORED PEOPLE (NAACP) officer and militant activist.

Williams was the president of the Monroe, North Carolina, chapter of the NAACP during the emergence of the CIVIL RIGHTS MOVEMENT in the late 1950's. Faced with repeated acts of racial VIOLENCE, racially motivated HATE CRIMES, and efforts on the part of local white supremacists to terrorize supporters of the NAACP, Williams decided that the focus of the NAACP on the use of public activism to win constitutional and legislative reforms was not sufficient to ensure lasting freedom and protection for African Americans. Instead, he championed the principle of armed self-defense. He organized a rifle corps of African American men, who helped protect the home of a local NAACP officer when it was invaded by members of the KU KLUX KLAN, and he urged other local NAACP groups to similarly prepare themselves in order to be able to protect members from racial attack. Williams' radical approach disturbed the national leadership of the organization; in 1959 both he and his chapter were expelled from the NAACP. Williams continued to advocate the use of armed resistance to protect African Americans from racial harm and argued that equal rights would never be achieved without open rebellion. He published his views in *Negroes with Guns* in 1962.

—*Barbara Bair*

Wilson, Margaret Bush

Born Jan. 30, 1919, St. Louis, Mo.: NATIONAL ASSOCIATION FOR THE ADVANCEMENT OF COLORED PEOPLE (NAACP) chairperson and Missouri civil rights leader.

Wilson chaired the national board of the NAACP from 1974 to 1983. Mary White Ovington, one of the founders of the NAACP, had served as the first female chairperson of the organization from 1917 to 1932, but Wilson was the first black woman appointed to that position. In the early 1980's she came into internal administrative conflict with NAACP executive director Benjamin HOOKS, raising questions about SEXUAL DISCRIMINATION within the rights organization.

Both of Wilson's parents were active NAACP members in St. Louis, and she herself grew up surrounded by organization activism. As a young lawyer in the 1940's she helped her father, James T. Bush, draft the framework for SHELLEY V. KRAEMER, an NAACP test case which in 1948 resulted in the U.S. Supreme Court ruling that RESTRICTIVE COVENANTS in residential real estate contracts were unconstitutional. In 1948 she made an unsuccessful run for Congress on the Progressive Party ticket, while becoming the first black woman to be a candidate for Congress in Missouri. Afterward she specialized in real estate law and worked in private practice before becoming an assistant attorney general in St. Louis in 1961.

Wilson meanwhile remained dedicated to leadership in the NAACP. In 1958 she was elected president of the local NAACP chapter, and in 1962 she became president of the conference overseeing all the branches in the state of Missouri. She joined the NAACP national executive board in 1963, the same year she participated in the MARCH ON WASHINGTON. In the mid-1960's she worked on special task forces on housing and urban reform issues as part of the Lyndon B. JOHNSON administration's War on Poverty. She was a founder of the Model Housing Corporation and deputy directory of the St. Louis Model Cities Agency in the late 1960's, as well as treasurer of the NAACP National Housing Corporation, helping minority community members gain federal help in housing construction. She also worked in a number of other capacities to further the cause of the black poor and provide affordable housing in Missouri, and she became involved in the campaign to desegregate the city school system in ATLANTA, GEORGIA. As chairperson of the NAACP, she called for the impeachment of President Richard M. NIXON and emphasized the organization's activism on employment, housing, and education issues. After she left her NAACP office, Wilson returned to private law practice in St. Louis.

—Barbara Bair

Wilson, Woodrow

Dec. 28, 1856, Staunton, Va.—Feb. 3, 1924, Washington, D.C.: Twenty-eighth PRESIDENT of the United States (1913-1921).

Regarded as a relatively strong advocate of civil rights for minorities and women during his time, President Wilson created the National War Labor Board to mediate labor disputes and to reduce the discrimination that was causing racial conflict and threatening the war effort During WORLD WAR I. He also supported the NINETEENTH AMENDMENT that gave women the right to vote. However, Wilson also shared some of the racial attitudes of his Southern background. Shortly after he was inaugurated to his first term as president, he stunned his African American supporters by signing an executive order to segregate the restrooms and eating facilities used by federal civil servants.

—William L. Waugh, Jr.

Woman suffrage movement

1848-1920: National movement to guarantee women the right to vote.

From 1848 until 1920 suffrage was the dominant issue in the WOMEN'S RIGHTS movement, as it was considered the key to effecting other reforms. Before the movement culminated in ratification of the NINETEENTH AMENDMENT to the U.S. CONSTITUTION in 1920, woman suffrage was not entirely unknown. In some early North American colonies women had exercised limited VOTING RIGHTS, and women had voted in New Jersey under its constitution of 1776. However, the idea of universal woman suffrage dates from the mid-nineteenth century.

Before the suffrage movement arose, American women had organized numerous reform societies, particularly within the temperance and ABOLITION movements. This was partly because women were often denied leadership roles in existing male-dominated organizations. The general attitude was that a woman's sphere was the private and domestic, a man's sphere the public. However, many male leaders supported women's reform activities. For example, Frederick DOUGLASS and William Lloyd Garrison encouraged abolitionist activities by women such as Angelina GRIMKÉ and Sarah GRIMKÉ. The Quakers even accorded religious leadership roles to women such as Lucretia MOTT.

In 1840 a World Anti-Slavery Convention took place in London, England. American delegates included Mott and her husband, James Mott, as well as Garrison, Henry Stanton, and the latter's wife, Elizabeth Cady STANTON. A major controversy erupted over seating the American women delegates on the floor of the convention. Lucretia and other women delegates, as well as visitors like Elizabeth, were relegated to a spot behind a curtain and were not allowed to participate. Garrison objected to such discrimination and sat with the women. Mott and Stanton spent much of their time in London discussing women's position in society, agreeing that they must organize women to bring about change, just as the abolition movement had been organized to abolish SLAVERY. After their returned to the United States, they corresponded for several years, but with no opportunity for action. Stanton was busy raising children. Things changed in 1848, however. That year the organized women's movement, begat by the abolition movement, was born at the Seneca Falls Convention.

Located in upstate New York, Seneca Falls was the home of the Stanton family. There, in the summer of 1848, Mott and Stanton renewed their commitment of 1840. With three other friends they planned a convention on women's rights, announcing it through a local newspaper. Their agenda touched on all the disabilities of women that they had previously discussed, such as the property rights and legal status of married women, EMPLOYMENT DISCRIMINATION, and the status of women in the churches. Over Mott's rather scandalized opposition, Elizabeth insisted on adding woman suffrage to the list of issues. Frederick Douglass, a prominent black abolitionist leader from nearby Rochester, had arrived on the scene and promised to speak in favor of the suffrage proposal. Thus began a tradition of mutual support between abolitionists and suffragists.

When the convention took place in late July, its attendance astounded everyone. More than three hundred people from fifty miles around attended; they were mainly women but included forty men. James Mott, a revered abolitionist leader, was asked to preside over the convention the first day because none of the women felt competent to do so. On the second day, however, Stanton came into her own as speaker and leader. She began by describing the need for new roles for women and by presenting the Seneca Falls DECLARATION OF SENTIMENTS pre-

pared by the planning committee. Adapting the form and style of the DECLARATION OF INDEPENDENCE, this document affirmed that all men and women are created equal, but that men have usurped the citizenship and other rights of women. The subsequent resolutions, agreed upon by the committee, were nearly all adopted unanimously. However, the resolution that called for giving women the vote passed by only the smallest of margins. Politics was then considered a man's world of rough talk and dirty deals, through which women, as guardians of the good, should not sully themselves by voting. Woman suffrage as a cause in its own right would be many years in gaining acceptance.

After Seneca Falls women's rights soon developed into a recognized movement. From 1848 to 1860 a host of national, state, and local women's rights meetings took place, coordinated by a central committee of women leaders. The movement never took root in the South—probably because it was closely associated with the abolitionist movement. The newspapers reporting on the women's rights meetings often ridiculed them; cartoonists in particular made fun of them. Meanwhile many new leaders joined the movement; among them were Lucy STONE, Ernestine Rose, Amelia Bloomer, and Antoinette Brown. A number of early speakers and organizers were free black women, such as Harriet Purvis, Sarah Remond, and evangelist Sojourner TRUTH—who understood that emancipation would not be complete without the vote.

The most important new leader was Susan B. ANTHONY, whose name would eventually be attached to the Nineteenth Amendment. As a teacher and a temperance worker in Rochester, she had encountered discrimination in both fields. While visiting friends in Seneca Falls in 1851, she met Stanton and the two women began a lifelong friendship and partnership in the cause of women's rights. Anthony was the research person, the collector of information, the organizer; Stanton the creative orator and speech writer. However, Anthony also became a powerful speaker in her own right. Both women were indefatigable campaigners who would dominate the nineteenth century movement. The press gradually abandoned its hostile ridicule in favor of factual coverage. But public opinion changed only gradually.

Post-Civil War Militancy After the CIVIL WAR began in 1861, the Union war effort crowded out women's rights. Meanwhile, Stanton and Anthony tried to keep abolition and women's rights before the public as twin issues, to be resolved together. In 1863 they formed the National Woman's Loyal League to campaign for abolition of slavery throughout the whole country—including the South. Their league was instrumental in getting the THIRTEENTH AMENDMENT passed. However, the close cooperation of women and abolitionists shattered when the FOURTEENTH and FIFTEENTH AMENDMENTS guaranteed CITIZENSHIP rights, including the vote, to males of all races, but not to women. The league protested strenuously, but Douglass told them this was "the Negro's hour." If women demanded suffrage at the same time as recently emancipated slaves, probably no one would receive the vote. Sojourner Truth disagreed, maintaining that black women should have the vote along with black men, but to no avail. The American Equal Rights Association was formed in 1866 to promote universal suffrage for all men and women; but it soon divided into woman suffrage and black suffrage wings. By 1870 the FIFTEENTH AMENDMENT was ratified, without woman suffrage. The women felt betrayed, after their long support of abolition. The achievement of abolition left votes for women the sole issue.

Two new organizations were formed in 1869, the NATIONAL WOMAN SUFFRAGE ASSOCIATION (NWSA) and the American Woman Suffrage Association (AWSA). The NWSA, led by Stanton and Anthony, went so far as to campaign against ratification of the Fifteenth Amendment because it omitted women. Thereafter its program was eclectic, promoting not only a federal amendment for woman suffrage, but divorce right reform and church reform for women, antagonizing traditionalists who feared assaults on the sanctity of the home. The NWSA accepted the support of free love advocate Victoria Woodhull, of anti-immigrant "nativists," and of racist Democrat George Train. In the outraged eyes of Stanton and Anthony, educated white women deserved the right to vote more than "ignorant" former slaves and CHINESE AMERICANS. This would continue to be a theme of the NWSA, which accepted support from anyone who would support woman suffrage.

The AWSA, led by Lucy Stone, had the larger membership, including mainstream suffragists who eschewed other more radical women's causes and concentrated solely on the vote. It warmly welcomed African American women. It campaigned for suffrage from state to state, seeing a federal constitutional amendment as impracticle. The goal of enfranchising women in a particular state, however, seemed to be achievable within the foreseeable future.

In the later nineteenth century, various approaches to achieving woman suffrage were tried in different parts of the country. Manifold organizations were created to promote the cause, sometimes in conflict with one another.

The "New Departure" In 1869 Francis Minor and Virginia Minor, a suffragist couple from Missouri announced the so-called "New Departure" interpretation of the Constitution. The Minors maintained that women, as citizens, already had a constitutional right to vote and should exercise it. Their approach found wide support; numerous women attempted to vote, and some succeeded. Anthony, for example, registered and voted in Rochester, New York, in 1872; however, afterward she was arrested, tried, and fined. When she announced she would never pay the fine, the court took no further action in order to avoid publicity. Virginia Minor herself tried to vote in Missouri in 1872; when she was refused she took the Missouri registrar to court in MINOR V. HAPPERSETT. After she lost her case, she appealed to the U.S. Supreme Court, which upheld Missouri, invalidating the Minors' New Departure.

By this time two attempts in Congress had been made to introduce a woman suffrage amendment, in 1868 and 1869; however, nothing resulted from them. The year 1878 was a landmark: the so-called "Anthony Amendment," stating that the right to vote must not be abridged because of sex, was introduced into Congress by Senator A. A. Sargent, a good friend of Anthony. Afterward it was periodically reintroduced and reported out of committee; hearings were held and covered by the press, and an increasing number of Congressmen favored it. In 1886 it reached the Senate floor but was voted down. Eventually, however, it would become the Nineteenth Amendment.

Meanwhile Kansas held a referendum on woman suffrage in 1867. It lost, but the referendum method was tried again many times in numerous states, though with only a few positive results. The Rocky Mountain territories gave the suffrage movement its first successes. In efforts to attract more settlers and investors, promises of elevated political roles for women looked progressive. The Wyoming territorial legislature enfranchised women in 1869. The following year Utah's territorial legislature followed suit—motivated in part by the desire of MORMONS to counter the negative publicity their plural marriage

**States in Which Women Gained Suffrage
Before Ratification of the Nineteenth Amendment**

1890	Wyoming	1918	Oklahoma
1893	Colorado		South Dakota
1896	Idaho		Tennessee*
	Utah		Texas
1910	Washington	1919	Illinois*
1911	California		Indiana*
1912	Kansas		Iowa*
1913	Arizona		Maine*
	Oregon		Minnesota*
1914	Montana		Missouri*
	Nevada		Wisconsin*
1917	Arkansas		Kentucky*
	Nebraska*		
	New York		
	North Dakota*		
	Rhode Island		

*Right to vote only in presidential elections.

gave their church in other parts of the country. Both territories later kept woman suffrage in their constitutions after they achieved statehood. Meanwhile, both Colorado and Idaho amended their state constitutions during the 1890's to include woman suffrage. In those mountain states racism was a factor: Many white male voters thought that giving women the vote would help counteract the presumably uncivilized voting power of Chinese and African American men.

Organized opposition to woman suffrage was strong. Southern Democrats feared that it would add more black voters to the rolls; liquor interests feared women voters because of the female-led temperance movement. Women's reform groups seeking to improve wages and conditions of working women drew opposition from business. The traditional Protestant clergy saw giving women the vote as an attack on the Christian home and the subordinate role of women in the churches. In a growing array of women's antisuffrage societies, many women themselves claimed that they could best continue their existing reform activities by keeping aloof from politics.

By 1890 the goals and tactics of the NWSA and AWSA had largely converged: Both organizations engaged in state campaigns and both favored a federal suffrage amendment. Merger negotiations in that year resulted in the new National American Woman Suffrage Association (NAWSA), which

would continue as a major leader of the movement until suffrage was achieved. It gained some wealthy backers, although much of the financing came from small contributions by working women and the modestly situated. The early leadership was being superseded by newcomers such as Carrie Chapman CATT and Anna Howard Shaw.

In 1896 another new organization joined the suffrage movement: the National Association of Colored Women (NACW), with educator Mary Church TERRELL as its first president. With the motto "Lifting As We Climb," the NACW proclaimed woman suffrage as a major goal. Prominent among the members were journalist Ida B. WELLS, famous for her antilynching campaign, and Margaret Murray Washington, principal of the Tuskegee Institute's secondary school. The NACW coordinated the activities of more than a thousand black women's clubs that promoted suffrage.

From Militancy to Ratification Despite the positive developments during the 1890's, the suffrage movement was almost at a standstill. New states were not being won to the cause, nor was there progress toward a federal amendment. It appeared that the cause might be lost despite all the efforts. New strategies were developed after 1900. Catt, the president of the NAWSA in 1900, put into action the "society plan." Suffrage leaders sought out society leaders, persuading them to hold suffrage meetings with prominent business and professional figures as speakers. Wealthy women of leisure became activists, held suffrage meetings in their parlors, and attracted favorable press coverage. Some old-time suffragists complained of the new elitism. Another group significant for the future was wooed by the NAWSA: students. Beginning in 1906, NAWSA conventions included "College Evenings," inviting students to become active suffragists, learn the history of the movement, and venerate its pioneers.

The NAWSA and the NACW ostensibly worked together for suffrage; however, the NAWSA discriminated against black women and the NACW both subtly and overtly. Black women rarely were welcome to participate in its events—with the exception of Adella Hunt Logan of Tuskegee Institute, who was so light-skinned that only a few top NAWSA leaders knew she was classified as a "Negro." The larger question involved the NAWSA's strategy of attracting southern white women to the movement, which was considered a necessity for

Louise Hall and Susan Fitzgerald post notices promoting the vote for women in Cincinnati in 1912. (*Library of Congress*)

passing a federal suffrage amendment. Southern white women were as eager as their men to maintain white supremacy. Votes for white women would help them achieve this goal, but votes for black women would not. Accordingly the NAWSA endorsed a states' rights approach at its 1903 convention in New Orleans, allowing state organizations to formulate their own approaches to woman suffrage. This policy ensured white supremacy in the southern branches of the NAWSA. As a result, black suffragists felt betrayed, much as white women had felt when the Fifteenth Amendment had extended suffrage only to men.

In the SOUTHERN STATES white suffrage organizations campaigned for state constitutional amendments that would extend the vote to white women only. They also campaigned for changing the proposed federal amendment to specify white women. However, in NORTHERN STATES black men voted—and their votes would be needed in support of woman suffrage. This fact gave the NACW and its affiliates a certain leverage in confronting the hypocrisy of the NAWSA. These issues continued through the final stages of the suffrage movement. Meanwhile, the state-by-state approach did, in fact, add several more suffrage states to the total, though not in the South: California in 1911, and Arizona, Kansas, and Oregon in 1912. They raised the national total to ten states with woman suffrage, a bare beginning.

In 1913, while the NAWSA was pursuing its discriminatory strategy, black leader Ida B. Wells and her white colleague Belle Squire established the Alpha Suffrage Club in Chicago. Wells had noted how little the masses of black women on the South Side, where she lived, understood about the vote and its importance in bringing about change. The club set out to raise political consciousness. It was an opportune time; that same year the Illinois legislature gave presidential suffrage to women.

The year 1907 marked the beginning of what has been termed the "new militancy" under the leadership of Harriot Stanton Blatch and Alice PAUL. Blatch, the Vassar-educated daughter of Elizabeth Cady Stanton, had married an Englishman and only returned to the United States during her mother's last illness in 1902. In England she had become associated with the militant suffrage movement led by Emmeline Pankhurst and Christabel Pankhurst. These women, who called themselves "suffragettes," used civil disobedience, public demonstra-

tions, and even violence to convince the government that women must have the vote. (In the United States "suffragettes" later became a derogatory term for suffragists.)

Meanwhile, Anna Howard Shaw became NAWSA's president in 1904. Noted primarily as a suffrage orator, she was not an organizer for a new age. The NAWSA was about to be eclipsed by the militants. Distressed at the lack of action by American suffragists and seeing a need to draw more working-class women into the movement, Blatch organized the Equality League of Self-Supporting Women. This new organization enrolled both professional women and activists from the Women's Trade Union League, whose members understood militancy. The Blatch group began their actual militant suffrage activities in 1907 with a series of open-air meetings and parades in New York City.

These projects were mild compared to those of Alice Paul, a Quaker woman who had spent three years in England as a social caseworker and who, like Blatch, had joined the British militants. She had joined hunger strikes, had been jailed, and had been subjected to brutal forced feeding at the hands of male jailers. Upon her return to the United States in 1910, she joined the NAWSA and headed its Congressional Committee, formed to work in Washington for the federal suffrage amendment.

Borrowing from British suffragist tactics, the NAWSA and its Congressional Committee sponsored a parade of five thousand suffragists in Washington, D.C., on the day before President Woodrow WILSON's March, 1913, inauguration. With thousands of visitors in town, maximum publicity could be expected. Hostile onlookers shoved and jeered the marchers, who pushed on doggedly along Pennsylvania Avenue. Police protection was inadequate. Ida B. Wells took advantage of the disorder to slip into line beside white friends, instead of marching at the rear where the NAWSA had relegated black contingents. The parade reaped immense publicity for suffrage, and public opinion ultimately sympathized with the marchers. Suffrage petitions poured in to the Congressional Committee from all over the country.

The Congressional Committee and its militant members soon separated from the NAWSA to become the CONGRESSIONAL UNION, and, three years later, the NATIONAL WOMAN'S PARTY, still headed by Alice Paul. By then women had the vote in twelve states, so a party could actually function. January,

1917, saw a new campaign: picketing the White House. This accorded with Paul's conviction, borrowed from the British militants, that the party in power should be held responsible for the nation's policies in regard to woman suffrage. The picketers were nonviolent and even attractive, with banners proclaiming woman suffrage as essential to democracy. Such activity by the National Woman's Party helped keep the Anthony Amendment before Congress.

Improbably, the NAWSA revived. Former president Carrie Chapman Catt was drafted again for the office in 1915 and held the post until 1920. She proved herself the great organizer and strategist. Her "Winning Plan" of 1916 combined centralized control and state actions. In order to ratify a federal amendment, the NAWSA needed at least thirty-six state boards—which Catt called thirty-six "state armies"—to campaign for the Anthony Amendment under the national organization. Only this could ensure that it would pass Congress and be ratified by thirty-six states. Some southern members were unhappy at the centralization, but the plan was adopted.

The major suffrage organizations had sharply contrasting leadership styles. The NAWSA's Catt loved order and organization, and shunned conflict and confrontation. Paul of the National Women's Party thrived on confrontation and its attendant publicity. Relations between the two leaders were often rancorous, but each was devoted to the cause, and historians agree that their combined efforts were responsible for the final success. With United States entry into World War I in 1917, many suffragists threw themselves into activities such as war bond drives and Red Cross work. Although personally Catt leaned toward pacifism, she took every opportunity to publicize the NAWSA's patriotism in the well-founded belief that the reward would be passage of the suffrage amendment by a grateful nation. Paul, on the other hand, refused to participate in the war effort. Regarding war as an immoral activity of the male sex, she believed that women should concentrate on achieving suffrage. Her picketing campaign continued with slogans such as "Democracy Should Begin at Home" and references to "Kaiser Wilson." Mob violence resulted, with the suffragists being labelled traitors by onlookers and servicemen. By June, 1917, picketers were being arrested, jailed, and subjected to rough treatment, until Wilson thought it wise to release them in November. Widespread publicity once more created sympathy for the picketers and for suffrage.

In 1917 New York State instituted suffrage for women, becoming the only full suffrage state east of the Mississippi River. By then a number of states had enacted "partial suffrage," for some elections but not for all. President Wilson had for some time favored woman suffrage, but as a Democrat responsive to the South he chose to endorse individual state action on the issue. On January 9, 1918, however, he announced to Congress his support of the Anthony Amendment. The next day the amendment came to the floor of Congress. Three years earlier—the only previous time that the federal amendment had actually come to a vote in Congress—it had been defeated by a wide margin. In 1918 the amendment passed the House with exactly the two-thirds majority required. Much of the remaining opposition was from the South. Nationwide, the NAWSA "Winning Plan" and the militancy of the Woman's Party had succeeded—in the first round. However, the Senate voted the amendment down, despite Wilson's direct appeal for passage.

The NAWSA and the Woman's Party swung into high gear once again, despite fatigue, war work, and the influenza epidemic, to elect prosuffrage senators in the November, 1918, general election. The next year the process began all over again. In May the House once again approved the amendment; this time the Senate followed suit in June. By August, 1920, thirty-five states had ratified the amendment. However, getting the necessary thirty-sixth state's ratification proved difficult. Tennessee had the best chance, and suffrage leaders brought in their troops there. Success came in August, when Tennessee's Senator Harry Burn changed his vote to "aye" on the instructions of his elderly mother. The state's official ratification, on August 26, 1920, made the Nineteenth Amendment official, touching off huge victory celebrations in Washington, D.C., New York City, and elsewhere. A few months later women voted nationwide for the first time.

SUGGESTED READINGS:

Barry, Kathleen. *Susan B. Anthony: A Biography of a Singular Feminist.* New York: Ballantine Books, 1988.

Flexner, Eleanor. *Century of Struggle: The Woman's Rights Movement in the United States.* Rev. ed. Cambridge, Mass.: The Belknap Press of Harvard University Press, 1975.

Giddings, Paula. *When and Where I Enter: The Impact of Black Women on Race and Sex in America*. New York: Bantam Books, 1984.

Griffin, Elizabeth. *In Her Own Right: The Life of Elizabeth Cady Stanton*. New York: Oxford University Press, 1984.

Lunardini, Christine A. *From Equal Suffrage to Equal Rights: Alice Paul and the National Woman's Party, 1910-1928*. New York: New York University Press, 1986.

Van Voris, Jacqueline. *Carrie Chapman Catt: A Public Life*. New York: Feminist Press, 1987.

Wheeler, Marjorie S., ed. *One Woman, One Vote: Rediscovering the Woman Suffrage Movement*. Troutdale, Ore.: New Sage Press, 1995.

_____, ed. *Votes for Women! The Woman Suffrage Movement in Tennessee, the South, and the Nation*. Knoxville: University of Tennessee Press, 1995.

—*Elizabeth C. Adams*

Women of All Red Nations

WARN: Pantribal AMERICAN INDIAN women's organization founded in 1978.

WARN is a grassroots organization launched in 1978 by Lakota Sioux women residents of the Pine Ridge RESERVATION in South Dakota. Lorelie Means, the wife of Indian activist Ted Means and Madonna Means, the sister of Ted and Russell MEANS, founded this association, which has sought to address local problems through autonomous and self-reliant action. WARN has worked to organize local chapters throughout the United States and has urged women to assume leadership positions in both government and community affairs.

From the outset, women's health and health care, economic, environmental, and legal issues became WARN's central focus. In the early 1980's, WARN demanded that the federal government implement a plan to deliver safe drinking water to the Pine Ridge Reservation, where water contaminated by uranium and other pollutants was causing cancer, miscarriages, and birth defects. The organization also announced that sterilization of about 25 percent of the reservation's women was tantamount to genocide. WARN has also raised political and economic issues such as abuses in the CRIMINAL JUSTICE system and has tried to protect community interests by carefully monitoring energy re-

sources development on Indian land. WARN has promoted its agenda through annual conferences and publications.

—*David A. Crain*

Women's rights

The political, economic, and social movement advocating women's equality with men.

The women's rights movement originated during the eighteenth century within the French and American democratic revolutions when the idea that "all men were created equal" caught fire in the minds of some women. Women also, they came to believe, were created equal. During this era, women had virtually no political rights. Wives could not own property, they were prohibited from leaving their husbands, and mothers were barred from gaining custody of their own children. Occupations for women were few and were largely limited to nurses, domestic servants, and minor shop-clerk positions. Females were identified solely with the physiological roles of wife and mother. AFRICAN AMERICAN women held in SLAVERY were expected to care for their own families as well as laboring for their masters.

Abigail Adams—the wife of future president John Adams—had women's rights in mind when she prompted her husband to "think of the ladies" when he was helping to frame the U.S. CONSTITUTION in 1787. Mary Wollstonecraft's famous 1792 tract, *A Vindication of the Rights of Women*—a work that help start an avalanche of social propaganda revolving around women's rights—described women as without any sort of rights, political or domestic.

Growth in the Nineteenth Century Thanks to a decline in the birth rate that allowed women longer periods of freedom from childbearing, during the nineteenth century women became more concerned with social reform and improvement of their own position. This era of rapid industrial expansion saw poor young white women leave the farms and gravitate toward the cities to work in urban factories, while many African American women sought jobs as domestic servants. In *Woman in the Nineteenth Century* (1845)—considered the most impressive early American feminist work—Sarah Margaret FULLER encouraged women to help themselves and not rely solely on men in the effort toward independence.

Although women saw gradual improvement in property rights, divorce, and child custody as the nineteenth century progressed, it was not until the Seneca Falls Convention in July, 1848, the first women's rights assembly in the United States, that women began enthusiastically to fight for their rights. Women such as Lucretia MOTT and Elizabeth Cady STANTON campaigned to secure women's rights in voting, education, and employment. At the convention, Stanton and Mott drafted the DECLARATION OF SENTIMENTS that paralleled the wording of the American DECLARATION OF INDEPENDENCE by proclaiming that "all men and women are created equal." Although acquiring VOTING RIGHTS was not a primary issue at the time, Stanton advocated a woman suffrage resolution. Without the right to vote, she maintained, legislation for other rights could not be enacted. As a result, the focus of the women's movement from the 1850's to 1920 shifted to the WOMAN SUFFRAGE MOVEMENT. After 1851 Stanton and Susan B. ANTHONY worked together for the women's rights movement.

Opportunities for women began to increase. Women were granted the vote in Wyoming Territory in 1869, Utah Territory in 1870, and the states of Colorado (1893) and Idaho (1896). The first American woman lawyer was admitted to the bar in Iowa in 1869. In 1872 as part of the newly founded Equal Rights Party, Victoria Woodhull, became the first American woman to run for the U.S. PRESIDENCY. Earlier, she and her sister had opened the first female brokerage house on Wall Street. In 1890 Wyoming became the first state to allow woman suffrage. Stanton's *Woman's Bible* (1895), which attacked what she called the male bias of the Judeo-Christian Bible, was published in 1895. By the turn of the century, women were attending college to become teachers, librarians, and social workers.

Abolition and Temperance Movements During the nineteenth century, the ABOLITION and temperance movements influenced the women's movement. With the North's victory in the CIVIL WAR, women abolitionists hoped their hard work would result in suffrage for women as well as for the emancipated slaves. However, the FOURTEENTH and FIFTEENTH AMENDMENTS that granted citizenship and suffrage to African American men failed to grant the same rights to women of any color. Charismatic evangelist Sojourner TRUTH, a freed slave, abolitionist, and the first African American woman to speak publicly to large audiences, challenged women's

double difficulty of slavery and sexual discrimination: "Ain't I a woman?" she cried, baring her breasts in response to a public criticism about her aggressive manner. Similarly, the Quaker sisters Angelina GRIMKÉ and Sarah GRIMKÉ campaigned for both abolitionism and women's rights. Escaped slave and writer Frederick DOUGLASS fought for the Fifteenth Amendment that gave African American men the right to vote and supported women's rights as well. At the Seneca Falls Convention he demanded that women be allowed to vote. It was at the International Abolitionism Conference in London in 1840 that women such as Stanton and Mott were refused seating. Incensed, the women came to realize the similarity of the cause of abolitionism and their own repressed situation as women.

In a manner similar to the abolitionist movement, the temperance movement also played a strong part in women's rights. In the 1870's women started to parade publicly singing and praying against the evils of liquor. Under founder president Frances Willard, the Women's Christian Temperance Union (WCTU) fought to make saloons illegal. This political organizational experience was to set the stage for the woman suffrage movement.

The Right to Vote In the twentieth century women claimed equal rights and control over their own reproductive powers. Margaret SANGER, who helped found Planned Parenthood, helped women to control pregnancy. The term "New Woman" came to be used, but the struggle to win the vote was slow and disappointing. By 1910 only six states had granted women the vote. Woman suffrage amendments to the U.S. Constitution were presented to every Congress after 1878, and they always failed to pass. In time, the cause of women's suffrage attracted influential women with solid organizational skills who marched in parades and became fiery propagandists. When the United States entered WORLD WAR I in April, 1917, suffragists folded bandages and worked in hospitals and government offices with the hope that after the war they would be rewarded with the vote. Although President Woodrow WILSON at first declined, he eventually declared woman suffrage to be an emergency war measure, and Congress passed a woman suffrage amendment on June 4, 1919. Although it took forty years from draft to ratification, the NINETEENTH AMENDMENT—named the Anthony Amendment—became law in 1920, in time for twenty-five million women to vote in the presidential election.

Although women won the right to vote in 1920, immediately afterward, the women's movement diminished and did not re-emerge until the 1960's. When Alice PAUL of the NATIONAL WOMEN'S PARTY introduced the first EQUAL RIGHTS AMENDMENT (ERA) in 1923, it failed to pass. Groups such as the League of Women Voters, a nonpartisan organization dedicated to educating women on political issues, and the National Council of Negro Women were instrumental in supporting reforms related to the rights of both men and women.

Although both world wars prompted a mass movement of women into traditional male jobs, the shift was short-lived as women were encouraged, through official propaganda machines, to give up their jobs to returning vets. Motherhood and homemaking were glamorized after both wars. The ERA bill gained support during the 1950's, but suffered union opposition. Simone de Beauvoir's popular feminist manifesto *The Second Sex* (1953) helped put in motion the women's movement of the turbulent 1960's.

The Women's Liberation Movement During the 1960's, a decade of feminist activism spurred on by the CIVIL RIGHTS MOVEMENT, the next wave of the women's movement crested. Accurate knowledge of BIRTH CONTROL gave women greater control over their own destinies. In the 1960 presidential election, while the Republican Party endorsed the ERA, Democrats ignored it. The EQUAL PAY ACT OF 1963 stipulated that women and men workers must have equal pay for equal work and the CIVIL RIGHTS ACT OF 1964 prohibited EMPLOYMENT DISCRIMINATION on the basis of race or gender. The EQUAL EMPLOYMENT OPPORTUNITIES COMMISSION (EEOC) was set up to enforce the act.

During this decade, women, particularly women educated on a par with men, grew dissatisfied with the roles of wife and mother. By 1964 thirty-two states had set up commissions on the status of women. Outspoken women, such as psychologist and political activist Betty Friedan, soon took on the title of "feminist." Her best-selling, highly propagandistic book, *The Feminine Mystique* (1963), disclosed society's restrictions of women, adding fuel to the fire. In addition, she revealed how the EEOC had failed to enforce the Civil Rights Act by keeping women in low-paying jobs. In 1966 the NATIONAL ORGANIZATION FOR WOMEN (NOW) under Friedan, was founded. Militant women's groups sprang up and the social phenomenon known as the Women's Liberation Movement became evident in the newspaper headlines and public demonstrations that helped heighten awareness of discriminatory attitudes.

For some women, however, NOW's political stance was too stringent, particularly in the area of birth control and ABORTION. In 1969 the more conservative Women's Equity Action League (WEAL), which focused on women's involvement in government sprang up. Women of all ages came to desire recognition for their economic contributions and for changes in mass media concepts of women that fostered denigration and contempt. While some women liberationists were hostile to men, most wanted relationships based on equality and respect. Magazines and television shows featured articles on the need for reforms.

The beginning of the next decade saw the women's movement evolve into a well-run political power. Although the 1960's legislation mandated equal pay for women, women were still earning 45 percent less than men for the same jobs. In 1970, on the fiftieth anniversary of the adoption of the Nineteenth Amendment, women across the nation joined the Women's Strike for Equality. The National Women's Political Caucus touted such well-known feminists as Bella Abzug, Shirley CHISHOLM, and Gloria Steinem. Steinem, the editor of *Ms.* magazine, campaigned for the political, economic, and sexual liberation of women from traditional roles. Legislators such as Pat Schroeder, a member of Congress from Colorado beginning in 1972, worked diligently for women's reproductive and military-status rights. Authors such as Robin Morgan (*Sisterhood Is Powerful*, 1970) and Kate Millett (*Sexual Politics*, 1970), opened the floodgates of feminist cultural criticism.

Seven-hundred chapters strong by 1974 and active in ten countries, NOW sought to gain equal economic rights and enhance women's reproductive rights, including the right to ABORTION. In 1973 the U.S. SUPREME COURT decision in ROE V. WADE legalized abortion. A Women's Decade, 1975 to 1985, began with the International Women's Year (IWY). Some ten thousand delegates from 123 nations participated in the IWY conference in Mexico City in 1975. Working within the existing political system, NOW campaigned against sexual and domestic violence and negative media depictions of women. Its members criticized traditional definitions of gender roles—men were doctors and women were nurses—and campaigned to eliminate

Seventy rights groups joined to mount a massive march in support of the Equal Rights Amendment in Washington, D.C., in August, 1977. (*AP/Wide World Photos*)

gender bias in language. They also pressured corporations to eliminate discriminatory practices. Women infiltrated restaurants, bars, and professional clubs, and gained admittance to law and medical schools.

Although the passage of the Civil Rights Act of 1964 granted women equal employment opportunities, the ERA made headlines again when it was approved by the U.S. House of Representatives in 1971, and by the Senate in 1972. The amendment read:

> Equality of rights under the law shall not be denied or abridged by the United States or any State on account of sex.

The ERA was ratified by thirty states and First Lady Betty Ford flew an ERA flag at the White House in 1973; however, the ERA amendment eventually fell short of the three-quarter majority of states it required for ratification by June, 1982.

Terms such as "women's lib" and "feminist," came to be perceived negatively, with activist women becoming negative stereotypes. In 1984 Geraldine Ferraro became the first woman nominated for vice president of the United States by a major party. Meanwhile, many women's groups turned their attention to such economic issues as the "feminization of poverty," noting that female-headed families accounted for nearly half of all families living in poverty. Abortion came under attack, and the increasing divorce rate contributed to women's increasing poverty. Women's studies as an academic discipline focusing on women's issues became available in higher institutions.

By the 1990's much of women's rights activism had come to focus on women's health and SEXUAL HARASSMENT issues. In 1991 the televised Senate hearings on Clarence Thomas' appointment to the Supreme Court were dominated by Anita Hill's allegations of sexual harassment—an event that helped focus public attention on the issues of power in the workplace. By then the idea of equal education and choosing both a career and family life for women seemed normal. Although they had more opportunities than ever before, many women in corporate America came to feel that they had hit a "glass ceiling" that kept them out of the boardrooms of top companies. However, women's near exclusion from the most powerful positions and highest incomes, feminists maintain, is closely related to the

persistence of traditional religious, cultural, and family values. Few women, with such exceptions as India's Indira Gandhi, Israel's Golda Meir, Great Britain's Margaret Thatcher, Pakistan's Benazir Bhutto, and Nicaragua's Violeta Barrios de Chamorro had ever attained high political office.

SUGGESTED READINGS:

Beauvoir, Simone de. *The Second Sex*. New York: Alfred A. Knopf, 1953. Written by an internationally respected philosopher, the 1949 landmark study *Le Deuxieme sexe* became the classic of post-World War II feminism.

Buhle, Mari Jo, and Paul Buhle, eds. *The Concise History of Woman Suffrage: Selections from the Classic Work of Stanton*. Urbana: University of Illinois Press, 1978. Condensation of a classic work on the women's rights movements.

Friedan, Betty. *The Feminine Mystique*. New York: W. W. Norton, 1983. Twentieth anniversary edition of the women's rights classic that demonstrates society's discrimination against women.

Hoff, Joan. *Law, Gender, and Injustice: A Legal History of U.S. Women*. New York: New York University Press, 1991. Detailed account of the history and legal aspects of women's rights.

Trager, James. *The Women's Chronology*. New York: Henry Holt, 1994. Comprehensive summary of women's history. Excellent cross-references.

Wollstonecraft, Mary. *A Vindication of the Rights of Woman*. Edited by Carol H. Poston. New York: W. W. Norton, 1988. Authoritative text provides information regarding not just Wollstonecraft's classic feminist tract, but historical background information on the women's movement.

Zophy, Angela Howard, ed. *American Women's History*. New York: Garland, 1990. Good starting point for any research project—large fact-filled chronological account of women's history.

—*M. Casey Diana*

Wong Kim Ark, United States v.

1898: U.S. SUPREME COURT decision holding that the FOURTEENTH AMENDMENT'S guarantee of equal treatment under state laws extended to citizens without respect to their ethnic heritage.

Wong Kim Ark was born in the United States to CHINESE parents who were permanent residents, but not citizens, of the United States. After visiting China and returning to the United States, he applied to the commissioner of customs for permission to land in San Francisco. The commissioner refused, however, ruling that Wong Kim Ark was not a citizen of the United States.

In a majority opinion by Justice Horace Gray, the Supreme Court found Wong Kim Ark's exclusion from the country a contravention of the Fourteenth Amendment. That amendment declared authoritatively that "all persons born or naturalized in the United States, and subject to the jurisdiction thereof, are citizens of the United States." The Court recognized that the framers of this amendment had as their principal focus assuring citizenship to AFRICAN AMERICANS. The Court noted, however, that the words of the Fourteenth Amendment have a broader scope, one that applied to the case at hand. The amendment guaranteed citizenship to all of those born in the United States, without regard to their ethnic backgrounds.

—*Timothy L. Hall*

Wong Wing v. United States

1896: U.S. SUPREME COURT decision holding that a federal law providing for the sentencing of illegal CHINESE aliens to up to a year of hard labor without indictment or trial violated the rights to a grand jury indictment and to a trial by jury.

At issue in *Wong Wing* was a federal statute that provided that illegal Chinese aliens could be sentenced without a jury trial to up to a year of hard labor prior to being deported. The Supreme Court had previously upheld the constitutionality of federal attempts to deport or exclude Chinese aliens from entry into the United States, such as the CHINESE EXCLUSION ACT OF 1882. In *Wong Wing*, however, Justice George Shiras, Jr., writing for the Court, held that the federal sentencing law was unconstitutional. According to the Court, the mere detention of illegal aliens prior to their deportation did not present a constitutional violation. The Court also declared that CONGRESS had the power to make it a criminal offense to enter or remain in the United States illegally and to punish those guilty of this offense after a proper trial. The federal act in question had added the element of hard labor to detention, however, and had attempted to inflict this

sentence without indictment or trial. The infliction of this punishment thus, the Court found, violated the Fifth Amendment's right to indictment by a grand jury and the Sixth Amendment's guarantee of the right to trial by jury.

—*Timothy L. Hall*

Workers, rights of

Protection of workers from exploitative and unsafe working conditions, unfair hiring and promotion practices, and all forms of discriminatory treatment based on race, ethnicity, religion, age, or other characteristics.

Workers' rights in the United States and elsewhere clearly include basic civil rights, such as freedom of speech and freedom of assembly, as well as other rights that have only gradually come to be recognized as equally fundamental. These rights include the right not to be exploited and the right to be considered for employment on one's qualifications, such as education or experience, rather than on one's gender or ethnic background.

Worker's rights can be broadly classified in two categories: conditions for employment and conditions of employment. Conditions for employment include what factors an employer can consider in hiring workers, while conditions of employment include the wages that should be paid and the safety of the work environment. As in many other aspects of life, the notion that workers have certain rights in either area is primarily a product of the twentieth century. In addition, the extent to which workers enjoy certain rights has varied widely from country to country.

A Brief History of Labor Many of the rights workers in the Western industrialized nations take for granted, such as the right to join a LABOR UNION and the right to STRIKE, were not recognized by either governments or management until the twentieth century. What has come to be recognized as the worker's basic right to freedom of assembly and freedom of association was often decried in the nineteenth century as being seditious, or even treasonous, behavior. In the United States workers began forming workers' organizations almost simultaneously with the start of industrialization, but employers generally ignored the demands they presented. Workers who organized to obtain better working conditions were fired and immediately replaced. Some industries, such as mining and steel manufacturing, became notorious for the brutality with which they suppressed labor strikes. Both state and federal governments cooperated closely with industry in suppressing strikes well into the twentieth century. The most violent management-labor confrontations occurred in isolated mining communities, such as Ludlow, Colorado, where National Guard troops fired bullets into a crowd of striking miners and their families, and were scarcely noticed by the country as a whole. It was not until the 1930's, when workers in the automobile industry began organizing, that both sides of labor issues began to be well publicized on a national level. Prior to that time, strikes led by organizations such as the Industrial Workers of the World (IWW) were generally condemned in the press as being the work of "red," or unpatriotic and possibly communist, agitators not truly representative of working people.

Despite the violence organized labor encountered, however, unions representing workers in the textile industries, mining, and other manufacturing jobs gradually made progress in reforming working conditions. Following a disastrous fire in a garment industry sweatshop in New York in 1911, news reports exposing the horrendous conditions endured by working women and children helped to push through state and federal regulations outlawing the use of child labor. The number of hours in a legal working day was also gradually reduced, although the eight-hour work day that most Americans came to accept as standard was not achieved until the 1930's.

At the end of the nineteenth century it was not unusual to find children as young as eight years old working fourteen hours a day, six days a week, in textile factories in Massachusetts and New York. Passage of mandatory education laws requiring children to remain in school until they were sixteen, coupled with legislation making it illegal to employ children under the age of fourteen except in a family business, eliminated most child labor in the United States by the 1920's. Sweatshops in which women earned a pittance for doing piecework (they were paid for each item completed, rather than by the hour) persisted longer.

Sweatshops operated on a system of debt peonage in which owners sold workers materials at inflated prices that they were supposed to pay for from what they received for finished goods. Work-ers often found themselves unable to quit because owners would tell them that they still owed money. Similar systems existed in isolated mining and lumbering towns, where workers were paid in company scrip redeemable only at company-operated stores. The workers' pay was usually inadequate to cover the costs of groceries and other goods at the company stores. Encouraged to charge goods, they found themselves sinking even deeper in debt to the companies and thus unable to leave.

Reforms in Working Conditions Workers in Western Europe led the way in eliminating the worst abuses of workers in industrialized countries, followed quickly by the United States. By the 1930's most industrialized nations had established basic guarantees of workers' rights. The right to be free from exploitation was protected by the passage of minimum wage laws and the abolition of debt peonage, which was shown to be a form of SLAVERY. Federal labor laws also eliminated the piecework system that had been used to exploit women in sweatshops.

In the United States, passage of the Wagner Act in 1935 guaranteed workers the right to collective bargaining. Under the provisions of the act, which established the National Labor Relations Board, workers could not be dismissed or otherwise punished for their participation in union activities. Although employers could engage in publicity campaigns to discourage workers from participating in unions, workers nonetheless still had the right to freedom of assembly and freedom of speech.

Reforms in labor law also protected the rights of employees who did not belong to unions. If an employee worked in an industry where workers were not covered by a collective bargaining agreement, the law still presumed an unwritten contract, an agreement referred to in law as a covenant of good faith and fair dealing, existed. Employment might be considered to be "at will," that is, that either the employer or the employee could terminate the working relationship at any time, but if the employer fired an employee without just cause, the employee would then be entitled to receive compensation in the form of UNEMPLOYMENT INSURANCE. By the mid-twentieth century in the United States it was taken as a basic civil right that workers should not be victims of employers' whims. By requiring all employers to pay unemployment insurance premiums, government exerted pressure on employers to treat employees fairly. Employers also paid insurance premiums to provide workers with income in the event of disabling on-the-job injuries as society recognized the right of workers to be compensated for the loss of their ability to support themselves.

Reforms in Hiring and Promotion The right to be considered for employment or for promotion based on one's abilities and education, rather than on criteria such as gender or ethnic background has come to be viewed—at least in the United States—as a fundamental civil right. Equal employment opportunity is, however, an even more recent development than the right to collective bargaining or a minimum wage. Until the mid-twentieth century the right of employers to hire (or not hire) whomever they chose was rarely challenged. In the nineteenth century African Americans and new immigrants alike experienced blatant discrimination. Help-wanted signs in U.S. cities in the nineteenth century often included statements such as "No Irish Need

Apply." Hiring offices for factories and mines would bluntly inform would-be workers that they did not hire ALIENS or blacks, or, if they did, such people were eligible for only the most menial, low-paying, and dirty jobs.

Women were similarly discriminated against. The help-wanted sections of newspapers routinely divided employment advertisements into two sections: "Help Wanted Male" and "Help Wanted Female. "Women's work," like that allocated to African Americans and recent immigrants, tended to be low-paying. On-the-job opportunities for advancement were also limited by gender. In education, a field in which women held many of the teaching jobs, promotion to administrative positions such as principal almost always went to men.

Passage of the CIVIL RIGHTS ACT OF 1964 forced changes in both hiring and promotion practices. The act made it illegal for employers to discriminate

African Americans demonstrate for equality in the workplace during the late 1950's. (*Schomburg Center for Research in Black Culture, New York Public Library*)

based on race, religion, or gender. Following passage of the act, women and minorities were able to move more easily into occupational fields previously closed to them. As a consequence, the gap between average earnings for men and women began gradually narrowing. Many women and minority workers continued to experience discrimination in employment, but heightened awareness by employers made blatantly racist or sexist practices less likely.

Freedom from Sexual Harassment In the 1990's, as the typical work place in the United States became more mixed, with men and women working side by side in a variety of settings, women began to assert that the rights of workers included the right to work in a nonthreatening environment. Many women reported being made to feel uncomfortable by male co-workers or supervisors who made sexual propositions or told lewd jokes. Ironically, one sign of progress in the advancement of women in the workplace is that while women initially raised the issue of SEXUAL HARASSMENT, following passage of federal legislation several men filed successful lawsuits alleging that female supervisors had sexually harassed them.

The Global Situation The rights of workers around the world often differ widely from the model set by the United States and the Western European countries. Differences in the dominant cultures and religions can mean that the gender stereotyping forbidden in the United States is actively supported by the government of another country. For example, the strong gender segregation mandated by Islam means that in Muslim countries such as Saudi Arabia certain occupations may never be open to women. Nonetheless, there are certain fundamental rights recognized as universal to all workers. One such right is the right to be free from coercion. Most governments recognize the right of workers to be free to work or not to work as they choose. Coerced work, or forced labor, may be demanded of criminals, but ordinary citizens are presumed to be at liberty to walk away from jobs if they so desire.

Another right is the right to receive a basic minimum wage. While minimum wage levels vary from country to country, depending on the local economies, by the end of the twentieth century almost all countries had enacted minimum wage laws. Investigations by international labor unions and human rights organizations have often uncovered violations of those laws, both in the United States and elsewhere, but nonetheless official recognition of the workers' right to just compensation for their labor has existed.

Similarly, a workers' right to safe working environments has also become universally recognized. Reports of unsafe working conditions in factories in developing countries have been met with disapproval by other nations and have often led to either threats of BOYCOTTS of specific products or, more generally, economic sanctions of offending countries.

Finally, the right of children to be children and not to be forced to work at a young age began gaining international support in the 1990's. The age at which a child ceases to be a child and can instead be expected to begin work still varies greatly from country to country, but it has become widely accepted that no children should be expected to leave school and work before they enter adolescence. Reports of children as young as eight years old being chained to rug looms and forced to work as weavers in Asian countries have been met with universal condemnation. Human rights organizations have worked with government agencies in a variety of countries in an attempt to eliminate the practice of child labor, although the practice still persisted well into the 1990's in some developing nations.

Summary Although workers' civil rights have gradually expanded, granting them more opportunities and greater protection from both workplace hazards and financial uncertainty, for many workers these rights continue to be abused. Despite the passage of civil rights acts, many workers in the United States have continued to experience discrimination, illegally low pay, or other abuses on the job, just as workers throughout the world endure unsafe conditions or coercive employers. News media reports of ongoing investigations of sexual harassment cases, sweatshop working conditions, and other abuses have indicated that the rights of workers have been so recently won that some employers still believe those rights can be revoked or ignored. As in other areas of civil rights, mere passage of legislation guaranteeing employee rights has not led automatically to universal changes in employer behavior.

SUGGESTED READINGS:

Boris, Eileen, and Nelson Lichenstein, eds. *Major Problems in the History of American Workers.*

Lexington, Mass.: D. C. Heath, 1991. Interesting collection of essays devoted to U.S. labor history.

Ernst, Daniel R. *Lawyers Against Labor: From Individual Rights to Corporate Liberalism*. Urbana: University of Illinois Press, 1995. Examination of the evolution of labor policy by major corporations as they attempt to reduce the influence of labor unions.

Innes, Stephen, ed. *Work and Labor in Early America*. Chapel Hill: University of North Carolina Press, 1988. Looks at working conditions in colonial and revolutionary era times.

Jones, Green C. *Growing Up Hard in Harlan County*. Lexington: University of Kentucky Press, 1985. Engrossing personal history from Kentucky's coal mining region that describes the brutality miners experienced at the hands of mine operators.

Leader, Sheldon. *Freedom of Association: A Study in Labor Law and Political Theory*. New Haven, Conn.: Yale University Press, 1992. Discussion of the rights of workers to organize and engage in collective action.

Millis, Harry A. *From the Wagner Act to Taft Hartley*. Chicago: University of Chicago Press, 1950. History of the political process leading from one piece of legislation that empowered workers to another piece of legislation empowering employers.

Weiss, Donald. *Fair, Square, and Legal: Safe Hiring, Managing, and Firing Practices to Keep You & Your Company Out of Court*. New York: AMACON, 1991. Concise guide to what employers can and cannot do under U.S. labor law.

—*Nancy Farm Mannikko*

World War I

1914-1918: Military conflict into which the United States entered in early 1917.

Although Americans protested infringements on their civil rights during an undeclared war with France in 1798-1800, and during the U.S. Civil War, no precedents were established that carried over into the postwar years. American participation in World War I introduced an attitudinal change toward civil rights, the consequences of which were experienced thereafter with increasing, albeit varying, levels of intensity. The change consisted of two categories of civil rights manipulation. One was promoting support for the war effort by managing American minds. The other was aimed at preventing and punishing designated disloyal behavior through direct surveillance.

Promoting the War Effort The government's most effective wartime promotional effort was the Committee on Public Information (CPI), established by President Woodrow Wilson on April 14, 1917, eight days after Congress declared war on Germany. George Creel, a personal friend of Wilson's and a strong supporter of Wilsonian Progressivism was appointed chairman. The CPI's broad charge stressed the preparation and distribution of news extolling the ethical rectitude of the U.S. role as a belligerent in the war. Operating on a wartime budget of about $9,500,000, most of which was CPI-generated income, it issued news releases, printed propaganda, films, and even issued its own newspaper. The CPI arranged for exhibits in public places, especially at state fairs. It advertised Liberty Loans, trained "Four-Minute Men" to deliver short public addresses on war themes, and made special efforts to reach women and foreign-born Americans.

Although Creel claimed "expression, not suppression" for the CPI, the agency issued veiled threats against the news media for not practicing voluntary censorship. In the absence of specific guidelines, the CPI suggested to newspaper editors that they should submit questionable articles to it for approval; otherwise they would be reported to the appropriate governmental agency.

Creel's role as the CPI representative on the Censorship Board enabled him to review magazine articles presented to the board for clearance, and to limit the export of proscribed publications. The CPI also provided special war-study courses to elementary schools, stressing patriotism, heroism, and sacrifice. However, Creel and the CPI did practice measured restraint. They helped turn minds toward support of the Allied war effort, but usually not at the expense of squelching dissent.

Curbing Dissent More serious attacks on civil rights were taken by the federal government through the passage of proscriptive legislation aimed at muzzling dissent. The Espionage Act, passed in June, 1917, provided that anyone convicted of aiding the enemy, obstructing recruitment for the armed forces, or causing insubordination, disloyalty, or refusal to serve in the armed forces, would be subject to imprisonment for up to twenty years or a ten-thousand-dollar fine, or both. Moreover, all letters, circulars, postal cards, pictures, prints, newspapers, pamphlets, books, or other materials that violated the Espionage Act were barred from the U.S. mails. Postmaster General Albert S. Burleson could and did prohibit use of the mails for any material he deemed subject to the purview of the act. A number of socialist publications were banned, including *The American Socialist, The Masses,* and *The Milwaukee Leader,* along with assorted anti-British and pro-Irish publications. Socialist Party leader Eugene Debs was convicted two months before the end of the war for violating the Espionage Act because he publicly opposed the American war effort. He was sentenced to ten years in prison, but was pardoned by President Warren Harding on Christmas Day, 1921.

On October 6, 1917, Burleson's censorship power was extended when Congress passed the Trading with the Enemy Act, which authorized the postmaster general to scrutinize all foreign-language publications. One journal was suppressed because it suggested financing the war by raising taxes and borrowing less. Another was censored for reprinting Thomas JEFFERSON's opinion that Ireland should become a republic, because it might be offensive to the British.

Ironically, the high point of civil rights repression during the war, the Sedition Act of May 16, 1918, was thought by Wilson and his attorney general, Thomas Gregory, as heading off individual vigilantism. Gregory argued that the Espionage Act needed to be amended so that it would replace vigilant excesses with government agents acting under legal sanction. The result was the Sedition Act, which made it easier for the government to prosecute individual acts of perceived antiwar behavior. Its broad application included prohibition of any forms of interference with American military or naval forces such as conveying false statements; obstructing the sale of war bonds; inciting disloyalty in the armed forces, including recruiting; using abusive language in referring to the U.S. government, the Constitution, or the American flag; promoting the enemy's cause by displaying an enemy flag; using language in any form directed at curtailment of war production; or favoring the enemy's cause or opposing that of the United States. Anyone found guilty could be fined up to ten thousand dollars or imprisoned up to twenty years.

To assuage vigilante efforts, Gregory employed the American Protective League (APL), an organization he had been instrumental in establishing shortly after U.S. entrance into the war. Made up of private citizens, the APL assisted the Bureau of Investigation by spying on possible disloyal persons and arresting those who might be guilty of anti-American behavior. By the end of the war, there were 250,000 members in the APL. Many had been especially useful in carrying out "slacker raids" in large cities. During 1918 they raided places where draft-age men congregated, such as theaters, ballparks, union halls, hotels, and occasionally even residences. The raids netted forty thousand men, who were taken to detention centers; however, the uncertainty and confusion caused by the regulations made it difficult to decide what to do with them.

Two additional federal acts were less often used by government enforcers. The Sabotage Act, passed in April, 1918, resulted in prosecutions of more businessmen than saboteurs. Less than a month before the armistice, the Alien Act was passed aimed at anarchists attempting to enter the United States.

Enforcement of federal laws depended not only upon Burleson, Gregory, and the attitudes of federal judges and government employees, but also on state and local citizens and officials. The states were eager to contribute to the war effort by promoting the sale of Liberty Bonds. The behavior of persons who apparently could afford to purchase Liberty Bonds and refused might be interpreted as opposition to the war effort and dealt with accordingly. In Iowa, for example, summons were issued to individuals to appear before so-called "courts" to explain why they had not subscribed to their "quota" of Liberty Bonds.

Resistance to Government Attacks on Rights Organized opposition to attacks on civil rights came from the National Civil Liberties Bureau (NCLB). This group was originally a unit within the American Union Against Militarism and later the AMERICAN CIVIL LIBERTIES UNION (ACLU), but on October 1, 1917, it was an independent organization headed by Roger Baldwin, a civil rights activist. The NCLB was dedicated to defending conscientious objectors, challenging prosecutions under the Espionage and Sedition acts, publicly arguing against mob violence perpetrated against dissenters and aliens, and attempting to achieve evenhanded justice for victims of government oppression. When the NCLB aggressively supported the Industrial Workers of the World (IWW), it incurred the wrath of the government which regarded both the IWW and the NCLB as left-wing, pacifist, antiwar, and obstructionist organizations. With the NCLB's reputation and influence in decline, its nadir was reached when Baldwin was sentenced to eleven months in prison for refusing to serve in the military.

The NCLB provided support to conscientious objectors (CO's) by publicizing their mistreatment and urging the government to intervene in their behalf. There were 2,700 hard-core CO's during U.S. participation in World War I. Although death sentences were given to seventeen of them, none was carried out. However, a similar number of CO's died in prison for health reasons, which may have been caused or exacerbated by prison conditions. In 1933 newly elected President Franklin D. Roosevelt pardoned the last 142 CO's who were serving life sentences.

American racist attitudes were not ameliorated during World War I. If anything, they became more deeply entrenched. Black soldiers received inferior and inadequate training and were often assigned to labor units, where they made up more than a third of the total manpower. White attitudes remained the same: Black men were at best incapable, at worst inferior, and no change was in the offing.

There is little doubt that civil rights were weakened, and in some cases obliterated, during World War I. There were more than two thousand prosecutions of wartime critics, and 2,300 ALIENS were detained. However, there was a war to be won. In *Schenck v. United States* (1919), Supreme Court justice Oliver Wendell Holmes, Jr., spoke for the majority in upholding Schenck's guilt for attempting to persuade army inductees to oppose CONSCRIPTION. Holmes stated that during wartime individual expression that constitutes a "clear and present danger" to the national interest must be suppressed. A majority of Americans both during and after World War I strongly agreed.

SUGGESTED READINGS:

Higham, John. *Strangers in the Land: Patterns of American Nativism, 1860-1925.* New York: Atheneum, 1963.

Kennedy, David M. *Over Here: The First World War and American Society.* New York: Oxford University Press, 1980.

Murphy, Paul L. *World War I and the Origin of Civil Liberties in the United States.* New York: W. W. Norton, 1979.

Peterson, Horace C., and Gilbert C. Fite. *Opponents of War, 1917-1918.* Seattle: University of Washington Press, 1968

Schaffer, Ronald. *America in the Great War: The Rise of the War Welfare State.* New York: Oxford University Press, 1991.

Vaughn, Stephen. *Holding Fast the Inner Line: Democracy, Nationalism and the Committee on Public Information.* Chapel Hill: University of North Carolina Press, 1980.

Walker, Samuel. *In Defense of American Liberties: A History of the ACLU.* New York: Oxford University Press, 1990.

—*John Quinn Imholte*

World War II

1939-1945: Global conflict in which the United States, Great Britain, and the Soviet Union combined to defeat Germany, Italy, and Japan.

Because defeat would have meant incalculable harm to the American nation, the U.S. government was forced to dig deeply into its social resources in order to survive. The brutal necessities of conducting the war made previous social distinctions such as race and gender less rigid and accelerated the process of breaking down many social barriers.

African Americans and World War II After the German invasion of Poland, the event that triggered the war in Europe, President Franklin D. Roosevelt operated under the assumption that the United States would eventually be drawn into the conflict. To be prepared, he used his position to encourage American economic growth, especially in those industries concerned with national defense.

Most defense industries, like much of the rest of American business, discriminated against African Americans, concentrating them at the bottom of the economic spectrum. A. Philip RANDOLPH, president of the BROTHERHOOD OF SLEEPING CAR PORTERS, organized a march on Washington, D.C., during the summer of 1941 in order to protest the lack of black participation in the growing American defense industry. By mid-summer, thousands of African Americans were prepared to march on the nation's capital.

President Roosevelt began to fear the effect of thousands of disgruntled Americans in the capital during that period of international crisis. Also, his advisers informed him that communist agitators might attend the march, as well as German or Japanese agents. To defuse that situation, Roosevelt offered Randolph a deal: If the march were called off, the president would issue an executive order prohibiting discrimination in the war industry and in the U.S. government. Randolph accepted the deal, and on June 25, 1941, Roosevelt issued EXECUTIVE ORDER 8802, which established the Fair Employment Practices Committee. The March on Washington movement was important because it anticipated the CIVIL RIGHTS MOVEMENT of the 1960's in several ways. First, as an all-black movement, it represented the first large-scale "self-help" effort. Second, it used direct action: The movement represented a subtle threat by a minority group to disrupt the general society by taking grievances to the streets. Finally, the beneficiaries of the movement were the black working class. Before the movement, most civil rights gains had primarily benefited the black middle class.

During World War II, about one million African Americans served in the armed forces. Another consequence of the March on Washington movement was the War Department's decision to draft African Americans in direct proportion to their presence in the general population (about 10 percent). The decision was a milestone in civil rights because it represented the first time that any American government agency had even hinted at the concept of equality.

African Americans served in segregated units, usually officered by whites. In this regard, the U.S. military in World War II mirrored the general society in that blacks worked in secondary roles while whites held leadership positions. The War Department, however, also decided in 1941 that blacks could be trained as combat aircraft pilots—tacit recognition that black men were as able to perform complex tasks as white men. The Ninety-Ninth Pursuit Squadron, an all-black fighter squadron serving in North Africa, subsequently distinguished itself as one of the finest units to have served in combat in any of America's wars.

On the home front, the migration of blacks from southern rural areas to northern urban areas—a movement that began during World War I—was given additional stimulus by World War II. In their quest for defense-industry jobs, many African Americans moved to the cities where the defense industries were located. Because there were fewer barriers to voting in the northern states, the inner cities in the north began to represent blocks of black political power. The effect of these black voting areas proved important in the postwar era, when national politicians began to cater to the "black vote"—a political voice that, increasingly, called for enhanced black participation in American society.

Despite the many gains made by African Americans during the war, there were also many instances of friction between the whites and blacks. RACE RIOTS occurred with regularity throughout the war; one riot in Detroit during the summer of 1943 left thirty-four dead. White soldiers assaulted black soldiers and sailors frequently; in North Carolina, a white bus driver killed a black soldier in full view of the passengers and was found not guilty. Incidents such as these caused many blacks to question their participation in the war, as did the widely noted fact that the Red Cross segregated blood as either "White" or "Colored." Many African Americans argued that World War II was a "white man's war" and claimed that there was little difference between Nazi racial theories and domestic American racism.

In response to such criticisms, the federal government typically replied that it had few resources to spend on civil rights. The first priority, government officials argued, was to win the war; all social problems would have to be put on the "back burner." Yet despite such failures, the war was a major turning point in African American civil rights. Perhaps the single most important long-term effect of African American participation in World War II was that, having been used as an important resource in a war to save the American nation from defeat at the hands of the Germans and the Japanese, blacks would no longer accept exclusion from mainstream American society.

Women in World War II American entry into the war following the Japanese attack on Pearl Harbor affected the civil rights of women at a basic level. The industrial build-up started by President Roosevelt required millions of workers. Because men were being mobilized to serve as soldiers and sailors, the only alternative was to recruit women as factory workers. Some women served in the military with distinction during the war, but it was principally their role as industrial workers that effected a change in women's status. The war's growth in industrial production gave many American women their first taste of decent wages and the social independence that accompanies enhanced income. Moreover, as women became proficient in welding, riveting, and myriad other necessary production jobs, they gradually became imbued with self-confidence and an independent attitude that would not go away at war's end.

Six million U.S. women went to work during World War II, increasing their representation on the workforce by about 57 percent. The war represented a dramatic change in the demographics of working women. Because 75 percent of women entering the workforce were married, the average female worker changed from a single, unmarried woman under the age of thirty-five to a married

mother over the age of thirty-five.

Working women during the war had to face a social attitude that cast working women in a dim light. During the early months of the war, many industrialists shied away from hiring female workers. It took battlefield reverses and a severe shortage of industrial goods to accomplish the temporary change of attitude that allowed women into war production.

When the war ended, the men came home and reclaimed their jobs. Most women who wanted to remain in higher-paying jobs were either fired or quit at the insistence of their husbands. It would be just a matter of a few years, however, before women went back into industrial production in larger num-

At a time when the loyalty of immigrant groups was under suspicion, many Chinese Americans bought war bonds to demonstrate their loyalty to the United States in World War II. (*Asian American Studies Library, University of California at Berkeley*)

bers than ever. America was going to discover that, like African Americans, women would not quietly go back into second-class status after answering the call to duty during the war.

Native Americans and Latinos During the war, about twenty-five thousand American Indians served in the U.S. military in functions ranging from combat soldiers to signal corps specialists. Many others left their reservations for the first time to work in war industries. Wartime stress on national unity caused many Native Americans to blend more fully into mainstream American culture, helping to break down the already tenuous tribal identity that held native cultures together.

About 300,000 LATINOS served in the U.S. military during the war. In 1942, the governments of the United States and Mexico developed a policy that would allow Mexican workers to enter America to alleviate the labor shortage. That policy increased the numbers of Hispanics in American cities and contributed to ethnic tensions; in June, 1943, such tensions erupted into a four-day disturbance in Los Angeles known as the Zoot Suit Riots.

Chinese Americans and Japanese Americans Because of the American alliance with China, CHINESE AMERICANS experienced reduced discrimination during the war. To curry favor with the Chinese government, the United States in 1943 repealed the CHINESE EXCLUSION ACT OF 1882. The changed policy allowed Chinese people to emigrate to America in larger numbers. Of equal importance was the government's effort to improve the image of the typical Chinese person through "positive imaging" propaganda.

Japanese Americans, on the other hand, had an especially difficult time during the war because of the fact that Japan was one of America's principal enemies. Suspicion grew to the point where it became official U.S. policy to sequester Japanese Americans in special camps away from the West Coast. There were only 130,000 people of Japanese descent in the United States, but because of the perceived threat, in February, 1942, the War Relocation Authority (WRA) was formed. The WRA interned about 110,000 Japanese Americans in camps where they were to be "Americanized." Their property was seized or abandoned, and the conditions in the camps were harsh. In 1945, the Japanese Americans were allowed to return to what homes they had left, but they faced continuing discrimination through the following decades. It was not until

1988 that Congress voted to reimburse them for their loss by passing the CIVIL LIBERTIES ACT OF 1988.

SUGGESTED READINGS:

Garfinkel, Herbert. *When Negroes March: The March on Washington Movement in the Organizational Politics of FEPC.* Glencoe, Ill.: Free Press, 1959. Discusses the movement's importance and its key role in the creation of the Fair Employment Practices Committee.

Milkman, Ruth. *Gender at Work: The Dynamics of Job Segregation by Sex During World War II.* Urbana: University of Illinois Press, 1987. A provocative examination of gender rights issues in the American workforce and the role of U.S. women during the war.

Potter, Lov, with William Miles and Nina Rosenblum. *Liberators: Fighting on Two Fronts in World War II.* New York: Harcourt Brace Jovanovich, 1992. A study of minority participation in U.S. combat forces and related home-front discrimination.

Smith, Page. *Democracy on Trial: The Japanese American Evacuation and Relocation in World War II.* New York: Simon & Schuster, 1995. Offers a detailed narrative of Japanese American internment during the war.

Terkel, Studs. *"The Good War": An Oral History of World War Two.* New York: Pantheon Books, 1984. Collection of interviews with a cross-section of the war's participants.

U.S. Commission on Wartime Relocation and Internment of Civilians. *Personal Justice Denied.* Washington, D.C.: Government Printing Office, 1992. An official examination of the wartime internment of Japanese Americans.

Willmott, H. P. *The Great Crusade: A New Complete History of the Second World War.* New York: Free Press, 1990. Contains a comprehensive explanation of the war's events. Useful for understanding American social development during the war.

—*Tim Palmer*

Wounded Knee occupation

1973: Occupation of Wounded Knee, South Dakota, by members of the AMERICAN INDIAN MOVEMENT (AIM).

The occupation of Wounded Knee that began on February 28, 1973, was among the most militant of

Russell Means watches fellow AIM officer Dennis Banks burn a federal government offer to permit Indians occupying Wounded Knee to leave without being arrested. (*AP/Wide World Photos*)

the activities undertaken by AIM. From the outset, AIM's founders targeted tribal governments as much as federal authorities as obstacles to improving the lives of AMERICAN INDIANS. In AIM's eyes, the latter enforced unjust laws; the former collaborated with them to protect their own corrupt hold on power.

In 1973 AIM activists focused their assault on Richard Wilson, one of whose first acts after being elected tribal chairman on South Dakota's Pine Ridge RESERVATION was to challenge AIM's influence on his reservation. AIM responded by occupying the Wounded Knee area on reservation grounds. Wounded Knee was the site of the 1890 massacre of Sioux by the United States Army.

Six weeks later, following sporadic exchanges of gunfire between AIM activists and the federal agents who positioned themselves around the small town, AIM negotiated a withdrawal of its protesters.

—*Joseph R. Rudolph, Jr.*

Y

Yasui, Minoru

Oct. 19, 1916, Hood River, Oreg.—Nov. 14, 1986, Denver, Colo.: Victim of the federal government's JAPANESE AMERICAN INTERNMENT program during WORLD WAR II who resisted curfew rules.

An attorney and a reserve officer in the U.S. Army, Yasui was working for Japan's Chicago consulate when Japan attacked Pearl Harbor in December, 1941. He immediately resigned his consulate job and asked to be activated by the U.S. army; however he was denied permission because of his Japanese ancestry.

In early 1942 the federal government began restricting the rights of Japanese Americans living along the West Coast. Yasui was the first person openly to challenge the legality of a curfew that the government imposed on Japanese Americans on March 28, 1942. He immediately challenged the curfew in Portland, Oregon, by wandering the city's streets in the evening, hoping to be arrested. He was picked up by police only five hours after the curfew became law. He did not dispute curfew laws that applied to aliens, but he regarded curfew laws imposed only on Japanese Americans as unjust. An Oregon federal judge, James Alger Fee, found Yasui guilty of violating the curfew, asserting that because Yasui had worked for a Japanese consulate, he owed allegiance to Japan and was no longer an American citizen.

The U.S. SUPREME COURT did not rule on Yasui's appeal, but sent it back to the Portland court for review. Judge Fee then altered his decision to fit an earlier Supreme Court case, involving a man named Gordon Hirabayashi, in which the Court had ruled that civil rights were not the issue, it was simply a question of whether the United States had the power to wage war successfully. Yasui spent nine months in solitary confinement and more than a year in detention centers during the course of the war for his curfew violation.

—Larry N. Sypolt

Yatabe, Thomas T.

1897, San Francisco, Calif.—? Cofounder and first elected president of the JAPANESE AMERICAN CITIZENS LEAGUE (JACL).

Later trained as a dentist, Yatabe was at the center of controversy as a child, when he was forced to attend a segregated school in San Fran-

Four of the original members of the Japanese American Citizens League in 1972; from left to right: George Togasaki, Saburo Kido, Thomas T. Yatabe, and George Inagaki. (*Pacific Citizen*)

cisco in 1906. During WORLD WAR I he helped create the American Loyalty League, and later, the league's Fresno, California, branch. A cofounder of the JACL in 1930, he became the organization's first elected president in 1934. As a staunch advocate of loyalty to the United States during the JAPANESE AMERICAN INTERNMENT of World War II, Yatabe—like Saburo KIDO—was attacked by a *kibei* gang for his stand. After he resettled in the Midwest, he founded the Chicago branch of the JACL in 1943.

—*Charles A. Desnoyers*

Yick Wo v. Hopkins

1886: U.S. SUPREME COURT decision holding a local government's discriminatory application of its zoning laws against CHINESE AMERICANS in violation of the EQUAL PROTECTION CLAUSE of the FOURTEENTH AMENDMENT.

In 1880 San Francisco enacted a LAUNDRY ORDINANCE requiring all laundry operators not housed in brick or stone buildings to obtain licenses from the city. It so happened that 240 of the city's 320 laundries were operated by people of Chinese descent and that some 310 of these laundries were housed in wooden buildings. When the operators in wooden buildings applied for licenses, virtually none of the Chinese operators obtained one, while all but one non-Chinese operators obtained licenses.

Confronted with these facts, the Supreme Court found that the actions of the San Francisco officials had violated the equal protection clause of the Fourteenth Amendment. In an opinion by Justice Thomas Stanley Matthews, the Court unanimously agreed that the equal protection clause safeguarded the rights of both citizens and ALIENS. Furthermore, the Court found that the San Francisco ordinance, although perhaps unobjectionable on its face, had been administered in a discriminatory manner against people of Chinese descent and was, therefore, unconstitutional.

—*Timothy L. Hall*

Young, Andrew Jackson, Jr.

Born Mar. 12, 1932, New Orleans, La.: Civil rights activist, politician, and diplomat.

The son of a dentist and a schoolteacher, Andrew Young graduated from Howard University with a premedical degree in 1951, but decided instead to enter the ministry. After he was ordained by the United Church of Christ in 1955, he began organizing community action groups and voter registration drives in the churches he served. In 1957 he was hired as a youth director by the National Council of Churches, for whom he later directed a national voter registration project. In that role, he worked with Martin Luther KING, JR., and the SOUTHERN CHRISTIAN LEADERSHIP CONFERENCE (SCLC).

In 1961 Andrew Young joined the SCLC staff; he was named executive director three years later. Although he frequently marched with King and was arrested during three marches, his most important contributions to the CIVIL RIGHTS MOVEMENT were not often highly visible. An able organizer and strategist, he was deeply involved in the unsuccessful protest in Albany, Georgia, and the later, eventful protests in BIRMINGHAM and SELMA, Alabama. He was particularly instrumental in organizing the BIRMINGHAM CHILDREN'S CRUSADE and the first march on Selma. He also helped draft the CIVIL RIGHTS ACT OF 1964 and the VOTING RIGHTS ACT OF 1965. After King's assassination in 1968, Young and Ralph ABERNATHY led the POOR PEOPLE'S CAMPAIGN on Washington, D.C.

Believing that the Civil Rights movement needed to move from the streets into the political structure, Young left the SCLC in 1970 in order to run for CONGRESS. Unsuccessful in his first try, he was elected in 1972 and served in the House of Representatives until 1977, when President Jimmy CARTER appointed him ambassador to the United Nations. He was later mayor of ATLANTA, GEORGIA, from 1982 until 1989, but was defeated in his 1990 try for the Democratic nomination for governor.

—*Richard W. Leeman*

Young, Whitney

July 31, 1921, Lincoln Ridge, Ky.—March 11, 1971, Lagos, Nigeria: Director of the NATIONAL URBAN LEAGUE from 1961 to 1971.

After earning an M.A. in social work from the University of Minnesota in 1947, Whitney Moore Young, Jr., became industrial relations secretary for the St. Paul Urban League. His success in broadening employment opportunities for blacks led to his promotion in 1950 to executive director of the Omaha Urban League, where he also lectured in local colleges. In 1954 he became dean of the

Whitney Young, director of the National Urban League from 1961 to 1971. (*Library of Congress*)

School of Social Work at Atlanta University, where he instituted curricular changes, expanded the faculty, and enhanced the reputation of the school. While he was in Georgia he was an officer of the state branch of the NATIONAL ASSOCIATION FOR THE ADVANCEMENT OF COLORED PEOPLE and he advised student protest groups.

Chosen to lead the National Urban League in 1961, Young continued the league's traditional stress on employment and social service, but involved the league more directly in the CIVIL RIGHTS MOVEMENT. He convinced his board of directors to make the Urban League one of the major sponsors of the 1963 MARCH ON WASHINGTON. Young's conciliatory personality and mediation skills helped hold together the movement's traditional and militant elements through the 1960's.

Young used the Urban League's contacts with leaders of major American corporations to raise increasing sums of money for the league and to convince corporations to hire and promote more blacks. In speeches, newspaper columns, and his 1964 book, *To Be Equal*, Young called for a "domestic Marshall Plan" with massive aid programs designed to close the economic, educational, and social gaps among the races—a proposal that influenced President Lyndon B. JOHNSON's War on Poverty legislation. In *Beyond Racism: Building an Open Society* (1969) Young described his hopes for the future.

Young's success in raising money from wealthy white individuals and foundations aroused the enmity of some radical black activists, who accused him of being controlled by whites. However, Young never lost his faith in integration as the fundamental black goal.

In 1971, while attending a conference in Lagos, Nigeria, Young drowned while swimming in the ocean.

—Milton Berman

Z

Zoot suit riots

1943: RACE RIOT involving MEXICAN AMERI-CANS and white servicemen in Los Angeles, California.

During the late 1930's young Los Angeles Mexican Americans adopted a style of dress that included baggy pants; long, loose-fitting jackets with heavily padded shoulders; low, wide-brimmed hats; and draped key chains. Known as "zoot suits," these outfits became symbols of pride for young Chicano men. WORLD WAR II brought new prosperity to the Mexican American areas of Los Angeles, as defense-related industries employed local residents. The resulting changes increased the antipathy of many whites toward Mexican Americans. Fearing violence, young Mexican American men patrolled their neighborhoods, and this added to an already volatile situation. On June 3, 1943, white sailors on liberty in Los Angeles entered the Mexican American community and attacked young men wearing zoot suits. Over the next several days tensions mounted until military authorities declared the entire area off-limits to servicemen.

—*Duncan R. Jamieson*

The Declaration of Independence

In Congress, July 4, 1776
The unanimous declaration of the thirteen
United States of America

When in the Course of human Events, it becomes necessary for one People to dissolve the Political Bands which have connected them with another, and to assume among the Powers of the Earth, the separate and equal Station to which the Laws of Nature and of Nature's God entitle them, a decent Respect to the Opinions of Mankind requires that they should declare the causes which impel them to the Separation.

We hold these Truths to be self-evident, that all Men are created equal, that they are endowed by their Creator with certain unalienable Rights, that among these are Life, Liberty, and the Pursuit of Happiness—That to secure these Rights, Governments are instituted among Men, deriving their just Powers from the Consent of the Governed, that whenever any Form of Government becomes destructive of these Ends, it is the Right of the People to alter or to abolish it, and to institute new Government, laying its Foundation on such Principles, and organizing its Powers in such Form, as to them shall seem most likely to effect their Safety and Happiness. Prudence, indeed, will dictate that Governments long established should not be changed for light and transient Causes; and accordingly all Experience hath shewn, that Mankind are more disposed to suffer, while Evils are sufferable, than to right themselves by abolishing the Forms to which they are accustomed. But when a long Train of Abuses and Usurpations, pursuing invariably the same Object, evinces a Design to reduce them under absolute Despotism, it is their Right, it is their Duty, to throw off such Government, and to provide new Guards for their future Security. Such has been the patient Sufferance of these Colonies; and such is now the Necessity which constrains them to alter their former Systems of Government. The History of the present King of Great-Britain is a History of repeated Injuries and Usurpations, all having in direct Object the Establishment of an absolute Tyranny over these States. To prove this, let Facts be submitted to a candid World.

He has refused his Assent to Laws, the most wholesome and necessary for the public Good.

He has forbidden his Governors to pass Laws of immediate and pressing Importance, unless suspended in their Operation till his Assent should be obtained; and when so suspended, he has utterly neglected to attend to them.

He has refused to pass other Laws for the Accommodation of large Districts of People, unless those People would relinquish the Right of Representation in the Legislature, a Right inestimable to them, and formidable to Tyrants only.

He has called together Legislative Bodies at Places unusual, uncomfortable, and distant from the Depository of their public Records, for the sole Purpose of fatiguing them into Compliance with his Measures.

He has dissolved Representative Houses repeatedly, for opposing with manly Firmness his Invasions on the Rights of the People.

He has refused for a long Time, after such Dissolutions, to cause others to be elected; whereby the Legislative Powers, incapable of Annihilation, have returned to the People at large for their exercise; the State remaining in the mean time exposed to all the Dangers of Invasion from without, and Convulsions within.

He has endeavoured to prevent the Population of these States; for that Purpose obstructing the Laws for Naturalization of Foreigners; refusing to pass others to encourage their Migrations hither, and raising the Conditions of new Appropriations of Lands.

He has obstructed the Administration of Justice, by refusing his Assent to Laws for establishing Judiciary Powers.

He has made Judges dependent on his Will alone, for the Tenure of their Offices, and the Amount and Payment of their Salaries.

He has erected a Multitude of new Offices, and sent hither Swarms of Officers to harass our People, and eat out their Substance.

He has kept among us, in Times of Peace, Standing Armies, without the consent of our Legislatures.

He has affected to render the Military independent of and superior to the Civil Power.

He has combined with others to subject us to a Jurisdiction foreign to our Constitution, and unacknowledged by our Laws; giving his Assent to their Acts of pretended Legislation:

For quartering large Bodies of Armed Troops among us:

For protecting them, by a mock Trial, from Punishment for any Murders which they should commit on the Inhabitants of these States:

For cutting off our Trade with all Parts of the World:

For imposing Taxes on us without our Consent:

For depriving us, in many Cases, of the Benefits of Trial by Jury:

For transporting us beyond Seas to be tried for pretended Offences:

For abolishing the free System of English Laws in a neighbouring Province, establishing therein an arbitrary Government, and enlarging its Boundaries, so as to render it at once an Example and fit Instrument for introducing the same absolute Rule into these Colonies:

For taking away our Charters, abolishing our most valuable Laws, and altering fundamentally the Forms of our Governments:

For suspending our own Legislatures, and declaring themselves invested with Power to legislate for us in all Cases whatsoever.

He has abdicated Government here, by declaring us out of his Protection and waging War against us.

He has plundered our Seas, ravaged our Coasts, burnt our Towns, and destroyed the Lives of our People.

He is, at this Time, transporting large Armies of foreign Mercenaries to compleat the Works of Death, Desolation, and Tyranny, already begun with circumstances of Cruelty and Perfidy, scarcely paralleled in the most barbarous Ages, and totally unworthy the Head of a civilized Nation.

He has constrained our fellow Citizens taken Captive on the high Seas to bear Arms against their Country, to become the Executioners of their Friends and Brethren, or to fall themselves by their Hands.

He has excited domestic Insurrections amongst us, and has endeavoured to bring on the Inhabitants of our Frontiers, the merciless Indian Savages, whose known Rule of Warfare, is an undistinguished Destruction, of all Ages, Sexes and Conditions.

In every stage of these Oppressions we have Petitioned for Redress in the most humble Terms: Our repeated Petitions have been answered only by repeated Injury. A Prince, whose Character is thus marked by every act which may define a Tyrant, is unfit to be the Ruler of a free People.

Nor have we been wanting in Attentions to our British Brethren. We have warned them from Time to Time of Attempts by their Legislature to extend an unwarrantable Jurisdiction over us. We have reminded them of the Circumstances of our Emigration and Settlement here. We have appealed to their native Justice and Magnanimity, and we have conjured them by the Ties of our common Kindred to disavow these Usurpations, which, would inevitably interrupt our Connections and Correspondence. They too have been deaf to the Voice of Justice and of Consanguinity. We must, therefore, acquiesce in the Necessity, which denounces our Separation, and hold them, as we hold the rest of Mankind, Enemies in War, in Peace, Friends.

We, therefore, the Representatives of the UNITED STATES OF AMERICA, in General Congress, Assembled, appealing to the Supreme Judge of the World for the Rectitude of our Intentions, do, in the Name, and by Authority of the good People of these Colonies, solemnly Publish and Declare, That these United Colonies are, and of Right ought to be, FREE AND INDEPENDENT STATES; that they are absolved from all Allegiance to the British Crown, and that all political Connection between them and the State of Great-Britain, is and ought to be totally dissolved; and that as FREE AND INDEPENDENT STATES, they have full Power to levy War, conclude Peace, contract Alliances, establish Commerce, and to do all other Acts and Things which INDEPENDENT STATES may of right do. And for the support of this Declaration, with a firm Reliance on the Protection of divine Providence, we mutually pledge to each other our Lives, our Fortunes, and our sacred Honor.

Signed by Order and in Behalf of the Congress,
JOHN HANCOCK, PRESIDENT.

The Constitution of the United States of America

We the People of the United States, in Order to form a more perfect Union, establish Justice, insure domestic Tranquility, provide for the common defence, promote the general Welfare, and secure the Blessings of Liberty to ourselves and our Posterity, do ordain and establish this Constitution for the United States of America.

ARTICLE I.

SECTION 1. All legislative Powers herein granted shall be vested in a Congress of the United States, which shall consist of a Senate and House of Representatives.

SECTION 2. The House of Representatives shall be composed of Members chosen every second Year by the People of the several States, and the Electors in each State shall have the Qualifications requisite for Electors of the most numerous Branch of the State Legislature.

No Person shall be a Representative who shall not have attained to the Age of twenty five Years, and been seven Years a Citizen of the United States, and who shall not, when elected, be an Inhabitant of that State in which he shall be chosen.

Representatives and direct Taxes shall be apportioned among the several States which may be included within this Union, according to their respective Numbers, which shall be determined by adding to the whole Number of free Persons, including those bound to Service for a Term of Years, and excluding Indians not taxed, three fifths of all other Persons. The actual Enumeration shall be made within three Years after the first Meeting of the Congress of the United States, and within every subsequent Term of ten Years, in such Manner as they shall by Law direct. The number of Representatives shall not exceed one for every thirty Thousand, but each State shall have at Least one Representative; and until such enumeration shall be made, the State of New Hampshire shall be entitled to chuse three, Massachusetts eight, Rhode-Island and Providence Plantations one, Connecticut five, New-York six, New Jersey four, Pennsylvania eight, Delaware one, Maryland six, Virginia ten, North Carolina five, South Carolina five, and Georgia three.

When vacancies happen in the Representation from any State, the Executive Authority thereof shall issue Writs of Election to fill such Vacancies.

The House of Representatives shall chuse their Speaker and other Officers; and shall have the sole Power of Impeachment.

SECTION 3. The Senate of the United States shall be composed of two Senators from each State, chosen by the Legislature thereof, for six Years; and each Senator shall have one Vote.

Immediately after they shall be assembled in Consequence of the first Election, they shall be divided as equally as may be into three Classes. The Seats of the Senators of the first Class shall be vacated at the Expiration of the second Year, of the second Class at the Expiration of the fourth Year, and of the third Class at the Expiration of the sixth Year, so that one third may be chosen every second Year; and if Vacancies happen by Resignation, or otherwise, during the Recess of the Legislature of any State, the Executive thereof may make temporary Appointments until the next Meeting of the Legislature, which shall then fill such Vacancies.

No Person shall be a Senator who shall not have attained to the Age of thirty Years, and been nine Years a Citizen of the United States, and who shall not, when elected, be an Inhabitant of that State for which he shall be chosen.

The Vice President of the United States shall be President of the Senate, but shall have no Vote, unless they be equally divided.

The Senate shall chuse their other Officers, and also a President pro tempore, in the Absence of the Vice President, or when he shall exercise the Office of President of the United States.

The Senate shall have the sole Power to try all Impeachments. When sitting for that Purpose, they shall be on Oath or Affirmation. When the President of the United States is tried, the Chief Justice shall preside: And no Person shall be convicted without the Concurrence of two thirds of the Members present.

Judgment in Cases of Impeachment shall not extend further than to removal from Office, and disqualification to hold and enjoy any Office of honor, Trust or Profit under the United States: but the Party convicted shall nevertheless be liable and subject to Indictment, Trial, Judgment and Punishment, according to Law.

SECTION 4. The Times, Places and Manner of holding Elections for Senators and Representatives, shall be prescribed in each State by the Legislature thereof; but the Congress may at any time by Law make or alter such Regulations, except as to the Places of chusing Senators.

The Congress shall assemble at least once in every Year, and such Meeting shall be on the first Monday in December, unless they shall by Law appoint a different Day.

SECTION 5. Each House shall be the Judge of the Elections, Returns and Qualifications of its own Members, and a Majority of each shall constitute a Quorum to do Business; but a smaller Number may adjourn from day to day, and may be authorized to compel the Attendance of absent Members, in such Manner, and under such Penalties as each House may provide.

Each House may determine the Rules of its Proceedings, punish its Members for disorderly Behaviour, and, with the Concurrence of two thirds, expel a Member.

Each House shall keep a Journal of its Proceedings, and from time to time publish the same, excepting such Parts as may in their Judgment require Secrecy; and the Yeas and Nays of the Members of either House on any question shall, at the Desire of one fifth of those Present, be entered on the Journal.

Neither House, during the Session of Congress, shall, without the Consent of the other, adjourn for more than three days, nor to any other Place than that in which the two Houses shall be sitting.

SECTION 6. The Senators and Representatives shall receive a Compensation for their Services, to be ascertained by Law, and paid out of the Treasury of the United States. They shall in all Cases, except Treason, Felony and Breach of the Peace, be privileged from Arrest during their Attendance at the Session of their respective Houses, and in going to and returning from the same; and for any Speech or Debate in either House, they shall not be questioned in any other Place.

No Senator or Representative shall, during the Time for which he was elected, be appointed to any civil Office under the Authority of the United States, which shall have been created, or the Emoluments whereof shall have been encreased during such time; and no Person holding any Office under the United States, shall be a Member of either House during his Continuance in Office.

SECTION 7. All Bills for raising Revenue shall originate in the House of Representatives; but the Senate may propose or concur with Amendments as on other Bills.

Every Bill which shall have passed the House of Representatives and the Senate, shall, before it becomes a Law, be presented to the President of the United States; If he approve he shall sign it, but if not he shall return it, with his Objections to that House in which it shall have originated, who shall enter the Objections at large on their Journal, and proceed to reconsider it. If after such Reconsideration two thirds of that House shall agree to pass the Bill, it shall be sent, together with the Objections, to the other House, by which it shall likewise be reconsidered, and if approved by two thirds of that House, it shall become a Law. But in all such Cases the Votes of both Houses shall be determined by yeas and Nays, and the Names of the Persons voting for and against the Bill shall be entered on the Journal of each House respectively. If any Bill shall not be returned by the President within ten Days (Sundays excepted) after it shall have been presented to him, the Same shall be a Law, in like Manner as if he had signed it, unless the Congress by their Adjournment prevent its Return, in which Case it shall not be a Law.

Every Order, Resolution, or Vote to which the Concurrence of the Senate and House of Representatives may be necessary (except on a question of Adjournment) shall be presented to the President of the United States; and before the Same shall take Effect, shall be approved by him, or being disapproved by him, shall be repassed by two thirds of the Senate and House of Representatives, according to the Rules and Limitations prescribed in the Case of a Bill.

SECTION 8. The Congress shall have Power To lay and collect Taxes, Duties, Imposts and Excises, to pay the Debts and provide for the common Defence and general Welfare of the United States; but all Duties, Imposts and Excises shall be uniform throughout the United States;

To borrow Money on the credit of the United States;

To regulate Commerce with foreign Nations, and among the several States, and with the Indian Tribes;

To establish an uniform Rule of Naturalization, and uniform Laws on the subject of Bankruptcies throughout the United States;

To coin Money, regulate the Value thereof, and of foreign Coin, and fix the Standard of Weights and Measures;

To provide for the Punishment of counterfeiting the Securities and current Coin of the United States;

To establish Post Offices and post Roads;

To promote the Progress of Science and useful Arts, by securing for limited Times to Authors and Inventors the exclusive Right to their respective Writings and Discoveries;

To constitute Tribunals inferior to the supreme Court;

To define and punish Piracies and Felonies committed on the high Seas, and Offenses against the Law of Nations;

To declare War, grant Letters of Marque and Reprisal, and make Rules concerning Captures on Land and Water;

To raise and support Armies, but no Appropriation of Money to that Use shall be for a longer Term than two Years;

To provide and maintain a Navy;

To make Rules for the Government and Regulation of the land and naval Forces;

To provide for calling forth the Militia to execute the Laws of the Union, suppress Insurrections and repel Invasions;

To provide for organizing, arming, and disciplining, the Militia, and for governing such Part of them as may be employed in the Service of the United States, reserving to the States respectively, the Appointment of the Officers, and the Authority of training the Militia according to the discipline prescribed by Congress;

To exercise exclusive Legislation in all Cases whatsoever, over such District (not exceeding ten Miles square) as may, by Cession of particular States, and the Acceptance of Congress, become the Seat of the Government of the United States, and to exercise like Authority over all Places purchased by the Consent of the Legislature of the State in which the Same shall be, for the Erection of Forts, Magazines, Arsenals, dock-Yards and other needful Buildings;—And

To make all Laws which shall be necessary and proper for carrying into Execution the foregoing Powers, and all other Powers vested by this Constitution in the Government of the United States, or in any Department or Officer thereof.

SECTION 9. The Migration or Importation of such Persons as any of the States now existing shall think proper to admit, shall not be prohibited by the Congress prior to the Year one thousand eight hundred and eight, but a Tax or duty may be imposed on such Importation, not exceeding ten dollars for each Person.

The Privilege of the Writ of Habeas Corpus shall not be suspended, unless when in Cases of Rebellion or Invasion the public Safety may require it.

No Bill of Attainder or ex post facto Law shall be passed.

No Capitation, or other direct, Tax shall be laid, unless in Proportion to the Census or Enumeration herein before directed to be taken.

No Tax or Duty shall be laid on Articles exported from any State.

No Preference shall be given by any Regulation of Commerce or Revenue to the Ports of one State over those of another: nor shall Vessels bound to, or from, one State, be obliged to enter, clear, or pay Duties in another.

No Money shall be drawn from the Treasury, but in Consequence of Appropriations made by Law; and a regular Statement and Account of the Receipts and Expenditures of all public Money shall be published from time to time.

No Title of Nobility shall be granted by the United States: And no Person holding any Office of Profit or Trust under them, shall, without the Consent of the Congress, accept of any present, Emolument, Office, or Title, of any kind whatever, from any King, Prince, or foreign State.

SECTION 10. No State shall enter into any Treaty, Alliance, or Confederation; grant Letters of Marque and Reprisal; coin Money; emit Bills of Credit; make any Thing but gold and silver Coin a Tender in Payment of Debts; pass any Bill of Attainder, ex post facto Law, or Law impairing the Obligation of Contracts, or grant any Title of Nobility.

No State shall, without the Consent of the Congress, lay any Imposts or Duties on Imports or Exports, except what may be absolutely necessary for executing it's inspection Laws: and the net Produce of all Duties and Imposts, laid by any State on Imports or Exports, shall be for the Use of the Treasury of the United States; and all such Laws shall be subject to the Revision and Control of the Congress.

No State shall, without the Consent of Congress, lay any Duty of Tonnage, keep Troops, or Ships of War in time of Peace, enter into any Agreement or Compact with another State, or with a foreign Power, or engage in War, unless actually invaded, or in such imminent Danger as will not admit of delay.

ARTICLE II.

SECTION 1. The executive Power shall be vested in a President of the United States of America. He shall hold his Office during the Term of four Years, and, together with the Vice President, chosen for the same Term, be elected, as follows

Each State shall appoint, in such Manner as the Legislature thereof may direct, a Number of Electors, equal to the whole Number of Senators and Representatives to which the State may be entitled in the Congress: but no Senator or Representative, or Person holding an Office of Trust or Profit under the United States, shall be appointed an Elector.

The Electors shall meet in their respective States, and vote by Ballot for two Persons, of whom one at least shall not be an Inhabitant of the same State with themselves. And they shall make a List of all the Persons voted for, and of the Number of Votes for each; which List they shall sign and certify, and transmit sealed to the Seat of the Government of the United States, directed to the President of the Senate. The President of the Senate shall, in the Presence of the Senate and House of Representatives, open all the Certificates, and the Votes shall then be counted. The Person having the greatest Number of Votes shall be the President, if such Number be a Majority of the whole Number of Electors appointed; and if there be more than one who have such Majority, and have an equal Number of Votes, then the House of Representatives shall immediately chuse by Ballot one of them for President; and if no Person have a Majority, then from the five highest on the List the said House shall in like manner chuse the President. But in chusing the President, the Votes shall be taken by States, the Representation from each State having one Vote; A quorum for this Purpose shall consist of a Member or Members from two thirds of the States, and a Majority of all the States shall be necessary to a Choice. In every Case, after the Choice of the President, the Person having the greatest Number of Votes of the Electors shall be the Vice President. But if there should remain two or more who have equal Votes, the Senate shall chuse from them by Ballot the Vice President.

The Congress may determine the Time of chusing the Electors, and the Day on which they shall give their Votes; which Day shall be the same throughout the United States.

No Person except a natural born Citizen, or a Citizen of the United States, at the time of the Adoption of this Constitution, shall be eligible to the Office of the President; neither shall any person be eligible to that Office who shall not have attained to the Age of thirty five Years, and been fourteen Years a Resident within the United States.

In Case of the Removal of the President from Office, or of his Death, Resignation, or Inability to discharge the Powers and Duties of the said Office, the Same shall devolve on the Vice President, and the Congress may by Law provide for the Case of Removal, Death, Resignation or Inability, both of the President and Vice President, declaring what Officer shall then act as President, and such Officer shall act accordingly, until the Disability be removed, or a President shall be elected.

The President shall, at stated Times, receive for his Services, a Compensation, which shall neither be increased nor diminished during the Period for which he shall have been elected, and he shall not receive within that Period any other Emolument from the United States, or any of them.

Before he enter the Execution of his Office, he shall take the following Oath or Affirmation:—"I do solemnly swear (or affirm) that I will faithfully execute the Office of President of the United States, and will to the best of my Ability, preserve, protect and defend the Constitution of the United States."

SECTION 2. The President shall be Commander in Chief of the Army and Navy of the United States, and of the Militia of the several States, when called into the actual Service of the United States; he may require the Opinion, in writing, of the principal Officer in each of the executive Departments, upon any Subject relating to the Duties of their respective Offices, and he shall have Power to grant Reprieves and Pardons for Offenses against the United States, except in Cases of Impeachment.

He shall have Power, by and with the Advice and Consent of the Senate, to make Treaties, provided two thirds of the Senators present concur; and he shall nominate, and by and with the Advice and Consent of the Senate, shall appoint Ambassadors, other public Ministers and Consuls, Judges of the supreme Court, and all other Officers of the United States, whose Appointments are not herein otherwise provided for, and which shall be established by Law: but the Congress may by Law vest the Appointment of such inferior Officers, as they think proper, in the President alone, in the Courts of Law, or in the Heads of Departments.

The President shall have Power to fill up all Vacancies that may happen during the Recess of the Senate, by granting Commissions which shall expire at the End of their next Session.

SECTION 3. He shall from time to time give to the Congress Information of the State of the Union, and recommend to their Consideration such Measures as he shall judge necessary and expedient; he may, on extraordinary Occasions, convene both Houses, or either of them, and in Case of Disagreement between them, with Respect to the Time of Adjournment, he may adjourn them to such Time as he shall think proper; he shall receive Ambassadors and other public Ministers; he shall take Care that the Laws be faithfully executed, and shall Commission all the Officers of the United States.

SECTION 4. The President, Vice President and all civil Officers of the United States, shall be removed from Office on Impeachment for, and Conviction of, Treason, Bribery, or other high Crimes and Misdemeanors.

ARTICLE III.

SECTION 1. The judicial Power of the United States, shall be vested in one supreme Court, and in such inferior Courts as the Congress may from time to time ordain and establish. The Judges, both of the supreme and inferior Courts, shall hold their Offices during good Behaviour, and shall, at stated Times, receive for their Services, a Compensation, which shall not be diminished during their Continuance in Office.

SECTION 2. The judicial Power shall extend to all Cases, in Law and Equity, arising under this Constitution, the Laws of the United States, and Treaties made, or which shall be made, under their Authority;—to all Cases affecting Ambassadors, other public Ministers and Consuls;—to all Cases of admiralty and maritime jurisdiction;—to Controversies to which the United States shall be a Party;—to Controversies between two or more States; between a State and Citizens of another State; between Citizens of different States,—between Citizens of the same State claiming Lands under Grants of different States, and between a State, or the Citizens thereof, and foreign States, Citizens or Subjects.

In all Cases affecting Ambassadors, other public Ministers and Consuls, and those in which a State shall be Party, the supreme Court shall have original Jurisdiction. In all the other Cases before mentioned, the supreme Court shall have appellate Jurisdiction, both as to Law and Fact, with such Exceptions, and under such Regulations as the Congress shall make.

The Trial of all Crimes, except in Cases of Impeachment, shall be by Jury; and such Trial shall be held in the State where the said Crimes shall have been committed; but when not committed within any State, the Trial shall be at such Place or Places as the Congress may by Law have directed.

SECTION 3. Treason against the United States, shall consist only in levying War against them, or in adhering to their Enemies, giving them Aid and Comfort. No Person shall be convicted of Treason unless on the Testimony of two Witnesses to the same overt Act, or on Confession in open Court.

The Congress shall have Power to declare the Punishment of Treason, but no Attainder of Treason shall work Corruption of Blood, or Forfeiture except during the Life of the Person attainted.

ARTICLE IV.

SECTION 1. Full Faith and Credit shall be given in each State to the public Acts, Records, and judicial Proceedings of every other State; And the Congress may by general Laws prescribe the Manner in which such Acts, Records and Proceedings shall be proved, and the Effect thereof.

SECTION 2. The Citizens of each State shall be entitled to all Privileges and Immunities of Citizens in the several States.

A Person charged in any State with Treason, Felony, or other Crime, who shall flee from Justice, and be found in another State, shall on Demand of the executive Authority of the State from which he fled, be delivered up, to be removed to the State having Jurisdiction of the Crime.

No person held to Service or Labour in one State, under the Laws thereof, escaping into another, shall, in Consequence of any Law or Regulation therein, be discharged from such Service or Labour, but shall be delivered up on Claim of the Party to whom such Service or Labour may be due.

SECTION 3. New States may be admitted by the Congress into this Union; but no new State shall be formed or erected within the Jurisdiction of any other State; nor any State be formed by the Junction of two or more States, or Parts of States, without the Consent of the Legislatures of the States concerned as well as of the Congress.

The Congress shall have Power to dispose of and make all needful Rules and Regulations respecting the Territory or other Property belonging to the United States; and nothing in this Constitution shall be so construed as to Prejudice any Claims of the United States, or of any particular State.

SECTION 4. The United States shall guarantee to

every State in this Union a Republican Form of Government, and shall protect each of them against Invasion; and on Application of the Legislature, or of the Executive (when the Legislature cannot be convened) against domestic Violence.

ARTICLE V.

The Congress, whenever two thirds of both Houses shall deem it necessary, shall propose Amendments to this Constitution, or, on the Application of the Legislatures of two thirds of the several States, shall call a Convention for proposing Amendments, which, in either Case, shall be valid to all Intents and Purposes, as Part of this Constitution, when ratified by the Legislatures of three fourths of the several States, or by Conventions in three fourths thereof, as the one or the other Mode of Ratification may be proposed by the Congress; Provided that no Amendment which may be made prior to the Year One thousand eight hundred and eight shall in any Manner affect the first and fourth Clauses in the Ninth Section of the first Article; and that no State, without its Consent, shall be deprived of it's equal Suffrage in the Senate.

ARTICLE VI.

All Debts contracted and Engagements entered into, before the Adoption of this Constitution, shall be as valid against the United States under this Constitution, as under the Confederation.

This Constitution, and the Laws of the United States which shall be made in Pursuance thereof; and all Treaties made, or which shall be made, under the Authority of the United States, shall be the supreme Law of the Land; and the Judges in every State shall be bound thereby, any Thing in the Constitution or Laws of any State to the Contrary notwithstanding.

The Senators and Representatives before mentioned, and the Members of the several State Legislatures, and all executive and judicial Officers, both of the United States and of the several States, shall be bound by Oath or Affirmation, to support this Constitution; but no religious Test shall ever be required as a Qualification to any Office or public Trust under the United States.

ARTICLE VII.

The Ratification of the Conventions of nine States, shall be sufficient for the Establishment of this Constitution between the States so ratifying the Same.

Done in Convention by the Unanimous Consent of the States present the Seventeenth Day of September in the Year of our Lord one thousand seven hundred and Eighty seven and of the Independence of the United States of America the Twelfth. In Witness whereof We have hereunto subscribed our Names,

G^o: Washington—Presid^t and deputy from Virginia

New Hampshire	John Langdon
	Nicholas Gilman
Massachusetts	Nathaniel Gorham
	Rufus King
Connecticut	Wm Saml Johnson
	Roger Sherman
New York	Alexander Hamilton
New Jersey	Wil: Livingston
	David Brearley
	Wm Paterson
	Jona: Dayton
Pennsylvania	B Franklin
	Thomas Mifflin
	Robt Morris
	Geo. Clymer
	Thos. FitzSimons
	Jared Ingersoll
	James Wilson
	Gouv Morris
Delaware	Geo: Read
	Gunning Bedord jun
	John Dickinson
	Richard Bassett
	Jaco: Broom
Maryland	James McHenry
	Dan of St Thos. Jenifer
	Danl Carroll
Virginia	John Blair—
	James Madison Jr.
North Carolina	W^m. Blount
	Richd Dobbs Spaight.
	Hu Williamson

South Carolina	J. Rutledge
	Charles Cotesworth Pinckney
	Charles Pickney
	Pierce Butler
Georgia	William Few
	Abr Baldwin

Attest William Jackson Secretary

AMENDMENTS TO THE
U.S. CONSTITUTION

AMENDMENT I.

Congress shall make no law respecting an establishment of religion, or prohibiting the free exercise thereof; or abridging the freedom of speech, or of the press, or the right of the people peaceably to assemble, and to petition the Government for a redress of grievances.   [ratified December, 1791]

AMENDMENT II.

A well regulated Militia, being necessary to the security of a free State, the right of the people to keep and bear Arms, shall not be infringed.
[ratified December, 1791]

AMENDMENT III.

No Soldier shall, in time of peace be quartered in any house, without the consent of the Owner, nor in time of war, but in a manner to be prescribed by law.   [ratified December, 1791]

AMENDMENT IV.

The right of the people to be secure in their persons, houses, papers, and effects, against unreasonable searches and seizures, shall not be violated, and no Warrants shall issue, but upon probable cause, supported by Oath or affirmation, and particularly describing the place to be searched, and the persons or things to be seized.
[ratified December, 1791]

AMENDMENT V.

No person shall be held to answer for a capital, or otherwise infamous crime, unless on a presentment or indictment of a Grand Jury, except in cases arising in the land or naval forces, or in the Militia, when in actual service in time of War or public danger; nor shall any person be subject for the same offence to be twice put in jeopardy of life or limb, nor shall be compelled in any criminal case to be a witness against himself, nor be deprived of life, liberty, or property, without due process of law; nor shall private property be taken for public use without just compensation.   [ratified December, 1791]

AMENDMENT VI.

In all criminal prosecutions, the accused shall enjoy the right to a speedy and public trial, by an impartial jury of the State and district wherein the crime shall have been committed; which district shall have been previously ascertained by law, and to be informed of the nature and cause of the accusation; to be confronted with the witnesses against him; to have compulsory process for obtaining witnesses in his favor, and to have the assistance of counsel for his defence.   [ratified December, 1791]

AMENDMENT VII.

In Suits at common law, where the value in controversy shall exceed twenty dollars, the right of trial by jury shall be preserved, and no fact tried by a jury shall be otherwise re-examined in any Court of the United States, than according to the rules of the common law.   [ratified December, 1791]

AMENDMENT VIII.

Excessive bail shall not be required, nor excessive fines imposed, nor cruel and unusual punishments inflicted.   [ratified December, 1791]

AMENDMENT IX.

The enumeration in the Constitution, of certain rights, shall not be construed to deny or disparage others retained by the people.
[ratified December, 1791]

AMENDMENT X.

The powers not delegated to the United States by the Constitution, nor prohibited by it to the States, are reserved to the States respectively, or to the people.   [ratified December, 1791]

AMENDMENT XI.

The Judicial power of the United States shall not be construed to extend to any suit in law or equity, commenced or prosecuted against one of the United States by Citizens of another State, or by Citizens or Subjects of any Foreign State.

[ratified February, 1795]

AMENDMENT XII.

The Electors shall meet in their respective states, and vote by ballot for President and Vice President, one of whom, at least, shall not be an inhabitant of the same state with themselves; they shall name in their ballots the person voted for as President, and in distinct ballots the person voted for as Vice-President, and they shall make distinct lists of all persons voted for as President, and of all persons voted for as Vice-President, and of the number of votes for each, which lists they shall sign and certify, and transmit sealed to the seat of the government of the United States, directed to the President of the Senate;—The President of the Senate shall, in the presence of the Senate and House of Representatives, open all the certificates and the votes shall then be counted;—The person having the greatest number of votes for President, shall be the President, if such number be a majority of the whole number of Electors appointed; and if no person have such majority, then from the persons having the highest numbers not exceeding three on the list of those voted for as President, the House of Representatives shall choose immediately, by ballot, the President. But in choosing the President, the votes shall be taken by states, the representation from each state having one vote; a quorum for this purpose shall consist of a member or members from two-thirds of the states, and a majority of all the states shall be necessary to a choice. And if the House of Representatives shall not choose a President whenever the right of choice shall devolve upon them, before the fourth day of March next following, then the Vice-President shall act as President, as in the case of the death or other constitutional disability of the President.—The person having the greatest number of votes as Vice-President, shall be the Vice-President, if such number be a majority of the whole number of Electors appointed, and if no person have a majority, then from the two highest numbers on the list, the Senate shall choose the Vice-President; a quorum for the purpose shall consist of two-thirds of the whole number of Senators, and a majority of the whole number shall be necessary to a choice. But no person constitutionally ineligible to the office of President shall be eligible to that of Vice-President of the United States. [ratified June, 1804]

AMENDMENT XIII.

SECTION 1. Neither slavery nor involuntary servitude, except as a punishment for crime whereof the party shall have been duly convicted, shall exist within the United States, or any place subject to their jurisdiction.

SECTION 2. Congress shall have power to enforce this article by appropriate legislation.

[ratified December, 1865]

AMENDMENT XIV.

SECTION 1. All persons born or naturalized in the United States and subject to the jurisdiction thereof, are citizens of the United States and of the State wherein they reside. No State shall make or enforce any law which shall abridge the privileges or immunities of citizens of the United States; nor shall any State deprive any person of life, liberty, or property, without due process of law; nor deny to any person within its jurisdiction the equal protection of the laws.

SECTION 2. Representatives shall be apportioned among the several States according to their respective numbers, counting the whole number of persons in each State, excluding Indians not taxed. But when the right to vote at any election for the choice of electors for President and Vice President of the United States, Representatives in Congress, the Executive and Judicial officers of a State, or the members of the Legislature thereof, is denied to any of the male inhabitants of such State, being twenty-one years of age, and citizens of the United States, or in any way abridged, except for participation in rebellion, or other crime, the basis of representation therein shall be reduced in the proportion which the number of such male citizens shall bear to the whole number of male citizens twenty-one years of age in such State.

SECTION 3. No person shall be a Senator or Representative in Congress, or elector of President and Vice President, or hold any office, civil or military, under the United States, or under any State, who, having previously taken an oath, as a member of Congress, or as an officer of the United States, or as a member of any State legislature, or as an executive or judicial officer of any State, to support the Constitution of the United States, shall have engaged in insurrection or rebellion against the same, or given aid or comfort to the enemies thereof. But Congress may by a vote of two-thirds of each House, remove such disability.

SECTION 4. The validity of the public debt of the United States, authorized by law, including debts incurred for payment of pensions and bounties for services in suppressing insurrection or rebellion, shall not be questioned. But neither the United States nor any State shall assume or pay any debt or obligation incurred in aid of insurrection or rebellion against the United States, or any claim for the loss or emancipation of any slave; but all such debts, obligations and claims shall be held illegal and void.

SECTION 5. The Congress shall have power to enforce, by appropriate legislation, the provisions of this article. [ratified July, 1868]

AMENDMENT XV.

SECTION 1. The right of citizens of the United States to vote shall not be denied or abridged by the United States or by any State on account of race, color, or previous condition of servitude.

SECTION 2. The Congress shall have power to enforce this article by appropriate legislation.

[ratified February, 1870]

AMENDMENT XVI.

The Congress shall have power to lay and collect taxes on incomes, from whatever source derived, without apportionment among the several States, and without regard to any census or enumeration.

[ratified February, 1913]

AMENDMENT XVII.

The Senate of the United States shall be composed of two Senators from each State, elected by the people thereof, for six years; and each Senator shall have one vote. The electors in each State shall have the qualifications requisite for electors of the most numerous branch of the State legislatures.

When vacancies happen in the representation of any State in the Senate, the executive authority of such State shall issue writs of election to fill such vacancies: *Provided*, That the legislature of any State may empower the executive thereof to make temporary appointments until the people fill the vacancies by election as the legislature may direct.

This amendment shall not be so construed as to affect the election or term of any Senator chosen before it becomes valid as part of the Constitution.

[ratified April, 1913]

AMENDMENT XVIII.

SECTION 1. After one year from the ratification of this article the manufacture, sale, or transportation of intoxicating liquors within, the importation thereof into, or the exportation thereof from the United States and all territory subject to the jurisdiction thereof for beverage purposes is hereby prohibited.

SECTION 2. The Congress and the several States shall have concurrent power to enforce this article by appropriate legislation.

SECTION 3. This article shall be inoperative unless it shall have been ratified as an amendment to the Constitution by the legislatures of the several States, as provided in the Constitution, within seven years from the date of the submission hereof to the States by the Congress.

[ratified January, 1919, repealed December, 1933]

AMENDMENT XIX.

The right of citizens of the United States to vote shall not be denied or abridged by the United States or by any State on account of sex.

Congress shall have power to enforce this article by appropriate legislation. [ratified August, 1920]

AMENDMENT XX.

SECTION 1. The terms of the President and Vice President shall end at noon on the 20th day of January, and the terms of Senators and Representatives at noon on the 3d day of January, of the years in which such terms would have ended if this article had not been ratified; and the terms of their successors shall then begin.

SECTION 2. The Congress shall assemble at least once in every year, and such meeting shall begin at noon on the 3d day of January, unless they shall by law appoint a different day.

SECTION 3. If, at the time fixed for the beginning of the term of the President, the President elect shall have died, the Vice President elect shall become President. If a President shall not have been chosen before the time fixed for the beginning of his term, or if the President elect shall have failed to qualify, then the Vice President elect shall act as President until a President shall have qualified; and the Congress may by law provide for the case wherein neither a President elect nor a Vice President elect shall have qualified, declaring who shall then act as President, or the manner in which one who is to act shall be selected, and such person shall act accordingly until a President or Vice President shall have qualified.

SECTION 4. The Congress may by law provide for the case of the death of any of the persons from whom the House of Representatives may choose a

President whenever the right of choice shall have devolved upon them, and for the case of the death of any of the persons from whom the Senate may choose a Vice President whenever the right of choice shall have devolved upon them.

SECTION 5. Sections 1 and 2 shall take effect on the 15th day of October following the ratification of this article.

SECTION 6. This article shall be inoperative unless it shall have been ratified as an amendment to the Constitution by the legislatures of three-fourths of the several States within seven years from the date of its submission.　　　　[ratified January, 1933]

AMENDMENT XXI.

SECTION 1. The eighteenth article of amendment to the Constitution of the United States is hereby repealed.

SECTION 2. The transportation or importation into any State, Territory, or possession of the United States for delivery or use therein of intoxicating liquors, in violation of the laws thereof, is hereby prohibited.

SECTION 3. This article shall be inoperative unless it shall have been ratified as an amendment to the Constitution by conventions in the several States, as provided in the Constitution, within seven years from the date of the submission hereof to the States by the Congress.　　　　[ratified December, 1933]

AMENDMENT XXII.

SECTION 1. No person shall be elected to the office of the President more than twice, and no person who has held the office of President, or acted as President, for more than two years of a term to which some other person was elected President shall be elected to the office of the President more than once. But this Article shall not apply to any person holding the office of President when this Article was proposed by the Congress, and shall not prevent any person who may be holding the office of President, or acting as President, during the term within which this Article becomes operative from holding the office of President or acting as President during the remainder of such term.

SECTION 2. This article shall be inoperative unless it shall have been ratified as an amendment to the Constitution by the legislatures of three-fourths of the several States within seven years from the date of its submission to the States by the Congress.

[ratified February, 1951]

AMENDMENT XXIII.

SECTION 1. The District constituting the seat of Government of the United States shall appoint in such manner as the Congress may direct:

A number of electors of President and Vice President equal to the whole number of Senators and Representatives in Congress to which the District would be entitled if it were a State, but in no event more than the least populous State; they shall be in addition to those appointed by the States, but they shall be considered, for the purposes of the election of President and Vice President, to be electors appointed by a State; and they shall meet in the District and perform such duties as provided by the twelfth article of amendment.

SECTION 2. The Congress shall have power to enforce this article by appropriate legislation.

[ratified March, 1961]

AMENDMENT XXIV.

SECTION 1. The right of citizens of the United States to vote in any primary or other election for President or Vice President, for electors for President or Vice President, or for Senator or Representative in Congress, shall not be denied or abridged by the United States or any State by reason of failure to pay any poll tax or other tax.

SECTION 2. The Congress shall have power to enforce this article by appropriate legislation.

[ratified January, 1964]

AMENDMENT XXV.

SECTION 1. In case of the removal of the President from office or of his death or resignation, the Vice President shall become President.

SECTION 2. Whenever there is a vacancy in the office of the Vice President, the President shall nominate a Vice President who shall take office upon confirmation by a majority vote of both Houses of Congress.

SECTION 3. Whenever the President transmits to the President pro tempore of the Senate and the Speaker of the House of Representatives his written declaration that he is unable to discharge the powers and duties of his office, and until he transmits to them a written declaration to the contrary, such powers and duties shall be discharged by the Vice President as Acting President.

SECTION 4. Whenever the Vice President and a majority of either the principal officers of the executive departments or of such other body as Congress may by law provide, transmit to the President pro tempore of the Senate and the Speaker of the House of Representatives their written declaration that the President is unable to discharge the powers and duties of his office, the Vice President shall immediately assume the powers and duties of the office as Acting President.

Thereafter, when the President transmits to the President pro tempore of the Senate and the Speaker of the House of Representatives his written declaration that no inability exists, he shall resume the powers and duties of his office unless the Vice President and a majority of either the principal officers of the executive department or of such other body as Congress may by law provide, transmit within four days to the President pro tempore of the Senate and the Speaker of the House of Representatives their written declaration that the President is unable to discharge the powers and duties of his office. Thereupon Congress shall decide the issue, assembling within forty-eight hours for that purpose if not in session. If the Congress, within twenty-one days after receipt of the latter written declaration, or, if Congress is not in session, within twenty-one days after Congress is required to assemble, determines by two-thirds vote of both Houses that the President is unable to discharge the powers and duties of his office, the Vice President shall continue to discharge the same as Acting President; otherwise, the President shall resume the powers and duties of his office.

[ratified February, 1967]

AMENDMENT XXVI.

SECTION 1. The right of citizens of the United States, who are eighteen years of age or older, to vote shall not be denied or abridged by the United States or by any State on account of age.

SECTION 2. The Congress shall have power to enforce this article by appropriate legislation.

[ratified July, 1971]

AMENDMENT XXVII.

No law, varying the compensation for the services of the Senators and Representatives, shall take effect, until an election of Representatives shall have intervened. [ratified May 7, 1992]

Table of Court Cases

Compiled by Timothy L. Hall

Year	Case	Court	Citation	Decision
1833	Barron v. Baltimore	U.S. Sup.Ct.	32 U.S. 243	The Fifth Amendment's just compensation clause does not apply to action against a city for the taking of property without compensation, and the provisions of the Bill of Rights do not limit the actions of state or local governments.
1842	Prigg v. Pennsylvania	U.S. Sup.Ct.	41 U.S. 539	State statute prohibiting anyone from removing African Americans from a state by force to enslave them is unconstitutional as a violation of the fugitive slave clause of Article IV, section 2 of the Constitution.
1854	People v. Hall	Cal. S.Ct.	4 Cal. Rpts. 399	All nonwhites, including persons of Chinese ancestry, are prohibited from offering testimony against whites in civil and criminal proceedings.
1857	Dred Scott v. Sandford	U.S. Sup.Ct.	60 U.S. 393	African Americans are not citizens of the United States, and the Missouri Compromise is unconstitutional.
1870	Cherokee Tobacco case	U.S. Sup.Ct.	78 U.S. 616	Congress has power to enact a law taxing tobacco in territories occupied by the Cherokee even though a previous treaty with the Cherokee specified that no such taxes would be levied.
1873	Bradwell v. Illinois	U.S. Sup. Ct.	83 U.S. 130	State law providing that women cannot be licensed to practice law does not violate the Fourteenth Amendment's equal protection clause.
1873	Slaughterhouse Cases	U.S. Sup.Ct.	83 U.S. 36	State law giving one slaughterhouse a monopoly on business within a particular area does not violate any provision of the Fourteenth Amendment.
1874	Minor v. Happersett	U.S. Sup.Ct.	88 U.S. 162	State constitutional provision limiting the right to vote to men does not violate the Fourteenth Amendment.

Year	Case	Court	Citation	Decision
1875	Chy Lung v. Freeman	U.S. Sup.Ct.	92 U.S. 275	State law requiring owners of vessels carrying foreign nationals to post bonds to indemnify the state should the state later find it necessary to pay for the support or relief of such persons usurps the power of Congress under the commerce clause and is therefore unconstitutional.
1879	Ho Ah-kow v. Nunan	Cir. Ct. Cal.	12 F. Cas. 252	Ordinance providing that all jail inmates are to have their hair cut to within an inch of their scalps intends to discriminate against Chinese prisoners, thereby violating the equal protection rights of a Chinese person arrested on a misdemeanor charge whose queue is cut off pursuant to the ordinance.
1879	Strauder v. West Virginia	U.S. Sup.Ct.	100 U.S. 303	Exclusion of African Americans from jury service violates equal protection.
1880	In re Ah Chong	Cir. Ct. D. Cal.	2 F. 733	State law prohibiting aliens from fishing in waters of the state violates equal protection.
1880	In re Tiburcio Parrott	Cir. Ct. Cal.	1 F. 481	State constitutional provision prohibiting corporations from hiring persons of Chinese ancestry violates the U.S. Constitution.
1886	Yick Wo v. Hopkins	U.S. Sup.Ct.	118 U.S. 356	Discriminatory application of zoning laws against persons of Chinese ancestry violates the equal protection clause of the Fourteenth Amendment.
1888	United States v. Jung Ah Lung	U.S. Sup.Ct.	124 U.S. 621	Writ of *habeas corpus* is appropriately issued to a free person of Chinese descent who left the U.S. for a time and returned without an identification certificate needed for re-entry to the U.S. because the certificate was stolen from him.
1893	Fong Yue Ting v. United States	U.S. Sup.Ct.	149 U.S. 698	Congress has constitutional power to deport Chinese resident aliens.

Table of Court Cases

Year	Case	Court	Citation	Decision
1895	Lem Moon Sing v. United States	U.S. Sup.Ct.	158 U.S. 538	Federal law providing for exclusion of certain aliens from the United States and making decisions of immigration officials final in such matters deprived the federal courts of the power to review an exclusion order directed toward a person of Chinese ancestry.
1896	Plessy v. Ferguson	U.S. Sup.Ct.	163 U.S. 537	State requirement of segregated railway cars does not violate equal protection, so long as separate facilities are "equal."
1896	Talton v. Mayes	U.S. Sup.Ct.	163 U.S. 376	Proceedings in Indian tribal courts are not subject to protections afforded by the Bill of Rights.
1896	Wong Wing v. United States	U.S. Sup.Ct.	163 U.S. 228	Federal law sentencing Chinese immigrants to nearly a year of hard labor without trial by jury prior to being deported violates the Fifth Amendment's right to a grand jury indictment and the Sixth Amendment's right to a trial by jury.
1898	United States v. Wong Kim Ark	U.S. Sup.Ct.	169 U.S. 649	Fourteenth Amendment's declaration that all persons born in the United States are subject to its jurisdiction means that children of permanent Chinese residents in the United States are U.S. citizens.
1899	Cumming v. Richmond County Board of Education	U.S. Sup.Ct.	175 U.S. 528	Local school district's failure to offer a high school education to African Americans when it does so for whites does not violate the equal protection clause in the absence of proof that local officials have been motivated in their actions solely by hostility to African Americans.
1905	United States v. Ju Toy	U.S. Sup.Ct.	198 U.S. 253	Federal statute giving the executive branch conclusive authority to determine the right of persons of Chinese descent to enter the United States is binding on federal courts in *habeas corpus* proceedings and does not violate the Constitution.

Year	Case	Court	Citation	Decision
1908	Berea College v. Kentucky	U.S. Sup.Ct.	211 U.S. 45	State statute prohibiting the operation of schools in which both African Americans and whites are students does not violate constitutional rights of institution, since institution is a corporation and does not have all the constitutional rights of a person.
1908	Muller v. Oregon	U.S. Sup.Ct.	208 U.S. 412	State law imposing maximum work hours for women is not unconstitutional.
1914	McCabe v. Atchison, Topeka & Santa Fe Railway	U.S. Sup.Ct.	235 U.S. 151	State law requiring segregated railway cars but authorizing railroads to carry sleeping, dining, and chair cars for use by whites only violates the equal protection clause.
1915	Guinn v. United States	U.S. Sup.Ct.	238 U.S. 347	State voter literacy requirement intended to prevent African Americans from voting violates Fifteenth Amendment.
1917	Buchanan v. Warley	U.S. Sup.Ct.	245 U.S. 60	Municipal ordinance requiring residential segregation by race violates the Fourteenth Amendment's prohibition against taking of property without "due process of law."
1922	Ozawa v. United States	U.S. Sup.Ct.	260 U.S. 178	Federal naturalization law denying the possibility of citizenship to persons other than "free white persons" or aliens of African descent effectively excluded the possibility of U.S. citizenship for Japanese resident aliens who have applied for such citizenship.
1923	Frick v. Webb	U.S. Sup.Ct.	263 U.S. 326	State law prohibiting ownership of land by persons of Japanese descent does not violate either due process or equal protection clauses.
1923	Porterfield v. Webb	U.S. Sup.Ct.	263 U.S. 225	State law prohibiting certain aliens from leasing real estate does not violate due process or equal protection clauses.

Table of Court Cases

Year	Case	Court	Citation	Decision
1923	Terrace v. Thompson	U.S. Sup.Ct.	263 U.S. 197	State laws prohibiting land ownership by aliens are justified by considerations other than racial or national hostility and thus do not violate the due process and equal protection clauses of the Fourteenth Amendment.
1923	United States v. Bhagat Singh Thind	U.S. Sup.Ct.	261 U.S. 204	A high caste Hindu is not a "white person" as defined by federal naturalization law and is thus not entitled to U.S. citizenship.
1925	Cockrill v. People of the State of California	U.S. Sup.Ct.	268 U.S. 258	State law making it illegal for certain resident aliens to own agricultural real estate does not violate due process or equal protection clauses.
1925	Toyota v. United States	U.S. Sup.Ct.	268 U.S. 402	Person of Japanese ancestry is not entitled to U.S. citizenship under federal naturalization laws.
1926	Corrigan and Curtis v. Buckley	U.S. Sup.Ct.	271 U.S. 323	District of Columbia's enforcement of a restrictive real estate covenant barring sale of property to African Americans does not violate any constitutional right.
1927	Buck v. Bell	U.S. Sup.Ct.	274 U.S. 200	State's sterilization of a mentally impaired female does not violate due process clause.
1927	Gong Lum v. Rice	U.S. Sup.Ct.	275 U.S. 78	Refusal of school district to admit Chinese American student to school established for whites rather than one for "colored" children does not violate the Fourteenth Amendment.
1927	Nixon v. Herndon	U.S. Sup.Ct.	273 U.S. 536	Exclusion of African Americans from voting in state Democratic Party primaries is unconstitutional.
1935	Grovey v. Townsend	U.S. Sup.Ct.	295 U.S. 45	State Democratic Party's limitation of membership to whites does not violate equal protection.
1938	Missouri ex rel. Gaines v. Canada	U.S. Sup.Ct.	305 U.S. 337	State law requiring racial segregation in education and providing tuition for African Americans to attend school out of state when no in-state school for African Americans is available violates the equal protection rights of black students who wish to attend the state law school.

Year	Case	Court	Citation	Decision
1943	Hirabayashi v. United States	U.S. Sup.Ct.	320 U.S. 81	Curfew for Japanese Americans during World War II does not violate equal protection clause.
1944	Korematsu v. United States	U.S. Sup.Ct.	323 U.S. 214	Relocation of Japanese Americans to internment camps during World War II does not violate the equal protection clause.
1944	Smith v. Allwright	U.S. Sup.Ct.	321 U.S. 649	Exclusion of African Americans from party primaries violates Fourteenth and Fifteenth Amendments.
1946	Morgan v. Commonwealth of Virginia	U.S. Sup.Ct.	328 U.S. 373	State statute requiring racial segregation in public motor carriers imposes an unconstitutional burden on interstate commerce in violation of the commerce clause.
1947	Westminster School District v. Mendez	9th Cir.	161 F.2d 774	School district's policy of segregating Latino children in separate public school facilities violates due process and equal protection clauses.
1948	Goesaert v. Cleary	U.S. Sup. Ct.	335 U.S. 464	State law prohibiting women from serving as bartenders unless they are the wives or daughters of male owners of the bars does not violate equal protection.
1948	Perez v. Sharp	Cal. S.Ct.	32 Cal. 2d 711	State statute prohibiting interracial marriage violates the Fourteenth Amendment.
1948	Shelley v. Kraemer	U.S. Sup.Ct.	334 U.S. 1	Use of state courts to enforce racially restrictive real estate covenants violates equal protection.
1950	McLaurin v. Oklahoma State Regents	U.S. Sup.Ct.	339 U.S. 637	State practice of segregating black graduate student in special seating areas in an otherwise all-white school violates equal protection.
1950	Sweatt v. Painter	U.S. Sup.Ct.	339 U.S. 629	State decision to create a separate law school for African Americans rather than admit African Americans to state law school violates equal protection clause.
1952	Okimura v. Acheson	U.S. Sup.Ct.	342 U.S. 899	Remanding case for determination of whether the circumstances are such as to justify loss of citizenship by Japanese American who served in Japanese army and voted in Japanese elections.

Table of Court Cases

Year	Case	Court	Citation	Decision
1954	Bolling v. Sharpe	U.S. Sup.Ct.	347 U.S. 497	Segregation of public school children in the District of Columbia violates the due process clause of the Fifth Amendment, which implicitly guarantees the same right to equal treatment expressed in the equal protection clause of the Fourteenth Amendment.
1954	Brown v. Board of Education of Topeka, Kansas	U.S. Sup.Ct.	347 U.S. 483	Segregation of public school children according to race violates the equal protection clause of the Fourteenth Amendment.
1958	Cooper v. Aaron	U.S. Sup.Ct.	358 U.S. 1	State government officials are bound by the Supreme Court's decision declaring racial segregation in public schools unconstitutional and cannot claim anticipated racial unrest as a justification for delaying school desegregation.
1958	Nishikawa v. Dulles	U.S. Sup.Ct.	356 U.S. 129	Japanese American cannot be stripped of his U.S. citizenship for having served in a foreign army when he was involuntarily drafted into the Japanese army.
1960	Daisy Bates et al. v. City of Little Rock et al.	U.S. Sup.Ct.	361 U.S. 516	Attempt by two municipalities to force local NAACP chapters to disclose their membership lists violates freedoms of speech and association.
1960	Gomillion v. Lightfoot	U.S. Sup.Ct.	364 U.S. 339	Law altering a town's boundaries so it has twenty-five sides and, by excluding all black voters, a permanent white voting majority amounts to racial discrimination on its face without the necessity of proof of a facially discriminatory motive.
1961	Hoyt v. Florida	U.S. Sup. Ct.	368 U.S. 57	Jury selection system excluding women who do not affirmatively express a desire to serve on a jury does not violate equal protection.
1962	Baker v. Carr	U.S. Sup.Ct.	369 U.S. 186	A claim that the boundaries of state voting districts are inequitably drawn can only be heard by the federal courts and is not a "political question" immune from constitutional challenge.

Year	Case	Court	Citation	Decision
1963	Gideon v. Wainwright	U.S. Sup.Ct.	372 U.S. 335	States are required by the due process clause to provide attorneys to defendants charged with serious crimes.
1964	Griffin v. Prince Edward County School Board	U.S. Sup.Ct.	377 U.S. 218	School district's attempt to close public schools rather than comply with desegregation order violates equal protection clause.
1964	Heart of Atlanta Motel v. United States	U.S. Sup.Ct.	379 U.S. 241	Congress has power under the commerce clause to prohibit racial discrimination in privately owned places of public accommodation.
1964	New York Times v. Sullivan	U.S. Sup.Ct.	376 U.S. 254	First Amendment prevents actions for defamation against public officials unless a speaker or publisher acted with actual malice.
1964	Reynolds v. Sims	U.S. Sup.Ct.	377 U.S. 533	Equal protection requires states to draw voting districts in accordance with the "one person, one vote" formula.
1965	Griswold v. Connecticut	U.S. Sup.Ct.	381 U.S. 479	Constitutional right of privacy prevents states from punishing married couples for the use of contraceptive devices.
1965	Swain v. Alabama	U.S. Sup.Ct.	380 U.S. 202	Proof that prosecutors have deliberately excluded racial minorities from juries through use of peremptory challenges can be demonstrated by showing that prosecutors have excluded members of a racial minority from jury service in a series of cases.
1966	Harper v. Virginia Board of Elections	U.S. Sup.Ct.	383 U.S. 663	State poll tax is unconstitutional under the equal protection clause.
1966	Katzenbach v. Morgan	U.S. Sup.Ct.	384 U.S. 641	Congress has power under the Fourteenth Amendment to provide in Voting Rights Act of 1965 that persons who have completed the sixth grade in a Puerto Rican school cannot be denied the right to vote because of inability to read English, regardless of whether such a literacy requirement violates the equal protection clause.

Year	Case	Court	Citation	Decision
1966	Miranda v. Arizona	U.S. Sup.Ct.	384 U.S. 436	Statements obtained from criminal defendants during interrogation by police who do not advise defendants of their constitutional rights are inadmissible because the statements are obtained in violation of the Fifth Amendment's privilege against self-incrimination.
1966	United States v. Price	U.S. Sup.Ct.	383 U.S. 787	To the extent that private persons act in concert with public officials to have victims released from jail and thereafter intercepted and murdered, then private persons can be found to have violated federal statute prohibiting actions that deprive persons of civil rights under color of state law.
1967	Loving v. Virginia	U.S. Sup.Ct.	388 U.S. 1	State laws prohibiting interracial marriages violate equal protection.
1967	Reitman v. Mulkey	U.S. Sup.Ct.	387 U.S. 369	Provision in state constitution barring state from interfering with racial discrimination by private persons in sale or lease of property violates equal protection.
1967	Walker v. City of Birmingham	U.S. Sup. Ct.	388 U.S. 307	Conviction of civil rights leaders for leading a march against which an arguably unconstitutional injunction has been issued does not violate freedom of speech, since an injunction must be obeyed pending its appeal, and a claim that the injunction is unconstitutional will not serve as a defense to a criminal contempt proceeding arising out of the violation of the injunction.
1968	Green v. County School Board	U.S. Sup.Ct.	391 U.S. 430	Adoption of "freedom of choice" plan for students to attend public school of their choice does not satisfy school district's obligation to desegregate schools.
1968	Jones v. Alfred H. Mayer Co.	U.S. Sup.Ct.	392 U.S. 409	Congress has power to prohibit racial discrimination in housing sales.
1968	Levy v. Louisiana	U.S. Sup.Ct.	391 U.S. 68	State law denying recovery to an illegitimate child for the wrongful death of the child's mother violates equal protection.

Year	Case	Court	Citation	Decision
1969	Alexander v. Holmes County Board of Education	U.S. Sup.Ct.	396 U.S. 1218	Finding that no circumstances justify continued maintenance of racially segregated schools.
1969	Bowe v. Colgate-Palmolive	7th Cir. U.S. Ct. App.	416 F.2d 711	Job requirements limiting women to positions that do not require lifting any more than thirty-five pounds violate antidiscrimination provisions of federal civil rights law.
1969	Glover et al. v. St. Louis-San Francisco Railway Co. et al.	U.S. Sup.Ct.	393 U.S. 324	Union members who allege that they have been denied promotions because of racial discrimination are entitled to bring civil action without exhausting normal administrative remedies.
1971	Graham v. Richardson	U.S. Sup.Ct.	403 U.S. 365	Discrimination against aliens in connection with distribution of welfare benefits violates the equal protection clause.
1971	Griffin v. Breckenridge	U.S. Sup.Ct.	403 U.S. 88	Congress is constitutionally authorized to punish racially motivated assaults on public highways.
1971	Griggs v. Duke Power Company	U.S. Sup.Ct.	401 U.S. 424	Congress has power under the Constitution to prohibit racial discrimination in employment and to require that job tests be related to job skills.
1971	North Carolina State Board of Education v. Swann	U.S. Sup.Ct.	402 U.S. 43	State law prohibiting the assignment of students to public schools on the basis of race or to achieve some measure of racial balancing violates the equal protection clause.
1971	Palmer v. Thompson	U.S. Sup.Ct.	403 U.S. 217	Decision of city council to close municipal swimming pools rather than desegregate them does not violate the equal protection clause.
1971	Reed v. Reed	U.S. Sup.Ct.	404 U.S. 71	State law generally preferring men over women as administrators of a decedent's estate violates the equal protection clause.
1971	Swann v. Charlotte-Mecklenburg Board of Education	U.S. Sup.Ct.	402 U.S. 1	Upon determining that a school district has engaged in racial segregation, a federal court has authority to make flexible use of racial quotas and busing to integrate schools.

Year	Case	Court	Citation	Decision
1972	Moose Lodge No. 107 v. Irvis	U.S. Sup.Ct.	407 U.S. 163	State's grant of a liquor license to a racially discriminatory private club does not violate equal protection.
1973	Adams v. Richardson	D.C. Cir.	480 F.2d 1159	Federal courts have authority to review whether federal officials have complied with their obligations under civil rights laws of desegregating public schools.
1973	Espinoza v. Farah Manufacturing	U.S. Sup.Ct.	414 U.S. 86	Discrimination by private employer on the basis of U.S. citizenship does not violate provisions of federal civil rights law.
1973	Frontiero v. Richardson	U.S. Sup.Ct.	411 U.S. 677	Federal military dependent benefits awarded differently depending upon whether males or females are involved violates the equal protection clause.
1973	In re Griffiths	U.S. Sup. Ct.	413 U.S. 717	State's exclusion of aliens from membership in the bar is unconstitutional.
1973	Keyes v. Denver School District Number One	U.S. Sup.Ct.	413 U.S. 189	Upon proof that one part of a school district has engaged in racial segregation, a federal court has power to implement desegregation remedies throughout the district.
1973	Roe v. Wade	U.S. Sup.Ct.	410 U.S. 113	State laws prohibiting abortions violate constitutional right of privacy.
1974	Cleveland Board of Education v. LaFleur	U.S. Sup. Ct.	414 U.S. 632	Regulations requiring pregnant teachers to take maternity leave well before their anticipated delivery dates violate the due process clause.
1974	Lau v. Nichols	U.S. Sup.Ct.	414 U.S. 563	School district's failure to provide English language instruction to students of Chinese ancestry denied them a meaningful education in violation of the Civil Rights Act of 1964.
1974	Milliken v. Bradley	U.S. Sup.Ct.	418 U.S. 717	Multidistrict remedies for racially segregated schools are not permissible unless each district involved has engaged in purposeful segregation.

Year	Case	Court	Citation	Decision
1974	Serna v. Portales	10th Cir.	499 F.2d 1147	School district failing to meet the educational needs of Mexican American children violates federal civil rights laws and is ordered to implement bilingual education program and other programs to enhance educational opportunities of Mexican American children.
1975	Taylor v. Louisiana	U.S. Sup. Ct.	419 U.S. 522	Exclusion of women from jury duty deprives criminal defendant of Sixth Amendment right to fair and impartial jury.
1976	Hampton v. Wong Mow Sun	U.S. Sup.Ct.	426 U.S. 88	Civil service regulations limiting employment in most federal civil service positions to U.S. citizens and natives of Samoa violate the Fifth Amendment's due process clause.
1976	Massachusetts Board of Retirement v. Murgia	U.S. Sup.Ct.	427 U.S. 307	State law mandating retirement for state police officers does not violate the equal protection clause.
1976	Pasadena City Board of Education v. Spangler	U.S. Sup.Ct.	427 U.S. 424	District court has no authority to order yearly adjustments to maintain racial balances in public schools after official segregation has been remedied.
1976	Runyon v. McCrary	U.S. Sup.Ct.	427 U.S. 160	Federal law prevents racially segregated private school from refusing to admit black students.
1976	Washington v. Davis	U.S. Sup.Ct.	426 U.S. 229	Test required of police officer candidates does not violate equal protection, even though more African Americans than whites fail the test.
1978	Regents of the University of California v. Bakke	U.S. Sup.Ct.	438 U.S. 265	Equal protection clause prevents state from using racial quotas in medical school admissions process but not from considering race as one factor in attempting to achieve diversity in the student body.
1979	United Steelworkers of America v. Weber	U.S. Sup.Ct	443 U.S. 193	Affirmative action program adopted voluntarily by employer and union does not violate federal civil rights law prohibiting racial discrimination in employment.

Table of Court Cases

Year	Case	Court	Citation	Decision
1979	Addington v. Texas	U.S. Sup.Ct.	441 U.S. 418	In involuntary commitment proceedings that might commit an adult to a psychiatric institution, the Constitution requires the state to satisfy a standard of proof greater than the preponderance of evidence standard used in normal civil cases in demonstrating that an adult is a danger to self or to others.
1979	Vance v. Bradley	U.S. Sup.Ct.	440 U.S. 93	Mandatory retirement provision for officials in foreign service does not violate the equal protection clause.
1980	Fullilove v. Klutznick	U.S. Sup.Ct.	448 U.S. 448	Congressional affirmative action program involving grants of federal public works contracts does not violate the equal protection clause.
1980	Mobile v. Bolden	U.S. Sup.Ct.	446 U.S. 55	Without proof that at-large voting districts are adopted to minimize the voting strength of minorities, the mere fact that at-large districts have the effect of minimizing minority voting strength does not violate the equal protection clause.
1981	Michael M. v. Superior Court of Sonoma County	U.S. Sup. Ct.	450 U.S. 464	Statutory rape provision, which made it a crime for a male minor to have sexual intercourse with a female minor violates the defendant's right to be free from discrimination on the basis of gender under the equal protection clause.
1981	Rostker v. Goldberg	U.S. Sup.Ct.	453 U.S. 57	Exclusion of women from the draft does not violate equal protection.
1982	Plyler v. Doe	U.S. Sup.Ct.	457 U.S. 202	States denial of public education to children of illegal aliens violates the equal protection clause.
1984	Grove City College v. Bell	U.S. Sup.Ct.	465 U.S. 555	Receipt by some of the college's students of federal financial assistance makes the college subject to federal laws prohibiting sexual discrimination, but only as to the college's financial aid program, not as to other aspects of the college.

Year	Case	Court	Citation	Decision
1984	Palmore v. Sidoti	U.S. Sup.Ct.	466 U.S. 429	Where judge awards custody of a child to the mother—who, along with the father, is white—but later awards custody to the father when the mother remarries a black man, the custody order violates the equal protection clause.
1984	Roberts v. United States Jaycees		468 U.S. 609	Application of state law barring gender discrimination to Junior Chamber of Commerce (Jaycees) membership does not violate freedom of association.
1985	City of Cleburne v. Cleburne Living Center	U.S. Sup.Ct.	473 U.S. 432	Municipality's denial of a zoning permit for a home for the mentally infirm violates the equal protection clause.
1985	Hunter v. Underwood	U.S. Sup.Ct.	421 U.S. 222	State constitutional provision denying the right to vote to persons convicted of crimes involving moral turpitude violates the equal protection clause because the provision is partially motivated by a desire to disfranchise African Americans.
1986	Batson v. Kentucky	U.S. Sup.Ct.	476 U.S. 79	Prosecutor's use of peremptory challenges to disqualify potential jurors because of their race violates the equal protection clause.
1986	Ford v. Wainwright	U.S. Sup.Ct.	477 U.S. 399	Constitution prevents state from executing an insane prisoner.
1986	Meritor Savings Bank v. Vinson	U.S. Sup.Ct.	477 U.S. 57	Company permitting a sexually hostile working environment violates the antidiscrimination provisions of federal civil rights law.
1986	Vasquez v. Hillery	U.S. Sup.Ct.	474 U.S. 254	Defendant who proves purposeful discrimination in the selection of members of grand jury on the basis of race is entitled to have conviction overturned.
1986	Wygant v. Jackson Board of Education		476 U.S. 267	School district's practice of supporting affirmative action goals by laying off white teachers with greater seniority than black teachers violates the equal protection clause.

Year	Case	Court	Citation	Decision
1987	McCleskey v. Kemp	U.S. Sup.Ct.	481 U.S. 279	Statistics showing that the death penalty has been imposed disproportionately upon African Americans does not, standing alone, amount to proof of an equal protection violation.
1987	United States v. Paradise	U.S. Sup.Ct.	480 U.S. 149	District court order that state Department of Public Safety award 50 percent of promotions to qualified black candidates, if available, to remedy persistent employment discrimination against African Americans does not violate the equal protection clause.
1989	Richmond v. J. A. Croson Co.	U.S. Sup.Ct.	488 U.S. 469	Affirmative action program adopted by municipality requiring the prime contractor for the city to subcontract at least 30 percent of the value of contracts with the city to minority-owned businesses violates the equal protection clause.
1989	Wards Cove Packing Co. v. Atonio	U.S. Sup.Ct.	490 U.S. 642	Federal civil rights law allows an employer to rebut evidence that minorities are underrepresented in the workplace by demonstrating a reasonable business justification for this underrepresentation.
1990	Board of Education of Westside Community Schools v. Mergens	U.S. Sup. Ct.	496 U.S. 226	Federal Equal Access Act, which guarantees right of religious students to form religious clubs in public schools if other noncurricular clubs are permitted, does not violate the establishment clause.
1990	Cruzan v. Director, Missouri Department of Health	U.S. Sup. Ct.	457 U.S. 261	In case involving a patient whom a coma has left in a persistent vegetative state, although the Constitution may protect a "right to die," a state's requirement that artificial nutrition and hydration procedures not be discontinued for the patient without "clear and convincing" evidence that this is the patient's desire does not violate the right to die.

Year	Case	Court	Citation	Decision
1990	Missouri v. Jenkins	U.S. Sup.Ct.	495 U.S. 33	Federal district court has no authority to raise property tax rates within a school district to support desegregation remedies, but the court can order the school district to raise the tax rates itself.
1991	Oklahoma City Board of Education v. Dowell	U.S. Sup.Ct.	498 U.S. 237	A petition by a school district to end a desegregation decree may be granted when the school district has complied in good faith with the desegregation decree since it was entered and when vestiges of past discrimination have been eliminated to the extent practicable.
1991	Edmonson v. Leesville Concrete Co.	U.S. Sup.Ct.	500 U.S. 614	Use of race-based peremptory challenge by private litigant violates the equal protection clause.
1991	Rust v. Sullivan	U.S. Sup.Ct.	500 U.S. 173	Federal regulations prohibiting abortion counseling in federally funded clinics do not violate either freedom of speech or the constitutional right to an abortion.
1992	Foucha v. Louisiana	U.S. Sup.Ct.	504 U.S. 71	State statute allowing a person who has been confined in a mental health facility after being acquitted of a crime by virtue of insanity to remain confined after a hospital review committee has reported no evidence of mental illness and recommended conditional discharge violates the due process clause.
1992	R.A.V. v. City of St. Paul	U.S. Sup.Ct.	505 U.S. 377	Municipal ordinance prohibiting "hate speech" involving race, color, creed, religion, or gender violates freedom of speech.
1992	United States v. Fordice	U.S. Sup.Ct.	505 U.S. 717	Use by a state higher education system of educational practices originally implemented to achieve segregation of races and which continue to produce a segregating effect violates the equal protection guarantee if the practices can be eliminated without jeopardizing sound educational policy.

Table of Court Cases

Year	Case	Court	Citation	Decision
1993	Shaw v. Reno	U.S. Sup.Ct.	509 U.S. 630	Voting district plans designed solely to increase minority voting strength violate the equal protection clause.
1993	Wisconsin v. Mitchell	U.S. Sup.Ct.	508 U.S. 476	Enhancement of punishment for crimes motivated by racial hatred does not abridge freedom of speech.
1995	Adarand Constructors v. Peña	U.S. Sup. Ct.	115 S.Ct. 2097	Federal affirmative action program in awarding construction contracts can be justified only by a showing that the program serves some "compelling" interest and is narrowly tailored to achieve this interest.
1995	Jenkins v. Missouri	U.S. Sup.Ct.	115 S.Ct. 2038	Federal district court has no authority to order salary increases for educational personnel as part of a plan to attract nonminority students from outside the district to support desegregation orders.
1995	Miller v. Johnson	U.S. Sup. Ct.	115 S.Ct. 2475	State congressional district deliberately drawn to include a majority of African American residents violates the equal protection clause.
1996	Romer v. Evans	U.S. Sup.Ct.	116 S.Ct. 1620	State constitutional amendment prohibiting localities within the state from passing laws prohibiting discrimination against homosexuals violates the equal protection clause.
1996	United States v. Virginia	U.S. Sup.Ct.	116 S.Ct. 2264	Categorical exclusion of women from attendance at the Virginia Military Institute, a state institute of higher learning, violates the equal protection clause.

Chronology

Compiled by Timothy L. Hall

1619 First African Americans arrive in Jamestown, Virginia, as indentured servants.

1641 Massachusetts Colony recognizes legality of slavery.

1662 Virginia legislature rules that children of unions of slave and free parents are slave or free according to their mothers' status.

1664 Maryland enacts first law outlawing marriage between white women and black men.

1688 Pennsylvania Mennonites protest slavery.

1691 Virginia law calls for restricting manumissions to prevent growth of free black class.

1705 Virginia debars African Americans and Indians from holding ecclesiastic, civil, or military offices.

1712 Slave revolt in New York results in the execution of twenty-one slaves and suicides of six others.

1723 Virginia denies African Americans the right to vote.

1775 First abolitionist organization in the United States, the Pennsylvania Society for the Abolition of Slavery, is formed.

1776 Declaration of Independence.

1783 Great Britain recognizes American independence.

1787 U.S. Constitution is drafted and sent to the states for ratification.

1791 Bill of Rights is ratified as the first ten amendments to the U.S. Constitution.

1793 Passage of the Fugitive Slave Act requires return of escaped slaves to their owners.

1793 Invention of the cotton gin encourages the spread of slavery in the South.

1793 Virginia outlaws entry of free African Americans into the state.

1798 Federal Alien Act is passed as part of the Alien and Sedition Acts of 1798, granting the president power to arrest and deport aliens viewed as dangerous.

1808 Federal government bans importation of slaves into the United States, but illegal importation continues.

1820 Congress enacts the Missouri Compromise, under which Missouri is admitted to the Union as a slave state, Maine is admitted as a free state, and slavery is prohibited in the territory north of Missouri's southern boundary.

1822 Denmark Vesey is executed for conspiring to lead a slave insurrection in South Carolina.

1827 First African American newspaper, *Freedman's Journal*, is published.

1831 Supreme Court's *Cherokee Nation v. Georgia* decision results in forcible removal of Cherokees from Georgia to present-day Oklahoma.

1831 Nat Turner leads slave insurrection in Virginia.

1832 New England Anti-Slavery Society is organized.

1841 Oberlin College becomes first U.S. institution to confer college degrees to women.

1842 U.S. Supreme Court's *Prigg v. Pennsylvania* decision holds that a state statute prohibiting anyone from removing African Americans from the state by force to enslave them violates the fugitive slave clause of the Constitution.

1843 Jewish organization B'nai B'rith is founded.

1843 Sojourner Truth begins giving abolitionist lectures.

1848   Seneca Falls Convention focusing on women's rights is held.

1850   Compromise of 1850 results in California's admission to the Union as a nonslave state and the entrance of Utah and New Mexico as undecided on the issue.

1852   Harriet Beecher Stowe publishes *Uncle Tom's Cabin*, which attacks slavery.

1853   American Labor Union is formed.

1854   Republican Party is founded by antislavery members of the Whig, Democrat, and Free Soil parties.

1857   Supreme Court's *Dred Scott* decision declares that African Americans are not citizens of the United States and that the Missouri Compromise is unconstitutional.

1859   Abolitionist John Brown is hanged after his raid on the federal arsenal at Harper's Ferry, Virginia.

1861   Civil War begins (April).

1863   Lincoln issues Emancipation Proclamation, declaring slaves in states still in rebellion against the Union to be free (January 1).

1865   Civil War ends (April 9).

1865   Ratification of the Thirteenth Amendment to the U.S. Constitution prohibits slavery or other involuntary servitude (December).

1865   Southern states begin to enforce black laws, which severely limit liberties of newly freed African Americans.

1865   Ku Klux Klan is founded in Tennessee.

1866   Congress enacts Civil Rights Act of 1866, declaring that persons born in the United States are, without regard to race, citizens of the United States and requiring that all citizens receive the equal protection of the laws.

1868   Ratification of the Fourteenth Amendment to the U.S. Constitution grants citizenship to all persons born in the United States, without regard to race, and requires states to accord individuals equal protection of the laws and due process of the law (July).

1869   Elizabeth Cady Stanton founds the National Woman Suffrage Association.

1870   Ratification of the Fifteenth Amendment to the U.S. Constitution guarantees the right to vote without regard to race, color, or previous condition of servitude (February).

1871   Congress enacts the Ku Klux Klan Act in an attempt to restrain the violence perpetrated by the organization.

1872   Victoria Claflin Woodhull is the first woman candidate for U.S. president.

1873   Supreme Court's *Bradwell v. Illinois* decision upholds the power of states to exclude women from the practice of law.

1875   Congress enacts the Civil Rights Act of 1875, prohibiting racial discrimination in transportation, hotels, inns, theaters, and places of public amusement.

1877   Reconstruction ends after President Rutherford B. Hayes withdraws the last Union troops from the South.

1879   Supreme Court's *Strauder v. West Virginia* decision holds that exclusion of African Americans from jury service violates the equal protection clause.

1879   Supreme Court's *Reynolds v. United States* decision upholds a federal law banning polygamy in the territories in the face of Mormon protests.

1881   Booker T. Washington founds the Tuskegee Institute.

1882   Federal Chinese Exclusion Act halts the immigration of Chinese laborers to the United States.

1883 Supreme Court's *Civil Rights Cases* decision declares the Civil Rights Act of 1875 unconstitutional.

1886 American Federation of Labor (AFL) is founded.

1886 Supreme Court's *Yick Wo v. Hopkins* decision finds unconstitutional a municipality's discriminatory application of zoning laws against persons of Chinese ancestry.

1890 Federal troops massacre two hundred Sioux at Wounded Knee, South Dakota.

1896 Supreme Court's *Plessy v. Ferguson* decision establishes the separate-but-equal principle by holding that a legally mandated provision for separate railway cars for whites and blacks does not violate the equal protection clause.

1898 Supreme Court's *United States v. Wong Kim Ark* decision finds that the Fourteenth Amendment provides that children of permanent Chinese residents of the United States are U.S. citizens.

1899 Supreme Court's *Cumming v. Richmond County Board of Education* decision holds that a school district can provide high school education for white students even though it does not provide one for blacks.

1900 International Ladies Garment Workers Union is founded.

1905 Niagara Movement, predecessor of the National Association for the Advancement of Colored People, is organized with the help of W. E. B. Du Bois.

1907 Charles Curtis becomes the first Native American senator.

1908 Supreme Court's *Muller v. Oregon* decision upholds a state law limiting the working hours of women.

1909 National Association for the Advancement of Colored People (NAACP) is founded.

1911 National Urban League is organized to protect the rights of African Americans who migrate to northern cities from the South.

1915 Supreme Court's *Guinn v. United States* decision invalidates state voter literacy requirements intended to prevent African Americans from voting.

1916 Marcus Garvey arrives in the United States from Jamaica and becomes a leading advocate of black nationalism.

1916 National Women's Party is founded.

1919 Communist Party of the United States is founded.

1920 Ratification of the Nineteenth Amendment to the U.S. Constitution guarantees women the right to vote (August).

1920 American Civil Liberties Union (ACLU) is founded.

1922 Supreme Court's *Ozawa v. United States* decision upholds a federal law that denies resident aliens the opportunity to obtain U.S. citizenship because of their race.

1922 Rebecca L. Felton is appointed a senator from Georgia, becoming the first woman U.S. senator.

1923 Supreme Court's *Frick v. Webb* decision upholds a state law that prohibits persons of Japanese descent from owning real estate in the state.

1923 Supreme Court's *United States v. Bhagat Singh Thind* decision finds that a high caste Hindu is not a "white person" as defined in federal citizenship laws and thus is not entitled to U.S. citizenship.

1924 Society for Human Rights, a gay rights organization, is founded in Chicago.

1925 Wyoming elects Nellie Tayloe Ross the first woman governor in the United States.

1927 Supreme Court's *Gong Lum v. Rice* decision allows a state to segregate Chinese American students in schools with other "colored" students rather than in schools for whites.

1927   Supreme Court's *Nixon v. Herndon* decision finds unconstitutional the exclusion of blacks from voting in state Democratic primaries.

1927   Supreme Court's *Buck v. Bell* decision allows state to sterilize a mentally disabled woman.

1930   Wallace Fard founds the Nation of Islam.

1931   Trial of the Scottsboro Nine begins in Alabama.

1932   Tennessee makes Hattie Caraway the first woman elected to the U.S. Senate.

1935   Supreme Court's *Grovey v. Townsend* decision upholds state Democratic Party's limitation of membership to whites.

1935   Congress enacts the National Labor Relations Act, which recognizes the right of workers to organize and to bargain collectively.

1935   Mary McLeod Bethune founds the National Council of Negro Women.

1938   Supreme Court's *Missouri ex rel. Gaines v. Canada* decision holds that refusal of a state to allow African Americans to attend a state's only public law school violates the equal protection clause, although the state has offered to pay tuition to send the student to law school outside the state.

1939   NAACP creates the Legal Defense and Educational Fund to oppose racially discriminatory laws, and Thurgood Marshall takes charge of these efforts.

1940   Congress passes the Alien Registration Act.

1941   In response to A. Philip Randolph's call for African Americans to march on Washington to protest racial discrimination in the armed forces, defense industries, and federal employment generally, President Franklin D. Roosevelt issues an executive order that temporarily establishes the Fair Employment Practices Committee.

1942   President Roosevelt signs executive order forcibly to remove Japanese Americans from the West Coast (February 19).

1942   James Farmer and students at the University of Chicago establish the Congress of Racial Equality (CORE).

1943   Supreme Court's *Hirabayashi v. United States* decision upholds curfew for Japanese Americans during World War II.

1944   Supreme Court's *Korematsu v. United States* decision holds that Japanese American internment during World War II does not violate the equal protection clause.

1944   Supreme Court's *Smith v. Allwright* decision finds that exclusion of African Americans from participation in party primaries violates the Constitution.

1946   President Harry S Truman issues an executive order establishing the President's Committee on Civil Rights.

1947   Jackie Robinson becomes the first African American to play major league baseball when he plays for the Brooklyn Dodgers.

1947   President's Committee on Civil Rights produces report titled *To Secure These Rights*, which condemns racial discrimination in the United States.

1947   House Committee on Un-American Activities begins public hearings on the alleged infiltration of Hollywood by Communists.

1948   When Democratic Party National Convention adopts a strong civil rights plank, Southern Democrats withdraw to form the Dixiecrat Party with Strom Thurmond as their presidential candidate.

1948 Supreme Court's *Shelley v. Kraemer* decision holds that the Constitution prevents state courts from enforcing racially restrictive real estate covenants.

1948 President Harry S Truman signs Executive Order 9981 prohibiting racial discrimination in the armed forces and other federal employment.

1950 Supreme Court's *Sweatt v. Painter* decision holds that Texas' attempt to establish a separate law school for blacks rather than admit black applicants to the University of Texas Law School violates the equal protection clause.

1951 Gay rights Mattachine Society is founded in California.

1952 Passage of the McCarran-Walter Act eliminates racial and ethnic proscriptions against naturalization but retains national origins quotas.

1954 Supreme Court's *Brown v. Board of Education of Topeka, Kansas* decision finds that racial segregation in public schools violates the equal protection clause (May 17).

1954 Senate censures Senator Joseph McCarthy for his treatment of other senators and his accusations against army officials in connection with his investigations of domestic communism.

1955 Interstate Commerce Commission bans racial segregation on interstate buses and trains.

1955 Fifteen-year-old African American Emmett Till is murdered in Mississippi after allegedly flirting with a white woman; jury ultimately acquits two white men charged with his murder.

1955 Supreme Court issues a second opinion in the *Brown v. Board of Education* case (*Brown II*), requiring desegregation of public schools "with all deliberate speed."

1955 Merger of American Federation of Labor and Congress of Industrial Organizations creates the AFL-CIO.

1955 Rosa Parks's defiance of segregated seating rules on a Montgomery, Alabama, bus touches off a year-long bus boycott and leads to formation of the Southern Christian Leadership Conference in 1957.

1956 Most southern members of Congress sign the "Southern Manifesto," denouncing the Supreme Court's *Brown v. Board of Education* decision.

1957 Martin Luther King, Jr., and other African American leaders found the Southern Christian Leadership Conference (SCLC).

1957 Congress passes the first civil rights act since Reconstruction, banning discrimination in public places based on race, color, religion, or national origin.

1957 After Arkansas' governor uses National Guard troops to block African American children from entering Little Rock's Central High School, President Dwight D. Eisenhower federalizes the guard and mobilizes additional federal armed forces to ensure that the school is peacefully integrated.

1958 Supreme Court's *Cooper v. Aaron* decision rejects state's attempt to delay desegregation of public schools because of potential racial turmoil.

1960 Student sit-ins begin at lunch counters in Greensboro, North Carolina.

1960 Passage of the Civil Rights Act of 1960 expands protections of voting rights.

1960 Student Non-Violent Coordinating Committee (SNCC) is founded.

1961 Supreme Court's *Hoyt v. Florida* decision rules that a jury selection system excluding women who do not affirmatively express a desire to serve does not violate the equal protection clause.

1961 President John F. Kennedy issues an executive order establishing the Equal Employment Opportunity Commission.

1961 Freedom rides sponsored by CORE test ban on segregation in interstate buses, with riders being beaten and a bus burned in Birmingham, Alabama.

1962 President John F. Kennedy signs an executive order banning racial discrimination in federally financed housing.

1962 Voter registration drives begin in southern states under the direction of the Council of Federated Organizations (COFO).

1962 James Meredith enrolls in the University of Mississippi over the defiant protest of Governor Ross R. Barnett and in the face of mob violence.

1963 Congress passes the Equal Pay Act, which requires that men and women be paid the same when they perform substantially similar work.

1963 During demonstrations in Birmingham, Alabama, Police Commissioner Eugene (Bull) Connor orders the use of dogs and fire hoses against demonstrators.

1963 Medgar W. Evers, field secretary for the Mississippi NAACP, is assassinated by Byron De La Beckwith (June 12).

1963 March on Washington is undertaken by civil rights, labor, and religious organizations, at which Martin Luther King, Jr., delivers his "I Have a Dream" speech (August 28).

1963 Newly elected governor of Alabama, George C. Wallace, declares in his inaugural address, "Segregation now, segregation tomorrow, segregation forever."

1963 Bombing of the Sixteenth Street Baptist Church in Birmingham, Alabama, kills four African American girls (September 15).

1963 President John F. Kennedy is assassinated in Dallas, Texas (November 22).

1964 Supreme Court's *New York Times v. Sullivan* decision accords expansive First Amendment protection against claims of libel by southern police officials implicated in civil rights violations by paid advertisement in a newspaper.

1964 Council of Federated Organizations, a group of associated civil rights groups, organizes the Freedom Summer project to register African Americans to vote in Mississippi.

1964 Ratification of the Twenty-fourth Amendment prohibits poll taxes in federal elections.

1964 Civil rights workers James Chaney, Michael Schwerner, and Andrew Goodman are killed near Philadelphia, Mississippi (June).

1964 Supreme Court's *Griffin v. Prince Edward County School Board* decision finds that school districts cannot simply close public schools in an attempt to avoid desegregating them.

1964 Congress passes Civil Rights Act of 1964, which prohibits racial, religious, sexual, and other forms of discrimination in a variety of contexts.

1964 Martin Luther King, Jr., is awarded the Nobel Peace Prize.

1964 Supreme Court's *Heart of Atlanta Motel v. United States* decision upholds the power of Congress to prohibit racial discrimination in privately owned hotels and inns.

1965 Malcolm X is assassinated (February 21).

1965 Martin Luther King, Jr., leads march from Selma to Montgomery, Alabama, to protest discrimination against African American voting rights (March).

1965 Congress passes Voting Rights Act.

1965 Supreme Court's *Griswold v. Connecticut* decision holds that states cannot prohibit the use of contraceptives by married couples.

1965   Race riots in Watts area of Los Angeles ultimately require National Guard to restore order (August).

1965   Thurgood Marshall becomes solicitor general of the United States.

1965   Congress amends the McCarran-Walter Act to abolish the national origins quota system.

1966   Supreme Court overrules the attempt by Georgia's legislature to deny Julian Bond a seat in the legislature because of his association with SNCC.

1966   Massachussetts makes Edward W. Brooke the first black U.S. senator elected since Reconstruction.

1966   Black Panther Party is organized in Oakland, California, by Bobby Seale and Huey P. Newton.

1966   Constance Bake Motley becomes the first African American woman appointed to serve as a federal judge.

1966   National Organization for Women (NOW) is formed by Betty Friedan and others.

1966   Stokely Carmichael takes over leadership of SNCC and coins the phrase "Black Power" to advocate more militant responses to continued racial discrimination.

1967   Thurgood Marshall is appointed by President Lyndon B. Johnson as the first African American justice of the Supreme Court.

1967   Congress enacts the Age Discrimination Act, which prohibits various forms of employment discrimination based on age.

1967   Summer race riots disrupt many northern cities.

1967   Supreme Court's *Loving v. Virginia* decision holds that a state law barring interracial marriages is unconstitutional.

1968   Supreme Court's *Green v. County School Board* decision finds that a "freedom of choice" plan adopted by a school district does not satisfy the district's constitutional obligation to desegregate public schools.

1968   National Advisory Committee on Civil Disorders (the Kerner Commission) releases its report concerning urban riots, claiming as key reasons white racism and increasing racial and economic stratification.

1968   Supreme Court's *Jones v. Alfred H. Mayer Co.* decision finds that Congress has the power to prohibit racial discrimination in housing sales.

1968   Martin Luther King, Jr., is assassinated in Memphis, Tennessee, by James Earl Ray a few days after leading a protest march for striking sanitation workers (April 4).

1968   Congress passes the American Indian Civil Rights Act, which guarantees to residents of reservations a variety of rights with respect to tribal authorities.

1968   Congress passes the Civil Rights Act of 1968, which prohibits discrimination in the sale and rental of housing and in home financing.

1968   Supreme Court's *Levy v. Louisiana* decision holds unconstitutional a state law that denies recovery to an illegitimate child for the wrongful death of his mother.

1968   American Indian Movement is founded.

1968   Women's rights groups interrupt Miss America Pageant.

1968   Shirley Chisholm is elected congressional representative from New York and becomes the first African American woman elected to Congress.

1969   After police in New York City raid a gay bar in Greenwich Village, the Stonewall Inn riots launch the modern gay rights movement.

1969 Native Americans seize Alcatraz Island and hold it for eighteen months, demanding that it be made into a center of Native American culture.

1970 President Richard M. Nixon names the first woman generals.

1970 Chicano activists found La Raza Unida Party.

1971 Supreme Court's *Griffin v. Breckenridge* decision upholds a federal law punishing racially motivated assaults on public highways.

1971 Native American Rights Fund is created.

1971 Jesse Jackson organizes Operation PUSH.

1971 Supreme Court's *Reed v. Reed* decision holds unconstitutional a state statute that discriminates in favor of men over women in the selection of estate administrators.

1971 Attica Prison riots end, leaving over forty people dead.

1971 Ratification of the Twenty-sixth Amendment to the U.S. Constitution lowers the minimum voting age to eighteen.

1971 Supreme Court's *Swann v. Charlotte-Mecklenburg Board of Education* decision authorizes busing to desegregate school district.

1971 Supreme Court's *Graham v. Richardson* decision invalidates state discrimination against aliens in the distribution of welfare benefits.

1972 Congress proposes Equal Rights Amendment (ERA) for adoption as a constitutional amendment, but enough states to ratify the amendment are never secured.

1972 African American Angela Davis, a former UCLA professor, is acquitted of charges that she aided and abetted a courtroom shootout in California two years before.

1972 Five hundred Native Americans travel to Washington in the Trail of Broken Treaties to protest federal policy toward Native Americans.

1973 Supreme Court's *Roe v. Wade* decision finds that women have a constitutional right to an abortion (prior to the last trimester of pregnancy) that is protected from most forms of government regulation.

1973 Members of the American Indian Movement occupy a trading post and church in Wounded Knee, South Dakota, to protest Native American grievances (February).

1973 Supreme Court's *In re Griffiths* decision holds that a state cannot deny resident aliens the right to become lawyers.

1973 Supreme Court's *Frontiero v. Richardson* decision holds that federal law cannot award military dependent benefits differently depending upon whether men or women are involved.

1974 Coalition of Labor Union Women is founded.

1974 Supreme Court's *Lau v. Nichols* decision finds that a school district's failure to provide bilingual education for Chinese American students violates federal civil rights law.

1974 Supreme Court's *Cleveland Board of Education v. LaFleur* decision invalidates a regulation requiring pregnant teachers to take maternity leave substantially before their expected delivery dates.

1975 Supreme Court's *Taylor v. Louisiana* decision holds that the exclusion of women from a jury violates a criminal defendant's constitutional rights.

1976 Supreme Court's *Hampton v. Wong Mow Sun* decision finds unconstitutional federal regulations limiting most federal civil service positions to U.S. citizens and natives of Samoa.

1976   Episcopal Church approves the ordination of women as priests.

1976   Supreme Court's *Washington v. Davis* decision holds that laws having a disproportionately burdensome effect on racial minorities are not subject to the same rigorous review as laws purposefully discriminating on grounds of race.

1976   Supreme Court's *Massachusetts Board of Retirement v. Murgia* decision rules that a state law that discriminates against police officers on the basis of age by mandating retirement at a particular age does not violate equal protection.

1978   Three hundred Native Americans begin the "longest walk" to safeguard treaty rights.

1978   Supreme Court's *Regents of the University of California v. Bakke* decision prohibits the use of racial quotas in university admissions programs, but permits the consideration of race as one factor in a school's attempt to promote educational diversity.

1978   Congress passes the American Indian Religious Freedom Act.

1979   Supreme Court's *United Steel Workers of America v. Weber* decision upholds the ability of private employers to adopt affirmative action plans.

1980   Supreme Court's *Fullilove v. Klutznick* decision approves the constitutionality of a federal affirmative action program for public contractors.

1980   Race riots leave eighteen people dead in Miami after four Miami police officers are acquitted of charges of beating a black insurance executive to death.

1981   Supreme Court's *Rostker v. Goldberg* decision upholds the exclusion of women from the draft.

1981   President Ronald Reagan appoints Sandra Day O'Connor the first woman justice on the U.S. Supreme Court.

1982   Deadline passes for the ratification of the Equal Rights Amendment.

1982   Congress extends the effect of the Voting Rights Act of 1965.

1982   Supreme Court's *Plyler v. Doe* decision holds that a state's denial of public education to illegal aliens violates the equal protection clause.

1984   Congress enacts the Equal Access Act, which grants to religious children in public secondary schools the same rights to organize religious clubs as enjoyed by other extracurricular student groups.

1984   Civil Rights Commission ends the use of quotas in employment promotions for African Americans.

1984   Supreme Court's *Roberts v. United States Jaycees* decision upholds a state statute prohibiting gender discrimination from the claim that it violates freedom of association.

1984   Geraldine A. Ferraro runs as the Democratic Party's vice presidential candidate, becoming the first woman candidate on a major party ticket.

1985   Supreme Court's *City of Cleburne v. Cleburne Living Center* decision holds that a city cannot discriminate against a home for the mentally infirm by refusing to allow it to locate in a residential neighborhood.

1985   United States halts trade with South Africa after sustained public protests concerning the South African regime's racist policies.

1986   Supreme Court's *Batson v. Kentucky* decision holds that a prosecutor's attempt to disqualify possible jurors because of their race violates the equal protection clause of the Fourteenth Amendment.

1986   Supreme Court's *Bowers v. Hardwick* decision finds that consensual acts of homosexual sodomy are not protected by a fundamental right of sexual privacy.

1986 Martin Luther King, Jr., holiday celebrated officially for the first time.

1986 Supreme Court's *Wygant v. Jackson Board of Education* decision invalidates a school district's policy of supporting affirmative action goals by laying off white teachers with greater seniority than black teachers.

1986 Federal immigration reform law grants legal status to immigrants who entered the United States before 1982 but strengthens penalties against employers who hire illegal aliens.

1986 Supreme Court's *Ford v. Wainwright* decision bars state from executing an insane prisoner.

1987 Supreme Court's *McCleskey v. Kemp* decision holds that mere proof of a racially disproportionate impact of death penalty sentences on African Americans does not violate the Constitution.

1988 Congress passes law providing for reparations to Japanese-Americans interned during World War II.

1989 Supreme Court's *Richmond v. J. A. Croson, Co.* decision holds that state and local affirmative action programs must be subject to "strict scrutiny," a constitutional standard requiring the most compelling government justifications.

1990 Supreme Court's *Westside Community Schools v. Mergens* decision upholds the Equal Access Act, which allows students to organize religious clubs in public secondary schools.

1991 Clarence Thomas is confirmed to fill the vacant seat on the Supreme Court left by the retirement of Thurgood Marshall, but only after highly charged confirmation proceedings involving allegations that he had sexually harassed a former colleague center public attention on sexual harassment in the workplace.

1991 Supreme Court's *Board of Education of Oklahoma City Public Schools v. Dowell* decision holds that a school district is entitled to have a desegregation order lifted when it has complied in good faith with a desegregation decree since it was entered and when vestiges of past discrimination have been eliminated to the extent practicable.

1992 By a narrow margin, the Supreme Court's *Casey v. Planned Parenthood* decision reaffirms the constitutional right of abortion, but allows states greater ability to regulate aspects of abortion.

1992 After jury acquits four California police officers of having illegally beaten African American motorist Rodney King, riots break out in Los Angeles, leaving fifty people dead and an estimated two billion dollars of property damage.

1992 Supreme Court's *R.A.V. v. City of St. Paul* decision invalidates a "hate speech" statute, which makes it a crime to use racist or sexist speech.

1993 President Bill Clinton lifts the "gag rule" against abortion counseling in federally funded family-planning clinics and ends a previous ban on fetal tissue research.

1993 Janet Reno becomes first woman attorney general of the United States.

1993 President Bill Clinton orders "Don't ask, don't tell" policy for gays in the military, which permits gays to serve as long as they do not engage in homosexual conduct and do not openly admit their sexual orientation.

1993 U.S. Holocaust Memorial Museum opens in Washington, D.C.

1993 Congress passes the Family and Medical Leave Act, which requires large companies to provide unpaid leave for medical or family emergencies.

1993 Supreme Court's *Wisconsin v. Mitchell* decision upholds law enhancing punishment for crimes motivated by racial hatred.

1993 Congress passes law which allows voters to register to vote at the time they apply for a driver's license.

1993 Pentagon reveals allegations that eighty-three women were sexually harassed at the Navy's Tailhook Convention in Las Vegas.

1994 Seventy-three-year-old white supremacist Byron De La Beckwith is finally convicted of murdering civil rights leader Medgar Evers in 1963 and is sentenced to life in prison.

1994 Pope John Paul II circulates letter declaring that women cannot be ordained as priests in the Catholic Church.

1995 Verdict of acquittal ends lengthy trial of African American sports personality O. J. Simpson for allegedly murdering his wife.

1995 Supreme Court's *Miller v. Johnson* decision finds that state congressional districts deliberately drawn to include a majority of African-American residents violates equal protection.

1995 Nation of Islam minister Louis Farrakhan organizes march of more than 800,000 African American men on Washington.

1995 Shannon Faulkner is ordered admitted to the Citadel, a previously all-male public military academy, but she withdraws shortly afterward.

1995 Supreme Court's *Adarand Constructors v. Peña* decision holds that federal affirmative action programs must be subjected to "strict scrutiny."

1996 U.S. Fifth Circuit Court of Appeals decision in *Hopwood v. Texas* bars the University of Texas Law School from considering race as a factor in the admissions process.

1996 Rash of church burnings strike numerous African American churches.

1996 Supreme Court's *Romer v. Evans* decision finds that a state constitutional amendment that prohibits localities from passing laws prohibiting discrimination against homosexuals violates equal protection.

1996 Passage of California's Proposition 209, the Civil Rights Initiative, bans a variety of affirmative action programs (November).

1996 Supreme Court's *United States v. Virginia* decision holds that a state cannot exclude women from attendance at a publicly owned military school.

1997 Madeleine Albright is confirmed as the first woman secretary of state of the United States.

Rights Organizations
Compiled by Daniel G. Graetzer

ALABAMA

Klanwatch
400 Washington Ave.
Montgomery, Ala., 36104
Founded: 1980
Klanwatch gathers and disseminates information about the Ku Klux Klan and works to create a body of law to protect the rights of those whom the Klan attacks.

Southern Poverty Law Center (SPLC)
P.O. Box 2087
Montgomery, Ala., 36102
Founded: 1971
The SPLC works to protect and advance the legal and civil rights of poor people, regardless of race, through education and litigation. It does not accept fees from its clients.

ARIZONA

First Amendment Press (FAP)
8129 North 35th Ave., No. 134
Phoenix, Ariz., 85051-5892
Founded: 1993
The FAP provides information on citizen's rights and alleged government misconduct, offers legal advice and solution, conducts investigations, and maintains a speakers' bureau.

CALIFORNIA

Always Causing Legal Unrest (ACLU)
P.O. Box 2085
Rancho Cordova, Calif., 95741
Founded: 1990
This association includes feminists, antipornography activists, and other persons interested in an "alternative to First Amendment Fundamentalism." It urges corporations to place public safety and welfare and women's rights over profit and "conservative values," including trademark laws, private property rights, individual privacy, and profits.

Center for the Advancement of the Covenant
San Francisco University Philosophy Department
1600 Holloway Ave.
San Francisco, Calif., 94132
Founded: 1992
The center publicizes U.S. ratification of the 1992 International Covenant on Civil and Political Rights and the rights it contains by organizing an effective network of nongovernmental organizations to work toward federal, state, and local government compliance with the covenant.

Center for Third World Organizing (CTWO)
1218 East 21st St.
Oakland, Calif., 94606-3132
Founded: 1980
The CTWO provides training, issue analyses, and research to low-income minority organizations including welfare, immigrant, and Native American rights groups and monitors and reports on incidents of discrimination against people of color.

Chinese for Affirmative Action (CAA)
17 Walter U. Lum Place
San Francisco, Calif., 94108
Founded: 1969
The membership of the CAA includes individuals and corporations seeking equal opportunity for and the protection of the civil rights of Asian Americans. The organization works with the larger community to insure fair treatment under the law in employment matters; it has cooperated with state and local governmental agencies to help develop bilingual materials to aid Asian American job applicants; and it has encouraged the appointment of Asian Americans to public boards and commissions.

Death with Dignity Education Center (DDEC)
P.O. Box 1238
San Mateo, Calif., 94401-0816
Founded: 1994
The membership of the DDEC is a diverse group of people who believe that human beings have an inherent right to make their own choices regarding their heath care and end-of-life decisions. The organization informs and educates the pub-

lic about physician aid-in-dying so that they can make informed decisions themselves.

First Amendment Foundation (FAF)
1313 West 8th St., Ste. 313
Los Angeles, Calif., 90017
Founded: 1986
The FAF works to protect the rights of free expression for individuals and organizations and disseminates educational information on the First Amendment.

Freedom of Expression Foundation (FOEF)
5220 South Marina Pacifica
Long Beach, Calif., 90803
Founded: 1983
The membership of the FOEF includes corporations, foundations, broadcasters, and publishers whose purpose is to provide information to Congress and the public concerning freedom of speech as guaranteed by the First Amendment.

John Brown Anti-Klan Committee (JBAKC)
P.O. Box 14422
San Francisco, Calif., 94114
The membership of the JBAKC includes activists fighting racism and sexism. The committee supports gay rights and advocates freedom for political prisoners. Abolitionist John Brown, after whom the organization is named, is best known for leading twenty-one men on a raid of the federal arsenal at Harpers Ferry, Virginia (now part of West Virginia) in 1859 in order to further the fight against slavery.

National Committee Against Repressive Legislation (NCARL)
1313 West 8th St., Ste. 313
Los Angeles, Calif., 90017
Founded: 1960
The NCARL promotes First Amendment rights and opposes repressive laws and inquisitorial activities of government. Its notable activities have included promoting reforms of federal criminal laws and federal intelligence-gathering agencies and seeking to ban covert operations by the Central Intelligence Agency and political spying and harassment by the Federal Bureau of Investigation.

DISTRICT OF COLUMBIA

A. Philip Randolph Educational Fund (APREF)
1444 Eye St. NW, No. 300
Washington, D.C., 20005
Founded: 1964
The APREF works to eliminate prejudice and discrimination from all areas of life, educate individuals and groups on their rights and responsibilities, defend human and civil rights, and assist in the employment and education of the underprivileged.

American-Arab Anti-Discrimination Committee (ADC)
4201 Connecticut Ave. NW, Ste. 500
Washington, D.C., 20008
Founded: 1980
This grassroots organization represents Arab Americans and works to protect the rights of people of Arab descent, promote and defend the Arab American heritage, and serve the needs of the Arab American community. Through its Action Network and Media Monitoring Groups the organization works to counter the stereotyping of Arabs in the media and discrimination against Arab Americans in employment, education, and politics. It operates ADC Research Institute, conducts an internship program for college students, and organizes protests against racism in advertisements and other media.

Citizens' Commissions on Civil Rights (CCCR)
2000 M St. NW, Ste. 400
Washington, D.C., 20036
Founded: 1982
The CCCR is a bipartisan organization of former federal cabinet officials concerned with achieving the goal of equality of opportunity with objectives being to monitor the federal government's enforcement of laws barring discrimination on the basis of race, sex, religion, ethnic background, age, or disability; it also works to foster understanding of civil rights issues and to formulate constructive policy recommendations.

Citizens for Sensible Safeguards (CSS)
1742 Connecticut Ave. NW
Washington, D.C., 20009
Founded: 1995
A coalition of more than two hundred organizations

concerned with environmental, educational, civil rights, disability, health, and social services issues, the CSS works to improve laws and safeguards that protect citizens.

Commission for Social Justice (CSJ)

219 East St. NE
Washington, D.C., 20002
Founded: 1979

The CSJ serves as the antidefamation arm of the Order Sons of Italy in America and monitors businesses, schools, and the media to combat negative portrayals of Italian Americans.

Department of Civil Rights, AFL-CIO

815 16th St. NW
Washington, D.C., 20006
Founded: 1955

This staff arm of the AFL-CIO serves as an official liaison with women's and civil rights organizations and government agencies working in the field of equal opportunity. It also assists in the implementation of state and federal laws and AFL-CIO civil rights policies.

Freedom to Advertise Coalition (FAC)

2550 M St. NW, Ste. 500
Washington, D.C., 20037
Founded: 1988

The membership of FAC includes members of the American Advertising Federation, the American Association of Advertising Agencies, the Association of National Advertisers, the Magazine Publishers of America, the Outdoor Advertising Association of America, and the Point of Purchase Advertising Institute who unite to protect the rights of advertisers "truthfully and nondeceptively [to] advertise all legal products." Protection of the rights of commercial free speech as guaranteed by the U.S. Constitution and opposition of proposed legislation that would ban or restrict tobacco, alcohol, and other legal product advertising are among FAC's chief activities.

Judge David L. Bazelon Center for Mental Health Law

1101 15th St. NW, Ste. 1212
Washington, D.C., 20005
Founded: 1972

This organization's purpose is to clarify, establish, and enforce the legal rights of people with men-

tal and developmental disabilities by providing technical assistance and training to lawyers, consumers, providers of mental health and special education services, and policymakers at federal, state, and local levels.

Leadership Conference on Civil Rights (LCCR)

1629 K St. NW, Ste. 1010
Washington, D.C., 20006
Founded: 1950

The LCCR is a coalition of national organizations working to promote passage of civil rights, social, and economic legislation and to promote full enforcement of laws already on the books.

People for the American Way (PFAW)

2000 M St. NW, Ste. 400
Washington, D.C., 20036
Founded: 1980

The PFAW is a nonpartisan constitutional liberties organization whose members are religious, business, media, and labor figures committed to reaffirming the traditional American values of pluralism, diversity, and freedom of expression and religion.

United States Privacy Council (USPC)

P.O. Box 15060
Washington, D.C., 20003

The membership of USPC comprises individuals and groups committed to strengthening privacy rights in the United States by working to protect medical, insurance, and employee records, and update legislation, including the Fair Credit Reporting Act, the Privacy Act of 1974, and the Electronic Communications Privacy Act. The group also works to improve public access to governmental information.

GEORGIA

Center for Democratic Renewal (CDR)

P.O. Box 50469
Atlanta, Ga., 30302
Founded: 1979

The CDR advocates federal prosecution of the Ku Klux Klan and other groups or individuals involved in racist violence by seeking to build public opposition to racist groups and their activities and assist victims of bigoted violence by working with trade unions, public officials, and religious, women's, civil rights, and grassroots organizations.

Southern Christian Leadership Conference (SCLC)

334 Auburn Ave. NE
Atlanta, Ga., 30303
Founded: 1957

Organized by Martin Luther King, Jr., Ralph Abernathy, and other leaders in the Civil Rights movement, the SCLC is a nonsectarian coordinating and service agency for local organizations seeking full citizenship rights, equality, and the integration of African Americans in all aspects of life in the United States. Its members subscribe to King and Mohandas Gandhi's philosophy of nonviolence.

Southern Regional Council (SRC)

1900 Rhodes Haverty Bldg,
134 Peachtree St. NW
Atlanta, Ga., 30303-1825
Founded: 1944

The membership of the SRC includes leaders in education, religion, business, labor, the community, and the professions who are interested in improving race relations and combating poverty in the South.

ILLINOIS

Association Executives Human Rights Caucus (AEHRC)

P.O. Box 6001
Chicago, Ill., 60660-0001
Founded: 1983

The membership of the AEHRC includes individuals in the field of association management and employees of suppliers of goods and services to associations. The organization's goal is to foster greater appreciation and acceptance of the personal worth of all individuals, regardless of their sexual orientation.

INDIANA

Cuban American Legal Defense and Education Fund (CALDEF)

2513 South Calhoun St.

Fort Wayne, Ind., 46807-1305
Founded: 1980

CALDEF strives for equal treatment and opportunity for Cuban Americans and Hispanics in the fields of education, employment, housing, politics, and justice by discouraging negative stereotyping of Latinos and works to educate the public about problems of Cuban Americans and Latin Americans.

MARYLAND

Americans for Religious Liberty (ARL)

P.O. Box 6656
Silver Spring, Md., 20916
Founded: 1980

The membership of the ARL is composed of individuals dedicated to preserving religious, intellectual, and personal freedom. The organization supports the constitutional principle of separation of church and state, democratic secular public education, reproductive rights, and the Jefferson-Madisonian ideal of a pluralistic secular democracy.

National Association for the Advancement of Colored People (NAACP)

4805 Mt. Hope Drive
Baltimore, Md., 21215
Founded: 1909

The membership of the NAACP includes persons of all races and religions who believe in the organization's objectives and methods of achieving equal rights through the democratic process and eliminating racial prejudice by removing racial discrimination in housing, employment, voting, schools, the courts, transportation, recreation, prisons, and business enterprises.

MASSACHUSETTS

American Coordinating Committee for Equality in Sport and Society (ACCESS)

360 Huntington Ave., 161 CP
Boston, Mass., 02115
Founded: 1976

A coalition of thirty national civil rights, religious, political, and sports organizations, ACCESS works for equality in sports as a reflection of society as a whole. In the past it worked to end

U.S. sports contacts with South Africa until the latter country's apartheid system was abolished.

Gay and Lesbian Advocates and Defenders (GLAD)

P.O. Box 218
Boston, Mass., 02112
Founded: 1978

The membership of GLAD includes attorneys working to defend the civil rights of lesbians, gay men, and people with the HIV virus by operating an AIDS Law Project and speaker's bureau, conducting educational programs, and undertaking litigation.

Institute for First Amendment Studies (IFAS)

P.O. Box 589
Great Barrington, Mass., 01230
Founded: 1984

The membership of IFAS is made up of former members of Christian Fundamentalist churches and others dedicated to the constitutional principle of separation of church and state. The group monitors and reports on the activities of Fundamentalist groups.

MICHIGAN

Asian American Center for Justice of the American Citizens for Justice (ACJ)

P.O. Box 2735
Southfield, Mich., 48037-2735
Founded: 1983

The membership of the ACJ comprises Asian Americans and Pacific Islander Americans and other persons concerned with discrimination against ethnic groups. The ACJ works to combat and prevent racial intolerance, operates the Asian American Center for Justice, monitors legislation and law enforcement, works for civil rights in the areas of mental health, safety, and health and welfare, and promotes education of Asian Pacific American history and culture.

Trade Union Leadership Council (TULC)

8670 Grand River Ave.
Detroit, Mich., 48204
Founded: 1957

The membership of TULC includes mostly Michigan African American trade unionists who seek to eradicate injustices perpetrated upon people because of race, religion, sex, or national origin while seeking increased leadership and job opportunities for blacks.

MISSOURI

Protect Equality (PE)

6301 Rockhill Road, Ste. 315
Kansas City, Mo., 64131
Founded: 1965

PE is a nationwide interfaith program enabling religious organizations, institutions, and others to support equal opportunity employers with their purchasing power.

NEBRASKA

Anti-Fascist Network

P.O. Box 4824
Omaha, Nebr., 68104-0824
Founded: 1994

To ensure that the growth of government does not cancel out individual rights, this organization collects and researches information and reports on any groups, organizations, or government agencies that irresponsibly use inaccurate information to further their own goals at the expense of individual rights.

NEW YORK

American-Arab Relations Committee (AARC)

Box 416
New York, N.Y., 10017
Founded: 1964

The membership of AARC includes persons who wish to improve American-Arab relations and see the establishment of a peaceful and democratic Palestine. The AARC does not take stands on problems of the Arab world and inter-Arab relations or on domestic issues within the United States but opposes fascism, anti-Semitism, and Zionism. It pursues its goals through such activities as picketing and demonstrations, filing lawsuits, and registering complaints with the Federal Communications Commission about slanted portrayal of Arabs by the communication media.

American Civil Liberties Union (ACLU)

132 West 43rd St.

New York, N.Y., 10036

Founded: 1920

The organization champions the rights set forth in the Bill of Rights of the U.S. Constitution and works to advance equality before the law. ACLU activities have included litigation, advocacy, and public education, and sponsorship of litigation projects relating to women's rights, gay and lesbian rights, and children's rights. In 1996 the ACLU had 275,000 members and a staff of 125. That same year it established the American Civil Liberties Union Foundation as a tax- exempt arm with the purposes of legal defense, research, and public education.

American Israeli Civil Liberties Coalition (AICLC)

275 7th Ave., Ste. 1776

New York, N.Y., 10001

Founded: 1981

The objectives of the AICLC have been to aid Israelis in education, to teach Israelis about civil liberties, and to promote practice of basic civil liberties such as freedom of religion, speech, press, due process in civil and criminal proceedings, equal protection under the law, academic freedom, racial, ethnic, religious, and sexual equality. The organization has served as a source of financial and moral supports and has worked to keep Americans informed on the status of civil liberties in Israel.

Anti-Defamation League (ADL)

823 United Nations Plaza

New York, N.Y., 10017

Founded: 1913

The ADL has worked to stop the defamation of Jewish people and to secure justice and fair treatment to all citizens. It has also worked to educate Americans about Israel, promote better interfaith and intergroup relations, oppose anti-Semitism, counteract antidemocratic extremism, and strengthen democratic values and structures.

Asian American Legal Defense and Education Fund (AALDEF)

99 Hudson St.

New York, N.Y., 10013

Founded: 1974

The membership of AALDEF includes attorneys, legal workers, and others who seek to employ legal and educational methods to attack problems in Asian American communities. It has provided bilingual legal counseling and representation for people who cannot obtain access to legal assistance with areas of concern including immigration employment, voting rights, racially motivated violence against Asian Americans, environmental justice, and Japanese American redress.

Catholic Interracial Council of New York (CIC)

899 10th Ave.

New York, N.Y., 10019

Founded: 1934

The CIC works in cooperation with local parishes and governmental and voluntary groups to combat bigotry and discrimination and to promote social justice for all racial, religious, and ethnic groups.

Center for Constitutional Rights (CCR)

666 Broadway, 7th Floor

New York, N.Y., 10012

Founded: 1966

The CCR is a legal and educational organization dedicated to advancing and protecting the rights guaranteed by the U.S. Constitution and the United Nations' Universal Declaration of Civil Rights. It is committed to the "creative use of law" as a positive force for social change.

Children's Rights

132 West 43rd St., 6th Floor

New York, N.Y., 10036

Founded: 1995

This organization, which has only a staff of fifteen, fights for the rights of poor children who are dependent on government systems. Formerly called the Children's Rights Project of the American Civil Liberties Union.

Commission for Racial Justice (CRJ)

475 Riverside Drive, 16th Floor

New York, N.Y., 10115

Founded: 1963

The CRJ is a racial justice agency representing the 1.7 million members of the United Church of Christ. It promotes human rights programs and strategies that foster racial justice in African American and other minority communities.

The Generation After (TGA)
Box 14, Homecrest Sta.
Brooklyn, N.Y., 11229
Founded: 1979
The membership of TGA includes individuals working to eradicate anti-Semitism by exhorting human rights and social justice. The organization's goals are to accumulate and store data about neo-Nazi groups and to share such information with law-enforcement authorities in order to prevent violence that might be caused by such groups and to monitor neo-Nazi newspapers in the United States.

International Committee Against Racism (ICAR)
150 West 28th St., Room 301
New York, N.Y., 10001
Founded: 1973
The ICAR is dedicated to fighting all forms of racism and to building a multiracial society by opposing racism in all its economic, social, institutional, and cultural forms. It has worked to achieve these goals by sponsoring on-the-job, community, college, and high school workshops.

National Alliance Against Racist and Political Repression (NAARPR)
11 John St., Room 702
New York, N.Y., 10038
Founded: 1973
The NAARPR is a coalition of political, labor, church, civic, student, and community organizations dedicated to protecting the right to organize and is seeking to mobilize people to unite in word and action against many forms of repression of human rights in the United States.

National Urban League (NUL)
500 East 62nd St.
New York, N.Y., 10021
Founded: 1910
The NUL is a voluntary nonpartisan community service agency whose membership is made up largely of civic, professional, business, labor, and religious leaders. With its staff of trained social workers and other professionals, the league works to eliminate racial segregation and discrimination in the United States and to achieve parity for African Americans and other minorities in every phase of American life.

Workers' Defense League (WDL)
218 West 40th St., Room 203-204
New York, N.Y., 10018
Founded: 1936
The WDL is a labor-oriented human rights organization that provides counseling to workers on employment-related problems, conducts educational campaigns to defend and advance workers' rights, and maintains a speakers bureau.

PENNSYLVANIA

Anti-Repression Resource Team (ARRT)
P.O. Box 8040
State College, Penn., 16803-8040
Founded: 1979
ARRT combats all forms of political repression including police violence and misconduct, Ku Klux Klan and Nazi terrorism, spying and covert action by secret police and intelligence agencies while focusing on research, writing, lecturing, organizing, publishing, and conducting community workshops.

Association for the Sexually Harassed (ASH)
860 Manatawna Ave.
Philadelphia, Penn., 19128-1113
Founded: 1988
The membership of ASH includes employers, attorneys, organizations, schools, victims of sexual harassment, and other interested persons. The organization works to promote national awareness of sexual harassment by offering experts to appear on television and radio talk shows, mediation trouble-shooter services to resolve sexual harassment problems between employers and employees, telephone counseling, and consultation services.

VIRGINIA

Citizens for a Better America (CBA)
P.O. Box 356
Halifax, Va., 24558
Founded: 1975
The membership of CBA includes churches and individuals united to create a better America by strengthening individual rights in the United

States. It serves as a public advocacy organization that lobbies for civil rights and environmental legislation.

National Association to Protect Individual Rights (NAPIR)

5015 Gadsen
Fairfax, Va., 22032-3411
Founded: 1991

The NAPIR conducts research on issues including information privacy and government budgeting and provides information to public officials and the press.

WASHINGTON

Citizens Committee for the Right to Keep and Bear Arms (CCRKBA)

Liberty Park
12500 NE 10th Pl
Bellevue, Wash., 98005
Founded: 1971

The membership of CCRKBA includes citizens interested in defending the Second Amendment who conduct educational and political activities and studies on gun legislation.

Second Amendment Foundation (SAF)

James Madison Bldg.
12500 NE 10th Pl.
Bellevue, Wash., 98005
Founded: 1974

The membership of SAF includes individuals dedicated to promoting a better understanding of the Second Amendment right to "keep and bear arms."

WISCONSIN

Jews for the Restoration of Firearms Ownership (JPFO)

2872 South Wentworth Ave.
Milwaukee, Wis., 53207
Founded: 1989

The membership of JPFO includes individuals dedicated to advancing the right of law-abiding citizens to bear arms. It works to destroy the concept that "gun control is a beneficial policy."

Museums and Memorials

Compiled by K. L. A. Hyatt

ALABAMA

Birmingham Civil Rights Institute

520 Sixteenth St., North
Birmingham, Alabama
Description: Museum chronicling the history of the Civil Rights movement in Birmingham during the 1960's. Its permanent exhibits include a self-directed tour through some of the main events of that era.

The Civil Rights Memorial

400 Washington Ave.
Montgomery, Alabama
Description: Designed by Maya Ying Lin, who designed Washington, D.C.'s Vietnam War Memorial, this monument features a pair of circular stones on which are incised the names of forty martyred civil rights activists, including such well-known persons as Martin Luther King, Jr., and Medgar Evers, as well as little-known figures. The monument was commissioned by the Southern Poverty Law Center and stands before its main office.

Tuskegee Institute National Historic Site

1212 Old Montgomery Rd.
Tuskegee, Alabama
Description: Site administered by the National Park Service that preserves the history and significance of the Tuskegee Institute. The museum has significant holdings from the papers of both Booker T. Washington and the scientist George Washington Carver.

CALIFORNIA

César Chávez Monument

Peace Garden
California State University
Fresno, California
Description: Nine-foot-tall statue of the founder of the United Farm Workers of America and lifelong activist for the rights of farmworkers. The site also includes photographs from Chávez's life. The statue joins a bust of Mahatma Gandhi in the university's Peace Garden.

Japanese American National Museum

369 East First St.
Los Angeles, California
Description: Museum promoting awareness of the Japanese American experience as an important part of the heritage of the United States. It houses a comprehensive collection of Japanese American objects, images, and documents and offers a multifaceted program of exhibitions, films, and publications.

Manzanar National Historic Site

Owens Valley
Inyo County, California
Description: The site of one of the Japanese American internment camps during World War II, Manzanar has been preserved as a historic park. Since 1969 Japanese Americans of all ages have conducted an annual pilgrimage to the site to clean and restore the camp's cemetery and to highlight current Japanese American civil rights issues.

Simon Wiesenthal Center

9760 West Pico Blvd.
Los Angeles, California
Description: International center and museum for Holocaust remembrance and defense of human rights and the Jewish people. The center is named after its founder, a Holocaust survivor who dedicated his life to bringing Nazi war criminals to justice.

GEORGIA

The Martin Luther King Jr. Memorial Historic District

Auburn Ave.
Atlanta, Georgia 30312
Description: Five-block section of Atlanta dedicated to the memory of King and his followers. The historic site includes King's birthplace, his tomb, the Ebenezer Baptist Church, and a museum.

New Echota

State Historic Site
Calhoun, Georgia

Description: New Echota was established in 1825 as the capital of the independent Cherokee nation. The reconstructed historic site houses information on the Trail of Tears in 1838-1839, when the Cherokee were forcibly removed from the East Coast to what is now Oklahoma.

HAWAII

Queen Liliuokalani Statue
State Capitol Building
Honolulu, Hawaii
Description: Statue honoring Hawaii's last monarch, as well as the role that women have played in public offices.

INDIANA

Madame Walker Urban Life Center
617 Indiana Ave.
Indianapolis, Indiana
Description: This four-story brick building was the site of black entrepreneur Madame C. J. Walker's beauty supply business in the early twentieth century. It is now a historic landmark and serves as a community center.

KANSAS

Mid America All Indian Center
650 N. Seneca
Wichita, Kansas
Description: Preserves and promotes Native American culture by teaching history and culture to Native American youth and the non-Indian population. Represents the Native American population's needs for social services, cultural events, and social activities.

MARYLAND

Great Blacks in Wax Museum, Inc.
1601 E. North Ave.
Baltimore, Maryland
Description: Community-based educational and community center that promotes the study and preservation of African American history through the representation of historical figures and tableaus of historical events in lifelike wax statues.

MINNESOTA

Minnesota Historical Society-Lower Sioux History Center
Morton, Minnesota
Description: Repository of information on the clash of rights between the Dakota and American settlers from the mid-nineteenth century to the present.

The Roy Wilkins Memorial
Minneapolis, Minnesota
Description: Monument dedicated to Minnesota native Roy Wilkins, who was an officer in the National Association for the Advancement of Colored People for forty-six years, including twenty-two years as chief executive.

MONTANA

Jeannette Rankin Park
Madison St.
Missoula, Montana
Description: Named after the first woman member of Congress, this park is located near her childhood home. Rankin was first elected to Congress in 1916, two years after woman suffrage was approved in her state and four years before the Nineteenth Amendment was ratified.

NEBRASKA

Great Plains Black Museum
2213 Lake St.
Omaha, Nebraska
Description: Museum that promotes awareness of the role of African Americans, especially African American women, in the shaping of the Midwest.

NEVADA

Sarah Winnemucca Birthplace Site
Humboldt Sink
Lovelock, Nevada
Description: Memorial to the Paiute Indian woman Winnemucca, who was displaced from her birthplace at Lovelock when the Paiute were forcibly removed by federal mandate. She spent much of her life trying to regain the Paiutes' rights to their homeland and traveled widely on lecture tours to educate white people about the repressive operations of the Bureau of Indian Affairs.

NEW YORK

Home of Margaret Sanger
17 West 16th St.
New York, New York
Description: Residence and priviate research center of birth control pioneer Sanger, a central leader in the movement to make birth control education and devices legally available to women of all walks of life. The Margaret Sanger Birth Control Clinic is located at 46 Aboy Street in New York City.

Site of the Triangle Shirtwaist Company Fire
Brown Building
Washington Place and Green St.
New York, New York
Description: Now a New York University classroom building, this is the site in which hundreds of women workers were trapped by a fire that killed amost a third of their number on March 25, 1911. The tragedy caused reformers to spearhead labor legislation to regulate safety conditions in American workplaces.

The Statue of Liberty
Liberty Island
New York Harbor
Description: A colossal sculpture of the female figure of Liberty, this monument was given to the United States by France in 1886. Since then it has served as a welcoming beacon to visitors and immigrants, whose contributions to America its presence honors.

Women's Rights National Historic Park
Seneca Falls, New York
Description: Site of the 1848 Seneca Falls Women's Rights Convention, which spawned the nineteenth century women's movement. The park has a visitor's center and nineteen life-size bronze statues of the leaders who attended the conference. These figures include Elizabeth Cady Stanton, whose home is also part of the park.

OHIO

Sojourner Truth Monument
Donner Press Building
Akron, Ohio
Description: Stone monument honoring a speech that Truth delivered at the second National Woman Suffrage Convention in 1852. Though best known as an abolitionist leader guide for the Underground Railroad, Truth was also an active feminist.

OKLAHOMA

National Hall of Fame for Famous American Indians
Anadarko, Oklahoma
Description: Outdoor museum with bronze portraits of important American Indian figures.

SOUTH DAKOTA

Crazy Horse Memorial Foundation
Avenue of the Chiefs
Crazy Horse, South Dakota
Description: Colossal carving on the top of a granite mountain of Lakota leader Crazy Horse mounted on a horse. The unfinished monument has been designed as a Native American equivalent to Mount Rushmore, also in South Dakota, and to enhance awareness of Native American struggles.

TENNESSEE

National Civil Rights Museum
450 Mulberry St.
Memphis, Tennessee

Description: Museum located in the Lorraine Motel, in which Martin Luther King, Jr., was assassinated on April 4, 1968. Its exhibits include one of the first attempts at a comprehensive overview of the Civil Rights movement.

TEXAS

Dr. Héctor P. García Plaza
Texas A&M University
Corpus Christi, Texas
Description: Memorial honoring the founder of the American GI Forum. A well-known humanitarian and activist against Hispanic discrimination, García also served as a U.S. diplomat to the United Nations and as a member of the U.S. Commission on Civil Rights and was awarded the Presidential Medal of Freedom.

El Paso Holocaust Museum and Study Center
401 Wallenberg Drive
El Paso, Texas
Description: Museum memorializing the Jewish Holocaust of World War II, with an educational center that works to fight prejudice and bigotry throughout the world. The museum also has a garden dedicated to Gentiles who risked their lives to save Jews from Germany's Nazi regime, as well as an exhibit of photographs taken by Nazis themselves.

VIRGINIA

Booker T. Washington National Monument
Hardy, Virginia
Description: The site of the birthplace of Washington, this park is a living historic farm re-created to preserve the tobacco plantation on which Washington worked as a slave.

WASHINGTON

Wing Luke Asian Museum
407 Seventh Ave. South
Seattle, Washington
Description: Named afer the first Asian American elected official in the Pacific Northwest, this museum has permanent exhibits on the immigration and settlement of Asians in the Northwest and a model of a World War II-era Japanese American internment camp.

WASHINGTON, D.C.

Frederick Douglass National Historical Site
Cedar Hill
1411 West St. SE
Washington, D.C.
Description: Memorial housed in the last home of African American abolitionist, editor, and orator Frederick Douglass.

Mary McLeod Bethune Memorial
Lincoln Park
13th and East Capitol Streets
Washington, D.C.
Description: Memorial to Bethune and her accomplishments as an educator and founder of the National Council of Negro Women. Its statue of Bethune is the first of an African American woman erected in a public park in the nation's capital. The Bethune Museum and Archives for Black Women's History is located at 1319 Vermont Ave., NW, in Washington, D.C.

United States Holocaust Memorial Museum
Washington, D.C.
Description: National museum dedicated to preserving and promoting awareness of the genocide perpetrated by Germany's Nazi regime against Jews and other peoples during World War II.

Filmography

Compiled by Christine J. Catanzarite

1909 *A Corner in Wheat* Exploitation of the poor was the subject of this early D. W. Griffith film, in which he used the innovative technique of cross-cutting between scenes of a lush banquet and poor people waiting for bread.

1914 *Your Girl and Mine* Woman suffragist film made by Lewis J. Selznick's World Film Company, which later backed out of commercial distribution.

1915 *The Birth of a Nation* D. W. Griffith's controversial depiction of the Civil War and Reconstruction, in which the Ku Klux Klan is celebrated for its role as a bastion of white southern values and African Americans are depicted as simple-minded and dangerous.

1917 *The Immigrant* Charles Chaplin short in which the Little Tramp crosses the Atlantic with other impoverished immigrants to the United States, only to discover that the streets of America are not paved with gold.

1932 *Cabin in the Cotton* Class warfare results when poor sharecroppers and rich land-owners clash in this film directed by Michael Curtiz.

1934 *Massacre* An educated Sioux man (Richard Barthelmess) battles the injustices against his people.

Our Daily Bread King Vidor's Depression-era back-to-the-land saga about a family that escapes city life for communal living on a farm. Despite an overall left-wing tone, the film presents some contradictory political messages.

1935 *Black Fury* Coal miners are caught between moderate union workers and radical agitators. Directed by Michael Curtiz, this film was one of early Hollywood's few realistic depictions of labor unrest.

Riffraff Sometime comedic treatment of West Coast fishermen involved in labor disputes lured to strike by a charismatic union leader.

1936 *Black Legion* Blue-collar worker Humphrey Bogart joins the Klan-like Black Legion after losing a promotion to a Polish co-worker, only to discover that the legion profits from exploiting its members.

Modern Times Charles Chaplin's silent satire about the dehumanizing effects of the industrial revolution, in which his Little Tramp character is literally and figuratively consumed by the machinery of progress.

1940 *The Grapes of Wrath* John Ford's superb film version of the John Steinbeck novel abut the Joad family, Depression-era Okies traveling from the Dust Bowl to California. One of Hollywood's most successful social-problem films.

One Tenth of Our Nation Documentary showing inadequate educational conditions among African Americans in the South.

1941 *A Place to Live* Documentary focusing on substandard housing conditions among African Americans in Philadelphia.

1947 *Crossfire* Anti-Semitism leads to murder when a drunken World War II veteran beats a Jewish man to death in Edward Dmytryk's film about intolerance in America.

Gentleman's Agreement Gregory Peck portrays a writer masquerading as a Jew in order to experience anti-Semitism at first hand. Directed by Elia Kazan, adapted from the Laura Z. Hobson novel.

1949 *Home of the Brave* A black soldier in World War II suffers abuse from his fellow soldiers.

Intruder in the Dust Adaptation of the William Faulkner novel—in which a black man accused of murder faces a lynch mob in his southern town.

Lost Boundaries Examination of segregation in New England, where a light-skinned African American doctor and his family "pass" for white.

1950 *The Jackie Robinson Story* Robinson plays himself in this biography of the first black man to play major-league baseball in the modern era. The film includes a serious examination of the racial issues surrounding baseball's color barrier.

The Lawless Study of racial discrimination and mistreatment of Mexican American farmworkers in Southern California.

No Way Out This first film for Sidney Poitier, Ruby Dee, and Ossie Davis is a violent story of a bigot who instigates race riots. Directed by Joseph L. Mankiewicz.

1951 *Jim Thorpe—All American* Burt Lancaster plays the celebrated American Indian athlete, who became a controversial figure after he was stripped of his Olympic medals because he had played semi-professional baseball.

1952 *Big Jim McLain* John Wayne plays a Federal Bureau of Investigation agent tracking a communist spy ring for the House Committee on Un-American Activities. This fervently pro-HUAC film features a credit thanking the committee for their cooperation and their efforts in eradicating communism.

1953 *Salt of the Earth* Directed by Herbert Biberman and written by Michael Wilson, both of whom were blacklisted (along with several others involved in the production), this film tells the story of Latino union activity among miners in New Mexico. Much of the story is told from a feminist perspective.

1961 *The Intruder* A racist white southerner goes from town to town starting riots by protesting the court-ordered integration of schools. (Also released as *I Hate Your Guts!* and *Shame.*)

A Raisin in the Sun The politics of racism are examined in the adaptation of Lorraine Hansberry's play, in which a black family moves into a white Chicago neighborhood.

1962 *To Kill a Mockingbird* An Alabama lawyer (Gregory Peck) defends a poor black man (Brock Peters) accused of rape during the 1930's, and he tries to explain the racially charged case to his children. Adapted from the novel by Harper Lee.

1963 *The Cardinal* Otto Preminger directed this story of a cardinal's rise in the Roman Catholic Church. In a subplot, a black catholic priest travels to Rome to ask for the pope's assistance in desegregating a school in Georgia.

1964 *Black Like Me* Based on the true story of John Howard Griffin, a white journalist takes medication to darken his skin so he can experience racism in the South at first hand. Among the people he encounters on his journey is a young civil rights activist.

Nothing but a Man A black railroad worker and his schoolteacher wife encounter prejudice in the South when they try to settle down there.

One Potato, Two Potato Exploration of the problems faced by an interracial married couple (Barbara Barrie and Bernie Hamilton), centering on the custody battle waged by the white woman's former husband over their daughter. Among the first films to depict the problems of interracial marriage.

1967 *Guess Who's Coming to Dinner* The liberal convictions of a prosperous white couple (Katharine Hepburn and Spencer Tracy) are tested when their daughter brings home her black fiancé (Sidney Poitier).

Hotel This soap opera drama about the workings of a luxury hotel in New Orleans includes a subplot about the hotel's refusing accommodations to a black couple.

Sweet Love, Bitter Story of the friendship between a declining college professor and a troubled jazz musician (loosely based on Charlie Parker). The film contains several powerful scenes of civil rights-themed material.

1968 *Madigan* This film about the day-to-day life of a New York City detective contains a subplot about police brutality directed against African Americans.

Up Tight The first film about the militant black revolution examines the inner workings of a radical group and the relationships among its diverse members. Co-written by Ruby Dee and novelist Julian Mayfield, who also star in the film.

1969 *Change of Habit* Elvis Presley is a doctor and Mary Tyler Moore is a nun in this film, which features black and white nuns working together to provide free health care to disadvantaged African Americans and Latinos in the inner city.

The Lost Man A crook plans a heist to get money for the families of imprisoned black activists. One of his gang, a civil right protester, stages a demonstration to distract police during the robbery.

Medium Cool A fictional television news cameraman is involved in the police riots at the 1968 Democratic National Convention in Chicago.

Slaves Drama about a Kentucky plantation owner's relationship with his slave mistress and a slave (Ossie Davis) who asserts his rights. In addition to its revisionist views, which espouse the values of the modern Civil Rights movement, this film is notable for being directed and co-written by Herbert Biberman, who had been blacklisted and imprisoned as one of the Hollywood Ten.

1970 *King: A Filmed Record—Montgomery to Memphis* Documentary about the life of Martin Luther King, Jr., from 1955 until his 1968 assassination, using news footage and interviews.

My Sweet Charlie A black activist lawyer (Al Freeman, Jr.), on the run from a murder connected with a civil rights demonstration, becomes romantically involved with an unmarried, pregnant white woman (Patty Duke) in the South.

R.P.M. Campus radicals demand the appointment of a black trustee at their university.

Watermelon Man Melvin Van Peebles directed this story of a white racist, Godfrey Cambridge, who is transformed into a black man and forced to experience bigotry.

1971 *Sweet Sweetback's Baadasssss Song* Successful revolutionary independent film about a political outlaw on the run after injuring two policemen for beating a black radical. Produced, written, and directed by Melvin Van Peebles, who also stars in the film.

1972 *Malcolm X* Documentary about the black leader, with excerpts from his autobiography read by James Earl Jones. Produced and written by the same team behind Spike Lee's 1992 film of the same name.

1974 *Lenny* Bob Fosse directed this biography of comedian Lenny Bruce (Dustin Hoffman), including an examination of his arrests for public obscenity in the 1950's.

1976 *Union Maids* Documentary by Julia Reichert, James Klein, and Miles Mogulescu, examining the labor movement using Depression-era footage and interviews with women who participated in the struggle.

1977 *The Greatest* Muhammad Ali plays himself in this biography of the heavyweight boxing champion and civil rights activist.

1978 *King: The Martin Luther King, Jr., Story* Made-for-television biography of the civil rights leader, starring Paul Winfield as King and Cicely Tyson as his wife, Coretta.

1979 *Norma Rae* Poor southern textile family worker (Sally Field) becomes an assertive union organizer in this story of women and labor rights.

1980 *Eyes on the Prize: America at the Racial Crossroads, 1964-1972* Epic documentary about the Civil Rights movement, including film footage and still photographs that had never before been shown. A complex portrait of the struggle for civil rights in America.

The Life and Times of Rosie the Riveter Director Connie Fields's documentary about women on the production front during World War II, emphasizing the poor treatment of women workers, and particularly black women, as they broke gender barriers in the workplace.

1981 *Zoot Suit* Luis Valdez wrote and directed this stylized musical about Los Angeles' zoot suit riots during World War II, focusing on the Mexican American street gangs who were framed for murder and imprisoned by an unjust legal system.

1983 *The Lords of Discipline* Adaptation of Pat Conroy's novel about the mistreatment of the first black cadet at a South Carolina military school in 1964.

Miles of Smiles, Years of Struggle Documentary directed by Jack Santino and Paul Wagner about black Pullman porters and their contributions to American life, in spite of lack of opportunities in pre-civil rights America.

1984 *A Soldier's Story* Adaptation of a Pulitzer Prize-winning stage play about the murder of a black officer in the South in the 1940's. Most of the cast, which includes Howard E. Rollins, Jr., and Denzel Washington, is from the Negro Ensemble Company.

1985 *The Color Purple* Steven Spielberg's adaptation of Alice Walker's novel about the hard times of a poor black woman (Whoopi Goldberg) in the segregated South.

1987 *Hollywood Shuffle* Robert Townsend (who also wrote and directed) stars as a young black actor trying to make it in Hollywood. Instead of fame and fortune, he finds prejudice and typecasting.

1988 *Hairspray* Teenagers on a popular *American Bandstand*-like show in Baltimore clash when the show attempts to integrate in 1962. Directed by cult favorite John Waters.

The Milagro Beanfield War Mexican American farmers protest against the powerful white land developers who want to profit from their fields in this film directed by Robert Redford.

Mississippi Burning After three civil rights workers in Mississippi disappear mysteriously in 1964, two white FBI agents (Gene Hackman and Willem Dafoe) are assigned to investigate the case. Fictionalized account of real-life events that were also featured in the television film *Murder in Mississippi* (1990).

1989 *Common Threads: Stories from the Quilt* Social and governmental prejudices against homosexuals and individuals with AIDS are exposed in this powerful documentary, which examines the lives and deaths of five AIDS victims, who followed different paths to end up memorialized in panels of the AIDS Memorial Quilt.

Cross of Fire Made-for-television docudrama abut Ku Klux Klan Grand Dragon and politician D. C. Stephenson in 1920's Indiana.

Do the Right Thing Director Spike Lee's examination of the explosive racial situation at a white-owned pizza parlor in Brooklyn on a hot summer day.

Driving Miss Daisy Adaptation of Alfred Uhry's play about the relationship between a wealthy white woman (Jessica Tandy) and her black chauffeur (Morgan Freeman), set in Georgia before and during the Civil Rights movement.

Roe v. Wade Made-for-television film about the landmark U.S. Supreme Court decision that upheld a woman's right to choose abortion. Despite the controversial subject matter, the film remains politically neutral.

We Shall Overcome Documentary tracing the song that became the anthem of the Civil Rights movement.

1990 *The Court-Martial of Jackie Robinson* Cable television drama in which the future baseball star (Andre Braugher) confronts bigotry and discrimination in the military.

The Long Walk Home A wealthy white housewife (Sissy Spacek) and her black housekeeper (Whoopi Goldberg) struggle with the emergence of civil rights and feminism during the Montgomery bus boycott.

Murder in Mississippi Made-for-television film about the murders of three young civil rights activists in the summer of 1964.

1991 *Fried Green Tomatoes* An elderly woman reflects upon the lives of two young women in the South in the 1920's and 1930's. Includes an examination of racial injustices and Ku Klux Klan activities when a black man is accused of murder.

Jungle Fever Spike Lee's examination of interracial romance, involving a successful, married black man (Wesley Snipes) who has an affair with his white secretary (Annabella Sciorra).

Separate But Equal Made-for-television film with Sidney Poitier, as Thurgood Marshall, arguing the landmark *Brown v. Board of Education* case in 1954.

1992 *Incident at Oglala* Documentary examining the alleged framing of Native American Leonard Peltier for the deaths of two FBI agents at South Dakota's Pine Ridge Reservation in 1975. Produced and narrated by Robert Redford; directed by Michael Apted, who also directed *Thunderheart* (1992), a fictionalized account of the event.

A League of Their Own Director Penny Marshall's film about the professional women's baseball league that was formed during World War II. Includes some serious examination of women's roles in the pre-feminist era.

Malcolm X Spike Lee's biography of Malcolm X (Denzel Washington) shows the revolutionary leader's rise from his street origins to national power. Co-written by Lee, who also appears in the film.

A Private Matter Made-for-cable television film with Sissy Spacek as Sherri Finkbine, the real-life host of a children's television show who sparked controversy in the early 1960's when, after discovering that she had been exposed to thalidomide, she sought an abortion.

Thunderheart An FBI agent (Val Kilmer) confronts his American Indian heritage when he is assigned to investigate a murder on a reservation. Directed by Michael Apted, who also directed a documentary, *Incident at Oglala*, about the real case on which this film is based.

1993 *For Us, the Living* Made-for-television film about the life of slain civil rights activist Medgar Evers. Adapted from the biography by Evers' widow, Myrlie.

Philadelphia A promising gay attorney (Tom Hanks) is fired when it is discovered that he has AIDS, and he sues with the reluctant help of a homophobic black lawyer (Denzel Washington). Jonathan Demme's film was the first major studio production to address the AIDS epidemic.

1994 *Disclosure* Barry Levinson's film adaptation of the Michael Crichton novel, with a twist on the sexual harassment debate. Demi Moore plays the aggressive female boss who is sued by employee Michael Douglas after a sexual encounter.

Oleanna David Mamet directed his adaptation of his own play, which centers on the relationship between a male professor and his vulnerable female student and the consequent charges of sexual harassment.

The Vernon Johns Story Southern minister Vernon Johns, who helped inspire the Civil Rights movement and preceded Martin Luther King, Jr., as its leader, is depicted in this made-for-television film. James Earl Jones plays Johns.

1995 *The Celluloid Closet* Documentary, based on a book by Vito Russo, examining Hollywood's depiction of homosexuality. Narrated and co-produced by Lily Tomlin.

Higher Learning A large university is torn by racial and sexual conflicts, which escalate with the appearance of skinhead extremists in John Singleton's drama.

The Incredibly True Adventures of Two Girls in Love Teenage lesbians encounter social prejudices and the homophobia of their high school classmates in this independent film.

The K.K.K. Boutique Ain't Just Rednecks Depictions of racism, using documentary footage and fictional materials. Includes a salesman modeling a hooded robe.

Panther Traces the rise of the Black Panther Party in the 1960's. Directed by Mario Van Peebles, from a script written by his father, director Melvin Van Peebles.

Serving in Silence: The Margarethe Cammermeyer Story Made-for television film with Glenn Close as the real-life Cammermeyer, a distinguished career military officer who is released from the U.S. Army when it is revealed that she is a lesbian.

The Tuskegee Airmen Made-for-cable television film about the first black squadron in World War II, the "Fighting 99th," as they encounter social and military prejudice.

1996 *Blacklist: Hollywood on Trial* Documentary about the HUAC investigations in Hollywood during the late 1940's and 1950's, and the formation of a First Amendment advocacy group by prominent actors and directors. Includes footage from the hearings and interviews with blacklisted figures.

Citizen Ruth A street-smart pregnant woman (Laura Dern) becomes a pawn in the debate over reproductive rights.

Get on the Bus Spike Lee's film about a diverse group of black men on their way by bus to the "Million Man March" in Washington, D.C.

Ghosts of Mississippi Rob Reiner's film about the 1992 retrial of Byron de la Beckwith, who killed civil rights activist Medgar Evers in 1963. After two acquittals in the 1960's, Beckwith was found guilty of the murder.

If These Walls Could Talk Made-for-cable television film with Cher, Demi Moore, and Sissy Spacek as women involved in the issue of abortion both before and after its legalization. In the final portion of the film, set in 1996, "pro-life" activists break into a clinic and kill a doctor.

Once Upon a Time When We Were Colored Director Tim Reid examines the life of a Mississippi Delta family during the decades leading up to the Civil Rights movement.

The People v. Larry Flynt Milos Forman's film about *Hustler* magazine publisher Larry Flynt (Woody Harrelson), whose peddling of pornography led to numerous court battles over his First Amendment rights.

Soul of the Game The integration of major league baseball is examined in this made-for-cable television film, centering on the careers of Jackie Robinson, Satchel Paige, and Josh Gibson.

A Time to Kill Shades of *To Kill a Mockingbird*: A liberal white southern lawyer defends the black man who killed his daughter's rapist, amid rioting and racism.

1997 *Miss Evers' Boys* Made-for-cable television drama based on the true story of the U.S. government's medical studies of syphilis, in which a group of infected black men were denied medical treatment for their illness.

Rosewood John Singleton directed this film set in 1923 in a small Florida town, when a false accusation of assault leads to racially motivated riots and lynching. Based on real-life incidents.

Bibliography

Compiled by Kevin J. Bochynski

These listings are a guide to books on civil rights-related topics. Entries are organized under broad subject headings, and some titles are listed under more than a single heading. Reference materials are listed first; otherwise, subject headings are arranged alphabetically, with their page numbers listed below. For additional sources—and particularly for articles and books on more specialized topics—see the notes on suggested readings appended to many of the essays in the main text.

REFERENCE MATERIALS

Auerbach, Susan, ed. *Encyclopedia of Multiculturalism*. 6 vols. New York: Marshall Cavendish, 1994.

Bergman, Peter M. *The Chronological History of the Negro in America*. New York: Harper & Row, 1969.

Bessette, Joseph M., ed. *Ready Reference: American Justice*. 3 vols. Pasadena, Calif.: Salem Press, 1996.

Chabrán, Richard, and Raphael Chabrán, eds. *The Latino Encyclopedia*. 6 vols. New York: Marshall Cavendish, 1996.

Cowan, Tom, and Jack Maguire. *Timelines of African-American History: 500 Years of Black Achievement*. New York: Roundtable Press/ Perigree Press, 1994.

Gates, Henry Louis, ed. *Black Biography, 1790-1950: A Cumulative Index*. Alexandria, Va.: Chadwick-Healey, 1991.

Graham, Hugh D., ed. *Civil Rights in the United States*. University Park: Pennsylvania State University Press, 1994.

Hall, Kermit L., ed. *The Oxford Companion to the Supreme Court of the United States* New York: Oxford University Press, 1992.

Hine, Darlene Clark, Elsa Barkley Brown, and Rosalyn Terborg-Penn, eds. *Black Women in America: An Historical Encyclopedia*. Bloomington: Indiana University Press, 1994.

Hornsby, Alton, Jr. *The Chronology of African-American History: Significant Events and People from 1619 to the Present*. Detroit: Gale, 1991.

Low, W. Augustus, and Virgil A. Clift. *Encyclopedia of Black America*. New York: McGraw-Hill, 1981.

Luker, Ralph E. *Historical Dictionary of the Civil Rights Movement*. Lanham, Md.: Scarecrow Press, 1997.

McFadden, Margaret, ed. *Ready Reference: Women's Issues*. 3 vols. Pasadena, Calif.: Salem Press, 1996.

Mack, Kibibi Voloria, ed. *The African American Encyclopedia: Supplement*. 2 vols. New York: Marshall Cavendish, 1997.

Markovitz, Harvey, ed. *Ready Reference: American Indians*. 3 vols. Pasadena, Calif.: Salem Press, 1995.

Maxwell, John A., James J. Friedberg, and Deirdre A. DeGolia, eds. *Human Rights in Western Civilization: 1600 to the Present*. Dubuque, Iowa: Kendall/Hunt, 1994.

Murray, Paul T. *The Civil Rights Movement: References and Resources*. New York: G. K. Hall, 1993.

Newton, David E. *Gay and Lesbian Rights: A Reference Handbook*. Santa Barbara, Calif.: ABC-CLIO, 1994.

Ng, Franklin, ed. *The Asian American Encyclopedia*. 6 vols. New York: Marshall Cavendish, 1995.

Tuck, Richard. *Natural Rights Theories: Their Origin and Development*. Cambridge: Cambridge University Press, 1979.

Williams, Michael W., ed. *The African American Encyclopedia*. 6 vols. New York: Marshall Cavendish, 1993.

Wilson, Charles Reagan, and William Ferris, eds. *Encyclopedia of Southern Culture*. 4 vols. Chapel Hill: University of North Carolina Press, 1989.

ACTIVISTS AND LEADERS

Buni, Andrew. *Robert L. Vann of the "Pittsburgh Courier": Politics and Black Journalism*. Pittsburgh, Pa.: University of Pittsburgh Press, 1974.

Burner, Eric. *And Gently Shall He Lead: Robert Parris Moses and Civil Rights in Mississippi*. New York: New York University Press, 1994.

Cagin, Seth, and Philip Dray. *We Are Not Afraid: The Story of Goodman, Schwerner, and Chaney in the Civil Rights Campaign for Mississippi*. New York: Macmillan, 1988.

Capeci, Dominic J., Jr., and Martha Wilkerson. *Layered Violence: The Detroit Rioters of 1943*. Jackson: University of Mississippi Press, 1991.

Chappell, David L. *Inside Agitators: White Southerners in the Civil Rights Movement*. Baltimore: Johns Hopkins University Press, 1994.

Crawford, Vicki L., Jacqueline A. Rouse, and Barbara Woods, eds. *Women in the Civil Rights Movement: Trailblazers and Torchbearers, 1941-1965*. Bloomington: Indiana University Press, 1993.

Davis, Lenwood G. *A Paul Robeson Research Guide: A Selected, Annotated Bibliography*. Westport, Conn.: Greenwood Press, 1982.

Duffy, Susan. *Shirley Chisholm: A Bibliography of Writings by and About Her*. Metuchen, N.J.: Scarecrow Press, 1988.

Eagles, Charles W. *Outside Agitator: Jon Daniels and the Civil Rights Movement in Alabama*. Chapel Hill: University of North Carolina Press, 1993.

Erikson, Erik H. *Gandhi's Truth: On the Origins of Militant Nonviolence*. New York: W. W. Norton, 1969.

Evers, Charles, and Andrew Szanton. *Have No Fear: The Charles Evers Story*. New York: J. Wiley & Sons, 1997.

Frady, Marshall. *Jesse: The Life and Pilgrimage of Jesse Jackson*. New York: Random House, 1996.

Gregory, Dick. *Nigger: An Autobiography*. New York: Dutton, 1964.

Griswald del Castillo, Richard, and Richard A. Garcia. *César Chávez: A Triumph of Spirit*. Norman: University of Oklahoma Press, 1995.

Hall, Jacquelyn D. *Revolt Against Chivalry: Jessie Daniel Ames and the Women's Campaign Against Lynching*. New York: Columbia University Press, 1979.

Hardy, Gayle J. *American Women Civil Rights Activists: Biobibliographies of Sixty-eight Leaders, 1825-1992*. Jefferson, N.C.: McFarland, 1993.

Harris, William H. *Keeping the Faith: A. Philip Randolph, Milton P. Webster, and the Brotherhood of Sleeping Car Porters, 1925-37*. Reprint. Urbana: University of Illinois Press, 1977.

Haygood, Wil. *King of the Cats: The Life and Times of Adam Clayton Powell, Jr*. Boston: Houghton Mifflin, 1993.

Hill, Robert A., et al., eds. *The Marcus Garvey and Universal Negro Improvement Association Papers*. 7 vols. Berkeley: University of California Press, 1983-1990.

Hughes, Langston. *Langston Hughes and the "Chicago Defender": Essays on Race, Politics, and Culture, 1942-1962*. Edited by Christopher C. De Santis. Urbana: University of Illinois Press, 1995.

Jones, Beverly W. *Quest for Equality: The Life and Writings of Mary Eliza Church Terrell, 1863-1954*. Brooklyn, N.Y.: Carlson, 1990.

Karcher, Carolyn L. *The First Woman in the Republic: A Cultural Biography of Lydia Maria Child.* Durham, N.C.: Duke University Press, 1994.

Keppel, Ben. *The Work of Democracy: Ralph Bunche, Kenneth B. Clarke, Lorraine Hansberry, and the Cultural Politics of Race.* Cambridge, Mass.: Harvard University Press, 1995.

Koch, Thilo. *Fighters for a New World: John F. Kennedy, Martin Luther King, Robert F. Kennedy.* New York: Putnam, 1969.

Kotz, Nick, and Mary L. Kotz. *A Passion for Equality: George A. Wiley and the Movement.* New York: W. W. Norton, 1977.

Lewis, David L. *W.E.B. Du Bois: Biography of a Race, 1868-1919.* New York: Henry Holt, 1993.

Martin, Tony. *Race First: Idealogy and Organizational Struggles of Marcus Garvey and the Universal Negro Improvement Association.* Westport, Conn.: Greenwood Press, 1976.

Matthiessen, Peter. *Sal Si Puedes: César Chávez and the New American Revolution.* New York: Random House, 1969.

Means, Russell. *Where White Men Fear to Tread: The Autobiography of Russell Means.* New York: St. Martin's Press, 1995.

Meier, August, and John Hope Franklin. *Black Leaders of the Twentieth Century.* Urbana: University of Illinois Press, 1982.

Mills, Kay. *This Little Light of Mine: The Life of Fannie Lou Hamer.* New York: E. P. Dutton, 1993.

Neary, John. *Julian Bond: Black Rebel.* New York: William Morrow, 1971.

Parks, Rosa, and Gregory J. Reed. *Quiet Strength: The Faith, the Hope, and the Heart of a Woman Who Changed a Nation.* Grand Rapids, Mich.: Zondervan, 1994.

Patterson, Lillie. *A. Philip Randolph: Messenger for the Masses.* New York: Facts On File, 1996.

Powell, Adam Clayton, Jr. *Adam by Adam: The Autobiography of Adam Clayton Powell, Jr.* New York: Dial Press, 1971.

Ramdin, Ron. *Paul Robeson: The Man and His Mission.* London: P. Owen, 1987.

Robbins, Richard. *Sidelines Activist: Charles S. Johnson and the Struggle for Civil Rights.* Jackson: University Press of Mississippi, 1996.

Rudwick, Elliott. *W.E.B. Du Bois: A Study in Minority Group Leadership.* Philadelphia: University of Pennsylvania Press, 1960.

Sales, William W., Jr. *From Civil Rights to Black Liberation: Malcolm X and the Organization of Afro-American Unity.* Boston: South End Press, 1994.

Stetson, Erlene, and Linda David. *Glorying in Tribulation: The Lifework of Sojourner Truth.* East Lansing: Michigan State University, 1993.

Streitmatter, Rodger. *Raising Her Voice: African-American Women Journalists Who Changed History.* Lexington: University Press of Kentucky, 1994.

Thornbrough, Emma L. *T. Thomas Fortune, Militant Journalist.* Chicago: University of Chicago Press, 1972.

Urquhart, Brian. *Ralph Bunche: An American Life.* New York: W. W. Norton, 1993.

Wells-Barnett, Ida B. *Crusade for Justice: The Autobiography of Ida B. Wells.* Edited by Alfreda M. Duster. Chicago: University of Chicago Press, 1970.

White, Walter F. *A Man Called White: The Autobiography of Walter White.* New York: Viking Press, 1948. Reprint. Athens: University of Georgia Press, 1995.

Wilkins, Roy, with Tom Mathews. *Standing Fast: The Autobiography of Roy Wilkins.* New York: Viking Press, 1982.

Young, R. J. *Antebellum Black Activists: Race, Gender, and Self.* New York: Garland, 1996.

AFRICAN AMERICANS

Aptheker, Herbert. *Abolitionism: A Revolutionary Movement.* Boston: Twayne, 1989.

Bardolph, Richard, ed. *The Civil Rights Record: Black Americans and the Law, 1849-1970.* New York: Thomas Y. Crowell, 1970.

Bell, Howard H. *A Survey of the Negro Convention Movement.* New York: Arno Press, 1970.

Bennett, Lerone, Jr. *Before the Mayflower: A History of the Negro in America, 1619-1962.* Chicago: Johnson Publishing, 1962.

Bergman, Peter M. *The Chronological History of the Negro in America*. New York: Harper & Row, 1969.

Berry, Mary Frances. *Black Resistance, White Law: A History of Constitutional Racism in America*. East Norwalk, Conn.: Appleton-Century-Crofts, 1971.

Bracey, John H., August Meier, and Elliott Rudwick, comps. *Black Nationalism in America*. Indianapolis, Ind.: Bobbs-Merrill, 1970.

Cashman, Sean D. *African-Americans and the Quest for Civil Rights, 1900-1990*. New York: New York University Press, 1991.

Cowan, Tom, and Jack Maguire. *Timelines of African-American History: 500 Years of Black Achievement*. New York: Roundtable Press/ Perigree Press, 1994. (Senior Consultant, Richard Newman, W. E. B. Du Bois Inst.)

Cripps, Thomas. *Making Movies Black: The Hollywood Message Movie from World War II to the Civil Rights Era*. New York: Oxford University Press, 1993.

Du Bois, W. E. B. *The Souls of Black Folk*. 1903. New York: Penguin, 1989.

Ford, Nick A., and Harry L. Faggett, eds. *"Baltimore Afro-American": Best Short Stories by Afro-American Writers, 1925-1950*. Reprint. New York: Kraus, 1969.

Franklin, John Hope, and Genna R. McNeil, eds. *African Americans and the Living Constitution*. Washington: Smithsonian Institution Press, 1995.

Franklin, John Hope, and Alfred Moss, Jr. *From Slavery to Freedom*. 7th ed. New York: Alfred A. Knopf, 1994.

Fredrickson, George M. *The Black Image in the White Mind: The Debate on Afro-American Character and Destiny, 1817-1914*. New York: Harper, 1971.

Gaines, Kevin K. *Uplifting the Race: Black Leadership, Politics, and Culture in the Twentieth Century*. Chapel Hill: University of North Carolina Press, 1996.

Gates, Henry Louis, ed. *Black Biography, 1790-1950: A Cumulative Index*. Alexandria, Va.: Chadwick-Healey, 1991.

Gates, Henry Louis, and Nellie Y. McKay, eds. *The Norton Anthology of African American Literature*. New York: W. W. Norton, 1997.

Hornsby, Alton, Jr. *The Chronology of African-American History: Significant Events and People from 1619 to the Present*. Detroit: Gale, 1991.

Horton, James Oliver. *Free People of Color: Inside the African American Community*. Washington, D.C.: Smithsonian Institution, 1993.

Hutton, Frankie. *The Early Black Press in America, 1827-1860*. Westport, Conn.: Greenwood Press, 1993.

Lerner, Gerda, ed. *Black Women in White America: A Documentary History*. New York: Vintage Books, 1972.

Levine, Michael L. *African Americans and Civil Rights: From 1619 to the Present*. Phoenix, Ariz.: Oryx Press, 1996.

Litwack, Leon F. *Been in the Storm So Long: The Aftermath of Slavery*. New York: Vintage Books, 1979.

Logan, Rayford W. *The Betrayal of the Negro: From Rutherford B. Hayes to Woodrow Wilson*. New York: Collier, 1965.

Low, W. Augustus, and Virgil A. Clift. *Encyclopedia of Black America*. New York: McGraw-Hill, 1981.

Luker, Ralph E. *The Social Gospel in Black and White: American Racial Reform, 1885-1912*. Chapel Hill: University of North Carolina Press, 1991.

Marable, Manning. *Race, Reform, and Rebellion: The Second Reconstruction in Black America, 1945-1982*. Jackson: University Press of Mississippi, 1984.

Meier, August. *Negro Thought in America, 1880-1915*. Ann Arbor: University of Michigan Press, 1963.

Morgan, Edmund S. *American Slavery, American Freedom: The Ordeal of Colonial Virginia*. New York: W. W. Norton, 1975.

Myrdal, Gunnar. *An American Dilemma: The Negro Problem and Modern Democracy*. 2 vols. New York: Harper & Brothers, 1944.

Peterson, Carla. *Doers of the Word: African-American Women Speakers and Writers in the North, 1830-1880*. New York: Oxford University Press, 1995.

Rediger, Pat. *Great African Americans in Civil Rights*. New York: Crabtree, 1996.

Sitkoff, Harvard. *A New Deal for Blacks: The Emergence of Civil Rights as a National Issue*. New York: Oxford University Press, 1978.

Smith, Clay, Jr. *Emancipation: The Making of the Black Lawyer, 1844-1944*. Foreword by Thurgood Marshall. Philadelphia: University of Pennsylvania Press, 1993.

Smith, Robert C. *We Have No Leaders: African-Americans in the Post-Civil Rights Era*. Albany: University of New York Press, 1996.

Streitmatter, Rodger. *Raising Her Voice: African-American Women Journalists Who Changed History*. Lexington: University Press of Kentucky, 1994.

Suggs, Henry L., ed. *The Black Press in the South, 1865-1979*. Westport, Conn.: Greenwood Press, 1983.

Vaz, Kim M., ed. *Black Women in America*. Thousand Oaks, Calif.: Sage Publications, 1995.

Wepman, Dennis. *The Struggle for Freedom: African-American Slave Resistance*. New York: Facts On File, 1996.

Williams, Michael W., ed. *The African American Encyclopedia*. 8 vols. New York: Marshall Cavendish, 1993.

Wolseley, Roland E. *The Black Press, U.S.A.* 2d ed. Ames: Iowa State University, 1990.

Yellin, Jean Fagan. *Women and Sisters: The Antislavery Feminists in American Culture*. New Haven: Yale University Press, 1989.

AMERICAN INDIANS

Deloria, Vine, Jr., and Clifford M. Lytle. *American Indians, American Justice*. Austin: University of Texas Press, 1983.

_____. *The Nations Within: The Past and Future of American Indian Sovereignty*. New York: Pantheon Books, 1984.

Grossman, Mark. *The ABC-CLIO Companion to the Native American Rights Movement*. Santa Barbara, Calif.: ABC-CLIO, 1996.

Markovitz, Harvey, ed. *Ready Reference: American Indians*. 3 vols. Pasadena, Calif.: Salem Press, 1995.

Means, Russell. *Where White Men Fear to Tread: The Autobiography of Russell Means*. New York: St. Martin's Press, 1995.

Pevar, Stephen L. *The Rights of Indians and Tribes: The Basic ACLU Guide to Indian and Tribal Rights*. 2d ed. Carbondale: Southern Illinois University Press, 1992.

Prucha, Francis P. *The Great Father: The United States Government and the American Indians*. Lincoln: University of Nebraska Press, 1986.

Smith, Michael R. *American Indian Civil Rights Handbook*. Washington: United States Commission on Civil Rights, 1972.

Taylor, Graham D. *The New Deal and American Indian Tribalism: The Administration of the Indian Reorganization Act, 1934-45*. Lincoln: University of Nebraska Press, 1980.

Thompson, William N. *Native American Issues: A Reference Book*. Santa Barbara, Calif.: ABC-CLIO, 1996.

Wilkinson, Charles F. *American Indians, Time, and the Law: Native Societies in a Modern Constitutional Democracy*. New Haven: Yale University Press, 1987.

Wunder, John R. *"Retained by the People:" A History of American Indians and the Bill of Rights*. New York: Oxford University Press, 1994.

ASIAN AMERICANS

Chan, Sucheng, ed. *Entry Denied: Exclusion and the Chinese Community in America, 1882-1943*. Philadelphia: Temple University Press, 1991.

Cordova, Fred. *Filipinos, Forgotten Asian Americans: A Pictorial Essay, 1763-circa 1963*. Dubuque, Iowa: Kendall/Hunt, 1983.

Daniels, Roger. *Prisoners Without Trial: Japanese Americans in World War II*. New York: Hill and Wang, 1993.

Foner, Philip S., and Daniel Rosenberg. *Racism, Dissent and Asian Americans from 1850 to the Present: A Documentary History*. Westport, Conn.: Greenwood Press, 1993.

Hatamiya, Leslie T. *Righting a Wrong: Japanese Americans and the Passage of the Civil Liberties Act of 1988.* Stanford, Calif.: Stanford University Press, 1993.

Kim, Hyung-chan, ed. *Asian Americans and the Supreme Court: A Documentary History.* New York: Greenwood Press, 1992.

Ng, Franklin, ed. *The Asian American Encyclopedia.* 6 vols. New York: Marshall Cavendish, 1995.

Smith, Page. *Democracy on Trial: The Japanese-American Evacuation and Relocation in World War II.* New York: Simon & Schuster, 1995.

Tsuchida, Nobuya. *American Justice: Japanese American Evacuation and Redress Cases.* Minneapolis: University of Minnesota, 1988.

BIOGRAPHIES AND PERSONAL NARRATIVES

Abernathy, Ralph. *And the Walls Came Tumbling Down.* New York: Harper & Row, 1989.

Anderson, Jervis. *A. Philip Randolph: A Biographical Portrait.* New York: Harcourt Brace Jovanovich, 1973.

———. *Bayard Rustin: Troubles I've Seen: A Biography.* New York: HarperCollins, 1997.

Baker, Donald P. *Wilder: Hold Fast to Dreams: A Biography of L. Douglas Wilder.* Cabin John, Md.: Seven Locks Press, 1989.

Barry, Kathleen. *Susan B. Anthony: A Biography of a Singular Feminist.* New York: New York University Press, 1988.

Bass, Jack. *Taming the Storm: The Life and Times of Judge Frank M. Johnson, Jr., and the South's Fight over Civil Rights.* New York: Doubleday, 1993.

Braden, Anne. *The Wall Between.* New York: Monthly Review, 1958.

Brown, Elaine. *A Taste of Power: A Black Woman's Story.* New York: Anchor, 1992.

Chafe, William. *Never Stop Running: Allard Lowenstein and the Struggle to Save American Liberalism.* New York: Basic Books, 1993.

Clark, Septima. *Echo in My Soul.* New York: E. P. Dutton, 1962.

———. *Ready from Within: Septima Clark and the Civil Rights Movement.* Navarro, Calif: Wild Trees, 1986.

Douglass, Frederick. *The Life and Times of Frederick Douglass.* 1881. New York: Citadel Press, 1984.

Evers, Charles, and Andrew Szanton. *Have No Fear: The Charles Evers Story.* New York: J. Wiley & Sons, 1997.

Evers, Myrlie B., and William Peters. *For Us, the Living.* Jackson: University Press of Mississippi, 1996.

Falkner, David. *Great Time Coming: The Life of Jackie Robinson from Baseball to Birmingham.* New York: Oxford University Press, 1995.

Farmer, James. *Lay Bare the Heart: An Autobiography of the Civil Rights Movement.* New York: Arbor House, 1985.

Forman, James. *The Making of Black Revolutionaries: A Personal Account.* New York: Macmillan, 1972.

Fox, Stephen R. *The Guardian of Boston: William Monroe Trotter.* New York: Atheneum, 1971.

Frady, Marshall. *Jesse: The Life and Pilgrimage of Jesse Jackson.* New York: Random House, 1996.

Gates, Henry Louis, ed. *Black Biography, 1790-1950: A Cumulative Index.* Alexandria, Va.: Chadwick-Healey, 1991.

Gossett, Thomas. *Race: The History of an Idea in America.* 1963. Rev. ed. Edited by Arnold Rampersad and Shelley Fisher Fishkin. New York: Oxford University Press, 1997.

Gray, Fred D. *Bus Ride to Justice: Changing the System by the System: The Life and Works of Fred D. Gray, Preacher, Attorney, Politician.* Montgomery, Ala.: Black Belt Press, 1995.

Gregory, Dick. *Nigger: An Autobiography.* New York: Dutton, 1964.

Hamby, Alonzo L. *Man of the People: A Life of Harry S Truman.* New York: Oxford University Press, 1995.

Haygood, Wil. *King of the Cats: The Life and Times of Adam Clayton Powell, Jr.* Boston: Houghton Mifflin, 1993.

Hayman, John. *Bitter Harvest: Richmond Flowers and the Civil Rights Revolution.* Montgomery, Ala.: Black Belt Press, 1996.

Karcher, Carolyn L. *The First Woman in the Republic: A Cultural Biography of Lydia Maria Child.* Durham, N.C.: Duke University Press, 1994.

King, Coretta Scott. *My Life with Martin Luther King, Jr.* New York: Holt, Rinehart and Winston, 1969.

Kotz, Nick, and Mary L. Kotz. *A Passion for Equality: George A. Wiley and the Movement.* New York: W. W. Norton, 1977.

Lewis, David L. *W.E.B. Du Bois: Biography of a Race, 1868-1919.* New York: Henry Holt, 1993.

Lewis, Walker. *Without Fear or Favor: A Biography of Chief Justice Roger Brooke Taney.* Boston: Houghton Mifflin, 1965.

Logan, Rayford W., and Michael R. Winston, eds. *Dictionary of American Negro Biography.* New York: Norton, 1982.

McFeeley, William. S. *Frederick Douglass.* New York: Simon & Schuster, 1991.

McNeil, Genna Rae. *Groundwork: Charles Hamilton Houston and the Struggle for Civil Rights.* Philadelphia: University of Pennsylvania Press, 1983.

Means, Russell. *Where White Men Fear to Tread: The Autobiography of Russell Means.* New York: St. Martin's Press, 1995.

Mills, Kay. *This Little Light of Mine: The Life of Fannie Lou Hamer.* New York: E. P. Dutton, 1993.

Moody, Anne. *Coming of Age in Mississippi.* New York: Dial Press, 1968.

Oates, Stephen B. *Let the Trumpet Sound: The Life of Martin Luther King, Jr.* New York: Harper & Row, 1982.

Parks, Rosa, and Gregory J. Reed. *Quiet Strength: The Faith, the Hope, and the Heart of a Woman Who Changed a Nation.* Grand Rapids, Mich.: Zondervan, 1994.

Patterson, Lillie. *A. Philip Randolph: Messenger for the Masses.* New York: Facts On File, 1996.

Powell, Adam Clayton, Jr. *Adam by Adam: The Autobiography of Adam Clayton Powell, Jr.* New York: Dial Press, 1971.

Robinson, Jo Ann Gibson. *The Montgomery Bus Boycott and the Women Who Started It: The Memoir of Jo Ann Gibson Robinson.* David J. Garrow, ed. Knoxville: University of Tennessee Press, 1987.

Rollins, Judith. *All Is Never Said: The Narrative of Odette Harper Hines.* Philadelphia: Temple University Press, 1995.

Rosengarten, Theodore *All God's Dangers: The Life of Nate Shaw.* New York: Alfred A. Knopf, 1974.

Sally Belfrage. *Freedom Summer.* 1965. Charlottesville: University of Virginia Press, 1990.

Urquhart, Brian. *Ralph Bunche: An American Life.* New York: W. W. Norton, 1993.

Wells-Barnett, Ida B. *Crusade for Justice: The Autobiography of Ida B. Wells.* Edited by Alfreda M. Duster. Chicago: University of Chicago Press, 1970.

White, Walter F. *A Man Called White: The Autobiography of Walter White.* New York: Viking Press, 1948. Reprint. Athens: University of Georgia Press, 1995.

Wilkins, Roy, with Tom Mathews. *Standing Fast: The Autobiography of Roy Wilkins.* New York: Viking Press, 1982.

Williams, Cecil J. *Freedom and Justice: Four Decades of the Civil Rights Struggle as Seen by a Black Photographer of the Deep South.* Macon, Ga.: Mercer University Press, 1995.

Young, Andrew. *An Easy Burden: The Civil Rights Movement and the Transformation of America.* New York: HarperCollins, 1996.

BROWN V. BOARD OF EDUCATION

Atkinson, Pansye S. *Brown v. Topeka: An African American's View: Desegregation and Miseducation.* Chicago: African American Images, 1993.

Bass, Jack. *Unlikely Heroes: The Dramatic Story of the Southern Judges of the Fifth Circuit Who Translated the Supreme Court's Brown Decision into a Revolution for Equality.* New York: Simon & Schuster, 1981.

Kluger, Richard. *Simple Justice: The History of "Brown v. Board of Education" and Black America's Struggle for Equality.* New York: Alfred A. Knopf, 1976.

Lagemann, Ellen C., and LaMar Miller, eds. *Brown v. Board of Education: The Challenge for Today's Schools.* New York: Teacher's College Press, 1996.

Orfield, Gary, Susan E. Eaton, and the Harvard Project on School Desegregation. *Dismantling Desegregation: The Quiet Reversal of Brown v. Board of Education*. New York: New Press, 1996.

Speer, Hugh W. *The Case of the Century: A Historical and Social Perspective on Brown v. Board of Education of Topeka, with Present and Future Implications*. Kansas City: University of Missouri Press, 1968.

Wilkinson, J. Harvie, III. *From Brown to Bakke: The Supreme Court and School Integration, 1954-1978*. New York: Oxford University Press, 1979.

Wilson, Paul E. *A Time to Lose: Representing Kansas in Brown v. Board of Education*. Lawrence: University Press of Kansas, 1995.

CIVIL RIGHTS AND LIBERTIES

Abraham, Henry J., and Barbara A. Perry. *Freedom and the Court: Civil Rights and Liberties in the United States*. 6th ed. New York: Oxford University Press, 1994.

Barnes, Catherine. *A Journey from Jim Crow: The Desegregation of Southern Transit*. New York: Columbia University Press, 1983

Black, Earl. *Southern Governors and Civil Rights: Racial Segregation as a Campaign Issue in the Second Reconstruction*. Cambridge: Harvard University Press, 1976.

Branscomb, Anne W. *Who Owns Information? From Privacy to Public Access*. New York: Basic Books, 1994.

Condit, Celeste Michelle, and John Louis Lucaites. *Crafting Equality: America's Anglo-African Word*. Chicago: University of Chicago Press, 1993.

Domino, John C. *Civil Rights and Liberties: Toward the Twenty-first Century*. New York: HarperCollins College Publishers, 1994.

Donohue, William A. *The Politics of the American Civil Liberties Union*. New Brunswick, N.J.: Transaction, 1985.

Fiscus, Ronald J. *The Constitutional Logic of Affirmative Action*. Durham, N.C.: Duke University Press, 1992.

Gates, Henry L., ed. *Speaking of Race, Speaking of Sex: Hate Speech, Civil Rights, and Civil Liberties*. New York: New York University Press, 1994.

Goldwin, Robert A., and William A. Schambra, eds. *How Does the Constitution Secure Rights?* Washington: American Enterprise Institute, 1985.

Graham, Hugh D., ed. *Civil Rights in the United States*. University Park: Pennsylvania State University Press, 1994.

Greenawalt, Kent. *Discrimination and Reverse Discrimination*. New York: Alfred A. Knopf, 1983.

Hatamiya, Leslie T. *Righting a Wrong: Japanese Americans and the Passage of the Civil Liberties Act of 1988*. Stanford, Calif.: Stanford University Press, 1993.

Levy, Robert M., Leonard S. Rubenstein, Bruce J. Ennis, and Paul R. Friedman. *The Rights of People with Mental Disabilities: The Authoritative ACLU Guide to the Rights of People with Mental Illness and Mental Retardation*. Carbondale: Southern Illinois University Press, 1996.

McDonald, Laughlin, John A. Powell, and E. Richard Larson. *The Rights of Racial Minorities: The Basic ACLU Guide to Racial Minority Rights*. 2d ed. Carbondale: Southern Illinois University Press, 1993.

Marcus, Laurence R. *Fighting Words: The Politics of Hateful Speech*. Westport, Conn.: Praeger, 1996.

Markmann, Charles L. *The Noblest Cry: A History of the American Civil Liberties Union*. New York: St. Martin's Press, 1965.

Maxwell, John A., James J. Friedberg, and Deirdre A. DeGolia, eds. *Human Rights in Western Civilization: 1600 to the Present*. Dubuque, Iowa: Kendall/Hunt, 1994.

Pevar, Stephen L. *The Rights of Indians and Tribes: The Basic ACLU Guide to Indian and Tribal Rights*. 2d ed. Carbondale: Southern Illinois University Press, 1992.

Rudovsky, David, Alvin J. Bronstein, and Edward I. Koren. *The Rights of Prisoners: The Basic ACLU Guide to a Prisoner's Rights*. Rev. ed. New York: Bantam Books, 1983.

Stoner, Madeleine R. *The Civil Rights of Homeless People: Law, Social Policy, and Social Work*. New York: Aldine de Gruyter, 1995.

Tedford, Thomas L. *Freedom of Speech in the United States*. New York: McGraw-Hill, 1993.

Woodward, C. Vann. *The Strange Career of Jim Crow*. 3d ed. New York: Oxford University Press, 1974.

CIVIL RIGHTS MOVEMENT

Abernathy, Ralph. *And the Walls Came Tumbling Down*. New York: Harper & Row, 1989.

Anderson, Alan B., and George W. Pickering. *Confronting the Color Line: The Broken Promise of the Civil Rights Movement in Chicago*. Athens: University of Georgia Press, 1986.

Anderson, Terry H. *The Movement and the Sixties*. New York: Oxford University Press, 1995.

Ashmore, Harry S. *Civil Rights and Wrongs: A Memoir of Race and Politics, 1944-1994*. New York: Pantheon Books, 1994.

Bass, Jack. *Taming the Storm: The Life and Times of Judge Frank M. Johnson, Jr., and the South's Fight over Civil Rights*. New York: Doubleday, 1993.

Bender, Leslie. *Power, Privilege, and Law: A Civil Rights Reader*. St. Paul, Minn.: West Publishing, 1995.

Blumberg, Rhoda L. *Civil Rights: The 1960s Freedom Struggle*. Rev. ed. Boston: Twayne, 1991.

Branch, Taylor. *Parting the Waters: America in the King Years, 1954-1963*. New York: Simon & Schuster, 1988.

Brooks, Roy L. *Integration or Separation?: A Strategy for Racial Equality*. Cambridge, Mass.: Harvard University Press, 1996.

Brooks, Thomas R. *Walls Come Tumbling Down: A History of the Civil Rights Movement, 1940-1970*. Englewood Cliffs, N.J.: Prentice-Hall, 1974.

Campbell, Georgetta M. *Extant Collections of Early Black Newspapers: A Research Guide to the Black Press, 1880-1915, with an Index to the "Boston Guardian," 1902-1904*. Troy, N.Y.: Whitson, 1981.

Carawan, Guy, and Candie Carawan, comps. *We Shall Overcome!: Songs of the Southern Freedom Movement*. New York: Oak, 1963.

Chafe, William. *Civility and Civil Rights: Greensboro, North Carolina and the Black Struggle for Freedom*. New York: Oxford University Press, 1981.

_____. *The Unfinished Journey: America Since World War II*. 3d edition. New York: Oxford University Press, 1995.

Crawford, Vicki L., Jacqueline Anne Rouse, and Barbara Woods, eds. *Women in the Civil Rights Movement: Trailblazers and Torchbearers, 1941-1965*. Bloomington: Indiana University Press, 1993.

Cripps, Thomas. *Making Movies Black: The Hollywood Message Movie from World War II to the Civil Rights Era*. New York: Oxford University Press, 1993.

Dent, Thomas C. *Southern Journey: A Return to the Civil Rights Movement*. New York: William Morrow, 1996.

Dittmer, John. *Local People: The Struggle for Civil Rights in Mississippi*. Urbana: University of Illinois Press, 1994.

Dittmer, John, George C. Wright, W. Marvin Dulaney, and Kathleen Underwood, eds. *Essays on the American Civil Rights Movement*. College Station: Texas A&M University Press, 1993.

Domino, John C. *Civil Rights and Liberties: Toward the Twenty-first Century*. New York: HarperCollins College Publishers, 1994.

Egerton, John. *Speak Now Against the Day: The Generation Before the Civil Rights Movement in the South*. New York: Alfred A. Knopf, 1994.

Ewing, Preston, and Jan P. Roddy. *Let My People Go: Cairo, Illinois, 1967-1973: Civil Rights Photographs*. Carbondale: Southern Illinois University Press, 1996.

Fager, Charles E. *Selma, 1965: The March That Changed the South*. 2d ed. Boston: Beacon Press, 1985.

Gale, Dennis E. *Understanding Urban Unrest: From Reverend King to Rodney King*. Thousand Oaks, Calif.: Sage Publications, 1996.

Garrow, David J., ed. *Atlanta, Georgia, 1960-1961: Sit-ins and Student Activism*. Brooklyn, N.Y.: Carlson, 1989.

_____. *Birmingham, Alabama, 1956-1963: The Black Struggle for Civil Rights*. Brooklyn, N.Y.: Carlson, 1989.

_____. *Chicago 1966: Open Housing Marches, Summit Negotiations, and Operation Breadbasket*. Brooklyn, N.Y.: Carlson, 1989.

Gates, Henry L., ed. *Speaking of Race, Speaking of Sex: Hate Speech, Civil Rights, and Civil Liberties*. New York: New York University Press, 1994.

Geschwender, James A., ed. *The Black Revolt: The Civil Rights Movement, Ghetto Uprisings and Separatism*. Englewood Cliffs, N.J.: Prentice-Hall, 1971.

Goldfield, David R. *Black, White, and Southern: Race Relations and Southern Culture, 1940 to the Present*. Baton Rouge: Louisiana State University Press, 1990.

Graham, Hugh D. *The Civil Rights Era: Origins and Development of a National Policy, 1960-1972*. New York: Oxford University Press, 1990.

Haines, Herbert H. *Black Radicals and the Civil Rights Mainstream, 1954-1970*. Knoxville: University of Tennessee Press, 1988.

Hampton, Henry, and Steve Fayer. *Voices of Freedom: An Oral History of the Civil Rights Movement from the 1950s Through the 1980s*. New York: Bantam Books, 1990.

Hemphill, Paul. *Leaving Birmingham: Notes of a Native Son*. New York: Viking Press, 1993.

Hunter, Floyd. *Community Power Succession: Atlanta's Policy-Makers Revisited*. Chapel Hill: University of North Carolina Press, 1980.

Johnson, Charles S. *Backgrounds to Patterns of Negro Segregation*. Rev. ed. New York: Crowell, 1970.

Kasher, Steven. *The Civil Rights Movement: A Photographic History, 1954-68*. New York: Abbeville Press, 1996.

Lawson, Steven F. *Running for Freedom: Civil Rights and Black Politics in America Since 1941*. 2d ed. New York: McGraw-Hill, 1997.

Levine, Michael L. *African Americans and Civil Rights: From 1619 to the Present*. Phoenix, Ariz.: Oryx Press, 1996.

Lewis, David L., and Charles W. Eagles. *The Civil Rights Movement in America: Essays*. Jackson: University Press of Mississippi, 1986.

Luker, Ralph E. *Historical Dictionary of the Civil Rights Movement*. Lanham, Md.: Scarecrow Press, 1997.

Lynd, Staughton., and Alice Lynd, eds. *Nonviolence in America: A Documentary History*. Rev. ed. Maryknoll, N.Y.: Orbis Books, 1995.

McAdam, Doug. *Freedom Summer*. New York: Oxford University Press, 1988.

McCord, William M. *Mississippi: The Long Hot Summer*. New York: W. W. Norton, 1965.

Marable, Manning. *Race, Reform, and Rebellion: The Second Reconstruction in Black America, 1945-1982* Jackson: University Press of Mississippi, 1984.

Meier, August, John Bracey, Jr., and Elliott Rudwick, eds. *Black Protests in the Sixties*. New York: Marcus Weiner, 1991.

Murray, Paul T. *The Civil Rights Movement: References and Resources*. New York: G. K. Hall, 1993.

Myrdal, Gunnar. *An American Dilemma: The Negro Problem and Modern Democracy*. 2 vols. New York: Harper & Brothers, 1944.

Patterson, Charles. *The Civil Rights Movement*. New York: Facts On File, 1995.

Powledge, Fred. *Free at Last?: The Civil Rights Movement and the People Who Made It*. Boston: Little, Brown, 1991.

Rogers, Kim L. *Righteous Lives: Narratives of the New Orleans Civil Rights Movement*. New York: New York University Press, 1993.

Sanger, Kerran L. *"When the Spirit Says Sing!": The Role of Freedom Songs in the Civil Rights Movement*. New York: Garland, 1995.

Sitkoff, Harvard. *A New Deal for Blacks: The Emergence of Civil Rights as a National Issue*. New York: Oxford University Press, 1978.

Weisbrot, Robert. *Freedom Bound: A History of America's Civil Rights Movement*. New York: W. W. Norton, 1990.

Wexler, Sanford. *The Civil Rights Movement: An Eyewitness History*. New York: Facts On File, 1993.

Williams, Cecil J. *Freedom and Justice: Four Decades of the Civil Rights Struggle as Seen by a Black Photographer of the Deep South*. Macon, Ga.: Mercer University Press, 1995.

Williams, Juan. *Eyes on the Prize: America's Civil Rights Years, 1954-1965*. New York: Viking Penguin, 1987.

Wright, Roberta H. *The Birth of the Montgomery Bus Boycott*. Southfield, Mich.: Charro Press, 1991.

Young, Andrew. *An Easy Burden: The Civil Rights Movement and the Transformation of America*. New York: HarperCollins, 1996.

COURT CASES

Bell, Derrick A., Jr. *Race, Racism, and American Law*. 2d ed. Boston: Little, Brown, 1980.

Brooks, Roy L., Gilbert P. Carrasco, and Gordon A. Martin. *Civil Rights Litigation: Cases and Perspectives*. Durham, N.C.: Carolina Academic Press, 1995.

Dreyfuss, Joel, and Charles Lawrence, III. *The Bakke Case: The Politics of Inequality*. New York: Harcourt Brace Jovanovich, 1979.

Lagemann, Ellen C., and LaMar Miller, eds. *Brown v. Board of Education: The Challenge for Today's Schools*. New York: Teacher's College Press, 1996.

Olsen, Otto H., comp. *The Thin Disguise: Turning Point in Negro History: Plessy v. Ferguson; A Documentary Presentation, 1864-1896*. New York: Humanities Press, 1967.

Orfield, Gary, Susan E. Eaton, and the Harvard Project on School Desegregation. *Dismantling Desegregation: The Quiet Reversal of Brown v. Board of Education*. New York: New Press, 1996.

Schwartz, Bernard. *Swann's Way: The School Busing Case and the Supreme Court*. New York: Oxford University Press, 1986.

Williams, Lou F. *The Great South Carolina Ku Klux Klan Trials, 1871-1872*. Athens: University of Georgia Press, 1996.

CRIMINAL JUSTICE

Austern, David. *The Crime Victim's Handbook: Your Rights and the Role in the Criminal Justice System*. New York: Viking Press, 1987.

Hook, Donald D., and Lothar Kahn. *Death in the Balance: The Debate over Capital Punishment*. Lexington, Mass.: Lexington Books, 1989.

Karmen, Andrew. *Crime Victims: An Introduction to Victimology*. 3d ed. New York: Wadsworth, 1996.

Mushlin, Michael B. *Rights of Prisoners*. 2d ed. Colorado Springs, Colo.: Shepard's/McGraw-Hill, 1993.

Radelet, Michael L., ed. *Facing the Death Penalty: Essays on Cruel and Unusual Punishment*. Philadelphia: Temple University Press, 1989.

Rudovsky, David, Alvin J. Bronstein, and Edward I. Koren. *The Rights of Prisoners: The Basic ACLU Guide to a Prisoner's Rights*. Rev. ed. New York: Bantam Books, 1983.

Stark, James H., and Howard W. Goldstein. *The Rights of Crime Victims*. New York: Bantam Books, 1985.

Unseem, Burt, and Peter Kimball. *States of Siege: U.S. Prison Riots, 1971-1986*. New York: Oxford University Press, 1989.

Viano, Emilio C., ed. *The Victimology Handbook: Research Findings, Treatment, and Public Policy*. New York: Garland, 1990.

Wilson, Debra J. *The Complete Book of Victim's Rights*. Highlands Ranch, Colo.: ProSe Associates, 1995.

DISABILITIES, PEOPLE WITH

Driedger, Diane. *The Last Civil Rights Movement: Disabled Peoples' International*. New York: St. Martin's Press, 1989.

Goldman, Charles D. *Disability Rights Guide*. 2d ed. Lincoln, Nebr.: Media Publishing, 1991.

Kent, Deborah. *The Disability Rights Movement*. New York: Children's Press, 1996.

Percy, Stephen L. *Disability, Civil Rights, and Public Policy: The Politics of Implementation*. Tuscaloosa, Ala.: University of Alabama Press, 1989.

Scotch, Richard K. *From Good Will to Civil Rights: Transforming Federal Disability Policy*. Philadelphia: Temple University Press, 1984.

Shapiro, Joseph P. *No Pity: People with Disabilities Forging a New Civil Rights Movement*. New York: Times Books, 1993.

ECONOMIC ISSUES

Acker, Joan. *Doing Comparable Worth: Gender, Class, and Pay Equity*. Philadelphia: Temple University Press, 1989.

Belknap, Michal R., ed. *Combatting Housing Discrimination*. New York: Garland, 1991.

Berkowitz, Edward D. *America's Welfare State: From Roosevelt to Reagan*. Baltimore: Johns Hopkins University Press, 1991.

Blum, Linda M. *Between Feminism and Labor: The Significance of the Comparable Worth Movement*. Berkeley: University of California Press, 1991.

Bullard, Robert D., J. Eugene Grigsby, III, and Charles Lee, eds. *Residential Apartheid: The American Legacy*. Los Angeles: CAAS, 1994.

Draper, Alan. *Conflict of Interests: Organized Labor and the Civil Rights Movement in the South, 1954-1968*. Ithaca, N.Y.: ILR Press, 1994.

Haar, Charles M. *Suburbs Under Siege: Race, Space, and Audacious Judges*. Princeton, N.J.: Princeton University Press, 1996.

Honey, Michael K. *Southern Labor and Black Civil Rights: Organizing Memphis Workers*. Urbana: University of Illinois Press, 1993.

Kahn, Peggy, and Elizabeth M. Meehan, eds. *Equal Value/Comparable Worth in the U.K. and the U.S.A.* New York: St. Martin's Press, 1992.

Kirp, David L., John P. Dwyer, and Larry A. Rosenthal. *Our Town: Race, Housing, and the Soul of Suburbia*. New Brunswick, N.J.: Rutgers University Press, 1995.

Marmor, Theodore R., Jerry L. Mashaw, and Phillip L. Harvey. *America's Misunderstood Welfare State*. New York: Basic Books, 1990.

Reskin, Barbara F., ed. *Sex Segregation in the Workplace: Trends, Explanations, Remedies*. Washington: National Academy Press, 1984.

Stoner, Madeleine R. *The Civil Rights of Homeless People: Law, Social Policy, and Social Work*. New York: Aldine de Gruyter, 1995.

Turner, Margery A., Raymond Fix, and Raymond J. Struyk. *Opportunities Denied, Opportunities Dismissed: Racial Discrimination in Hiring*. Washington: Urban Institute, 1991.

Yinger, John. *Closed Doors, Opportunities Lost: The Continuing Costs of Housing Discrimination*. New York: Russell Sage Foundation, 1995.

EDUCATION

Anderson, James D. *The Education of Blacks in the South, 1860-1935*. Chapel Hill: University of North Carolina Press, 1988.

Bosmajian, Haig. *Academic Freedom*. New York: Neal-Schuman, 1988.

Buell, Emmett H. *School Desegregation and Defended Neighborhoods: The Boston Controversy*. Lexington, Mass.: Lexington Books, 1982.

Butchart, Ronald E. *Northern Schools, Southern Blacks, and Reconstruction: Freedmen's Education, 1862-1875*. Westport: Greenwood, 1980.

Clark, E. Culpepper. *The Schoolhouse Door: Segregation's Last Stand at the University of Alabama*. New York: Oxford University Press, 1993.

Crawford, James. *Bilingual Education: History, Politics, Theory, and Practice*. 3d ed. Los Angeles: Bilingual Educational Services, 1995.

Ernst, Benjamin, and Donald R., eds. *Academic Freedom: An Everyday Concern*. San Francisco, Calif.: Jossey-Bass, 1994.

Fischer, Louis, and David Schimmel. *The Civil Rights of Teachers*. New York: Harper & Row, 1973.

Gaillard, Frye. *The Dream Long Deferred*. Chapel Hill: University of North Carolina Press, 1988.

Hochschild, Jennifer. *The New American Dilemma: Liberal Democracy and School Desegregation*. New Haven: Yale University Press, 1984.

Lessow-Hurley, Judith. *The Foundations of Dual Language Instruction*. New York: Longman, 1990.

McNeil, Genna Rae. *Groundwork: Charles Hamilton Houston and the Struggle for Civil Rights*. Philadelphia: University of Pennsylvania Press, 1983.

Malloy, Ione. *Southie Won't Go: A Teacher's Diary of the Desegregation of South Boston High School*. Urbana: University of Illinois Press, 1986.

Margo, Robert. *Disfranchisement, School Finances, and Economics of Segregated Schools in the United States South, 1890-1916*. New York: Garland, 1985.

_____. *Race and Schooling in the South, 1880-1950: An Economic History*. Chicago: University of Chicago Press, 1991.

Porter, Rosalie P. *Forked Tongue: The Politics of Bilingual Education*. 2d ed. New York: Transaction, 1996.

Schimmel, David, and Louis Fischer. *The Civil Rights of Students*. New York: Harper & Row, 1975.

Shoemaker, Don, ed. *With All Deliberate Speed: Segregation-Desegregation in Southern Schools*. New York: Harper & Brothers, 1957.

Wilkinson, J. Harvie, III. *From Brown to Bakke: The Supreme Court and School Integration, 1954-1978*. New York: Oxford University Press, 1979.

Zigler, Edward, and Susan Muenchow. *Head Start: The Inside Story of America's Most Successful Educational Experiment*. New York: Basic Books, 1992.

GENDER, GAY, AND FAMILY ISSUES

Abramovitz, Mimi. *Regulating the Lives of Women: Social Welfare Policy from Colonial Times to the Present*. Boston: South End Press, 1988.

Archard, David. *Children: Rights and Childhood*. London: Routledge, 1993.

Duberman, Martin, Martha Vicinus, and George Chauncey, Jr., eds. *Hidden from History: Reclaiming the Gay and Lesbian Past*. New York: New American Library, 1989.

Gordon, Linda. *Pitied but Not Entitled: Single Mothers and the History of Welfare, 1890-1935*. New York: The Free Press, 1994.

Hawes, Joseph M. *The Children's Rights Movement: A History of Advocacy and Protection*. Boston: Twayne, 1991.

Mason, Mary Ann. *From Father's Property to Children's Rights: The History of Child Custody in the United States*. New York: Columbia University Press, 1994.

Mohr, Richard D. *A More Perfect Union: Why Straight America Must Stand Up for Gay Rights*. Boston: Beacon Press, 1994.

Nava, Michael, and Robert Dawidoff. *Created Equal: Why Gay Rights Matter to America*. New York: St. Martin's Press, 1994.

Newton, David E. *Gay and Lesbian Rights: A Reference Handbook*. Santa Barbara, Calif.: ABC-CLIO, 1994.

Sidel, Ruth. *Woman and Children Last: The Plight of Poor Women in Affluent America*. New York: Penguin Books, 1987.

Williamson, Joel. *New People: Miscegenation and Mulattoes in the United States*. New York: New York University Press, 1984.

GOVERNMENT AND POLITICS

Bentley, George R. *A History of the Freedmen's Bureau*. New York: Octagon Books, 1970.

Bessette, Joseph M., ed. *Ready Reference: American Justice*. 3 vols. Pasadena, Calif.: Salem, 1996.

Branscomb, Anne W. *Who Owns Information? From Privacy to Public Access*. New York: Basic Books, 1994.

Couto, Richard A. *Lifting the Veil: A Political History of Struggles for Emancipation*. Knoxville: University of Tennessee Press, 1993.

Fariello, Griffin. *Red Scare: Memories of the American Inquisition: An Oral History*. New York: W. W. Norton, 1995.

Ferrell, Claudine L. *Nightmare and Dream: Anti-Lynching in Congress, 1917-1922*. New York: Garland, 1986.

Franklin, John Hope, and Genna R. McNeil, eds. *African Americans and the Living Constitution*. Washington: Smithsonian Institution Press, 1995.

Fried, Richard M. *Nightmare in Red: The McCarthy Era in Perspective*. New York: Oxford University Press, 1990.

Goldwin, Robert A., and William A. Schambra, eds. *How Does the Constitution Secure Rights?* Washington: American Enterprise Institute, 1985.

Humphrey, Hubert H. *The Civil Rights Rhetoric of Hubert H. Humphrey, 1911-1978*. Edited by Paula Wilson. Lanham, Md.: University Press of America, 1996.

Kaczorowski, Robert J. *The Politics of Judicial Interpretation: The Federal Courts, Department of Justice, and Civil Rights, 1866-1876*. Dobbs Ferry, N.Y.: Oceana, 1985.

Kennedy, Robert F. *Rights for Americans: The Speeches of Robert F. Kennedy*. Edited by Thomas A. Hopkins. Indianapolis, Ind.: Bobbs-Merrill, 1964.

Magdol, Edward. *A Right to the Land: Essays on the Freedmen's Community*. Westport, Conn.: Greenwood Press, 1977.

Marmor, Theodore R., Jerry L. Mashaw, and Phillip L. Harvey. *America's Misunderstood Welfare State*. New York: Basic Books, 1990.

Martin, John F. *Civil Rights and the Crisis of Liberalism: The Democratic Party, 1945-1976*. Boulder, Colo.: Westview Press, 1979.

Nieman, Donald G. *To Set the Law in Motion: The Freedmen's Bureau and the Legal Rights of Blacks, 1865-1868*. Millwood, N.Y.: KTO Press, 1979.

Oubre, Claude F. *Forty Acres and a Mule: The Freedmen's Bureau and Black Land Ownership*. Baton Rouge: Louisiana State University Press, 1978.

HEALTH ISSUES

Appelbaum, Paul S. *Almost a Revolution: Mental Health Law and the Limits of Change*. New York: Oxford University Press, 1994.

Chapman, Audrey R., ed. *Health Care Reform: A Human Rights Approach*. Washington: Georgetown University Press, 1994.

Cottin, Lou. *Elders in Rebellion: A Guide to Senior Activism*. Garden City, N.Y.: Anchor Books, 1979.

Craig, Barbara H., and David M. O'Brien. *Abortion and American Politics*. Chatham, N.J.: Chatham house, 1993.

Dickerson, Neal A. *Civil Rights: HIV Testing, Contact Tracing, and Quarantine*. Las Colinas, Tex.: Monument Press, 1993.

Dudley, William, ed. *Death and Dying: Opposing Viewpoints*. San Diego, Calif.: Greenhaven Press, 1992.

Koop, C. Everett. *The Right to Live, the Right to Die*. Wheaton, Ill.: Tyndale House, 1976.

Levy, Robert M., Leonard S. Rubenstein, Bruce J. Ennis, and Paul R. Friedman. *The Rights of People with Mental Disabilities: The Authoritative ACLU Guide to the Rights of People with Mental Illness and Mental Retardation*. Carbondale: Southern Illinois University Press, 1996.

Nurcombe, Barry, and David F. Partlett. *Child Mental Health and the Law*. New York: The Free Press, 1994.

HISTORY, U.S.

Aptheker, Herbert. *A Documentary History of the Negro People in the United States*. 6 vols. New York: Citadel Press, 1951.

Ayers, Edward L. *The Promise of the New South: Life After Reconstruction*. New York: Oxford University Press, 1992.

————. *Vengeance and Justice: Crime and Punishment in the Nineteenth-Century American South*. New York: Oxford University Press, 1984.

Bailyn, Bernard, et al. *The Great Republic*. Lexington, Mass.: D. C. Heath, 1977.

Bergman, Peter M. *The Chronological History of the Negro in America*. New York: Harper & Row, 1969.

Black, Earl. *Southern Governors and Civil Rights: Racial Segregation as a Campaign Issue in the Second Reconstruction*. Cambridge: Harvard University Press, 1976.

Brundage, W. Fitzhugh. *Lynching in the New South: Georgia and Virginia, 1880-1930*. Urbana: University of Illinois Press, 1993.

Carter, Dan T. *Scottsboro: A Tragedy of the American South*. Rev. ed. Baton Rouge: Louisiana State University Press, 1979.

Chafe, William. *The Unfinished Journey: America Since World War II*. 3d edition. New York: Oxford University Press, 1995.

Couto, Richard A. *Lifting the Veil: A Political History of Struggles for Emancipation*. Knoxville: University of Tennessee Press, 1993.

Eastland, Terry, and William J. Bennett. *Counting by Race: Equality from the Founding Fathers to Bakke and Weber*. New York: Basic Books, 1979.

Egerton, John. *Speak Now Against the Day: The Generation Before the Civil Rights Movement in the South*. New York: Alfred A. Knopf, 1994.

Fehrenbacher, Don E. *The Dred Scott Case: Its Significance in American Law and Politics*. New York: Oxford University Press, 1978.

Foner, Eric. *Reconstruction: America's Unfinished Revolution, 1863-1877*. New York: Harper & Row, 1988.

Franklin, John Hope. *The Emancipation Proclamation*. Garden City, N.Y.: Doubleday, 1963.

Higham, John. *Strangers in the Land: Patterns of American Nativism, 1860-1925*. New York: Atheneum, 1970.

Hornsby, Alton, Jr. *The Chronology of African-American History: Significant Events and People from 1619 to the Present*. Detroit: Gale, 1991.

Kousser, J. Morgan. *The Shaping of Southern Politics: Suffrage Restriction and the Establishment of the One-Party South, 1880-1910*. New Haven, Yale University Press, 1974.

Morris, Thomas D. *Southern Slavery and the Law, 1619-1860*. Chapel Hill: University of North Carolina Press, 1996.

Painter, Nell Irvin. *Standing at Armageddon: The United States, 1877-1919*. New York: W. W. Norton, 1987.

Rable, George C. *But There Was No Peace: The Role of Violence in the Politics of Reconstruction*. Athens: University of Georgia Press, 1984.

Rasmussen, R. Kent. *Farewell to Jim Crow: The Rise and Fall of Segregation in America*. New York: Facts On File, 1997.

Rudwick, Elliott M. *Race Riot at East St. Louis, July 2, 1917*. Carbondale: Southern Illinois University Press, 1964.

Scott, Lawrence P., and William M. Womack. *Double V: The Civil Rights Struggle of the Tuskegee Airmen*. East Lansing: Michigan State University Press, 1994.

Takaki, Ronald. *Iron Cages: Race and Culture in Nineteenth-Century America*. New York: Knopf, 1979.

Woodward, C. Vann. *The Burden of Southern History*. Baton Rouge: Louisiana State University Press, 1960.

_____. *Origins of the New South, 1877-1913*. Baton Rouge: Louisiana State University Press, 1971.

_____. *Reaction and Reunion: The Compromise of 1877 and the End of Reconstruction*. Boston: Little, Brown, 1951.

_____. *The Strange Career of Jim Crow*. 3d ed. New York: Oxford University Press, 1974.

JUDICIAL ISSUES

Abraham, Henry J., and Barbara A. Perry. *Freedom and the Court: Civil Rights and Liberties in the United States*. 6th ed. New York: Oxford University Press, 1994.

Bardolph, Richard, ed. *The Civil Rights Record: Black Americans and the Law, 1849-1970*. New York: Thomas Y. Crowell, 1970.

Belknap, Michal R. *Federal Law and Southern Order: Racial Violence and Constitutional Conflict in the Post-Brown South*. Rev. ed. Athens: University of Georgia Press, 1995.

Bell, Derrick A., Jr. *Race, Racism, and American Law*. 2d ed. Boston: Little, Brown, 1980.

Berry, Mary Frances. *Black Resistance, White Law: A History of Constitutional Racism in America*. East Norwalk, Conn.: Appleton-Century-Crofts, 1971.

Braeman, John. *Before the Civil Rights Revolution: The Old Court and Individual Rights*. New York: Greenwood Press, 1988.

Davidow, Robert P., ed. *Natural Rights and Natural Law: The Legacy of George Mason*. Fairfax, Va.: George Mason University Press, 1986.

Greenawalt, Kent. *Discrimination and Reverse Discrimination*. New York: Alfred A. Knopf, 1983.

Greenberg, Jack. *Crusaders in the Courts: How a Dedicated Band of Lawyers Fought for the Civil Rights Revolution*. New York: Basic Books, 1994.

Grofman, Bernard, ed. *Political Gerrymandering and the Courts*. New York: Agathon Press, 1990.

Morris, Thomas D. *Southern Slavery and the Law, 1619-1860*. Chapel Hill: University of North Carolina Press, 1996.

Nieman, Donald G., ed. *Black Southerners and the Law, 1865-1900*. New York: Garland, 1994.

Sickels, Robert J. *Race, Marriage, and the Law*. Albuquerque: University of New Mexico Press, 1972.

Spence, Gerry. *From Freedom to Slavery: The Rebirth of Tyranny in America*. New York: St. Martin's Press, 1993.

KING, MARTIN LUTHER, JR.

Abernathy, Ralph. *And the Walls Came Tumbling Down*. New York: Harper & Row, 1989.

Baldwin, Lewis V. *There Is a Balm in Gilead: The Cultural Roots of Martin Luther King, Jr.* Minneapolis: Fortress Press, 1991.

Branch, Taylor. *Parting the Waters: America in the King Years, 1954-1963*. New York: Simon & Schuster, 1988.

Calloway-Thomas, Carolyn, and John L. Lucaites, eds. *Martin Luther King, Jr., and the Sermonic Power of Public Discourse*. Tuscaloosa: University of Alabama Press, 1993.

Garrow, David J. *Bearing the Cross: Martin Luther King, Jr., and the Southern Christian Leadership Conference*. New York: William Morrow, 1986.

_____. *Protest at Selma: Martin Luther King, Jr., and the Voting Rights Act of 1965*. New Haven, Conn.: Yale University Press, 1978.

King, Coretta Scott. *My Life with Martin Luther King, Jr.* New York: Holt, Rinehart and Winston, 1969.

King, Martin Luther, Jr. *I Have a Dream: Writings and Speeches That Changed the World*. Edited by James M. Washington. San Francisco, Calif.: HarperCollins, 1992.

Moses, Greg. *Revolution of Conscience: Martin Luther King, Jr., and the Logic of Nonviolence*. New York: Guilford Press, 1997.

Oates, Stephen B. *Let the Trumpet Sound: The Life of Martin Luther King, Jr.* New York: Harper & Row, 1982.

Ralph, James R., Jr. *Northern Protest: Martin Luther King, Jr., Chicago, and the Civil Rights Movement*. Cambridge, Mass.: Harvard University Press, 1993.

KU KLUX KLAN

Blee, Kathleen M. *Women of the Klan: Racism and Gender in the 1920s*. Berkeley: University of California Press, 1991.

Chalmers, David M. *Hooded Americanism: The History of the Ku Klux Klan*. 3d ed. Durham N.C.: Duke University Press, 1987.

Ezekiel, Raphael S. *The Racist Mind: Portraits of American Neo-Nazis and Klansmen*. New York: Viking Press, 1995.

Maclean, Nancy. *Behind the Mask of Chivalry: The Making of the Second Ku Klux Klan*. New York: Oxford University Press, 1994.

Stanton, Bill. *Klanwatch: Bringing the Ku Klux Klan to Justice*. New York: Weidenfeld, 1991.

Trelease, Allen W. *White Terror: The Ku Klux Klan Conspiracy and Southern Reconstruction*. New York: Harper and Row, 1971.

Tucker, Richard K. *The Dragon and the Cross: The Rise and Fall of the Ku Klux Klan in Middle America*. Hamden, Conn.: Archon Books, 1991.

Williams, Lou F. *The Great South Carolina Ku Klux Klan Trials, 1871-1872*. Athens: University of Georgia Press, 1996.

LATINOS

Chabrán, Richard, and Raphael Chabrán, eds. *The Latino Encyclopedia*. 6 vols. New York: Marshall Cavendish, 1996.

Garza, Catarino, ed. *Puerto Ricans in the U.S.: The Struggle for Freedom*. New York: Pathfinder Press, 1977.

Griswald del Castillo, Richard, and Richard A. Garcia. *Cesar Chavez: A Triumph of Spirit*. Norman: University of Oklahoma Press, 1995.

Matthiessen, Peter. *Sal Si Puedes: Cesar Chavez and the New American Revolution*. New York: Random House, 1969.

Olson, James S., and Judith E. Olson. *Cuban Americans: From Trauma to Triumph*. New York: Twayne, 1995.

Weyr, Thomas. *Hispanic U.S.A.: Breaking the Melting Pot*. New York: Harper & Row, 1988.

LEGISLATION

Belknap, Michal R. *Federal Law and Southern Order: Racial Violence and Constitutional Conflict in the Post-Brown South*. Rev. ed. Athens: University of Georgia Press, 1995.

Belz, Herman. *Equality Transformed: A Quarter-Century of Affirmative Action*. New Brunswick, N.J.: Transaction, 1991.

Bolick, Clint. *The Affirmative Action Fraud: Can We Restore the American Civil Rights Vision?* Washington: Cato Institute, 1996.

Cathcart, David A. *The Civil Rights Act of 1991*. Philadelphia: American Law Institute-American Bar Association Committee on Continuing Professional Education, 1993.

Davidson, Chandler, and Bernard Grofman, eds. *Quiet Revolution in the South: The Impact of the Voting Rights Act, 1965-1990*. Princeton, N.J.: Princeton University Press, 1994.

Eisenberg, Theodore. *Civil Rights Legislation*. 3d ed. Charlottesville, Va.: Michie, 1981.

Garrow, David J. *Protest at Selma: Martin Luther King, Jr., and the Voting Rights Act of 1965*. New Haven, Conn.: Yale University Press, 1978.

Halpern, Stephen C. *On the Limits of the Law: The Ironic Legacy of Title VI of the 1964 Civil Rights Act*. Baltimore: Johns Hopkins University Press, 1995.

Hatamiya, Leslie T. *Righting a Wrong: Japanese Americans and the Passage of the Civil Liberties Act of 1988*. Stanford, Calif.: Stanford University Press, 1993.

Kennedy, Stetson. *Jim Crow Guide to the U.S.A.: The Laws, Customs, and Etiquette Governing the Conduct of Nonwhites and Other Minorities as Second-Class Citizens*. 1959. Reprint. Westport Conn.: Greenwood Press, 1973.

Levy, Leonard W., and Douglas L. Jones, eds. *Jim Crow in Boston: The Origin of the Separate but Equal Doctrine*. New York: Da Capo Press, 1974.

Loevy, Robert D. *To End All Segregation: The Politics of the Passage of the Civil Rights Act of 1964*. Lanham, Md.: University Press of America, 1990.

Lopez, Ian F. Haney. *White by Law: The Legal Construction of Race*. New York: New York University Press, 1996.

Rasmussen, R. Kent. *Farewell to Jim Crow: The Rise and Fall of Segregation in America*. New York: Facts On File, 1997.

Ritz, Susan. *The Civil Rights Act of 1991: Its Impact on Employment Discrimination Litigation*. New York: Practicing Law Institute, 1992.

Rosenfeld, Michael. *Affirmative Action and Justice: A Philosophical and Constitutional Inquiry*. New Haven, Conn.: Yale University Press, 1991.

Silverberg, Louis G., ed. *The Wagner Act: After Ten Years*. Washington: Bureau of National Affairs, 1945.

Stone, Clarence N. *Regime Politics: Governing Atlanta, 1946-1988*. Lawrence: University of Kansas Press, 1988.

Taylor, Graham D. *The New Deal and American Indian Tribalism: The Administration of the Indian Reorganization Act, 1934-45*. Lincoln: University of Nebraska Press, 1980.

Wilson, Theodore B. *The Black Codes of the South*. Tuscaloosa: University of Alabama Press, 1965.

Woodward, C. Vann. *The Strange Career of Jim Crow*. 3d ed. New York: Oxford University Press, 1974.

ORGANIZATIONS AND MOVEMENTS

Anderson, John, and Hilary Hevenor. *Burning Down the House: MOVE and the Tragedy of Philadelphia*. New York: W. W. Norton, 1987.

Carson, Clayborne. *In Struggle: SNCC and the Black Awakening of the 1960s*. Cambridge, Mass.: Harvard University Press, 1995.

Donohue, William A. *The Politics of the American Civil Liberties Union*. New Brunswick, N.J.: Transaction, 1985.

Findlay, James F. *Church People in the Struggle: The National Council of Churches and the Black Freedom Movement, 1950-1970*. New York: Oxford University Press, 1993.

Garrow, David J. *Bearing the Cross: Martin Luther King, Jr., and the Southern Christian Leadership Conference*. New York: William Morrow, 1986.

Kaplan, William. *State and Salvation: The Jehovah's Witnesses and Their Fight for Civil Rights*. Toronto: University of Toronto Press, 1989.

McDonald, Laughlin, John A. Powell, and E. Richard Larson. *The Rights of Racial Minorities: The Basic ACLU Guide to Racial Minority Rights*. 2d ed. Carbondale: Southern Illinois University Press, 1993.

McPherson, James M. *The Abolitionist Legacy: From Reconstruction to the NAACP.* 2d ed. Princeton, N.J.: Princeton University Press, 1995.

Manis, Andrew M. *Southern Civil Religions in Conflict: Black and White Baptists and Civil Rights, 1947-1957.* Athens: University of Georgia Press, 1987.

Markmann, Charles L. *The Noblest Cry: A History of the American Civil Liberties Union.* New York: St. Martin's Press, 1965.

Mooney, Patrick H., and Theo J. Majka. *Farmers and Farm Workers' Movements: Social Protest in American Agriculture.* New York: Twayne, 1995.

Ovington, Mary W. *Black and White Sat Down Together: The Reminiscences of an NAACP Founder.* Edited by Ralph Luker. New York: Feminist Press, 1995.

Payne, Charles M. *I've Got the Light of Freedom: The Organizing Tradition and the Mississippi Freedom Struggle.* Berkeley: University of California Press, 1995.

Smith, Robert C. *We Have No Leaders: African-Americans in the Post-Civil Rights Era.* Albany: University of New York Press, 1996.

Stoper, Emily. *The Student Non-Violent Coordinating Committee: The Growth of Radicalism in a Civil Rights Organization.* Brooklyn, N.Y.: Carlson Publishers, 1989.

Van Deburg, William L. *New Day in Babylon: The Black Power Movement and American Culture, 1965-1975.* Chicago: University of Chicago Press, 1992.

Wagner-Pacifici, Robin E. *Discourse and Destruction: The City of Philadelphia Versus MOVE.* Chicago: University of Chicago Press, 1994.

Zangrando, Robert L. *The NAACP Crusade Against Lynching, 1909-1950.* Philadelphia: Temple University Press, 1980.

Zinn, Howard. *SNCC: The New Abolitionists.* 2d ed. Boston: Beacon Press, 1965.

PRESIDENCY, THE

Amaker, Norman C. *Civil Rights and the Reagan Administration.* Washington: Urban Institute Press, 1988.

Berman, William C. *The Politics of Civil Rights in the Truman Administration.* Columbus: Ohio State University Press, 1970.

Burk, Robert Fredrick. *The Eisenhower Administration and Black Civil Rights.* Knoxville: University of Tennessee Press, 1984.

Caro, Robert A. *The Years of Lyndon Johnson.* 2 vols. New York: Alfred A. Knopf, 1982-1990.

Detlefsen, Robert R. *Civil Rights Under Reagan.* San Francisco, Calif.: ICS Press, 1991.

Fleming, Harold C., and Virginia Fleming. *The Potomac Chronicle: Public Policy and Civil Rights from Kennedy to Reagan.* Athens: University of Georgia Press, 1996.

Kearns, Doris. *Lyndon Johnson and the American Dream.* New York: Harper & Row, 1976.

Mann, Robert. *The Walls of Jericho: Lyndon Johnson, Hubert Humphrey, Richard Russell, and the Struggle for Civil Rights.* New York: Harcourt Brace, 1996.

Riddlesperger, James W., Jr., and Donald W. Jackson, eds. *Presidential Leadership and Civil Rights Policy.* Westport, Conn.: Greenwood Press, 1995.

Shull, Steven A. *A Kinder, Gentler Racism?: The Reagan-Bush Civil Rights Legacy.* Armonk, N.Y.: M. E. Sharpe, 1993.

_____. *The President and Civil Rights Policy: Leadership and Change.* New York: Greenwood Press, 1989.

Wolk, Allan. *The Presidency and Black Civil Rights: Eisenhower to Nixon.* Rutherford, N.J.: Farleigh Dickinson University Press, 1971.

Wolters, Raymond. *Right Turn: William Bradford Reynolds, the Reagan Administration, and Black Civil Rights.* New Brunswick: Transaction, 1996.

RACIAL AND ETHNIC GROUPS

Auerbach, Susan, ed. *Encyclopedia of Multiculturalism.* 6 vols. New York: Marshall Cavendish, 1994.

Clayton, Obie. An American Dilemma *Revisited: Race Relations in a Changing World.* New York: Russell Sage Foundation, 1996.

Davidson, Osha G. *The Best of Enemies: Race and Redemption in the New South.* New York: Charles Scribner's Son, 1996.

Gossett, Thomas. *Race: The History of an Idea in America.* 1963. Rev. ed. Edited by Arnold Rampersad and Shelley Fisher Fishkin. New York: Oxford University Press, 1997.

Gunning, Sandra. *Race, Rape, and Lynching: The Red Record of American Literature, 1890-1912.* New York: Oxford University Press, 1996.

Kallen, Evelyn. *Ethnicity and Human Rights in Canada.* 2d ed. New York: Oxford University Press, 1995.

Kymlicka, Will. *Multicultural Citizenship: A Liberal Theory of Minority Rights.* New York: Oxford University Press, 1995.

_____, ed. *The Rights of Minority Cultures.* New York: Oxford University Press, 1995.

Lopez, Ian F. Haney. *White by Law: The Legal Construction of Race.* New York: New York University Press, 1996.

Mallea, Paula. *Aboriginal Law: Apartheid in Canada?* Brandon, Manitoba: Bearpaw, 1994.

Walker, James W. St. G. *Racial Discrimination in Canada: The Black Experience.* Ottawa: Canadian Historical Association, 1985.

Williamson, Joel. *The Crucible of Race: Black-White Relations in the American South Since Emancipation.* New York: Oxford University Press, 1984.

_____. *New People: Miscegenation and Mulattoes in the United States.* New York: Free Press, 1980.

Winks, Robin W. *The Blacks in Canada: A History.* Montreal: McGill-Queen's University Press, 1971.

SCHOOL BUSING

Bolner, James. *Busing: The Political and Judicial Process.* New York: Praeger, 1974.

Cottle, Thomas J. *Busing.* Boston: Beacon Press, 1976.

Davison, Douglas, ed. *School Busing: Constitutional and Political Development.* 2 vols. New York: Garland, 1994.

Dimond, Paul R. *Beyond Busing: Inside the Challenge to Urban Segregation.* Ann Arbor: University of Michigan Press, 1985.

Mills, Nicholaus, ed. *Busing U.S.A.* New York: Teachers College Press, 1979.

Rossell, Christine. *The Carrot or the Stick for School Desegregation Policy: Magnet Schools or Forced Busing.* Philadelphia: Temple University Press, 1990.

Rubin, Lillian B. *Busing and Backlash: White Against White in a California School District.* Berkeley: University of California Press, 1972.

Schwartz, Bernard. *Swann's Way: The School Busing Case and the Supreme Court.* New York: Oxford University Press, 1986.

Teele, James E. *Evaluating School Busing: Case Study of Boston's Operation Exodus.* New York: Praeger, 1973.

SUPREME COURT, U.S.

Davis, Abraham L., and Barbara L. Graham. *The Supreme Court, Race, and Civil Rights.* Thousand Oaks, Calif.: Sage Publications, 1995.

Hall, Kermit L., ed. *The Oxford Companion to the Supreme Court of the United States.* New York: Oxford University Press, 1992.

Kim, Hyung-chan, ed. *Asian Americans and the Supreme Court: A Documentary History.* New York: Greenwood Press, 1992.

Spann, Girardeau A. *Race Against the Court: The Supreme Court and Minorities in Contemporary America.* New York: New York University Press, 1993.

Tucker, David F. B. *The Rehnquist Court and Civil Rights.* Aldershot; Brookfield, Vt.: Dartmouth, 1995.

Tushnet, Mark V. *Making Civil Rights Law: Thurgood Marshall and the Supreme Court, 1936-1961.* New York: Oxford University Press, 1994.

Wilkinson, J. Harvie, III. *From Brown to Bakke: The Supreme Court and School Integration, 1954-1978.* New York: Oxford University Press, 1979.

WOMEN'S RIGHTS

Barry, Kathleen. *Susan B. Anthony: A Biography of a Singular Feminist.* New York: New York University Press, 1988.

Becker, Susan D. *The Origins of the Equal Rights Amendment*. Westport, Conn.: Greenwood Press, 1981.

Blum, Linda M. *Between Feminism and Labor: The Significance of the Comparable Worth Movement*. Berkeley: University of California Press, 1991.

Boles, Janet K. *The Politics of the Equal Rights Amendment: Conflict and the Decision Process*. New York: Longman, 1979.

Crawford, Vicki L., Jacqueline A. Rouse, and Barbara Woods, eds. *Women in the Civil Rights Movement: Trailblazers and Torchbearers, 1941-1965*. Bloomington: Indiana University Press, 1993.

Du Bois, Ellen Carol. *Feminism and Suffrage: The Emergence of an Independent Women's Movement in America, 1848-1869*. Ithaca, N.Y.: Cornell University Press, 1978.

Evans, Sara. *Personal Politics: The Roots of Women's Liberation in the Civil Rights Movement and the New Left*. New York: Vintage Books, 1979.

Flexner, Eleanor. *Century of Struggle: The Woman's Rights Movement in the United States*. Rev. ed. Cambridge, Mass.: The Belknap Press of Harvard University Press, 1975.

Frost-Knappman, Elizabeth, and Kathryn Cullen-DuPont. *Women's Suffrage in America: An Eyewitness History*. New York: Facts On File, 1992.

Goldstein, Leslie F. *Contemporary Cases in Women's Rights*. Madison: University of Wisconsin Press, 1994.

Hall, Jacquelyn D. *Revolt Against Chivalry: Jessie Daniel Ames and the Women's Campaign Against Lynching*. New York: Columbia University Press, 1979.

Hardy, Gayle J. *American Women Civil Rights Activists: Biobibliographies of Sixty-eight Leaders, 1825-1992*. Jefferson, N.C.: McFarland, 1993.

Hine, Darlene Clark, Elsa Barkley Brown, and Rosalyn Terborg-Penn, eds. *Black Women in America: An Historical Encyclopedia*. Bloomington: Indiana University Press, 1994.

Hoff-Wilson, Joan, ed. *The Rights of Passage: The Past and the Future of the ERA*. Bloomington: Indiana University Press, 1986.

Jones, Beverly W. *Quest for Equality: The Life and Writings of Mary Eliza Church Terrell, 1863-1954*. Brooklyn, N.Y.: Carlson, 1990.

Kaminer, Wendy. *A Fearful Freedom: Women's Flight from Equality*. Reading, Mass.: Addison-Wesley, 1990.

Karcher, Carolyn L. *The First Woman in the Republic: A Cultural Biography of Lydia Maria Child*. Durham, N.C.: Duke University Press, 1994.

Kraditor, Aileen. *The Ideas of the Woman Suffrage Movement, 1890-1920*. Garden City, N.Y.: Doubleday, 1971.

Lee, Rex E. *A Lawyer Looks at the Equal Rights Amendment*. Provo, Utah: Brigham Young University, 1980.

Lerner, Gerda, ed. *Black Women in White America: A Documentary History*. New York: Vintage Books, 1972.

McFadden, Margaret, ed. *Ready Reference: Women's Issues*. 3 vols. Pasadena, Calif.: Salem Press, 1996.

Milkman, Ruth. *Gender at Work: The Dynamics of Job Segregation by Sex During World War II*. Urbana: University of Illinois Press, 1987.

Peterson, Carla. *Doers of the Word: African-American Women Speakers and Writers in the North, 1830-1880*. New York: Oxford University Press, 1995.

Reskin, Barbara F., ed. *Sex Segregation in the Workplace: Trends, Explanations, Remedies*. Washington: National Academy Press, 1984.

Sellen, Betty-Carol, and Patricia Young. *Feminists, Pornography, and the Law: An Annotated Bibliography of Conflict, 1970-1986*. Hamden, Conn.: Library Professional Publications, 1987.

Slavin, Sarah, ed. *The Equal Rights Amendment: The Politics and Process of Ratification of the 27th Amendment to the U.S. Constitution*. New York: Haworth Press, 1982.

Steiner, Gilbert Y. *Constitutional Inequality: The Political Fortunes of the Equal Rights Amendment*. Washington D.C.: Brookings Institution, 1985.

Streitmatter, Rodger. *Raising Her Voice: African-American Women Journalists Who Changed History*. Lexington: University Press of Kentucky, 1994.

Vaz, Kim M., ed. *Black Women in America*. Thousand Oaks, Calif.: Sage Publications, 1995.

Wheeler, Marjorie Spruill. *New Women of the New South: The Leaders of the Woman Suffrage Movement in the Southern States*. New York: Oxford University Press, 1994.

Yellin, Jean Fagan. *Women and Sisters: The Antislavery Feminists in American Culture*. New Haven: Yale University Press, 1989.

THE ENCYCLOPEDIA OF

CIVIL RIGHTS IN AMERICA

List of Entries by Category

Subject Headings

AFRICAN AMERICAN SUBJECTS

Abolitionism
Affirmative action
African Americans
Afro-American League
American Dilemma, An
American Negro Academy
Atlanta Compromise
Attica prison riot
Baltimore Afro-American
Birmingham Children's Crusade
Black laws
Black nationalism
Black Panther Party
Black Power movement
Black United Front (1968)
Black United Front (1980)
Boston Guardian
Brownsville incident
Cambridge, Maryland, race riot
Chicago Defender
Churches and the Civil Rights movement
Cincinnati race riots
Civil rights history
Civil Rights movement
Colored Women's League

Combahee River Collective Statement
Congress of Industrial Organizations
Congress of Racial Equality
Council of Federated Organizations
Crusade for Justice
Deacons for Defense and Justice
Detroit race riots
East St. Louis riots
Emancipation Proclamation
Freedom Now Party
Freedom riders
Grandfather clauses
Greensboro sit-ins
Jim Crow laws
King, Rodney, beating of
King Day
Little Rock, Arkansas
March on Washington
Miami riots
Mississippi civil rights workers murders
Mississippi Freedom Democratic Party
Mississippi Plan
Montgomery bus boycott
Mount Pleasant riots
MOVE Organization
National Association for the Advancement of
    Colored People

National Association for the Advancement of Colored People Legal Defense and Educational Fund

National Association of Colored Women

National Bar Association

National Urban League

Negro Convention movement

New York Age

Newspapers, African American

Niagara Movement

Operation PUSH

Operation Rescue

Pittsburgh Courier

Poll taxes

Project Confrontation

Providence race riots

Race riots

Reconstruction era

Republic of New Africa

Scottsboro Nine

Selma, Alabama, march

Sit-ins

Slavery

Southern Christian Leadership Conference

Southwest Voter Registration Project

Student Non-Violent Coordinating Committee

TransAfrica

Voter Education Project

Watts riots

AFRICAN AMERICANS, NOTABLE

Abernathy, Ralph

Baker, Ella

Bethune, Mary McLeod

Bevel, James

Briggs, Cyril V.

Brown, Charlotte Hawkins

Brown, H. Rap

Carmichael, Stokely

Child, Lydia Maria Francis

Clark, Septima Poinsette

Cleage, Albert Buford, Jr.

Cleaver, Eldridge

Collins, Wayne Mortimer

Crummell, Alexander

Davis, Angela

Delany, Martin

Douglass, Frederick

Du Bois, W. E. B.

Edelman, Marian Wright

Evers, Charles

Evers, Medgar

Evers, Myrlie Beaseley

Farmer, James

Farrakhan, Louis

Forman, James

Fortune, T. Thomas

Franklin, C. L.

Fuller, Margaret

Gage, Matilda Joslyn

Garvey, Marcus

Gilman, Charlotte Perkins Stetson

Gregory, Dick

Hall, Prince

Hamer, Fannie Lou

Hampton, Fred

Hill, Herbert

Holman, M. Carl

Hooks, Benjamin Lawson

Innis, Roy Emile Alfredo

Jackson, Jesse

Jacob, John Edward

Johnson, Charles S.

Johnson, James Weldon

Jones, Eugene Kinckle

Jones, Nathaniel Raphael

Jordan, Barbara

Jordan, Vernon Eulion, Jr.

King, Coretta Scott

King, Martin Luther, Jr.

King, Martin Luther, Sr.

Lewis, John Robert

Lockwood, Belva Ann Bennett

McKissick, Floyd

Makino, Frederick Kinzaburo

Malcolm X

AGE, SEX, AND FAMILY SUBJECTS

AMERICAN INDIAN SUBJECTS

HISTORICAL EVENTS AND MOVEMENTS

LAWS AND GOVERNMENT POLICIES

Age Discrimination in Employment Act

Air Carriers Access Act

Alaska Native Claims Settlement Act

Alien and Sedition laws

Alien Land Law of 1920

Alien Registration Act of 1940

American Indian Civil Rights Act

American Indian Religious Freedom Act

Americans with Disabilities Act

Architectural Barriers Act

Bill of Rights, U.S.

Cable Act

California Civil Rights Initiative

Charter of the Virginia Company

Child Abuse Prevention and Treatment Act

Chinese Exclusion Act of 1882

Civil Liberties Act of 1988

Civil Rights Act of 1866 and the Civil Rights
    Act of 1875

Civil Rights Act of 1957

Civil Rights Act of 1960

Civil Rights Act of 1964

Civil Rights Act of 1968

Civil Rights Act of 1991

Civil Rights Restoration Act of 1988

Comprehensive Employment Training Act

Constitution, U.S.

Constitutions, state

Declaration of Independence

Dred Scott case

Dyer antilynching bill

Education for All Handicapped Children Act

Equal Employment Opportunities Act

Equal Pay Act of 1963

Equal protection clause

Equal Rights Amendment

Executive Order 8802

Executive Order 9980

Executive Order 9981

Fifteenth Amendment

First Amendment

Fourteenth Amendment

Freedom of Information Act

Fugitive slave laws

Indian Bill of Rights

Indian Child Welfare Act

Indian Citizenship Act

Indian Reorganization Act

Laundry ordinances

McCarran-Walter Act

Nineteenth Amendment

Nontraditional Employment for Women Act

Rehabilitation Act of 1973

Scott Act

Social Security Act

Thirteenth Amendment

Twenty-fourth Amendment

Twenty-sixth Amendment

Voting Rights Act of 1965

Voting Rights Act of 1975

Voting Rights Act of 1982

Wagner Act

MEDICAL, HEALTH, AND DISABILITY SUBJECTS

Addington v. Texas

AIDS/HIV victims

Air Carriers Access Act

American Coalition of Citizens with Disabilities

Americans with Disabilities Act

Architectural Barriers Act

Bill of Rights for the Handicapped

Crippled Children's Services

Disability rights movement

Education for All Handicapped Children Act

Foucha v. Louisiana

Health care

Mentally ill, rights of the

Rehabilitation Act of 1973

Right to die

ORGANIZATIONS

Afro-American League

Alaska Native Brotherhood and Alaska Native
    Sisterhood

Alianza Hispano-Americana
American Association of Retired Persons
American Birth Control League
American Citizens for Justice
American Civil Liberties Union
American Coalition of Citizens with Disabilities
American Indian Movement
American Negro Academy
Americans for Indian Opportunity
Amnesty International
Asian Americans for Equality
Black Panther Party
Black United Front (1968)
Black United Front (1980)
Brotherhood of Sleeping Car Porters
Chinese American Citizens Alliance
Chinese for Affirmative Action
Chinese Hand Laundry Alliance
Colored Women's League
Communist Party of the U.S.A.
Congress of Industrial Organizations
Congress of Racial Equality
Congressional Union for Woman Suffrage
Council of Federated Organizations
Crusade for Justice
Cuban American Legal Defense and Education
  Fund
Daughters of Bilitis
Deacons for Defense and Justice
Farm Labor Organizing Committee
Freedom Now Party
Fuerzas Armadas de Liberación Nacional
Gray Panthers
Heart Mountain Fair Play Committee
Indian Rights Association
Japanese American Citizens League
Ku Klux Klan
League of United Latin American Citizens
Mattachine Society
Mexican-American Anti-Defamation Committee
Mexican American Legal Defense and Education
  Fund
Mexican American Political Association
Mississippi Freedom Democratic Party

MOVE Organization
Movimiento Estudiantil Chicano de Aztlán, El
Mutualistas
National Abortion and Reproductive Rights Action
  League
National Alliance of Spanish-Speaking People for
  Equality
National Asian Pacific American Legal Consortium
National Association for the Advancement of
  Colored People
National Association for the Advancement of
  Colored People Legal Defense and Educational
  Fund
National Association of Colored Women
National Association of Cuban-American Women
National Bar Association
National Chinese Welfare Council
National Coalition for Redress/Reparations
National Committee for Redress
National Conference of Puerto Rican Women
National Congress for Puerto Rican Rights
National Congress of American Indians
National Council for Japanese American Redress
National Council of American Indians
National Council of Hispanic Women
National Council of La Raza
National Farm Workers Association
National Indian Association
National Organization for Women
National Puerto Rican Coalition
National Puerto Rican Forum
National Urban League
National Woman Suffrage Association
National Woman's Party
National Women's Trade Union League
Native American Rights Fund
Niagara Movement
9 to 5, National Association of Working Women
Older Women's League
Operation PUSH
Operation Rescue
Organization of Chinese Americans
Project Confrontation
Puerto Rican Legal Defense and Education Fund

Raza Unida Party, La
Republic of New Africa
Society of American Indians
Southern Christian Leadership Conference
Southwest Voter Registration Project
Student Non-Violent Coordinating Committee
TransAfrica
United Farm Workers of America
Voter Education Project
Women of All Red Nations

PLACES

Albuquerque walkout
Alcatraz occupation
Atlanta, Georgia
Attica prison riot
Bellingham incident
Birmingham, Alabama
Brownsville incident
Cambridge, Maryland, race riot
Canada
Chicago
Cincinnati race riots
Delano grape strike
Detroit race riots
East St. Louis riots
Greensboro sit-ins
Hawaii
Little Rock, Arkansas
March on Washington
Mexico
Miami riots
Mississippi
Mississippi civil rights workers murders
Montgomery bus boycott
Mount Pleasant riots
Northern states
Providence race riots
Reservations, Indian
Rhode Island Charter
Rock Springs riot
Salinas lettuce strike
Sleepy Lagoon case

Snake River massacre
Southern states
Tacoma incident
Virginia Declaration of Rights
Watsonville incident
Watts riots
Wounded Knee occupation

RELIGION

American Indian Religious Freedom Act
Anabaptists
Churches and the Civil Rights movement
First Amendment
Jews
Mormons
Religion, freedom of
Rhode Island Charter
Roman Catholics
Southern Christian Leadership Conference
Virginia Declaration of Rights

WOMEN, NOTABLE

Anthony, Susan B.
Báez, Joan
Baker, Ella
Bethune, Mary McLeod
Bolin, Jane Matilda
Brown, Charlotte Hawkins
Catt, Carrie Chapman
Child, Lydia Maria Francis
Chisholm, Shirley
Clark, Septima Poinsette
Davis, Angela
Deer, Ada Elizabeth
Edelman, Marian Wright
Evers, Myrlie Beaseley
Fuller, Margaret
Gage, Matilda Joslyn
Gilman, Charlotte Perkins Stetson
Hamer, Fannie Lou
Hernández, Antonia
Jones, Eugene Kinckle
Jordan, Barbara

WOMEN'S ISSUES

Court Case Index

Page numbers in boldface type indicate full articles devoted to the topic.

Index

Page numbers in boldface type indicate full articles devoted to the topic. Page numbers in italic type indicate photographs. The author of written works is identified in parenthesis after the title of the work.